# THE ECONOMIC
# ANALYSIS
# OF INDUSTRIAL
# PROJECTS

PRENTICE-HALL INTERNATIONAL SERIES
IN INDUSTRIAL AND SYSTEMS ENGINEERING

*W. J. Fabrycky and J. H. Mize, Editors*

# THE ECONOMIC ANALYSIS OF INDUSTRIAL PROJECTS

LYNN E. BUSSEY

*Kansas State University*

Prentice-Hall, Inc., *Englewood Cliffs, New Jersey*   07632

*Library of Congress Cataloging in Publication Data*

Bussey, Lynn E.   (date)
   The economic analysis of industrial projects.

   (Prentice-Hall international series in industrial
and systems engineering)
   Includes bibliographies and index.
   1. Capital investments.   2. Corporations—Finance.
I. Title.
HG4028.C4B83        658.1'52        77-26808
ISBN   0-13-223388-6

Printed in the United States of America

10   9   8   7   6   5   4   3

PRENTICE-HALL INTERNATIONAL, INC., *London*
PRENTICE-HALL OF AUSTRALIA PTY. LIMITED, *Sydney*
PRENTICE-HALL OF CANADA, LTD., *Toronto*
PRENTICE-HALL OF INDIA PRIVATE LIMITED, *New Delhi*
PRENTICE-HALL OF JAPAN, INC., *Tokyo*
PRENTICE-HALL OF SOUTHEAST ASIA PTE. LTD., *Singapore*
WHITEHALL BOOKS LIMITED, *Wellington, New Zealand*

**To the memory of**

HEZEKIAH LEWIS BUSSEY
*Father, instiller of curiosity, seeker of truth*


LESTER EDMUND COX
*Practical resource allocator, humanitarian*


WILSON JOSEPH BENTLEY
*Engineer, educator, superior executive, humanist*

# AN ECONOMICS CATECHISM

You cannot pay yourself more money unless you do more work;
You cannot print more money unless you produce more goods;
You cannot have more jobs unless you have more investment;
You cannot have more investment unless you have more savings;
You cannot have more savings unless you keep faith with the saver;
You cannot keep faith with the saver unless you have sound money;
You cannot have sound money if you spend beyond your means;
But you can't increase your means unless you increase your effort.
And that takes you right back to the beginning of the catechism.

*—Eric Sevareid,*
quoting a leading British politician,
from the CBS EVENING NEWS WITH WALTER CRONKITE.*

# CONTENTS

**part two**  DETERMINISTIC
             INVESTMENT ANALYSIS      187

**7**  Evaluating a Single Project—
Deterministic Criteria and Techniques      188

## 8 Multiple Projects and Constraints I (The Lorie-Savage Problem)  244

## 9 Multiple Projects and Constraints II (Extended Deterministic Formulations)  286

# PREFACE

This book is concerned with the economic analysis and selection of industrial projects. Its aim is to provide the reader with reasonably detailed and *theoretically correct* information about the economic process of internal investment within the firm, extended insofar as possible into the domain of practical application. In developing this book, two purposes have motivated the presentation. First, the book should be usable as a reading text to teach engineers, engineering students, and others with suitable mathematical backgrounds some advanced concepts in intrafirm economic analysis and intertemporal exchange. Second, it attempts to summarize the major developments reported in the research literature over the last 20 years, or approximately so, on intrafirm capital expenditure theory and methodology. In limiting the intended audience to technically trained persons, it has been possible to provide an expanded coverage of the topics presented and yet at the same time to retain where necessary a relatively rigorous analytic protocol in deriving principles or emphasizing results.

The level of presentation is designed for advanced undergraduate and graduate students in engineering and the "hard" sciences. While others may certainly undertake a reading of it, the book presumes a working knowledge of differential calculus, linear programming, and statistical theory through regression analysis. A background in economics, at least equivalent to an introductory course *plus* a course in engineering economy, or as an alternative a course in intermediate microeconomics would be helpful. Some undergraduate business students will find the economics presented here somewhat redundant but probably more rigorous from the standpoint of fundamental assumptions and development than they are accustomed to.

The book is organized into three major parts. Part I, consisting of Chapters 1 through 6, deals with some fundamental topics. These are the organization of the firm, economic exchange and valuation, perfect capital markets and the exchange of funds (as *dated* commodities with *time* preferences) between periods, the function of interest as the mediating variable in intertemporal exchange, interest calculations, depreciation models, corporate income tax effects, cash flow streams, and the firm's cost of capital. These chapters, possibly with the exception of Chapter 5 (corporate income tax effects and cash flow streams), can be used as review material for those who have been previously introduced to similar topics.

Part II, consisting of Chapters 7, 8, and 9, deals with the deterministic analysis and selection of both single and multiple projects under conditions of certainty. The fundamental assumptions underlying net present value, internal rate of return (and return on invested capital), and benefit-cost ratio are developed within the bounds of a perfect capital market, for both the unconstrained and constrained cases. The constrained case is shown to be the Lorie-Savage model, which is often trivial in a perfect capital market but which serves as an excellent teaching model. In Chapter 9, the perfect capital market assumption is dropped, and some models of the selection process under imperfect capital market assumptions are examined. One of the models presented is an extensive goal programming formulation of a capital allocation problem, in which incompatible goals are sought and an ordinal utility ranking replaces the time-value of money (interest).

In Part III, consisting of Chapters 10, 11, and 12, the certainty assumption is relaxed. Methods are developed in these chapters for evaluating and selecting projects under conditions of explicit risk. Considerable attention is paid to the theoretical bases underlying the expected utility principle and the correlative interactions of synergistic projects. One of the features of Part III, not known to be published elsewhere in a text, is the application of the Sharpe-Lintner-Mossin capital market model to the selection of *discrete* industrial projects for both public and *private* firms.

This book can be used in several ways. Since it contains over 60 worked-out examples, many of which are treated as comprehensive applications, it can be used directly as a teaching text for undergraduate course work in advanced engineering economy. Also, because the principal journal sources are cited for all the major topics discussed in the book, it can be used in graduate courses that require supplementary readings for in-depth coverage of selected topics, where the instructor wants to place special emphasis. Third, it can be used as a text in applied financial theory, for technically trained persons who do not have an extensive background in the economic theory of the firm. Fourth, it can be used by the practitioner to acquaint himself with some of the more recent developments in the area of resources allocation within the firm.

Over the last two decades tremendous advances have been made in the area of financial theory. At first, as with all advances in "new" knowledge, tentative thrusts were made in many directions simultaneously. Not all of these thrusts have been sterile; indeed, a surprising number have proved to be fruitful. Lately, perhaps in the last seven to ten years, there has been a pronounced effort to integrate the well-founded developments into a unified, *prescriptive* theory of finance of the firm, based on sound economic principles.

Even while the finance theorists have been forging a new and useful body of knowledge, however, it appears that little of this knowledge has been accepted and adopted into the technical area of *engineering economy*—the interfacial area between engineering and economics, where the engineering specialist must deal with the economic aspects of his technical creations. Modern financial theory has a great deal to say about the traditional methods used in engineering economic analysis, and engineers in all disciplines would be well counseled to heed the economist's *caveats*. Thus, one of the implied objectives in this book is to hasten the transfer of the "new" knowledge from financial economics to engineering, so that the technically trained specialist can continue to solve society's problems *within the constraints imposed by our economic system.*

## Acknowledgments

A book such as this is not the product of one person, even though it bears a single author's name. I have learned much from my teachers, co-workers, and students. I am most grateful, of course, to the many authors who are cited as direct references in nearly all the chapters here. It is their hard labor in "breaking new ground" that makes this book possible. Also, I am grateful to my former teachers—particularly Andrew Schultz, Jr., and the late William C. Andrae of Cornell University, the late Wilson Bentley of Oklahoma State University, and G. T. Stevens, Jr., now of The University of Texas (Arlington)—who nurtured a "need to know" in me when it was needed.

But I owe a special debt of gratitude to Richard H. Bernhard of North Carolina State University, for the help he has given me over a period of several years. In all my associations with Professor Bernhard, I have experienced in him an implicit insistence for precision and intellectual honesty which I have tried to reflect in this book. Moreover, I have always found him to be a "critic's critic"—not one who merely excises faulty material, but rather one who courteously and politely points the way to better information or perhaps a better method of presentation or expression. Dick Bernhard has read an earlier version of this manuscript and has helped immeasurably to improve its content and style of presentation, for which I am most grateful. He is not to be held accountable for the results in any way, however; they are totally my responsibility.

As a point of special recognition, I should like to acknowledge the very considerable talent and dedication of Joyce Rickstrew Reich, who, as an undergraduate some years ago, began typing the original chapter of this book and who has now finished the book as my editorial assistant. I gratefully acknowledge her assistance, especially in keeping me from making many errors of omission and commission. Also, I would like to note that Jan Gaines typed a considerable portion of the manuscript, and Kim Reinhardt and her staff cheerfully made innumerable copies of the drafts for me. I thank them all.

*Kansas State University*
*Manhattan, Kansas*

Lynn E. Bussey

part one

BASIC
CONCEPTS

# INTRODUCTION

There are three fundamental and essential decisions that must be continually made within the industrial firm if it is to survive. The first is to decide upon the objective of the firm—what service or product is to be produced, what market is to be served, and basically how the firm is to go about doing these. The second decision is concerned with whom to hire and retain—which persons, which skills, which abilities, which personalities, how many, and so forth. The third decision is about how the available resources of the firm—particularly money—shall be allocated: for which programs, to which departments, in what amounts, and under what conditions. All other decisions that take place within the firm are derivatives of these main three, and it is these main three that give the "set," direction, and "flavor" to the individual firm—and generally spell its success or failure.

This book is concerned with the manner in which the *third* type of decision is made. It is concerned, in detail, with how money *ought* to be allocated within the firm in order to improve the ultimate worth of the shareholders' holdings. We say *ought* because in recent years the thrust of investment research has swung away from being merely descriptive of what is or was done and has moved toward what should be done within the firm in order to attain certain goals. Investment analysis has become goal-oriented. This book reflects that orientation.

Furthermore, at the outset we should recognize that the three fundamental decisions mentioned above are certainly not made in isolation. One should not think for a moment that they can be separated completely or that there is no dependence

# 1

among the three decisions. Obviously there is a relationship, because the whole concept of *organization* implies an interrelated *system* of persons, structures, machines, tools, materials, methods, money, and other inputs. Certainly this system is physically and temporally *organized* to produce some output or service of value—i.e., accomplish a stated objective. So all three decisions concerning the organizational objective, persons and their skills, and how money is to be allocated are in reality very much related.

Nevertheless, we have attempted to separate the resource allocation decision and treat it in isolation. There must be good reasons for doing this, and there are. First, the subject is one that is generally factual, its data are generally stated in numerical quantities, and its processes are generally amenable to mathematical formulation. Moreover, it is a repetitive decision in most firms, and the format of the decision remains somewhat constant over time (i.e., virtually the same facts are elicited, they are typically analyzed in the same manner, and generally the same persons, or their successors, make the decisions).

The most important consideration, however, is that the resource allocation decision is generally made about things that give a long-time "set" to the thrust of the organization. Capital expenditure decisions are made about *capital* items—what plants will be built, where they will be located, what processes will be used, how the plants will be equipped, what product will be made, what capacity the process will have, and so forth. In short, the consequences of capital expenditure decisions usually extend far into the future and typically shape the basic character of the firm. Furthermore, although capital expenditure decisions can usually be modified to some extent after they are made, they are seldom reversible. There is virtually no secondhand market for many types of industrial capital goods—only the scrap dealer. Thus, the alternative to a "bad" resource allocation decision is to scrap the project, recognize the loss, and start again.

Because of these two factors—longevity and irreversibility—the resource allocation decision not only effectively commits the firm to a fixed technology but largely determines the level of future operating expenses as well. The importance of the decision goes far beyond the initial outlay.

This book is concerned with the economic analysis of industrial projects. An industrial project, or capital investment project, may be defined as any candidate project that involves the outlay of cash in exchange for an anticipated return flow of future benefits. Returns or benefits may be monetary, or they may be nonmonetary if they can be expressed in money terms. It is the exchange of a present expenditure for future benefits that is the distinctive feature of the economic analysis of projects.

There is a fundamental difference between what engineers know as *engineering economy* and the *economic analysis of projects*. Because of its heritage, derived principally from Wellington's early railroad location economics and also the economics of early transcontinental telephone lines ("Bell" economics), engineering economy as historically taught is chiefly concerned with economic choices between *executable* alternative solutions. Thus, some sort of economic criterion, such as minimum annual cost or maximum present value, is invoked to delineate the preferred choice among feasible alternatives. Note, however, that generally the implicit *intent* is to *select and execute at least one* of the feasible alternatives.

In the last decade or so, it has become increasingly apparent that the choice is not always solely between *executable* alternatives. For one reason or another (usually restrictions of available capital), it is now generally impossible to execute all worthy (i.e., cost-saving or profit-improving) projects. Even though all candidate projects at the decision level may be technically feasible and economically attractive, some must be selected and some rejected, typically because of a restriction in money or other resources. The real question facing the firm then, as a proxy representative of its owners, is *whether or not a project should be accepted at all*. This is a much different economic question—one that is *based on a different decision criterion*—than the typical economic alternative question answered by engineering economy. The economic analysis of industrial projects addresses itself to this fundamental question of whether a project should be selected at all. In effect, industrial project evaluation and selection uses economic and mathematical principles to answer the question, "Given a set of defined alternatives, what projects, *if any*, should the firm undertake?" While the analytic methodology of project analysis has its roots in engineering economy, the traditional limited horizons of engineering economy have been pushed back much farther by project analysis. Now the question is, "What is best for the firm, *overall*," rather than, "Which of these alternatives should we do?"

Thus, the effect of this methodology is to shift the emphasis of the capital expenditure decision away from an insular and myopic viewpoint within, say, a department toward the point of view that expenditure decisions should be made on a firm-wide basis. Industrial project selection takes a firm-wide stance toward *all* projects and requires them to compete for resources not only against each other but, more importantly, against the *overall* benefits that will accrue to the firm. More to the point, the competition for resources is not based so much on the requirement of an economic comparison of alternatives pair by pair but more so on the requirement that a *subset of projects* be chosen that will maximize *something of overall benefit to the firm*—generally, for example, its net worth. This is the fundamental difference between engineering economy and industrial project selection.

Finally, it should be mentioned that there is no chapter included in this book that deals with so-called *public sector* project selection. The reason is simple. Basically this is a prescriptive book about the economic analysis and selection of projects. At the present time, there is no generally agreed method—or at least, no generally accepted method—for measuring the benefits of public projects in money terms. In the private sector, the effect of good or bad project acceptance methods inevitably shows up in the future balance sheets and income statements of the firm. These financial statements are usually prepared according to rather standardized and generally accepted accounting methods and reflect the ultimate outcomes of historically accepted projects that operate in more or less free markets. There is no comparable market or form of accounting in the public sector, and there are no generally agreed standards for measuring the intangible benefits of undertaking public projects. Where attempts to define such standards have been made, they are invariably the caveats of legislative or administrative bodies and may or may not actually measure the benefits they purport to. In other words, no free market intervenes to establish the impartial *value* of the future benefits. Even so, it *may* be possible to establish a *social rate of discount* that would be free of bias; in such a case, project selection methods could be used. We recognize that much has been written on so-called *benefit-cost* methodologies for public sector projects, where the benefits are often intangibles, and we recognize that mathematical and economic manipulations are used to evaluate the benefit-cost aspects of projects. But in the absence of an *unbiased* estimate of a social discount rate (for money,) or at least a *consensus* utility-of-money function, the whole area of *public sector* project selection methodology is not meaningful.

The general format of the remainder of the book will deal with the investment decision in the context of the industrial firm. Considerable emphasis will be directed toward principles and depth of understanding of these principles. The first topics are basic ones concerning the nature of the firm, its objectives, how the time value of money affects decisions, and how income taxes affect decisions. The exposition proceeds thence to deterministic project evaluation and selection methods, in which all factors are considered *known with certainty*. Finally, this assumption is relaxed, and the effects of an uncertain future on the investment decision are examined.

# THE FIRM—
# ECONOMIC EXCHANGES AND OBJECTIVES

## 2.1. Introduction

In this chapter, we are concerned with building an integrated concept of what the word *firm* means in economic terms. A firm is simply an idea or a concept that exists in the mind—it is not an actual, real thing. It is a very specific economic idea, however, based on some well-defined assumptions and many well-reasoned conclusions. The economic concept of the ideal firm, although it is merely a mental and mathematical fabrication, often enables us to interpret and understand, with great insight, the economic behavior of actual businesses. Moreover, we can often make surprisingly accurate decisions and predictions by using the economic concept of the firm. An understanding of the economic firm is fundamental to any undertaking involving entrepreneurial analysis or project evaluation.

Our development of the concept of the firm will be based first on an input-output analysis of economic exchange. Economic exchange is the fundamental mechanism by which we observe the firm's actions. Once economic exchange is thoroughly understood, we can then progress to a discussion of the economic functions of the firm; namely, financing, investing, and producing. Knowing these functions, we then inquire into the objectives the firm attempts to pursue in its functions. Since actual firms generally measure their functions and progress toward objectives in money terms, we then consider the firm's sources and uses of its funds as the means of

# 2

*measuring* the behavior of the firm. We then see that the firm pursues its objectives with regard to the future by examining investment opportunities, or *projects*, on the basis of their financial inputs and outputs.

## 2.2. Economic Exchange—The Input-Output Basis of the Firm

In economic analyses of the functions of financing, project evaluation and selection (investment), replacement, and divestment, we are basically concerned with the economic behavior of an economic entity called the *firm*. A firm may be an individual person, or sole proprietorship; a group of partners, or partnership; or a legally defined entity called a *corporation*. It may also be a *joint venture* consisting of several individual persons, partners, or corporations; a complex of corporations owned by another corporation (a *holding company*); or it can be any other social organization that, *as an entity, engages in economic exchanges for consideration or for things of economic value*. For economic analysis purposes, it matters little what the legal or social structure of the firm is. What is important, is that the *firm* acts as an *entity* when it engages in economic exchange.

The focus of our study is on the *exchanges* of goods and services between firms (organizations, companies, individuals). For example, for a grocery store the economic analyst is interested in the exchanges that take place when the store purchases bread, milk, and other commodities [the store's *cash* is exchanged to the wholesaler for the *commodities* (goods) *purchased*]. The analyst is also interested in the exchanges that take place when the grocery store sells bread, milk, and other economic goods to the public in exchange for cash. Similarly, for a home-appliance manufacturing company, the analyst is interested in the economic exchanges that take place when the *inputs* of steel, electrical parts, labor, and machinery are acquired by the firm. The analyst is also interested in the economic exchanges that take place when the *outputs* (refrigerators, stoves, washers, and dryers) are sold. Thus, to the economic analyst it matters not what the size or social organization of the firm is—only that the firm behave as an economic entity and engage in economic exchange in order to acquire its inputs and dispose of its outputs.

All firms acquire a diverse group of inputs, consisting of goods and services, money, and credit, in order to be able to provide outputs of goods and services to other economic entities. Thus, *exchanges* of goods and services are the basic activities common to all firms. *Exchanges* are the processes by which firms acquire the inputs of goods and services they need and by which they provide the outputs of goods and services that other firms require. Although each party to an exchange may think that he has increased his utility (benefited) from the exchange, the economist takes the position (with respect to both parties) that the objects, or things of value or the considerations exchanged, were equivalent in value at the time of the exchange.

In a pure barter economy (where there is no common medium of exchange such as money), firms would be limited to exchanges of economic goods and services *in kind* for other goods and services *in kind*. Thus, a farmer might exchange a dozen chickens and a pig with his neighbor for a month's supply of milk. (As recently as the early 1900's, it was a common custom in northern Arkansas and southern Missouri, where numerous water-powered mills were located, for farmers to trade a portion of their grain to the mill owner in exchange for the miller's service of grinding the grain to flour). In a complex economy, however, the barter system is obviously unusable because of its lack of flexibility.

In modern complex economies an artificial medium of exchange, called *money*, provides the flexibility that the barter system lacks. Money is basically cash and promises. Cash, both in the United States and many foreign nations, is merely the social promise of the State to provide, at some future date or upon demand an economic equivalent. Similarly, bonds, notes, accounts payable, and other kinds of future intents are simply promises of *firms* to provide, at some future date or upon demand, an economic equivalent. Together, the economist views *cash* and *promises to pay* as *credit*. Fundamentally, any complex society operates, in an economic sense, on the faith it places in its sources of credit (cash and promises to pay).

In a modern complex society, firms normally give up ownership of cash and promises (credit), which they possess, when economic goods and services are received from others; and they take in (acquire possession of) cash and promises in exchange for economic goods and services provided to others. Furthermore, the *value* of the economic goods and services exchanged in both directions (input and output) is usually quantified in terms of the customary monetary unit in local use (dollar, franc, pound sterling, etc.). A firm, or economic entity, may therefore *receive* or *give* in exchange any of the following objects, considerations, or "things:"

1. Economic goods and services,
2. Cash,
3. Promises to be satisfied in the future.

Thus, *exchange* can be defined as the reciprocal movement of economic elements of equivalent value between entities, which are firms, or in a special sense, households.

There are two equivalent halves to every exchange. One half, which the firm receives, is an input to the firm. The other half, which the firm gives up, is an output from the firm. Accountants refer to the considerations or goods that are received (or to be received) as *debits* and to the considerations or goods that are given up (or to be given up) as *credits*. Thus, when a grocery store receives cash for groceries sold, the cash received is a debit to the firm's *cash receipts*, and the equivalent value of the groceries given up is a credit to the firm's *sales*. Note in this example that an economic good (groceries) was exchanged for a promise (cash, which is the promise of the State to provide an equivalent economic good at some time in the future, upon demand). In all cases, accountants record both halves of the economic exchange in their books—one half as debits, the other half as credits. This is called *double-entry bookkeeping*, from the fact that every economic exchange undertaken by the firm is composed of two halves, one an input and the other an output.

At this point, let us summarize what has been postulated about the firm and its exchange processes. *First*, the economic analyst is interested in and deals with particular economic entities, called *firms*. A firm may be a person, a partnership, a corporation, or any combination of these social organizations. *Second*, the firm engages in exchanges of consideration or *things* of economic value. *Third*, the exchanges themselves provide the information necessary for economic analysis. *Fourth*, the assumption that each half of any given exchange is equal to the other in value, and measurable in money terms, allows the analyst to state and measure the economic position of the firm in terms of inputs and outputs at desired intervals of time.

**Example 2.2.1.** *Input-output exchange of a firm.* To demonstrate the concepts stated above, it will be helpful to use a numerical example of the history of a small firm. We shall analyze the economic whole life of this firm, from its inception to final dissolution. This example follows the analytical method presented by Schrader, Malcolm, and Willingham ([5], pp. 6–14), although it uses a somewhat different terminology and different numbers.

Tom Barnaby and Ron Perkins were students in the School of Forestry at Landgrant University in Excelsior City. Both had limited resources and had to work in order to attend the university. In their sophomore year, they realized that there was a growing market for fireplace wood, due to the housing boom in Excelsior City. They also discovered that several of the new housing developments were located in wooded areas, so that they could acquire the right to cut timber from the landowner for practically no cost. They reasoned that if they acquired the necessary equipment and if they worked together full time during the summer and part time during the fall, they could cut and sell fireplace wood and make enough profit to cover their expenses for the following year. On a handshake, they agreed to share all expenses and divide any profits equally and to try it for a year.

Subsequently, in order to get started, Tom and Ron each withdrew $200 from his savings account (a total of $400) and borrowed $800 from the bank to purchase a chain saw, axes, and a secondhand pickup truck, the last being for transportation and deliveries. Their pricing policy was to charge $20 per cord of wood, cash in advance, for wood ordered between June 1 and September 1 but delivered after September 1, and to charge $30 per cord for orders received on or after September 1 and delivered on an as-available basis. For wholesale deliveries (principally to supermarkets) a discount of 20% was allowed.

Their receipts of cash (net) from the sale of firewood amounted to $6,000 in their first year of operation. Since they judged their operation to be successful, they continued it a second year; in that year their net sales amounted to $8,000. They spent $1,000 for gasoline and oil the first year and $1,200 in the second year. Advertising in the local newspaper cost $150 the first year and $200 the second. Liability insurance was $100 each year, and repairs were $400 in the first year and $700 in the second year. Other incidental costs, including licenses and rental of land space to store the cut firewood, amounted to $100 per year. Timber rights were acquired from the housing developers for $100 in each year.

At the end of their second year of operation, their impending graduation the following June dictated that they dissolve their enterprise, so on December 31 they sold their used chain saw, axes, and pickup truck for $300. They also paid off their note to the bank, plus $144 interest for the 2 years.

We shall now make a simple accounting of Tom and Ron's business venture, with emphasis on economic exchanges. *First*, we note that they joined together as an informal partnership, but with a definite understanding about expenses and anticipated profits, as an economic entity—that is, they acted *as if* the entity was a firm. *Second*, the *firm* engaged in exchanges of considerations and things of economic value, as distinguished from what Tom and Ron did as individuals. *Third*, we should be able to make an economic analysis of the *firm* by examining the exchanges (inputs and outputs) in which it engaged over the 2-year period of its life. The major economic question to be asked by an analyst would probably be "Was the firm profitable?" This, indeed, is probably the major focus of economic analyses not only in going concerns but also in regard to possible future activities a firm may undertake in future time periods.

With the information given above, it should be easy enough to answer the profitability question for Tom and Ron's firm. In a money economy (that is, one in which the value of money remains constant), the firm was a profitable venture for Tom and Ron since it returned more *money* to them than they put into the firm. Together, they put in $400 and got back a net total of $8,706, as the tabulation of *cash* received and disbursed in Table 2.1 illustrates. For the time being, we shall assume that their money profit is also their economic profit, although this statement may be far from the truth as we shall later see.

**Table 2.1.** STATEMENT OF CASH RECEIPTS AND REIMBURSEMENTS FOR THE TOM-RON FIREWOOD FIRM—COMPLETE HISTORY

| | | |
|---|---:|---:|
| Cash received from | | |
| Tom's savings account | | $ 200 |
| Ron's savings account | | 200 |
| Bank loan | | 800 |
| Sale of firewood (net) | | 14,000 |
| Sale of used equipment | | 300 |
| Total cash receipts | | $15,500 |
| Cash disbursed for | | |
| Chain saw, axes, used pickup truck | $1,200 | |
| Gasoline and oil | 2,200 | |
| Advertising | 350 | |
| Liability insurance | 200 | |
| Repairs | 1,100 | |
| Miscellaneous | 200 | |
| Timber rights | 200 | |
| Bank loan repayment | 800 | |
| Interest on bank loan | 144 | 6,394 |
| Net cash receipts | | $ 9,106 |
| Cash returned to Tom and Ron | | 9,106 |
| Cash balance | | $ –0– |
| Cash returned to Tom and Ron | | $ 9,106 |
| Less cash invested by Tom and Ron | | 400 |
| Net Income to Tom and Ron | | $ 8,706 |

It is very important to note that the economic exchanges made by Tom and Ron's firm were with outside (third) parties and *not* between Tom and Ron. These dealings consisted of exchanges of objects and considerations of economic value between Tom's and Ron's *firm* and *other* parties, in terms of goods, cash, and promises. Let us now reexamine the exchanges of the firm in detail and concentrate on the nature of the inputs and outputs described by the exchanges in each transaction.

    1. First, Tom and Ron each invested $200 in the enterprise. From the firm's standpoint, $400 in cash is received as an input in exchange for a rather indefinite commitment to pay back this money to Tom and Ron at some undefined time in the future. In an economic sense, no service or utility is created by this exchange. The *use* of cash by the

firm *through time* has utility both to the *lender* (Tom and Ron, as individuals) and the *borrower* (the firm), but since no time has yet elapsed at the moment of the investment exchange, no economic benefit or cost is incurred by the firm. We would simply record the exchange for the firm as follows:

(1)

| | | |
|---|---|---|
| Object received (input): cash | $ 400 | |
| Object given (output): promise to repay owners | | $ 400 |

In the terminology used by accountants, items received by the firm (inputs) are called *debits* and items given up by the firm (outputs) are called *credits*. Thus, the exchange could also be recorded as follows:

| | | |
|---|---|---|
| Debit: cash | $ 400 | |
| Credit: promise to repay owners | | $ 400 |
| (Explanation: investment of $200 by Tom and $200 by Ron in the firm.) | | |

2. Additional cash was received by the firm as a result of the bank loan for $800. In exchange, a written promissory note was given to the bank by Tom and Ron, acting as the firm. In this case, the written promise to pay would be specific as to the time of repayment of the money and as to the interest to be paid for the use of it. Again no time has elapsed, however, so no economic benefit or cost *yet* results from this exchange. The basic nature of this exchange is, therefore, the same as the first exchange examined:

(2)

| | | |
|---|---|---|
| Debit (input): cash | $ 800 | |
| Credit (output): promise to repay bank | | $ 800 |
| (Explanation: executed promissory note for $800 to the First State Bank, payable in 2 years, and bearing simple interest at the rate of 9% per year. Interest is due on repayment of the note.) | | |

3. The firm purchased a used pickup truck, a chain saw, and axes for use in the business, paying cash for these items of equipment. This exchange is somewhat different from the preceding two exchanges, in that physical items essential to the business are now the inputs, and the output is cash. Cash is acceptable and useful to others only because it represents a general promise, or *future* receivable, from society in general (the State) for objects having present economic value. In transactions 1 and 2, the exchanges consisted of promises and cash. The third transaction

here, however, records an exchange of an economic good for a social promise, cash. We would record this exchange as follows:

(3)

| | | |
|---|---|---|
| Debit (input): truck and equipment | $ 1,200 | |
| Credit (output): cash | | $ 1,200 |
| (Explanation: to record purchase of pickup truck, chain saw, and two axes.) | | |

Social promises (cash and other promises to pay cash in the future) are often distinguished as *financial* objects from other goods and services, which are termed *economic* objects. The apparent need for distinguishing the two categories is that the economic value of a good or service is usually stated, at a given point in time, by the magnitude and kind of financial object given or received in exchange for the economic good or service. Hence, we hereafter refer to cash and promises to pay as financial objects and to products, materials, labor, and so forth as economic objects (goods and services).

4. Tom and Ron's firm sold an economic good (fireplace wood) to its customers in exchange for $6,000 in cash the first year and $8,000 in cash the second year. This exchange is similar to transaction 3, except that the input and output are reversed. Here, an economic good is the output, and a financial object (cash) is the input. Together, these two exchanges are recorded as follows:

(4)

| | | |
|---|---|---|
| Debit (input): cash | $14,000 | |
| Credit (output): sale of firewood | | $14,000 |
| (Explanation: to record sale of fireplace wood, $6,000 in Year 1 and $8,000 in Year 2, and receipt of cash.) | | |

5–10. The next group of 12 exchanges (6 kinds in each of 2 years) are all similar in nature. In each case, various economic objects (things of value) were received as inputs by the firm, and cash was given up as outputs in each exchange. These exchanges can be recorded (collectively) as follows:

(5)

| | | |
|---|---|---|
| Debit (input): gasoline and oil | $ 2,200 | |
| Credit: (output): cash | | $ 2,200 |

(6)

| | | |
|---|---|---|
| Debit (input): advertising service | $ 350 | |
| Credit (output): cash | | $ 350 |

(7)

| | | |
|---|---|---|
| Debit (input): liability insurance (a service) | $ 200 | |
| Credit (output): cash | | $ 200 |

(8)

| | | |
|---|---|---|
| Debit (input): repair parts and service | $ 1,100 | |
| Credit (output): cash | | $ 1,100 |

(9)

| | | |
|---|---|---|
| Debit (input): Licenses (an economic good of the State); rental of land space (an economic good) | $ 200 | |
| Credit (output): cash | | $ 200 |

(10)

| | | |
|---|---|---|
| Debit (input): purchase of right to cut timber (an economic good) | $ 200 | |
| Credit (output): cash | | $ 200 |
| (Explanation: To record amounts of economic goods and services received as inputs, and exchanges of each as outputs.) | | |

11. At the end of their second year of operation, Tom and Ron decided to dissolve their firm. They ceased business and sold their tangible equipment for $300 in cash. This exchange is the opposite of exchange 3 because here the firm has an input of cash and an output of economic goods (the used equipment). The firm may record this exchange as follows:

(11)

| | | |
|---|---|---|
| Debit (input): cash | $ 300 | |
| Credit (output): truck and equipment | | $ 300 |
| (Explanation: to record disposal of truck, chain saw, and axes.) | | |

12–13. Tom and Ron, acting as the firm, repaid the bank loan plus the interest due. The repayment of the $800 loan itself is simply an exchange of financial objects and is recorded as follows:

(12)

| | | |
|---|---|---|
| Debit (input): cancellation of promise to repay bank | $ 800 | |
| Credit (output): cash | | $ 800 |
| (Explanation: to record repayment of bank loan.) | | |

Although the interest payment of $144 will be recorded in a similar manner, the reasoning for the exchange is somewhat different. In return for the use of the bank's $800 over a period of time, Tom and Ron agreed to make a payment to the bank *in addition* to the $800. This additional payment, for the *use* of borrowed money over a period of time, is called *interest*. It is payment for an economic service rendered by another party; namely, the right to use the other party's money for a period of time. Cash paid by the firm to another party for the use of money is an output, whereas the input is the economic service itself (the use of the money), in the same sense that advertising *services* and insurance protection *service* are economic inputs to the firm, and the cash payments for these services are outputs. Thus, this exchange would be recorded as follows:

(13)

| | | |
|---|---|---|
| Debit (input): use of borrowed money (interest) | $ 144 | |
| Credit (output): cash | | $ 144 |
| (Explanation: to record the economic value of the use of borrowed money in exchange for a cash payment.) | | |

14. To conclude the exchange history of this firm, we need to take into account the return of the initial investments, $200 to Tom and $200 to Ron, which they advanced to the firm from their savings accounts. This exchange is the opposite of transaction 1, and it would be recorded as follows:

(14)

| | | |
|---|---|---|
| Debit (input): promise to repay owners | $ 400 | |
| Credit (output): cash | | $ 400 |

15. With reference now to the bottom three lines of Table 2.1, it is more difficult economically to analyze or evaluate the *net income* of $8,706 returned by the firm to the partners. In simplistic or naive economic terms, Tom and Ron provided *three* distinct economic services for the firm: (a) They provided the initial investment of $400 with which to begin business (the bank probably would not have lent them $800 without some personal investment); (b) they provided labor for the firm; and (c) they undertook an entrepreneurial or risk-taking venture.

Just as the bank is entitled to a cash payment for interest on its loan to the firm, Tom and Ron are entitled to a cash payment for interest on their own money lent to the firm (invested in it). In taking their money out of their savings account, the opportunity for them to collect interest payments on their $400 was precluded—that is, in economic language, the opportunity to keep $400 at interest in the bank was foreclosed, or foregone, in favor of investing it in the firm. In economic principle, it is proper for Tom and Ron to assess this foregone opportunity to collect bank interest as a *cost* against the firm. To the firm, this is called an *opportunity cost*, that is, a cost incurred by one alternative course of action as a result of foregoing another opportunity that would otherwise yield a benefit. So, part of the $8,706 is due to Tom and Ron simply as an equivalent interest payment on their investment of $400.

Since they both provided direct labor to the firm, they are also entitled to fair compensation for the number of hours they worked. In addition, under a simplistic interpretation of our enterprise economic system, if anything remains as positive net income after providing for labor and interest on investment, then the remainder belongs to the owners. In the same system, if a deficiency exists, then the owners must bear that loss, first as a loss of imputed interest on their investment and next as a loss of some or all of their original investment.

The first two services provided by Tom and Ron are evaluated by the opportunity cost principle. Assuming that the bank would have paid 5% simple interest for 2 years on their savings accounts had they left their money on deposit, then their investment of $400 in the firm would incur an imputed interest charge of $40 against the net return of $8,706 from the firm. Also, if they each worked an equivalent of, say, 20 weeks per year at half time each (20 hours per week), then together in 2 years they would have put in 1,600 man-hours of labor to the firm. To obtain an opportunity cost (imputed) wage rate for their firm, Tom and Ron would compare the *kind* of work they did with similar jobs in their geographical area and impute a wage rate for their labor. Cutting timber, manufacturing firewood, and delivering it is a skill only somewhat more advanced than unskilled labor. Assuming that a comparable wage rate for this skill in Excelsior City was $3.50 per man-hour, they would figure their second service of providing labor as being worth $5,600 = (20 wk/yr)(20 hr/wk)(2 men) (2 years)($3.50/man-hr).

By definition in a naive economy, the third (risk-taking) service is residual. Hence, the economic net income made by Tom and Ron is determined by difference:

| | | |
|---|---:|---:|
| Net income to Tom and Ron | | $ 8,706 |
| Less imputed interest on | | |
| investment | $ 40 | |
| Imputed Labor services | 5,600 | 5,640 |
| Difference = economic net income | | $ 3,066 |

We may now summarize what this example illustrates. *First*, to analyze an entity called a firm we look at the economic exchanges undertaken by the firm. *Second*, the whole-life exchanges of the firm sum to the total of the economic objects received (inputs) and given (outputs) by the firm over its life. The substance and nature of Tom and Ron's firm is illustrated in Fig. 2.1. Note that in every instance an exchange of a good or service is exactly offset by some amount of cash flowing in the direction *opposite* to the flow of the good or service. Note also that the economic *output* service of selling firewood required several other *inputs* of *economic goods and services*, which are exactly balanced by cash flows in the direction opposite to the flow of goods and services. This graphically illustrates the simple dynamic economic structure of the firm, in terms of its economic inputs and outputs and offsetting cash flows.

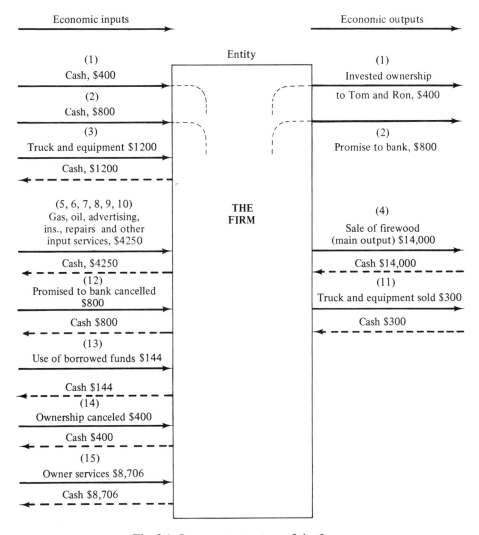

**Fig. 2.1.** Input-output nature of the firm.

## 2.3. Functions of the Firm:
### Financing, Investing, Producing

There are three fundamental types of exchange in which entrepreneurial firms engage, which in turn define the firm's basic functions. These exchanges are those by which the firm secures the capital it needs (financing), those by which it employs its available capital (investing), and those by which it generates financial returns on its invested funds (producing). Thus, the entrepreneurial firm is an entity that engages in economic exchanges in order to perform the functions of financing, investment, and production.

For our purposes, we may illustrate the firm and its financial exchanges in Fig. 2.2. The firm acquires capital funds from a source or sources of funds, called the *investor* or *lender*; invests the capital in one or more *investments*; hopefully receives returns from the investments over time; and then periodically pays *returns on capital* to the sources of capital. While this process is defined sequentially here, in actuality the typical business firm carries out these functions simultaneously and almost continuously, so that the process is a recursive one of seeking possible sources of funds, making investments, generating returns on the investments, and paying returns on capital.

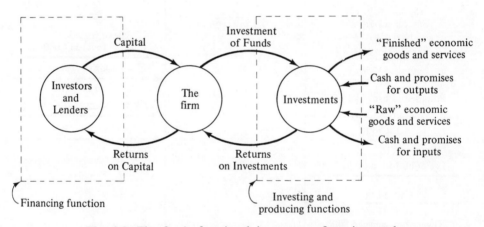

**Fig. 2.2.** The firm's functional investment, financing, and producing cycle.

The securing of capital from investors and lenders and the paying of returns on capital to these sources of the firm's funds is called the *financing function* of the firm. The capital funds that the firm obtains are of two types: equity funds and borrowed funds. Equity funds are obtained by the firm when it sells shares of stock, representing *ownership* of portions of the firm, to investors in exchange for cash or its equivalent. Investors invest their money for shares in the ownership of a firm in the expectation

18

of receiving returns on their invested capital. These returns on *equity* capital are generally called *dividends*, and in certain cases the returns may also include some preferential right or rights due to ownership, such as the right to convert one type of shares to another type or the right to preferential purchase of additional shares at a below-market price. In general, not only do owners of equity shares in a firm stand to receive dividends (and perhaps other preference items of ownership) if the firm is profitable, but also they stand to lose a part or all of their capital invested in the firm if the firm fails. Hence, the burden of uncertainty and risk is borne principally by the equity shareholders.

Capital is also secured by the firm from lenders. The term *lenders* includes all others who furnish money to the firm on a *lending* basis, that is, without ownership attributes being exchanged. Lenders retain title to the funds that are furnished to the firm. A firm may borrow funds from lenders such as banks, insurance companies, mortgage loan companies, bondholders, and any others who give the firm the right to use, but *not* own, a given sum of money (or other financial promises) for a stated period of time, in exchange for the payment of *interest* by the firm. Interest is the return on lent capital.

Capital may also be secured by the firm by retaining a portion of the *returns on capital* that it generates. This method of securing capital is called *retaining earnings*. Because the net earnings of the firm are themselves presumably the result of a prior equity capital investment by some investor or investors, however, it is conceptually proper to say that *all* net earnings of the firm belong totally to the equity investors. Hence, the retention of earnings by the firm is, in effect, a sequestering of something that rightfully belongs to the equity investors anyway. From this line of reasoning, a process that is equivalent to retaining earnings would be to pay out *all* the firm's net earnings to the equity investors and then promptly to *re*acquire new capital in the same amount from the same investors. Thus, we say that retention of earnings is a form of *raising* new capital for the firm, and retaining earnings is considered to be a part of the financing function of the firm.

Turning now to the investment and producing functions of the firm (see Fig. 2.2), we may suppose that at any given point in time the firm has available to it a finite number of opportunities for investing the funds that it has previously acquired from equity investors and lenders. Each such investment opportunity is termed an *investment project* or, simply a *project*. *In addition*, at the *same* point in time there may already be in operation a number of *production activities*, which are merely projects that existed at earlier points in time but which have been previously selected and executed. In other words, the distinction between a *project* and a *production activity* is simply this: A project is a *future* opportunity to generate a return on a *contemplated* investment, while a production activity is a *present* means already in existence of generating a return on an *actual* investment. Thus, the investment and production functions of the firm are interrelated, somewhat as follows.

At any given point in time, the set of unselected, available opportunities for investment is called the *candidate set* of projects, while the previously selected and executed set of projects is called the *production activities* set or *executed set of pro-*

*jects*. It is the *executed* set that accounts for the ongoing, day-to-day activities of the firm; that is, the set of production activities is what generates *present* sales, expenses, net income, and returns on investment. On the other hand, it is the *candidate* set of projects that is the opportunity set—the unselected set that offers opportunities for *new* projects (investments) that will generate *future* sales, expenses, and net incomes and opportunities for discontinuing unprofitable activities and projects (divestments).

The firm generally identifies investors and lenders, makes contractual arrangements with them, and obtains capital from them for the purpose of investing these funds in *future* projects. The firm does this with the express expectation of receiving returns on its investments from the projects that exceed, in the aggregate, the amounts of capital obtained and invested. *Only in this way* can the firm provide a return on capital to the investors and lenders and thereby assure a continuing source of new capital. *The firm itself owns no capital*; it merely employs the capital furnished to it by equity shareholders and lenders. The firm's managers, therefore, are simply stewards to the owners and lenders (investors). Management's stewardship includes not only the custody of and legal responsibility for the firm's physical and financial assets but also the moral and ethical responsibility to use the investors' capital efficiently and with integrity. Such moral and ethical responsibility is called *fiducial* responsibility. Fiducial integrity and stewardship in management requires that decisions regarding investment opportunities (projects) be made not only from the *standpoint of the firm*, so as to benefit the firm's investors, but also so that the firm's investors may be benefited as greatly as possible.

The decisions concerning investment projects and productive activities include then, in the most general sense, (1) whether to accept any, some, or all of the candidate set of *new* projects and (2) whether to continue with any, some, or all of the existing productive activities (investments) of the firm. These decisions are made from the *point of view of the firm*, by managers who stand as fiducial representatives of the firm's investors and lenders.

In some cases, such as small firms owned and managed by members of the same family group, ownership and management are vested in the same persons. In these cases, the fiducial responsibility problems resulting from separation of ownership and management do not exist. Large, long-established organizations tend to employ professional managers who actually own little of the firm's shares, however, and the managerial function becomes separated from the investor-owner. This is especially true of firms whose stocks are listed on the various stock exchanges and whose shares are widely held.

When the owner-investor function is separated from the managerial function (as in Fig. 2.2), the owner-investors do not necessarily exist as a cohesive group and often can exercise little actual control over the project selection policies of the firm. At best, their collective action is expressed in the stock market through the prices established for the firm's shares. At least theoretically, if the price of a firm's shares go down, the present owners are offering more shares for sale than the market can absorb. A possible cause would be dissatisfaction with the investment policies of the firm. Conversely, if the market price of a firm's shares increases, then potential buyers in effect are expressing confidence in the firm's future returns on capital, by demanding more of the firm's shares than the market can supply.

This leads us then to consider especially the *investment* function of the firm, which is illustrated in Fig. 2.3, and also to consider the *goals* (objectives) of the firm, which are discussed in the next section. Typically, the investment function of the firm is embodied in making a decision as to whether the firm should invest in a future project, in order to generate future returns on the investment, as depicted in Fig. 2.3. In order to make this decision, the firm examines the proposed project in terms of its required investment, its anticipated cash flows, and intangible factors that cannot be expressed in quantitative terms, such as social and environmental effects. The decision is then made to execute or to abandon the proposed project in accordance with some evaluation criterion or criteria that are consistent with the goals and objectives of the firm. This entire investment procedure is the subject of industrial project evaluation and selection.

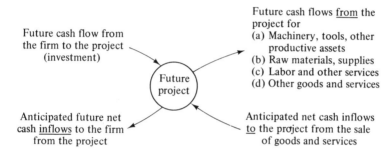

**Fig. 2.3.** Net cash flows in the investment function of the firm.

## 2.4. Objectives of the Firm

Firms are the basic building blocks of an entrepreneurial economy. It should be obvious from a layman's point of view and from everyday observation that individuals associate themselves with each other voluntarily in some form of organization, with objectives or ends that appear to be economic in nature, that is, for the purpose of economic gain. Having demonstrated that firms exist by their economic exchanges, it is now proper to ask the specific question, "What is, or should be, the nature of the firm's objectives in pursuing some kind of economic gain?" The answer is not nearly so simple as the question, however, since there are at least five distinct approaches in looking for answers to this question, each of which leads to a different kind of objective.

The first approach to determining the firm's objectives is given by *organization theory*, a body of knowledge accumulated by human behaviorists interested in explaining the firm in terms of organizational variables. As an example of this theory, we cite first an organizational concept due to Chester I. Barnard [1]. Essentially, Barnard develops the idea that man forms organizations by his willingness to coordinate his physical activities, in order to overcome environmental or physical (biological) limitations, so that a common purpose can be accomplished.

In Barnard's concept, three essentials must be present for an organization to exist in the short run: namely, (1) an agreed or commonly accepted purpose for the organization of human activity, (2) willingness and ability to provide economic goods and services on the part of the contributors, and (3) organizational communication. For long-run survival of the organization, Barnard requires that the utility (value) produced by the organization and distributed to its contributors shall exceed the costs incurred by the organization. For the simplified exchange model illustrated in Fig. 2.1, the equivalent of Barnard's requirement is that the persons or firms who *receive* the cash or other outputs from the firm *value* these payments more highly than the cash and economic goods and services that they provide to the firm.

A criticism of Barnard's concept, however, can be raised because it does not provide us with any specific organizational objective other than long-run organizational *survival* nor does it tell us how this is to be accomplished. In passing, it should also be noted that in many instances *organizational survival* is a pathologic state for *some* organizations and represents a dysfunctional departure from the original purpose, say, of providing a service to the public. Governmental organizations are particularly susceptible to this organizational disease of goal displacement toward pure *survival*.

Along a somewhat parallel vein, Simon [6] conceives of the principal objective of the firm as one of survival also—to survive comfortably and securely as a good-size organization—which it does by making "satisficing" decisions, not optimizing ones. Baumol [2] presents a compromise position for oligopoly cases (dominance in a market by relatively few producing firms). Again, however, the human behavior approach leads us to the conclusion that the firm tries to optimize no *quantifiable* variable whatsoever, thus leaving unexplained the commonly observed propensity for real firms to earn something called *profit*, which *is* quantifiable.

The second approach toward identifying the firm's objectives comes from simplistic or naive economic theory. The naive view has the rational entrepreneur maximizing his net profit—that which is left over after the firm has provided for the other production costs connected with the inputs of land, labor, and capital. According to the naive concept, the entrepreneur supposedly provides organizing, decision-making, and ultimate risk-taking functions as additional service inputs to the firm and is therefore entitled to a *profit* as a result of rendering these services. Hence, according to this concept, a firm should maximize its net profit in order to realize the optimum return on the decision-making, organizing, and risk-taking services provided.

There are several major problems with the naive theory. First, the ultimate risk taken by the firm belongs not to the firm itself but to its owners. Second, *ownership* is often separated from *control* of the firm, in that control is frequently vested in professional managers who bear little, if any, ultimate *risk* for the firm's success or failure. How does one then separate *net profit* as a reward between risk-taking and managerial control? Third, a theoretical deficiency exists in the naive theory. This deficiency was pointed out by Knight [4], who demonstrated that profit is equivalent to a difference between incomes in an economy in equilibrium and in disequilibrium rather than as compensation for risk-taking. In Knight's analysis, *profits* and *losses* are borne by *all* members of an economy and not by a special entrepreneurial class, so there is no profit element in the theory of income distribution. As a result, the attempt to locate some entrepreneur who has a prior claim to profit is equivalent to "looking in a dark room for a black cat which is not there" (Bronfenbrenner [3], p. 361). Hence, according to Knight (and others) the naive entrepreneurial-service theory is sterile and not workable—profit simply does not belong to the entrepreneur but to all members of the economy.

The third major approach in economic theory toward identifying the objectives of the firm comes from Knight [4], who has the firm maximizing net *revenue* (the accountant's *gross profit*). This is a corollary of Knight's opposition to the naive theory mentioned above. In the Knightian system, the firm supposedly maximizes *enterprise net income* on all implicit (nonpurchased) productive services lumped together—that is, it attempts to maximize gross profit.

The fourth principal approach toward identifying the firm's economic objective is due to Bronfenbrenner [3]. In this concept, profit is considered as compensation for only that subset of uncertainties that arises from having no *contractual* claim to one's income, per hour of labor, per piece of product, or per unit of land or capital. Bronfenbrenner concentrates, therefore, upon the incomes of those persons who accept, as *residual* claimants, part or all of what is left after contractual claims against the firm are honored and contractual claimants paid. Examples of residual claimants are the common and preferred stockholders (who hold only contingent claims to income), the salaried partner (who holds a contractual claim as to his salary, but only a residual claim as to his share of partnership net income), and the executive on the bonus list (who holds a contractual claim on his salary but only a residual claim on a possible bonus). From the contractual-residual concept of profit, Bronfenbrenner shows that a firm will adopt a profit-making objective *between* the extremes given by the naive theory (maximizing net profit) and the Knightian theory (maximizing gross profit). That is, the Bronfenbrenner firm will tend to use less entrepreneurial service input than the firm that maximizes gross profit and more entrepreneurial service input than the firm that maximizes net profit. Bronfenbrenner also shows that this type of objective, between the extremes of maximizing gross and net profits, is analogous to Simon's sociological concept of the organization adopting a "satisficing" mode of decision-making. It probably also lends weight to Simon's hypothesis that "businessmen do not know how to optimize, and even if they did, they wouldn't."

The fifth major source for identifying the goals of a firm lies in financial theory. *Finance* is an area of economic study that is concerned with (1) determining the amount of funds to employ in a firm, (2) allocating these funds efficiently among various assets, and (3) obtaining the best mix of financing in relation to the overall value of the firm (Solomon [7], Chapter 1). Originally a part of economics, finance evolved in the 1920's and 1930's as a separate area of study, and in the last 10 to 15 years it has progressed even further from a descriptive discipline (one that merely describes how firms are financed) to a normative discipline (one that describes how firms *ought* to be financed). In this evolutionary development, most of the modern authorities in the field of finance have come to reject the profit maximization theory that some economists still prefer.[1] Modern financial theory is somewhat closer to Bronfenbrenner's position.

What many modern financial authorities hold is that the objective of the firm should be to maximize the *future value of the firm* to its shareholders. If we assume that shareholders are the only ones among interested parties who have no contractual claims on the firm's income, then the value maximization concept is closely related to Bronfenbrenner's profit theory; however, it is not exactly the same thing. The reason is that Bronfenbrenner's theory does not take into account the *value of the firm* as it changes over time, whereas modern financial theory does exactly that.

The value of the firm is represented by the market value of the firm's shares, which, in turn, is a reflection of the firm's financing, investment, and dividend decisions. Financial value theory is broader than the profit theories because it includes not only Bronfenbrenner's concept of a residual net income return for noncontractual claims against income but also the ultimate effect of receiving these returns *over time* against a background of subjectively evaluated financing and investment decisions.

Thus, from the finance authority's point of view, all the profit maximization theories are found inferior, essentially because of the following reasons:

1. They do not specify the *timing* of expected net income, nor do they take into account the time value of money (the interest effect).
2. Profit theories do not consider the risk or uncertainties of the prospective net income streams. Some investment projects are far more risky than others. As a result, the firm's prospective net income stream may be more uncertain if these projects were undertaken.
3. Profit theories do not account for the risk differences that exist between firms as a result of the methods by which they are financed. This risk is known as *financial* risk and is a subjective function of the ratio of debt-to-equity capital used in a particular firm's capital structure.
4. Finally, profit theories do not allow for the effect of a firm's dividend policy on the market value of the firm's shares. If the firm were merely to maximize net earnings, it would never pay a dividend or, in general terms, never distribute a portion of net income to noncontractual claimants. As a minimum course of action, the firm could *always* improve net income simply by retaining earnings and investing them in Treasury bills or bonds. In that case, the market value of the firm's stock would be seriously reduced because of the lack of dividends, and the overall *value* of the firm would be less than if dividends were paid.

For these reasons, the maximization of any kind of net income is *not* the same as maximization of the *value* of the firm over time. The latter objective, according to

---

[1]See, for example, Solomon [7], Chapter 2.

financial theorists, is a more desirable one and is the one currently advanced by most authorities in this field. Maximization of shareholder wealth (the market value of the firm), *over time*, is now apparently the appropriate objective for an entrepreneurial-type firm (Solomon [7], Chapter 2). In the balance of this book, we shall assume that a firm's objective is the maximization of the *present value* shareholders' future wealth, as represented by the market prices and dividends related to the firm's shares. Future wealth is *directly* related to the future *cash flows* of projects accepted by the firm.

## 2.5. Sources and Uses of Funds

For the evaluation of a candidate project, we need a model of the cash flows of the project, year by year, over the life of the project. In essence, we need to construct a cash flow model, similar to Fig. 2.3, in which the elements that go to establish the *net* cash flows each year are identified year by year, from the time of inception of the project until its final life-end. To do this, a simple investment model will be described.

Projects usually are started with an investment, which is an estimated cash flow or flows moving *from* the firm *to* the project. Investment-type net cash flows, moving from the firm to the project, are arbitrarily given a negative sign. Thus, the net cash flow "$-100,000$" would indicate that $100,000 flows from the firm to the project at a particular point in time, and this is interpreted as a net investment of funds *by* the firm in the project.

More than one increment of investment by the firm can occur in the same project. For example, because of the lead time involved in designing and constructing a production facility and placing it "on stream," the investment of funds in the project may occur over several years. As an example, a refinery costing $100 million might require approximately 4 years to design and construct, so that the initial investment cash flows might be distributed somewhat as follows:

| Year | Net Cash Flow |
|------|---------------|
| 1 | $ −5,000,000 (design) |
| 2 | −10,000,000 (cost of site and initial land work) |
| 3 | −50,000,000 (construction costs) |
| 4 | −35,000,000 (construction costs and start-up) |

Initial investment costs are usually determined by skilled estimators and engineers who are experts in the process technology and construction methodology for a particular industry. Consulting engineering firms, who repeatedly design and specify processing equipment and plants for a given industry, are good examples, such as engineering firms who design electrical generating plants for private and public utilities concerns.

Smaller projects are often analyzed by in-house experts, provided, of course, that they have no vested interest in getting a project accepted. It is in this area that design and cost engineers are of particular value since their training and experience usually qualify them in the technology of their employer. Additionally they need only a knowledge of and emphasis in basic economic principles to equip them for making estimates not only for initial investments in small projects but also for the net cash inflows generated by the projects. Obviously, for a project to be worth the investment of funds, it should return to the firm over the life of the project a series of net cash inflows much greater than the initial investments.

Periodic cash inflows (from the project to the firm) are assumed to be generated by the *production function* of the project, given that the initial investments are made. In discrete cash flow analysis, these cash inflows are usually assumed to occur at specific points in time, equidistant apart, for example, at the end of each operating year. In continuous cash flow analysis (*funds flow* method), the cash flows are taken as flow *rates*, for example, in dollars per year. Cash flows *from* a project to the firm are considered to be positive valued (+). The discrete case is somewhat easier to describe and illustrate, which we do by example.

**Example 2.5.1.** *Periodic cash flow of a project.* Consider a typical project being considered by the ABC Company that is expected to develop a cash flow for the year 19xx as illustrated in Fig. 2.4.

ABC Company, Inc.

*CASH FLOW STATEMENT—TRANSFORMER PROJECT*

for the year ended December 31, 19xx

**SOURCE OF FUNDS**

| | | |
|---|---:|---:|
| Operating Revenues (Sales) | | $3,000,000 |
| Less: | | |
|     Cash operating costs (except | | |
|         interest paid) | $1,640,000 | |
|     Interest paid on debt | 60,000 | |
|     Income tax paid | 493,000 | 2,193,000 |
| Net Funds Generated from Operations | | $ 807,000 |
| Add: | | |
|     Sale of excess equipment and plant | | |
|         (net) | | 50,000 |
|     New borrowed capital (loan) | | 60,000 |
| Total Cash Inflow to Project: | | $ 917,000 |

**APPLICATION OF FUNDS**

| | |
|---|---:|
| Increase in Working Capital | |
|     of the Project During the Period | $ 167,000 |
| Repayment of Debt (Old Loan) | 140,000 |
| Capital Expenditures for New Equipment | 320,000 |
| Net Cash Return (Cash Inflow to ABC Company) | 290,000 |
| Total Cash Outflow from Project: | $ 917,000 |

**Fig. 2.4.** Funds flow statement for a project.

The statement in Fig. 2.4 indicates that the project is expected to develop $807,000 net income from its operations, to which other cash inflows of $50,000 and $60,000 are to be added representing the sale of excess equipment and proceeds from a new loan, respectively, for a total cash inflow *to the project* of $917,000. In the same period, $167,000 of this net cash inflow is to be retained in the project as an increase in its working capital, $140,000 is a cash outflow from the project to repay the principal on a former loan, $320,000 is a cash outflow for new equipment purchased, and the *balancing* amount of $290,000 is the net cash return *to* the firm (the ABC Company) from the project. Cash returns from a project to the firm, by arbitrary convention, are taken as positively signed (+). Thus, the net cash *in*flow to the firm from ABC's Transformer Project would be $ + 290,000 for 19xx.

The general nature of cash flow generation and application can be illustrated by a flow diagram, such as Fig. 2.5. Here the project itself generates $807,000 in cash from the operation of the project, called *net funds generated from operations*. This item is the result left from the *cash* inflow of operating revenues ($3,000,000) less *cash* outflows for operating costs ($1,640,000), interest ($60,000), and income taxes ($493,000). To the net funds generated by the project ($807,000), one adds $50,000 from the sale of excess equipment and $60,000 received from a new loan, making a total cash inflow to the project of $917,000. This is the total funds inflow, or *source*.

The total funds inflow to the project, $917,000, is used for several purposes. For example, it is used here for the purchase of new equipment ($320,000), which would result, for example, from the expansion of the project or from replacing existing worn-out equipment. It is also used here to retire an old loan ($140,000) and to increase working capital ($167,000). The balance remaining of $917,000 − 320,000 − 140,000 − 167,000 = $290,000 is called the *net* cash flow from the project for the year 19xx. This is the *cash flow* that remains after *all* cash inflows and outflows for the project are taken into account for a particular year. If it is positively signed, the flow is from the project to the firm; if it is negative, the net cash flow is from the firm to the project.

When we combine the investment cash flows *to* a project and the return cash flows *from* a project, the result is a series of net cash flows distributed by periods. This series is often called the *net cash flow stream* for the project, and it is upon this estimated stream that the firm decided whether to engage in the project. A typical *net* cash flow stream for a project might be illustrated as follows:

| End-of-Year: | 0 | 1 | 2 | 3 | 4 |
|---|---|---|---|---|---|
| Net Cash Flow: | $−50,000 | −10,000 | + 3,000 | +30,000 | +40,000 |

Even though the cash flows may actually take place throughout the year, each flow is often typically assumed to occur instantaneously at the *end* of each year, in order to simplify calculations when interest is considered. Calculations with interest and interest factors will be discussed in Chapter 3.

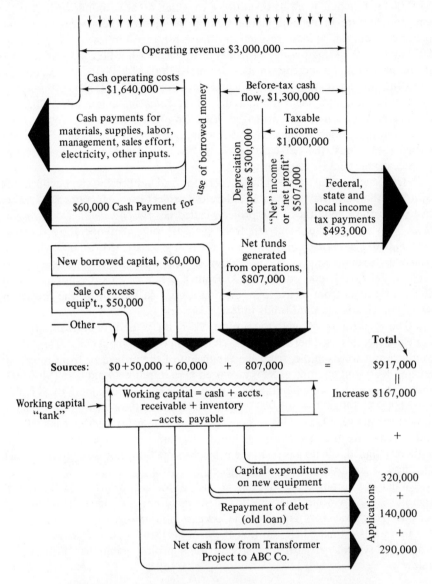

**Fig. 2.5.** Illustration of cash flow generation and application. (Adapted by permission from *Engineering Economy* by Gerald W. Smith, 2nd ed., (c) 1973 by Iowa State University Press, Ames, Iowa 50010.)

## 2.6. Summary

In this chapter we have developed some important economic concepts about the entrepreneurial firm. We shall now summarize these concepts.

*First*, the firm was defined as an entity that engages in economic exchanges for the purpose of making a gain. This concept was illustrated by an example using a series of economic exchanges to delineate the economic life of a simple firm. The economic exchanges were described as a series of inputs and outputs of the firm, from which an ultimate net gain was realized for the owners of the firm. The nature of the final gain was then analyzed by using the concept of *opportunity cost*, by which we factored the gain into a return on input investment, a return on input labor, and an economic profit.

*Second*, the three functions of the entrepreneurial firm were described and illustrated. These three functions (financing, investment, and production) are in reality merely classifications of *particular* economic exchanges in which the firm engages. *Financing* includes all those exchanges by which the firm acquires funds from owners and lenders in exchange for future promises to pay returns on capital (dividends and interest on equity and borrowed capital). *Investing* includes all the anticipated exchanges by which the firm expects to invest funds in projects, in anticipation of receiving returns from each executed project on the invested funds. The investing function is described by the economic exchanges that result in a *net cash flow stream* for each project. *Production* is seen as the function that includes all the economic exchanges pertaining to the operation of a group of projects after they have been selected and placed in operation by the firm.

*Third*, the objectives of the firm were examined in detail, from both sociological and economic standpoints. It is finally urged, for purposes of economic analysis, that the firm's objective should be maximization of the shareholder's wealth over time.

*Fourth*, the concept of *funds flow*, or generation of cash flow by a project, was considered in detail in order to demonstrate how production activities generate net cash inflows to the firm from executed projects. The net cash flow stream, a discrete or continuous function of time, is the basic economic measure of a project used to determine its profitability to the firm.

## REFERENCES

[1] BARNARD, CHESTER I., *The Functions of the Executive* (Cambridge, Mass.: Harvard University Press, 1938).

[2] BAUMOL, WILLIAM J., *Business Behavior, Value and Growth* (New York: Macmillan, 1959), Chapters 4, 6–8.

[3] BRONFENBRENNER, MARTIN, "A Reformulation of Naive Profit Theory," *Southern Economic Journal*, **26** (4) (April, 1960); also reprinted in Breit, Wm., and H. M. Hochman

(ed.), *Readings in Microeconomics* (New York: Holt, Rinehart and Winston, 1968), pp. 359–370.

[4] KNIGHT, FRANK H., *Risk, Uncertainty, and Profit* (Boston: Houghton-Mifflin, 1921).

[5] SCHRADER, WILLIAM J., ROBERT E. MALCOLM, and JOHN J. WILLINGHAM, *Financial Accounting: An Input/Output Approach* (Homewood, Ill.: Richard D. Irwin, Inc., 1970).

[6] SIMON, HERBERT, *Models of Man* (New York: Wiley, 1957), Chapter 10.

[7] SOLOMON, EZRA, *The Theory of Financial Management* (New York: Columbia University Press, 1963).

# PROBLEMS

**2-1.** From an economic standpoint, what is a firm?

**2-2.** Define the following terms: (a) economic good, (b) service, (c) input, (d) output, (e) commodity, (f) exchange, (g) money, (h) cash, (i) credit.

**2-3.** Describe an economic *exchange*.

**2-4.** The exchanges of the U-Drive-Em Golf Range Company are as follows:

19XX

| | |
|---|---|
| January | (1) Two men invest $16,000 each to form the company. |
| | (2) The company purchases a 200 × 750 ft lot adjacent to a developing shopping center for $8,000. |
| February | (3) The company purchases the necessary lighting and equipment for $12,000. |
| | (4) The company purchases 4,000 golf balls, paying $2,000 in cash. |
| March–June | (5) Second quarter revenue is $5,000. |
| | (6) Expenses for the second quarter are electricity, $750; repairs and maintenance, $260. |
| July | (7) The company purchases 2,000 additional golf balls, paying $1,000 cash. |
| July–Sept. | (8) Revenue in the third quarter is $6,000. |
| | (9) Expenses in the third quarter are electricity, $900; repairs and maintenance, $300. |
| October | (10) A large department store wants to locate in the shopping center and offers the company $24,000 for the lot. |
| November | (11) The company sells its lighting and equipment for $8,000 and accepts the offer from the department store. |
| December | (12) The remaining cash is distributed to the owners. |

*Requirements:*

(a) Record the exchanges as debit and credit transactions.

(b) Prepare an income statement (per Fig. 2.1) from your record of the transactions.

(c) If each owner spent an average of 30 hr per week, from March 1 to November 15, operating the range and if comparable wages in the area are $3.50 per hr for this kind of work (opening up, turning on lights, renting clubs and buckets of balls, picking up balls, etc.), how much net profit did each owner make?

**2-5.** What are the fundamental types of exchange that business firms engage in?

**2-6.** What is meant by *to invest*?

**2-7.** From the standpoint of project analysis, what is an *investment*?

**2-8.** What is the *financing function* of the firm?

**2-9.** What relates the financing and the investing functions of the firm?

**2-10.** What is the difference between an *owner* and a *lender*?

**2-11.** How is an investment project defined?

**2-12.** What is meant by the *fiducial* responsibility of the management of a firm? Why is this responsibility carefully defined and protected under the laws of most states?

**2-13.** Describe three possible goals of an entrepreneurial firm.

**2-14.** Why is the goal of maximization of *net income* not the same as maximization of the *value of the firm* over time?

**2-15.** What is the principal difference (in words) between *net profit after taxes* and *net cash flow* for a firm in a particular year?

**2-16.** What is the reason for concentrating upon the expected *cash flows* in evaluating a proposed project rather than upon its anticipated *net incomes*?

**2-17.** From a recent annual report of a company whose stock is traded on one of the major stock exchanges, construct a funds flow (cash flow) statement from the balance sheets and income statement given in the report. Compare your funds flow statement to the one provided in the annual report (if it is given).

# INTEREST, INTEREST FACTORS,
# AND EQUIVALENCE

## 3.1. What Is Interest?

Most persons who approach the subject of economic evaluation for the first time do so with a simplistic notion of *interest*. Usually, the elementary idea is that interest is money paid by a borrower for the use of money borrowed from a lender or, from the standpoint of the lender, it is "hire" money received for the use of money lent. While it is true that interest *payments* are transacted in this manner, this *money payment* concept of interest is much too restricted and narrow for our purposes in making economy studies. What is needed is a more fundamental understanding of the concept of interest and of the function it plays in the formation of capital goods and productivity.

The real meaning of interest lies at a deeper conceptual level, and it is important for a student newly arrived in the field of economic evaluation to develop a correct grasp of the interest concept and the functions performed by interest in our economy. While interest rates are, in general, established by market conditions and are therefore part of the uncertain future with which we must deal in making economic evaluations of projects, nevertheless, we can gain considerable insight into the nature of interest and its functions by examining *interest theory* under what are called *perfect capital market* conditions. So that we can gain this insight, we shall briefly review here the traditional interest theory model under perfect capital market conditions, as initially developed by Irving Fisher [2] and later extended by J. Hirshleifer [4], [5].

# 3

**3.1.1.** *Perfect capital market assumptions.* The assumptions generally made about *perfect* capital markets can be summarized somewhat as follows:

1. *Financial markets are perfectly competitive.*

   In such a market, no individual or firm is considered to be large enough to affect prices (interest rates) by his actions in the market. Another way of interpreting this assumption is that every borrower and lender trades in such small amounts that no one borrower or lender has any appreciable effect on the level of interest rates.

2. *There are no transaction costs.*

   Because of this assumption, all transactions occur at market prices (interest rates), and furthermore there are no market costs or consequences associated with bankruptcies, brokers, middlemen, mergers, etc. Likewise, there are no transaction taxes.

3. *Information is complete, costless, and available to all.*

   Market prices (interest rates) and all other market factors must be fully known to all. Otherwise, for example, some would borrow (or lend) at rates other than the market rate (which would violate the fourth assumption below). Moreover, *complete* information implies perfect knowledge about future events and future outcomes, not only of one's own actions but also of all others operating in the market.

33

4. *All individuals and firms are able to borrow and lend on the same terms.*
Another way of stating this assumption is to say that there is but one interest rate; it is known with certainty at all times and all individuals and firms can borrow or lend at that rate. Such a market would be characterized by an unlimited supply of funds as well as an unlimited "sink" for funds, so that funds could be borrowed (or invested) as needed at the known interest rate.

While no financial market in reality meets the test of these assumptions four-square, nevertheless, many securities markets in which there is open trading come sufficiently close so that even our *perfect market* interest models give us good approximations to actual behavior.

**3.1.2.** *The consumption basis of single-period intertemporal exchange.* Considerable insight into the nature of *interest* can be gained by examining the consumption behavior of an individual, whose income is fixed, in a perfect capital market. To concentrate on the essential principles, assume that time may be expressed simply as *now* and *later*, so that only *one time period* exists between the two instants. Thus, *now* is taken as time $t = 0$, and *later* is taken as time $t = 1$. Later might be tomorrow or next year or even 10 years from now. The essential point is that there is only *one* time period between $t = 0$ and $t = 1$. Suppose that the perfect capital market assumptions, stated in Section 3.1.1, are applicable, and suppose also that an individual is planning his consumption pattern over this single time period—i.e., he will consume some now and some later. Then, certain events, such as consumption, borrowing, and lending, will occur at time $t = 0$ and again at $t = 1$.

The individual's sole problem, we assume, is to choose from alternative combinations of total consumption. The only knowledge we assume about the individual's preferences is that he prefers more consumption to less at any given time. For example, if he has the choice of (1) consuming $100 worth of goods now and $100 worth later or (2) consuming $110 now and $100 later, he would choose alternative 2.

Now, in this system the individual is limited in the amount he can consume by two factors: (1) his income and (2) the available terms under which he can *transfer* income from time $t = 0$ to $t = 1$, and vice versa. For convenience, let us assume that prices are stable and also that the amount of the individual's consumption can be measured in dollars. In a world of certainty the individual would know his income exactly (for example, $100 now and $100 later). Thus, his income is limited but known in amount. As to the second factor (transferal of income from one instant in time to another), there exists a capital *market* that governs the individual's opportunities for transferal. Just as there is a market for trading fruits, vegetables, and other produce, there is also a market for trading this year's income for next year's. Such a market is called an *intertemporal funds* or *capital market*, and its operation is assumed to be governed by the perfect capital market conditions stated in Section 3.1.1.

The terms of trade in the capital market obey the forces of supply and demand for intertemporal shifts in income, just as the terms for trading fruits and vegetables depend on the forces of supply and demand for those commodities. Unlike other markets, however, Fisher [2] tells us that in the intertemporal capital market man displays an inherent tendency to consume his income immediately and not to postpone the purchase of goods and services. If, however, he abstains from spending all his present income, the difference between his present income and his present consumption is said to be *savings*.

Man saves, Fisher says, only because there is an inducement to do so. The inducement is that *tomorrow's consumption is made more attractive (more valuable) than today's consumption*. The premium for saving today—and thus transferring consumption from today to tomorrow—is provided by the capital market and specifically is the *interest rate* established for valuing the intertemporal transfer of funds. As an example, one might forego spending $1 of this year's income in exchange for being able to spend an additional $1.07 next year. Such a trade can be thought of as *lending* since present ($t = 0$) consumption is reduced by $1, which is then lent in the intertemporal capital market, in order to receive an increase of $1.07 in next year's ($t = 1$) spendable income. Alternatively, one might forego $1.07 of next year's income at $t = 1$ in order to increase his present ($t = 0$) consumption by $1. This trade can be thought of as *borrowing*.

Transaction costs, or imperfections in the market that might cause a difference in the rates of interest for borrowing and lending, would result in differences in the *terms* (conditions) for borrowing and lending in the market. Hence, in a *perfect* capital market, we speak only of *the* terms by which present consumption is traded for future consumption, or vice versa. The concept of *the* terms is totally encompassed in and expressed as the *rate of interest*. In the foregoing example, $1 of present income (consumption) is traded for $1.07 of future income (consumption), and the *rate of interest* is expressed as a fraction of the present amount, thus:

$$\text{Rate of interest} = \frac{\$1.07 - \$1.00}{\$1.00} = 0.07.$$

Much of the foregoing discussion can be illustrated advantageously by an example and a simple graphical model. Consider the situation faced by Mr. A, whose income *stream* in a simple world of a single time period would consist of $Y_0 = \$100$ at time $t = 0$ (now) and $Y_1 = \$100$ at time $t = 1$ (next year). It is assumed that Mr. A's entire *wealth* is represented by his basic income stream. Thus, Mr. A's initial income position is represented by point $Y$ in Fig. 3.1. The point $Y$ is called the intertemporal *endowment position* and represents the anticipated current and future incomes *endowed* on Mr. A before he enters into trading in the capital market.

It would appear that Mr. A's consumption pattern is completely dictated by his fixed income stream—i.e., he could spend $100 now and $100 next year. In the presence of a capital market, however, this is not necessarily the case. In fact, Mr. A can *transfer* income and consumption from one time to another, anywhere along the *market line X-W, as he chooses*. He can trade this year's consumption for next year's by lending some or all of this year's income. If he reduces current consumption to zero and *lends* all this year's income, then next year he can consume not only his next year's endowment income of $100 ($t = 1$) but also the $107 equivalent of *this year's* endow-

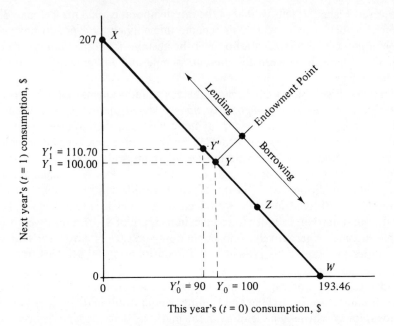

**Fig. 3.1.** Intertemporal borrowing and lending.

ment income. His consumption pattern, therefore, would be zero at time $t = 0$ and $207 at time $t = 1$, which corresponds to point $X$ in Fig. 3.1. Similarly, he could *borrow* against next year's income, receiving $100/(1 + 0.07) = \$93.46$ now, and thereby increase his present consumption upward from $100 (his present income endowment) to $193.46. His next year's endowment income ($100) would just repay his borrowing, however, so his consumption pattern would be $193.46 at time $t = 0$ and zero at time $t = 1$. This situation corresponds to point $W$ in Fig. 3.1. If, however, he lends or borrows only a portion of his endowment income, he can consume *any combination* lying on the line $X$-$W$. Thus, for example, if Mr. A reduces his consumption (see Fig. 3.1) at time $t = 0$ to $Y'_0 = \$90$, then he is said to *save* the difference ($10) between his endowment income at $t = 0$, $Y_0 = \$100$, and his actual consumption, $Y'_0 = \$90$. By *lending* his present savings of $10 in the capital market now, he can receive back $10.70 next year, which will increase his next year's consumption to $110.70. This consumption pattern corresponds to point $Y'$ in Fig. 3.1. In a similar fashion, he might wish to increase his present consumption by *borrowing* from future income, in which case he would arrive at a consumption pattern corresponding to some point, say $Z$, on the market line.

Which consumption pattern—i.e., which point on the market line—should Mr. A choose? In a perfect market situation where borrowing and lending can occur at the same rate of interest, he should choose the point on the market line he likes best. Thus, *the choice of a particular consumption pattern is independent of the market rate of interest* in a perfect capital market. Mr. A would not, however, choose an *interior* consumption point inside the area $OXWO$ since such a choice would correspond to his giving away some of his consumption opportunity. Because consumption is assumed to be desirable, any interior consumption point is inferior to points lying on the market line; thus, rational consumption combinations lie only on the market line.

The market line can be described by its slope and an intercept. The *slope* corresponds geometrically to the rate of exchange at which the market permits the trading of current consumption for future consumption, i.e., to the *rate of interest*. Specifically, the one-period rate of interest, $i$, is defined as the *premium* on the relative value of current over one-year-in-the-future consumption claims. Looking at it another way, if current consumption is sacrificed (i.e., saved, or negatively enhanced) in the amount $Y_0' - Y_0 = -\Delta Y_0$ and if future consumption is thereby enhanced through operation of the market in the amount $Y_1' - Y_1 = \Delta Y_1$, then the *rate* of enhancement (per unit of $-\Delta Y_0$) is

$$(1 + i) = - \frac{\Delta Y_1}{\Delta Y_0}$$

and consequently the slope of the market line is $\Delta Y_1/\Delta Y_0 = -(1 + i)$. Since the market rate of interest is assumed to be applicable to all persons and firms in both borrowing and lending situations, in a one-period model ($t = 0, 1$) any given individual's set of consumption patterns at $t = 0$ and $t = 1$ can be fully described by the *intercept* of a market line passing through his *endowment position*. The convention is to use the horizontal intercept—the amount, for example, Mr. A could consume this year by foregoing all claims to future income. This is the *present value* of his endowed income stream or alternatively, his *wealth*. In Fig. 3.1, Mr. A's wealth is $193.46, signified by point $W$.

How is *present value*, or *wealth*, determined in general? It is simply the *market value* of the individual's endowment of present and future consumption claims (income). In Fig. 3.1, if $Y_0$ is a present endowed income amount (a claim to present consumption) and $Y_1$ is a similar endowed claim to next year's income, then the present market value, $W$, is by geometry

$$W = Y_0 + \frac{Y_1}{1 + i}. \tag{3.1}$$

To summarize the foregoing development, the capital market establishes the rate of transformation of current and future consumption, and this rate is equal to $(1 + i)$. That is, future consumption can be increased by a factor of $(1 + i)$ for each unit by which current consumption is reduced or, conversely, present consumption can be increased by one unit if future consumption is decreased by $(1 + i)$. The line representing the consumption opportunities available to an individual is fixed by his income *endowment* and the *market rate of interest* at which he can borrow and lend.

Given an individual's particular income endowment, the intercept of the market line on the present consumption axis is called the individual's *present value*, or *wealth*. All income streams that have the same present value, *regardless of initial endowment* (e.g., $Y_a$, $Y_b$, $Y_c$, ..., in Fig. 3.2) lie on the *same* present value line, e.g., on $XW$. Different initial income endowments (e.g., $Y'$) *with different present values*, such as $W'$

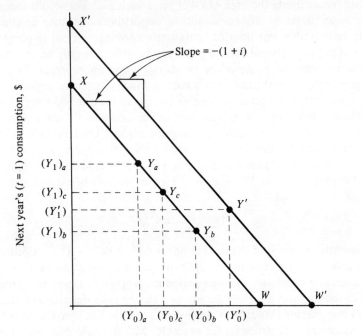

**Fig. 3.2.** Market model with different endowments.

in Fig. 3.2, will lie on different present value lines, e.g., $X'W'$. The present value lines through both $XW$ and $X'W'$ have a common slope of $-(1 + i)$ and are therefore parallel.

**3.1.3. *Multiperiod intertemporal exchange.*** The single-period capital exchange model can be extended in a rather straightforward manner by analogy to several periods. For the two-period case, consider Fig. 3.3 and the following discussion.

The individual has an income stream, represented by the vector **OY**, consisting of income amounts $\mathbf{Y} = (Y_0, Y_1, Y_2)$ to be received at times $t = (0, 1, 2)$, respectively. The market rate of interest in effect between $t = 0$ and $t = 1$ (period 1) is $i_1$, and the rate between $t = 1$ and $t = 2$ (period 2) is $i_2$. Perfect conditions are assumed to apply so that borrowing and lending can take place freely at those rates. The opportunities for consumption available to the individual under these conditions (assuming no give away of income) are defined by a *plane* in space, such as the plane bounded by points **WXZ** in Fig. 3.3. The point **Y** of the endowment income vector, **OY**, lies in this plane. By analogy with the single-period model, the angles $\phi_{0,1}$ and $\phi_{1,2}$ are defined as

$$\phi_{0,1} = \tan^{-1}(1 + i_1), \qquad \phi_{1,2} = \tan^{-1}(1 + i_2).$$

Point **W**, the point at which the plane intersects the $t = 0$ axis, indicates the maximum amount available for consumption at time zero if nothing is consumed at times $t = 1$

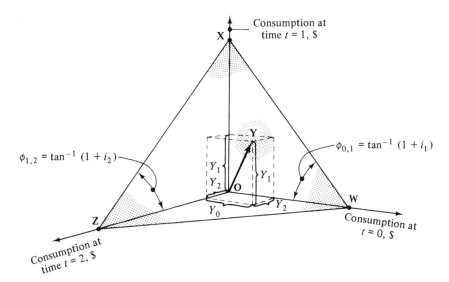

**Fig. 3.3.** Two-period intertemporal exchange.

and $t = 2$. Hence, the numerical value at point **W** is the *present value* of the income stream $(Y_0, Y_1, Y_2)$. To determine the equivalent value of **W**, the equivalent components of income vector **OY** are summed along the $t = 0$ axis. Thus:

$$\mathbf{W} = Y_0 + \frac{Y_1}{\tan \phi_{0,1}} + \frac{Y_2}{(\tan \phi_{0,1})(\tan \phi_{1,2})}$$

$$= Y_0 + \frac{Y_1}{(1+i_1)} + \frac{Y_2}{(1+i_1)(1+i_2)}.$$

Hence, by simply knowing the endowment income vector $\mathbf{OY} = (Y_0, Y_1, Y_2)$ and the interest rates, we may find the present value of the endowment vector. Since the terminus of this vector, **Y**, is a point in the present value *plane*, all other points in the plane will have the same present value. Then by analogy with the single-period model, all present value planes for other endowments will lie parallel to each other, and the one most remote from the origin will have the largest present value.

This line of reasoning and development extends directly to the $N$-period case. The present value, or wealth, of the individual is then given by

$$\mathbf{W} = Y_0 + \frac{Y_1}{(1+i_1)} + \frac{Y_2}{(1+i_1)(1+i_2)} + \cdots + \frac{Y_N}{(1+i_1)(1+i_2)\cdots(1+i_N)}$$

$$= \sum_{t=0}^{N} \frac{Y_t}{\prod_{j=0}^{t}(1+i_j)} \tag{3.2}$$

where $Y_t$ is the income stream at time $t$ and $i_j$ is the assumed known interest rate in effect during period $j$, i.e., from $t = j - 1$ to $t = j$. (Note that, by definition, $i_0 = 0$ since there is no period corresponding to $t = -1$ to $t = 0$.)

In general, then, we can state that under perfect market conditions any two income streams with the same present value are exactly equivalent since they provide the same potential consumption alternatives to an individual. If one income stream has a greater present value than another, however, it will provide *increased* consumption alternatives *in all combinations* relative to the smaller. The converse is also true. Hence, present value is also referred to as *wealth* since two persons with the same wealth are assumed to have the *same consumption opportunities*, even though one may choose a different combination of spending than the other.

Two further observations should be made concerning Eq. (3.2). In most practical investment applications it is generally customary to assume that the current market interest rate will maintain itself into the future without change, so then all the $i_j$ are equal to a common value, $i$, and Eq. (3.2) for present value becomes simply

$$\mathbf{W} = Y_0 + \frac{Y_1}{(1+i)} + \frac{Y_2}{(1+i)^2} + \cdots + \frac{Y_N}{(1+i)^N}$$

$$= \sum_{t=0}^{N} Y_t(1+i)^{-t}. \tag{3.3}$$

Second, it is obvious from Eq. (3.2) and (3.3) that the *compound* interest method is the economically (theoretically) correct one to use for calculation procedures in economic evaluation—not simple interest, as some writers claim.

**3.1.4. *The equilibrium market price concept of interest rates.*** A complete understanding of the function of capital markets and interest cannot be gained by simply examining the *consumption* behavior of an individual who makes intertemporal trades in a *perfect* capital market. This is only half the story. The other half arises because of the *productive* function supplied by the capital market. To motivate a discussion of the productive aspects of the capital market, let us begin by reviewing some concepts about production-type organizations.

For convenience, the *generalized factor inputs* to any productive-type organization may be categorized as (1) *land*, or natural resources;[1] (2) labor; and (3) capital.[2] *Natural resources* (land) are assumed to be provided by Nature in fixed supply. The amount paid, or *return*, for the use of land is termed *economic rent* by the economist. *Human labor*, the second input factor to the productive process, is assumed to be determined by biological and social determinants. The *return* to the laborer, whether he be ditchdigger or corporation executive, is called *wages*—the amount paid for the labor consumed in the productive process. These two factors taken together—natural resources and labor—are called (in economic terms) the *primary factors of production*, since their supply is largely determined *outside* the economic system itself.

---

[1]Natural resource inputs of all kinds, including land, are often called simply *land* (in a generic sense) by the economist.

[2]As Hirshleifer ([5], pp. 399–400) points out, however, these three classifications are arbitrary and traditional only, probably originating among early English economists in the 18th and 19th centuries when there was an obvious three-class society in England (the landowning aristocracy, the working peasant, and the capital-lending middle class). In economic terms, these separate factor inputs are today not functionally defensible.

The third input, *capital*, is produced *within the economic system proper*, however. It is an *intermediate* factor in the productive process. Capital is both an *output* of the productive process and an *input* to it also. Capital, in the form of *real capital* or *capital goods*, is produced by the productive system. For example, an injection molding machine is a machine tool. In economic parlance, it is called a *real-capital* item, or a capital good, and it is the *output* of certain manufacturing operations (a productive process) used to make it. Once a real-capital item has been produced, it can then be *rented out* (leased or sold) for *hire money* in the market place, just as the primary productive inputs can. The real-capital item is then used as an input in another productive process. For example, the injection molding machine can be used to produce ball-point pens, which are then sold to consumers. The services of the molding machine are thus an *input* into a productive process also. Hence, we say in economic terms that real capital is an input factor to the productive system, as well as being an output of it also.

Why, and how, are the intermediate factors of production—i.e., real capital or capital goods—produced? The question, "How?", can be answered as follows. Quite simply, all intermediate productive factors (capital) are produced by a process in which the following occur:

1. Some individuals in the economy refrain from *total* consumption of goods and services produced within the economic system, thereby generating savings.
2. Other individuals in the economy employ the resulting *savings* to produce and use real-capital items, such as tools, buildings, and equipment, that can, in turn, produce other consumption goods.

The answer to the question, "Why?", is somewhat more difficult. In general, the economist takes it as a *technological fact of life* that society can realize more future consumption, *in total and in the long run*, by using indirect or roundabout production methods. This requires the use of tools and concentration of productive effort in factories. As Fisher [2] indicates, however, man displays an inherent tendency to consume immediately and *not* to postpone consumption from today until tomorrow.

If this is so, what is it that induces man to postpone consumption, thereby creating savings, and then to invest his savings in the production of intermediate capital goods? Quite obviously, the inducement must be the expectation of receiving *more* tomorrow than he *saves* today. In other words, the inducement is that tomorrow's consumption can be made larger (more valuable) than that which is foregone today. *This is the basic function of interest to the consumer:* to make tomorrow's goods relatively more valuable than today's. But the supply of interest *is generated from the "rental" of the intermediate capital goods.* That is, while some individuals in the economy postpone consumption and thereby create savings, others in the economy *use* these savings, in the converted form of machines and other capital goods, as intermediate productive inputs. They (the users of the intermediate goods) in turn, pay *rent* for the use of these goods, and this rent becomes the *interest* paid to the savers. Thus, *from a productive standpoint*, interest is looked upon as a *return* on an investment in intermediate capital goods. In Fisher's words ([2], pp. 14–15), the process is as follows:

... The *value* of capital [goods] must be computed from the value of its estimated future net income, not *vice versa.*

This statement may at first seem puzzling, for we usually think of causes and effects running forward not backward in time. It would seem that income is derived from capital; and in a sense, this is true. Income [i.e., services] *is* derived from capital *goods*. But the *value* of the income is not derived from the *value* of the capital goods. On the contrary, the value of the capital [goods] is derived from the value of the income. . . .

These relations are shown in the following scheme in which the arrows represent the order of sequence—(1) from capital goods to their future services; that is, income; (2) from these services to their value; and (3) from their value back to capital value:

Capital goods $\longrightarrow$ flow of services (income)

$$\downarrow$$

Capital value $\longleftarrow$ income value

Not until we know how much income an item of capital will probably bring us can we set any valuation on that capital at all. It is true that the wheat crop depends on the *land which yields it*. But the *value* of the crop does not depend upon the value of the land. On the contrary, the *value of the land depends upon the expected value of its crops*. (Italics supplied).

From a *productive* standpoint, the interest rate is viewed as a *return rate*—i.e., the ratio of the *income value* produced to the *capital value* of the intermediate goods. From the *consumer's* standpoint, the interest rate is viewed as an inducement to save—the thing that makes postponement of consumption an attractive policy. Thus, in the capital market we have two opposing forces operating to establish *the* interest rate: (1) on the part of the consumer, a demand for interest payments as an inducement to postpone consumption and to save, and (2) on the part of the producer, a limited ability to generate *income value* from the intermediate capital goods he employs. When these two forces reach equilibrium, a market price for *interest* is established— this market price is simply the *rate of interest* for the intertemporal exchange of funds. But note that in the economic evaluation of projects, we are attempting to set *capital values* on the productive assets (intermediate capital goods). So it is, from Fisher's incisive analysis above, we must establish *capital value* from the *income* value of the products and/or services produced. It is simply an intertemporal exchange problem.

## 3.2. Interest Factors and Notation

Calculations of present value, such as those required by the form of Eq. (3.3), and by other types of calculations involving interest rates are generally made easier by the use of *interest factors*. Such factors can be rationally derived from assumptions concerning the timing and amounts of money flows, and values of the interest factors are often tabulated to facilitate calculations involving interest rates. Interest factors, as well as the timing and money flows from which they are derived, are generally stated in a standardized notation. Interest-type equivalence problems are often stated in the same notation also.

**3.2.1. Notation and cash flow diagrams.** The following notation is generally used in this book for interest calculations (unless modified otherwise at a particular place in the book), and the notation generally follows the *American National Standard for Industrial Engineering Terminology for Engineering Economy, ANSI Z94.5 — 1972* (Ref. [7]):

$r$ = nominal interest rate per period.
$i$ = effective interest rate per interest period.
$N$ = number of compounding periods.
$P$ = present sum of money; that is, the *equivalent* worth, at a relative point in time called the *present*, of one or more cash flows or money amounts that occur in the *future*. $P$ occurs at the end of Period 0 or at the start of Period 1.
$F$ = future sum of money, that is, the *equivalent* worth, at a relative point in time called the *future*, of one or more cash flows or money amounts that occur either at the present or in the future, or both. $F$ occurs at the *end* of some period, e.g., at $t = 1, 2, 3, \ldots, N$.
$A$ = *end-of-period* cash flow amount (or equivalent end-of-period amount) in a *uniform series* continuing for a specified number of periods. $A$ is one of a series of *equal* amounts, say $A_1 = A_2 = A_3 = \cdots = A$, *each* of which occurs at the end of a period in an uninterrupted series of periods, e.g., at $t = 1, 2, 3, \ldots$, and so forth.
$G$ = uniform period-by-period *increase* or *decrease* in cash flow or money amount (the arithmetic gradient). $G$ is assumed to occur instantaneously at the *end* of a given period.

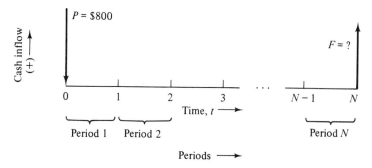

**Fig. 3.4.** Cash flow diagram for generalized bank loan problem.

In addition to the use of a standard notation, equivalence relationships and calculations can frequently be made clearer by the use of *cash flow* (or equivalence) *diagrams*. These diagrams depict the time-occurrence of cash flows or money amounts and are analogous to *free body diagrams* used to solve statics problems. Figure 3.4 shows a cash flow diagram for the problem in the last section involving an unknown future worth, *F*, of a present amount, $P = \$800$, at $i = 5\%$ per annum compounded annually. The cash flow diagram utilizes several conventions:

1. The horizontal line is a *uniform time scale* on which *time* is assumed to move from left to right. Time *intervals*, or *periods*, are numbered sequentially 1, 2, 3, ..., indicating equal periods sequentially placed. Alternatively, the *discrete* value of time, *t*, may also be used to mark the *end* of one period and *beginning* of the succeeding period; that is, $t = 0, 1, 2, \ldots, n$. In the latter case, *Period 1* occurs between $t = 0$ and $t = 1$; *Period 2*, between $t = 1$ and $t = 2$; and so forth.
2. The arrows signify cash flows or money amounts. Normally, arrows directed in a *negative* direction indicate disbursements (negative cash *inflows*), and those directed in a *positive* direction indicate cash inflows or receipts. *Positive* may be either upward or downward, so that the positive direction must be specified with each diagram.
3. In project evaluation work, the cash flow diagram is conventionally taken from the standpoint of the firm, that is, from the standpoint of the *lender* to the *project*. This is the case in Fig. 3.4, where the lender is the bank and the project is the Ron & Tom Enterprise. (If the roles were reversed, of course the directions of the cash flows would also be reversed.)

**3.2.2. *Example of simple interest calculation.*** In the Ron & Tom Enterprise described in Example 2.2.1, the partners borrowed $800 from the bank at 9% simple interest for 2 years. The amount borrowed, $800, for the *use* of which the interest is paid, is known as the *principal*. It is generally a present amount, denoted by the symbol *P*. The *rate of interest* (denoted by *r*) is the amount of interest accrued (earned) by a *unit of principal* over a *unit of time*. Thus, in the Tom-Ron Enterprise example, 800 units of principal earned 144 units of interest in 2 years, so the rate of interest was

$$r = \frac{144}{800(2)} = 0.09$$

or 9% *per annum*. This is the usual way of expressing *simple* interest rates—*percent per annum*.

The simplest kind of equivalence problem can be illustrated by a bank loan involving simple interest (see Fig. 3.4). Here, a present amount *P* is borrowed from the bank, to be repaid *n* years hence by a future amount *F*, where $F > P$. Now the difference, $F - P$, is simply the *interest* (*I*) owed to the bank for the use of *P* dollars, which is calculated as

$$I = F - P = Pnr$$

because the interest earned is directly proportional to the principal involved (*P*), the interest rate (*r*), and the number of periods (*n*) during which the principal was used. Thus, the future amount, *F*, is *equivalent* to the present amount, *P*, when simple interest is considered:

$$F = P + I = P + Pnr = P(1 + nr)$$

or, conversely, the *present value* (of the loan) is made equivalent to a larger *future value* (loan + interest) by subtracting interest:

$$P = F - I = \frac{F}{(1 + nr)}.$$

## 3.3. Compound Interest

Suppose that the terms of the Ron & Tom Enterprise loan had been changed somewhat, so that instead of being required to pay simple interest at the end of the 2-year period, they were required to pay interest at 9% per annum at the end of *each* year. Suppose also that they did not pay the interest installment becoming due at the end of the first year, and by agreement with the bank this first interest installment was simply added to their loan—that is, during the *second* year, the bank lent them not only the principal ($P = \$800$) but also the interest due at the beginning of the second year ($I_1 = Pnr = (800)(1)(0.09) = \$72$). If interest is treated in this manner, it is said to be *compounded*, since in the second year there is interest being earned on the first year's interest as well as on the principal (and so forth for the third, fourth, and any succeeding years). The effect of compounding the Tom-Ron loan can be shown by the following table.

| End of Period | Amount Owed at Beginning of Period | Interest Charge for Period | Amount Owed at End of Period |
|---|---|---|---|
| 0 | $–0– | $–0– | $800.00 |
| 1 | $800.00 | 72.00 | 872.00 |
| 2 | 872.00 | 78.48 | 950.48 |

Thus, $F = \$950.48$ would be due the bank at the end of the second period under this plan, whereas under the simple interest plan the amount was $F = \$944.00$. The difference of $6.48 is due to *compounding* (or, interest on interest). Because compound interest methods have been shown to be the theoretically correct ones (see Section 3.1) for making equivalence calculations in project evaluation, they are of great importance and are used throughout this book.

## 3.4. Discrete Compound Interest Factors

Equivalence calculations are considerably simplified by the use of compound interest *factors*. For cash flows occurring discretely, that is, using the convention that flows occur instantaneously at the ends of given time periods, there are eight such interest factors. All eight employ the convention that the length of the compounding period is equal to the interest rate period. That is, *effective* interest rates are utilized.

For example, the same factors may be used where $i$ (the effective interest rate) is stated as *percent per annum compounded annually, percent per quarter compounded quarterly, percent per month compounded monthly,* or in general *percent per period compounded per period.* The basis of these factors, then, is that *the compounding period is equal in length of time to the interest period.* If some other basis is used for stating interest, then one must first make the conversion to an effective interest rate, $i$ (see Section 3.6), before using the interest factors.

**3.4.1.** *Single-payment compound amount factor (finding F, given P).* In the example given in Section 3.3, the interest at $9\%$ per annum on the principal amount of \$800 was permitted to accumulate for 2 years so that the future amount of \$950.48 at the end of the second year was made equivalent to the present amount of \$800. The relationship between a future amount and a present amount can be derived in general terms and is called the *single-payment compound amount* factor.

If an amount $P$ dollars exists at a point in time and $i\%$ is the *effective* interest (or growth) rate per period compounded per period, then $P$ will grow to a future amount $F_1 = P + Pi = P(1 + i)$ by the end of one period. As seen from the following table, by the end of two periods, $F_2 = P(1 + i)^2$; by the end of three periods, $F_3 = P(1 + i)^3$; and so forth:

| End of Period ($t$) | Amount at Beginning of Period | Interest (or Growth) During Period | Compound Amount at End of Period |
|---|---|---|---|
| 1 | $P$ | $Pi$ | $P + Pi = P(1 + i) = F_1$ |
| 2 | $P(1 + i)$ | $P(1 + i)i$ | $P(1 + i) + P(1 + i)i = P(1 + i)^2 = F_2$ |
| 3 | $P(1 + i)^2$ | $P(1 + i)^2 i$ | $P(1 + i)^2 + P(1 + i)^2 i = P(1 + i)^3 = F_3$ |
| . | . | . | . |
| . | . | . | . |
| . | . | . | . |
| $N$ | $P(1 + i)^{N-1}$ | $P(1 + i)^{N-1} i$ | $P(1 + i)^{N-1} + P(1 + i)^{N-1} i = P(1 + i)^N = F_N$ |

The general relationship between $P$ and $F_N$, that is, $(1 + i)^N$, is commonly known as the *single-payment compound amount factor* ($F$):

$$F = F_N = P(1 + i)^N. \tag{3.4}$$

Numerical values for this factor are tabulated in Appendix A for a wide range of values of $i$ and $N$. In this book, we use the ANSI standard notation $(F/P, i\%, N)$ for the interest factor $(1 + i)^N$. Hence, Eq. (3.4) can be stated

$$F = P(F/P, i\%, N) \tag{3.5}$$

where the factor in parentheses, $(F/P, i\%, N)$, designates the *value* of the factor $(1 + i)^N$. When writing the mnemonic for this factor, we note that the sequence of $F$ and $P$ in $F/P$ is *in the same order* as the *unknown* $F$ and the *known* $P$ in Eq. (3.5). This type of sequencing is true for all the functional interest factors used in this book.

As an example of the use of the single-payment compound amount factor, consider again the example in Section 3.3. There $P = \$800$, $i = 9\%$ per annum compounded annually, $N = 2$ years, and it was desired to find the equivalent value, $F$, at the end of 2 years. In factor notation, the *unknown* amount $F$ is placed on the *left* side of the equation, the *known* amount $P$ on the *right* side, and the required factor can then be written directly from the indicated sequential relationship of $F$ and $P$, thus:

$$F = P(F/P, i\%, N)$$
$$= 800(F/P, 9\%, 2).$$

From Appendix A the value of the factor $(F/P, 9\%, 2)$ is 1.1881, so the calculation becomes

$$F = 800(\overset{(F/P,9\%,2)}{1.1881}) = \$950.48.$$

The equivalence diagram of this calculation is illustrated in Fig. 3.5.

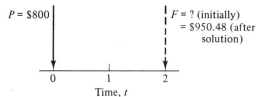

**Fig. 3.5.** Cash flow diagram for Ron-Tom loan.

**3.4.2. Single-payment present worth factor (finding P, given F).** Equation (3.4) may be solved for an unknown $P$, assuming $F$ given, thus:

$$P = F\left(\frac{1}{1+i}\right)^{N}. \tag{3.6}$$

The resulting factor, $(1 + i)^{-N}$, is known as the *single-payment present worth factor*, and its tabular values are used to find a present amount $P$, *given* a future amount $F$ that occurs $N$ periods in the future. The equivalence diagram is similar to Fig. 3.5, except the values of $F$ and $P$ are now known and unknown, respectively. Thus, the $P/F$ factor is

$$(P/F, i\%, N) = \frac{1}{(1+i)^{N}} = (1+i)^{-N} \tag{3.7}$$

and it is used to find an unknown $P$, given a known $F$:

$$P = F(P/F, i\%, N). \tag{3.8}$$

Tabulated values of this factor appear in Appendix A.

An example of the use of this factor is to find the *present* equivalent at $i = 9\%$ of a future amount $F = \$950.48$ that occurs 2 years hence. Thus:

$$P = F(P/F, i\%, N) = 950.48(\overset{(P/F,9\%,2)}{0.8417}) = \$800.$$

Note that the single-payment compound amount factor and the single-payment present worth factor are reciprocals.

### 3.4.3. *Uniform-series compound amount factor (finding F, Given A).* Frequently a series of uniform amounts, each of amount $A$, will occur at the *end* of *each* period for several consecutive periods. Such a uniform series is often called an *annuity* and is illustrated in Fig. 3.6.

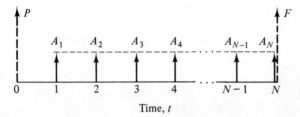

Fig. **3.6.** Equivalent periodic amount cash flow diagram.

In Fig. 3.6, two important facts should be noted. These facts are the basis for the derivation of all the *uniform series* interest factors in this book:

1. The equivalent *present* value, $P$, of the series occurs one interest period *before* the first $A$ of the uniform amounts,
2. The equivalent future value, $F$, of the series occurs *at the same time* as the last $A$, which is $N - 1$ periods after the *first $A$*.

When a flow of $A$ dollars occurs at the end of each period, from $t = 1$ to $t = N$, the future value, $F$, at the end of the $N$th period ($t = N$) is obtained by summing the future values of each of the $N$ flows of amounts $A$ each. Thus, to find $F$ in Fig. 3.4, we would sum the future values, $\Delta F_t$, of $A_1, A_2, A_3, \ldots, A_N$, in this manner:

$$\Delta F_N = A_N(1 + i)^0 = A_N$$

$$\Delta F_{N-1} = A_{N-1}(1 + i)^1$$

$$\Delta F_{N-2} = A_{N-2}(1 + i)^2$$

$$\vdots \qquad \qquad \vdots$$

$$\Delta F_3 = A_3(1 + i)^{N-3}$$

$$\Delta F_2 = A_2(1 + i)^{N-2}$$

$$\Delta F_1 = A_1(1 + i)^{N-1}$$

or, since $A_1 = A_2 = A_3 = \cdots = A_N$ by the assumption of $A$ being a *uniform* series, then

$$F = A[1 + (1 + i) + (1 + i)^2 + \cdots + (1 + i)^{N-1}]. \qquad (3.9)$$

This equation should be recognized as a geometric series with common ratio $(1 + i)$. The sum of the first $N$ terms of this kind of series can be found by multiplying the equation by the common ratio, thus:

$$F(1 + i) = A[(1 + i) + (1 + i)^2 + (1 + i)^3 + \cdots + (1 + i)^N] \qquad (3.10)$$

and then subtracting Eq. (3.9) from Eq. (3.10) term by term:

$$F(1 + i) - F = A[(1 + i)^N - 1];$$

and upon solving for $F$ we have

$$F = A\left[\frac{(1 + i)^N - 1}{i}\right]. \tag{3.11}$$

The term in brackets is the *uniform-series compound amount* factor:

$$(F/A, i\%, N) = \left[\frac{(1 + i)^N - 1}{i}\right].$$

This factor expresses the equivalence between a uniform series of $N$ *end-of-period* amounts, $A$, and a future value, $F$, at the end of the $N$th period.

As an example, suppose that equal cash flows of $1,000 each occur at the ends of five successive years. If interest is 10% per year compounded annually, what is the equivalent future amount of these cash flows at the end of the fifth year? The solution is

$$\overset{(F/A,10\%,5)}{F_5 = A(F/A, 10\%, 5) = \$1,000( \ 6.1051 \ ) = \$6,105.10.}$$

Values of the $(F/A, i\%, N)$ factor appear in Appendix A.

### 3.4.4. *Uniform-series present worth factor (finding P, given A).*

To find the factor that relates a series of uniform end-of-period amounts, $A$, to their present value, we combine two relationships already developed. From Eq. (3.4), we know that $F = P(1 + i)^N$, and upon substituting this value of $F$ in Eq. (3.11) we have

$$F = P(1 + i)^N = A\left[\frac{(1 + i)^N - 1}{i}\right];$$

and upon dividing both sides by $(1 + i)^N$, we have

$$P = A\left[\frac{(1 + i)^N - 1}{i(1 + i)^N}\right]. \tag{3.12}$$

Equation (3.12) is the relationship for finding the present equivalent, $P$, of a uniform series of $N$ *end-of-period* amounts, $A$, when the effective interest rate is $i$. Note that each amount, $A$, occurs at the *end* of periods 1, 2, 3, . . . , $N$, and the present equivalent, $P$, *occurs at time zero* (at the *beginning* of the first period). This factor is called the *uniform-series present worth factor* and is denoted

$$(P/A, i\%, N) = \left[\frac{(1 + i)^N - 1}{i(1 + i)^N}\right].$$

Tabulated values of this factor appear in Appendix A.

An example of the use of this factor would be to find the present equivalent of five equal cash flows of $1,000 each that occur at the ends of years 1, 2, 3, 4, and 5, with effective interest $i = 10\%$ per year compounded annually. The solution is

$$\overset{(P/A,10\%,5)}{P = A(P/F, i\%, N) = \$1,000( \ 3.7908 \ ) = \$3,790.80.}$$

**3.4.5.** *Uniform-series capital recovery factor (finding A, given P).* This factor establishes the equivalence between a given *present* amount, $P$ (occurring at time $t = 0$) and a series of $N$ uniform (equal) but unknown amounts, $A$, that occur at the ends of periods 1, 2, 3, . . . , $N$. The factor is obtained directly by solving Eq. (3.12) for the unknown, $A$, by multiplying both sides of the equation by the inverse of the terms in parentheses. Thus,

$$A = P\left[\frac{i(1 + i)^N}{(1 + i)^N - 1}\right].$$  (3.13)

The *uniform-series capital recovery* factor is the quantity in brackets, or

$$(A/P, i\%, N) = \left[\frac{i(1 + i)^N}{(1 + i)^N - 1}\right].$$

Tabulated values of this factor appear in Appendix A.

An example of the use of this factor would be to find the value of the uniform series of five equal cash flows, each flow occurring at the end of Periods 1, 2, 3, 4, and 5, that is equivalent to a present value $P = \$3,790.80$, with effective interest $i = 10\%$ per period compounded each period. The solution is

$$A = P(A/P, i\%, N) = \$3,790.80(\overset{(A/P,10\%,5)}{0.2638}) = \$1,000.00.$$

Note that the $A/P$ factor is the inverse of the $P/A$ factor developed in Section 3.4.4.

**3.4.6.** *Uniform-series sinking fund factor (finding A, given F).* Taking. Eq. (3.11) and solving for $A$, we have

$$A = F\left[\frac{i}{(1 + i)^N - 1}\right]$$  (3.14)

and the quantity in brackets is called the *sinking fund factor*, or

$$(A/F, i\%, N) = \left[\frac{i}{(1 + i)^N - 1}\right].$$

Equation (3.14) is the relationship for finding the amount, $A$, of a *uniform series* of amounts occurring at the *end* of $N$ interest periods, which would be equivalent to a total future amount, $F$, also occurring at the end of the last ($N$th) period.[3] Tabulated values of this factor appear in Appendix A.

As an example of the use of this factor, we ask the question, what is the periodic amount, $A$, occurring in a uniform series of five such amounts at the ends of the

---

[3] Before the days of income taxes (prior to 1913) and inflation, it was a common industrial practice for a company to set aside a portion of its profits each month, in cash, equal to the amount of depreciation reckoned on its depreciable assets. Depreciation expense was thus said to be *funded* out of profits. As they occurred, these monthly cash flows were invested in a bank account at interest. The purpose of this practice was to provide a fund of sufficient size ($F$) at the end of $N$ years so that the depreciated machines could be replaced from the available cash fund. Such a fund was called a *sinking fund*, and the amount of the periodic deposit ($A$) was determined by the use of this factor, hence its name. The practice of funding depreciation expense is no longer in wide use, but the name has remained attached to this equivalence factor.

Periods 1, 2, 3, 4, and 5, that is equivalent to a *future* amount $F = \$6,105$ occurring at the end of the fifth period, if the effective interest rate $i = 10\%$? The solution is

$$A = F(A/F, i\%, N) = \$6,105(\overset{(A/F,10\%,5)}{0.1638}) = \$1,000.$$

Note that the $A/F$ factor is the inverse of the $F/A$ factor developed in Section 3.4.3.

### 3.4.7. Uniform-series gradient conversion factor.

Sometimes money amounts can be represented by a series of flows that are projected to *increase* or *decrease* by a *uniform amount* each period. Such a series constitutes an arithmetic series, and an equivalent annual amount can be calculated for the series. For example, maintenance and repair expenses often increase with the age of an asset. Another example is that a particular type of depreciation expense calculation *decreases* in amount as the asset becomes older. Quite often these calculations can be simplified (in equivalence amounts) by the gradient conversion factor.

Figure 3.7 is a diagram of a series of end-of-period amounts, $G, 2G, 3G, \ldots,$ that *differ* by a constant amount, $G$, each period. The $G$ is known as the *gradient amount*.

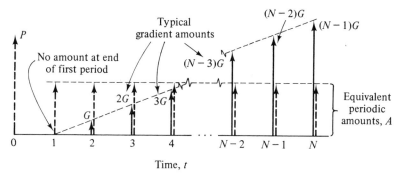

Fig. 3.7. Flow diagram for gradient conversion factor.

Note that the *timing* of the gradient amounts (flows), on which the derived formulas and tabular values are based, is as follows:

| End of Period | Amount |
| --- | --- |
| 1 | 0 |
| 2 | $G$ |
| 3 | $2G$ |
| . | |
| . | |
| . | |
| $N - 1$ | $(N - 2)G$ |
| $N$ | $(N - 1)G$ |

To find the value of an interest factor that will convert this arithmetic series of amounts into a *uniform* series, $A$, we simply find the present equivalent of the gradient series, $P$, and then convert this present amount into an equivalent uniform amount. Thus, when we sum the compounded gradient series, we have the equivalent present amount:

$$P = \frac{G}{(1+i)^2} + \frac{2G}{(1+i)^3} + \frac{3G}{(1+i)^4} + \cdots + \frac{(N-2)G}{(1+i)^{N-1}} + \frac{(N-1)G}{(1+i)^N}. \quad (3.15)$$

Now, multiply Eq. (3.15) by $(1+i)^N$ on both sides, giving

$$P(1+i)^N = G(1+i)^{N-2} + 2G(1+i)^{N-3} + 3G(1+i)^{N-4} + \cdots$$
$$+ (N-2)G(1+i) + (N-1)G. \quad (3.16)$$

Note that this sequence contains $N-1$ terms and can be recomposed by factoring into the sequence

$$P(1+i)^N = G[(1+i)^{N-2} + (1+i)^{N-3} + (1+i)^{N-4} + \cdots + (1+i)^2 + (1+i)^1 + 1]$$
$$+ G[(1+i)^{N-3} + (1+i)^{N-4} + \cdots + (1+i)^2 + (1+i)^1 + 1]$$
$$+ G[(1+i)^{N-4} + \cdots + (1+i)^2 + (1+i)^1 + 1]$$
$$+ \cdots + G[(1+i)^2 + (1+i)^1 + 1]$$
$$+ G[(1+i)^1 + 1]$$

$$= G(F/A, i\%, N-1) + G(F/A, i\%, N-2) + G(F/A, i\%, N-3) \cdots$$
$$+ G(F/A, i\%, 2) + G(F/A, i\%, 1)$$

$$= G\left[\frac{(1+i)^{N-1} - 1}{i} + \frac{(1+i)^{N-2} - 1}{i} + \cdots\right.$$
$$\left. + \frac{(1+i)^2 - 1}{i} + \frac{(1+i)^1 - 1}{i}\right]$$

$$= \frac{G}{i}[(1+i)^{N-1} + (1+i)^{N-2} + \cdots + (1+i)^2 + (1+i) - (N-1)1];$$

and if we move the $NG/i$ term (on the right-hand side) outside the brackets, then

$$P(1+i)^N = \frac{G}{i}[(1+i)^{N-1} + (1+i)^{N-2} + \cdots + (1+i)^2 + (1+i) + 1] - \frac{NG}{i}. \quad (3.17)$$

The terms inside the brackets in Eq. (3.17) define the $(F/A, i\%, N)$ factor for $N$ periods; hence Eq. (3.17) becomes

$$P(1+i)^N = \frac{G}{i}\left[\frac{(1+i)^N - 1}{i}\right] - \frac{NG}{i}. \quad (3.18)$$

Now $P(1+i)^N$ is simply $F_N$; in order to find an equivalent end-of-period amount in an equal series, $A$, we multiply Eq. (3.18) on both sides by the $A/F$ factor:

$$A = F(A/F, i\%, N) = P(1 + i)^N(A/F, i\%, N) = P(1 + i)^N\left[\frac{i}{(1 + i)^N - 1}\right]$$

$$= \left\{\frac{G}{i}\left[\frac{(1 + i)^N - 1}{i}\right] - \frac{NG}{i}\right\}\left[\frac{i}{(1 + i)^N - 1}\right]$$

$$= \frac{G}{i} - \frac{NG}{(1 + i)^N - 1} = \frac{G}{i} - \frac{NG}{i}\left[\frac{i}{(1 + i)^N - 1}\right] \qquad (3.19)$$

$$= G\left[\frac{1}{i} - \frac{N}{(1 + i)^N - 1}\right].$$

The resulting factor, $\{(1/i) - [N/(1 + i)^N - 1]\}$, is called the *uniform-series gradient conversion factor* and converts a series of uniformly increasing (or decreasing) end-of-period amounts, the first (or last) of which is zero, into an equivalent series of *equal end-of-period* amounts. The gradient conversion factor is denoted

$$(A/G, i\%, N) = \left[\frac{1}{i} - \frac{N}{(1 + i)^N - 1}\right]$$

and is tabulated in Appendix A.

Note that the gradient conversion factor is derived from an assumption of a *zero* cash flow at the beginning (or the end) of the gradient (time $t = 1$ or $t = N$). In case the initial flow is not zero, it and the succeeding flows can be decomposed into two *equivalent* flows; that is,

$$A_t = A_1 + A_2$$

where $A_1 = $ the initial *nonzero* flow at $t = 1$. Then the resulting equivalence is simply

$$A_t = A_1 + G(A/G, i\%, N) \qquad (3.20)$$

where $G$ is the gradient difference. For a *decreasing* gradient series, the sign of $G$ simply becomes negative, and $A_1$ is still the *initial* amount at $t = 1$:

$$A_t = A_1 - G(A/G, i\%, N). \qquad (3.21)$$

**Example 3.4.1.** Suppose that estimates of certain end-of-year expenses are $0 at the end of the first year, $2,000 for the second year, $4,000 for the third year, and $6,000 for the fourth year. If the effective interest rate is 15%, what is the equivalent annual end-of-period amount ($A$)?

*Solution:* Since the difference between end-of-period amounts is constant ($G = \$2,000$) and the beginning amount is zero at $t = 1$, these data fit the gradient model [Eq. (3.20)] in which $A_1 = 0$ and $N = 4$. Thus,

$$A = 0 + G(A/G, i\%, N) = 2,000(\overset{(A/G,15\%,4)}{1.3263}) = \$2,653.$$

Note that $A_1 = A_2 = A_3 = A_4 = \$2,653$, and that this amount replaces the actual amounts $g_1 = 0$, $g_2 = G = \$2,000$, $g_3 = 2G = \$4,000$, and $g_4 = 3G = \$6,000$.

**Example 3.4.2.** *Initial amount not zero.* In the preceding example, suppose that the expense estimates had been as follows:

| End of Period, t | Expense |
|:---:|:---:|
| 1 | $3,000 |
| 2 | 5,000 |
| 3 | 7,000 |
| 4 | 9,000 |

If the effective interest rate were still 15%, what is the equivalent end-of-period amount of these expenses?

*Solution:* The initial amount at $t = 1$ is $A_1 = \$3,000$, and the constant difference is G = $2,000 per period. Applying Eq. (3.20),

$$A = A_1 + G(A/G, i\%, N)$$

$$A = \$3,000 + \$2,000 \overset{(A/G, 15\%, 4)}{(\;1.3263\;)} = \$5,653.$$

**Example 3.4.3.** *Decreasing gradient.* Suppose the amounts in Example 3.4.2 were reversed:

| End of Period, t | Expense |
|:---:|:---:|
| 1 | $9,000 |
| 2 | 7,000 |
| 3 | 5,000 |
| 4 | 3,000 |

At 15% effective interest rate, what is the equivalent end-of-period amount?

*Solution:* Here, $A_1 = \$9,000$ and the gradient is negative ($G = -\$2,000$ per period). Applying Eq. (3.21),

$$A = A_1 - G(A/G, i\%, N)$$

$$= \$9,000 - \$2,000 \overset{(A/G, 15\%, 4)}{(\;1.3263\;)} = \$6,348.$$

**3.4.8.** *Gradient present worth factor.* If we divide Eq. (3.18) by $(1 + i)^N$, we can derive the form of the gradient present worth factor, thus:

$$P = \frac{G}{i}\left[\frac{(1+i)^N - 1}{i(1+i)^N}\right] - \frac{NG}{i(1+i)^N}$$

or,

$$P = \frac{G}{i}\left[\frac{(1+i)^N - 1}{i} - N\right]\left[\frac{1}{(1+i)^N}\right]$$

where the gradient present worth factor is

$$(P/G, i\%, N) = \frac{1}{i}\left[\frac{(1+i)^N - 1}{i} - N\right]\left[\frac{1}{(1+i)^N}\right]. \qquad (3.22)$$

This factor is useful in converting a uniform *gradient* series into a present equivalent amount. The timing of *P* occurs one period *before* the initial value of the gradient.[4] Values for the gradient present worth factor are tabulated in Appendix A.

## 3.5. Nominal and Effective Interest Rates

In most equivalence applications, the interest period (time period during which interest is applied) is the same as the compounding period. For example, 5% *compound interest* is interpreted as an interest rate of 5% *per year, compounded yearly.* It is possible, however, for the compounding to be done more frequently than the interest period. In these cases the compounding frequency per interest period is greater than unity. Some applications of different compounding frequencies are listed in Table 3.1, where the interest period is taken to be annual.

**Table 3.1.** EXAMPLE OF SEVERAL INTEREST COMPOUNDING FREQUENCIES

| Frequency of Compounding | Example |
|---|---|
| Annual | Economy studies, long-term loans |
| Semiannual | Certain types of savings bonds |
| Quarterly | Small bank savings accounts |
| Monthly | Credit union deposits; mortgage loans |
| Weekly or | Large bank savings accounts (day-in day-out interest); |
| Daily | savings and loan accounts |

If an interest rate is compounded more frequently than its nominal interest period, then the *effective* interest rate is higher than the *nominal* rate. For example, if the *nominal interest rate* is 8% per annum but the compounding is done twice a year (semiannually), then the *effective interest rate* (or, *actual* annual rate) is 8.16%. This can be seen easily if we consider $100 as the principal at the beginning of the year; then the interest during the first 6 months is

$$I_1 = \$100\left(\frac{0.08}{2}\right) = \$4.00$$

and the total principal at the beginning of the second six-month period is

$$P + Pi = \$100 + \$4 = \$104.$$

The interest during the second 6 months is

$$I_2 = \$104\left(\frac{0.08}{2}\right) = \$4.16$$

---

[4]As with the derivation of the gradient-to-uniform-series factor in Section 3.4.7, the *initial* value of an *ascending* gradient is zero so *P* would occur with such a gradient *one period prior* to the occurrence of the zero value in the gradient.

so that the principal plus interest at year's end is

$$P + I_1 + I_2 = \$100 + \$4.00 + \$4.16 = \$108.16$$

and the *effective rate* of interest is simply

$$i = \frac{I_1 + I_2}{P} = \frac{\$8.16}{\$100} = 8.16\%;$$

we note that $i$ now has units of *percent per year compounded yearly*. That is, when applied to the same principal amount, an interest rate of 8.16% per year compounded yearly *produces the same total interest* $(I)$ *per year* as does the nominal interest rate of 8% per year compounded twice yearly. In short, the *effective rate*, $i$, when compounded per period, has the same *effect* (in producing interest) as does the nominal rate compounded more often.

In this book, effective interest rates are designated by $i$ and are interpreted as $i$ *percent per period compounded per period*. Nominal interest rates are designated by $r$ and are interpreted as $r$ *percent per period* (no compounding). For most cases in economic analysis $i = r$ numerically; that is, the nominal and effective rates are equal because the compounding period equals the interest period. In cases where the compounding and interest periods are not equal, an effective rate can be determined, as outlined in the following paragraph.

For noncomparable compounding and interest periods, the effective interest rate follows by analogy from the numerical example above, where $r$ is now the nominal *rate per year*:

Semiannual Compounding: $\quad i = \left(1 + \dfrac{r}{2}\right)^2 - 1$

Quarterly Compounding: $\quad i = \left(1 + \dfrac{r}{4}\right)^4 - 1$

Weekly Compounding: $\quad i = \left(1 + \dfrac{r}{52}\right)^{52} - 1$

or in general for $c$ periods per year

$$i = \left(1 + \frac{r}{c}\right)^c - 1. \tag{3.23}$$

In the limit, interest may be considered to be compounded an infinite number of times per year, that is, continuously in time. Under this assumption, the effective interest rate may be derived as follows. From the fact that

$$\left(1 + \frac{r}{c}\right)^c - 1 = \left[\left(1 + \frac{r}{c}\right)^{c/r}\right]^r - 1$$

and realizing that

$$\lim_{c \to \infty} \left(1 + \frac{r}{c}\right)^{c/r} = e,$$

then

$$i = \lim_{c \to \infty} \left[\left(1 + \frac{r}{c}\right)^{c/r}\right]^r - 1 = e^r - 1. \tag{3.24}$$

Hence, when interest at nominal rate $r$ is compounded continuously, the effective rate $i$ is $e^r - 1$.

In economy studies, *only those interest rates placed on a comparable basis* may be compared one with another. For example, one might be asked to decide whether or not it is better to receive interest at a rate of $17\%$ per year compounded annually or at $16\%$ per year compounded monthly. The effective rate of $17\%$ per year compounded annually is of course $17\%$; while for $16\%$ compounded monthly the *effective annual rate* is

$$ i = \left(1 + \frac{0.16}{12}\right)^{12} - 1 = 0.1722 $$

or $17.22\%$.

The compound interest factors derived in Section 3.4 are all derived *on the basis of an effective interest rate*—that is, for an $i$ expressed as *percent per period compounded per period*. Thus, the tables in Appendix A may be used whenever the interest period and compounding period correspond; for example, whenever $i$ is expressed as

a. percent per annum compounded annually.
b. percent per quarter compounded quarterly.
c. percent per week compounded weekly.

$$ \vdots $$

percent per period compounded per period.

Whenever the interest period and the compounding period do NOT correspond, then the conversion in Eq. (3.23) must be made before the interest tables can be used.

## 3.6. Continuous Interest Factors

In certain cases, interest may be considered to compound continuously, as indicated by the derivation of the continuous rate equation in Eq. (3.24). This concept of *continuous generation of interest* leads to the derivation of another separate family of interest factors, similar in nature to the discrete compounding factors developed in Section 3.4. Such factors are known as *discrete amount, continuous compounding factors* and involve various combinations of the argument, $e^{rN}$. Moreover, if funds are considered as *distributed* flows in time instead of discrete amounts at one point in time, then yet another family of continuous amount, continuous compounding interest factors can be derived. Such factors are often called *funds flow* factors.

While in some instances these latter two families of continuous interest factors have some advantages over the discrete-event factors (e.g., they can be functionally integrated, while the discrete factors cannot); nevertheless, the development of the continuous interest factors will be omitted from this book. At the present time, virtually all the research work in economic analysis of the firm has been done with discrete analytic methods. Nearly all the important theoretical developments that have taken place in the last 20 years in capital budgeting utilize discrete cash flow methodology. The balance of this book uses discrete cash event timing. Thus, we feel it is an unnecessary burden to ask the student to familiarize himself with continuous interest methodology merely for the mathematical exercise. Adequate references to these concepts and the methodology can be found in Ref. [1] and [6], if they are needed.

## 3.7. Application of the Equivalence Concept

The equivalence concept is given depth of meaning when one fully understands *how* to establish equivalence among money amounts by performing the required calculations quickly and accurately. The following examples illustrate some of the many economic calculations that involve the *timing* of money amounts, their *amounts*, and the *interest factors* that operate to establish equivalence. In following these examples and in working equivalence problems generally, the important points made in Section 3.2.1 concerning *notation* and *timing* of cash flows should be strictly observed.

### 3.7.1. *Present worth calculations*

**Example 3.7.1.** Suppose that maintenance costs in a shop are expected to occur as follows:

| End of Year | Maintenance During Year |
|:-----------:|:-----------------------:|
| 0 | $ –0– |
| 1 | 1,000 |
| 2 | 1,200 |
| 3 | 1,400 |
| 4 | 1,600 |
| 5 | 1,800 |

At an effective interest rate of 10% per annum compounded annually, what is the present equivalent (present *worth*) of this series of costs?

*Solution:* The cash flow diagram for this series of costs is illustrated in Fig. 3.8. Note that the cash flows are outward from the firm, so the arrows are taken

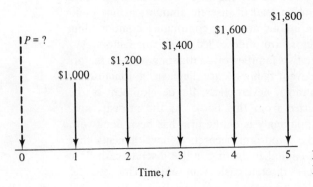

Fig. 3.8. Cash flow diagram for Example 3.7.1.

in the negative direction. The present equivalent is also in the negative direction, since it is merely the *equivalent* of the future cash flows. The present worth of this series of costs may be found by converting each cost to its present equivalent using $(P/F, i\%, N)$ factors and summing the equivalent amounts:

$$P = \$909.10 + 991.68 + 1{,}051.82 + 1{,}092.80 + 1{,}117.62 = \$5{,}163.02.$$

$$(P_1)_0 = \$1{,}000(\overset{(P/F,10\%,1)}{0.9091})$$

$$(P_2)_0 = \$1{,}200(\overset{(P/F,10\%,2)}{0.8264})$$

$$(P_3)_0 = \$1{,}400(\overset{(P/F,10\%,3)}{0.7513})$$

$$(P_4)_0 = \$1{,}600(\overset{(P/F,10\%,4)}{0.6830})$$

$$(P_5)_0 = \$1{,}800(\overset{(P/F,10\%,5)}{0.6209})$$

Note especially that $P_0 = \$5{,}163.02$ is *NOT* an amount that is *expended* now; it is merely the *present equivalent* of the *expenditures as they occur* when the time value of money is 10% per year compounded yearly.

**Example 3.7.2.** Given the following estimates of future royalties to be paid for the use of a patented device, what is the present value of these royalties if the time value of money is calculated at the rate of 8% per year compounded yearly?

| End of Year | Royalty to Be Paid |
|:---:|:---:|
| 0 | \$15,000 (down payment) |
| 1 | 3,000 |
| 2 | 2,000 |
| 3 | 1,000 |

*Solution:*

$$P = \$15{,}000 + \$3{,}000(\overset{(P/F,8\%,1)}{0.9259}) + \$2{,}000(\overset{(P/F,8\%,2)}{0.8573}) + \$1{,}000(\overset{(P/F,8\%,3)}{0.7938})$$

$$= \$15{,}000 + \$2{,}777.70 + \$1{,}714.60 + \$793.80 = \$20{,}286.10.$$

**3.7.2. *Future value calculations.*** Using the data in Example 3.7.1, the future value at time $N = 5$ can be calculated in a manner similar to that for present value, except that the future value (compound amount) interest factors are used and the unknown equivalent amount is $F$ at $N = 5$:

$$(F_1)_5 = \$1,000(\overset{(F/P,10\%,4)}{1.4641}) =$$

$$(F_2)_5 = \$1,200(\overset{(F/P,10\%,3)}{1.3310}) =$$

$$(F_3)_5 = \$1,400(\overset{(F/P,10\%,2)}{1.2100}) =$$

$$(F_4)_5 = \$1,600(\overset{(F/P,10\%,1)}{1.1000}) =$$

$$F = \$1,800(\overset{(F/P,10\%,0)}{1.0000}) + \$1,760. + \$1,694. + \$1,597.20 + \$1,464.10 = \$8,315.$$

**Example 3.7.3.** Using the data in Example 3.7.2, the future value of the royalties at the end of the third year is

$$F = \$15,000(\overset{(F/P,8\%,3)}{1.2597}) + \$3,000(\overset{(F/P,8\%,2)}{1.1664}) + \$2,000(\overset{(F/P,8\%,1)}{1.0800}) + \$1,000$$

$$= \$18,895. + \$3,499. + \$2,160. + \$1,000. = \$25,554.$$

It should also be noted that the present value can be found from the equivalent future value:

$$P = \$25,554(\overset{(P/F,8\%,3)}{0.7938}) = \$20,285.59,$$

which agrees with the result obtained in Example 3.7.2, $P = \$20,286.10$, within a few cents difference. The difference is attributable to roundoff errors caused by four-place values in the interest tables. Had six-place interest tables been used, so as to preserve the five-place significance of the cash amounts, the results would have been in very close agreement.

    **3.7.3.** *Equivalent periodic amounts.* The calculation of an equivalent annual (periodic) amount $(A)$ always proceeds from either a *single* present equivalent $(P)$ or a *single* future equivalent $(F)$ since the factors relating $A$ are either the $(A/P, i\%, N)$ and $(A/F, i\%, N)$ factors or their inverses, the $(P/A, i\%, N)$ and $(F/A, i\%, N)$ factors. That is, given a single amount in the present, $P$, or a single amount in the future, $F$, (at time $t = N$), we can calculate an equivalent $A$ or the reverse; namely, given a series of payments $A$, we can calculate a single $P$ or a single $F$. Examples of these calculations were given in Sections 3.4.3 and 3.4.4.

    If we recognize that the calculation of a single $P$ or a single $F$ is an *intermediate* step, however, we can calculate a second series of amounts, say $A_2$, that is equivalent to a first series of amounts $A_1$. The following example will illustrate this point.

    **Example 3.7.4.** As a result of a prior loan on a home, there remains 15 equal annual payments of \$2,200 due to the bank. The interest rate on the prior loan is 8% per annum compounded annually. The house has just been sold to a new owner, who now wishes to renegotiate the loan to lower the annual payments. The bank is willing to do this but wants 10% equivalent interest. If the new payments are to be paid over 30 years, what is the amount of each new annual payment?

*Solution:* The present value of the remaining payments on the old loan, at 8% interest, is

$$
P = A_1(P/A, i\%, N) = \$2,200(\overset{(P/A,8\%,15)}{8.5595}) = \$18,831.00
$$

and the equivalent annual amount, $A_2$, of the new payments for 30 years at 10% interest is

$$
A_2 = P(A/P, i\%, N) = \$18,831(\overset{(A/P,10\%,30)}{0.1061}) = \underline{\underline{\$1,998}} \text{ per year.}
$$

Note that while under the original loan the total amount of principal plus interest remaining is 15($2,200) = $33,000, under the new loan the total payments amount to 30($1,998) = $59,940. Yet the two series of payments, $A_1 = \$2,200$ per year for 15 years, and $A_2 = \$1,998$ per year for 30 years, are *equivalent;* and *both* are equivalent to the present amount $P = \$18,831$, which is common to both series.

**3.7.4.** *Use of the gradient conversion factor.* In Example 3.7.1, the series of maintenance costs were treated as individual end-of-period amounts, and a present equivalent amount $P$ was found using separate $(P/F, i\%, N)$ factors. The same problem can be solved using the gradient conversion factor $(A/G, i\%, N)$.

**Example 3.7.5.** Consider the annual maintenance costs in Example 3.7.3 as being composed of a *constant* amount, say $A_1$, plus a *varying* amount in a gradient series. Then, we have the problem of finding the present value, $P$, of the following amounts:

| End of Year | Maintenance Cost (A) |
|:-----------:|:--------------------:|
| 1 | $1,000 + $–0– |
| 2 | 1,000 + 200 |
| 3 | 1,000 + 400 |
| 4 | 1,000 + 600 |
| 5 | 1,000 + 800 |
|   | ↑        ↑ |
|   | $A_1$   Gradient series, |
|   |        $G = \$200$/year |

The gradient conversion factor $(A/G, i\%, N)$ converts the gradient series into a second *equivalent annual amount*, say $A_2$, thus:

$$A_2 = G(A/G, i\%, N) = \$200(\overset{(A/G,10\%,5)}{1.8101}) = \$362.02 \text{ per year}$$

so that the total series is then an *equal* amount $A$ for all five periods:

$$A = A_1 + A_2 = \$1,000 + \$362.02 = \$1,362.02;$$

and then the present equivalent can be found, thus:

$$P = A(P/A, i\%, N) = \$1,362.02(\overset{(P/A,10\%,5)}{3.7908}) = \$5,163.$$

In compact form this relationship can be written directly as

$$P = [A + G(A/G, i\%, N)](P/A, i\%, N)$$
$$= [\$1,000 + \$200(1.8101)](3.7908) = \$5,163.$$

In a similar fashion the future value of the series is

$$F = [A + G(A/G, i\%, N)](F/A, i\%, N)$$
$$= [\$1,000 + \$200(1.8101)](6.1051) = \$8,315.$$

**3.7.5. Equivalence involving several factors.** In most economy studies, an equivalent amount of a nonuniform distribution of money flows is needed. Here, the problem is simply separated into its elemental forms. *Intermediate* equivalent amounts are used to make the transitions needed. The following example will illustrate the method.

**Example 3.7.6.** We are required to calculate the present equivalent of the following schedule of cash flows, at an effective interest rate $i = 15\%$ per annum compounded annually:

| End of Year | Cash Flow in Year |
|:---:|:---:|
| 0 | $- 200 |
| 1 | 900 |
| 2 | 1,000 |
| 3 | 1,000 |
| 4 | 1,000 |
| 5 | 1,200 |
| 6 | 1,300 |
| 7 | 1,400 |
| 8 | 1,600 |

The cash flow diagram is illustrated in Fig. 3.9.

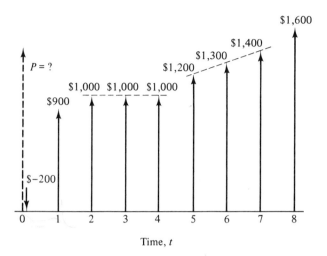

**Fig. 3.9.** Cash flow diagram for Example 3.7.6.

*Anatomical Solution:* The equivalence at present time ($t = 0$) is established by the following calculations:

*End of Year*

| | |
|---|---|
| 0: | $P = \$-200 \qquad +\$782.64 \qquad\qquad +\$1,985.30 \qquad\qquad + \$1,684.92 + \$523.04$ |
| 1: | $\$900(\underset{(P/F,15\%,1)}{0.8696}) =\qquad \$2,283(\underset{(P/F,15\%,1)}{0.8696}) =$ |
| 2: | $\$1,000$ |
| 3: | $\$1,000 \quad = \$1,000(\underset{(P/A,15\%,3)}{2.283}) =$ |
| 4: | $\$1,000$ |
| 5: | $\$1,200 \qquad\qquad (A/G,15\%,3)\ (P/A,15\%,3) \qquad \$2,946.69(\underset{(P/F,15\%,4)}{0.5718}) =$ |
| 6: | $\$1,300 \quad = [\$1,200 + \$100(0.9071)](2.283) =$ |
| 7: | $\$1,400$ |
| 8: | $\$1,600(\underset{(P/F,15\%,8)}{0.3269}) =$ |

or

$$P = \$-200 + \$782.64 + \$1,985.30 + \$1,684.92 + \$523.04 = \underline{\$4,775.90}.$$

Having established the equivalent present value of this nonuniform series of cash flows, we may now establish (a) a future equivalent amount ($F$) at *any* time $t$ ($t = 1, 2, 3, \ldots$) or (b) an equivalent periodic amount ($A$). Thus, for example, the future equivalent at the end of year 3 is.

$$F_3 = P(F/P, i\%, N)$$

$$= \$4,775.90(\ \overset{(F/P,15\%,3)}{1.5209}\ ) = \$7,264.$$

Likewise, the equivalent annual amount over the 8-year period is

$$A_{1\rightarrow 8} = \$4,775.90(\ \overset{(A/P,15\%,8)}{0.2229}\ ) = \$1,064.55 \text{ per year.}$$

**3.7.6. Uniform payments with noncomparable compounding periods.** Situations may occur in a series of equal periodic amounts ($A$) in which there are several compounding periods between each end-of-period amount, and it is desired to calculate the equivalent worth of those payments in the present or at some time in the future. This problem is posed in Example 3.7.7.

**Example 3.7.7.** Suppose there are five end-of-year cash flows of $1,000 each, and interest is to be compounded at 12% per annum compounded *monthly*. The present value of these flows is to be determined. The problem is depicted in Fig. 3.10.

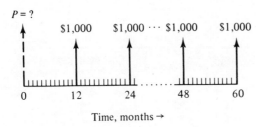

**Fig. 3.10.** Cash flows with noncomparable compounding.

*Solution:* The number of compounding periods is $12N = 12(5 \text{ years}) = 60$ months. The effective interest rate is $12\%/12 = 1\%$ per month, compounded monthly. The cash flows do not occur *monthly*, however, but rather every 12 months. There are three methods of solving this problem, each of which is correct.

The first method is to take a typical cycle of periods in which a payment occurs (here, 1 cycle = 12 months) and convert the end-of-cycle payment into its equivalent end-of-*period* series of payments. Thus, in Fig. 3.10, the end-of-year payment ($1,000) is converted to its end-of-month equivalent with $i = 1\%$ per month compounded monthly, so that

$$A_{\text{monthly}} = F(A/F, 1\%, 12) = \$1,000(0.0788) = \$78.80.$$

Since $78.80 would then occur (equivalently) not only at the ends of months 1, 2, ..., 12 but also at the ends of months 13, 14, 15, ..., 60, then the present value would be

$$P = A_{\text{monthly}}(P/A, 1\%, 60)$$
$$= \$78.80(44.9550) = \underline{\underline{\$3,542.45}}.$$

Hence, the original problem of five \$1,000 end-of-year payments is converted to an equivalent problem of 60 end-of-month payments of \$78.80 each.

The second method is to find the *equivalent* periodic (here, annual) interest rate via Eq. (3.23) and apply this equivalent rate directly to the \$1,000 payments. Thus, from Eq. (3.23), the equivalent interest rate of 1% per month compounded monthly is

$$i = \left(1 + \frac{0.12}{12}\right)^{12} - 1 = 0.126825,$$

the units of which are (fractionally) *per year, compounded yearly.*[5] The present value of \$1,000 at the end of each of 5 years then can be found, using this new effective rate, thus:

$$P = \$1,000(P/A, 12.68\%, 5).$$

Because interest factors are not commonly tabulated for 12.68%, one must either calculate the factor value from its derived formula or make linear interpolations in available tables. If the exact value of

$$(P/A, 12.68\%, 5) = \left[\frac{(1.1268)^5 - 1}{0.1268(1.1268)^5}\right] = 3.54465$$

is used, then $P = \$1,000(3.54465) = \$3,544.65$ is the result. If one makes a linear interpolation, however, between, say, the 12% factor table and the 15% factor table,

$$(P/A, 12.68\%, 5) = \frac{0.1268 - 0.1200}{0.1500 - 0.1200}[(P/A, 12\%, 5) - (P/A, 15\%, 5)]$$
$$+ (P/A, 15\%, 5)$$
$$= 0.2267(3.6048 - 3.3522) + (3.3522)$$
$$= 3.4095,$$

then the approximate present value is

$$P' = \$1,000(3.4095) = \underline{\underline{\$3,409.50}}.$$

Linear approximations of nonlinear functions are only approximate, but due to

---

[5]This same result can be obtained from the relationship $i = (F/P, r/M, M) - 1$, where $r =$ nominal interest rate and $M =$ number of compounding periods per cycle. Thus, for $r = 12\%$ per annum, $M = 12$ months per cycle,

$$i = (F/P, 1\%, 12) - 1 = 1.1268 - 1 = 0.1268,$$

which is the same result obtained by Eq. (3.23).

the inexact knowledge concerning *future* cash flows these linear approximations are usually precise enough.

The third method, and most time-consuming, is to treat each of the periodic cash flows as a single amount and find the present value directly using the *comparable* compounding rate and period. Thus:

$$P = \$1,000[(P/F, 1\%, 12) + (P/F, 1\%, 24) + \cdots + (P/F, 1\%, 60)]$$
$$= \$1,000(0.8874 + 0.7876 + 0.6989 + 0.6203 + 0.5504)$$
$$= \$1,000(3.5446) = \underline{\underline{\$3,544.60.}}$$

The first and third methods are precise if enough significant digits are carried in the calculations. Thus, in the first method the factors $(P/A, 1\%, 60) = 44.9550384119$ and $(A/F, 1\%, 12) = 0.078848788661$ when 12 significant figures are carried in the calculations; in the third method $(P/A, 12.6825030160\%, 5) = 3.54465032312$. The first method then results in a value of

$$P = \$1,000\overset{(A/F,1\%,12)}{(0.078848788661)}\overset{(P/A,1\%,60)}{(44.9550384119)} = \underline{\underline{\$3,544.65}}$$

and the third method results in a value of

$$P = \$1,000\overset{(P/A,12.68+\%,5)}{(3.54465032312)} = \underline{\underline{\$3,544.65.}}$$

The second method (linear interpolation) always results in an approximation since the equations for the interest factors are, *in general*, nonlinear functions of the interest rate.

## 3.8. Economic Interpretation of Equivalent Annual Amount

It has been argued by some analysts that industrial project economy studies can be satisfactorily made by using *simple* interest rates to convert future amounts to present amounts or to convert present and future amounts to *equivalent annual amounts*. The advocated method is to use straight-line depreciation plus average (simple) interest to calculate an approximation to the equivalent annual amount, $A$. At least as early as 1938, Grant ([3], pp. 83–92) showed this method to be only an approximation; it is useful only when one is going from a *known P* to an *unknown A*, and then only when the life $N$ and the interest rate $i$ are both small.

It is not difficult to show that the *rational* (i.e., theoretically correct) calculation of the equivalent annual amount leads to an equation that is frequently very useful but is also the basis of an economic interpretation of the equivalent cost of capital recovery—i.e., that portion of an equivalent $A$ that is due to capital investment.

Consider a project with depreciable assets having the following characteristics:

$P =$ initial cost of the assets at time $t = 0$.

$F =$ salvage value of assets at time $t = N$.
$N =$ life of the depreciable assets, periods.
$i =$ the effective interest rate (percent per period, compounded per period), stated as a decimal amount.

Note that $(P - F)$ is the depreciable amount, and this amount is to be *recovered* over $N$ periods. Applying Eq. (3.13) and (3.14), the net equivalent annual *cost of capital recovery* is simply

$$A = P(A/P, i\%, N) - F(A/F, i\%, N). \qquad (3.25)$$

Our objective is to cast Eq. (3.25) in another form that will enable us to obtain an economic meaning from it. To do so, add and subtract the term $F(A/P, i\%, N)$ to the right side of Eq. (3.25), obtaining

$$A = (P - F)(A/P, i\%, N) + F[(A/P, i\%, N) - (A/F, i\%, N)],$$

and then reduce as follows:

$$A = (P - F)(A/P, i\%, N) + F\left[\frac{i(1 + i)^N}{(1 + i)^N - 1} - \frac{i}{(1 + i)^N - 1}\right]$$

$$= (P - F)(A/P, i\%, N) + Fi\left[\frac{(1 + i)^N - 1}{(1 + i)^N - 1}\right] \qquad (3.26)$$

$$= (P - F)(A/P, i\%, N) + Fi.$$

This is an important and frequently useful form for calculating the uniform amount that represents the *annual equivalent cost of capital recovery* $(P - F)$. An economic interpretation of Eq. (3.26) is that the annual equivalent cost of capital recovery, $A$, is composed of two factors:

1. The term $(P - F)(A/P, i\%, N)$, which is the annual equivalent of the *depreciable* value of the asset.
2. The term $Fi$, which is simply the return required, at simple interest, on the amount invested in the salvage value, over the life of the asset.

Note that the first term, $(P - F)(A/P, i\%, N)$, provides for the ratable recovery of the invested capital, $(P - F)$, *at interest*, over the life of the asset. This can be shown to be equivalent to "annual depreciation plus interest on the *unrecovered* depreciable balance" (see, for example, [6], pp. 143–46). The second term, $Fi$, is the return on the salvage value of the investment. Even though salvage value is not a cost that can be recovered against income, the investor is entitled to an annual return (at simple interest) on his investment in the salvage value, and this annual return is expressed by $Fi$.

In making so-called annual cost estimates for a project, one thus *explicitly* and simultaneously provides for both the *recovery of the capital invested* plus *interest (return) on the unrecovered capital balances*, when annual costs include the equivalent amount, $A$, found by Eq. (3.26). An example will amplify this point.

**Example 3.8.1.** A paint spraying booth is to be purchased for $4,700. The delivery and installation charges are $300, so that the installed cost is estimated to be $5,000. It is estimated that the equipment will have a useful life of 5 years and the salvage value at the end of that time will be \$1,000. If interest is calculated at 6% per annum compounded annually, what is the annual amount that should be charged as a productive cost of this asset—that is, what is the equivalent amount that will provide for both recovery of invested capital plus interest on the unrecovered investment?

*Solution:* (a) The first, and preferable method, is simply to calculate the annual equivalent amount, $A$, by Eq. (3.26):

$$A = (P - F)(A/P, i\%, N) + Fi$$

$$= (\$5,000 - \$1,000)(\overset{(A/P,6\%,5)}{0.2374}) + \$1,000(0.06)$$

$$= \$1,009.60 \text{ per year.}$$

(b) It is easy to show that the method in (a) is exactly equivalent numerically to the direct method below, in which interest at 6% is calculated each period on the unrecovered investment balance:

$$\text{Annual recovery } without \text{ interest} = \frac{P - F}{N} = \frac{\$5,000 - \$1,000}{5 \text{ years}}$$

$$= \$800 \text{ per year.}$$

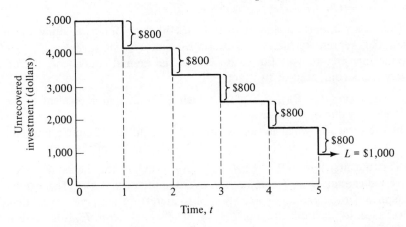

| End of Period, $t$ | Investment Recovered during Period | Investment at Beginning of Period | Interest (Return) on Unrecovered Investment | Recovery Plus Interest (Return) |
|---|---|---|---|---|
| 1 | \$ 800 | $P = \$5,000$ | $(0.06)(5,000) = \$\ 300$ | \$1,100 |
| 2 | | 4,200 | $(0.06)(4,200) =\ \ \ 252$ | 1,052 |
| 3 | | 3,400 | 204 | 1,004 |
| 4 | | 2,600 | (etc.)   156 | 956 |
| 5 | | 1,800 | 108 | 908 |
| | \$4,000 | | \$1,020 | \$5,020 |

Now, finding the *equivalent* annual amount of the last column in the table, that is, of the investment recovery *plus* interest on the unrecovered investment balances, we have

$$A = [\$1,100( \overset{(P/F,6\%,1)}{0.9434} ) + \$1,052( \overset{(P/F,6\%,2)}{0.8900} ) + \$1,004( \overset{(P/F,6\%,3)}{0.8396} )$$
$$+ \$956( \overset{(P/F,6\%,4)}{0.7921} ) + \$908( \overset{(P/F,6\%,5)}{0.7473} )]( \overset{(A/P,6\%,5)}{0.2374} ) = \$1,009.50 \text{ per year.}$$

Note again that it is *compound* interest (in the interest factors) that establishes the relationship between the net investment in the capital goods to be recovered $(P - F)$ and the periodic amount $(A)$ that is to be deducted as economic *cost* against the future output of the capital goods.

## REFERENCES

[1] DEGARMO, E. PAUL, and JOHN R. CANADA, *Engineering Economy*, 5th ed. (New York: The Macmillan Company, 1973).

[2] FISHER, IRVING, *The Theory of Interest* (New York: The Macmillan Company, 1930; reprinted, New York: Kelley and Millman, Inc., 1954).

[3] GRANT, EUGENE L., *Principles of Engineering Economy*, revised ed. (New York: The Ronald Press Company, 1938).

[4] HIRSHLEIFER, J., "On the Theory of Optimal Investment Decision," *Journal of Political Economy*, LXVI (5) (October, 1958).

[5] ————, *Price Theory and Applications* (Englewood Cliffs, N.J.: Prentice-Hall, Inc., 1976).

[6] THUESEN, H. G., W. J. FABRYCKY, and G. J. THUESEN, *Engineering Economy*, 5th ed. (Englewood Cliffs, N.J.: Prentice-Hall, Inc., 1976).

[7] *American National Standard, Industrial Engineering Terminology, Engineering Economy*, ANSI Z94.5–1972. (New York: The American Institute of Industrial Engineers, Inc., The American Society of Mechanical Engineers; 1973).

## PROBLEMS

**3-1.** How much money would have to be invested today to provide a balance of $1,000 at the end of 10 years if the investment earns 5% simple interest per annum?

**3-2.** For what period of time will $1,000 have to be invested to amount to a future amount of $1,500 if the investment earns 6% simple interest per annum?

**3-3.** What is the simple rate of interest per annum if $1,000 invested today amounts to $1,250 at the end of 4 years?

**3-4.** If $1,000 is borrowed now for 10 years and if the interest is to be paid at the end of each year at the rate of 8% per annum simple interest on the entire loan, what is the total amount of repayment during the 10-year period including the principal repayment at the end of the tenth year?

**3-5.** If $1,000 is borrowed now for 10 years and if the interest is paid at the end of the tenth year at the rate of 8% per annum compounded annually, what is the total amount of repayment at the end of the tenth year including the principal repayment at the end of the tenth year?

**3-6.** What is the total amount of repayment in Problem 3-5 if the rate of interest was 8% per annum compounded quarterly?

**3-7.** What is the effective interest rate per year for
(a) 8% per annum compounded annually?
(b) 8% per annum compounded semiannually?
(c) 8% per annum compounded quarterly?
(d) 2% per quarter compounded quarterly?

**3-8.** What is the present value of these future payments?
(a) $5,000 in 10 years from now at 15% per annum compounded annually?
(b) $1,000 in 10 years from now at 10% per annum compounded semiannually?
(c) $2,000 in 5 years from now at 8% per annum compounded quarterly?

**3-9.** At 8% per annum compounded annually, what is the annual end-of-the-year payment that will provide a future amount of $10,000 in 10 years?

**3-10.** How much money at 8% per annum compounded annually can be loaned today on the agreement that $1,000 will be paid 6 years from now?

**3-11.** At 10% per annum compounded annually, what single payment 10 years from now is equivalent to a payment of $2,000 at the end of 3 years?

**3-12.** A lending institution offers to lend $300 now on a contract in which the borrower must pay back $10 at the end of each week for the next 35 weeks. What is the effective interest rate expressed in percent per year compounded annually?

**3-13.** What present amount is equivalent to $5,000 in 10 years from now using an interest rate of 6% per annum compounded semiannually?

**3-14.** Using an interest rate of 8% per annum compounded annually, convert the following sequence of end-of-year amounts to
(a) Present worth amount.
(b) Annual equivalent amount.
(c) Equivalent amount at the end of year 5.
(d) Future sum at the end of the sequence.

| EOY | Amount | EOY | Amount | EOY | Amount |
|---|---|---|---|---|---|
| 0 | — | 5 | 500 | 10 | 600 |
| 1 | 100 | 6 | 500 | 11 | 500 |
| 2 | 100 | 7 | 500 | 12 | 500 |
| 3 | — | 8 | 600 | 13 | 1000 |
| 4 | — | 9 | 600 | | |

**3-15.** Using an interest rate of 8% per annum compounded annually, convert the following series of end of year amounts to
(a) Present worth amount $(P)$.
(b) Annual equivalent amount $(A)$.

(c) Equivalent amount at the beginning of year 8.

(d) Future sum at the end of the sequence $(F)$.

| EOY | Amount | EOY | Amount | EOY | Amount |
|-----|--------|-----|--------|-----|--------|
| 0 | 100 | 4 | 200 | 8 | 500 |
| 1 | 200 | 5 | 200 | 9 | 800 |
| 2 | 200 | 6 | 300 | 10 | 900 |
| 3 | — | 7 | 400 | 11 | 1000 |

**3-16.** Using an interest rate of 8% per annum compounded annually, convert the following series of end of year amounts to

(a) Present worth amount $(P)$.

(b) Annual equivalent amount $(A)$.

(c) Future sum at the end of the sequence $(F)$.

| EOY | Amount | EOY | Amount | EOY | Amount |
|-----|--------|-----|--------|-----|--------|
| 0 | — | 4 | 1400 | 8 | 800 |
| 1 | 2000 | 5 | 1200 | 9 | 700 |
| 2 | 1800 | 6 | 1000 | 10 | 600 |
| 3 | 1600 | 7 | 900 | | |

**3-17.** Suppose that 9 years ago you started putting $20 per month into a bank at the beginning of each month at 6% per annum compounded monthly. You made 71 continuous payments and then stopped but left the accumulated deposit in the bank. One year from now you plan to buy a house, paying $100 per month for 10 years with payments to begin at the end of the first month. For how many months can you make the housing payments using the money in the bank?

# DEPRECIATION:
# TECHNIQUES AND STRATEGIES

## 4.1. Introduction

In estimating the future cash flows from a project to the firm, three items are considered that, in themselves, are *not* cash flows:

1. *Depreciation*, which is a provision for the retirement of a productive asset,
2. *Depletion*, which is a provision for the wasting of an irreplaceable natural resource,
3. *Amortization*, which is a provision for the recognition of a prepaid expense.

While these items are not cash flows, they dramatically alter the amounts expended for income taxes, which are cash flows. Thus, depreciation, depletion, and amortization are *mediators* of the net cash flow from a project since they affect the amount of the income tax cash flow from the project.

The original reason for considering these noncash items was not tax-oriented, as it is now. The original reason was an economic one. Economically, depreciation (for example) is viewed as a ratable using up or devaluation of an intermediate good (productive asset), which has a finite span of utility, i.e., a finite productive life. Thus, depreciation is viewed economically as a proper charge against the future income produced by the intermediate good. In other words, depreciation in the economic sense represents the ratable cost of a wasting asset that is being used up in producing

# 4

its throughput. For example, a sewing machine may be rendered virtually valueless in producing, say, 300,000 pairs of shoes. Economically, the initial *cost* of the machine (an intermediate economic good) should be charged ratably against the 300,000 pairs of shoes, pair by pair. This is the original, or economic, concept of depreciation.

Since 1913, when the Sixteenth Amendment was adopted and the first Federal income tax statutes were passed by Congress, the income tax law (consisting of both statute and trial law) has become more intricate and more interwoven with the conduct of business affairs. Indeed, the tax law is now so intimately involved in virtually every aspect of business and industrial operations that it would be equivalent to industrial "suicide" to ignore the effects of the income tax in our industrial decision-making systems.

Certain kinds of depreciation allowances are deductible under the Federal (and most state) income tax laws. That is, an allowance for the wasting of the asset can be deducted from gross income by the firm before calculating the income tax due. This deduction, while of a noncash nature, nevertheless results in a *reduction* of the tax due (a *cash* outflow) because the tax is calculated on the *net* income amount *after* the depreciation allowance is factored in. Thus, the cash outflow of the firm is reduced when depreciation deductions are claimed. The same is true for depletion deductions and, where allowable, for amortization deductions also. So now the reason for examining depreciation methods and calculations in economic analyses is that *the firm can increase the cash inflows* from projects by taking advantage of depreciation, depletion, and amortization deductions, not only as to amounts but also by affecting the timing of the deductions.

This chapter presents a summary of the principal depreciation and depletion methodologies *as they exist in 1976 under the Federal income tax laws*.[1] A number of methods for computing depreciation allowances are permitted by law. In addition, switching from one method to another is possible under certain circumstances. The particular method of depreciation that is optimal under a particular set of conditions depends in part on the reinvestment rate at which the generated funds (cash flows) can be invested.

It is a major purpose of this chapter, among others, to derive decision rules which select from among the various depreciation alternatives that method which is optimal in a given situation.

## 4.2. Optimal Depreciation Strategies

*The original author of much of the material in Sections 4.2 through 4.9 is B. Alva Schoomer, Jr.*[2]

There are several definitions of depreciation, not all of which are equivalent. For income tax purposes, the most useful view is that an investment is a prepaid expense, and depreciation is the allocation of that expense to future years. Since reporting depreciation to the Internal Revenue Service (IRS) results in tax savings to the taxpayer, the way in which an investment is allocated over its lifetime is of importance to most taxpayers and of critical importance to many.

The amount of tax savings generated through depreciation by industry in the

---

[1]While the information contained in this chapter and the format of its presentation are designed to provide accurate and authoritative information concerning the subject matter covered, it should be understood that no attempt is being made here to render legal, accounting, or other professional service. If legal advice or other expert assistance is required, the services of a competent professional person (attorney or accountant) should be sought.

[2]Sections 4.2 through 4.9 (except 4.8.1) are based on B. Alva Schoomer, Jr., "Optimal Depreciation Strategies for Income Tax Purposes," *Management Science*, **12** (August, 1966), pp. B552–B579. Most of the material from the source article is reprinted here, with permission from the original author and from the original publisher. Some notational changes have been made from the original article, however, in order to be consistent with ANSI Z94.5–1972, "American National Standard, Industrial Engineering Terminology for Engineering Economy." Moreover, the original article has been conformed to the provisions of the Internal Revenue Code of 1954, as amended by the various acts of Congress up to and including the *U.S. Revenue Act of 1964* [5], the *Tax Reform Act of 1969*, the *Revenue Act of 1971*, and the *Revenue Adjustment Act of 1975*. This conformation has resulted in a considerable number of changes from the original article in the numerical examples, and especially in the treatment of the 10% Investment Credit and the *additional* 20% first year depreciation, together with the illustrations (figures) associated with these topics. Several numerical examples also have been added.

United States is very large. Studies indicate that depreciation, amortization, and depletion deductions are considerably more than *twice* the retained earnings for many U. S. corporations. In recent years, depreciation reported by U. S. firms has increased considerably, due to the liberalization of depreciation allowances made available by the 1962 and 1964 tax laws and by recent IRS guidelines.

If the funds generated through depreciation can be invested profitably, a very substantial enhancement of corporate earnings can result. (Indeed, in the automotive industry, profits can be regarded as arising entirely from earnings on the tax savings due to depreciation.) For this reason, depreciation policy is increasingly the concern of all corporate management, not merely that portion of management that traditionally has been responsible for the financial aspects of the concern. Even so, most firms still fail to take full advantage of the possibilities inherent in the current tax law.

Several types of depreciation procedures are acceptable to the Treasury Department. The three procedures in most common use are those allowed specifically by the Internal Revenue Code [3]: the straight-line method, the declining-balance method, and the sum-of-the-years' digits method. These three methods differ not so much in the amount of total depreciation allowable over the life of the asset as in the fraction of the total depreciation that may be taken in the early years of the asset's useful life. In general, it is desirable to take as much depreciation as possible as early as possible so that the funds thus generated can be invested for a longer period of time. The purpose of the present chapter is to provide some quantitative guidelines for use by management in establishing depreciation policy for new investments.

Clearly, the desirability of using an accelerated depreciation schedule depends on the amount of profit that can be made by investing the funds thus generated. For this reason, a quantitative comparison of the various depreciation procedures requires that a measure of profitability for the invested funds be available. For present purposes, we shall use a present worth analysis. Strictly speaking, the present worth method is the uniquely correct method to use only when a perfect capital market exists. In practice, of course, this is not true; nevertheless, for most firms it is true enough to make present worth a highly practical measure of profitability.

The Treasury Department recognizes both item accounting and class accounting procedures for depreciation. In the former, depreciation is computed separately for each depreciable capital asset. The individual results are then added to find the total depreciation deductible by that corporation for the year. In class accounting, each capital asset owned by the firm is put into one of several asset classes. Depreciation is then computed separately for each class of assets on the basis of the average life of the assets within the class. Whether item or class accounting is used, depreciation procedures are similar and the results of the present chapter apply. For ease of presentation, however, we shall speak as though item accounting only were being carried out.

The analysis presented herein is applicable to property held for the production of income, not for capital gains. Due to the somewhat different legal restrictions involved, setting quantitative guidelines for the latter-type property would require a slightly different form of analysis. Furthermore, we shall restrict our attention to the usual corporate situation, in which the incremental tax rate is constant over time and depreciation is fully covered by pretax earnings.

The remainder of the present exposition is divided into four major parts: (1) a description of the Investment Tax Credit and of the various procedures that are commonly used for depreciation accounting, their characteristics, and the legal restrictions on their use; (2) a derivation of the discounted tax savings resulting from use of the straight-line and accelerated depreciation methods; (3) certain conditions under which one method of depreciation is preferable to another; and (4) a consideration of depreciation policies that involve switching from one method to another. Finally, a small section at the end of the chapter recapitulates the results in a form suitable for day-to-day use.

The definitions given below are necessary for the subsequent discussion and are consistent with the current version of the Internal Revenue Code [6].

## 4.3. Definitions

**4.3.1.** *Depreciable property.* Any property, personal[3] or real, tangible or intangible, which is used in the conduct of a trade or business or which is held to produce income, which was acquired in a bona fide transaction and which has a limited and estimable life exceeding 1 year (property having a useful life of 1 year or less is expensed, not depreciated).

**4.3.2.** *Basis of property.* For purposes of computing depreciation, the basis of any item of depreciable property purchased by the taxpayer is the cost of the property plus the cost of any capital additions made to the property; that of property inherited is equal to the fair market value of the property at the time of inheritance. Determination of the basis of an asset obtained in other ways can be quite intricate; see Chapter I, Subchapters O, C, K, and B of the Internal Revenue Code of 1954, as amended.

**4.3.3.** *Useful life.* The useful life of the property that is used for purposes of calculating depreciation can be estimated by the taxpayer subject to review and possible disallowance by the Internal Revenue Service. Alternatively, one may obtain from the IRS an agreement in writing fixing the useful life of the property in question. Such an agreement is binding both upon the IRS and the taxpayer.

**4.3.4.** *Salvage value.* The salvage value of an asset is the taxpayer's estimate of the market value of the asset at the end of its useful life. The Revenue Act of 1962 stipulates that in calculating depreciation for certain property the taxpayer may elect to

---

[3]Personal property is used here in the legal sense, that is, as any property that is not realty.

reduce the salvage value by up to *10% of the basis* of the property. In order to qualify for this election the property must be depreciable personal property acquired after October 16, 1962, having a useful life of at least 3 years [4]. The election may be applied only in tax years beginning after January 1, 1962. Clearly, it is to the taxpayer's advantage to make this election whenever possible.

Salvage value enters explicitly into calculations of depreciation by the straight-line and sum-of-the-years' digits methods but not in computing depreciation by means of the declining balance method. No matter which method is used for calculating depreciation, however, the total depreciation taken may not exceed the basis minus the salvage value.

**4.3.5. Symbols and notation.** Throughout this chapter we shall use the following symbolic notation:

$N$ = depreciable life of the asset (years).

$B$ = original installed cost, or *basis*, of the asset.

$L$ = estimated salvage value of the asset after its useful life of $N$ years, possibly reduced by $0.1B$ in accordance with the 1962 Code.

$i$ = the effective interest rate applicable to cash flows (for finding equivalence).

$T$ = the effective income tax rate.

$T_0$ = the first-year 20% additional depreciation rate.

$F_t$ = the undepreciated balance remaining at the end of period $t$.

$D_t$ = the depreciation taken (claimed) during period $t$.

$t$ = a subscript referring to a given period ($t = 0, 1, 2, ..., N$).

$P$ = the present value of a tax savings due to depreciation of assets. The subscript used on $P$ indicates the mode of depreciation used:

$P_0$ = the present value using the straight-line depreciation method.

$P_\alpha$ = the present value using the declining balance method.

$P_S$ = the present value using the sum-of-years' digits method.

$\alpha/N$ = the depreciation rate used for the declining balance method; $\alpha = 1.5$ for used property and $\alpha = 2$ for new property.

$M$ = some period (number of years) where $M < N$.

$\Pi$ = the combined depreciation and discount factors for any depreciation method (SL, DB, or SYD).

$\Delta v$ = definition in Eq. (4.13).

$\omega$ = the right-hand side of Inequality (4.19).

$\chi$ = the right-hand side of Inequality (4.20).

$P(M)$ = the present value of the cash flow resulting from taking depreciation over the first $M$ years.

$C(M)$ = the cumulative depreciation over the first $M$ years.

$\lambda(M)$ = definition in Eq. (4.32).

$\mu(M)$ = definition in Eq. (4.33).

## 4.4. Allowable Methods of Depreciation

**4.4.1.** *20% first year depreciation.* On qualifying property, 20% of the first $10,000 of the cash cost (or the first $20,000 of the cash cost if a joint return is filed) of newly purchased property may be deducted the first year. In order to qualify, property must be tangible personal property with a useful life of at least 6 years and must be acquired by purchase after December 31, 1957.

If the property was purchased on trade-in, the cash cost does not include that portion of the basis of the new property that is due to the residual basis of the property traded in but rather includes that portion paid for in cash or its equivalent. The basis of the new property is reduced by the amount of the first year depreciation; the property is then depreciated by some suitable method using the new basis. The total amount of first year depreciation is shown in Fig. 4.1 as a function of the cash cost of the

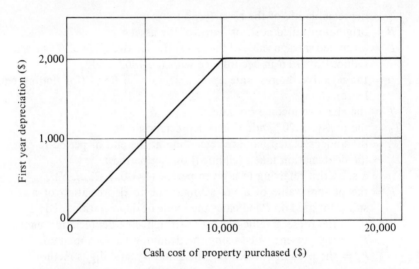

Cash cost of property purchased ($)

**Fig. 4.1.** First year depreciation as a function of cash cost of property purchased during the year.

property. In Fig. 4.2 the effective rate of first year depreciation is shown as a function of the cash cost of the property. Buildings and structural components (such as elevators and escalators) are not eligible for the 20% first year "bonus" depreciation since they are *real* property.

**4.4.2.** *The straight-line method.* Of all the procedures for computing depreciation, the straight-line method is the most widely usable. It may be used on any depreciable property and is the only method that may be used on intangible property. For the straight-line method, the *rate* of depreciation is constant and equal to the reciprocal

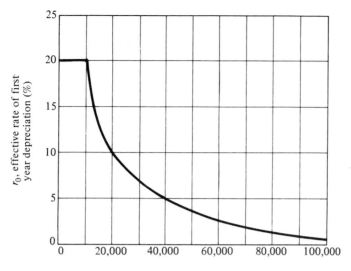

Cash cost of property purchased ($)

**Fig. 4.2.** The effective rate of first year depreciation as a function of the cash cost of property purchased during the year. The rate is constant at 20% up to a cash cost of $10,000. Thereafter it declines hyperbolically.

of the depreciable life of the asset in years. The annual depreciation deduction is computed by dividing the basis minus the salvage value by $N$. Obviously, the deduction is constant over the life of the asset, also. Thus:

$$D_t = \frac{1}{N}(B - L) \tag{4.1}$$

where $1/N$ is called the *straight-line rate*.[4]

---

[4]It is not difficult to show that the straight-line depreciation formula in Eq. (4.1) devolves directly from the famous equation [Eq. (3.26)] that provides for the recovery of capital plus a return on the unrecovered investment, when $i = 0$. Recalling Eq. (3.26),

$$A = (P - L)\left[\frac{i(1 + i)^N}{(1 + i)^N - 1}\right] + Li,$$

the depreciation portion is $D_t = A - Li$, or

$$D_t = (P - L)\left[\frac{i(1 + i)^N}{(1 + i)^N - 1}\right]$$

in which, if $i = 0$, we have the indeterminate form $D_t = 0/0$. Applying l'Hôpital's rule,

$$\lim_{i \to 0} D_t = \lim_{i \to 0} (D_t') = (P - L)\lim_{i \to 0}\left[\frac{Ni(1 + i)^{N-1} + (1 + i)^N}{N(1 + i)^{N-1}}\right],$$

or

$$D_t\Big|_{i=0} = (P - L)\left(\frac{1}{N}\right).$$

No other method of depreciation is of universal applicability. For example, in order to use the declining balance method, *the asset must be tangible property with a useful life of at least 3 years.* All the other methods have in common the property that they produce more cash than the straight-line method early in the life of the asset. For this reason, they are generally more profitable than the straight-line method, everything else being equal.

**4.4.3.** *The declining balance method.* The declining balance method may be used on any tangible property having a useful life of at least 3 years. Depreciation for any 1 year is computed by multiplying the depreciation *rate*, which is constant throughout the life of the asset, by the current basis of the asset. The basis is then reduced by the amount of the depreciation taken during that year, and the procedure is repeated for the next year. This cycle continues until either the useful life of the asset is expended or the total depreciation taken is equal to the original basis minus the salvage value. Thus the current basis of the asset declines with time. The depreciation rate is larger than that used for the straight-line method. The maximum rate that can be used with the declining balance method is twice that of the straight-line method or $2/N$. This rate applies only if the property was acquired *new* by the taxpayer after December 31, 1953; otherwise, the maximum rate is $1.5/N$. The latter rate is used if the property was acquired *used* or *acquired before January 1, 1954.*

We shall now calculate the amount of the declining balance left after the $t$th year and the amount of depreciation allowable using the declining balance method during the $t$th year [1], [6]. Let $\alpha/N$ be the *rate of depreciation* to be used with the declining balance method. The value of $\alpha$ is indicated above. If $\alpha$ is equal to 2, the method is called the *double declining balance method*, or less commonly, the *200% declining balance method*; if $\alpha$ is equal to 1.5, the method is called the *150% declining balance method.* Let $F_t$ be the amount of the declining balance after the $t$th year and $D_t$ be the depreciation taken during the $t$th year. Then

$$\left.\begin{aligned} F_1 &= B - B\frac{\alpha}{N} = B\left(1 - \frac{\alpha}{N}\right), \\ F_2 &= F_1 - F_1\frac{\alpha}{N} = B\left(1 - \frac{\alpha}{N}\right)^2, \\ &\quad\cdot \\ &\quad\cdot \\ &\quad\cdot \\ F_t &= F_{t-1} - F_{t-1}\frac{\alpha}{N} = B\left(1 - \frac{\alpha}{N}\right)^t, \end{aligned}\right\} \tag{4.2}$$

and

$$D_t = F_{t-1}\frac{\alpha}{N} = B\frac{\alpha}{N}\left(1 - \frac{\alpha}{N}\right)^{t-1}. \tag{4.3}$$

Since $F_n \neq 0$, there is a salvage value of the asset implicit in the declining balance

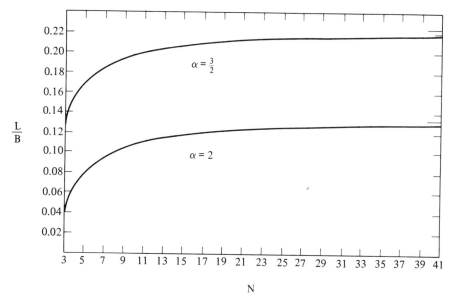

**Fig. 4.3.** The salvage value implicit in the declining balance method as a function of the estimated life of the asset, and the limit as $N$ increases without bound.

method [2]. This salvage is different for different values of $\alpha$ and $N$. Its variation with $N$ for the two most common values of $\alpha$ is shown in Fig. 4.3 and in Table 4.1. For a given basis and $\alpha$, the salvage value increases monotonically as $N$ increases, gradually approaching the limit:

$$\lim_{N \to \infty} F_t = \lim_{N \to \infty} B \left(1 - \frac{\alpha}{N}\right)^N = Be^{-\alpha}. \qquad (4.4)$$

**Example 4.4.1.** Suppose the initial basis of a depreciable asset is \$10,000 and that the estimated economic life is 5 years. For the double declining balance method, $\alpha = 2$, and the end-of-period balances for the first 5 years are

$$F_1 = \$10,000(1 - \tfrac{2}{5}) = \$6,000$$
$$F_2 = \$10,000(1 - \tfrac{2}{5})^2 = \$3,600$$
$$F_3 = \$10,000(1 - \tfrac{2}{5})^3 = \$2,160$$
$$F_4 = \$10,000(1 - \tfrac{2}{5})^4 = \$1,296$$
$$F_5 = \$10,000(1 - \tfrac{2}{5})^5 = \$\ \ 778.$$

Hence, the salvage value at the end of 5 years is $L = F_5 = \$10,000(0.077760)$

**Table 4.1.** THE SALVAGE VALUE THAT IS INHERENT IN THE DECLINING BALANCE METHOD, AS A FRACTION OF THE BASIS.

| $N$ | $\alpha$ | |
|---|---|---|
|  | $\frac{3}{2}$ | 2 |
| 3 | 0.125000 | 0.037037 |
| 4 | 0.152588 | 0.062500 |
| 5 | 0.168070 | 0.077760 |
| 6 | 0.177979 | 0.087792 |
| 7 | 0.184864 | 0.094865 |
| 8 | 0.189927 | 0.100113 |
| 9 | 0.193807 | 0.104160 |
| 10 | 0.196874 | 0.107374 |
| 11 | 0.199361 | 0.109989 |
| 12 | 0.201417 | 0.112157 |
| 13 | 0.203146 | 0.113983 |
| 14 | 0.204620 | 0.115543 |
| 15 | 0.205891 | 0.116891 |
| 16 | 0.206999 | 0.118067 |
| 18 | 0.208836 | 0.120020 |
| 20 | 0.210298 | 0.121577 |
| 25 | 0.212910 | 0.124364 |
| 30 | 0.214639 | 0.126213 |
| 35 | 0.215867 | 0.127528 |
| 40 | 0.216785 | 0.128512 |
| 45 | 0.217497 | 0.129276 |
| 50 | 0.218065 | 0.129886 |
| $\infty$ | 0.223130 | 0.135335 |

= \$777.60, which rounds to \$778. The corresponding depreciation schedule for the \$10,000 asset would be

$$D_1 = B_0 - F_1 = \$10,000 - \$6,000 = \$4,000$$
$$D_2 = F_1 - F_2 = \$\ 6,000 - \$3,600 = \$2,400$$
$$D_3 = F_2 - F_3 = \$\ 3,600 - \$2,160 = \$1,440$$
$$D_4 = F_3 - F_4 = \$\ 2,160 - \$1,296 = \$\ 864$$
$$D_5 = F_4 - F_5 = \$\ 1,296 - \$\ 778 = \underline{\$\ 518}$$

$$\sum_{t=1}^{5} D_t = \$9,222$$

and the sum of the depreciation amounts, \$9,222, plus the salvage value, $F_5 = L$ = \$778, is the original basis, $B = \$10,000$.

**4.4.4. *The sum-of-the-years' digits method.*** The sum-of-the-years' digits method may be used on *personal* property and, in general, on property used as a part of manufacturing, production, or extraction. With this method, the current year's depreciation deduction is calculated by subtracting the salvage value from the original basis of the property and multiplying this quantity by a fraction that differs from year to year. The fraction has a denominator which is constant with time and which is equal to the sum of the digits representing the number of years of useful life of the asset. For example, for $N = 5$, the denominator equals $1 + 2 + 3 + 4 + 5 = 15$. The numerator changes each year and is equal to the number of useful years of life left in the asset at the beginning of the current year. For example, if an asset originally had a useful life of 5 years, at the end of the second year it has 3 years' useful life remaining so that the fraction for the third year would be $\frac{3}{15}$ or $\frac{1}{5}$. In general, for an asset with $N$ years' useful life the denominator of the fraction is equal to $N(N + 1)/2$ and the numerator of the fraction is equal to $N - t + 1$, so that the entire fraction is equal to $2(N - t + 1)/N(N + 1)$. Thus,

$$D_t = \frac{2(B - L)(N - t + 1)}{N(N + 1)} \tag{4.5}$$

and the amount of depreciation deducted in any given year is proportional to the useful remaining life of the asset at the beginning of that year [2], [7].

The *book value* (undepreciated balance) remaining at any time $t$ can easily be found by subtracting from the original basis, $B$, the cumulative depreciation to time $t$, or

$$F_t = B - \sum_{t=1}^{t} D_t = B - \frac{2(B - L)}{N(N + 1)} \sum_{t=1}^{t} (N - t + 1)$$

$$= B - \frac{2(B - L)}{N(N + 1)} [(N) + (N - 1) + (N - 2) + \cdots + (N - t + 1)]$$

$$= B - \frac{2(B - L)}{N(N + 1)} \left[ \sum_{t=1}^{N} t - \sum_{t=1}^{N-t} t \right]$$

$$= B - \frac{2(B - L)}{N(N + 1)} \left[ \frac{N(N + 1)}{2} - \frac{(N - t)(N - t + 1)}{2} \right]$$

$$= B - (B - L) + (B - L) \left[ \frac{(N - t)(N - t + 1)}{N(N + 1)} \right];$$

or

$$F_t = (B - L) \left[ \frac{N - t}{N} \right] \left[ \frac{N - t + 1}{N + 1} \right] + L. \tag{4.6}$$

**Example 4.4.2.** Consider again Example 4.4.1 with an asset whose basis $B = \$10{,}000$ and life $N = 5$ years. With a salvage value $F_s = \$778$ (the same as for the DDB method) the sum-of-years' digits method yields the following depreciation schedule and undepreciated balances:

$$D_1 = \frac{2(\$10,000 - \$778)(5)}{30} = \$3,074$$

$$D_2 = \frac{2(\$10,000 - \$778)(4)}{30} = \$2,459$$

$$D_3 = \frac{2(\$10,000 - \$778)(3)}{30} = \$1,844$$

$$D_4 = \frac{2(\$10,000 - \$778)(2)}{30} = \$1,230$$

$$D_5 = \frac{2(\$10,000 - \$778)(1)}{30} = \$\ 615$$

$$\sum_{t=1}^{5} D_t = \$9,222$$

$$F_1 = (\$10,000 - \$778)(\tfrac{4}{5})(\tfrac{5}{6}) + \$778 = \$6,926$$
$$F_2 = (\$10,000 - \$778)(\tfrac{3}{5})(\tfrac{4}{6}) + \$778 = \$4,467$$
$$F_3 = (\$10,000 - \$778)(\tfrac{2}{5})(\tfrac{3}{6}) + \$778 = \$2,622$$
$$F_4 = (\$10,000 - \$778)(\tfrac{1}{5})(\tfrac{2}{6}) + \$778 = \$1,393$$
$$F_5 = (\$10,000 - \$778)(0)(\tfrac{1}{6}) + \$778 = \$\ 778$$

Note that the final salvage value $L = F_5 = \$778$, as in the DDB model, and that the depreciation amounts for the SYD method are smaller than the DDB amounts in the early years but larger in the later years.

These are the three methods of depreciation that are specifically allowed by law. In addition, the Internal Revenue Code states that "any other consistent method productive of an annual allowance which when added to all allowances for the period commencing with the taxpayer's use of the property and including the taxable year, does not, during the first two-thirds of the useful life of the property, exceed the total of such allowances which would have been used had such allowances been computed under the method described in paragraph (2)." The method described in the paragraph referenced is the declining balance method. Thus, the *declining balance method produces as fast a write-off as is allowable* during the early life of the asset. *In this sense, it is a limiting method of depreciation.*

## 4.5. The Investment Tax Credit

The so-called Investment Tax Credit was originally instituted by the Revenue Act of 1962 in order to encourage investment in new plants and equipment. That act provided that a certain fraction of the amount of money invested by an individual or a firm in new capital assets is deductible as an investment credit from the taxpayer's income tax liability. The basis of the asset was then reduced by the amount of the investment credit. In 1966, the investment credit was suspended for a 15-month period because it was considered to have been a stimulus to inflation. After 5 months of suspension, the credit was restored in 1967 because it was felt the inflationary pressures had eased. Next, the credit was repealed by the Tax Reform Act of 1969 [6] on the grounds that it was contributing a great deal to the inflationary spiral and that it was administratively difficult to "turn on and off." Finally, to provide a stimulus to the lagging economy, the investment credit was restored by the Revenue Act of 1971, increased in amount to the level of 10% in 1975, and reduced to 7% for property purchased after December 31, 1976.

In order to qualify for the investment credit, property must be "Section 38" property, which is tangible personal property or other tangible property (but not including buildings or their structural components) that (a) is used as an integral part of manufacturing, production, or extraction or to furnish transportation, communication, electricity, gas, water, or sewage disposal services; (b) constitutes a research or storage facility used in connection with the above; or (c) is elevators and escalators. It now includes only depreciable property with a usable life of at least 3 years constructed or acquired by the taxpayer after December 31, 1976. Under certain conditions, the investment credit is also available to *owners* of leased property (lessors), and the right to receive the credit may be passed to the lessee if he is the original user. Under certain conditions, used property may also qualify.

The amount of the investment credit is not always simply 7% of the total amount invested by the taxpayer during the current tax year in new plant and equipment.[5] The effective rate used for computing the investment credit varies with the estimated life of the asset as shown in Table 4.2. Moreover, the maximum amount of investment credit that is allowable in a single year depends on the taxpayer's *total tax liability* during that year in the manner illustrated in Fig. 4.4. Thus, in practice, the effective rates used for computing the investment credit may not be those shown in Table 4.2 under some circumstances. In addition, only $100,000 of *used* property may be subject to the investment credit.

**Table 4.2.** VARIATION WITH ESTIMATED LIFE OF THE FRACTION OF THE BASIS THAT IS SUBJECT TO THE 7% INVESTMENT CREDIT AND (AS A CONSEQUENCE) OF THE EFFECTIVE RATE FOR COMPUTING THE CREDIT

| *Life (Years)* | *Fraction of Basis Subject to Credit* | $r_0$, *Effective Rate* (%) |
|:---:|:---:|:---:|
| Less than 3 | 0 | 0 |
| 4–5 | $\frac{1}{3}$ | $2\frac{1}{3}$ |
| 6–7 | $\frac{2}{3}$ | $4\frac{2}{3}$ |
| At least 8 | 1 | 7* |

*10% if property was purchased and placed in service after January 22, 1975, and before December 31, 1976; otherwise 7%.

[5] The investment tax credit rate for public utilities is 4% instead of 7%.

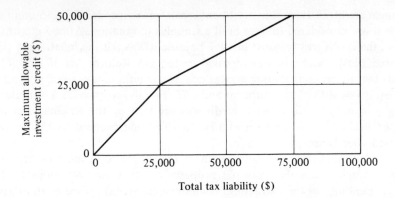

**Fig. 4.4.** The maximum investment credit that is allowed as a function of the taxpayer's total income tax liability. Past $25,000, the maximum allowable credit is $25,000 + 0.5 (Tax liability—$25,000).

**Example 4.5.1.** Suppose a manufacturing company purchased a new machine tool on January 1, 1978, for $65,000 cash. Clearly, its basis in the property is $65,000. The tool has a useful life, $N$, of 10 years. The manufacturer estimates that at the end of its useful life the machine will have a salvage value of $14,000. The manufacturer elects to reduce this salvage value by 10% of the basis of the asset, however, so that $L = \$14,000 - \$6,500 = \$7,500$.

On its 1978 tax return, the manufacturer reports so-called 20% first year depreciation amounting to $2,000 and, as a consequence, reduces its original basis in the property by this amount to a total of $63,000. In addition, he reports a 7% investment credit of $4,550; *this does not affect its basis in the property.* Using the new basis, the company then proceeds to depreciate the property throughout its life by the straight-line method, the double declining balance method, or the sum-of-the years' digits method, giving rise to the following further deductions:

| Year | Straight-Line Method | Double Declining Balance Method | Sum-of-the-Years' Digits Method |
|------|----------------------|--------------------------------|----------------------------------|
| 1978 | $5,550 | $12,600 | $10,091 |
| 1979 | 5,550 | 10,080 | 9,082 |
| 1980 | 5,550 | 8,064 | 8,073 |
| 1981 | 5,550 | 6,451 | 7,064 |
| 1982 | 5,550 | 5,161 | 6,055 |
| 1983 | 5,550 | 4,129 | 5,045 |
| 1984 | 5,550 | 3,303 | 4,036 |
| 1985 | 5,550 | 2,641 | 3,027 |
| 1986 | 5,550 | 2,114 | 2,018 |
| 1987 | 5,550 | 1,691 | 1,009 |

At the corporate tax rate (48% on all income over $50,000) the tax savings produced by reporting these depreciation deductions and investment credit are $5,510 in 1978 due to the 20% first year depreciation and the 7% investment credit, plus:

| Year | Straight-Line Method | Double Declining Balance Method | Sum-of-the-Years' Digits Method |
|------|---------------------|--------------------------------|--------------------------------|
| 1978 | $2,664 | $ 6,048 | $ 4,844 |
| 1979 | 2,664 | 4,838 | 4,359 |
| 1980 | 2,664 | 3,870 | 3,875 |
| 1981 | 2,664 | 3,096 | 3,391 |
| 1982 | 2,664 | 2,477 | 2,906 |
| 1983 | 2,664 | 1,982 | 2,422 |
| 1984 | 2,664 | 1,585 | 1,937 |
| 1985 | 2,664 | 1,268 | 1,453 |
| 1986 | 2,664 | 1,015 | 969 |
| 1987 | 2,664 | 812 | 484 |

Discounting these tax savings at 10% per year yields a present value of $21,378 for the tax savings due to reporting depreciation using the straight-line method, $24,334 for the double declining balance method, and $23,684 for the sum-of-the-years' digits method. As we shall see later, even greater tax savings often can be obtained by using the declining balance method for the first several years of the asset's life and then switching to the straight-line method.

If a taxpayer owns a depreciable asset for only a portion of the year, all the 20% first year depreciation and the 7% investment credit may be taken, but only a pro rata share of the regular depreciation allowance may be deducted.

Table 4.3 recapitulates the conditions under which the investment credit and the various methods of depreciation may be used in computing depreciation allowances for various kinds of assets. Figure 4.5 shows how cumulative depreciation calculated by the various methods varies throughout the life of a typical asset.

## 4.6. The Present Value of the Cash Flow Due to Depreciation

We shall now compute the present value of the cash flow due to depreciation deductions. Since the allowances for the first year depreciation and the 7% credit are deducted at the end of the first year of the asset's ownership, the present value of these allowances is clearly equal to the total amount of the deduction divided by $(1 + i)$.

**4.6.1. *Straight-line method.*** For the straight-line method, an amount $(B - L)/N$ is deducted for each of the $N$ years of the asset's useful life. This deduction gives rise to

**Table 4.3.** COMPUTING DEPRECIATION ALLOWANCES FOR VARIOUS KINDS OF ASSETS, USING THE INVESTMENT CREDIT, AND VARIOUS METHODS OF DEPRECIATION.

| Qualifying Property | Allowable Credit and Methods of Depreciation | | | | | |
|---|---|---|---|---|---|---|
| | 20% First Year Depreciation | Straight Line | Double Declining Balance | 150% Declining Balance | Sum-of-the-Years' Digits | 7% Investment Credit |
| I. Intangible Property | | X | | | | |
| II. Tangible Property | | | | | | |
|   A. Useful life 2 years | | X | | | | |
|   B. Useful life 3 years | | | | | | |
|     1. Constructed or acquired *new* after December 31, 1976: | | X | X | X | X | X |
|     2. Acquired *used*: | | X | | X | | X* |
|   C. Useful life 4 or 5 years | | | | | | |
|     1. Constructed or acquired *new* after December 31, 1976: | | | | | | |
|       a. Buildings used as an integral part of manufacturing, production, or extraction (Section 1231) | | X | X | X | X | |
|       b. Other property | | X | X | X | X | X |
|     2. Acquired *used*: | | | | | | |
|       a. Buildings used as an integral part of manufacturing, production or extraction (Section 1231) | | X | | X | | |
|       b. Other property | | X | | X | | X* |
|   D. Life of at least 6 years | | | | | | |
|     1. Constructed or acquired *new* after December 31, 1976: | | | | | | |
|       a. Buildings used as an integral part of manufacturing, production, or extraction (Section 1231) | | X | X | X | X | |
|       b. Other real property | | X | X | X | X | |
|       c. Personal property | X† | X | X | X | X | X |
|     2. Acquired *used*: | | | | | | |
|       a. Buildings used as an integral part of manufacturing, production, or extraction | | X | | X | | |
|       b. Other property | | X | | X | | X* |
|       c. Personal property | X† | X | | X | | X* |

*Only the first $100,000 of *used* property may be included for the investment tax credit.

†For corporations, the *maximum* amount of additional first year depreciation is limited to 0.20($10,000) = $2,000 in any one year.

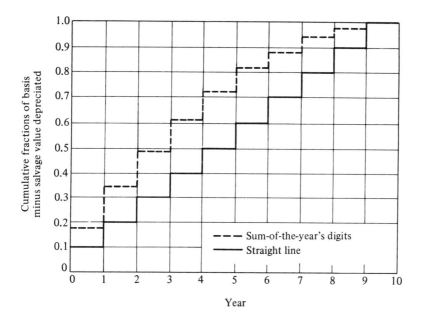

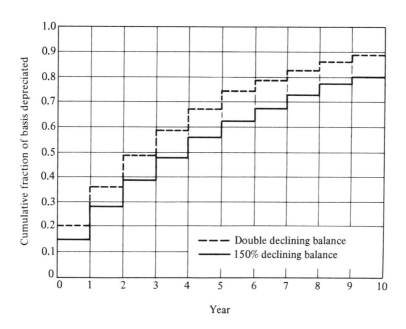

**Fig. 4.5.** The cumulative fraction of the basis (or basis minus salvage value) that is depreciated by the various methods for each year during the life of an asset whose useful life is 10 years.

(cash) tax savings in the amount of $T(B - L)/N$ each year, for a total present value of

$$P_0 = T\left(\frac{B-L}{N}\right) \sum_{t=1}^{N} (1 + i)^{-t} = T\left(\frac{B-L}{N}\right) \frac{1}{i} [1 - (1 + i)^{-N}] \qquad (4.7a)$$

$$= T\left(\frac{B-L}{N}\right) \frac{(1 + i)^N - 1}{i(1 + i)^N} = T\left(\frac{B-L}{N}\right)(P/A, i\%, N). \qquad (4.7b)$$

**Example 4.6.1.** We recall Example 4.5.1, in which a company purchased a new machine tool for $65,000 cash in 1978, estimated it to have a 10-year useful life and a salvage value of $14,000. Also, the company elected to reduce this salvage value by 10% of the basis of the asset ($65,000), so that the adjusted salvage value $L = \$14,000 - \$6,500 = \$7,500$. Moreover, the company exercised a 20% first year depreciation allowance of MIN $[(0.20)(\$65,000)$ or $\$2,000] = \$2,000$, thus reducing the basis to $63,000; and we recall the corporate effective income tax rate is 48%. The tax savings for 1978 and succeeding years are

| Year | Source | Tax Saving |
|------|--------|-----------|
| 1978 | 7% investment credit (see Fig. 4.4): | |
|  | $(0.07)(\$65,000) =$ (direct tax savings) $=$ | $4,550 |
| 1978 | 20% first year depreciation ($\leq \$2,000$): | |
|  | $T_0 = [0 \leq (0.20)(\$65,000) \leq \$2,000]$ | |
|  | Tax saving $= T(T_0) = 0.48(2,000) =$ | $960 |
| 1978 | Normal first year depreciation (S.L.): | |
|  | $D_1 = (B - L)/N = (\$63,000 - \$7,500)/10$ | |
|  | $= \$5,550/\text{yr}$ | |
|  | Savings $= TD_1 = (0.48)(\$5,550) =$ | $2,664 |
| 1979 through 1987 | $\begin{cases} D_t = (\$63,000 - \$7,500)/10 = \$5,550/\text{yr} \\ \text{Saving} = TD_t = (0.48)(\$5,550.) = \\ (t = 2, 3, \ldots, 10) \end{cases}$ | $2,664/\text{yr} |

Assuming the effective interest (discount) rate is $i = 10\%$ and that the tax savings accrue at the ends of the years enumerated, the present value (end of 1977) is

| Year | (Tax Saving)$(P/F, 10\%, t)$ | | Present Value, $\Delta P_0$ |
|------|------------------------------|---|----------------------------|
| 1978 | $8,174 (0.9091) | $=$ | $ 7,430.90 |
| 1979 | 2,664 (0.8264) | $=$ | 2,201.65 |
| 1980 | 2,664 (0.7513) | $=$ | 2,001.50 |
| 1981 | 2,664 (0.6830) | $=$ | 1,819.55 |
| 1982 | 2,664 (0.6209) | $=$ | 1,654.13 |
| 1983 | 2,664 (0.5645) | $=$ | 1,503.76 |
| 1984 | 2,664 (0.5132) | $=$ | 1,367.05 |
| 1985 | 2,664 (0.4665) | $=$ | 1,242.78 |
| 1986 | 2,664 (0.4241) | $=$ | 1,129.80 |
| 1987 | 2,664 (0.3855) | $=$ | 1,027.09 |
| | $P_0$ | $=$ | $21,378.21 |

The present value could also have been calculated using Eq.(4.7):

$$P_0(\text{S.L.}) = T\left(\frac{B-L}{N}\right)(P/A, i\%, N)$$

$$= 0.48\left(\frac{63,000 - 7,500}{10}\right)\overset{P/A,\,10\%,\,10}{(\;6.1446\;)}$$

$$= \$16,369.13$$

to which must be added the present value of the 7% investment credit and the tax saving due to the 20% first year depreciation, or

$$\overset{P/F,\,10\%,\,1}{(\$4,550 + \$960)(\;0.9091\;)} = \$5,009$$

so that the total $P_0' = \$16,369 + \$5,009 = \$21,378$.

**4.6.2. Declining balance method.** Equation (4.3) indicates the periodic depreciation for this method is

$$D_t = B\frac{\alpha}{N}\left(1 - \frac{\alpha}{N}\right)^{t-1}.$$

From this relationship, the present value of the tax savings due to the declining balance depreciation over the life of the asset ($N$ periods) is

$$P_\alpha = TB\frac{\alpha}{N}\sum_{t=1}^{N}\left(1 - \frac{\alpha}{N}\right)^{t-1}(1 + i)^{-t}.$$

This expression can be simplified as follows. First, multiply the right-hand side by $[1 - (\alpha/N)]/[1 - (\alpha/N)]$, to obtain

$$P_\alpha = TB\frac{\alpha/N}{1 - (\alpha/N)}\sum_{t=1}^{N}\left(1 - \frac{\alpha}{N}\right)^{t}(1 + i)^{-t}.$$

Second, let

$$C = TB\frac{\alpha/N}{1 - (\alpha/N)}\quad\text{(a constant)};$$

$$a = 1 - \frac{\alpha}{N}\quad\text{(another constant)};$$

$$b = 1 + i\quad\text{(a third constant)};$$

$$d = \frac{a}{b}\quad\text{(a fourth constant)}.$$

Then, making these substitutions

$$P_\alpha = C\sum_{t=1}^{N}\left(\frac{a}{b}\right)^{t} = C\sum_{t=1}^{N}d^{t},$$

the right-hand side of which is simply a constant ($C$) times the summation of the first $N$ terms of a partial geometric series (common ratio $= d$) whose form is

$$P_\alpha = C(d + d^2 + d^3 + \cdots + d^N)$$

and which, upon factoring $d$ on the right-hand side, becomes

$$P_\alpha = Cd(1 + d + d^2 + d^3 + \cdots + d^{N-1}). \tag{4.8}$$

The terms in parentheses in Eq. (4.8) form a geometric series of $N$ terms, the first one being unity, and with a common ratio $d$. This series can be summed by multiplying Eq. (4.8) through by the common ratio, $d$:

$$P_\alpha d = Cd(d + d^2 + d^3 + \cdots + d^N)$$

and subtracting from Eq. (4.8), thus:

$$P_\alpha - P_\alpha d = Cd(1 - d^N),$$

and then solving for $P_\alpha$:

$$P_\alpha = Cd\left(\frac{1 - d^N}{1 - d}\right).$$

We now back-substitute $d = a/b = [1 - (\alpha/N)]/(1 + i)$ and $C = (TB\alpha/N)/[1 - (\alpha/N)]$ to obtain

$$P_\alpha = TB\,\frac{\alpha/N}{1 - (\alpha/N)}\left[\frac{1 - (\alpha/N)}{1 + i}\right]\left\{\frac{1 - \left[\dfrac{1 - (\alpha/N)}{1 + i}\right]^N}{1 - \left[\dfrac{1 - (\alpha/N)}{1 + i}\right]}\right\}$$

or

$$P_\alpha = TB\,\frac{\alpha}{N}\,\frac{1 - \left[\dfrac{1 - (\alpha/N)}{1 + i}\right]^N}{i + (\alpha/N)}, \tag{4.9}$$

which is the expression for the present value of a series of declining balance depreciation amounts.

**Example 4.6.2.** Again reviewing the data in Example 4.5.1, we can calculate the present value of the tax savings resulting from the double declining balance depreciation deductions as

$$P_\alpha = (0.48)(63,000)(\tfrac{2}{10})\left[\frac{1 - \left(\dfrac{1 - \frac{2}{10}}{1 + 0.10}\right)^{10}}{0.10 + \frac{2}{10}}\right]$$

$$= \$19,325.42$$

to which we again add the present value of the tax savings due to the 20% first year depreciation and the 7% investment credit, or ($5,510)(0.9091) = $5,009, yielding a total present value $P_\alpha' = \$19,325 + \$5,009 = \$24,334$. Note that the present value due to using the double declining balance method of depreciation is nearly $3,000 greater than what could have been obtained by using the straight-line method (Example 4.6.1).

**4.6.3. *Sum-of-years' digits method.*** Equation (4.5) indicates the periodic sum-of-years' digits depreciation amount is

$$D_t = \frac{2(B - L)(N - t + 1)}{N(N + 1)}.$$

Assuming that these values of $D_t$ occur at the ends of periods $t = 1, 2, \ldots, N$, the present value of the series at interest (discount) rate $i$ is

$$P_S = T \frac{2(B - L)}{N(N + 1)} \sum_{t=1}^{N} \frac{N - t + 1}{(1 + i)^t}.$$

This relationship can be simplified as follows. Partition the numerator of the summation, $(N - t + 1)$, into two parts, one of the form $(N + 1)$ and the other of the form $(-t)$; thus:

$$P_S = \frac{2T(B - L)}{N(N + 1)} \left[ (N + 1) \sum_{t=1}^{N} (1 + i)^{-t} - \sum_{t=1}^{N} t(1 + i)^{-t} \right]. \tag{4.10}$$

Then letting $s = (1 + i)^{-1}$ and defining two arbitrary variables $Q$ and $R$ as

$$Q = \sum_{t=1}^{N} (1 + i)^{-t} = \sum_{t=1}^{N} s^t$$

$$= s + s^2 + s^3 + \cdots + s^N$$

and

$$R = \sum_{t=1}^{N} t(1 + i)^{-t} = \sum_{t=1}^{N} t s^t$$

$$= s + 2s^2 + 3s^3 + \cdots + N s^N,$$

we then recognize both $Q$ and $R$ as two geometric series whose finite sums are

$$Q = \frac{s(1 - s^N)}{1 - s}$$

and

$$R = \frac{s(1 - s^N) - (1 - s)Ns^{N+1}}{(1 - s)^2}.$$

Substituting these values of $Q$ and $R$ into Eq. (4.10) gives

$$P_S = \frac{2(B - L)T}{N + 1} \left[ \frac{N + 1}{N} Q - \frac{R}{N} \right],$$

which, after back substitution for $Q$, $R$, and $s$ and several intermediate steps of algebraic manipulation, yields

$$P_S = \frac{2(B - L)T}{(N + 1)i} \left\{ 1 + \frac{1}{Ni} [(1 + i)^{-N} - 1] \right\}, \tag{4.11}$$

which is the expression for the present value of the tax savings resulting from the depreciation amounts found by a sum-of-years' digits method.

**Example 4.6.3.** Returning again to the data in Example 4.5.1, the present value of the tax savings resulting from the SYD method may be calculated from Eq. (4.11) as follows:

$$P_S = \frac{2(63,000 - 7,500)(0.48)}{(10 + 1)(0.10)} \left\{ 1 + \frac{1}{10(0.10)} [(1 + 0.10)^{-10} - 1] \right\}$$

$$= \frac{2(55,500)(0.48)}{1.10} [1 + 1(-0.614460)]$$

$$= \$18,674.31$$

to which we again add \$5,009 (the tax savings due to 7% investment credit and 20% first year depreciation), to obtain a total present value $P'_s = \$18,674.31 + \$5,009 = \$23,683$ for the SYD method.

## 4.7. Simple Depreciation Strategies

Throughout the remainder of this chapter, we shall select as optimal that depreciation policy or strategy that *maximizes the present value of the resulting tax savings* since this is, in effect, an effective cash inflow to the firm.

We shall now investigate the circumstances under which one method of depreciation used throughout the life of an asset is more profitable than any other method of depreciation so used.

**4.7.1. *First year depreciation.*** As we have seen from Fig. 4.2, the *effective* depreciation rate for the first year is not always 20%. Thus, it might be advantageous *not* to take the additional first year depreciation, under certain circumstances. To show that this hypothesis is false, we proceed as follows.

Let $T_0$ be the *effective* additional 20% first year depreciation *rate*. Also, let $B\Pi$ be the present value of the method of regular depreciation to be used, where $B =$ the basis of the asset and $\Pi =$ the combined depreciation and discount factors for the method of depreciation used. Then we shall take the additional first year depreciation if, and only if, the present value of the *total* depreciation on the property, including the additional first year depreciation, is at least as great as the present value of the depreciation on the property without the additional first year depreciation.

In symbolic form, we take the additional first year depreciation if, and only if,

$$T_0 B(1 + i)^{-1} + (1 - T_0)B\Pi \geq B\Pi \tag{4.12}$$

or

$$T_0 B(1 + i)^{-1} + B\Pi - T_0 B\Pi \geq B\Pi$$

$$T_0 B(1 + i)^{-1} - T_0 B\Pi \geq 0$$

$$T_0(1 + i)^{-1} - T_0\Pi \geq 0$$

$$T_0 - T_0(1 + i)\Pi \geq 0;$$

that is, if

$$T_0[1 - (1 + i)\Pi] \geq 0, \tag{4.13a}$$

which is true if $T_0 > 0$ and if

$$(1 + i)\Pi = (1 + i)\sum_{t=1}^{N}(1 + i)^{-N} < 1. \tag{4.13b}$$

$T_0$ is, of course, always positive. It is also easy to prove that $(1 + i)\Pi$ is never greater than one, as follows:

a. For the straight-line method,

$$(1 + i)P_0 = \frac{1}{N} \sum_{i=1}^{N} (1 + i)^{-i+1} \leq 1$$

since there are $N$ terms, all but the first being less than zero.

b. For the declining balance method,

$$(1 + i)P_\alpha = \left[\frac{1 + i}{1 + (N/\alpha)i}\right]\left\{1 - \left[\frac{1 - (\alpha/N)}{1 + i}\right]^N\right\} < 1$$

since both factors are less than one.

c. For the SYD method,

$$(1 + i)P_S = \frac{2(1 + i)}{N(N + 1)i^2}[Ni - 1 + (1 + i)^{-N}];$$

but

$$(1 + i)^{-N} < \left[1 - Ni + \frac{N(N + 1)}{2}i^2\right]$$

so that $(1 + i)P_s < 1$. (See footnote 6.)

Thus, the Inequality (4.13) always holds, and it is always advantageous to take the additional 20% first year depreciation.

**4.7.2. *Optimal value of the estimated useful life of the asset.*** We shall now prove the well-known result that it is always preferable to use as small an estimated useful

---

[6]To show that $(1 + i)P_s < 1$, given $i < 1$, we first note that, by the binomial expansion, the complete series $(1 + i)^{-N}$ is always less than the sum of a finite number of terms in the expansion; e.g., say for the first three terms,

$$(1 + i)^{-N} < 1 - Ni + \frac{N(N + 1)i^2}{2}. \tag{1}$$

Now rewrite this expression for $-N + 1$, obtaining

$$(1 + i)^{-N+1} < 1 - (N - 1)i + \frac{(N - 1)Ni^2}{2}. \tag{2}$$

From the given SYD expression,

$$(1 + i)P_s = \frac{2(1 + i)}{N(N + 1)i^2}[Ni - 1 + (1 + i)^{-N}]$$

we have

$$(1 + i)P_S = \frac{2}{N(N + 1)i^2}[Ni(1 + i) - (1 + i) + (1 + i)^{-N+1}]$$

$$= \frac{2}{N(N + 1)i^2}[Ni + Ni^2 - 1 - i + (1 + i)^{-N+1}]. \tag{3}$$

But from Inequality (2) and Eq. (3) we have

$$(1 + i)P_s < \frac{2}{N(N + 1)i^2}\left[Ni + Ni^2 - 1 - i + 1 - (N - 1)i + \frac{(N - 1)Ni^2}{2}\right]$$

or

$$(1 + i)P_s < 1. \quad \text{Q.E.D.}$$

life of the asset as can be justified legally. We shall prove this fact by showing that either the first derivative (with respect to $N$) or the first difference of the present value is negative. Differentiating Eq. (4.7b) with respect to $N$ gives

$$\frac{dP_0}{dN} = T\frac{B-L}{i}\{-N^{-2}[1 - (1+i)^{-N}] - (1+i)^{-N}\log_e(1+i)\} < 0.$$

Similarly, the derivative of Eq. (4.9) is

$$\frac{dP_\alpha}{dN} = -TB\alpha\left\{i(Ni+\alpha)^{-2}\left[1 - (1+i)^{-N}\left(1 - \frac{\alpha}{N}\right)^N\right]\right.$$

$$+ (Ni+\alpha)^{-1}(1+i)^{-N}\left(1 - \frac{\alpha}{N}\right)^N\log_e(1+i)$$

$$+ (Ni+\alpha)^{-1}(1+i)^{-N}\left[\left(2 - \frac{\alpha}{N}\right)\left(1 - \frac{\alpha}{N}\right)^{N-1} + \left(1 - \frac{\alpha}{N}\right)^N\log_e\left(1 - \frac{\alpha}{N}\right)\right]\right\}$$

$$< 0.$$

Finally, we shall find it useful to define the quantity

$$\Delta v \equiv i^2 N(N+1)(N+2)\frac{P_S(N+1) - P_S(N)}{2T(B-L)}, \tag{4.14}$$

which is proportional to the first difference of Eq. (4.9). It follows from the definition above and from Eq. (4.9) that

$$\Delta v = (2 - Ni)(1+i)^{N+1} - (Ni+2+2).$$

But since $(1+i)^{N+1} > 1$,

$$\Delta v < 2 - Ni - Ni - 2i - 2 = -2i(N+1) < 0. \tag{4.15}$$

Thus, the present value of any of the three methods of depreciation becomes larger as the estimated useful life of the asset decreases.

**4.7.3. Sum-of-years' digits method versus the straight-line method.** We shall now prove that, when it can be used, the sum-of-the-years' digits method is always superior to the straight-line method.

Setting

$$P_S > P_0$$

gives

$$\frac{2}{i(N+1)}\left\{1 - \frac{1}{Ni}[1 - (1+i)^{-N}]\right\} > \frac{1}{Ni}[1 - (1+i)^{-N}],$$

or

$$2 + (N+1)i + (Ni - i - 2)(1+i)^N > 0. \tag{4.16}$$

Expanding the binominal yields

$$(N-1)i^{N+1} + N!\sum_{N=3}^{N}\frac{(N+1)(n-2)}{n!(N-n+1)!}i^n > 0, \tag{4.17}$$

an expression that is true for all positive values of $i$ and for all values of $N$ greater than

1. Therefore, when it is applicable, the sum-of-the-years' digits method is always superior to the straight-line method.

**4.7.4. *Declining balance method versus the straight-line method.*** We shall now examine the circumstances under which the declining balance method is preferable to the straight-line method. In contrast with the results of Section 4.7.3, we shall find that sometimes one method is preferable and sometimes the other, depending on the rate of return that can be earned and upon the ratio of the salvage value of the asset to its original basis. We shall find that, generally speaking, high rates of return and high values of the ratio of the salvage value to the basis favor the declining balance method. The former is not surprising; a high rate of return on the tax savings produced should favor an accelerated method of depreciation. The latter is true because there is a salvage value implicit in the declining balance method (see Fig. 4.3) that may be quite large with respect to the actual salvage value of the asset. Thus, considerably more depreciation *in toto* may be available if one uses the straight-line method. Obviously, this effect decreases as the actual salvage value of the asset increases.

Setting

$$P_\alpha > P_0$$

gives, by substitution,

$$B \frac{\alpha}{N} \frac{1 - \{[1 - (\alpha/N)]/(1 + i)\}^N}{(\alpha/N) + i} > (B - L) \frac{1}{Ni} [1 - (1 + i)^{-N}], \qquad (4.18)$$

which yields, after rearrangement, ·

$$\frac{L}{B} > 1 - \frac{\alpha i \{(1 + i)^N - [1 - (\alpha/N)]^N\}}{[(\alpha/N) + i][(1 + i)^N - 1]} \qquad (4.19)$$

as the condition under which the declining balance method is preferable to the straight-line method. We shall designate the right-hand side of the Inequality (4.19) by $\omega$. Then the declining balance method of depreciation is preferable to the straight-line method if the ratio of the salvage value to the original basis ($L/B$) of the asset is greater than $\omega$; whereas the straight-line method is preferable if the ratio $L/B$ is less than $\omega$. Values of $\omega$ are given in Fig. 4.6 as a function of $i$ for several values of $N$ and for $\alpha = \frac{3}{2}$. We are not concerned here with values of $\alpha$ greater than $\frac{3}{2}$ since whenever these values can be used, the sum-of-the-years' digits method can be used also, and the latter would be used in preference to the straight-line method. We shall consider the latter comparison in Section 4.7.5.

**4.7.5. *The declining balance method versus the sum-of-years' digits method.*** We shall now examine the conditions under which the declining balance method is superior to the sum-of-the-years' digits method. The derivation and the results are analogous with those given in Section 4.7.4. Which method is superior is determined by the rate of return that can be earned and by the ratio of the salvage value of the asset at the end of its useful life to its original basis. Again, we shall see that large values of the rate of return and of the ratio of salvage value to basis favor the declining balance method.

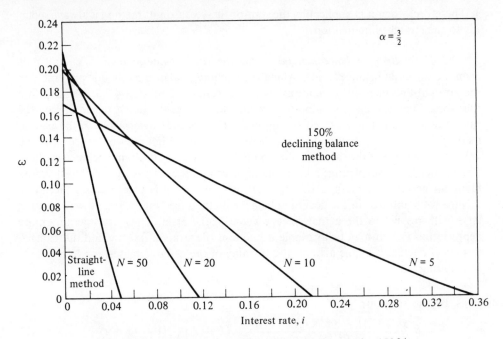

**Fig. 4.6.** The straight-line method is preferable to the 150%
declining balance method for those values of $L/B$ lying below
the appropriate line; the 150% declining balance method is
preferable for values of $L/B$ falling above the line.

Setting

$$P_\alpha > P_S$$

gives, by substitution of Eqs. (4.8) and (4.11),

$$B \frac{\alpha}{N} \frac{1 - \{[1 - (\alpha/N)]/(1 + i)\}^N}{(\alpha/N) + i} > (B - L) \frac{2}{i(N + 1)} \left\{1 - \frac{1}{Ni}[1 - (1 + i)^{-N}]\right\},$$

which yields, after rearrangement,

$$\frac{L}{B} > 1 - \frac{i^2\alpha(N + 1)\{(1 + i)^N - [1 - (\alpha/N)]^N\}}{2[(\alpha/N) + i][(Ni - 1)(1 + i)^N + 1]}, \qquad (4.20)$$

as the condition under which the declining balance method is preferable to the sum-of-the-years' digits method.

We define the variable $\chi$ as the right-hand side of Inequality (4.20). As before, the declining balance method is preferable if $L/B$ is greater than $\chi$, while the sum-of-the-years' digits method is preferable if $L/B$ is less than $\chi$.

Values of $\chi$ are given as a function of $i$ for several values of $N$ and for $\alpha = 2$ in Fig. 4.7. Obviously, we are not concerned with values of $\alpha$ less than 2 since a taxpayer

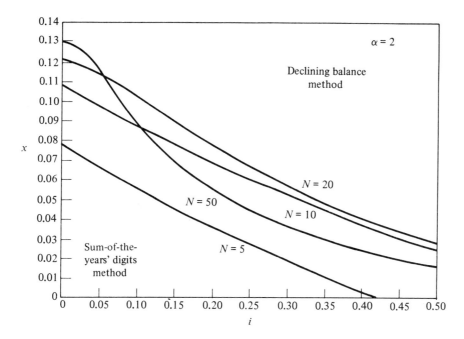

**Fig. 4.7.** The sum-of-the-years' digits method is preferable to the double declining balance method for those values of $L/B$ lying below the appropriate line; the opposite is true for those values of $L/B$ lying above the line.

will use as large a value of $\alpha$ as possible, and if the sum-of-the-years' digits method is allowable, so is the double declining balance method.

## 4.8. Depreciation Strategies Involving Switching

In the absence of an agreement to the contrary between the taxpayer and the Treasury Department, the taxpayer may at any time elect to change his method of depreciation from the declining balance method, or the sum-of-years' digits method, to the straight-line method.

As we shall see, it is to the taxpayer's advantage to switch from the declining balance method when the salvage value implicit in the declining balance method (see Fig. 4.3) is large with respect to the salvage value of the actual asset in question. Also, we shall point out that it is not advantageous to switch from the sum-of-years' digits method, under ordinary circumstances.

**4.8.1. *Switching from the declining balance method to the straight-line method.*** The present value of the cash flow resulting from declining balance depreciation over the first $M$ years ($M \leq N - 1$), similar to Section 4.6.2, is given by

$$P_\alpha(M) = TB\frac{\alpha}{N}\sum_{t=1}^{M}\left(1 - \frac{\alpha}{N}\right)^{t-1}(1 + i)^{-t}$$

$$= TB\frac{\alpha/N}{1 - (\alpha/N)}\sum_{t=1}^{M}\left(\frac{1 - (\alpha/N)}{1 + i}\right)^t,$$

which is a sum of the first $M$ terms of a geometric series, the closed form of which is

$$P_\alpha(M) = TB\left(\frac{\alpha}{B}\right)\left\{\frac{1 - [1 - (\alpha/N)/(1 + i)]^M}{1 + (\alpha/N)}\right\}. \tag{4.21}$$

At time $t = M$, we shall decide whether (a) to adopt a policy of switching to straight-line depreciation in the *next* and succeeding periods (i.e., from $t = M$ to $t = M + 1, M + 2, \ldots, N$) or (b) to continue with the declining balance depreciation policy for *one more period*. [We should note that at time $t = M$, the present value, $P_\alpha(M)$ (at $t = 0$) given by Eq. (4.21), is the same regardless of whether the switching policy is adopted or not since switching affects the *next* period.]

At $t = M$, the book value of the asset is

$$B_M = B - C(M) = B\left(1 - \frac{\alpha}{N}\right)^M$$

via Eq. (4.2), and given that $B_M > L$ (this requirement is always necessary since the IRS regulations prohibit the depreciation of an asset to a book value less than a reasonable salvage value). If the policy is to continue in the next period with the declining balance method, then the next period $(M + 1)$ depreciation amount would be

$$(D_{M+1})_{\text{DB}} = B_M\frac{\alpha}{N} = B\left(1 - \frac{\alpha}{N}\right)^M\left(\frac{\alpha}{N}\right);$$

thereafter, if the same decision is made, the declining balance depreciation amounts would be given by

$$(D_t)_{\text{DB}} = B\left(1 - \frac{\alpha}{N}\right)^{t-1}\left(\frac{\alpha}{N}\right) \quad (t = M + 2, M + 3, \ldots, N). \tag{4.22}$$

(We note that $0 < \alpha/N < 1$ always since $\alpha = 1.5$ or $2$ and $N \geq 3$.) Hence, $0 < [1 - (\alpha/N)] < 1$ also, and as a consequence

$$(D_{M+1})_{\text{DB}} > (D_{M+2})_{\text{DB}} > \cdots > (D_N)_{\text{DB}}. \tag{4.23}$$

On the other hand, if the policy in period $M + 1$ is to switch to the straight-line method, then the remaining periodic depreciation amounts would be given by

$$(D_t)_{\text{DBS}} = \frac{B[1 - (\alpha/N)]^M - L}{N - M} \quad (t = M + 1, M + 2, \ldots, N), \tag{4.24}$$

where $(D_t)_{\text{DBS}}$ = the (equal) periodic depreciation amounts due to the *switched* (DBS) policy.

Now, switching to a straight-line policy becomes attractive only if $(B_N)_{\text{DB}} > L$, i.e., if the implied book value due to the declining balance method at $t = N$ is greater than the salvage value, $L$. [Otherwise, at some other earlier point in time, say $t = M$, then

$(B_M)_{DB} = L$, and no further depreciation could be taken—this would be an optimal policy since we saw in Section 4.7.5 that the DB method is preferred to the SL method over the same life $(M)$]. Assuming thus that $(B_N)_{DB} > L$, then switching should occur if, and only if,

$$(D_{M+1})_{DBS} > (D_{M+1})_{DB}, \tag{4.25}$$

that is, if and only if the depreciation amount in the *next* period via the switched straight-line strategy (DBS) would exceed the depreciation amount via the declining balance, or *unswitched* (DB) method. The reasons are as follows:

1. Prior to and including time $t = M$, the $t = 0$ present value, $P_\alpha(M)$, is a fixed amount [see Eq. (4.21)].

2. At time $t = M$, if $(D_{M+1})_{DBS} > (D_{M+1})_{DB}$, then for $t = M + 2, M + 3, \ldots, N$, the *same* inequality will hold; that is

   $$(D_t)_{DBS} > (D_t)_{DB} \quad (t = M + 1, M + 2, M + 3, \ldots, N)$$

   since $(D_{M+1})_{DBS} = (D_{M+2})_{DBS} = (D_{M+3})_{DBS} = \cdots = (D_N)_{DBS} = (D_t)_{DBS}$ [from Eq. (4.24)], and also from Inequality (4.23):

   $$(D_{M+1})_{DB} > (D_{M+2})_{DB} > \cdots > (D_N)_{DB}.$$

   Hence, *period-by-period*, $(D_t)_{DBS} > (D_t)_{DB}$.

3. Because (2) holds, then the present value of the *switched* strategy at time $t = M$, $P_{DBS}(M)$, will always exceed the present value (at $t = M$) of the remaining declining balance depreciation amounts, $P_{DB}(M)$.

Since we need consider only the depreciation amounts in the next period $(M + 1)$, we can derive a criterion for switching from Eqs. (4.22), (4.24), and (4.25). The first requirement is that the salvage value of the asset be less than the imputed salvage value due to the declining balance method; i.e.,

$$L < (B_N)_{DB} = B \left( 1 - \frac{\alpha}{N} \right)^N$$

or

$$\frac{L}{B} < \left( 1 - \frac{\alpha}{N} \right)^N. \tag{4.26}$$

This is an upper limit on the value of $L/B$. The second requirement is that Inequality (4.25) be satisfied, into which we substitute Eqs. (4.22) and (4.24):

$$(D_{M+1})_{DBS} > (D_{M+1})_{DB}$$

or

$$\frac{B[1 - (\alpha/N)]^M - L}{N - M} > B \left( 1 - \frac{\alpha}{N} \right)^M \left( \frac{\alpha}{N} \right),$$

which, after some algebraic manipulations, reduces to

$$\frac{L}{B} < \left( 1 - \frac{\alpha}{N} \right)^M \left[ 1 - (N - M) \frac{\alpha}{N} \right]. \tag{4.27}$$

Combining Inequalities (4.26) and (4.27), we have the criterion

$$\frac{L}{B} < \left(1 - \frac{\alpha}{N}\right)^M \left[1 - (N - M)\frac{\alpha}{N}\right] < \left(1 - \frac{\alpha}{N}\right)^N. \tag{4.28}$$

Since $M$ is an unknown for any given $L/B$ and $N$, solving Inequality (4.28) for $M$ is essentially a problem in recursive approximation. The most efficient way to find the desired value of $M$ is to tabulate $P_{DB}(M)$ and $P_{DBS}(M)$ between zero and $N - 1$ and then to select the appropriate value of $M$ by inspection. Approximately optimal switching times are given in Fig. 4.8.

**4.8.2. Switching from sum-of-years' digits to the straight-line method.** The same type of reasoning and procedure used in Section 4.8.1 can be used to analyze the policy of switching from the sum-of-years' digits method to the straight-line method. In this case, however, it is tedious but not difficult to show that the time $t = M$ present value of the switched policy is always less than the $t = M$ present value of the remaining sum-of-years' digits depreciation; hence, no switching should take place. This demonstration is left as an exercise for the student.

**4.8.3. The declining balance method with switching versus the sum-of-years' digits method.** The derivation outlined in this section is analogous to that of Section 4.8.1, and the result is similar: The possibility of switching enhances the value of the declining balance method.

The declining balance method is preferable to the sum-of-years' digits method if

$$P_{DBS}(M) > P_S, \qquad \text{for some } M \text{ such that } 0 < M \leq N. \tag{4.29}$$

Also, the present value ($t = 0$) of the switched strategy (declining balance to straight line) is the sum of Eq. (4.21) and the $t = 0$ present value of the straight-line depreciation amounts in Eq. (4.24), or

$$
\begin{aligned}
P_{DBS}(M) = {} & TB\left(\frac{\alpha}{N}\right)\left\{\frac{1 - \left[\dfrac{1 - (\alpha/N)}{1 + i}\right]^M}{1 + (\alpha/N)}\right\} \\
& + (1 + i)^{-M} \sum_{t=M+1}^{N} \frac{B[1 - (\alpha/N)] - L}{N - M}(1 + i)^{-t} \\
= {} & TB\left(\frac{(\alpha/N)}{1 + (\alpha/N)}\right)\left\{1 - \left[\frac{1 - (\alpha/N)}{1 + i}\right]^M\right\} \\
& + \frac{1}{i(N - M)}\left[\left(1 - \frac{\alpha}{N}\right)^M - \frac{L}{B}\right][(1 + i)^{-M} - (1 + i)^{-N}]. \tag{4.30}
\end{aligned}
$$

Substituting into Eq. (4.29) from Eqs. (4.10) and (4.30) and solving for $L/B$ gives

$$\frac{L}{B} > \zeta(M) \equiv 1 + \frac{\begin{aligned}(N + 1)[(\alpha/N) + i][(1 + i)^{-M} - (1 + i)^{-N}] \times [1 - (\alpha/N)]^M \\ - [i(\alpha/N)](N + 1)(N - M)\{1 - [1 - (\alpha/N)^M(1 + i)]\}\end{aligned}}{\begin{aligned}2[(\alpha/N) + i](N - M)\{1 - (1/Ni)[1 - (1 + i)^{-N}]\} \\ - (N + 1)[(\alpha/N) + i][(1 + i)^{-M} - (1 + i)^{-N}]\end{aligned}}$$

$$\tag{4.31}$$

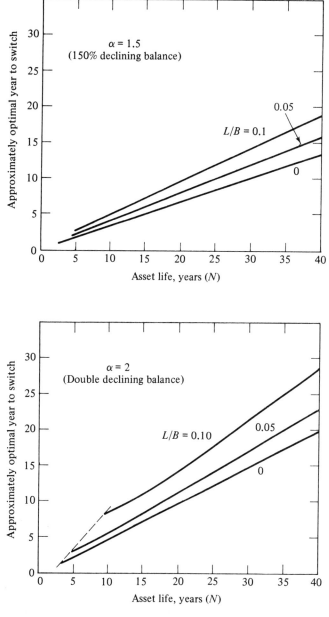

**Fig. 4.8.** Approximately optimal year to switch from the declining balance method to the straight-line method.

for some $M$ such that $0 < M \leq N$. Thus, the declining balance method with switching is preferable if

$$\frac{L}{B} > \zeta \equiv \min_{0 < M \leq N \zeta(M)}, \tag{4.32}$$

and the sum-of-the-years' digits method (without switching) is preferable if

$$\frac{L}{B} < \zeta. \tag{4.33}$$

The variation of $\zeta$ with $i$ for several values of $N$ is shown in Fig. 4.9.

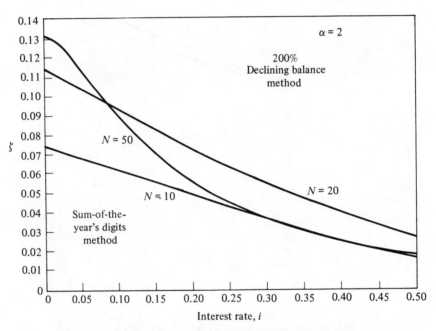

**Fig. 4.9.** The declining balance method with switching is preferable to the sum-of-the-years' digits method when $L/B > \zeta$; the sum-of-the-years' digits method is preferable if $L/B < \zeta$.

## 4.9. Summary of Conclusions: Depreciation

In this chapter we have derived several decision rules that maximize the present value of the income tax savings resulting from depreciation deductions, for the case in which the incremental tax rate of the taxpayer remains constant over the useful life of the asset. These rules fall into two categories as follows.

Rules applying whether switching is allowed or not:

1. Take the 20% first year depreciation deduction and the investment credit wherever possible.
2. Always use as small a value of $N$ as possible.
3. When using the declining balance method, use as large a value of $\alpha$ as possible.

Rules applying when switching is not allowed:

4. The sum-of-the-years' digits method is always preferable to the straight-line method.
5. The declining balance method without switching is preferable to the straight-line method if $L/B > \omega$; the straight-line method is preferable if $L/B < \omega$.
6. The declining balance method without switching is preferable to the sum-of-the-years' digits method if $L/B > \chi$; the sum-of-the-years' digits method is preferable if $L/B < \chi$.
7. It is never advantageous to switch from the sum-of-the-years' digits method to the straight-line method.
8. It is advantageous to switch from the declining balance method to the straight-line method if, and only if, the actual salvage value of the asset is less than the salvage value implied in the declining balance method.
9. The declining balance method with optimal switching is always preferable to the straight-line method.
10. The declining balance method with optimal switching is preferable to the sum-of-the-years' digits method if $L/B > \zeta$; the sum-of-the-years' digits method is preferable if $L/B < \zeta$.

These rules, together with currently existing legal restrictions on the use of the various methods, can be depicted as logical flow diagrams, as shown in Fig. 4.10

## 4.10. Depletion of Resources

Depletion operates to reduce the income tax cash outflow in the same general manner as depreciation, with one important difference. Whereas depreciation is applied to the basis of *tangible* property, depletion allowances are applied in reduction of the basis of *natural resources*, such as mines, wells, and timberlands. The allowance arises, in theory at least, because the resource is "severed" or produced and is irreplaceable. The deduction for depletion is aimed theoretically at compensating the taxpayer for his *capital* consumed in severance and production, and for his *loss* of the resource. Thus, *depletion* is to the owner of a produced natural resource what *depreciation* is to the owner of a depreciable asset.

**4.10.1. *Entitlement to depletion.*** Annual depletion deductions depend on the owner's economic interest. As a general rule, every person (firm, partnership, corporation, etc.) *receiving income from the exhaustion of a natural resource* is entitled to

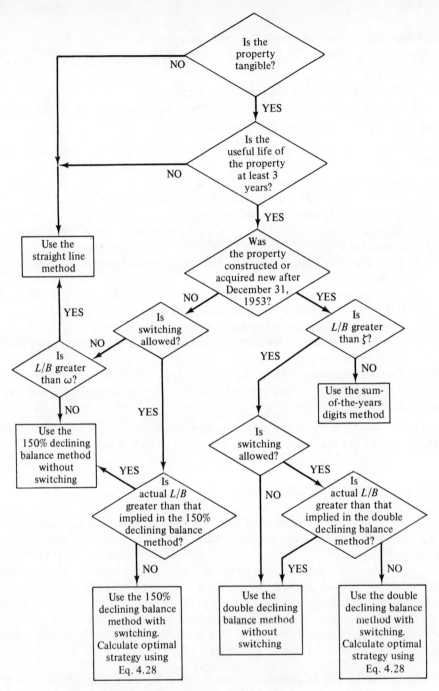

**Fig. 4.10.** Optimal depreciation strategies for income tax purposes when the tax rate is constant over time.

deduct an allowance for depletion as an expense on his tax return *according to his capital interest in the property.*

The right to a depletion deduction depends on two factors: (1) the economic interest (ownership of a capital investment, or a portion thereof) in the resource in place and (2) the actual production of the resource. If either of these two factors is absent, no depletion deduction is allowable.

**4.10.2.** *Methods for computing depletion deductions.* There are only two methods for calculating depletion deductions. The basic method for calculating depletion, applicable to all types of depletable assets, is known as *cost depletion.* The second method, applicable to all depletable assets except timber, is known as *percentage depletion.* These two methods will be described briefly.

Cost depletion is, simply stated, the cost of the mineral interest (or other interest, such as timber or gravel), divided by the estimated recoverable reserves, multiplied by the number of units sold during the taxable year. More specifically, cost depletion is found by first *estimating* the number of units (tons, barrels, board feet, etc.) that make up the resource deposit. Then the number of producible units is divided into the cost of the property (or that part of the total cost allocable to the resources deposit). The quotient is the *cost depletion per unit* of resource. This amount is multiplied by the number of units *sold* or, in the case of timber, the number of units *felled,* during the year. The product of the number of units times the cost depletion per unit establishes the *cost depletion deduction* for the year.

**Example 4.10.1.** The Empire Mining Company bought a mine for $65,000, and an engineer's estimate indicated that 600,000 tons of ore could be mined. The estimated value of the land, *excluding the ore deposit,* was $5,000. During the first year, 65,000 tons of ore were extracted, and 60,000 tons were sold. Cost depletion for the year is calculated as follows:

$$\text{Cost depletion per unit} = \frac{\text{net basis of resource}}{\text{estimated total reserve}}$$

$$= \frac{\$65,000 - \$5,000}{600,000 \text{ tons}}$$

$$= \$0.10 \text{ per ton.}$$

$$\text{Cost depletion} = (\$0.10/\text{ton})(60,000 \text{ tons})$$

$$= \$6,000.$$

The second method of calculating the depletion deduction is called the *percentage depletion* method and is limited to those who are otherwise entitled to *cost depletion.* It is *not* applicable to timber resources, nor is it generally applicable to petroleum and natural gas deposits. In general, percentage depletion is calculated by multiplying a percentage factor, fixed in amount by law, times the *gross income from the property—* that is, the *property* is the ore deposit or other *developed* resource producing the gross income. Percentage depletion, as calculated by a fixed percentage times the gross income from the property (deposit), is then limited to not more than 50% of the *net* income from the property. Net income is calculated without using the depletion deduction.

**Example 4.10.2.** The owner and operator of a sulfur well has gross receipts from the sale of crude sulfur of $100,000 during the taxable year. Operating expenses (labor, power, taxes, etc.) for operating the property are $60,000, leaving a taxable income of $40,000 before deduction of the depletion allowance. Although percentage depletion is allowed on sulfur deposits at a 22% rate, resulting in a tentative depletion deduction of (0.22)($100,000) = $22,000, his allowable percentage depletion is limited to (0.50)($100,000 − $60,000) = $20,000 for the year, which is 50% of the *net* income from the property.

**4.10.3.** *The depletion deduction.* For all depletable assets except timber, the taxpayer *must* use the depletion method that results in the *greater* depletion deduction; that is, depletion is calculated by both the *cost* and *percentage* methods each year, and the greater value for the year is the depletion deduction for the year. For timber, only the cost method may be used.

Because of the rule that the maximum of cost or percentage depletion be used, it is possible to deplete the basis (cost) of the resource deposit (except timber) to a *negative value*. That is, until the cost or basis of the property is recovered (reduced to zero), it is possible to use either cost or percentage depletion (whichever is greater in a particular year) as the means of depleting basis of the property; but once the *basis* is reduced to *zero*, and if the resource continues thereafter to produce, then percentage depletion is *still* allowable (to the extent of 50% of the net income from the property). These percentage depletion deductions, beyond the recovered basis of the resource, in effect drive the book value of the property to a negative amount. Rather than show negative values for producing resources on their balance sheets, most firms show the excess percentage depletion as a credit to their surplus or retained earnings.

**4.10.4.** *Typical percentage depletion rates.* Under the Internal Revenue Code [Section 613(b)], percentage depletion is allowed at specified rates on specified natural resources. The following are some typical rates applied to *gross income from the property* for the indicated resources:

a. 22%—sulfur, uranium, asbestos, bauxite, chromite, graphite, mica, quartz, and ores of antimony, beryllium, cadmium, cobalt, lead, manganese, mercury, molybdenum, nickel, platinum, tin (and others); when produced outside the United States the rate is reduced on some to 14% and others to 10%.
b. 22%—regulated natural gas, natural gas sold under a fixed contract, and any geothermal deposit determined to be a natural gas well.
c. 15%—United States deposits of gold, silver, copper, iron ore, oil shale.
d. 14%—Rock asphalt, vermiculite, ball clay, bentonite clay, refractory clay.
e. 10%—Asbestos (outside U.S.), coal, lignite, perlite, sodium chloride.
f. 7½%—Clay for sewer pipe and tile or for lightweight aggregates.

g. 5%—Gravel, peat, pumice, sand, clay for roofing tile and flower pots; bromine, calcium chloride from wells.

h. 14%—A general classification for nonmetallic minerals to which a *use* test applies. The use test is that it be sold or used for ornamental or dimensioned building stone; otherwise, the rate is 5%.

i. 22% to 15%—petroleum deposits producing less than 2,000 bbl per day and natural gas deposits producing less than 12 MMcf per day; either owned by independent producers.

## 4.11. Amortization of Prepaid Expenses

The *prepayment* of future expenses is generally recovered by expense deductions in future years against income, thus reducing the amounts on which the income tax is paid. Such a process is called *amortization*, and the expense deduction is called an *amortization expense*.

Recent modifications in the income tax laws have extended the deductibility of amortization expenses. The following are some representative categories of *prepaid items* that can (or must) be amortized over the life of the item, rather than deducted in total in the year of acquisition:

a. The expenses on an issue of bonds, such as printing, advertising, and legal fees (mandatory amortization).

b. Premium paid for the purchase of a bond in excess of its face value (amortization elective).

c. Expenses incurred in acquiring a lease (mandatory amortization).

d. Rapid amortization (60 months) of certain rolling stock for domestic railroads placed in service before 1976 (elective; in lieu of depreciation).

e. Rapid amortization (60 months) for pollution control facilities placed in service before 1976 (elective; in lieu of depreciation).

f. Rapid amortization (60 months) for coal mine safety equipment placed in service before 1976 (elective; in lieu of depreciation).

In general, the *method* of amortization is straight line, with zero salvage value.

## 4.12. Class or ADR Depreciation Methods

For assets placed in use after 1970, a taxpayer can calculate depreciation *under the general rules* using the estimated useful lives of the individual assets, *or* he can elect to use the ADR (*a*sset *d*epreciation *r*ange) system. The ADR system of depreciation groups similar assets into classes for the several SIC (*s*tandard *i*ndustrial *c*lassification) codes, applies fixed *ranges* of years as estimated lives to the different classes, and then specifies the methodology for calculating depreciation amounts.

The ADR system is intended to keep conflict between the taxpayer and the Government over individual asset lives at a minimum and to liberalize depreciation rates. A taxpayer thus does not have to justify his asset retirement and replacement policies. The ADR system, with its tabular method of fixing *ranges* for the lives of asset categories, takes the place of the former Bulletin F of the Internal Revenue Service, which was abandoned in 1962. The Revenue Act of 1971 gave statutory effect to the ADR system, which is quite complicated and detailed both in concept and computational detail, and particularly so for early asset retirements.

Once the classification of assets is accomplished and the ADR system is established, however, *then the statutory depreciation methods* (straight-line, declining balance, sum-of-years' digits, or any other truly representative method) *may be used, with one exception*: The ADR system assumes that the asset depreciation period (established by the asset classification) already takes salvage value into account. Accordingly, the *calculations* for the straight-line and sum-of-years' digits methods under ADR *have zero for the salvage value*. Note, however, that *no asset may be depreciated below a reasonable salvage value*, even though zero may have been used to establish the *annual* depreciation amount [Internal Revenue Service Regulations §1.167(a)–1(a)]. Because the *methodology* of ADR depreciation is basically the same as that for individual assets, the details of the ADR system will not be discussed here. The reader can find adequate discussions in the various income tax regulations and publications.

## REFERENCES

[1] MYERS, J. H., "Useful Formulae for DDB and SYD Depreciation," *Accounting Review*, **33** (1958), pp. 93–95.

[2] _____, "Influence of Salvage Value upon Choice of Tax Depreciation Methods," *Accounting Review*, **35** (1960), pp. 598–602.

[3] *U.S. Internal Revenue Code of 1954*, as amended and in force on January 3, 1961 (Washington, D.C.: U.S. Government Printing Office).

[4] *U.S. Revenue Act of 1962* (Washington, D.C.: U.S. Government Printing Office).

[5] *U.S. Revenue Act of 1964* (Washington, D.C.: U.S. Government Printing Office).

[6] *U.S. Revenue Act of 1969* (Washington, D.C.: U.S. Government Printing Office).

[7] VAN NESS, P. H., "The Mathematics of Accelerated Depreciation," *N.A.A. Bulletin* (April, 1961), pp. 5–14.

## PROBLEMS

**4-1.** A new machine is purchased Jan. 1, 197x for $9,000. Delivery and installation charges are $1,000. The expected life of the machine is 8 years at which time it will be sold for $1,000. Compute the book value and depreciation for the fourth year using the following depreciation methods: (a) straight line, (b) declining balance, (c) double declining balance, (d) sum-of-years' digits, and (e) straight line that will recover as much during the first 3 years as during the last 5 years of life.

**4-2.** An asset costs $25,000 and is expected to have a life of 8 years with a salvage value equal to $1,000. (a) What is the depreciation charge for the fifth year and the book value at the end of the fifth year using the declining balance method? (b) What is the depreciation charge for the fifth year and what is the book value at the end of the fifth year using the 200% declining balance method?

4-3. An asset costs $75,000 and is expected to have a life of 20 years with a salvage value of 20% of the initial cost. What is the accumulated depreciation for the first 10 years for each of the following depreciation methods: (a) straight line, (b) declining balance, (c) double declining balance, and (d) sum-of-the-years' digits?

4-4. An asset costs $10,000 and is expected to have a life of 5 years at which time it will have no salvage value. (a) What is the depreciation charge for the third year using sum-of-the-years' digits depreciation? (b) What is the book value at the end of the second year using declining balance depreciation?

4-5. An asset was purchased for $4,000. Shipping and nonrecurring installation costs amounted to $1,000. After 5 years the machine will be sold for $1,000 after paying $500 for dismantling it. (a) What is the book value at the end of the third year using double declining balance depreciation? (b) What is the depreciation charge for the third year using the 150% declining balance method? (c) What is the book value at the end of the third year using the 150% declining balance method?

4-6. An asset costs $600 and is expected to last 6 years at which time it will have a salvage value of $120. What is the book value at the end of the second and fourth year using the following depreciation methods: (a) straight line, which will recover 1.5 times as much during the first half of the life as the second half; (b) straight line, which will recover 2 times as much during the first half of life as the second half; (c) straight line, which will recover 3 times as much during the first 4 years as the last 2 years? Are (a), (b), and (c) "legal" methods of depreciation for tax purposes?

4-7. An asset costs $10,000 and has a life of 10 years with no salvage value. When do you switch from double declining balance depreciation to straight-line depreciation to obtain the *fastest* depreciation possible?

4-8. An asset costs $10,000 and is expected to have a life of 5 years at which time it will have a salvage value of $2,000. (a) Determine the depreciation charge for each year and the book value at the end of each year for the entire life of the asset using straight line, declining balance, double declining balance, and sum-of-the-years' digits depreciation. (b) What is the present value of each depreciation schedule where

$$PV = \sum_{t=1}^{n} D_t(P/F, i, t)$$

and the discount rate is 8%? (c) On the same graph, plot the book values for each of the depreciation methods used above.

4-9. In general, for certain assets, taxpayers may commence depreciation using the double declining balance method and then switch to sum-of-the-years' digits at a later date on a given asset. A company purchased an asset for $10,000 whose life is expected to be 10 years with no salvage value. Assume that the optimum time to switch from DDB to SOYD is in the third year. (a) What is the depreciation schedule using a DDB-switch-to-SOYD method? (b) What is the present value of the depreciation schedule in (a)? (c) What is the present value of the depreciation schedule using a double declining balance with a later (optimal) switch to straight line? [Note: for (b) and (c), assume an interest rate of 10%.]

# CORPORATE INCOME TAX
# CONSIDERATIONS

## 5.1. Introduction

This chapter is concerned with the effects of *income* taxes on the project evaluation problem. It is important at the outset that we distinguish *income* taxes from other types of taxes, as some confusion commonly exists concerning the different types of taxes levied in our economy. Some of the more common taxes are

a. *Property taxes*, often called *ad valorem* taxes, are levied against the *value of property*, that is, against the value of real estate or business and personal property. These taxes are commonly levied by school districts, municipalities, counties, and states.

b. *Sales* or *use taxes* are taxes assessed on the *transfer* of property from one owner to another. The tax is based on the value of the property transferred at the time of sale and is usually levied by a state or city.

c. *Excise taxes* are *Federal* taxes levied against the value of a commodity at a certain stage of manufacture or transfer. Originally (1792), excise taxes comprised the principal source of Federal revenue, and the levies were against commodities thought to be nonnecessities, such as whiskey and molasses. Over the years, this kind of Federal tax has been extended to a variety of items, until now such diverse commodities as gasoline, automobiles, tires, firearms, telephone and teletypewriter service, air transportation, liquors,

# 5

and civil aircraft are taxed. Generally, this tax is paid by the manufacturer or supplier and appears as a part of the price charged to the customer.

All the preceding taxes are independent of the *income* produced by the items taxed, if any. These taxes depend only on the *value* of the item or service at the time it is taxed. The fourth major tax, however, used not only by the Federal government but also by most states and many municipalities, is the *income* tax:

   d. *Income taxes* are assessed against the *taxable income* of individuals and corporations. "Taxable" income is the difference between gross income and certain deductions specified in the tax laws. The income tax due is generally calculated as a percentage of the taxable income.

The information in this chapter is concerned with *income* taxes. As far as industries and businesses are concerned, the other general categories of taxes are either included in the price of the product or service produced or included as an expense of production, so that the net effect of such taxes as far as the firm is concerned is recovered either in *gross income* or as a reduction of *income* tax paid.

In making economic studies of projects, there are basically two types of study that can be made. One type of study is the *before-tax* economic study, in which the effects of the income tax are simply ignored. Although this type of study is of long historical usage in *engineering economy* analyses, it is not necessarily the most desirable or the most informative type of study to make. In fact, modern capital budgeting theory indicates that before-tax studies are, in fact, limited to very special cases in the comparison of alternative choices of action. This topic will be covered in more detail in Chapters 6 and 7.

The other type of economic study is the *after-tax* study, in which the effect of income taxes is explicitly taken into account in the economic study. Income taxes affect all business and industrial firms except those owned by the government or specifically exempt from the tax, such as certain cooperatives and other not-for-profit organizations (e.g., hospitals and charitable organizations). *Unless there is a clear reason for ignoring income taxes, they should always be taken into account in economic studies for the firm.* The reason for this statement is simple: The income tax represents a major cash outflow for most firms, and it should be considered along with all other cash inflows and outflows. This is consistent with the objective stated in Chapter 2: The firm ought to maximize the present value of future *cash flows* since this is the equivalent of maximization of future wealth for the share owners—*even if* the "firm" be owned, in fact, by a not-for-profit cooperative or is a government project owned by the citizens.

The income tax statutes, regulations, and case law are all quite complex. Not only are the Federal laws and regulations difficult for a layperson to understand, but the interrelationships between the Federal and the various state income tax laws are also difficult to comprehend. Furthermore, due to the pressures for increased tax revenues at all levels of government, the income tax laws are in a state of almost constant flux from year to year. Add to this the number of tax procedures and methods that can be changed simply by executive order or by Internal Revenue Service regulation, and one has an impossible task before him if he tries to encapsulate all this into one chapter. What will be done here, then, is simply to present some income tax *principles* rather than the complete methodology. In general, the income tax principles, rates, and regulations are those in existence in 1977.

Furthermore, we see little benefit to be gained by discussing *individual* income taxes—that is, the income taxes assessed on an individual's income. While it is true that there are many businesses and small industries that pay income taxes as if they were individuals (e.g., a partnership or a "Subchapter S" corporation—a corporation whose shareholders elect under the tax laws to be taxed individually), nevertheless, the *major* difference between a business taxed as a corporation and one taxed as an "individual" (or group of individuals) is the *rate* of tax paid.

There are essentially no differences in the *procedures* used to determine taxable income; the only major difference lies in the amount of tax paid due to the *application of different rates.* While individuals pay Federal income taxes based on a sliding scale that increases from 14% to a maximum of 70% of taxable income, with 25 rate *steps* included in this range, a corporation pays its tax based on at most *two* rates. Thus, the calculations leading to taxable income are essentially the same for both individuals and corporations, whereas the number of rates is at most two for corporations versus a possible 25 for individuals. Hence, we shall omit consideration of *individual* income taxes and refer the reader to a more comprehensive source (e.g., [1] and [2]) for this information. It is to be understood, therefore, that what follows hereafter will be in respect to *corporate* income taxes, and specifically Federal income taxes, since these comprise the major income tax burden of business and industry.

## 5.2. Basic Principles of Federal Income Taxation[1]

For corporations, there are *five* basic *income* tax calculations that must be made in order to determine the *income tax liability* to be paid in any given year. These calculations are

1. The *ordinary* income tax liability—that portion of the total income tax determined by the ordinary income and applicable rates, as defined below. Ordinary income has a technical meaning that is quite restricted. It does not mean simply *customary* in the lay sense. Ordinary income is defined in the tax law as resulting, *in the broad sense*, from gross income minus the deductions *allowed by law*. Such deductions generally are the expenses (other than those that are capital in nature) that are connected with the *production of income*.

2. The *capital gains* income tax liability—that portion of the total income tax that results from the sale of certain specified assets at a *gain*, that is, for more than their book value at the time of sale.

3. For businesses, the *Section 1231* income tax liability—similar in nature to the capital gains tax, this portion of the tax liability arises if a *productive* asset (used in the production of income, e.g., a machine, tool, or other asset used in the productive process) is sold at a gain or a loss during the year.

4. The tax on *tax preference items*—a special 10% tax is imposed on certain items called *tax preference items* if *together* they exceed the sum of $30,000 plus the taxpayer's income tax liability for the year. Tax preference items are (a) capital gains (alternative tax method), (b) accelerated depreciation on buildings and other *real* property, (c) accelerated depreciation on personal property subject to a lease, (d) percentage depletion in excess of cost, (e) excess amortization (pollution control facilities, etc.), and (f) excess bad debt deductions for financial institutions.

5. The *accumulated earnings tax*—a special tax is imposed on all earnings *retained* by the corporation in excess of *reasonable needs of the business*. "Reasonable needs" have been defined by the courts to mean the amount of earnings retention required, or anticipated to be required, in one cycle of operation: that is, from the time of purchase of raw materials, through the necessary processing steps, through the sale of the manufactured items, and finally to

---

[1]Portions of the remainder of this chapter are extracted, condensed, and paraphrased from [3], by permission.

the time of collection of the outstanding accounts receivable. If earnings (surplus) are retained *in excess* of such a figure, the presumption is that the corporation retained the earnings to avoid paying dividends to its shareholders (which would then be taxable the *second* time to the shareholders as *individual* income). To forestall this practice, the accumulated earnings tax may be imposed on the corporation, for all retained earnings that are in excess of $100,000. The rates for this tax are $27\frac{1}{2}\%$ on the first $100,000 of *illegal* retention (i.e., on the first $100,000 in excess of the sum of reasonable needs plus $100,000) and $38\frac{1}{2}\%$ on the remainder.

While the *rates* of these several types of income taxes may change from time to time and while the specific method for calculating a particular tax may be altered by law or regulation from year to year, the general *principles* underlying these five basic income tax calculations seem to have survived over a considerable span of years. Hence, the principles of income tax calculation will be illustrated by the following sections, but anyone who undertakes or is responsible for economy studies should be sure that he is familiar with the *current* provisions of the income tax laws and regulations.

## 5.3. The *Ordinary* Income Tax Liability

The *ordinary* income tax is a function of *gross income* and certain specified deductions. Gross income is the total income of the firm that results from its *principal trade or business*. Business gross income is customarily taken as the total receipts from sales minus the cost of goods sold, plus "other" income (such as income from investments). Gross income should not be confused with the gross receipts from the business. Gross income is essentially gross receipts minus cost of goods sold plus "other" income.

The cost of goods sold for any year is determined by valuing the inventory at the beginning of the year, adding purchases during the year, and subtracting the value of the inventory at the end of the year.

In mercantile firms, cost of goods sold would include the purchase price of the articles bought for resale, less cash and trade discounts, plus delivery charges to get the articles into inventory (stock), all adjusted for beginning and ending inventories. In manufacturing firms, it would include the entire *factory* cost—that is, costs of materials used, direct labor, manufacturing overhead, and any other cost accounting items required to *convert* the raw materials into a finished product.

Since only the cost of goods sold is deducted from gross receipts in order to arrive at gross income, it is important to distinguish cost of goods sold from all other costs and expenses of operation allowed as deductions under the tax laws. These other costs and expenses are deducted from gross income in order to arrive at taxable income, on which the ordinary income tax is based.

The procedure of calculating taxable income closely follows the itemization used on a conventional income (profit and loss) statement. An example will illustrate the procedure for calculating taxable income.

**Example 5.3.1.** In Chapter 2, Figs. 2.4 and 2.5 were used to illustrate the cash flows from the Transformer Project of the ABC Company. The same data, now with more detail added, will be used in Fig. 5.1 to illustrate how a taxable income amount is calculated for this project from an income statement.

Several important details should be noted in Fig. 5.1. *First*, gross income is the result of several kinds of transactions, namely, gross *sales*, merchandise allowances and returns, cost of goods sold (includes material, direct labor, and factory overhead), and such other income items as interest and dividends received, plus royalties and rents received. *Second*, *cash* operating expenses (except interest paid) are deducted from gross income, such as those shown in Fig. 5.1. *Third*, *noncash* expense items (depreciation, depletion, and amortization deductions) are subtracted from gross income. *Fourth*, a special cash item—interest paid on indebtedness—is deducted from gross income. The gross income minus the total of these three classifications of *operating expenses* yields *taxable income*, on which the ordinary income tax is based.

Assuming that the following *ordinary* tax rates apply in this example,

$$\text{Federal}\begin{cases}\text{normal tax rate} = \begin{cases}20\% \text{ of first } \$25,000 \text{ taxable income, plus} \\ 22\% \text{ of all taxable income over } \$25,000\end{cases} \\ \text{surtax rate} = 26\% \times (\text{taxable income} - \$50,000)\end{cases}$$

State tax rate = 2.65% of taxable income (assumed)

the ABC Company would calculate its *ordinary* income tax liability as

$$\begin{aligned}\text{Ordinary tax} &= 0.20(\$25,000) + 0.22(\$1,000,000 - \$25,000) \\ &\quad + 0.26(\$1,000,000 - \$50,000) + 0.0265(\$1,000,000) \\ &= \$5,000 + \$214,500 + \$247,000 + \$26,500 \\ &= \$493,000.\end{aligned}$$

The corresponding *cash flow* from operating the Transformer Project would then be calculated by (1) deducting the income tax paid (a cash outflow) from taxable income, and (2) adding back the *noncash items* in the income statement:

| | |
|---|---:|
| Taxable income | $1,000,000 |
| Less ordinary income tax paid | 493,000 |
| After-tax income | $ 507,000 |
| Add: | |
| Depreciation deducted | |
| Depletion deducted | 300,000 |
| Amortization deducted | |
| Cash flow from operations | $ 807,000 |

ABC Company, Inc.

## INCOME STATEMENT—TRANSFORMER PROJECT

for the Year Ended December 31, 19xx

| | | |
|---|---:|---:|
| **GROSS SALES OF TRANSFORMERS** | | $3,100,000 |
| Less Merchandise Returns and Allowances | | 100,000 |
| **NET SALES** | | $3,000,000 |
| Less Cost of Goods Sold: | | |
| Inventory, 1/1/19xx | $ 686,000 | |
| Add Purchases, 19xx | 695,000 | |
| Direct Labor, 19xx | 250,000 | |
| Factory Overhead, 19xx | 250,000 | |
| | $1,881,000 | |
| Less Inventory 12/31/19xx | 496,000 | |
| Cost of Goods Sold: | | 1,385,000 |
| **INCOME FROM OPERATIONS** | | $1,615,000 |
| Add Interest Received | $ 25,000 | |
| Royalties Received | 10,000 | |
| Rents Received | 10,000 | 45,000 |
| **GROSS INCOME** | | $1,660,000 |

Less Operating Expenses:
1. *Cash Items* (such as):

   a. Compensation for personal services not included in direct labor (wages, salaries, bonuses, etc.)

   b. Rentals paid

   c. Repairs (*not* reconstructions)

   d. Losses due to bad debts

   e. Contributions for charitable purposes (limit: 5% of taxable income)

   f. Casualty losses (fire, wind, theft) not covered by insurance     300,000

   g. Advertising and sales promotion expenses

   h. Utilities and communications (electricity, power, heat, telephone, telegraph, postage)

   i. Record-keeping expenses (computer rental, supplies, etc.)

   j. Contributions to qualified employee retirement plans

2. *Noncash Items:*

   a. Depreciation deductions

   b. Depletion deductions     300,000

   c. Amortization deductions

3. *Special Cash Item:*

   Interest paid on borrowed money (i.e., interest paid on bonds, notes, and all other *indebtedness* of the firm)     60,000

**TAXABLE INCOME**     $1,000,000

Fig. 5.1. Typical itemized calculation of taxable income.

Now compare these actual cash flow items above, and in Fig. 5.1, to those in Fig. 2.4:

| *From Income Statement (Fig. 5.1)* | | | *From Cash Flow Statement (Fig. 2.4)* | |
|---|---|---|---|---|
| Net sales | | $3,000,000 | Operating revenues | $3,000,000 |
| Less: | | | Less: | |
| Cost of goods sold | $1,385,000 | | | |
| Operating expenses | 300,000 | | | |
| Other income | (45,000) | 1,640,000 | Cash operating costs | 1,640,000 |
| Interest paid | | 60,000 | Interest paid | 60,000 |
| Income tax paid | | 493,000 | Income tax paid | 493,000 |
| Cash flow from operations | | $ 807,000 | Net funds generated | $ 807,000 |

The essential point is that by adding noncash items back to *after-tax income* on the *operating* statement, we obtain the *same* cash flow result as if we deducted actual cash outflow items from cash inflow items on a *cash flow* statement.

## 5.4. Effective Ordinary Income Tax Rates

The Federal corporate tax rate structure is composed of two rates applied to ordinary income. A *normal* tax rate of 20% is applied to the first $25,000 of corporate ordinary taxable income, and all ordinary taxable income in excess of $25,000 is subject to a *normal* tax rate of 22%. In addition, a *surtax* rate of 26% is imposed on ordinary taxable income in excess of the first $50,000. Thus, for ordinary taxable incomes in excess of $50,000, *both* rates are applied; whereas, for incomes less than $50,000, only the normal tax rates (20% or 22%) apply. This leads to an *effective* Federal tax rate that varies with taxable income, as shown in Table 5.1 and Fig. 5.2.

**Table 5.1.** EFFECTIVE ORDINARY INCOME TAX RATES

| *Corporate Taxable Income* | *Normal Tax* | *Surtax* | *Total Ordinary Tax* | *Effective Rate* |
|---|---|---|---|---|
| $      1.00 | 0.20 | — | 0.20 | 0.200 |
| 1,000.00 | 200.00 | — | 200.00 | 0.200 |
| 10,000.00 | 2,000.00 | — | 2,000.00 | 0.200 |
| 25,000.00 | 5,000.00 | — | 5,000.00 | 0.200 |
| 35,000.00 | 7,200.00 | — | 7,200.00 | 0.206 |
| 50,000.00 | 10,500.00 | — | 10,500.00 | 0.210 |
| 100,000.00 | 21,500.00 | 13,000.00 | 34,500.00 | 0.345 |
| 500,000.00 | 109,500.00 | 117,000.00 | 226,500.00 | 0.453 |
| 1,000,000.00 | 219,500.00 | 247,000.00 | 466,500.00 | 0.467 |

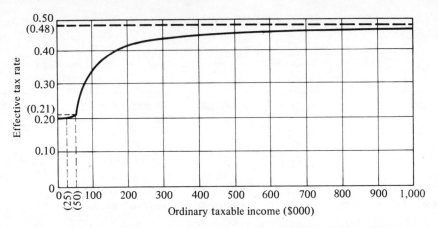

**Fig. 5.2.** Effective ordinary income tax rate as a function of taxable income.

As may be seen in Fig. 5.2, the *effective* Federal ordinary income tax rate approaches 48% asymptotically as the taxable income becomes *large*. Also, if state income taxes are a significant factor, the state income tax rate must be added into the calculation to find the total *effective* ordinary income tax rate to be applied to the corporation's taxable income.

In general, the effective ordinary income tax rate from all taxing sources can be estimated from

$$\text{effective ordinary income tax rate } (T_e) = \frac{\sum (\text{all ordinary income taxes})}{\text{taxable income}}$$

## 5.5. Generalized Cash Flows from Operations

The procedure illustrated in Example 5.3.1, plus the effective tax rate concept developed in Section 5.4, can be generalized to find cash flows from a project for any given period. Thus, for any given period $t$ in the sequence of the project life, $t = 1, 2, \ldots, N$, let

$G_t =$ the gross income from the project; this is a *cash inflow* to the project resulting from operating the project during period $t$.

$E_t =$ the *cash outflows* during $t$ for all deductible expenses, excluding interest paid on project indebtedness.

$D_t =$ the sum of all *noncash* items chargeable during $t$, such as depreciation, depletion, and amortization expenses.

$I_t =$ the *cash interest paid* during $t$ on borrowed funds.

$T_e =$ the effective *ordinary* income tax rate (Federal, state, and other).

$Y_t =$ the net cash flow from the project during $t$.

By analogy to Example 5.3.1, the ordinary income tax due is

$$(G_t - E_t - D_t - I_t)T_e \tag{5.1}$$

and the *after-tax* income is then simply taxable income minus the income tax payable, or

$$\underbrace{(G_t - E_t - D_t - I_t)}_{\text{Taxable income}} - \underbrace{(G_t - E_t - D_t - I_t)T_e}_{\text{Income tax}}$$

or,

$$\text{after-tax income} = (G_t - E_t - D_t - I_t)(1 - T_e). \tag{5.2}$$

The cash flow resulting from the project operation is after-tax income *plus* the noncash items (as in Example 5.3.1), or

$$Y_t = (G_t - E_t - D_t - I_t)(1 - T_e) + D_t. \tag{5.3}$$

Equation (5.3) for the project cash flow can be stated in an alternate form by combining the depreciation terms; thus:

$$Y_t = (G_t - E_t - I_t)(1 - T_e) + D_t T_e. \tag{5.4}$$

In passing, note that the last term in Eq. (5.4) is simply the effective tax rate, $T_e$, times the depreciation deduction, $D_t$, and this is the *equivalent cash contribution* of the *noncash* depreciation deduction to the total cash flow, $Y_t$. This term—the cash flow equivalent of the depreciation deduction—was used in Chapter 4 to evaluate the effectiveness of the different depreciation methods presented there.

**Example 5.5.1.** Consider a firm for which an estimator is forecasting cash flows for a certain project. The estimated gross incomes, operating expenses, interest payments on indebtedness, and depreciation deductions for the project are listed in Table 5.2 below. The effective ordinary income tax rate (state and Federal) is estimated to be 51% of taxable income for each of the years in the estimating period. Find the net cash flows for each of the years and find the present value of the net cash flows if the effective interest rate is 15% per year compounded yearly.

**Table 5.2.** DATA FOR EXAMPLE 5.5.1

| End of Year, $t$, | Gross Income, $G_t$ | Operating Expenses, $E_t$ | Interest Payments, $I_t$ | Depreciation Deduction, $D_t$ |
|---|---|---|---|---|
| 0 | –0– | –0– | –0– | –0– |
| 1 | $100,000 | $50,000 | $4,000 | $20,000 |
| 2 | 140,000 | 60,000 | 2,000 | 16,000 |
| 3 | 180,000 | 70,000 | 1,000 | 12,000 |
| 4 | 160,000 | 80,000 | –0– | 10,240 |
| 5 | 150,000 | 90,000 | –0– | 8,190 |

*Solution.* For the first year, the cash flow by Eq. (5.4) is

$$Y_1 = (\$100,000 - \$50,000 - \$4,000)(1 - 0.51) + \$20,000(0.51)$$
$$= \$46,000(0.49) + \$20,000(0.51) = \$32,740.$$

The cash flows for the second and third years are found in a similar manner. The cash flows for the fourth and fifth years are found similarly, except that $I_4 = I_5 = 0$. The resulting cash flows, $Y_t$ ($t = 1, 2, \ldots, 5$), are tabulated in Table 5.3, along with the $(P/F, 15\%, t)$ factors and incremental cash flows that produce the total present value of the cash flow *stream*, or $P_0 = \$145,043$.

**Table 5.3.** CASH FLOWS FOR EXAMPLE 5.5.1

| End of Year, t | Cash Flow, $Y_t$ | Present Value Factor $(P/F, 15\%, t)$ | Incremental Cash Flow Present Value |
|---|---|---|---|
| 0 | –0– | –0– | –0– |
| 1 | $32,740 | 0.8696 | $ 28,471 |
| 2 | 46,380 | 0.7561 | 35,068 |
| 3 | 59,938 | 0.6575 | 39,409 |
| 4 | 44,422 | 0.5718 | 25,401 |
| 5 | 33,576 | 0.4972 | 16,694 |
| | | | $P_0 = \$145,043$ |

## 5.6. The Capital Gains Tax Liability

In addition to the *ordinary* income tax, corporations are taxed on *gains* made on the sale of certain assets called *capital assets*. The *gain* on which the tax is based is generally the excess of the asset *sale or market value* over its adjusted *book value* at the time of disposition. Thus, if the sale value exceeds the adjusted book value of the asset at the time of sale, a taxable *gain* is the result; if, however, the adjusted book value exceeds the sale value, then a *capital loss* is the result. Hence, capital assets upon sale may have either *gains* or *losses* associated with them. The original purpose of this section of the income tax law was to give preferential tax treatment to the gains derived from the sale of the *tools* of industry as opposed to the profits derived from the *products* made by the tools (capital assets).

One must be very careful to distinguish *capital assets*, upon which gains and/or losses may result, from other assets. Capital assets, *in general*, are now defined by the law to include *all* property held by the taxpayer, *except*

1. Property held primarily for sale to customers in the ordinary course of business. Such property is said to be held *in trade*—that is, for *trading* purposes. Such property (held for sale or trade) is *inventory*, or *stock in trade*. It is *not* a capital asset. Such property is *not* depreciable.

2. Assets used to carry on the production process [including, for example, production machinery, tools, equipment, testing machines, and real property (buildings) *used in connection with the production process*]. Such assets are *not* capital assets. Instead, they are classified for income tax purposes as Section 1231 asstes (see Section 5.7), which are accorded capital gains tax *treatment* under Section 1231 of the Internal Revenue Code. These assets *are* depreciable, but they are *not* capital assets.

3. Short-term noninterest-bearing state or Federal obligations (notes) issued on a discount basis.

4. A copyright; literary, musical, or artistic composition; a letter, memorandum, or similar composition; or *similar* property held by the person who created it (and in the case of a letter, memorandum, or similar property) held also by a person for whom the property was prepared or by a transferee.

5. Accounts or notes receivable acquired in the ordinary course of business for services rendered or for sale of stock in trade.

According to the foregoing, it would appear that all property not specifically excepted above would be treated as a capital asset. Such is not the case, however, because the courts have put narrower interpretations on the exceptions named. Thus, *property* must be judged to be capital or noncapital on a property-by-property basis.

Some examples of property treated by court-interpreted cases are as follows:

*Stocks and securities*, except for the short-term securities mentioned in (3) above, are considered to be capital assets since they are generally held for the *production of income* (this is a principal test). They are *not* capital assets in the hands of securities *dealers*, however, but rather *stock-in-trade*, or inventory. Sale of a bond or stock by one not engaged in the securities business may result in a *capital* gain or loss, but the same sale by a bank or securities dealer would necessarily result in an *ordinary* gain or loss.

*Vacant real estate* held for investment (*not* as a real estate *dealer*) *is* a capital asset. Any gain on its sale is taxed as a capital gain, and any loss is a capital loss.

*Land* used *in the production process* is *not* a capital asset. It is a Section 1231 asset; however, it is *not* depreciable. *Land improvements* (e.g., grading for drainage, drainage structures, curbs, gutters, sewers, landscaping) *used in connection with the production process* are Section 1231 assets, just as the land is; likewise, they are *not* depreciable. Gains on the sale of Section 1231 assets are treated the same as gains on the sale of capital assets, but losses are not treated in the same manner (see Section 5.7).

**5.6.1.** *The capital asset holding period.* When gains or losses do result from the sale of a capital asset, the law provides that the gain or loss be recognized—i.e., taken into account for tax purposes—either *fully* at ordinary income tax rates or *alternatively* at the special 30% rate, depending on the *period of time during which the asset was held.*

If a capital asset is held for 6 months or less, then on its disposal any gain is termed a *short-term gain* and any loss is termed a *short-term loss*. If a capital asset is held for *more than 6 months* (not 6 months or more), then on its disposal any gain is termed a *long-term gain*, and any loss is termed a *long-term loss*.

**5.6.2. *Categorization of gains and losses.*** For *each* capital asset sold during a taxable year, the taxpayer must determine whether or not a gain or loss resulted, or neither; and if one did result, then whether it is a short- or long-term gain or loss. When this determination has been made for each capital asset sold, then certain types of gains and losses are combined. The manner in which the various gains and losses are combined is depicted in Table 5.4.

Referring to Table 5.4, the manner of *combining* gains and losses is as follows. *First*, long-term losses are subtracted from long-term gains. If the long-term gains exceed the long-term losses, then a *net long-term gain* is the result. The opposite leads to a *net long-term loss*. The *net* long-term gain or loss (or neither) defines the starting point in the first column of Table 5.4.

**Table 5.4.** CORPORATION TAX TREATMENT OF CAPITAL GAINS AND LOSSES

| *Net Combined Long-Term Transactions* | *Net Combined Short-Term Transactions* | *Net Result* | *Tax Treatment* | | |
|---|---|---|---|---|---|
| | | | *Capital Gain* | *Capital Loss* | *Ordinary Income* |
| L.T. Gain | None | L.T. Gain | X | | |
| | S.T. Gain | L.T. Gain and S.T. Gain | X | | X |
| | S.T. Loss | Net L.T. Gain or Net S.T. Loss | X | X | |
| L.T. Loss | None | L.T. Loss | | X | |
| | S.T. Gain | Net L.T. Loss or Net S.T. Gain | | X | X |
| | S.T. Loss | L.T. Loss and S.T. Loss | | X X | |
| None | S.T. Gain | S.T. Gain | | | X |
| | S.T. Loss | S.T. Loss | | X | |

*Second,* short-term losses are subtracted from short-term gains. If short-term gains exceed short-term losses, the result is called a *net short-term gain.* The opposite result is called a *net short-term loss.* The *net* short-term gain or loss (or neither) defines the position in the second column of Table 5.4.

*Third,* the result of the *net* values in Columns 1 and 2 is shown in Column 3 (Net Result) in Table 5.4, and the *dollar amounts* of the *net* gains and *net* losses are taxed as shown in Columns 4, 5, and 6. That is, the Net Result in Column 3 is (1) a *combination* of short-term and/or long-term gain and/or short-term and/or long-term loss, and (2) the *combination* is then *taxable* as shown in Columns 4, 5, and 6.

**Example 5.6.1.** During the taxable year, the ABC Company, Inc., had the following capital asset transactions:

| | | |
|---|---:|---:|
| Long-term capital gain | $6,800 | |
| Long-term capital loss | (2,000) | |
| Net long-term capital gain | | $4,800 |
| Short-term capital gain | $3,500 | |
| Short-term capital loss | (4,300) | |
| Net short-term capital loss | | ( 800) |
| Excess of net long-term gain over short-term loss | | $4,000 |

The $4,000 excess would be taxed as a long-term capital gain under the rule summarized in Table 5.4. The capital gain tax rates are explained in Section 5.7.

**5.6.3.** *Taxability of capital gains and losses.* In general, a long-term capital loss is used to reduce long-term capital gains, and a short-term capital loss is used to reduce short-term capital gains. In addition, any *net* long-term loss can be used to reduce *net* short-term gain, and *net* short-term loss can be used to reduce *net* long-term gain. If a *net* gain (short or long term) is the result, there will be a tax due according to Table 5.4.

If there is an overall *net* capital *loss* in a given year, however, then the corporation may use this loss only to *carry backward and forward* against past and future capital gains. *It cannot deduct the excess capital loss* from ordinary income (*individual* taxpayers are accorded this deduction privilege to a limited extent but not corporations). The carry backward and forward privilege works like this: Any excess capital loss not used in the current taxable year may be carried back (in time) to each of the 3 taxable years preceding the loss year, beginning with the most distant year, and then to the other 2 years in succession. The loss in the current year is, thus, first applied to reduce prior reported capital gains in the *third* previous year; then if excess loss remains, it is applied to reduce capital gains in the *second* previous year, and so forth. If all the current taxable year capital loss is not thus used up to reduce prior capital gains, then any excess capital loss may be carried forward for 5 successive years to reduce *future* capital gains, if any. Any capital loss not used up in the carry-back-carry-forward procedure is simply lost taxwise to the corporation. It should be mentioned here that the carryback feature can result in a partial refund by the Government of income tax paid for prior years, which is accomplished by filing an amended tax return for the year(s) in question (up to 3 years back).

The tax rates applied to *corporate* capital gains are as follows:

1. If the capital gain is taxed at *ordinary* income tax rates (Table 5.4), then the tax rate is 20, 22, or 48%, depending on whether the corporation is in the lower or upper normal tax bracket or in the surtax bracket (taxable income > $50,000).

2. If the capital gain is taxed at *capital gains rates*, then the tax rate is the lesser of 20% (or 22%), which are the ordinary tax rates for incomes less than $50,000, *or a special alternative tax rate* of 30% if the corporation is already in the surtax bracket (taxable income greater than $50,000).

**Example 5.6.2.** A corporation has taxable income of $200,000 that *includes* the following gains and losses in addition to its regular income from operations:

| | | |
|---|---:|---:|
| Long-term capital gain | $17,800 | |
| Long-term capital loss | ( 2,200) | |
|    Net long-term capital gain | | $15,600 |
| Short-term capital gain | $ 3,000 | |
| Short-term capital loss | ( 8,000) | |
|    Net short-term capital loss | | ( 5,000) |
|    Excess long-term capital gain | | $10,600 |

What income tax is to be paid?

*Solution.* The tax computation is accomplished in two parts. These are called the *regular tax computation* and the *alternative tax computation.* The corporation pays the *lesser* of the two taxes:

Regular Tax Calculation:

| | |
|---|---:|
| Normal tax, 0.20($25,000) + 0.22($200,000 − $25,000) = | $43,500 |
| Surtax, 0.26($200,000 − $50,000) = | 39,000 |
|    *Total regular (ordinary) tax* | $82,500 |

Alternative Tax Calculation:

| | | |
|---|---:|---:|
| Taxable income | $200,000 | |
| Less: Excess of net long-term capital | | |
|    gain over short-term capital | | |
|    loss (see above) | 10,600 | |
|    *Ordinary income* | $189,400 | |
| Tax on ordinary income: | | |
|    Normal tax, $5,000 + 0.22($189,400 − $25,000) = | | $41,168 |
|    Surtax, 0.26($189,400 − $50,000) = | | 36,244 |
|       *Total ordinary tax* | | $77,412 |
|    Tax on capital gain, 0.30($10,600) = | | 3,180 |
|       *Total alternative tax* | | $80,592 |

Since the alternative tax of $80,592 is less than the regular tax of $82,500, the corporation should pay the lesser amount ($80,592) as allowed by law.

## 5.7. The Section 1231 Tax Liability

In Section 5.6, it was mentioned that assets used *to carry on the production process* are not capital assets, and thus, it might appear that these assets would be denied the favorable tax treatment accorded to capital assets. Fortunately, this is not the case. In fact, production-type assets are accorded even more favorable treatment than capital assets, under Section 1231 of the Internal Revenue Code, as we shall see. The reason for this special exception was developed early in the tax law as a result of practical business pressures. For example, suppose a machine used in the business were classed as a *capital* asset. If the machine were then later sold at a loss before the end of its useful life, the loss would be a *capital* loss, which is deductible only to the extent that it reduces prior or future capital gains. But if the machine were classed as a *noncapital* asset, then such a loss would be an *ordinary* loss, which is fully deductible against gross income in the year of sale. Accordingly, *noncapital* asset treatment for *depreciable* property was extended initially by the Revenue Act of 1938 as an aid to business and industry.

This feature has remained in the law since 1938 but has been modified many times. The principal modifications have been to close some tax *loopholes*, in which favorable taxable gains treatment could result from the premature sale of assets that had been, in effect, overdepreciated due to the use of an accelerated depreciation method. The present version (1977) of Section 1231, however, is generally equitable, since post-1969 depreciation to the extent of the gain is recoverable as ordinary income in the year of disposal of the property (see Section 5.7.2.)

**5.7.1.** *What are Section 1231 assets?* The most convenient way to refer to this special concession for business is by the section of the law that incorporates it. Hence, this widely quoted capital gains provision and the assets it covers are commonly known as *Section 1231 assets*.

The asset items, properly called *property used in the trade or business*, that *are* included in Section 1231 (if held for more than 6 months) are

1. Property used in a trade or business *on which depreciation is allowable*. This category would include such items as buildings, structures, equipment, machinery, tools, materials handling devices, and other similar items used *in connection with the production* of the product or service being produced.
2. Real property used in the trade or business and not held regularly for sale to customers. This category would include, for example, the *land* on which a factory is built and also *improvements* to the land, such as new street pavements, sidewalks, grading, and landscaping. [Note, however, that the costs of road construction, excavating, grading, and dirt (and rock) removal for a

*specific* production-type building are *not* improvements to the land but rather costs that are directly connected with the construction of a particular production facility and *are*, therefore, depreciable as a part of the facility under item (1).] Thus, one must be careful in economic studies to determine *if* and *how much land improvements* may be attributed directly to a production facility before taking the decision to depreciate all or a portion of the cost of these improvements.

3. Coal, domestic iron ore, and timber *royalties*, that is, money royalties received as a result of the severance of the mineral or timber.
4. Certain other items not generally considered to be in the business domain, such as cut timber on which the taxpayer has elected to report the gain at the time of cutting; unharvested crops sold with the land; and livestock held for draft, breeding, dairy, or sporting purposes.

As far as industrial purposes are concerned, the primary interest centers on the first two classifications mentioned—depreciable property and real property *used in the trade or business*. These are the principal Section 1231 assets considered here.

**5.7.2.  *Tax treatment of Section 1231 depreciable assets.*** When Section 1231 assets are sold, one must first categorize the property as either *depreciable* or *non*depreciable Section 1231 assets. For depreciable Section 1231 assets, the tax law contains highly specialized rules that cut down or completely eliminate any capital gain that might result from the sale of these assets at more than their book value. In general, the law requires that prior depreciation deductions be "recaptured" as *ordinary income* in the year of sale, thus resulting in a tax in the year of disposal essentially equal to the taxes saved in prior years by taking the depreciation deductions.

This concept can be visualized better by referring to Fig. 5.3, which is a plot of book values of a Section 1231 asset that was purchased, say, for $P_0 = \$5,000$ and depreciated on a straight-line basis. We need also to assume that the asset was purchased after 1963 since complications arise if the asset was purchased before 1964 and if accelerated depreciation methods are used. With reference to Fig. 5.3, at the time of sale, four mutually exclusive events can happen, each of which has a different income tax consequence under Section 1231:

1. The asset is sold at its book value. In this case, no gain or loss is realized, and no tax consequence derives from the sale.
2. The asset is sold at a selling price, say $SP_1$, which is greater than book value but less than original cost. Here, let $SP_1 = \$2,500$. The tax treatment in the year of sale is as follows. The sale price less book value, $SP_1 - BV = \$2,500 - \$1,000 = \$1,500$, is recaptured depreciation, which is *added* to ordinary income in the year of sale and is taxed at *ordinary* income tax rates (20%, 22%, or 48%).
3. The asset is sold at a selling price, say $SP_2$, which is greater than the original cost of the asset. Here, let $SP_2 = \$6,000$. The tax treatment is as follows: The *gain* is $SP_2 - BV = \$6,000 - \$1,000 = \$5,000$. The depreciation

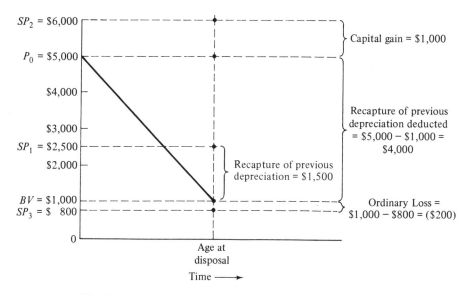

**Fig. 5.3.** Typical gain/loss situations resulting from the sale of Section 1231 assets.

claimed in prior years is $P_0 - BV = \$5,000 - \$1,000 = \$4,000$, however, so of the total gain of $5,000 realized on sale, $4,000 is recaptured depreciation, and $1,000 is "net gain on sale." Thus, $4,000 would be *added* to ordinary income in the year of sale and taxed at *ordinary* income rates (20%, 22%, or 48%), and $1,000 is taxed at *capital gain* rates (20%, 22%, or 30%).

4. The asset is sold at a selling price, say $SP_3$, which is less than the book value of the asset at the time of sale. Here, let $SP_3 = \$800$. The tax treatment is as follows. The *loss* is $SP_3 - BV = \$800 - \$1,000 = (\$200)$. Note that this is in the nature of a capital loss, *except* that in this instance (net loss on sale of a Section 1231 asset), *all Section 1231 assets are treated differently from capital assets: The net loss on the sale of Section 1231 assets is fully deductible as an ordinary loss* in the year of occurrence. This means a direct *ordinary* tax saving (20%, 22%, or 48%) in the year in which the loss occurs.

Thus, the principal differences in the tax consequences on the sale of a depreciable *capital* asset and a depreciable *Section 1231* asset lie in (1) the disallowance or recapture of prior depreciation for the Section 1231 asset if a gain *results* and its subsequent taxation as ordinary income and (2) the *ordinary* income deduction that results if a Section 1231 asset is sold at a loss.

**5.7.3. Tax treatment of Section 1231 nondepreciable assets.** For *non*depreciable Section 1231 assets, if a net *gain* results from the sale of such assets, the net gain is taxed at the *capital gain rate*, the same as any other capital gain realized from the sale of *capital* assets.

If a net *loss* results from the sale of nondepreciable Section 1231 assets, however, *the net loss is again fully deductible* by the corporation *as an ordinary loss* at ordinary income tax rates. Thus, the loss deductibility feature of Section 1231 is applied to *business related* assets, i.e., those used by the corporation for the production of income.

**5.7.4.** *What tax rate on Section 1231 transactions?* The exact tax rate that should be used in calculating a prospective Section 1231 tax (or benefit, if a Section 1231 loss is incurred) depends on the *prior history* of Section 1231 gains and losses in the tax year being examined. For the following analysis, which will illustrate the complexity of determining an *exact* rate, we assume the corporation is already in the surtax bracket (i.e., ordinary income from other sources is considerably greater than $50,000) for the year in question.

If such a corporation disposes of Section 1231 property at a sale price of, say, $4,000, resulting in a loss of $1,000, and there is no offsetting gain, the loss is fully deductible from income and there is a tax saving of $480 (with an assumed normal-plus-surtax rate of 48%). The $480 is an equivalent cash *in*flow to the firm in the year of sale, which is *added* to the price received (a cash inflow of $4,000) for the property or a total cash inflow of $4,480. Should such a sale result instead in a *gain* of $1,000, the gain would be taxed at only 30%, resulting in a net cash inflow in the years of sale of the sale price of $4,000 *less* $300 in capital gains tax paid on the Section 1231 gain, or a net cash inflow of $3,700.

Now, if a loss or gain on Section 1231 property had *already* occurred in the same tax year, the tax situation becomes more complicated. For example, assume another Section 1231 asset had already been sold for $2,000 and that a loss of $500 had occurred on this sale. Because of the associated tax of 48% on this transaction, a tax saving of 0.48($500) = $240 would have resulted with a total cash inflow due to the prior transaction of $2,000 + $240 = $2,240. This event is illustrated in Fig. 5.4(a). Now, if a subsequent sale is transacted, say, as we first illustrated with a sale price of $4,000 but resulting in a *gain* of $1,000, then the result is a *net gain* of $500, which is taxed at 30%, so that the year-end cash flow is *toward* the company in the amount of the *two* cash sales *less* the tax paid, or $2,000 + $4,000 − $150 = $5,850. This situation is depicted in Fig. 5.4(b).

In the first instance [Fig. 5.4(a)], the net change in the cash position due to *tax* alone would be an equivalent cash *inflow* of $240 on a loss of $500, or at a rate of 48%. In the second instance, the net change in the cash position due to the *tax* alone would be an equivalent *outflow* of $150 on a net gain of $500, or at a rate of 30%.

It should now be obvious that the gain of $1,000 and the loss of $500 could be reversed in sequence and the same tax consequence would result—namely, that a *net tax of $150* (a cash outflow) would come about from *both* transactions combined. Thus, we *cannot* say that a tax rate of 30% is associated *specifically* with the gain of $1,000 and another tax rate of 48% is associated *specifically* with the loss of $500, for such an association would result in a net cash *outflow* (due to taxes) of only (0.30) × ($1,000) − (0.48)($500) = $60, which is clearly in error. What *is* associated is the capital gains tax rate of 30% with the *net* gain of $500, which results from *both* transactions.

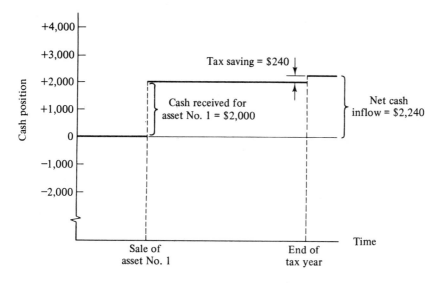

(a) After $500 loss but before $1,000 gain

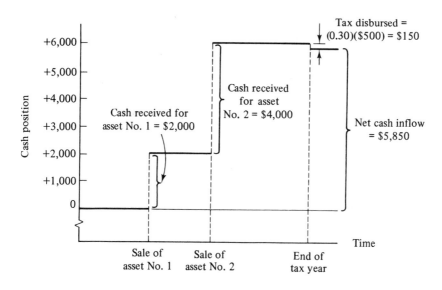

(b) After $500 loss and after gain of $1,000

**Fig. 5.4.** Cash flow position resulting from a $500 loss followed by a $1,000 gain.

It therefore follows that one cannot, *a priori*, associate any specific tax rate with a *specific* Section 1231 gain or loss, unless the entire history of gains and losses is known for the taxable year in question. Obviously, if the history of such gains and losses is known, then such knowledge should be used. As we have pointed out many times previously, however, in capital resource allocation we are dealing with *future* incomes and *future* expenses associated with projects *not yet executed*. In this kind of situation, it would be sheer foolishness to *predict* an assumed *history* of Section 1231 gains and losses in any given year. What is done, therefore, as a matter of practical expediency is to assume that all Section 1231 gains are taxed at the capital gains rate of 30% and that all Section 1231 losses are deductible from ordinary income at a normal-plus-surtax rate of 48%. This convention results in an incremental cash *in*flow due to the tax saving of 48% of any loss incurred or a decremental cash *out*flow due to tax of 30% of any gain that results from a Section 1231 sale.

## 5.8. The *Tax Preference Items* Tax Liability

Certain items reported on the Federal income tax return are specified by the Internal Revenue Code to be *tax preference items*. Loosely defined, tax preference items are those transactions that, for one reason or another, are accorded some kind of special or preferential tax treatment by one or more sections of the Internal Revenue Code. An incomplete but representative listing of tax preference items for corporations are

1. 37.5% of the amount of *capital gains* for the taxable year. (The 37.5% figure results from the difference in the 30% capital gains rate and the ordinary tax rate of 48%, or $\frac{18}{48} = \frac{3}{8} = 37.5\%$). Note that this category does *not* include *Section 1231* gains.
2. Accelerated depreciation on *real* property. With some limitations accelerated depreciation is allowed on buildings and other real estate that is otherwise not Section 1231 property. The *excess* of this accelerated depreciation over straight-line depreciation is a tax preference item. The same rule applies to the special 5-year amortization plan for rehabilitation expenditures. Note carefully, however, *that accelerated depreciation of Section 1231 assets does not* result in a tax preference item.
3. Accelerated depreciation on personal property subject to a lease. When personal property (defined as property *other* than real estate and buildings) is *leased* to another, the owner may deduct accelerated depreciation. To the extent that this accelerated depreciation exceeds straight-line depreciation, the excess is a tax preference item. Note again that this category does *not* include Section 1231 assets *used* and depreciated by the *owning* corporation in conducting the business of the corporation.
4. Percentage depletion on a mineral deducted in excess of the mineral cost is a tax preference item.
5. The rapid 5-year amortization of pollution control facilities, on-the-job training facilities, child-care facilities, and certain railroad rolling stock results in deductions in excess of what would normally be allowed by depreciating these assets. The *excess* of the rapid amortization over normal straight-line depreciation is a tax preference item.

**5.8.1.** *Taxation of tax preference items.* A special minimum tax, applied at the rate of 10% of all tax preference items in a given taxable year (less certain deductions), is imposed in addition to the other income taxes a corporation must pay. This tax is avowedly imposed in order to equalize the tax burden between those taxpayers who supposedly claim tax preference items (e.g., corporations and individual high-income taxpayers) and those who do not.

In figuring this tax, the total of the tax preference items [see items (1) to (5), above] is reduced by

1. A specific $30,000 annual exemption, plus
2. Income taxes for the taxable year, calculated without regard to the tax preference items tax.

The net result is then multiplied by 10% to obtain the tax preference items tax.

**Example 5.8.1.** In 1975, a corporate taxpayer reported a tax of $60,880, and his tax return contained a total of $110,000 of tax preference items. His *minimum*, or *tax preference*, tax for that year would be calculated as follows:

| | | |
|---|---:|---:|
| Total tax preference items: | | $110,000 |
| Less: | | |
|     Specific exemption | $30,000 | |
|     Income tax | 60,880 | 90,880 |
| Income subjected to 10% | | |
|     *minimum* or *tax* | | |
|     *preference* tax: | | $ 19,120 |
| Tax Liability: | | |
| Income tax: | | $ 60,880 |
| 10% *minimum* tax: | | 1,912 |
| Total tax due: | | $ 62,792 |

## 5.9. The Accumulated Earnings Tax

In addition to all other income taxes payable by a corporation, there may be imposed yet another special tax, called the *accumulated earnings tax*, if the corporation fails to meet certain tests concerning the payment of dividends during the taxable year. The purpose of this tax is punitive in nature, as the preface to the legislative act states, and the tax is imposed on any corporation that is used for the purpose of accumulating earnings in excess of its *reasonable needs* to avoid the payment of dividends to its shareholders.

One should realize that the earnings of corporations are normally taxed *twice* by the income tax. The *first* tax occurs when the taxable income of a corporation is taxed directly by the tax methods discussed in this chapter (i.e., the ordinary income tax, the capital gains tax, the Section 1231 tax, and the tax preference items tax). After this first income tax is paid, the law contemplates that the after-tax income of the corporation will normally be distributed to the shareholders as dividends on their investments in the shares of the corporations. The *second* tax then occurs when the shareholders pay income tax on the *dividend income* received from the corporation. Thus, the normal turn of events under the law contemplates *two* taxes upon the same net income, first as taxable income in the hands of the corporation and second as dividend income on the remainder in the hands of shareholders.

It is possible to *use* a corporation as a device to avoid, or substantially avoid, the payment of the second tax at the shareholder level. The method is simply to retain the after-tax earnings within the corporation instead of paying them out as dividends. This is particularly attractive for small corporations with a limited number of share-holders since they control the "wealth" of the corporation anyway.

The accumulated earnings tax, or as it is sometimes known, the Section 531 tax, is aimed at preventing this practice. Basically, the tax is imposed after two kinds of exclusions:

1. The first $100,000 of *all* accumulated earnings (over the cumulated time-history of the corporation) is arbitrarily excluded from the tax, plus
2. A *reasonable* accumulation of earnings is excluded from the tax. The word *reasonable* has acquired legal definition by various court decisions. In substance, however, it means that the corporation may retain sufficient earnings (in total) so that (a) it can carry on normal, day-to-day operations with funds invested in cash operating accounts, accounts receivable, inventory, and other assets used daily by the business and so that (b) it can reasonably *expand* its operations for the near future.

Earnings retained in excess of items (1) and (2) are said to be *unreasonably retained* and are subject to the following taxes:

1. For the first $100,000 of *un*reasonable retention, the tax rate is $27\frac{1}{2}\%$.
2. For all amounts in excess of the first $100,000 of *un*reasonable retention, the tax rate is $38\frac{1}{2}\%$.

Two conditions must be present to subject a corporation to the accumulated earnings tax. One of these is an *intent to avoid* the income tax that otherwise would be paid by the shareholders on the dividends if they had been distributed, and the second condition is an *accumulation of earnings and profits* during the year.

The courts have held that a *presumption of intent* arises when a corporation accumulates earnings and profits in excess of the reasonable needs of its business. This presumption can be overcome by a preponderance of evidence, however, that the accumulation was not motivated by a desire to avoid the second income tax on the shareholders.

Among the circumstances that tend to negate a tax avoidance intent are

1. The fact that little or no overall tax saving was achieved as a result of the corporation's retention of earnings.
2. The fact that the accumulation was for the reasonable needs of the business, *including such things as contemplated or planned expansion, debt retirement,*

*acquisition of another business, investments related to the business,* and *loans to suppliers or customers in furtherance of the business of the corporation.*

3. Absence of loans to shareholders.
4. Absence of investments that have no reasonable connection with the business.
5. A good dividend record over past years.

Thus, it is relatively simple to avoid the imposition of the accumulated earnings tax on a corporation, especially if the corporation is in an expanding mode and takes relatively good precautions to establish several of the other circumstances listed above that mitigate against *un*reasonable accumulation of earnings.

## 5.10. Illustrations of Typical Calculations for Corporate After-Tax Cash Flows

The following series of examples (Examples 5.10.1 through 5.10.6) illustrate the calculations involved in finding after-tax cash flows for some typical situations encountered in project estimation and evaluation. Certain assumptions are common to all of these examples; namely, (1) cash flows (including those due to income taxes) are assumed to occur at the end of the same year as the income or expense deduction that gives rise to the cash flow, and (2) unless otherwise noted all productive assets are Section 1231 assets, which are disposed of by the corporation through an "arm's length transaction" to a disinterested third party at the end of the project life.

Furthermore, the general basis of each after-tax cash flow calculation is Eq. (5.4), which is repeated here:

$$Y_t = (G_t - E_t - I_t)(1 - T_e) + D_t T_e \qquad (5.4)$$

where the symbols are defined on page 120. This equation is then modified, as necessary in each example, to reflect the effects of additional taxes paid, such as the Section 1231 gains tax, the capital gains tax, and the tax preference items tax. The modifications of this equation will be clearly stated in each example.

In general, the calculations required by Eq. (5.4) can be considerably simplified by using a tabular format, as follows:

| (1) Year, $t$ | (2) Gross Income, $G_t$ | (3) Cash Expenses (except interest), $E_t$ | (4) Interest Expense, $I_t$ | (5) Operational Income = (2) − [(3) + (4)] | (6) Ordinary Income Tax = (5)($T_e$) |
|---|---|---|---|---|---|

| (7) Operational Cash Flow = (5) − (6) | (8) Depreciation Expense, $D_t$ | (9) Tax-Saving Cash Flow = (8)($T_e$) | (10) Total Cash Flow = $Y_t$ = (7) + (9) |
|---|---|---|---|

Column 1 contains the end-of-year notation ($t = 0, 1, 2, \ldots, N$), beginning with the *end of year 0*, that is, the *present time* at which the decision to execute or not to execute the project is being taken. Column 2 contains the estimated values of the gross incomes, year by year; Column 3, the estimated cash expense deductions; and Column 4, the estimated cash interest deductions. Column 5 is called *operational income*, and it simply is gross income minus cash expenses, or Column 2 minus the sum of Columns 3 and 4. Column 6 is the cash outflow due to the ordinary income tax, or Column 5 times the effective tax rate, $T_e$. Column 7 is called the *operational cash flow* and is the operational income (Column 5) minus the tax cash outflow in Column 6. Depreciation expense and *other noncash expense items* are recorded in Column 8, or in a multicolumn equivalent of 8. Then, Column 9 is the equivalent cash *inflow* due to the savings in income taxes resulting from the noncash expenses in Column 8 and is calculated as Column 8 (as a total) times the effective tax rate, $T_e$. Column 10 is then simply the total cash flow, or Columns 7 plus 9.

**Example 5.10.1.** The proposed installation of some new machinery is estimated to cost $200,000 installed. The new machinery is expected to reduce net annual operating expenses by a cash amount of $50,000 per year for 10 years and to have a salvage value of $47,000 at the end of the tenth year. Assuming that the company's ordinary tax rate is 48%, that full advantage can be taken of the additional 20% first year depreciation, that the full benefit of the 7% investment tax credit can be used, and that the company exercises its option to reduce the salvage value by 10% of the original cost and sell the asset at that value at the end of its life, calculate the following: (a) the first year depreciation, (b) the annual depreciation for the second through tenth years if the straight-line method is used, (c) the net cash flows for each of the 10 years, and (d) the net present value of the cash flow stream if the discount rate is 10%.

*Solution:*

a. *First year depreciation*

$$\Delta D_1 = \text{additional first year depreciation}$$

$$= \text{lesser} \begin{cases} (0.20)(\$200,000) = \$40,000 \\ \text{limit} = 0.20(\$10,000) = \$2,000 \end{cases}$$

$$= \$2,000.$$

Reduced basis $= B_0 = \$200,000 - \$2,000 = \$198,000.$

Reduced salvage value $= L_{10} = \$47,000 - 0.10(\$200,000) = \$27,000.$

Normal first year depreciation (S.L.) $= \dfrac{B_0 - L_{10}}{N} = \dfrac{\$198,000 - \$27,000}{10 \text{ yr}}$

$$= \$17,100/\text{yr}.$$

$D_1 = $ additional first year depreciation $+$ normal first year depreciation

$$= \$2,000 + \$17,100 = \$19,100.$$

b. *Depreciation, second through tenth years*

$$D_t = \frac{B - L}{N} = \frac{\$198,000 - \$27,000}{10 \text{ yr}} = 17,100/\text{yr}.$$

c. *Net cash flow table*

| End of Year, t | Expense Savings before Tax* | Cash Flow from Savings | Depreciation Expense | Cash Flow from Depreciation | Section 1231 Cash Flow | 7% Investment Credit | Total Cash Flow |
|---|---|---|---|---|---|---|---|
| 0 | -0- | -0- | -0- | -0- | $-200,000 | $14,000 | $-186,000 |
| 1 | $50,000 | ($26,000) | $19,100 | $9,168 | -0- | -0- | + 35,168 |
| 2-9 | 50,000 | 26,000 | 17,100 | 8,208 | -0- | -0- | + 34,208 |
| 10 | 50,000 | 26,000 | 17,100 | 8,208 | + 27,000 | -0- | + 61,208 |

*Equivalent to a taxable cash *in*flow.

d. *Net present value*

$$P_0 = \$-186,000 + \$35,168(\overset{(P/F,10\%,1)}{0.9091}) + \$34,208(\overset{(P/A,10\%,8)(P/F,10\%,1)}{5.3349})(0.9091)$$
$$+ \$61,208(\overset{(P/F,10\%,10)}{0.3855})$$
$$= \$35,474.25.$$

**Example 5.10.2.** This is the same problem as Example 5.10.1, except that sum-of-years' digits depreciation is to be used.
*Solution:*

a. *First year depreciation*

$\Delta D_1$ = additional first year depreciation

= $2,000 (same as Example 5.10.1).

Normal first year depreciation (SYD):

$$B = \$200,000 - \$2,000 = \$198,000$$
$$L = \$47,000 - 0.10(\$200,000) = \$27,000$$
$$\text{Depreciable amount} = B - L = \$171,000.$$

By Eq. (4.4),

$$(D_B)_t = (B - L)\frac{2(N - t + 1)}{N(N + 1)}$$

$$\therefore \quad (D_B)_1 = (\$171,000)\frac{2(10 - 1 + 1)}{10(11)}$$

$$= \$31,091.$$

Total first year depreciation = $D_1$ = $2,000 + $31,091 = $33,091.

b. *Depreciation, second through tenth years*

    By Eq. (4.4),

$$(D_B)_t = (B - L)\frac{2(N - t + 1)}{N(N + 1)}.$$

| Year, $t$ | $2(N - t + 1)$ | $N(N + 1)$ | $(D_B)_t$ |
|-----------|----------------|------------|-----------|
| 2  | 18 | 110 | $27,982 |
| 3  | 16 |     | 24,873 |
| 4  | 14 |     | 21,764 |
| 5  | 12 |     | 18,655 |
| 6  | 10 |     | 15,545 |
| 7  | 8  |     | 12,436 |
| 8  | 6  |     | 9,327 |
| 9  | 4  |     | 6,218 |
| 10 | 2  |     | 3,109 |

c. *Net cash flow table*

| End of Year, $t$ | Expense Savings before Tax* | Cash Flow from Savings | Depreciation Expense | Cash Flow from Depreciation | Section 1231 Cash Flow | 7% Investment Credit | Total Cash Flow |
|---|---|---|---|---|---|---|---|
| 0  | –0–      | –0–      | –0–     | –0–     | $–200,000 | $14,000 | $–186,000 |
| 1  | $50,000  | $26,000  | $33,091 | $15,884 | –0–       | –0–     | 41,884 |
| 2  |          |          | 27,982  | 13,431  | –0–       | –0–     | 39,431 |
| 3  |          |          | 24,873  | 11,939  | –0–       | –0–     | 37,939 |
| 4  |          |          | 21,764  | 10,447  | –0–       | –0–     | 36,447 |
| 5  |          |          | 18,655  | 8,954   | –0–       | –0–     | 34,954 |
| 6  |          |          | 15,545  | 7,462   | –0–       | –0–     | 33,462 |
| 7  |          |          | 12,436  | 5,969   | –0–       | –0–     | 31,969 |
| 8  |          |          | 9,327   | 4,477   | –0–       | –0–     | 30,477 |
| 9  |          |          | 6,218   | 2,985   | –0–       | –0–     | 28,985 |
| 10 | 50,000   | 26,000   | 3,109   | 1,492   | + 27,000  | –0–     | 54,492 |

*Equivalent to a taxable cash *in*flow.

d. *Net present value*

$$P_0 = \$-186,000 + \$41,884(\overset{(P/F,10\%,1)}{0.9091}) + \$39,431(\overset{(P/F,10\%,2)}{0.8264})$$

$$+ \cdots + \$54,492(\overset{(P/F,10\%,10)}{0.3855})$$

$$= \underline{\$+42,578.}$$

**Example 5.10.3.** This is the same problem as Example 5.10.1, except that double declining balance depreciation is to be used. Note, however, that the asset *may not be depreciated below a reasonable salvage value* (here, the reduced salvage value of $27,000) even though the DDB method is used.

Solution:

a. *First year depreciation*

As before, the additional first year depreciation $\Delta D_1 = \$2,000$ (the lesser of $2,000 or 20% of first cost). Then

$$B = \$200,000 - \$2,000 = \$198,000$$

$$(D_D)_1 = B\frac{\alpha}{N} = \$198,000\left(\frac{2}{10}\right) = \$39,600$$

$$D_1 = \text{total first-year depreciation} = \$2,000 + \$39,600 = \underline{\underline{\$41,600.}}$$

b. *Depreciation and book values, second through tenth years*

| End of Year, $t$ | $\dfrac{BV_t}{B} = \left(1 - \dfrac{2}{N}\right)^t$ | Book Value, $BV_t$ | DDB Depreciation, $D_t = BV_{t-1} - BV_t$ |
|---|---|---|---|
| 1 | 0.800 | $158,400 | $39,600 |
| 2 | 0.640 | 126,720 | 31,680 |
| 3 | 0.512 | 101,376 | 25,344 |
| 4 | 0.411 | 81,378 | 19,998 |
| 5 | 0.328 | 64,944 | 16,434 |
| 6 | 0.262 | 51,876 | 13,068 |
| 7 | 0.210 | 41,580 | 10,026 |
| 8 | 0.168 | 33,264 | 8,586 |
| 9 | 0.134 | 27,000* | 6,264* |
| 10 | 0.107 | 27,000* | –0–* |

*Book value cannot be less than reduced salvage value, which limits depreciation ($D_t$) in nineth and tenth years.

c. *Net cash flow table*

| End of Year, $t$ | Expense Savings before Tax* | Cash Flow from Savings | Depreciation Expense | Cash Flow from Depreciation | Section 1231 Cash Flow | 7% Investment Credit | Total Cash Flow |
|---|---|---|---|---|---|---|---|
| 0 | –0– | –0– | –0– | –0– | $-200,000 | $14,000 | $-186,000 |
| 1 | $50,000 | $26,000 | $41,600 | $19,968 | –0– | –0– | + 45,968 |
| 2 | ↑ | ↑ | 31,680 | 15,206 | –0– | –0– | 41,206 |
| 3 | | | 25,344 | 12,165 | –0– | –0– | 38,165 |
| 4 | | | 19,998 | 9,599 | –0– | –0– | 35,599 |
| 5 | | | 16,434 | 7,888 | –0– | –0– | 33,888 |
| 6 | | | 13,068 | 6,273 | –0– | –0– | 32,273 |
| 7 | | | 10,026 | 4,812 | –0– | –0– | 30,812 |
| 8 | | | 8,586 | 4,121 | –0– | –0– | 30,121 |
| 9 | ↓ | ↓ | 6,264 | 3,007 | –0– | –0– | 29,007 |
| 10 | 50,000 | 26,000 | –0– | –0– | + 27,000 | –0– | 53,000 |

*Equivalent to a taxable cash *inflow.*

    d. *Net present value*

$$P_0 = \$-186{,}000 + \$45{,}968(\overset{(P/F,10\%,1)}{0.9091}) + \cdots + \$53{,}000(\overset{(P/F,10\%,10)}{0.3855})$$
$$= \$+44{,}690.$$

Some observations should now be made about Examples 5.10.1, 5.10.2 and 5.10.3. First, one should observe in all three problems that the *total* amount of depreciation deducted over the 10-year period is the same; namely, $200,000 − $27,000 = $173,000. Second, the equivalent cash inflows from the savings is the same ($26,000 per year); and third, the investment credit is the same for all three problems ($14,000). Nevertheless, the net present values of the cash flow streams are different:

    i. For the S.L. depreciation method, $35,474,

    ii. For the SYD depreciation method, $42,578,

    iii. For the DDB depreciation method, $44,690.

Obviously, the double declining balance method provides the highest net present value of the cash flow streams. The reason is the *timing* of the depreciation deductions. The DDB method forces a greater proportion of the *total* depreciation into the earlier years of the project, thereby creating larger increments of tax *savings* in the earlier years.

    **Example 5.10.4.** *Sale of Section 1231 asset at less than salvage value.* We now continue with Example 5.10.3, using the double declining balance method of depreciating the producing assets, but now we assume that the assets will be disposed of at a sale price of $20,000 at the end of year 10, instead of being disposed of at the reduced salvage value, $L = \$27{,}000$. (This is not a realistic problem from the standpoint of practical project evaluation since one would not deliberately plan in the *future* for a loss to occur upon asset disposal. In reality, the estimator would merely adjust his salvage value and correct the estimated depreciation table. This problem is included at this point, however, to show the tax treatment for an already *existing* asset that might have to be sold at a book loss.)

    *Solution*:

    a. The first year depreciation is calculated exactly as Example 5.10.3(a):

$$D_1 = \$41{,}600.$$

    b. The depreciation deductions are calculated exactly the same as Example 5.10.3(b):

$$D_2 = \$31{,}680$$
$$D_3 - \ 25{,}344$$
$$\vdots \quad\quad \vdots$$
$$\vdots \quad\quad \vdots$$
$$D_9 = \ \ 6{,}264^2$$
$$D_{10} = \quad -0-^2$$

---

[2]Note again, that depreciation *cannot* be taken below a reasonable salvage value (here, considered to be the reduced salvage value, $L = \$27{,}000$).

c. The *net cash flow table* is virtually the same as for Example 5.10.3(c), except there is an *extra transaction amount* for the tenth year in the Section 1231 Asset column, representing the *loss* of $7,000 between the salvage value ($L = \$27,000$) and the sale value ($SP = \$20,000$). This entry is explained below the table.

| End of Year, $t$ | Expense Savings before Tax | Cash Flow from Savings | Depreciation Expense | Cash Flow from Depreciation | Section 1231 Cash Flow | 7% Investment Credit | Total Cash Flow |
|---|---|---|---|---|---|---|---|
| 0 | –0– | –0– | –0– | –0– | \$–200,000 | \$14,000 | \$–186,000 |
| 1 | \$50,000 | \$26,000 | \$41,600 | \$19,968 | –0– | –0– | 45,968 |
| 2 | ↑ | ↑ | 31,680 | 15,206 | –0– | –0– | 41,206 |
| 3 | | | 25,344 | 12,165 | –0– | –0– | 38,165 |
| 4 | | | 19,998 | 9,599 | –0– | –0– | 35,599 |
| 5 | | | 16,434 | 7,888 | –0– | –0– | 33,888 |
| 6 | | | 13,068 | 6,273 | –0– | –0– | 32,273 |
| 7 | | | 10,026 | 4,812 | –0– | –0– | 30,812 |
| 8 | | | 8,586 | 4,121 | –0– | –0– | 30,121 |
| 9 | ↓ | ↓ | 6,264 | 3,007 | –0– | –0– | 29,007 |
| 10 | { 50,000 | 26,000 | –0– | –0– | + 20,000* + 3,360† | –0–} | 49,360 |

*$20,000 is the cash *inflow* resulting from selling the assets for that amount.

†The tax *saving* resulting from the *loss* of selling the asset is calculated at *ordinary* tax rates (since this is a Section 1231 loss):

Gain (loss) = selling price − book value

$\quad\quad$ = $20,000 − $27,000 = ($7,000)

Tax *saving* = (loss)$T_e$ = $7,000(0.48) = $3,360 (an equivalent cash *inflow*, since it is a tax *saving*).

(Thus, selling the asset at a *book* loss of $7,000 at the end of year 10 resulted in an actual *cash* loss of only $7,000 − $3,360 = $3,640.)

d. The *net present value* is

$$P_0 = \$-186,000 + \$45,968(\overset{(P/F,10\%,1)}{0.9091}) + \cdots + \$49,360(\overset{(P/F,10\%,10)}{0.3855})$$

$$= \$43,287.$$

**Example 5.10.5.** *Sale of Section 1231 asset at a gain.* Assuming that the Section 1231 assets in Example 5.10.4 were sold at the end of year 10 for a *gain* of $7,000 instead of a loss, the rule requires that the gain be taken into account as additional *ordinary* income, to the extent of the *total* depreciation taken in all prior years. Thus, if the sale price were $34,000 resulting in a gain of $34,000 − $27,000 = $7,000, the entries in the Section 1231 column for year 10 would be

$$\$+34,000$$
$$- 3,360$$

where $34,000 is the cash *in*flow due to the sale and the tax *out*flow due to the Section 1231 gain (at *ordinary* tax rate) is

$$\text{Tax} = (\text{gain})(T_e) = (\$34,000 - \$27,000)(0.48) = \$3,360,$$

which is then signed $(-)$ to indicate an *out*flow of cash (additional tax).

The remaining calculations are analogous to Example 5.10.4. We emphasize again, however, that a project evaluation engineer would not deliberately *plan* to sell assets *at a gain* in the future (this would bias the analysis by shifting cash flows due to depreciation from earlier years into the last year, thereby reducing net present value). Likewise, consistency requires that he also *not* plan to sell *at a loss*. This is equivalent to the shifting of cash flow from the last year of the project into earlier years, which would increase net present value, thereby making the project "look good." From an *estimating* standpoint, one should plan the project so that asset disposal occurs at the end of the project life *at a reasonably estimated salvage value*.

**Example 5.10.6. *Borrowed funds.*** The True Products Company is investigating the installation of two new tape-controlled milling machines (costing together, installed, $340,000), which are anticipated to replace four older, manually controlled machines. The old machines together generate $85,000 annually in gross income. While the new machines are being installed, it will be necessary to send an operator-trainee to a special instructional school to learn how to operate the new machines. The 30-day school will cost the company $3,600 in tuition, travel, and wages for the operator. After the new machines are installed, they will require the newly trained operator plus one helper to operate them. During the first year of operation, the operator will be paid wages plus fringe benefits of $10,000 per year and the helper, $8,000 per year. Thereafter, these costs are expected to rise at the rate of 4% per year.

Other cash operating costs on the two new machines are expected to be $5,000 per year for the first 5 years and then increase by $1,000 per year thereafter. Gross income on the new machines will exceed that of the old machines by 20% per year.

It is estimated that the machines will be obsolete in 10 years and that a reasonable salvage value, after applying the elective 10%-of-basis reduction, would be $40,000 for both machines together. Double declining balance depreciation is to be used. Extra first year depreciation will be claimed also, and the company can take full advantage of the investment credit against its income tax. At the end of the project life, both machines will be sold for their salvage value.

The initial purchase price of $340,000 will be financed as follows: Cash, in the amount of $240,000; plus a promissory note, in the amount of $100,000, bearing interest at the rate of 10% per year, with principal payments of $20,000 each to be made at the ends of years 1 through 5, with accrued interest paid annually at the same times.

*Requirements:*

a. Calculate the depreciation table,
b. Calculate the interest table,
c. Calculate the cash flow table, assuming that the effective ordinary tax
   rate is 48%,
d. Calculate the net present value for this project using a discount rate of
   12%.

*Solution:*

a. *Depreciation schedule*
   i. Additional first year depreciation $= D_0'$.

$$D_0' = \text{lesser of} \begin{cases} (\$340{,}000)(0.20) = \$68{,}000 \\ \text{limit of } 0.20(\$10{,}000) = \$2{,}000 \end{cases}$$

$$= \$2{,}000.$$

   ii. Double declining balance depreciation:

$$D_t = \text{deductible depreciation}$$

$$D_t = B\frac{\alpha}{N}\left(1 - \frac{\alpha}{N}\right)^{t-1}$$

where $B = \text{cost} - D_0' = \$340{,}000 - \$2{,}000 = \$338{,}000$

$\alpha = 2$ (for DDB method)

$N = 10$ years

$\therefore \quad D_t = (\$338{,}000)(\tfrac{2}{10})(1 - \tfrac{2}{10})^{t-1}$

| End of Year, t | Addtional First Year Depreciation | DDB Depreciation | Total Depreciation, $D_t$ | Book Value |
|---|---|---|---|---|
| 0 | –0– | –0– | –0– | $340,000 |
| 1 | $ 2,000 | $67,600 | $69,600 | 270,400 |
| 2 | –0– | 54,080 | 54,080 | 216,320 |
| 3 | –0– | 43,264 | 43,264 | 173,056 |
| 4 | –0– | 34,138 | 34,138 | 138,918 |
| 5 | –0– | 28,054 | 28,054 | 110,864 |
| 6 | –0– | 22,308 | 22,308 | 88,556 |
| 7 | –0– | 17,576 | 17,576 | 70,980 |
| 8 | –0– | 14,196 | 14,196 | 56,784 |
| 9 | –0– | 11,492 | 11,492 | 45,292 |
| 10 | –0– | 5,292* | 5,292* | 40,000* |

*$D_{10}$ is limited by the inability of the company to depreciate below the *reasonable* salvage value of $40,000. Hence $D_{10}$ is the *lesser* of $45,292 − $40,000 = $5,292, or $D_t = (\$338{,}000)(0.20)(0.8)^9 = \$9{,}126$ by the DDB method.

Table 5.5. NUMERICAL EXAMPLE OF NET CASH FLOW CALCULATIONS

| (1) End of Year, $t$ | (2) Gross Income, $G_t$ | (3) Operating Expenses Labor | (3) Other | (4) Interest Expense, $I_t$ | (5) Net Income before Depreciation | (6) Cash Flow from Operations = $(1 - T_e)(5)$ | (7) Depreciation Expense | (8) Cash Flow from Depreciation | (9) Section 1231 Cash Flow | (10) 7% Investment Credit | (11) Net Cash Flow, $Y_i$ |
|---|---|---|---|---|---|---|---|---|---|---|---|
| 0 | -0- | -0- | $ 3,600* | $ -0- | $-3,600 | $-1,872 | -0- | -0- | $\begin{cases}\$-340{,}000\dagger \\ +100{,}000\end{cases}$ | $23,800‡ | $-218,072 |
| 1 | $102,000 | $18,000 | $ 5,000 | $10,000 | 69,000 | 35,880 | $69,600 | $33,408 | − 20,000§ | -0- | 49,288 |
| 2 | | 18,720 | ← | 8,000 | 70,280 | 36,546 | 54,080 | 25,958 | − 20,000 | -0- | 42,504 |
| 3 | | 19,468 | | 6,000 | 71,532 | 37,197 | 43,264 | 20,767 | − 20,000 | -0- | 37,964 |
| 4 | | 20,248 | | 4,000 | 72,752 | 37,831 | 34,128 | 16,381 | − 20,000 | -0- | 34,212 |
| 5 | | 21,058 | 5,000 | 2,000 | 73,942 | 38,450 | 28,054 | 13,466 | − 20,000 | -0- | 31,916 |
| 6 | | 21,900 | 6,000 | -0- | 74,100 | 38,532 | 22,308 | 10,708 | -0- | -0- | 49,240 |
| 7 | | 22,776 | 7,000 | -0- | 72,224 | 37,556 | 17,576 | 8,436 | -0- | -0- | 45,992 |
| 8 | | 23,687 | 8,000 | -0- | 70,313 | 36,563 | 14,196 | 6,814 | -0- | -0- | 43,377 |
| 9 | | 24,634 | 9,000 | -0- | 68,366 | 35,550 | 11,492 | 5,516 | -0- | -0- | 41,066 |
| 10 | 102,000 | 25,620 | 10,000 | -0- | 66,380 | 34,518 | 5,292 | 2,540 | + 40,000 | -0- | 77,058 |

*The $3,600 for operator's salary, travel, and training is directly deductible as *ordinary* expense from income elsewhere in the company.

†Section 1231 cash flow is $-340,000 for the machines and $+100,000 *inflow* from the "bank" on the loan.

‡Investment credit = ($340,000)(.07) = $23,800, which is a *direct* credit against the income tax, to be treated for this project as an equivalent cash inflow.

§Principal amounts (cash *outflows*) paid on loan to "bank."

144

b. *Interest table*

| End of Year, t | Loan Balance at Beginning of Year | Interest Payment at End of Year | Principal Payment at End of Year | Loan Balance at End of Year |
|---|---|---|---|---|
| 0 | –0– | –0– | –0– | $100,000 |
| 1 | $100,000 | $10,000 | $20,000 | 80,000 |
| 2 | 80,000 | 8,000 | 20,000 | 60,000 |
| 3 | 60,000 | 6,000 | 20,000 | 40,000 |
| 4 | 40,000 | 4,000 | 20,000 | 20,000 |
| 5 | 20,000 | 2,000 | 20,000 | –0– |

c. *Cash flow characteristics*
   See Table 5.5.

d. *Net present value*

| End of Year, t | Net Cash Flow, $Y_t$ | $(P/F, 12\%, t)$ | Present Value Increment |
|---|---|---|---|
| 0 | $-218,072 | 1.0000 | $-218,072 |
| 1 | 49,288 | 0.8929 | 44,009 |
| 2 | 42,504 | 0.7972 | 33,884 |
| 3 | 37,964 | 0.7118 | 27,023 |
| 4 | 34,212 | 0.6355 | 21,742 |
| 5 | 31,916 | 0.5674 | 18,109 |
| 6 | 49,240 | 0.5066 | 24,945 |
| 7 | 45,992 | 0.4523 | 20,802 |
| 8 | 43,377 | 0.4039 | 17,520 |
| 9 | 41,066 | 0.3606 | 14,808 |
| 10 | 77,058 | 0.3220 | 24,813 |

Net present value $= \sum_0^{10} (Y_t)(P/F, 12\%, t) = \$29,583.$*

*It should be noted that the net present value of $29,583 results from the use of the *equity* capital of $240,000 used to finance the purchase and excludes considerations of the borrowed capital by $100,000, except for the *timing* of the initial loan, the *timing* and amounts of the principal payments, and the tax effects of the interest paid.

# REFERENCES

[1] *1974 Federal Tax Course* (New York: Commerce Clearing House, Inc., 1973).
[2] *United States Master Tax Guide* (New York: Commerce Clearing House, Inc., 1974).
[3] *Federal Tax Course, 1976* (Englewood Cliffs, N.J.: Prentice-Hall, Inc., 1976).

## PROBLEMS

√ **5-1.** During the year 19xx, a company in the warehouse business had operating expenses of $30,000, depreciation of $25,000, and interest expenses of $15,000. The cost of goods sold was $150,000. What is the ordinary taxable income (TI), ordinary tax, and the ordinary tax rate (TR) if the company had sales of (a) $235,000? (b) $320,000? Assume normal tax rates of 20% on the first $25,000 of taxable income, 22% on all over $25,000, and a surtax rate of 26% on all income over $50,000.

√ **5-2.** A company has a taxable income of $22,000 per year. It is considering a project that will result in an additional $15,000 per year for the next 10 years. The normal tax rate is 20% on the first $25,000 of taxable income, 22% on all over $25,000, and the surtax rate is 26% on all income over $50,000. (a) What is the effective tax rate and tax if the additional project is not attempted and the earnings remain $22,000? (b) What is the effective income tax rate and tax if the new project is attempted and results in the additional $15,000 per year? (c) What is the effective income tax rate applicable to the increment of earnings due to the new venture?

√ **5-3.** A machine that was purchased 3 months ago for $8,000 and used in production was sold by a company for $10,000. Assume a tax rate of 48% and a capital gains tax rate of 30%. How much tax will be paid as a result of this sale?

√ **5-4.** A company purchased a piece of land 10 years ago for $50,000. Today they sold the land for $100,000. Using a capital gains tax rate of 30% and a tax rate of 48%, (a) how much tax is paid as a result of the sale? (b) what is the after-tax cash flow due to the sale of the property?

√ **5-5.** A company purchased a machine at the end of year 0 for $10,000. It will be depreciated using double declining balance depreciation with a life of 10 years. Assume a capital gains tax rate of 30% and an ordinary tax rate of 48%. What is the after-tax cash flow due to the sale of the asset at the end of the tenth year for (a) $2,000? (b) zero (i.e., scrap)?

**5-6.** A company purchased a machine 10 years ago for $50,000. It was depreciated using sum-of-the-years' digits depreciation with a life of 20 years and no salvage value. If the machine is sold today for $2,000, what is the after-tax cash flow due to the sale if the tax rate is 40% and the capital gains tax rate is 30%?

**5-7.** A real estate company just purchased 500 acres of land for $600 per acre. The company has two options as to what they can do with the land. In 3 months, they can sell the land to a manufacturing firm for $800 per acre, or they can wait 5 years and sell the land on the open market for approximately $1,500 per acre. Assume that $30 per acre each year in property taxes must be paid on land kept over 1 year. Assuming a tax rate of 48%, a capital gains tax of 30%, and a discount rate of money of 10%, to whom should the company sell the land?

**5-8.** During the year, machines A and B were sold for $10,000 and $40,000, respectively. Machine A was purchased 20 years ago for $100,000 and was depreciated using double declining balance depreciation with a life of 25 years. Machine B was purchased 10 years ago for $150,000 and was depreciated using declining balance depreciation with a salvage value of $30,000 and a life of 8 years. Assuming these were the only sales of depreciable assets during the year, what is the tax that resulted from these sales using an effective tax rate of 48% and a capital gains tax rate of 30%?

**5-9.** During the past year, a company made the following sales. It sold 500 acres of land for $700 per acre. This land was purchased 5 years ago for $150 per acre. It sold 300 acres of land for $500 per acre. This land was purchased 2 months ago for $550 per acre. Assuming these were the only sales of capital goods during the year, a tax rate of 48%, and a capital gains tax rate of 30%, what is the net after-tax gain that resulted from the sales?

**5-10.** During the year, a corporation made transactions that resulted in the following capital gains and losses:

Long-term capital gain $= 20,000.$
Long-term capital loss $= 15,000.$
Short-term capital gain $= 5,000.$
Short-term capital loss $= 1,000.$

Assuming a tax rate of 48% and a capital gains tax rate of 30%, what is the amount of taxes paid?

**5-11.** A proposed project will require the use of four machines. The machines will all be depreciated using straight-line depreciation with no salvage value. The following table describes the machines.

| Machine Number | Purchase Cost | Depreciable Life (years) | Actual Life (years) | Selling Price |
|---|---|---|---|---|
| 1 | $100,000 | 6 | 7 | $1,000 |
| 2 | 24,000 | 6 | 7 | 0 |
| 3 | 32,000 | 8 | 8 | 2,000 |
| 4 | 20,000 | 5 | 7 | 1,000 |

Assume a tax rate of 48% and a capital gains rate of 30%. Assume the machines were all purchased at the beginning of the project. What are the cash flows due to the sale of these machines at the end of year 7 and at the end of year 8?

**5-12.** A proposed project will require the purchase of four machines described in the table below.

| Machine Number | Purchase Cost | Salvage Value | Depreciable Life (years) | Selling Cost | Actual Life (years) | Purchased at End of Year |
|---|---|---|---|---|---|---|
| 1 | $50,000 | $5,000 | 9 | $ 0 | 9 | 0 |
| 2 | 60,000 | 2,000 | 8 | 20,000 | 8 | 1 |
| 3 | 60,000 | 0 | 4 | 5,000 | 4 | 1 |
| 4 | 60,000 | 0 | 4 | 5,000 | 4 | 5 |

Machine 1 will be depreciated using straight-line depreciation. The other machines will be depreciated using declining balance depreciation. Assume a tax rate of 50% and a capital gains tax rate of 30%. What are the cash flows at the end of year 5 and at the end of year 9 due to the sale of these Section 1231 assets?

**5-13.** A project requires four machines. The machines will all be sold at the end of the eighth year. The following table gives other useful information about the machines.

| Machine Number | Depreciation Model | Purchase Cost | Depreciable Life (years) | Salvage Value | Selling Price at $t = 8$ |
|---|---|---|---|---|---|
| 1 | SL | $100,000 | 10 | $ 0 | $10,000 |
| 2 | DB | 50,000 | 10 | 0 | 10,000 |
| 3 | DDB | 50,000 | 10 | 10,000 | 20,000 |
| 4 | SOYD | 60,000 | 11 | 0 | 30,000 |

The machines will all be purchased at the beginning of the project (i.e., $t = 0$). What is the tax paid, and what is the cash flow due to the sale of these machines? Assume a tax rate of 52% and a capital gains tax rate of 30%.

SL = straight-line depreciation.
DB = declining balance depreciation.
DDB = double declining balance depreciation.
SOYD = sum-of-the-years' digits depreciation.

**5-14.** A large company is considering a 10-year project for manufacturing a new product. The project's estimated income and expenses are tabulated below. The machine needed to produce the new product costs $40,000 and has an economic life of 10 years with no appreciable salvage value. The company's effective tax rate is 52%, and no borrowed capital will be used to fund the project if it is undertaken. Project data:

| EOY | Income | Deductible Operating Expenses | EOY | Income | Deductible Operating Expenses |
|---|---|---|---|---|---|
| 1 | 10K | 25K | 6 | 60K | 30K |
| 2 | 20K | 20K | 7 | 60K | 30K |
| 3 | 20K | 15K | 8 | 40K | 25K |
| 4 | 30K | 15K | 9 | 30K | 25K |
| 5 | 50K | 25K | 10 | 25K | 20K |

(a) Determine the net cash flow stream if straight-line depreciation is used on the asset.
(b) Determine the net cash flow stream if SOYD depreciation is used on the asset. (c) Determine the net cash flow stream using straight-line depreciation and a machine salvage value of $10,000.

**5-15.** If a proposed 8-year project is accepted, land will be rented to provide space for a small building having the necessary production equipment. These Section 1231 assets (building and machines) will be purchased at the beginning of the first year for $60,000. The purchase price is to be allocated $20,000 to the building and $40,000 to the machines. They will have an economic life of 8 years and salvage values of $5,000 for the building and $10,000 for the machinery. Straight-line depreciation will be used on the building and double declining balance with switching to straight line used on the machinery. Equity capital will be used to fund the project. The expected gross income less cash operating expenses are expected to be as follows:

| End of Year: | 1 | 2 | 3 | 4 | 5 | 6 | 7 | 8 |
|---|---|---|---|---|---|---|---|---|
| GI-EXP: | 7K | 10K | 15K | 18K | 20K | 20K | 12K | 6K |

The company's effective tax rate is 48%, and capital gains are taxed at 30%. Assume the company is large enough to utilize any tax benefits that may result from this project. (a) Determine the net cash flows for the project. (b) Assume that the company borrows $30,000 at the beginning of the first year. The principal is to be paid back in six equal annual payments beginning at the end of year 1, together with 8% interest on the unpaid balance. Using the information above, calculate the net cash flow stream. (c) Instead of renting the land, assume that the land can be bought for $2,000 and, due to the location, the price of the land will increase to approximately $5,000 in 8 years. Also, due to heavy use, the Section 1231 machines are expected to have a salvage value of $5,000. Working capital totaling $7,000 will be needed at the beginning of year 2, and losses due to inventory shrinkage and bad debts are estimated to be $2,000 over the project life. Using this new information, determine the net cash flows for each year.

**5-16.** A manufacturer is considering the introduction of a new product. Income and expenditure forecasts have been made and are as follows:

| End of Year | Gross Income | Operating Expenses | Investment |
|---|---|---|---|
| 1 | $ 0 | $ 75K | $ |
| 2 | 0 | 50K | 380K |
| 3 | 150K | 100K | 200K |
| 4 | 200K | 120K | 80K |
| 5 | 300K | 110K | 70K |
| 6 | 450K | 160K | 30K |
| 7 | 550K | 170K | |
| 8 | 600K | 200K | |
| 9 | 575K | 220K | |
| 10 | 550K | 180K | 20K |
| 11 | 500K | 180K | |
| 12 | 500K | 160K | |
| 13 | 450K | 140K | |
| 14 | 400K | 120K | |
| 15 | 300K | 100K | |

The $75,000 expense in year 1 is for research and development, and since the company is large enough, this expenditure can be deducted as an expense. The investments are for the following items:

|  |  |  |
|---|---|---:|
| EOY 2 | Working capital | $ 50,000 |
|  | Building (20-year life, |  |
|  | salvage = $50,000) | 200,000 |
|  | Land for building (to be |  |
|  | sold in 20 years for $60K) | 30,000 |
|  | Machine (12-year life, |  |
|  | salvage = $20,000) | 100,000 |
|  |  | $380,000 |
|  |  |  |
| EOY 3 | Additional working capital | $ 70,000 |
|  | Machine (8-year life, |  |
|  | salvage = $30,000) | 130,000 |
|  |  | $200,000 |

The remaining investments are for additional working capital. The income cash flows are from the sale of the new product. To help fund the cost of the new building a loan for $100,000 is to be made at the beginning of year 3. The principal of the loan is to be paid back in 5 equal annual installments of $20,000 each, plus 8% interest on the remaining balance each year. Another loan of $150,000 is to be obtained at the beginning of year 4. The principal of this loan is to be paid back in 10 equal annual installments of $15,000 each, plus 6% on the remaining balance each year. The company's effective tax rate is 48%, and capital gains are taxed at a rate of 30%. (a) Determine the net cash flow stream for the proposed project, where all assets are depreciated by the straight-line method. (b) Determine the net present value of the *net* cash flow stream if the discount rate is 12%.

**5-17.** The Sawyer Chemical Company is considering a new process for making phosphoric acid, which they utilize in the manufacture of commercial fertilizer. The new process involves the purchase of new machinery and equipment that will have an installed cost of $200,000. The new process will result in excess productive capacity of phosphoric acid for Sawyer, but the excess can be sold to other fertilizer manufacturers, and the cost of in-house acid will be reduced. The total annual savings and excess acid sales together is estimated to be $150,000 per year. Operating expenses are estimated to be $50,000 per year. The equipment used in the new process has an estimated life of 6 years, with a salvage value of $20,000 at the end of that time. Sawyer has an effective income tax rate of 52% and requires a marginal investment rate of 8%. Assume that capital gains are taxed at 30% and that the new equipment will be sold for its salvage value at the end of 6 years. (a) Using the optimal method of depreciation, what is the net present value of the project? (b) What is the net present value of the project if a $30,000 investment in working capital is also required now? (Assume the working capital will be recovered at the end of the project life). (c) If the project (cost = $200,000) is financed

60% by borrowed funds and 40% by equity funds, what is the net present value of the equity portion? (Assume that the principal of the loan, obtained at the beginning of the project, will be paid back in six equal installments at the end of each year and that $5,000 interest will be paid annually. Include the working capital requirement).

# THE FINANCING FUNCTION

## 6.1. Introduction

Until now we have assumed for convenience that the interest (discount) rate relating future cash flows in a proposed project to present value is a *known* figure. As we have suggested before, however, the discount rate is also the vehicle by which we judge the attractiveness of an investment opportunity, or project. In reality, the discount rate is *not* a known figure, but it can be estimated with sufficient precision so that near-optimal investment decisions can be made. The result is that *two* decisions ought to be made simultaneously: the financing decision and the investment decision.

The investment decision is related to the financing decision because the acceptance or rejection of future investment projects depends on how the projects are to be financed. As we saw in Chapter 2, the firm is but an *intermediary* in the process of obtaining funds from owners and other investors and investing these funds in projects. The projects accepted by the firm must somehow be related to the methods of financing used by the firm to obtain the necessary funds for investment. In short, the *interest* or *discount rate* used in evaluating investment projects is a function of the *cost* of financing these projects. The cost of financing is commonly called the *cost of capital* and is usually expressed as a rate (e.g., percent per annum).

In this chapter, we take up the question of how to measure the cost of the capital used to finance projects. Without proof at this point, we recall from Chapter 2 that an

# 6

appropriate objective for the firm is maximization of the future wealth of the shareholders, which is equivalent to the maximization of the firm's *present value* (in a perfect capital market). Maximization of the present value of the firm involves discounting *future* cash flow streams at some determinable interest rate. Generally, this interest rate is taken at, or slightly above, the firm's *marginal cost of capital.*

Again, the principle of opportunity costing requires that the firm invest its funds, acquired from shareholders and lenders, in the best alternative use, that is, in projects whose *net present values* are positive when all cash flows are discounted at the marginal cost of capital. Alternatively, the same principle requires the firm to invest in future projects whose internal rates of return are greater than the firm's cost of capital (assuming no restrictions on the supply of capital or other dependencies among projects). If these rules are followed, supposedly the market price of the firm's shares will be maximized over time.

The cost of capital is no doubt the most difficult concept to articulate and demonstrate in the whole field of finance. It is also the most controversial topic because there are widespread theoretical differences as to how the cost of capital is to be measured. In this chapter, we shall simply adopt a pragmatic approach and investigate the *marginal* concept of the cost of capital—that is, we shall look at models that estimate the cost of capital from an incremental standpoint since it is principally *new* (or incremental) capital that finances *future* projects. We shall not go further into the

**153**

finance field to investigate the controversial area of *optimal* financial structure of the firm, in which the traditionalists still battle the modernists over whether or not an optimal financial structure for the firm is attainable. (The traditionalists, typified by such authors as Solomon [17] and Durand [6], maintain that an optimal balance can be struck between the amount of equity funds and the amount of borrowed funds at which the cost of capital is a minimum; whereas the modernists, typified by Modigliani and Miller [11], [12] advocate that the cost of capital is constant and independent of the ratio of borrowed funds to equity funds). This area of financial theory is beyond the scope of this chapter. For those interested in optimal financing theory, there are several excellent references (e.g., [19], [20], and [2]).

## 6.2. Costs of Capital for Specific Financing Sources

Although the funds used and invested by the firm are derived from three principal sources (debt, equity, and retained earnings), it is inappropriate to associate any one of these specific sources of capital with specific projects. The reason is that the firm raises capital as an *entity*. It cannot continually finance by borrowing (debt) without building its equity base also, either through the retention of earnings or by the sale of additional equity shares. Thus, the specific sources of funds for most firms vary somewhat over time. Moreover, since the focus of the *cost* of capital is fundamentally concerned with the *valuation of the firm as a whole*, we need to use an *overall* cost of capital as the acceptance criterion for proposed projects, even though the firm may employ one type of financing for one project and another type for another project. It is the *overall* cost of capital for the firm that establishes the lower boundary for the opportunity costs of the firm.

In order to measure the firm's overall cost of capital, however, it is necessary to consider the costs of specific methods of obtaining capital. In this sense, we are concerned with *explicit* costs rather than opportunity costs. For example, the explicit cost associated with debt capital is interest, and the explicit cost associated with equity capital is dividends. The explicit cost of any source of financing is a discount rate. Specifically, it is an interest rate that equates the present value of the funds *received* by the firm (net of underwriting and other costs at time $t = 0$) to the present value of the expected future funds outflows. Such outflows may be interest, repayment of debt principal, dividends, or premium redemptions of convertible securities. Thus, for *any* source of capital, the explicit *cost* of financing can be determined by solving the following equation for $k$:

$$P_0 = C_0 + \frac{C_1}{(1+k)} + \frac{C_2}{(1+k)^2} + \cdots + \frac{C_t}{(1+k)^t} \tag{6.1}$$

where $P_0$ = the net amount of funds received by the firm at time $t = 0$,
$\quad\quad C_0$ = underwriting and other flotation costs at time $t = 0$,
$\quad\quad C_t$ = future cash outflows at time $t$ connected with receiving $P_0$ now; the summation occurs from $t = 0, 1, \ldots, n$.

$k$ = the explicit cost of capital for the sources of capital giving rise to $P_0$, $C_0$, and $C_t$.

The remainder of this chapter is devoted to the measurement of the *explicit* costs of specified sources of capital and the combining of these costs into an *effective cost* for the firm. Note, however, that our attention is always fixed on the *present and future costs of capital* for the firm and not its historical costs. While historical costs can and do affect the ability of the firm to raise new capital, and hence its cost, what we are interested in is the *incremental* cost of capital for the firm. The use of incremental, or marginal, explicit costs is the required measure because we use this marginal cost of capital to decide whether to invest *incrementally* in a set of *new* projects. Except as they may affect the cost of any retained earnings used in calculating the overall cost of capital, past costs of financing have no bearing on this decision.

In calculating the explicit costs of the various sources of capital, we shall express all money amounts on an *after-tax* basis so that the firm's overall cost of capital is then on a comparable after-tax basis. Once the several explicit source costs are determined, we shall then combine these into a weighted average, or overall, cost of capital for the firm. The weighted average cost of capital then embodies the concept of a minimum attractive rate of return, or a threshold value for judging the acceptability of projects.

## 6.3. Cost of Debt Capital

Borrowed funding, or debt capital, is derived from many sources. For example, short-term loans are often obtained from banks and insurance companies by borrowing on promissory notes or open lines of credit; whereas long-term loans are obtained from financial underwriting firms and the public by offering the firm's bonds or equipment mortgage indentures for sale. As far as the cost of capital is concerned, there is no difference in the methodology of calculating the *cost* of a short-term or a long-term debt. The major difference between the cost of *debt* capital (in general) and the cost of other forms of funding lies in the fact that the *interest payments* on the amount of debt *are deductible from ordinary income*, and the *net* cost of this source of capital needs to be stated on an after-tax basis.

To calculate the cost of debt capital, we simply use Eq. (6.1) in an *after-tax* form. Thus, $C_0$ becomes the *after-tax* cash outflow of any *present* portion of flotation and underwriting costs, and $C_1, C_2, \ldots, C_n$ are the *after-tax* cash flows of interest payments, amortization costs, and principal amounts repaid over the life of the note or mortgage. $P_0$ then becomes the *net* cash inflow received by the firm at time $t = 0$, or the *net proceeds of the loan*. Solving Eq. (6.1) for $k$ then yields the required *cost of borrowed capital* for that particular source.

**6.3.1. *Short-term capital costs.*** The cost of short-term debt financing is the *effective* annual (periodic) interest rate, *after* income taxes. Where the interest payments on the loan are made more often than the period of comparison, then the effective rate must be calculated from the nominal interest rate. In a manner similar to Section 3.5, we let

> $r$ = the nominal interest rate per year on the loan,
> $c$ = the number of compounding periods per year,
> $k_i$ = the effective *after-tax* annual interest rate,
> $T_e$ = effective income tax rate.

Then

$$k_i = \left[\left(1 + \frac{r}{c}\right)^c - 1\right](1 - T_e) \tag{6.2}$$

gives the *effective* annual after-tax cost-of-capital rate on the loan.

**Example 6.3.1.** The sum of $20,000 is borrowed at an interest rate of 6% per annum, with interest to be paid *quarterly* over the the life of the loan. If the effective income tax rate is 52%, what is the effective interest rate of this loan (i.e., what is the effective *cost of capital* for this loan)?

*Solution:* From Eq. (6.2),

$$k_i = \left[\left(1 + \frac{0.06}{4}\right)^4 - 1\right](1 - 0.52) = \underline{\underline{2.94\%}}.$$

**6.3.2. *Capital costs for bonds.*** A bond is a written promise to pay; it is sold by the firm into the financial market, by which the firm receives immediate cash proceeds in exchange for a promise to pay a *sum certain* (the face value of the bond) at the end of the maturation of the bond (say, $N$ years hence), *plus* interest payments in the interim on a regular basis at a nominal rate of interest based on the face value of the bond. The interest payments may be specified in the bond to be made once annually or more often, such as semiannually or quarterly. When interest payments are made more often than the effective interest period, then the *effective* interest rate must be used, as for short-term securities in Section 6.3.1 and Example 6.3.1.

More often, however, the price actually received from the sale of a bond differs from its face value. If the price received is *less* than the face value of the bond, the bond is said to be *sold at a discount*, and if the price received is *greater* than its face value (this can happen if the *coupon* interest rate provides a yield greater than market interest value), the bond is said to be *sold at a premium*.

When the price paid for a bond differs from its face value, the premium or discount must be amortized by the issuer for Federal income tax purposes. In this case, the ratable portion of the total amortizable discount or premium is taken into account as an additional increment of expense or income for each year in the life of the bond. To put this more concretely, let $F$ be the future, or *face*, value of the bond at maturity ($t = N$) and $A_t$ be the annual amortization amount (either discount or premium). Then

$$A_t = \frac{1}{N}(F - P_0). \tag{6.3}$$

Note that if the bond is sold at a discount $(F > P_0)$, then $A_t$ is positive in Eq. (6.3); if the bond is sold at a premium $(P_0 > F)$, then $A_t < 0$. Note also that the annual amortization is calculated at the uniform rate $1/N$, as required by the income tax regulations. Also, let $I_t$ be the periodic interest paid at nominal rate $r$ on the loan over its life. The *net* cash outflow, including interest, then becomes

$$C'_t = \left[ I_t + \frac{1}{N}(F - P_0) \right](1 - T_e) \tag{6.4}$$

if the bond is sold at either a discount or a premium since the sign of the amortization term is determined by the magnitudes of $F$ and $P_0$.

The *approximate* after-tax cost of bonds sold at a discount or premium is then given by[1]

$$k_i = \frac{[I_t + (F - P_0)/N](1 - T_e)}{\frac{1}{2}(F + P_0)} \tag{6.5}$$

where $(F + P_0)/2$ is the average amount of bond outstanding. This equation implicitly assumes deductibility of the discount $(F - P_0)$, over the life of the bond at the firm's effective tax rate. It is approximate because it does not consider compounding of the rate $k_i$, and it does not consider the tax effect of initial issuance expenses.

An *exact* method of calculating the after-tax cost of capital for a bond involves the trial-and-error solution of a present value function that relates the present cash inflow due to the sale of the bond to future cash outflows and inflows arising from fulfilling the obligations stated in the bond. The present value function is stated in terms of an unknown *after-tax* equivalent cost-of-capital rate, $k_i$. In order to formulate this equation, let

$P_0 =$ the present *net* cash inflow to the firm due to the sale of the bond (i.e., the net cash realization of the bond from the underwriter),

$F =$ the *face value* of the bond, to be paid by the firm upon the maturity of the bond at the end of $N$ periods hence,

$k_i =$ the unknown *after-tax* effective cost of capital rate (percent per year compounded annually),

$N =$ the number of years to maturity,

$A =$ the periodic cost of issuing the interest payments (check writing, envelopes, postage, etc.),

$r =$ the *coupon* or nominal rate of interest (percent per year) at which periodic interest payments are paid on the face value, $F$,

$c =$ number of interest payment periods per year (e.g., for annual payments, $c = 1$; for semiannual payments, $c = 2$),

$S =$ *selling expenses* of the bond at time $t = 0$, such as printing, advertising, cost of stamps, and legal fees,

$T_e =$ effective tax rate of the firm.

---

[1] See G. David Quirin [14], pp. 100–101.

Now, upon sale of the bond(s) to the underwriter (and thence to the public), the issuing firm receives $P$ dollars from the underwriter and a bill for $S$ dollars of selling expenses, which is usually deducted from $P$ so that the *net* cash inflow amount received by the firm is $P_0 = P - S$ dollars. The $P_0$ dollars is a present net cash *inflow, after taxes*. The $S$ dollars of selling expense is not a deductible expense in the year of payment, however; instead, according to Federal tax law it must be *amortized* over the life of the bond. Thus, it is a prepaid expense that results in tax savings in future years.

Similarly, if the bond is sold at a discount, then the face value of the bond, $F$, exceeds its present selling price, $P_0$, and the difference $F - P_0$ is an *amortizable* expense over the life of the bond. Because this amortization expense is deductible from Federal income taxes, tax savings result in future years. Note that all amortization expenses are required to be deducted annually using a straight-line rate of $1/N$. Note also that the periodic interest payments paid by the firm to the bondholder are also deductible expenses against ordinary income, and this results in future tax savings.

Taking into account these cash flows and noncash items that result in tax savings cash flows, we may write the present value function in terms of the *unknown* cost of capital factors as follows:

$$P_0 = F(P/F, k\%, N) + \left[ A + F\left(\frac{r}{c}\right) \right](1 - T_e)(P/A, k/c\%, cN)$$

$$- \frac{1}{N}(F - P_0 + S)(T_e)(P/A, k\%, N). \tag{6.6}$$

This equation is then solved by trial-and-error iteration for the unknown *after-tax* cost of capital, $k$. Note that Eq. (6.6) consists of four cash flows (or their equivalents in terms of tax savings):

1. $P_0$, the present *net* cash *inflow* from the sale of the bond,
2. $F$, the future after-tax cash *outflow* (the face value of the bond to be paid upon maturity),
3. $[A + F(r/c)](1 - T_e) =$ the *net* after-tax cash *outflows* due to the periodic payment of interest at an annual rate $r$ every $c$ periods per year (the cash outflow is net after the ordinary tax savings),
4. $(F - P_0 + S)(T_e/N) =$ the annual after-tax cash equivalent of the tax *savings* due to the amortization of the bond discount, $F - P_0$, and the amortization of the *selling expenses*, $S$.

Each of the cash flow terms is multiplied by the appropriate interest factor in which the after-tax effective cost of capital, $k$ percent per year compounded annually, is an unknown. The method of solution is by trial and error, and the following example demonstrates the method.

**Example 6.3.2.** A series of bonds is to be issued by the Riley Manufacturing Company. Each bond has a face value of $1,000 and bears interest at the rate of 8% per year, with the interest being payable to the bondholder semiannually. The bond series matures in 10 years. The bonds have been put out for bid to several underwriters, and the highest bid received by the Riley Manufacturing Company has been \$910, less selling expenses of \$2.00 per bond. If the company's effective tax rate is 52%, what is the effective after-tax cost of this new borrowed capital to the Riley Manufacturing Company?

    *Solution:*

$P_0 = \$910 - \$2 = \$908$ per bond;
$S = \$2$ per bond;
$r = 0.08$ per year;
$c =$ two periods per year (semiannual interest payments);
$N = 10$ years;
$F = \$1,000$ per bond;
$T_e = 0.52; (1 - T_e) = 0.48.$

From Eq. (6.6), we write

$$\$908 = \$1,000(P/F, k\%, 10) + \$1,000\left(\frac{0.08}{2}\right)(0.48)\left[P/A, \frac{k}{2}\%, 2(10)\right]$$

$$- \frac{1}{10}(\$1,000 - \$908 + \$2)(0.52)(P/A, k\%, 10). \qquad (6.7)$$

Using a trial value of $k = 5\%$, we evaluate the right-hand side of Eq. (6.7):

$$\underset{(P/F,5\%,10)}{\$1,000(\ 0.6139\ )} + \underset{(P/A,2\frac{1}{2}\%,20)}{\$19.20(\ 15.5892\ )} - \underset{(P/A,5\%,10)}{\$4.89(\ 7.7217\ )} = \$875.45.$$

Since \$875.45 < \$908, we try a lower interest rate, say $k = 4\%$. Then the right-hand side becomes

$$\underset{(P/F,4\%,10)}{\$1,000(\ 0.6756\ )} + \underset{(P/A,2\%,20)}{\$19.20(\ 16.3514\ )} - \underset{(P/A,4\%,10)}{\$4.89(\ 8.1109\ )} = \$949.88.$$

The actual value, $P_0 = \$908$, lies between these two present values calculated at the assumed rates, so we make a linear interpolation for the unknown $k$, using the proportions of similar triangles:

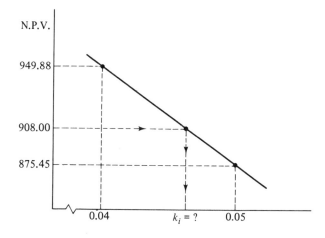

                           $i \longrightarrow$

$$\frac{\$949.88 - \$908.00}{\$949.88 - \$875.45} = \frac{k - 0.04}{0.05 - 0.04}$$

or

$$k = 0.04 + 0.01\left(\frac{41.88}{74.43}\right) = 0.0456, \text{ or } \underline{4.56\%}.$$

The after-tax equivalent cost of capital for this bond issue is 4.56% to the Riley Manufacturing Company.

## 6.4. Cost of Preferred Stock

Preferred stock is generally considered to be a security that is senior to common stock, at least in its claim on after-tax earnings of the firm. Unlike a bond, there is no guarantee of a return to the shareowner of preferred stock so there is no prior or preferential claim on the *assets* of the firm as there is with a bond; however, if dividends are declared from earnings by the firm, then preferred shareholders generally have prior claim to the after-tax *income* of the firm.

Because preferred stock represents a form of *ownership* in the firm and there is no contractual requirement for the redemption of stock, its cost may be represented by

$$k_p = \frac{D_p}{P_0} \tag{6.8}$$

where  $D_p$ = the preferred stock dividend, paid from *after-tax* earnings,
$P_0$ = the net proceeds of the preferred stock issue.

Thus, if a firm were able to sell a 9% preferred stock issue ($100 par value) and could realize proceeds of $96 per share, the cost of the preferred issue would be

$$k_p = \frac{0.09(\$100)}{\$96} = 0.09375, \text{ or } \underline{9.38\%}.$$

Note that this cost is *not* adjusted for income taxes because all *dividends* are paid from after-tax earnings. Thus, the explicit cost of preferred stock is usually substantially greater than the cost of debt financing.

Note also that Eq. (6.8) does not take into account the tax effect of the amortization of any issuance costs, such as printing, postage, and clerical costs, The reason is that there is no finite *life* for preferred stock, and the expenses of its sale are treated in the firm's hands as a reduction of the price received.

## 6.5. Cost of Equity Capital (Common Stock)

While the cost of equity capital is difficult to measure in theory,[2] it is comparatively easy to construct some valuation models, based on simplified assumptions, that make the measurement function rather easy to approximate. We shall present two

---

[2]See Van Horne [19], pp. 93–94.

such models here. One is a *dividend valuation* model in which a stream of constant-amount dividends are to be paid, and the other is a *growth* model that incorporates a growth requirement in the dividend stream.

**6.5.1. Dividend valuation model.** The financial stock market tends to establish the present *value* of a common stock by its daily trading activities, in which willing buyers and willing sellers exchange the ownership of shares at bargained prices. Presumably, the price paid for a stock is what the buyer and the seller believe it to be worth. If we consider the buyer to be nonspeculative, then he purchases the stock in the expectation of receiving *future* dividends. This is the basis of the valuation of common stock.

Because dividends are all that equity shareholders as a group receive from the firm as a result of their investment, this stream of income is the series of cash dividends to be paid in future periods. From the standpoint of the firm, then, the present traded price (value) of the stock, $P_0$, is related to the future dividends, $D_t$, by the functional relationship

$$P_0 = D_0 + \frac{D_1}{(1 + k_e)} + \frac{D_2}{(1 + k_e)} + \cdots + \frac{D_t}{(1 + k_e)^t} \tag{6.9}$$

and since there is no finite horizon for the stream of dividends to stop, this series is summed to $t = \infty$, or

$$P_0 = \sum_{t=0}^{\infty} \frac{D_t}{(1 + k_e)^t}. \tag{6.10}$$

If uniformity of dividends is assumed, that is $D_1 = D_2 = \cdots = D_t = D$, then Eq. (6.10) becomes

$$P_0 = D \sum_{t=0}^{\infty} (1 + k_e)^{-t} = \frac{D}{k_e} \tag{6.11}$$

for all values of $-1 < k_e < \infty$. In other words, from Eq. (6.11), the cost of equity capital is the dividend-price ratio, or

$$k_e = \frac{D}{P_0}. \tag{6.12}$$

This equation is based on the assumptions that future dividends will remain unchanged, investors are not speculative, and the tax situations of the shareholders themselves are ignored.

**6.5.2. The Gordon-Shapiro growth model.** The Gordon-Shapiro [7] model for estimating the equity cost of capital, like the dividend valuation model, uses a stream of dividends and the current market price to establish the cost of equity capital. Unlike the prior stream-of-dividends model in which dividends are assumed to remain constant over time, however, the Gordon-Shapiro model incorporates a growth factor for earnings. The basis for requiring a growth factor *along with* dividends is that prospective investors tend to value potential growth in earnings as a positive factor for the firm and thereby drive the present value, $P_0$, of the shares higher on the market than other shares without growth.

The starting point for the Gordon-Shapiro growth model is Eq. (6.10), repeated here:

$$P_0 = \sum_{t=0}^{\infty} D_t(1 + k_e)^{-t}.$$

Now, the dividend stream, $D_t$, arises from and is paid out of net earnings of the firm, and also out of earnings on retained earnings. That is, we assume that a portion of total annual earnings will be retained by the firm and the balance paid as dividends. Hence, earnings in the following year will be based in part on prior retained earnings, and hence, dividends in the next and succeeding years will be based, in part, on prior retained earnings.

Thus, let

$E_0$ = after-tax earnings per share at time $t = 0$.
$b$ = fraction of earnings retained by the firm (not paid as dividends).
$D_0$ = dividends paid at time $t = 0$.

Then the fraction of earnings retention is simply

$$b = \frac{E_0 - D_0}{E_0}, \tag{6.13}$$

and $b$ is assumed invariate over time, although it is subject to reevaluation each time the cost of capital calculation is made. Thus, retained earnings at $t = 0$ are simply $E_0 - D_0 = bE_0$, and the dividends paid are $(1 - b)E_0$.

We now let $B_0$ = the *book value* of the stock, per share, at $t = 0$; and $r$ = the simple rate of earnings to book value at $t = 0$, or $r = E_0/B_0$. Again, $r$ is assumed invariate over time but may be revalued each time the cost of capital is estimated.

Now, at time $t = 0$, we conceive that the retained earnings, $bE_0$, will be added to the book value of the stock and that the total earnings, $B_0 + bE_0$, will be placed at work for the firm in the ensuing period at the earnings rate $r$. Thus, the amount $r(bE_0)$ is the *earnings on retained earnings* during the time $0 < t < 1$, and consequently, at $t = 1$ we have

$$E_1 = E_0 + rbE_0 = E_0(1 + rb).$$

Similarly, at $t = 2, 3, \ldots, N$ we have

$$E_2 = E_1 + rbE_1 = E_1(1 + rb)$$
$$E_3 = E_2 + rbE_2 = E_2(1 + rb)$$
$$\vdots \qquad\qquad \vdots$$
$$E_n = E_{n-1} + rbE_{n-1} = E_{n-1}(1 + rb),$$

which leads to the recursive relationship

$$E_t = E_0(1 + rb)^t. \tag{6.14}$$

In general, the dividends paid are

$$D_t = E_t - bE_t = (1 - b)E_t; \tag{6.15}$$

and if Eq. (6.14) is multiplied by the factor $(1 - b)$, we have

$$(1 - b)E_t = (1 - b)E_0(1 + rb)^t. \tag{6.16}$$

Now, the left-hand side of Eq. (6.16) is simply $D_t = (1 - b)E_t$, or the dividends paid in the $t$th year; and the right-hand side is $(1 - b)E_0(1 + rb)^t = D_0(1 + rb)^t$, where $(1 - b)E_0 = D_0$, which is the dividend paid at time $t = 0$. Thus, the relationship between the dividend at time $t = 0$ and time $t$ is

$$D_t = D_0(1 + rb)^t. \tag{6.17}$$

Substituting this value for the dividend stream [Eq. (6.17)] into the valuation Eq. (6.10) gives the relationship

$$P_0 = \sum_{t=0}^{\infty} D_0(1 + rb)^t(1 + k_e)^{-t}, \tag{6.18}$$

which is the basic valuation equation of the Gordon-Shapiro model.

If we convert Eq. (6.18) to continuous compounding to simplify the summation, we have that

$$(1 + rb)^t \sim e^{rbt} \quad \text{and} \quad (1 + k_e)^{-t} \sim e^{-k_e t}$$

so that

$$P_0 = D_0 \int_{t=0}^{\infty} e^{rbt} e^{-k_e t} \, dt = D_0 \int_{t=0}^{\infty} e^{-t(k_e - rb)} \, dt$$

or

$$P_0 = D_0 \left(\frac{1}{k_e - rb}\right). \tag{6.19}$$

Solving Eq. (6.19) for $k_e$, we have

$$k_e = \frac{D_0}{P_0} + rb; \tag{6.20}$$

and if we substitute the equivalents $r = E_0/B_0$ and $b = (E_0 - D_0)/E_0$, we have the equivalent equation that

$$k_e = \frac{D_0}{P_0} + \frac{E_0 - D_0}{B_0}. \tag{6.21}$$

To interpret this finding, we note that the Gordon-Shapiro growth model for equity cost of capital consists of two terms, the first of which is simply the current dividend per share divided by the current market price per share, which corresponds to the basic model in Section 6.5.1; the second is the growth term, which is the ratio of current retained earnings per share $(E_0 - D_0)$ to current book value of the stock per share. In other words, if growth is to be provided for by retention of earnings, then the basic cost of equity capital is increased by the ratio of retained earnings to book value.

**6.5.3. The Solomon growth model.** A model similar to the Gordon-Shapiro growth model was suggested by Solomon ([17], pp. 55–62) to represent the inclusion of the growth term. In our present notation, Solomon's model is

$$k_e = \frac{D_0}{P_0} + \frac{E_0 - D_0}{P_0}. \tag{6.22}$$

The principal difference is that the growth term in Solomon's model, $(E_0 - D_0)/P_0$, is based on *market value* $(P_0)$ in the denominator rather than on *book value* $(B_0)$ as is the Gordon-Shapiro model [Eq. (6.21)].

The effect of this difference can be summarized as follows. If the firm's stock is valued on the market at a price higher than the book value of the stock (i.e., $P_0 > B_0$), then Solomon's estimate of the cost of capital, $k_e$, will be less than that due to Gordon-Shapiro. On the other hand, if the firm's shares are depressed in value on the market, Solomon's estimate of the cost of capital will be greater than that of Gordon-Shapiro. Since the market usually *anticipates* future earnings and growth capabilities of a firm by the current pricing of its stock, a *conservative* estimate (higher value) of the cost of capital, $k_e$, will result when one uses whichever model produces the higher value of $k_e$; that is, if $P_0 > B_0$, use the Gordon-Shapiro model, and if $B_0 > P_0$, use the Solomon model.[3]

**Example 6.5.1.** The present after-tax earnings of the Royal Machine Company are $3.40 per share on common stock, which sells for $36.00 per share. Current dividends are $1.67 per share. The ratio of retained earnings to total earnings is expected to remain constant in the future. The present book value of the stock is $19.50 per share. Calculate the firm's cost of equity capital (a) by the Gordon-Shapiro model and (b) by the Solomon model.

*Solutions*:

a. Gordon-Shapiro model

$$D_0 = \$1.67 \text{ per share}$$
$$P_0 = \$36.00 \text{ per share}$$
$$B_0 = \$19.50 \text{ per share}$$
$$E_0 = \$3.40 \text{ per share.}$$

From Eq. (6.21),

$$k_e = \frac{D_0}{P_0} + \frac{E_0 - D_0}{B_0} = \frac{\$1.67}{\$36.00} + \frac{\$3.40 - \$1.67}{\$19.50}$$

$$k_e = 0.0464 + 0.0887 = 0.1351, \text{ or } \underline{13.5\%}.$$

b. Solomon model

From Eq. (6.22),

$$k_e = \frac{D_0}{P_0} + \frac{E_0 - D_0}{P_0} = \frac{\$1.67}{\$36.00} + \frac{\$3.40 - \$1.67}{\$36.00}$$

$$k_e = 0.0464 + 0.0481 = 0.0945, \text{ or } \underline{9.45\%}.$$

---

[3]This rule results in a *conservative* value, which may not be an *optimal* strategy for the firm. In effect, a conservative value for cost of capital may be higher than necessary and thus preclude the selection of some profitable projects. This would act as a brake on expansion, which tends to be counterproductive in a growing firm.

Note that in both cases the equity cost of capital, $k_e$, is an *after-tax* rate since the earnings and dividends of the firm are both after-tax amounts.

**6.5.4. *Note on book value of stock.*** The balance sheet net worth of the firm's *common* stock may be defined as follows:

Net worth (common) = total assets — (current liabilities + long-term liabilities
+ bonds payable + defaulted dividends + preferred shares)

where all of these terms are stated in dollars and taken from the firm's balance sheet. The *book value*, $B_0$, per share of the common stock is then simply

$$B_0 = \frac{\text{net worth of common stock}}{\text{number of shares of common stock}}.$$

The use of $B_0$, defined in this manner, is sufficiently precise for use in calculating the cost of equity capital for the firm.

## 6.6. Cost of Retained Earnings

For many firms, a large portion of their *new* financing for expansion and for rebuilding existing assets is derived from retained earnings. On cursory examination, it might appear that retained earnings are *free* as far as the firm is concerned since the firm *generated* the retained earnings in the first place—they appear to be without cost to the firm. This is false logic for two reasons, however. First, the firm does not own the retained earnings—*the shareholders do.* Second, there is an opportunity cost involved, and this opportunity cost is simply the dividend foregone by the share-holders *out of their own earnings.*

In the absence of taxation, the *minimum* cost of retaining these undistributed earnings is the cost of equity capital itself, $k_e$, since the same amount of money could be obtained by the firm by first paying out *all* its earnings as dividends and then obtaining part of its earnings back as *new* common stock. The net result is the same: After-tax financing money in the same amount is obtained by the firm. In this case, the cost of retaining the earnings is obtained by solving Eq. (6.10) for $k_e$, only using the current market price for $P_0$. [If the growth model is to be used, then Eq. (6.21) or (6.22) should be considered.] In any case, $k_e$ represents the return that investors *expect* the firm to receive on its investments.

If the firm cannot generate projects that provide a return of at least $k_e$, then the shareholders presumably could find stocks of other companies in the market that could provide this return or better, and the firm should then distribute its current earnings to its shareholders to permit them to invest in other firms rather than invest the shareholders' retained earnings at lower returns. This statement is based on the reasoning that if the firm were to invest in projects with expected returns *lower* than $k_e$, the expected dividends to shareholders would decline (that is, $D_t/P_0$ would become smaller), and the shareholders would suffer a loss in expected future wealth. Thus, $k_e$

represents the *minimum* opportunity cost of a continuing stream of dividends that will provide at least the *current level* of expected future wealth of the shareholders.

With taxation, however, the shareholder may not obtain full use of his dividend since a portion is generally taxed away when he reports receipt of the dividend. The existence of *personal* income taxes on the incomes of shareholders tends to make the process of raising new equity capital more difficult and costly to the shareholders than retaining earnings by the firm. Bierman and Smidt ([3], pp. 154–155) give an example that illustrates this point. Assume that a particular shareholder pays a 60% income tax on marginal income and can earn a before-tax 10% return on common stock in a corporation whose only source of capital is equity common stock. If a corporation has $100 that it can invest to earn 4%, it will then have $104 at the end of a year. If it then pays the $104 to the shareholder as a dividend, he will have remaining $(1 - 0.60) \times (\$104) = \$41.60$ after personal income taxes. Alternatively, the corporation can pay the $100 immediately as a dividend, and the shareholder will have $(1 - 0.60)(\$100) = \$40$ to invest. During the year he will earn $4 of earnings before taxes at his return rate of 10% and will have remaining $(1 - 0.6)(\$4) = \$1.60$ after taxes, plus his $40, or $41.60 after-taxes at the end of the year. If the firm can earn more than 4% for the year, the shareholder will be better off with the firm reinvesting at *its* rate of return rather than paying the money out as a dividend. This conclusion is the result of two factors: (1) the deferral of personal income taxes and (2) the conversion of deferred *ordinary* income taxes into a possible future capital-gains tax (at lower rate) for the shareholder.

On the other hand, income taxation is of no consequence or, at worst, is only a minimum consideration to *some* shareholders as pension funds, tax-exempt foundations, and universities, for example. In such instances, these shareholders have access to investment opportunities that could approach or equal the *before-tax* return on equity capital of the firms in which they own stock. Thus, there is no one *minimum yield* of the firm at which *all* shareholders are better off if the firm reinvests its earnings instead of paying greater dividends.

A second general approach to the evaluation of the cost of retained earnings is Solomon's ([17], pp. 53–55) "external yield criterion." This approach is based on the notion that the firm should evaluate *external* investment opportunities as a possible use for retained earnings and use as an opportunity cost the yield presented by the best external investment opportunity that is foregone. To expand this idea, Solomon suggests that, in any reasonable financial market, opportunities should exist for the firm to invest its after-tax earnings, say, to acquire control in the assets of another operating enterprise (called here a *foreign* firm), either in the same or another industry, which would offer an earnings yield equal to (or greater than) and having the same degree of uncertainty as those offered by the firm's *existing* assets. A further condition is that sufficient control needs to be acquired in the other foreign firm to permit the filing of a consolidated tax return for both enterprises.

In that case, $k_e$ is the proper measure of the retained earnings invested in the foreign enterprise since if the purchasing firm had no projects of its own in which to invest its retained earnings, it would measure its earnings from the foreign enterprise by the simple model $k_e = D_t/P_0$, where $D_t$ is the foreign firm dividends and $P_0$ is the amount invested in the foreign firm. Thus, a foregone opportunity to invest in a comparable foreign firm produces an *opportunity cost of capital*, for the firm that retains a portion of its own earnings, which is independent of the personal tax consequences of the firm's own shareholders. The fundamental basis for this reasoning, in the face of income taxes, is that the incremental dividends from the foreign firm are *passed through* the owning firm to its shareholders and taxed *in the same manner* as if the owning firm itself had generated the income.

Thus, as Solomon ([17], p. 54) states:

> A precise formulation of the cost of retained funds based on the personal use approach presents formidable difficulties if the assumption of uniform [personal] tax rates is lifted. When stockholder tax brackets vary from zero to high percentage figures, a precise formulation is impossible. Happily it is unnecessary to pursue these refinements. The proper measure of the opportunity cost of any course of action, in this case the proposed internal investment, is the best alternative opportunity the course of action forces us to forego, and at minimum this is equal to $k_e$, the yield available on external investment. The exact measure for the *next* best alternative is not necessary to the analysis. In other words, so long as external opportunities are available, the minimum measure for the cost of internal funds [retained earnings] is $k_e$, regardless of the effect of personal taxes.

A word of caution should be added to remove any possible argument about *connecting* a particular project to an explicit cost of capital, such as retained earnings. None of the preceding analysis is to be used to imply, for example, that the use of funds for dividends *never* represents the best alternative to internal investment. Financial theorists are agreed that a *stable* dividend policy enhances the market value of a firm's stock and hence tends to reduce the cost of equity capital in the long run. So it does not follow that retention *must* take place as long as there are investment opportunities that provide returns better than $k_e$. What we are attempting to do here is to establish a correct *criterion* for investment in projects that must be exceeded if an internal project is to be approved. Once the project is approved, *then* it is a separate issue as to how the project is actually financed. For example, a project may pass the screening standard, $k_e$, but will not be financed from retained earnings even though these funds are available. Priority on retained funds may be given to the payment of dividends, and the project may actually be financed from external funds. But as far as the investment *decision* is concerned, the appropriate standard for measuring the cost of retained earnings is $k_e$.

## 6.7. Weighted Average Cost of Capital

Once the explicit costs of capital have been determined for each individual source (short-term debt, bonds, equity, and retained earnings), these costs may be combined to find an average or effective cost of capital for the firm. One method of combining the explicit costs of capital is by weighting each cost according to some standard and then calculating the weighted average cost of capital for the firm.

To illustrate the *mechanics* of calculating the weighted average cost of capital, suppose that a firm has the following capital structure at its most recent statement date:

|  | Amount | Proportion |
|---|---|---|
| Short-term debt | $    500,000 | 0.05 |
| Bonds | 1,000,000 | 0.10 |
| Preferred stock | 1,500,000 | 0.15 |
| Common stock | 6,000,000 | 0.60 |
| Retained earnings | 1,000,000 | 0.10 |
|  | $10,000,000 | 1.00 |

Suppose also the firm had computed the following *after-tax* explicit costs of capital for these sources of capital:

|  | After-Tax Cost |
|---|---|
| Short-term debt | 6.08% |
| Bonds | 5.56 |
| Preferred stock | 10.00 |
| Common stock | 11.56 |
| Retained earnings | 11.56 |

If the explicit source costs are weighted by the relative amounts of the sources, the weighted average cost of capital for the firm would be calculated as follows:

| (1)<br>Source of Financing | (2)<br>Proportion | (3)<br>Explicit Cost | (4)<br>Weighted Cost = (2)(3) |
|---|---|---|---|
| Short-term debt | 0.05 | 0.0608 | 0.00304 |
| Bonds | 0.10 | 0.0556 | 0.00556 |
| Preferred stock | 0.15 | 0.1000 | 0.01500 |
| Common stock | 0.60 | 0.1156 | 0.06936 |
| Retained earnings | 0.10 | 0.1156 | 0.01156 |
|  |  | Weighted average cost of capital: | 0.10452 |

Thus, one can approximate the *historic* cost of capital for the firm by using a weighted average method in which the weights are the relative proportions of the amount of capital from each source. In this example, the weighted average cost of capital is 10.45%.

## 6.8. Marginal Cost of Capital

When one has calculated the *historical* cost of capital (as in Section 6.7), the critical question then is whether or not this figure represents the firm's *real* (or true) *cost of capital* to be used for evaluating *new* projects. This question has been argued by many authors for some time. Several authors seem to argue that the weighted average cost is the correct value to use in judging the acceptability of new projects (see, for example, Bradley [4], p. 166; Committee [5], p. 127; Hunt, Williams, and Donaldson [9], p. 461). Other authors explicitly recommend the use of a *marginal* cost of capital as the correct value for finding new project acceptability (see, for example, Solomon [16]; Grunewald and Nemmers [8], p. 337; Prather and Wert [13], p. 192; Van Horne [19], pp. 91, 105–106; Weston and Brigham [20], p. 139; and Arditti and Tysseland [1]). In this text, we shall subscribe to the view that the *marginal* cost of capital is the minimum correct rate to use as a cutoff rate for accepting new projects. We take this position for two reasons, which we shall enumerate.

*First*, one very good reason for using the *marginal* cost of capital as a cutoff rate for new projects is that the use of a lower rate would permit acceptance of projects that would tend to lower the future value of the firm (or, equivalently, the value of its common stock). Since the weighted average cost of capital for a firm usually is *less* than its marginal cost of capital, the use of the lower weighted average cost figure to judge *new* project acceptability would thus reduce the value of the firm. This counter-vails the generally accepted goal of the firm to maximize shareholder wealth over time (Solomon [17], Chapter 2), which we discussed in Chapter 1.

*Second*, past costs of financing, used to calculate the weighted average cost of capital, have no bearing on the actual cost of financing *new* projects. In other words, it is the expected *rise* in *future* earnings that will contribute to the increased value of the firm. For future projects to cause a rise in the earnings and dividends of the firm (i.e., its future worth), the *last-added* future project—the one with the *lowest* rate of return in a group of projects—*must produce a rate of return at least equal to the cost of the last-added increment of capital used to finance it. Otherwise*, the future value of the firm would suffer a net decrease since in this case a project would have been accepted that would provide a return on the *incremental* investment *smaller* than the cost of the *incremental* capital used to finance it. In short, the rise in expected future earnings of the firm from the *new* projects must be sufficient to raise expected future worth *per share*, not just expected future worth.

The remainder of Section 6.8 will be devoted to an explanation of the marginal cost of capital concept, which has been adapted from an article by Arditti and Tysseland [1].

**6.8.1. *Marginal cost–marginal revenue approach.*** We assume that a number of investment projects, called $A, B, C, \ldots, H$, are available to the firm. We also assume that each of these projects is *independent*—that is, the net cash flow stream from each project is in no way dependent on that of any other project. A third assumption is that a unique rate of return[4] exists for each of the projects (e.g., $i_A, i_B, \ldots, i_H$) so that the projects may be ranked in the order $i_A > i_B > i_C > \cdots > i_H$. Also associated with each project is an initial expenditure, or cost, which is to be financed by the capital to be raised.

---

[4]Strictly, a *unique rate of return* means that there is a *unique*, real value of $i$ that satisfies, for any given project, the equality

$$NPV = \sum_{t=0}^{N} Y_t(1 + i)^{-t} = 0$$

where $NPV$ = net present value of the cash flow stream of the project.
  $Y_t$ = net cash flow at the end of year $t$ ($t = 0, 1, \ldots, N$).
  $i$ = the internal rate of return for the project ($-1 < i < \infty$).

Consider now that Fig. 6.1 represents a typical marginal cost–marginal revenue approach to the determination of the *cutoff* point for cost of capital and internal rate of return. The dollar costs of investment in the projects are given on the horizontal axis (cumulated), and the marginal revenue (i.e., the internal rate of return for each project, in descending order) is given on the vertical axis. Also plotted on the same graph are both *average* and *marginal* costs of capital. Note that through Project *C* the marginal cost of capital (*MCC*) and the average cost of capital (*ACC*) are equal; thereafter, the marginal cost of capital (*MCC*) increases at discrete intervals. The average cost of capital (*ACC*) also increases, but by smaller increments.

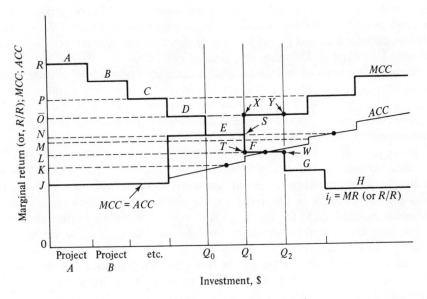

**Fig. 6.1.** Investment opportunities, marginal and average cost of capital.

Now, if one considers the instantaneous situation, the cutoff point for project selection should be the total funds expended at either $Q_0$ or $Q_1$, and one would be indifferent toward Project *E* since it is expected to return exactly the marginal cost of capital. At either $Q_0$ or $Q_1$, the *marginal* rate of return (the rate of return of the last-added project) first equals the *marginal* cost of capital (the cost of the last-added increment of capital to finance either Projects *D* and *E*, or simply *D* by itself). For convenience, we assume that *E* is actually accepted, but Project *F* definitely would *not* be accepted since its marginal cost of funds is greater than its expected rate of return.

**6.8.2. *A discounted cash flow approach.*** Referring again to Fig. 6.1, if one cuts off at $Q_1$, at the intersection of the project investment opportunity curve ($i_A, i_B, \ldots, i_H$) with the marginal cost of capital curve (*MCC*), he will accept Project *E* and reject Project *F*. At this point, the marginal cost of capital is $MCC_N$.

Looking at the effect on the value of the firm over time, then as a result of having accepted Projects *A* through *E*, the firm (and its shareholders) is better off by the sum of the *net present values* of the cash flows from Projects $(A + B + C + D + E)$, when discounted at the *average* cost of capital $ACC_K$. Thus, the *total* effect on the value of the firm is computed by using the *average* cost of capital since this is the *average* cost of the *bundle of funds* that financed this *bundle of projects. We do this even though $MCC_N$ is used as the marginal cutoff rate.*

Another way of looking at this fact is to view the *total* prospective return (in dollars) to the firm as the area $ORSQ_1$, which amounts to the sum of the incremental interest *return* rates times the funds used; the *cost* of the funds used by the firm as the area $OJSQ_1$, which is the dollar area under the marginal cost curve; and the *net* dollar return to the firm as the area $JRSJ$, which is simply the total dollar return from Projects $(A + B + C + D + E)$ less the dollar cost of the funds used for these projects. Hence, an *average* total internal rate of return for the project bundle could be calculated by dividing the area $ORSQ_1$ by the amount of funds used, $OQ_1$; and likewise, an *average* cost of capital could be calculated by dividing the area $OJSQ_1$ by the funds used, $OQ_1$; and finally, an *average* net rate of return could be calculated by dividing the area $JRSJ$ by the funds used, $OQ_1$. In every instance, the three *average* interest rates apply to the entire *bundle* of projects $(A + B + C + D + E)$, but the *cutoff* rate is the *marginal* cost of capital, *not* the average.

To repeat, the *marginal* cost of capital, at the particular point in the capital supply curve, is used as the *cutoff rate* in evaluating each individual project by comparing that rate with the project's rate of return. To evaluate the effect of accepting the entire project *bundle* upon the value of the firm, however, the *average* cost of capital is used, that is, the weighted average cost of all the explicit source funds that finance the *bundle* of accepted projects. This idea becomes clearer when we pose the opposite problem of what would happen if we were to cut off at the average cost rate.

For example, suppose we were to cut off at an investment of $Q_2$, using the *average* cost of capital rate, and accept Project *F*. Then the *total* contribution of Project *F* in dollars would be the area $Q_1TWQ_2$, or in terms of the rate of return and amount of capital used, $L(Q_2 - Q_1)$. The corresponding *total* cost of the funds used is the area $Q_1XYQ_2$, or in terms of the cost of capital and amount of capital used, $\bar{O}(Q_2 - Q_1)$. It is then obvious that the net benefit in dollars, obtained by adding Project *F*, is $(L - \bar{O})(Q_2 - Q_1)$; and since the cost rate of capital $(\bar{O})$ is greater then the benefit rate of return $(L)$, the net area represented by $(L - \bar{O})(Q_2 - Q_1)$ is *negative* and, hence, represents a *deduction* from the earlier net benefit that came from the selection of Projects $(A + B + C + D + E)$. Since Project *F* thus actually *reduces* the net present value of the previously accepted projects, it should be rejected, even though it appears marginally acceptable at the firm's *average* cost of capital. This conclusion is more precisely demonstrated in the next section.

### 6.8.3. *Mathematical approach to marginal cost of capital.* The market value of the firm at any time $t_0$ may be represented by

$$P_0 = \frac{\bar{Y}}{1 + k_0} \tag{6.23}$$

where $\bar{Y} =$ an abbreviation for the future expected net cash flow stream from the firm's activities (projects already accepted).

$k_0 =$ the firm's average cost of capital, or the equivalent discount rate used to capitalize the income stream $\bar{Y}$.

Now, the firm's value could also be represented by

$$P_0 = S_0^o + D_0^o \qquad (6.24)$$

where $S_0^o =$ the market value of the firm's common stock at $t_0$; and the superscript denotes *original*,

$D_0^o =$ the market value of its *original* debt at $t_0$.

We assume only these two types of security in its capital structure (common stock and debt). For simplicity, the model will be based on one time period. The more general $N$-period case can be derived straightforwardly, but it is cumbersome algebraically and not useful as a teaching device. The present formulation is a variation of that set forth by Modligliani and Miller [11], except that their income stream is a perpetuity and they assume a constant $k$.

The firm now supposedly makes an investment, $C$, in a project that will provide an expected rate of return, $r$. After this investment of $C$ dollars, the new value of the firm may be represented by

$$P_1 = \frac{\bar{Y} + C(1 + r)}{1 + k_1} \qquad (6.25)$$

where $k_1$ is the *new* average cost of capital or discount rate that capitalizes the *new* expected income stream.

The new value of the firm could also be represented by

$$P_1 = S_1^o + D_1^o + C \qquad (6.26)$$

where $S_1^o =$ the *new* market value of the *old* common stock.

$D_1^o =$ the *new* market value of the *old* bonds.

$C =$ either *new* stock or *new* debt, or both.

Now, we pose the question: Under what conditions will the investment project, $C$, be accepted? *Only if it will not diminish the value of the firm's common stock*, namely, if, and only if, this condition is satisfied:

$$S_1^o \geq S_0^o \quad \text{or} \quad S_1^o - S_0^o \geq 0.$$

Thus, there must be some rate of return, $r$, which the new investment $C$ must return to the firm to satisfy the condition.[5] To find this rate of return, we use the following sequence of operations.

First, subtract Eq. (6.24) from Eq. (6.26) to obtain

$$P_1 - P_0 = S_1^o + D_1^o + C - S_0^o - D_0^o.$$

---

[5]At this point, the usual *perfect capital markets* conditions are to be restated and applied. These may be found in Chapter 3. A discussion appears in [10].

We then *assume* that $D_1^Q = D_0^Q$, on the basis that the risk characteristics of the new project are *not sufficiently different* from the firm's present projects to change the market value of the *old bonds*. Thus, we drop the offsetting debts, and then transferring $C$ to the left side of the equation, we have

$$P_1 - P_0 - C = S_1^Q - S_0^Q.$$

In view of the shareholder benefit condition that we assumed earlier, namely, $S_1^Q \geq S_0^Q$, we now have that

$$P_1 - P_0 - C \geq 0$$

or

$$P_1 - P_0 \geq C \tag{6.27}$$

as being the *equivalent investment criterion* that a prospective project must meet in order to be judged acceptable. Then, substituting Eq. (6.25) for $P_1$ and Eq. (6.23) for $P_0$, we have

$$\frac{\bar{Y} + C(1+r)}{1+k_1} - \frac{\bar{Y}}{1+k_0} \geq C,$$

which may be written as

$$\left(\frac{\bar{Y}}{1+k_0}\right)\left(\frac{1+k_0}{1+k_1} - 1\right) + \frac{C(1+r)}{1+k_1} \geq C.$$

On multiplying through by $(1+k_1)$, we have

$$\left(\frac{\bar{Y}}{1+k_0}\right)[(1+k_0) - (1+k_1)] + C(1+r) \geq C(1+k_1).$$

Recalling that $\bar{Y}/(1+k_0) = P_0$ by definition, then

$$P_0[(1+k_0) - (1+k_1)] + C(1+r) \geq C(1+k_1).$$

Dividing through by $C$ and simplifying, we obtain

$$\frac{P_0}{C}(k_0 - k_1) + (1+r) \geq (1+k_1).$$

Finally, solving for $r$, we have

$$r \geq k_1 + \frac{P_0}{C}(k_1 - k_0). \tag{6.28}$$

We should now consider the content and meaning of Eq. (6.28). Recalling that $k_1$ was defined as the new *average* cost of capital after the incremental capital amount $(C)$ was raised and that $r$ was defined [Eq. (6.25)] as the minimum rate of return required on investment—that is, the cutoff rate or marginal cost of capital, then, from Eq. (6.28) r *is obviously greater than* k$_1$ by the increment $P_0(k_1 - k_0)/C$, if $k_1 > k_0$.

Two cases now need to be examined. First, if the new investment $C$ does not change the firm's risk characteristics, then the market will evaluate $k_1 = k_0$; where this so, then $r = k_1 = k_0$, and hence, from Eq. (6.28) the *marginal* cost of capital may be as low as $k_1$, which is also $k_0$. The second case comes about if the new investment, $C$, *changes the firm's risk characteristics* so that the market evaluates the firm's stock such that $k_1 > k_0$. Then, from Eq. (6.28) the rate of return from $C$ must be greater than $k_1$ (the *new* average cost of capital) by the increment $P_0(k_1 - k_0)/C$. In other words, the new project must generate not only additional income, but in actuality it must generate sufficient *additional* income to raise the expected return on *total* assets from $k_0$ to $k_1$.

This important point can be illustrated by an example. Suppose that the following values occurred for a particular firm:

$$k_0 = 0.145$$

$$k_1 = 0.150$$

$$P_0 = \$1,000,000$$

$$C = \$100,000$$

What would be the minimum rate of return for $C$ to be acceptable? The answer may be calculated from Eq. (6.28):

$$r \geq 0.150 + \frac{\$1,000,000}{\$100,000}(0.150 - 0.145)$$

or

$$r \geq 0.20,$$

which is also the *marginal* cost of capital.

Note that the firm must earn *more* than 15% on this new investment of $C = \$100,000$ because in addition it must earn an amount large enough to bring the *average* rate of return on *total* investment up from 14.5% to 15.0%. For each dollar invested in $C$, there are \$10 of old investments, each expected to return 14.5%. Therefore, the *extra* amount above 15% expected to be earned by each dollar of $C$ is 5% since one-tenth of this amount can be attributed to returns from assets that existed previously.

It can also be shown from this example that the acceptance of the investment $C$ at an expected rate of return of 15% would diminish the value of the firm. To prevent dilution of the common stock, i.e., to prevent the price of the common stock from falling, we must have $P_1 \geq P_0 + C$. Since $P_1 = P_0 + C = \$1,000,000 + \$100,000 = \$1,100,000$, we can write $P_1 \geq \$1,100,000$. But at a 15% rate of return on $C = \$100,000$, i.e., setting $r = 0.15$ in Eq. (6.25) and letting $\bar{Y} = (1 + k_0)P_0 = (1.145) \times (\$1,000,000)$, we have

$$P_1 = \frac{1.145(1,000,000) + 1.15(100,000)}{1.15} = \$1,095,652.$$

Consequently, the terminal value we obtain here, $P_1 = \$1,095,652$, is less than that required (\$1,100,000) to prevent the diminution of the firm's value.

When weighted with the old $k_0$, it is readily seen that this *required* $r = 0.20$ gives the *new* $k_1$, and therefore $r = 0.20$ must be the *marginal* cost of capital:

| Capital Amount | Relative Amount | Cost of Capital | Weighted Average |
|---|---|---|---|
| $1,000,000 | 0.909 | 0.145 | 0.1318 |
| 100,000 | 0.091 | 0.200 | 0.0182 |
| $1,100,000 | 1.000 | | $0.1500 = k_1$ |

Thus, the new project, if it returns only the *new average* cost of capital (15%), should be rejected; whereas if it returns the *marginal* cost of capital ($r = 0.20$), it should be accepted.

## 6.9. Numerical Example of the Marginal Weighted-Average Cost of Capital

This example is a sequential, two-part demonstration of (1) how a firm's weighted average *present* cost of capital may be determined from balance sheet and market data and (2) how its *marginal* cost of capital can be estimated from the amounts and explicit costs of *new* capital to be raised for a prospective *bundle* of new projects. Explanations of the methodology accompany the exposition.

**6.9.1. Calculation of the present weighted-average cost of capital.** The balance sheet of the ABC Company, for the year just ended, is illustrated in Fig. 6.2. The current market (traded) price for the common stock is $29 per share, and ABC has paid dividends on its common stock in the amount of $1.00 per share for the year just passed. Similar but somewhat lower dividend amounts were paid in prior years. Growth in dividends is expected over the next few years. The company's ordinary income tax rate is 56%, which includes Federal and state taxes. Calculate the present weighted-average cost of capital for the company.

*Solution.* The first step is to calculate the explicit costs of each capital source:

a. *Bonds:* From the balance sheet, the face value ($F$) is $10,000 per bond, the coupon interest rate is $r = 8\%$, and interest is paid semiannually. The maturity time is $N = 10$ years. Since no selling costs or amortizable discounts are mentioned, the explicit after-tax cost of the bonds may be calculated from Eq. (6.2):

$$k_i = \left[\left(1 + \frac{0.08}{2}\right)^2 - 1\right](1 - 0.56)$$

$$= 0.0359 = \underline{\underline{3.59\%}}.$$

b. *Preferred Stock.* From the balance sheet, the preferred dividend rate is 5% on the par value of $100 per share, which causes the preferred

*ABC Company*

BALANCE SHEET

Year Ended July 31, 19xx

### ASSETS

*Current Assets:*

| | | |
|---|---|---|
| Cash on hand and in banks | $ 102,000 | |
| Accounts receivable | 348,000 | |
| Raw material, in-process and finished goods inventories (at cost) | 300,000 | |
| Total, current assets | | $ 750,000 |

*Depreciable Assets:*

| | | |
|---|---|---|
| Plant and equipment (at cost) | 1,200,000 | |
| Less: Allowance for depreciation | 350,000 | 850,000 |
| Total Assets: | | $1,600,000 |

### LIABILITIES AND NET WORTH

*Current Liabilities:*

| | | |
|---|---|---|
| Accounts payable | $ 150,000 | |
| Employees' witholding taxes payable | 5,000 | |
| Federal income tax payable | 10,000 | $ 165,000 |

*Long-Term Liabilities:*

| | | |
|---|---|---|
| ABC Co. corporate bonds, face value $10,000 each; bearing 8% interest payable semiannually; maturity = 10 years | | 500,000 |
| Total Liabilities: | | $ 665,000 |

*Net Worth:*

| | | | |
|---|---|---|---|
| 1,000 shares (issued), 5% preferred stock, par value $100 per share | | 100,000 | |
| 30,000 shares (issued) common stock, par value $20 per share | | 600,000 | |
| *Surplus:* | | | |
| Retained earnings, year just ended | $ 40,000 | | |
| Retained earnings, prior years | 195,000 | 235,000 | |
| Total, net worth: | | | 935,000 |
| Total, Liabilities + Net Worth: | | | $1,600,000 |

**Fig. 6.2.** Balance sheet of the ABC Company.

dividend $D_p = (0.05)(\$100) = \$5$ per share. From Eq. (6.8), the cost of this source is

$$k_p = \frac{D_p}{P_O} = \frac{\$5}{\$100} = 0.05 = 5\%,$$

or the same as the preferred stock after-tax dividend rate.

c. *Common Stock.* To calculate the cost of common stock, we first need the book value of the common stock alone. This we obtain from the balance sheet:

$$BV_0 = \text{total assets} - \text{total liabilities} - \text{preferred stock}$$
$$= \$1,600,000 - \$665,000 - \$100,000$$
$$= \$835,000.$$

The book value *per share* is then $BV_0$ divided by the number of shares, or

$$BV'_0 = \frac{BV_0}{\text{No of. shares}} = \frac{\$835,000}{30,000} = \$27.83 \text{ per share.}$$

Next, we need *retained earnings per share*. This figure can be obtained from the balance sheet, recognizing that retained earnings equals total earnings $(E_0)$ minus common dividends $(D_0)$, or

$$E_0 - D_0 = \frac{\text{retained earnings}}{\text{No. of shares}} = \frac{\$40,000}{30,000 \text{ shares}}$$
$$= \$1.3333 \text{ per share.}$$

Then we may calculate *total earnings per share* $(E_0)$ by adding back the dividends paid:

$$E_0 = (E_0 - D_0) + D_0$$
$$= \$1.3333 + \$1.00 = \$2.3333.$$

Summarizing, we have available these data:

$$D_0 = \$1.00 \quad \text{(given in the problem)}$$
$$P_0 = \$29.00 \quad \text{(given in the problem)}$$
$$E_0 = \$2.3333 \quad \text{(calculated above)}$$
$$BV'_0 = \$27.83 \quad \text{(calculated above)}$$

Using the Gordon-Shapiro growth model [Eq. (6.21)], the cost of equity capital is

$$k_e = \frac{D_0}{P_0} + \frac{E_0 - D_0}{BV'_0}$$

$$= \frac{\$1.00}{\$29.00} + \frac{\$1.3333}{\$27.83} = 0.0824.$$

The last step is then to calculate the weighted-average cost of capital by the methodology presented in Section 6.7:

| Source of Financing | Amount | Proportion | Explicit After-Tax Cost of Source | Weighted Cost |
|---|---|---|---|---|
| Bonds | $ 500,000 | 0.348 | 0.0359 | 0.01249 |
| Preferred stock | 100,000 | 0.069 | 0.0500 | 0.00345 |
| Common stock | 835,000 | 0.583 | 0.0824 | 0.04804 |
| | $1,435,000 | 1.000 | | 0.06398 |

Here, then, the present weighted-average cost of capital is $k_0 = 0.06398 = 6.398\%$.

### 6.9.2. *The future weighted-average cost of capital after provision for new capital.* It
is commonly recognized in financial management practice that excess common stock
in a firm's capital structure, in relation to the amount of debt, can *lever* additional debt
without necessarily increasing the firm's overall cost of capital. In other words, additional debt capital can be obtained without adding equity capital, and the average cost
of capital to the firm will drop. At some point where the debt-to-equity ratio becomes
large enough, however, additional equity capital must be obtained because lending
institutions refuse more debt capital on the grounds that the equity (ownership) of the
firm is too "thin." Thus, the financing of a growing firm (one that continually needs
new capital) takes place in a time sequence in which additional funds are obtained
alternately by borrowing and by obtaining new equity capital, or by a combination of
both.

The particular *method* of raising new capital depends, first, on the prevailing
market rates for bonds, preferred stock, and common stock at the time the firm needs
the additional capital; second, on the financial history of the firm; third, on the
financial structure of the firm (current ratio of borrowed to equity capital); and
fourth, on a subjective evaluation by the market of the riskiness of the firm.

Various theories have been proposed about whether an *optimal* capital structure
exists or not—that is, whether a firm, by balancing its debt-to-equity ratio, can obtain
a minimum cost of capital. Two principal views prevail in financial theory. One, the
traditionalist theory, maintains that an optimal capital structure can be built that will,
in fact, minimize the firm's cost of capital. Proponents of this position are typified by
Solomon [17], Durand [6], Schwartz [15], and others who have attempted empirical
measurements of this proposition. The other principal theory is called the *Modigliani-Miller hypothesis*, which in effect says that the firm's cost of capital is independent of
its capital structure and, therefore, no minimum cost of capital exists. Proponents of
this view are Modigliani and Miller [10], [11], [12], who have attempted empirical
substantiation of it and found evidence supporting it.

When the Modigliani-Miller (M-M) hypothesis was first introduced, it caused a
furor among financial theorists, who attacked not only the theory developed by M-M
but also the empirical work offered in support of it. Thereafter, M-M added to their
theoretical developments and performed additional empirical investigations, which
again tended to support their theories. Now, more recent empirical tests, which
remedy the statistical defects in the earlier studies, tend to support the traditional
(minimum cost of capital) hypothesis. Thus, one can argue, probably successfully,
either way he chooses as to whether or not an optimal capital structure exists for the
firm.

For our purposes, however, this theoretical financial argument is not entirely
germane to our present development. It is mentioned only to acquaint the reader who

is not familiar with the theoretical financial literature that such developments are occurring, which *ultimately* will be incorporated into the project evaluation problem when they are more fully developed. Thus, we take the position now that what *is* germane to our purpose is a need to establish the *marginal cost of capital*, and we shall develop a method to do this without regard to the optimality of the resulting capital structure. That is, to find the marginal cost of capital for the firm, we shall simply assume that additional capital can be obtained on an arbitrary basis, without regard to the optimality of the resulting capital structure of the firm.

**Example 6.9.1.** Returning now to the problem in Section 6.9.1, suppose that the ABC Company proposes to obtain an additional $500,000 to finance a series of proposed projects that are expected to increase the earnings of the company. The $500,000 in additional capital is to be obtained as follows:

a. $100,000 is to be obtained by a new series of bonds that will bear interest at 9% on the face value of $100 per bond, with interest payable quarterly. Maturity dates average 20 years from now, and the bonds are expected to sell at par (face value).

b. $300,000 is to be obtained by a new issue of common stock, which, in the opinion of the company's financial advisors, can be sold at or above the present market price of the company's existing stock.

c. $100,000 is to be obtained from the retention of earnings from the company's existing operations.

The question then is, what is the weighted average cost of capital of the ABC Company *after* this proposed additional capital is provided?
*Solution*:

a. The explicit after-tax cost of capital of the *new* bonds [from Eq. (6.2)] is

$$k_i = \left[\left(1 + \frac{0.09}{4}\right)^4 - 1\right](1 - 0.56) = \underline{\underline{0.04096}}.$$

b. The explicit after-tax cost of capital for the new stock is the same as the old stock, on the assumption that (i) the price will not change and (ii) the dividends will continue to grow at the same rate as calculated earlier by the Gordon-Shapiro model. Thus,

$$k_e = 0.0824.$$

c. The explicit cost of retained earnings is assumed to be the same as the cost of equity capital, for the reasons stated in Section 6.6. Thus,

$$k_r = 0.0824.$$

d. The *new weighted-average cost of capital* is then calculated as follows:

| Source of Capital | Present Amount | Projected Increment | Future Amount | Future Ratio | Explicit After-Tax Cost | Weighted Cost |
|---|---|---|---|---|---|---|
| Bonds (1) | $ 500,000 | — | $ 500,000 | 0.2584 | 0.0359 | 0.0093 |
| Bonds (2) | — | $100,000 | 100,000 | 0.0517 | 0.04096 | 0.0021 |
| Preferred | 100,000 | — | 100,000 | 0.0517 | 0.0500 | 0.0026 |
| Common | 835,000 | 300,000 | 1,135,000 | 0.5866 | 0.0824 | 0.0483 |
| Retained earnings | — | 100,000 | 100,000 | 0.0516 | 0.0824 | 0.0043 |
|  | $1,435,000 | $500,000 | $1,935,000 | 1.0000 |  | 0.0666 |

Hence, after raising the $500,000 in new capital, the firm's *new* weighted-average cost of capital is 6.66%.

**6.9.3.** *The marginal cost of capital.* At this point, we have the firm's old cost of capital, $k_0 = 6.398\%$, and its new cost of capital, $k_1 = 6.66\%$, after obtaining the new increment of capital ($500,000). Both of these costs of capital are *weighted averages*, and neither is the firm's *marginal* cost of capital. We may estimate the marginal cost as follows.

First, we assume that the new capital budget of $500,000 will be entirely utilized (or nearly so) by a *bundle* of projects that will employ these available funds in an optimal manner. Consequently, we may view whatever bundle that accomplishes this objective as *one single project* with an *effective* rate of return equal to or greater than the *average* cost of the incremental capital. To calculate the *marginal cost of capital* for this entire bundle of projects, we use Eq. (6.28) to obtain

$$r \geq k_1 + \frac{P_0}{C}(k_1 - k_0).$$

Thus,

$$r \geq 0.0666 + \frac{(\$29.00/\text{share})(30,000 \text{ shares})}{\$500,000}(0.666 - 0.06398)$$

or

$$r \geq 0.0712.$$

Essentially, the same result could have been obtained by examining the *incremental* cost of the new capital, the values of which can be obtained from (d) above:

| Incremental Source of Capital | Incremental Capital Amount | Ratio | Explicit After-Tax Cost | Incremental Weighted Cost |
|---|---|---|---|---|
| Bonds (2) | $100,000 | 0.20 | 0.04096 | 0.0082 |
| Common | 300,000 | 0.60 | 0.0824 | 0.0494 |
| Retained earnings | 100,000 | 0.20 | 0.0824 | 0.0165 |
|  | $500,000 | 1.00 |  | 0.0741 |

Thus, *marginal* (or incremental) cost of capital for the $500,000 capital *increment* is 7.41%, which is of course higher than the *average* cost of capital of 6.66%. The principal reason for the *marginal* cost being greater than the *average* cost of capital is that as additional increments of capital are required, they often come at incrementally higher costs; hence, the project last-added (marginally) to the acceptable set (i.e., the project with the lowest acceptable rate of return) must produce a rate of return at least equal to the cost of the last-added increment of capital. In calculating the present value of a *bundle* of projects to be financed in total by an increment of new capital, it is the *marginal* cost of new capital that should be used as a *floor* discount rate.

## 6.10. Summary

In this chapter, we have considered the financing function of the firm: how it raises capital for investment in projects and how the *costs* of raising the capital can be identified. By applying the principle of opportunity costing, we identified *explicit* after-tax costs of capital for the various sources of capital available to the firm: short-term borrowing, long-term bonds, preferred stock, and equity (common) stock. For equity capital, two growth models of cost of capital were presented: the Gordon-Shapiro model and the Solomon model. The cost of retained earnings was shown to be the same as that for equity funding, principally on the basis that retained earnings rightfully belong to the shareholders, and retention is equivalent to paying the dividends out and then reacquiring them at current market price.

Thereafter, we showed how to obtain the weighted-average cost of capital for the firm, both before and after a new market offering for additional capital. Finally, we demonstrated how to find the firm's *marginal* cost of capital, which is the basis for establishing the *minimum rate of return* for new projects to be financed by the new capital.

## REFERENCES

[1] ARDITTI, FRED D., and MILFORD S. TYSSELAND, "Three Ways to Present the Marginal Cost of Capital," *Financial Management*, **2**, No. 2 (Summer, 1973), pp. 63–67.

[2] BARGES, ALEXANDER, *The Effect of Capital Structure on the Cost of Capital* (Englewood Cliffs, N.J.: Prentice-Hall, Inc., 1963).

[3] BIERMAN, HAROLD, JR., and SEYMOUR SMIDT, *The Capital Budgeting Decision*, 3rd ed. (New York: The Macmillan Company, 1971).

[4] BRADLEY, JOSEPH F., *Administrative Financial Management*, 2nd ed. (New York: Holt, Rinehart & Winston, 1969).

[5] COMMITTEE, THOMAS C., *Managerial Finance for the Seventies* (New York: McGraw-Hill Book Company, 1972).

[6] DURAND, DAVID, "Costs of Debt and Equity Funds for Business: Trends and Problems of Measurement," reprinted in [18].

[7] GORDON, MYRON J., and ELI SHAPIRO, "Capital Equipment Analysis: The Required Rate of Profit," *Management Science*, **III** (October, 1956); reprinted in [18].

[8] GRUNEWALD, ADOLPH E., and ERWIN ESSER NEMMERS, *Basic Managerial Finance* (New York: Holt, Rinehart & Winston, 1970).

[9] HUNT, PEARSON, CHARLES M. WILLIAMS, and GORDON DONALDSON, *Basic Business Finance* (Homewood, Ill.: Richard D. Irwin, Inc., 1966).

[10] MODIGLIANI, FRANCO, and MERTON H. MILLER, "Dividend Policy, Growth, and the Valuation of Shares," *Journal of Business* (October, 1961), pp. 411–433.

[11] _____, "The Cost of Capital, Corporation Finance, and the Theory of Investment," *American Economic Review*, **XLVIII** (June, 1958); reprinted in *Foundations for Financial Management*, ed., James C. Van Horne (Homewood, Ill.: Richard D. Irwin, Inc., 1966).

[12] _____, "The Cost of Capital, Corporation Finance, and the Theory of Investment: Reply," *American Economic Review*, **IL** (September, 1958); "Taxes and the Cost of Capital: A Correction," *Ibid.*, **LIII** (June, 1963); "Reply," *Ibid.*, **LV** (June, 1965); "Reply to Heins and Sprenkle," *Ibid.*, **LIX** (September, 1969).

[13] PRATHER, CHARLES L., and JAMES E. WERT, *Financing Business Firms* (Homewood, Ill.: Richard D. Irwin, Inc., 1971).

[14] QUIRIN, G. DAVID, *The Capital Expenditure Decision* (Homewood, Ill.: Richard D. Irwin, Inc., 1967).

[15] SCHWARTZ, ELI, "Theory of the Capital Structure of the Firm," *Journal of Finance*, **14** (March, 1959), pp. 18–39.

[16] SOLOMON, EZRA, "Measuring a Company's Cost of Capital," *Journal of Business*, **XXVIII** (October, 1955), pp. 240–252.

[17] _____, *The Theory of Financial Management* (New York: Columbia University Press, 1963).

[18] SOLOMON, EZRA (ed.), *The Management of Corporate Capital* (Glencoe, Ill.: The Free Press, 1959).

[19] VAN HORNE, JAMES C., *Financial Management and Policy*, 2nd ed., (Englewood Cliffs, N.J.: Prentice-Hall, Inc., 1968).

[20] WESTON, J. FRED, and EUGENE F. BRIGHAM, *Managerial Finance*, 4th ed., (New York: Holt, Rinehart & Winston, 1972).

## PROBLEMS

**6-1.** The sum of $100,000 is to be borrowed by the Shortcash Manufacturing Company from its bank, at an interest rate of 8% per year. The company's effective ordinary income tax rate is 48%. If interest payments are to be made as follows, calculate the effective after-tax annual interest rate of the loan:

(a) Interest payments are to be made quarterly.

(b) Interest payments are to be made monthly.

(c) Interest payments are to be made semiannually.

**6-2.** If Shortcash Manufacturing Company, in Problem 6-1, must keep at least $20,000 (in cash) on deposit in the bank at all times as a liquidity requirement, what is the effective annual after-tax interest rate being paid on the *available* portion of the loan, if the interest payments are made quarterly, monthly, or semiannually (as in Problem 6-1)?

**6-3.** What effective annual interest rate is being paid by savings and loan associations who pay their depositors "$5\frac{1}{4}\%$ interest from day in to day out, compounded daily"? (*Note:* A savings and loan association normally pays income taxes at corporate tax rates. Assume the effective tax rate is $40\%$).

**6-4.** Assume you borrowed $20,000 from a savings and loan association to finance a new house, and the association's terms were as follows: (a) The $20,000 is immediately discounted by 1% (i.e., you are charged "*one point*" at the time the loan is made) so that you actually receive $19,800 but owe $20,000. (b) The $20,000 is to be repaid at $9\frac{1}{2}\%$ annual interest, with both principal and interest payments to be paid in 240 *equal monthly* installments. Assuming you can deduct the *interest* portion of your payments and that your effective tax rate is $25\%$, what is the effective annual rate of interest you will pay?

**6-5.** Calculate the *before-tax* interest rate for Problem 6-4, and compare this to the *after-tax* cost of money for a savings and loan association you obtained in Problem 6-3. Estimate the annual gross profit of a savings and loan company that maintains an average of $25,000,000 in outstanding loans each year.

**6-6.** A new series of bonds to finance equipment is to be issued by Delay, Linger, and Wait Airlines. Each bond will have a face value of $10,000 and will bear a coupon (face) rate of interest of 8% per year. Interest is to be paid quarterly, and the bond series matures in 15 years. The bid price for the bonds by the successful underwriter is $9,000 per bond, less marketing expenses of $5.00 per bond. If the airline's effective income tax rate is $42\%$, what is the effective after-tax cost of this new borrowed capital to the company? (Use the exact method.)

**6-7.** Using Quirin's approximate method, what is the cost of capital for the bonds in Problem 6-6?

**6-8.** Corporations often obtain *new* money for undertaking projects by the sale of *convertible debentures*, which are basically bonds but with an additional right that permits the owner to convert the debenture into a stated number of shares of common stock at some specified future date. Because of this conversion right, the offering (i.e., initial) price of convertible debentures is frequently greater than a conventional bond of similar face value and interest rate. The *conversion premium* may be calculated as the difference between the initial offering price of the debenture and the present value of an equivalent conventional bond if held to maturity.

Consider yourself to be a prospective purchaser of a convertible debenture of the BCD Company. The debenture has a face value of $1,000 at maturity 10 years from now, and it will pay interest at the rate of 6% per annum, payable each 6 months. The initial offering price of the debenture (the market price) is now $1,000. If *your* time value of money is, say, 10% (before taxes) and your tax rate is 30%, how much would you be paying (cash outlay now) for the conversion premium if you bought the debenture?

**6-9.** The legal maximum interest rate on charge accounts (credit card accounts, etc.) is $1\frac{1}{2}\%$ per month on the unpaid balance.
(a) What is the corresponding *nominal* annual rate of interest?
(b) What is the corresponding *effective* annual rate of interest?

**6-10.** The common stock of General Spaceship Enterprises is presently traded on the New York Stock Exchange at a mean price of $65.00 per share. Last year, the company paid out a total of $720,000 in common stock dividends on 360,000 shares of common stock, and the present ratio of dividends to total earnings is expected to remain constant in the foreseeable future. The company's operating statement for the year just ended discloses that the company earned a profit of $1,440,000 after income taxes. The book value of the company's equity capital (common stock + retained earnings) is $24 per share. In addition to the foregoing equity structure, the company owes $5,000,000 in corporate bonds, which bear an interest rate of 6% per annum on the face value of the bonds. Interest on the bonds is paid quarterly, and the bonds mature in 8 more years. The company's effective ordinary income tax rate is 55%.

(a) What is the company's present cost of equity capital, using the Gordon-Shapiro model?

(b) What is the company's weighted-average cost of capital?

(c) What is the common stock dividend, in dollars per share, expected to be 3 years from now (i.e., payable at the end of the third year)?

**6-11.** The balance sheet of the B & B Company, as of the end of its current fiscal year, is as follows:

| *Assets* | | *Liabilities and Net Worth* | |
|---|---|---|---|
| *Current Assets:* | | *Current Liabilities:* | |
| Cash | $ 250,000. | Current installments on | |
| Receivables | 1,600,000. | long-term debt payable | $ 50,000. |
| Inventories | 1,950,000. | Accounts payable | 100,000. |
| | | Short-term bank loan | 250,000. |
| | | Federal income tax payable | 200,000. |
| *Fixed Assets:* | | *Other Liabilities:* | |
| Plant and equipment, | | 6.0% bonds due in 20 years* | 600,000. |
| net after depreciation | 1,700,000. | | |
| | | *Net Worth:* | |
| | | Preferred stock (100,000 | |
| | | shares)† | 800,000. |
| | | Common stock (1,000,000 | |
| | | shares outstanding) | 3,000,000. |
| | | Surplus and retained earnings | 500,000. |
| Total Assets | $5,500,000. | Total Liabilities and Net Worth | $5,500,000. |

*Bonds are each $1,000 face value, mature in 20 more years, bear interest at the rate of 6% per year, and interest is paid quarterly.

†Preferred stock pays a dividend of $0.47 per share annually.

Cash dividends have averaged $0.25 per share of common stock each year for the last 4 years. Earnings for the last 12 months were $825,000 after income taxes. The company's effective tax rate is 56%. Stock is traded on the American Exchange (Chicago), and the price for the company's common stock has ranged between $5.50 and $7.25 per share in the last 6 months, while the preferred stock price has averaged $9.05 per share in the same period.

What is the company's present estimated weighted-average cost of capital, using the Gordon-Shapiro model to estimate the cost of equity capital?

**6-12.** The B & B Company, whose capital structure is described in Problem 6-11, is contemplating a series of new investment-type projects whose cost is estimated to be $1,000,000. Financial consultants have recommended that the required capital for these projects be obtained as follows:

(i) $500,000 (nominal amount) by a new series of bonds (Series B), with face value of $1,000 each, bearing an interest rate of 8% per year and maturing in 15 years. Interest will be paid semiannually, and it will cost $1.50 per bond to prepare each interest check and mail it every 6 months. In addition, the successful bond underwriter has made a bid price of $960 per bond, less $10 selling expense, for this Series B issue.

(ii) $300,000 (actual amount) by the sale of a new preferred stock issue, to pay 6% dividends per year.

(iii) The balance of the $1,000,000 by retained earnings.

(a) After the proposed financing is accepted and marketed, what will the company's weighted-average cost of capital be?

(b) What is the company's marginal cost of capital for the $1,000,000 worth of new projects?

(c) How does your answer for (b) compare with that given by Eq. (6.28)? How do you explain the difference?

part two

DETERMINISTIC INVESTMENT
ANALYSIS

# EVALUATING A SINGLE PROJECT—
# DETERMINISTIC CRITERIA
# AND TECHNIQUES

## 7.1. Introduction

In some of the preceding chapters, in order to have a *figure of merit* for comparing one project with another, we calculated such *ad hoc* measures as *present value* (present worth) and *rate of return*. There we were not especially concerned with the appropriateness of the measuring criterion itself but rather with simply developing the *worth* of a project or a sequence of money flows by using some stated technique. Now, however, we are concerned with the *methods* used to evaluate and compare projects.

In the economic analysis of projects available to the firm, the objective is to decide, from the economic data available and from a managerial standpoint, whether or not a given project is acceptable to the firm. In other words, management needs to decide whether a project should be executed by the firm, thence to become a part of the productive activities of the firm, or whether it should be rejected as an investment opportunity. In making this decision, there are two general situations that surround the decision problem. The decision-making problem exists in one of two mutually exclusive milieu: The project selection problem either is *constrained* by certain stated (or implied) assumptions concerning the selection process or is *unconstrained*. To elaborate, for example, if the firm is attempting to select a number of executable projects from a larger set of candidate projects in the face of a limitation

# 7

on the amount of funds that can be expended, which in total will not permit execution of all candidate projects, then the selection problem is said to be *constrained*. The constraint is the total funds expenditure limitation. Similarly, if the firm is trying to judge whether to build a 10-, 12-, 14-, or 16-story building on a particular site, then the four alternatives are *mutually exclusive*, and the selection problem again is constrained by the nonindependence of the four alternatives (only one alternative can be executed). On the other hand, if there are *no* constraining factors in the selection problem, then the project selection problem is said to be *unconstrained*.

In the unconstrained selection problem, the objective is to determine the economic desirability of a single project in isolation, that is, without overt comparison to competing or alternative projects and in the absense of other constraints. While the attempt here is apparently to judge such a project on its own merits, one cannot escape using a particular type of comparative methodology to judge the merit of the project. The comparison is actually supplied by the firm's opportunity cost. While it appears to be absent, the principle of opportunity costing is *always* present, even in judging single projects under unconstrained conditions. The actual comparison the firm must make in this case is between the alternatives *accept the project* and *do nothing*. Choice of the latter always involves alternative use of the funds that would otherwise be invested in the project. Single unconstrained projects need always be measured by the best alternative use of the firm's funds: either the firm's cost of capital (as a minimum basis) or the opportunities for external investment presented by the market place for a similar risk investment. Thus, while we may on occasion seemingly decide to accept or reject a single, isolated project without *formal* stated comparison to other competing or relating projects, nevertheless, in doing so we really do (or ought to) make a direct comparison with the firm's opportunity cost base, which is its marginal investment rate.

In the *constrained* selection problem on the other hand, one frequently finds two or more projects (or alternatives) being compared to each other as competitors, with the objective being the elimination of all but one acceptable or most desirable alternative. Typically, textbook *engineering economy* problems emphasize this comparative selection technique: One "best" solution is to be selected from a set of mutually exclusive alternative solutions to a problem. The usual basic engineering economy problem posed to the undergraduate student, for example, is to find some minimum cost alternative from several possible solutions in a set, only one of which can be executed. This type of comparative analysis is always a *constrained* selection problem since it implies that the selection of one method or process automatically precludes the execution of *any* competing process or method. In other words, the selection of one project automatically eliminates the selection of all other alternative projects.

Now, the fundamental importance of the presence or absence of constraints in the selection process is that the *constrained* selection problem must be treated differently from the *unconstrained* problem, as we shall see in Chapter 8. While we may use any of several criteria, pretty much at will, to select an isolated project under *un*constrained conditions, it turns out that when constraints are present, our choice of criterion is severely limited. For this reason, not all project selection methodologies are usable under all conditions.

The major purpose of this chapter is to investigate some selection criteria that have theoretical merit, particularly from the standpoint of their underlying assumptions and limitations of application. Some of these criteria, such as payback, net present value, and internal rate of return, are rather widely used in industry and business as criteria for project selection, but often they are misapplied or misunderstood or misused. The reasons appear to be (1) that the *assumptions* underlying these criteria, which effectively limit their applicability, are not fully understood and (2) that the economic conditions *assumed to apply* in the economic analysis itself are not consistent with the assumptions underlying the criteria. Hence, this chapter is designed to investigate several of these useful criteria from a critical standpoint, with the aim of discovering the underlying assumptions and clarifying the conditions of application. We must always bear in mind that here we are considering *only* the *un*constrained case.

In all the methodologies presented in this chapter, certain basic assumptions need to be made concerning the investment projects and the firm. These assumptions are often called *perfect market conditions* and the *essential assumptions of certainty* and are generally stated somewhat as follows.

## 7.2. The Essential Assumptions of Certainty

The assumptions that underlie most deterministic project analyses are called the *essential assumptions of certainty* and are generally traced to the pioneer works of Irving Fisher, *The Theory of Interest* [9]; Friedrich and Vera Lutz, *The Theory of Investment of the Firm* [17]; and J. Hirshleifer, "On the Theory of Optimal Investment Decision" [11]. The essential assumptions can be briefly summarized as follows:

1. *There is a perfect capital market, and the supply of funds is unrestricted.*

The detailed conditions of a *perfect capital market* were presented and discussed in Section 3.1.1. The reader should review these at this time. The important factors to remember, however, can be summarized as follows: In a perfect capital market, each buyer or seller of securities is presumed to trade in such small amounts (relative to the total market) that no one buyer or seller has any appreciable effect on securities prices. This means that as a seller of securities, a firm can raise as much cash as it wants at the going rate of interest. Moreover, a perfect capital market means that the firm, as a buyer of securities, can invest as much surplus cash as it wants at the market rate of interest. Since the firm has (or can obtain) all the funds it needs to accept all *profitable* investments, there is no need to rank investment projects in order of their profitability. Since the firm, under these conditions, can be presumed to have made all the profitable investments it desires, then the market rate of interest accurately measures the firm's marginal investment opportunities. The second most important factor is that there are no costs associated with market transactions.

2. *There is complete certainty about investment outcomes.*

Complete certainty about investment outcomes means that the firm is in possession of all relevant *present and future* knowledge concerning not only (a) the projects and investment opportunities under present consideration but also (b) all possible projects and investment opportunities. Moreover, the relevant knowledge is *exact*, that is, without risk or uncertainty variations from deterministically certain values. This certainty applies to all factors and variables in the problem: cash flows, discounting rates, timing, economic lives, etc. Because of this certainty of knowledge, firms do not find it necessary to make an allowance for uncertainty in their analyses, nor do security buyers distinguish between bonds and stocks, for example. Since there is no uncertainty, all project returns will equal the risk-free (or *pure*) rate of interest, which we shall call *cost of capital* for present purposes.

3. *Investment projects are indivisible.*

Contrary to the type of investments that can be made in the stock or bond markets, in which purchases of *multiple* shares or bonds can be made at a constant per share price, a *project* is generally indivisible—that is, it must be executed in its entirety as a functional unit or not at all. This is the fundamental distinction between *portfolio* or *investment* analysis as practiced by financial practitioners for stock and bond investments and *project* analysis as practiced by engineers and industrial managers for industrial projects. In *project* analysis, each project is considered to be a functional entity, executable only in its entirety. Fractional parts of projects are not considered. (If it becomes necessary to consider a fractional part or parts of a large project, the large project can be broken down into smaller discrete, separately executable portions, thereby preserving the *executable entity principle*.) The financial implication of this assumption is that firms must commit funds by *discrete* amounts, each representing the investment for a particular project (or combination of projects).

> 4. *Investment projects are independent*.

In a given *set* of investment projects, each project is independent. This means that the profitability of one project does not *in any way* affect the profitability of any other project. The implication, therefore, is that there is *no* economic, technical, or other dependence between any two projects in *any* of the elements that define their cash flow streams. A further *key* implication is that this assumption precludes the existence of mutually exclusive projects, such as competing alternative solutions to the same technical problem, which are by definition *dependent* projects.

The four assumptions above describe what might be called the ideal situation, somewhat analogous in thermodynamics to the ideal Carnot cycle, useful but usually quite different from the real-world situation. In Chapters 10, 11, and 12 these assumptions will be relaxed, but in Chapters 7 and 8 they remain the fundamental assumptions underlying the analysis of projects. The practical result of these assumptions is that the firm makes a "go–no go" decision about *each* discrete project, without considering its relationship to any other project.

## 7.3. Some Measures of Investment Worth (Acceptance Criteria)

In this chapter, we shall describe and illustrate four different measures of investment worth, or acceptance criteria, that were chosen either because they are currently used in business practice or because good theoretical arguments can be advanced in their favor. The ones that we shall investigate are the *payback method*, *net present value* (sometimes called *net present worth*), *internal rate of return*, and *profitability index* (or *benefit-cost method*).

Obviously, these are not the only acceptance criteria that could be examined. Many practitioners will recognize the omission of others. For example, no discussion of the following criteria are included:

1. Proceeds per dollar of outlay (total proceeds divided by investment).
2. Average annual proceeds per dollar outlay (similar to 1, except proceeds and investments are averaged).
3. Average income on investment book value (an accounting measure based on the declining values of an investment due to depreciation).

4. Average income on cost (similar to 3, except that *cost* is substituted for *book value* of the investment).
5. Return on investment (ROI) procedures—generically, a typical procedure (or variant) in which a return on investment for each year is determined by dividing the annual income for the year by the average annualized investment for that year and then *averaging* the annual returns on investment to obtain an overall ROI for the project.

These methods are not investigated here because they are not acceptable as economic criteria. They either do not consider the time value of money or account for it incorrectly (e.g., the ROI methods). An interested reader can find a thorough discussion of these criteria, with examples, in Bierman and Smidt's *second* edition ([5], pp. 21–25) and in some managerial accounting texts.

While we are primarily concerned in this chapter with the *un*constrained selection problem, curiously enough most of these criteria have been advocated in the literature at one time or another for use in selecting *among competing projects* as well as in selecting isolated projects. For example, they have been suggested as being equally valid in discriminating between competing *alternative* projects (a typical constrained case) as well as selecting a single project in the absence of constraints. For many of the criteria above, claims of validity under *both* the constrained and unconstrained cases are simply not warranted, as we shall see.

## 7.4. The Payback Period

The so-called *payback* period is a relatively simple and frequently used criterion for judging the economic worth of an investment. The payback period is formally defined as the length of time required for the stream of cash inflows received by the firm from a project to extinguish the original cash outlay(s) required by the investment. Mathematically, the payback period, $\theta$, is defined by the relationship

$$\sum_{t=0}^{\theta} Y_t = 0 \qquad (7.1)$$

where $Y_t$ = net cash flows to or from the project at times $t = 0, 1, 2, \ldots, \theta$. (Normally, $Y_0 < 0$ and the other $Y_t > 0$, so that $\theta$ is then determinate. Futher, the periods 0–1, 1–2, etc., can be made sufficiently short so that $\theta$ can be estimated for fractional portions of a year.)

The ordinary decision procedure in using payback as a criterion is to use it as a *limit* rather than as a direct criterion. Thus, a firm might establish some maximum payback period for a given class of projects and then reject all projects having payback periods greater than the maximum. For example, the firm might adopt maximum payback periods of 10 years for new construction-type projects, 5 years on new laborsaving machinery, and 3 years on new product tooling. Projects displaying payback periods greater than these maxima would be rejected, whereas those with shorter payback periods would be accepted. Thus, the payback figure functions in this manner more as a measure against an upper *limit* decision criterion rather than as a criterion in its own right.

A second use for the payback period is to use it as a ranking device among projects. When used this way, those projects with the shortest payback periods are given the highest rankings. For example, four hypothetical projects, with the assumed investments and cash inflows shown in Table 7.1, would be ranked by the payback criterion [Eq. (7.1)] in the order given in Column 7 of the table.

**Table 7.1.** CASH FLOWS AND PAYBACK PERIODS OF FOUR HYPOTHETICAL PROJECTS

| Project | Initial Investment | Net Cash Proceeds | | Total Proceeds | $\theta$ = Payback Period (years) | Ranking |
|---|---|---|---|---|---|---|
| | | End of Year 1 | End of Year 2 | | | |
| A | $10,000 | $10,000 | — | $10,000 | 1 | 1 |
| B | 10,000 | 10,000 | $1,100 | 11,100 | 1 | 1 |
| C | 10,000 | 3,762 | 7,762 | 11,524 | 1.7* | 3 |
| D | 10,000 | 5,762 | 5,762 | 11,524 | 1.8* | 4 |

*The fractional parts of a year result from an assumption that the end-of-period cash flows can be prorated over the periods involved, for calculation purposes.

On the face of things, it would appear that the payback period, as an isolated selection criterion by itself, is not a very reliable one. For example, it fails to distinguish between Projects *A* and *B*, thus ignoring the longer cash flow stream of *B*. Obviously, to ignore the cash flows that occur *after* payback is not a very desirable characteristic in a selection criterion. A second defect arises because it appears not to consider the time value of money. This is a serious omission when a project involves the input of depreciable capital goods since the very existence of capital goods implies that interest is at work in the economy. Then, if this were not enough, yet a third defect is often displayed by the payback criterion: It may incorrectly rank projects in order of preference. For example, it ranks Projects *A* and *B* as being preferable to *C* or *D* (both *A* and *B* have shorter payback periods); whereas it is entirely possible that either *C* or *D* would be preferred to *A* or *B* because of the higher *total* cash inflows for *C* and *D* ($11,524 for *C* or *D* versus $10,000 for *A* and $11,100 for *B*). So, at least on the surface, it would appear that payback is not a very reliable selection criterion.

In spite of these shortcomings, however, payback continues to be one of the most widely applied quantitative concepts in making investment decisions. Its use has persisted over a long span of years, seemingly in disregard of some of the more sophisticated, rational criteria such as net present value and internal rate of return. While some academic writers have dismissed payback as misleading and worthless, for the reasons indicated, at the same time businessmen and other academicians have continued to advocate the payback concept as a selection methodology, at least as a *secondary* criterion. Why is there this inconsistency between the two positions?

Weingartner [32] originally posed this problem and offered some explanations, the substance of which goes as follows.

There are several different ways in which payback can be interpreted. We shall enumerate these briefly and then expand them. *First*, the reciprocal of the payback period, $1/\theta$, can be interpreted as a crude measure of the average rate of return on original investments. For example, if a given project displays a payback period of 4 years, then $1/\theta = 1/4 = 25\%$ of its original investment will be recovered per year, on the average. At the end of 4 years (the payback period), the project will have recovered $4(0.25) = 100\%$ of the firm's original investment. As we shall see, a form of this "interest" interpretation is the only one that has any significance in the context of certainty.

*Second*, the use of payback as a ranking device implies that the return of invested capital in a shorter period of time is somehow better than a return in a longer period of time. The explanation for this attribute, Weingartner says, is not necessarily a desire on the part of the firm to preserve an attitude of cash liquidity toward an uncertain future (which would improve the firm's ability to take advantage of unknown but attractive projects in the future), but rather the explanation may lie in the fact that a short payback period reduces an *un*certain future as quickly as possible to a known and certain position: complete recovery of the investment. Thereafter, uncertainty is of no consequence to the firm since the investment has been recovered and any proceeds derived after payback are simply profit. Thus, payback is a form of break-even analysis which makes no sense in the world of certainty that we have assumed but which probably functions to shortcut the process of generating information and evaluating it—at least, it is a basis for *subjective* evaluation by the firm's decision-maker.

*Third*, there are some inherent differences between financial investments, say, in the stock market, and investments in capital projects by the firm. With financial investments, especially where there is a ready and open trading market, the choice of the investor at any time revolves purely around the decision to leave the funds in an investment or withdraw them. The situation is different with physical assets and projects. Not only is the market value for used physical assets substantially below their *going concern* value *in the project*, but the range of alternatives with respect to operating the project is quite different. Basically, the firm is limited to (1) committing additional resources to the project (expanding its scope), (2) withdrawing resources from the project (contracting its scope), (3) leaving the resources at a static level, and (4) *always* operating the project within the confines and limits of the project's resources, regardless of their levels. The randomness and the timing of the economic outcomes focus the manager's attention on the financial restrictions placed on the resource levels, and for these reasons payout information is extremely important to the manager—it is the rate at which he can expect uncertainty concerning a project to be resolved, with a consequent lifting of the resource constraints. Again, under our assumptions of certainty, this concept has no meaning; nevertheless, as far as any single indicator *can* represent the necessary information, the payback period *does* provide relevant data, at least for subjective evaluation.

Now, returning to the one concept that has some validity under our conditions of certainty, we shall examine in detail the payback period as an economic measure of the rate of return on investment. The exposition of this concept is essentially that due to Gordon [10], which was later generalized by V. L. Smith [23].

**7.4.1.** *Payback rate of return.* Suppose the firm is considering an investment proposal (project) characterized by the following attributes:

$P$ = the initial investment at time $t = 0$.
$F$ = the salvage value at time $t = N$.
$N$ = the life of the project, years.
$i$ = the effective interest rate per year.
$t$ = time in periods ($t = 0, 1, 2, \ldots, N$).
$Y$ = uniform end-of-period *cash flow* generated by the project.

Thus, we describe a simple project that has a single investment of $P$ dollars at time $t = 0$ and returns a uniform stream of cash flows, each of $Y$ dollars per year, over the life of the project of $N$ years beginning with $t = 1$. This simplification is justified because our objective here is to build a demonstrative analytic model.

Now, in Chapter 3 we have already shown that the depreciable portion of an investment, $P - F$, is related to a series of uniform end-of-period money amounts, $A$, by the relationship given in Eq. (3.26), which is repeated here:

$$A = (P - F)\left[\frac{i(1 + i)^N}{(1 + i)^N - 1}\right] + Fi. \tag{3.26}$$

If the salvage value, $F$, is assumed to be minimal with respect to the amount of the investment, $P$, so that we can consider $F = 0$, then the entire investment $P$ is recovered, instead of just a portion ($P - F$), and Eq. (3.26) reduces to

$$A = P\left[\frac{i(1 + i)^N}{(1 + i)^N - 1}\right]. \tag{7.2}$$

Solving Eq. (7.2) in terms of $P/A$ and setting our project cash inflow $Y = A$, we can then define the ratio $\theta = P/Y$ from our known capital investment, $P$, and known annual cash flow, $Y$, so that finally we have from Eq. (7.2) that

$$\theta = \frac{P}{Y} = \left[\frac{(1 + i)^N - 1}{i(1 + i)^N}\right]. \tag{7.3}$$

We now note that $P/Y$ is simply the initial investment in dollars divided by the annual cash inflow in dollars per year, or the *payback period*, $\theta$. [The units of the equation, years, derives from the units of $i$ ($\$/\$$-year) in the denominator.] Thus, the ratio of investment to net cash inflow, or payback period, not only establishes the length of time for investment recovery but also *defines the value of an effective interest rate, $i$,* via Eq. (7.3).

What is the meaning of this interest rate? As we saw in Chapter 3, the effective interest rate defined by Eq. (7.3), or its reciprocal in Eq. (7.2), is the particular interest rate that assures one not only of the *return of his original capital* over the life of the project but also of receiving *interest on the unrecovered investment balances* in the interim periods at that interest rate.

Smith ([23], pp. 220–230) arrives at substantially the same economic interpretation of $\theta$ by using a continuous compounding approach in the cash flow stream. His method uses a capital constraint and Kuhn-Tucker conditions to indicate an optimal marginal solution, in which the *reciprocal* of the payback period defines an equilibrium intersection point between the cost of funds invested and the rate of return on funds inflow. The equilibrium point, defined by the payback reciprocal, is the interest rate

$$\longrightarrow \quad \frac{1}{\theta^*} = k + \frac{r}{1 - e^{-rN}} \qquad (7.4)$$

where $k =$ the marginal profitability of the last dollar's worth of available capital that is, the firm's marginal *cost of capital*.

$\dfrac{r}{1 - e^{-rN}} =$ *incremental capital recovery rate* on the last dollar's worth of investment

in the project, with annual interest rate $r$ realized on the project investment.

In summary, then, the payback ratio (or period), $\theta = P/Y$, or its reciprocal *defines an effective interest rate, i,* that provides for two simultaneous functions: (1) the recovery over the life of the project of the invested capital and (2) interest at rate $i$ on the periodic declining investment balances during the project life. If this interest rate is greater than the firm's marginal attractive rate of return (or, under conditions of certainty, the firm's cost of capital), then the project should be accepted. This statement is based on the fact that if the project's effective return rate, $i$, is equal to or greater than the firm's minimum attractive rate, then the project will provide for recovery of capital in $N$ years plus interest on the unrecovered project balances at a rate equal to or greater than the minimum attractive rate of return. This concept will be demonstrated by example.

**Example 7.4.1.** A project requires an initial investment of $10,000, and is estimated to return cash flows of $2,500 each year for 10 years. The firm's cost of capital is 15%. (a) What is the payback period? (b) What is the payback rate of return? (c) What is the effective return rate? (d) Should the project be accepted?

*Solution:*

a. Payback period $= \theta = \dfrac{P}{Y} = \dfrac{\$10,000}{\$2,500} = 4$ years.

b. Payback rate of return $= \dfrac{1}{\theta} = 0.25 = 25\%$ per year.

c. $\theta = \dfrac{P}{Y} = \left[ \dfrac{(1 + i)^{10} - 1}{i(1 + i)^{10}} \right] = 4.0 = (P/A, i\%, 10)$

where $i$ is the unknown. Hence, from tables,

$$(P/A, 20\%, 10) = 4.1925$$
$$(P/Y, i\%, 10) = 4.00$$
$$(P/A, 25\%, 10) = 3.5705$$

and by linear interpolation

$$\frac{4.1925 - 4.00}{4.1925 - 3.5705} = \frac{i - 0.20}{0.25 - 0.20}$$

or

$$i = 0.20 + \frac{0.1925}{0.6220}(0.05) = 0.215 \longrightarrow 21.5\%.$$

d. Since $(i = 21.5\%) > (\bar{k} = \text{cost of capital} = 15\%)$, the project should be accepted. Note that the decision is made on $i > \bar{k}$, *not* on $1/\theta > \bar{k}$.

## 7.5. Criteria Using Discounted Cash Flows

The major impediment that eliminates many project selection criteria from serious consideration is that the *magnitudes* and *timing* of *all* the cash flows, to and from a candidate project, are not correctly taken into account. This is essentially true of all but three—net present value, internal rate of return, and profitability index (or, as it is often called, *excess present value index* or *benefit-cost ratio*). Under certain conditions these three criteria can be *properly* applied to the selection problem. These criteria are the so-called *rational criteria* because they take into account the two attributes most often absent in other criteria: (1) the entire cash flow stream for the life of the project and (2) the time value of money.

Over the span of the last 20 years or so, there has been much advocacy, argument, and disagreement in the research literature concerning these three criteria (and others that are related). The root of much, if not all, of the disagreement lies in whether a project or set of projects is to be selected under *constrained* conditions or not. At first, the fundamental importance of a constraint in the selection problem was not realized at all, and until Weingartner [30] published his Ford Foundation prize-winning dissertation, "Mathematical Programming and the Analysis of Capital Budgeting Problems" in 1963, no substantial progress was really made toward solving the problem. When Weingartner pointed out, however, that a linear-programming type of formulation of the capital budgeting problem resulted in an *optimal* selection of projects (under certainty conditions) when the objective function *maximized the net present value criterion*, the path was opened up for further developments that clarified theoretically why the other criteria did not result in optimal solutions.

Since that time, several outstanding articles have appeared in the research literature that have carefully and critically examined these three rational criteria and their "relatives" from the standpoint of assumptions and limitations. Early examples of such published studies were those by Lorie and Savage [16], Solomon [24], Renshaw [22], Swalm [25], Bernhard [3], Weingartner [31], and Beranek [2], which compared two or more of these criteria but which, in general, did not develop any *comprehensive* evaluation and comparison of their assumptions and limitations. In 1971 this situation was remedied when Bernhard [4] published a comprehensive comparison and critique of eight criteria:

1a.  Present Worth [net present value]
1b.  Equivalent "Annual" Worth
2a.  Benefit-Cost Ratio[1]
2b.  Net Benefit-Cost Ratio
2c.  Solomon's Average Rate of Return
3a.  Internal Rate of Return [or, "yield," "investor's method," "marginal efficiency of capital," etc.]
3b.  MAPI Urgency Rating[2]
4.   Eckstein's Benefit-Cost Ratio[3]

Bernhard showed that criterion 1b is but a variation of 1a, that 2b and 2c are equivalent to 2a, and that 3b reduces to 3a, so we need consider here only the three basic criteria, namely, present worth, benefit-cost ratio, and internal rate of return. As for criterion 3b, the MAPI urgency rating, Bernhard showed it to be an inappropriate method for examining mutually exclusive alternatives, equivalent to 3a; therefore, we shall not consider it as a viable alternative since many project selection problems in reality involve mutually exclusive alternatives (in sets of candidate projects).

In addition to Bernhard's and Weingartner's work, three other noteworthy articles are the benchmarks generally accepted today by theoreticians as thorough analyses

---

[1]Several forms of the benefit-cost ratio exist, including the net benefit-cost ratio (Bernhard's method 2b) and Eckstein's benefit-cost ratio (Bernhard's method 4). The benefit-cost ratios are all generically derivable from net present value and are discussed more fully in Section 7.7 and Footnote 3.

[2]The MAPI (Machinery and Allied Products Institute) "Urgency Rating" [28] for a project, as interpreted by Dryden [7], is

$$UR = \frac{B_1 - K}{C}$$

where $B_1$ = cash *in*flow from the project to the firm in year 1.

$K = C - \sum_{t=2}^{N} B_t(1 + r)^{1-t}$ = first-period capital consumption.

$C$ = initial cash outflow to the project at time $t = 0$.
$B_t$ = cash inflow from the project at time $t = 2, 3, \ldots, N$.
$N$ = life of the project.
$r$ = the internal rate of return of the project.

[3]Eckstein's benefit-cost ratio is so called because it differs from the conventional benefit-cost ratio described in Section 7.7. The definition (in our notation) of Eckstein's benefit-cost ratio [8] is as follows: Let

$$b = \sum_{t=1}^{N} b_t(1 + i)^{-t} = \text{present value of cash } \textit{in}\text{flows from } t = 1 \text{ to } N.$$

$$c = \sum_{t=1}^{N} c_t(1 + i)^{-t} = \text{present value of cash } \textit{out}\text{flows from } t = 1 \text{ to } N.$$

$C$ = initial cost of project at $t = 0$.

$B = b - c$ = difference in present values of cash inflows and outflows.

Then, Eckstein's benefit-cost ratio is defined as

$$EBC = \frac{B + c}{C + c}.$$

and explanations of the three rational criteria. The first is the classic article by J. Hirshleifer, "On the Theory of Optimal Investment Decision" [11], which provides a fundamental explanation and justification of net present value as a selection criterion. The other two are articles published in 1965 by Teichroew, Robichek, and Montalbano [26], [27] that rigorously analyze the internal rate of return (IRR) criterion and specify the conditions under which IRR can and cannot be used as a selection criterion.

The remainder of this chapter is essentially an exposition of the information disclosed by those authors. As far as we know at this time, the articles mentioned in the preceding paragraph are the best sources of *fundamental* research information available concerning net present value, internal rate of return, and benefit-cost ratio.

## 7.6. The Net Present Value Criterion

The general form for expressing net present value was developed in Chapter 3, as Eq. (3.2), which is repeated here for convenience:

$$P_0 = \sum_{t=0}^{N} \frac{Y_t}{\prod_{j=0}^{t} (1 + i_j)} \tag{3.2}$$

where $P_0$ = the net present value.

$Y_t$ = the *net* cash flow at the end of period $t$, i.e., at time $t$.

$i_j$ = the interest (discount rate) for period $j$.

$N$ = the life of the project.

$j$ = points in time prior to $t$, i.e., $j = 0, 1, 2, \ldots, t$.

$t$ = the point in time under consideration; i.e., $t = 0, 1, 2, \ldots, N$.

Thus, *in the general form*, it is not necessary for the interest rates, $i_j$, to be equal, which permits one to assess the present value by using a period-by-period evaluation in which the interest rate can take on different values. For the usual purposes of project evaluation, however, one assumes $i_0 = 0$ and $i_1 = i_2 = i_3 = \cdots = i_N = i$, so that Eq. (3.2) reduces directly to Eq. (3.3), which is repeated here:

$$P_0 = \sum_{t=0}^{N} Y_t (1 + i)^{-t}. \tag{3.3}$$

In applying Eq. (3.3), one usually has available as input information the *net* cash flows, $Y_t$, for the project, which are assumed to occur instantaneously at the *ends* of the periods $t = 0, 1, 2, \ldots, N$ in the life of the project. Also, one usually has available an estimate, or other knowledge, of the discounting rate, $i$, to be used. Under these conditions, finding the net present value is straightforward. The result is a *point* estimate of $P_0$—i.e., a single value of $P_0$ at a particular interest rate $i$. While the point estimate of net present value is informative, in that one can determine if it is positive, negative, zero, or indeterminate, the behavior of the criterion *as a function* is more informative. For the unconstrained case, the general rule is to accept the project if net present value is positive; otherwise, reject it. We shall now examine the detailed development (due mainly to Hirshleifer [11]) that leads to this decision criterion.

### 7.6.1. *Production-consumption opportunities of the firm.*

In deriving the expression for net present value in Sections 3.1.2 and 3.1.3, under perfect market conditions, we saw that *one* activity in which a firm[4] can engage is to borrow and lend funds in the financial market. In this way, consumption opportunities can be shifted from one period to another, but because the borrowing and lending rates are identical in a perfect capital market, this activity in itself does *not* increase the present value, or worth, of the firm (see Section 3.1.2 and Fig. 3.1). The reason, of course, is that given an initial *endowment position* of incomes at times $t = 0$ and $t = 1$, the *market interest line* with constant slope $[= -(1 + i)]$, which passes through the endowment position, defines a *single* value of present value ($W$, in Fig. 3.1). Thus, while the firm can borrow and lend in order to shift its consumption capability at will from one period to another, it cannot increase its present worth above that initially fixed by its endowment position.

A *second* activity, however, is available to the productive firm that *will* increase its net worth (this is considered to be desirable—"more" is preferred to "less"). This activity is to acquire some intermediate factors of production—e.g., some buildings, equipment, tools, and other aids to production—which act also to shift income from one period to another but which will *also increase the worth of the firm*, as we shall see. How this second, or *productive opportunity*, is undertaken will now be described.

It is taken as a fact of life by the economist that roundabout production methods (i.e., those involving intermediate "tools") will produce more product, in the long run, than "hand" methods. Initially, investments in the intermediate tools often bring large returns, but eventually, a sort of diminishing return effect sets in so that additional increments of investment bring ever-decreasing returns.

Although the following explanation is not strictly analogous, it serves to help one visualize the diminishing returns effect that is present with investment in several productive opportunities. Suppose a firm has available several productive opportunities, or projects, in which it can invest funds and thereafter produce consumption products with the "tools" it purchased. In a time frame of *now* ($t = 0$) and *tomorrow* ($t = 1$), each productive project, $j$ ($j = 1, 2, 3, \ldots$), provides a *rate* of return to the firm of

$$i_j^* = \left(\frac{\Delta Y_1 - \Delta Y_0}{\Delta Y_0}\right)_j = \left(\frac{\Delta Y_1}{\Delta Y_0}\right)_j - 1 \qquad (7.5)$$

where $(\Delta Y_0)_j$ is the investment in project $j$ at time $t = 0$, $(\Delta Y_1)_j$ is the return cash

---

[4]Hirshleifer [11] makes no distinction in his analysis between an individual and a firm. He regards firms solely as agencies or instruments of individuals, as we do in this text.

flow at time $t = 1$, and $i_j^*$ is the simple one-period rate of return on the investment. If all the firm's potential production opportunities (projects) are arranged in order of decreasing rate of return and then plotted so that the *cumulative* cash flows, $\sum (\Delta Y_0)_j$ at time $t = 0$ and $\sum (\Delta Y_1)_j$ at $t = 1$, are represented on intertemporal exchange axes, we would have an *exchange map* of the investment opportunities available to the firm, such as the piecewise linear function $OZ$ in Fig. 7.1.

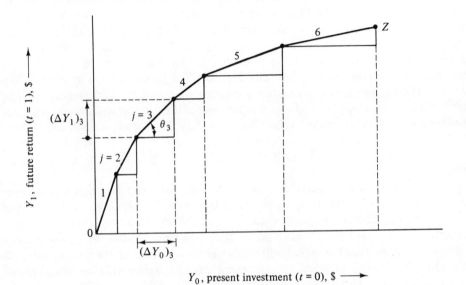

**Fig. 7.1.** Discrete productive opportunity curve.

The piecewise-linear curve $OZ$ is called the *productive opportunity curve* of the firm. Note that its slope, for any project, is defined by the ratio $(\Delta Y_1/\Delta Y_0)_j$ of that project. For example, for Project 3 ($j = 3$), the slope is defined as $(\Delta Y_1)_3/(\Delta Y_0)_3$, but this is related to the rate of return for that project by Eq. (7.5). That is, for any project, the slope $\theta_j = \tan^{-1}(\Delta Y_1/\Delta Y_0)_j = \tan^{-1}(1 + i_j^*)$. Hence, projects can be arranged in order of decreasing $i_j^*$, and the cumulative effect on the firm becomes one of diminishing returns with increasing total investment (the individual rates of return, proportional to $\theta_j$, approach zero as more and more projects are invested).

Let us now imagine that the number of productive opportunities available to the firm becomes "very large" (i.e., infinite in number) and that the cumulative cash flow required for investment, $\sum (\Delta Y_0)$ at $t = 0$, is derived solely from the *savings* the firm is able to effect. Under these assumptions, the productive opportunity curve, $OZ$ in Fig. 7.1, becomes continuous, and when it is placed on the firm's consumption exchange map, as in Fig. 7.2, the productive opportunity curve assumes a reverse or a left-handed shape since the concept of *positive* savings (the source of investment

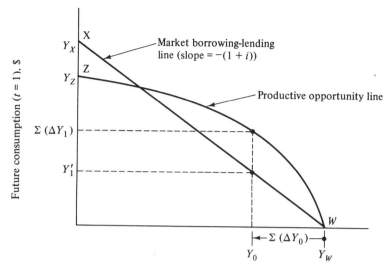

**Fig. 7.2.** Productive and borrowing–lending opportunities.

funds) is foregone consumption, or consumption in the negative direction. Thus, in Fig. 7.2, the *productive* opportunities for intertemporal exchange are expressed by the curve $WZ$. Assuming that the firm initially has at its disposal only present-time funds raised from its shareholders (i.e., its endowment is present wealth, $W$, on the $t = 0$ consumption potential axis), it can engage in *productive* activities by investing any portion of its current funds *saved*, say $Y_W - Y_0 = \sum (\Delta Y_0)$, and then receive after one period the increased future amount, $\sum (\Delta Y_1)$, at time $t = 1$. Note also that if the firm engages only in *lending activities* in the capital market by lending the same saved amount, $Y_W - Y_0$, it can receive at the end of "tomorrow" only the amount $Y_1'$ (this assumes the existence of at least *some* productive opportunities that will provide rates of return greater than the market rate of interest).

How much "savings" (e.g., $Y_W - Y_0$) should the firm devote to the purchase of intermediate productive tools? Well, to the extent that the *slope* of the productive opportunity line (1 + the marginal return rate) *exceeds* that of the market borrowing-lending line, it can devote any amount it chooses. In Fig. 7.3, for example, the firm could choose any investment-production alternative between $W$ and $R^*$, which is the point of tangency of the capital market line whose slope is $-(1 + i)$—the line that measures the attractiveness of the alternative investment opportunities (to lend) in the *capital* market. [At $R^*$, if the firm had further savings to invest, it would want to switch from a policy of investment in more capital (productive) goods to one of lending in the capital market—the rate of return there would be greater.]

Now, the *choice* of a particular investment-production exchange point can be fixed for a particular firm by its *indifference curves*,[5] which express the firm's indifference between combinations of "today's" and "tomorrow's" consumption (income) levels. Suppose that the firm's indifference curves were represented by the family $A_1$, $A_2, A_3, \ldots$, in Fig. 7.3. The firm's objective is to climb onto as high an indifference curve as possible—i.e., toward $A_3$, or beyond if possible. Moving along the productive opportunity line $WR^*Z$, the firm's decision-maker sees that the highest-valued indifference curve touched by the former is $A_2$, at point $A'$. Since the firm, as an isolated entity, can maximize its utility for intertemporal exchange at $A'$, it would invest its savings, $Y_W - Y_0$, in intermediate productive goods at $t = 0$, and thereafter (at $t = 1$), it would receive the amount $Y_1' - 0$ as income, which would result from the sale of the product produced by the purchased intermediate productive goods. We note that if the firm followed this policy, it would increase its net present value from $Y_W$ (the endowment point) to $Y_W'$.

But the solution at $A'$ is not the best alternative available to a firm that can also borrow in a perfect capital market. By continuing to invest more savings in capital goods, the firm can move from $A'$ along the productive opportunity line to the point $R^*$, which is the point of tangency of the financial market line and the productive opportunity line. (At this point, investment of $t = 0$ funds in capital equipment should cease since the alternative rate of return, $i$, provided by lending in the capital market, is greater than the marginal rate of return, $i^*$, provided by the next project.) The firm can now move *in a reverse direction* (borrowing) along the financial market line to point $A''$, which lies on a higher-level indifference curve ($A_3$) and which produces an even higher net present value, $Y_W''$.

---

[5]An *indifference curve* (or *isoquant*) is one that expresses a decision-maker's indifference of choice among combinations of two or more goods. Alternatively, an indifference curve is one of constant value or utility to the decision-maker. For example, in the sketch below, an individual would be indifferent between the *commodity sacks* of apples and oranges shown on indifference curve *A*—he would just as soon have sack $A_1$ as $A_2$ or $A_3$ or any other sack on the curve. Since "more is better," however, he would rather have any of the sacks represented by curve *B* than any represented by curve *A*. Indifference curves representing *intertemporal* choice are typically convex to the origin.

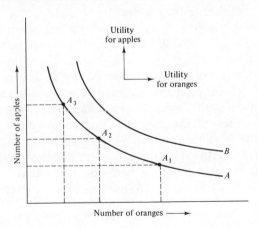

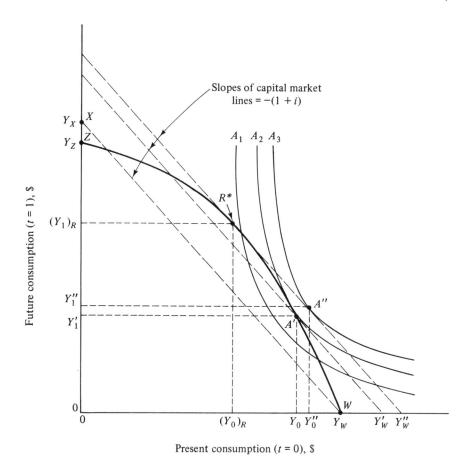

**Fig. 7.3.** Choice of productive exchange alternatives.

The firm, thus, can make the investment decision in two steps. The first step is the productive solution, in which the firm should continue to make investments until it reaches point $R^*$—the point at which the slope of the productive opportunity line is equal to that of the market line. That is, $R^*$ is the point at which

$$\frac{d\mathcal{Y}_1}{d\mathcal{Y}_0} = -(1 + i^*) = -(1 + i) \tag{7.6}$$

where $d\mathcal{Y}_1/d\mathcal{Y}_0$ is the slope of the productive opportunity line, $i^*$ is the incremental (marginal) rate of return, and $i$ is the market interest rate. From Eq. (7.6), $i^* = i$, which is to be interpreted that further investment in additional intermediate goods should cease when $i^* = i$ (i.e., at point $R^*$).

The second step of the decision is to "finance" the investment, or part of it, by borrowing (i.e., moving along the financial market line to point $A''$) where the firm's utility is maximized. Note that the investment in intermediate goods is accomplished by first "saving" (at $t = 0$) the amount $Y_W - (Y_0)_R$ and then following that action by borrowing the amount $Y_0'' - (Y_0)_R$ in the financial market so that the net "saving" —or equity funds—used in purchasing the intermediate goods is $Y_W - Y_0''$. The essential point of the whole derivation is the demonstration that the firm can reach a position of maximum utility by *maximizing net present value*, $Y_W''$.

An essential point of economic productive-consumptive optimization, as demonstrated above, is that the *productive optimum is independent* of the *firm's utilitarian choices*. No matter where the firm's indifference curves may lie, the optimal productive combination at $R^*$ remains unchanged since the location of $R^*$ is fixed solely by (1) the productive opportunity curve $WZ$ (the set of the firm's investment opportunities, or projects) and (2) the market rate of interest (which establishes the slope of the financial market line). The fact that the *production optimum* can be established independently of the firm's *choices* of its level of borrowing or lending in the financial market is called the *Separation Theorem*. It follows from the initial assumption of perfect and costless financial markets. Because *maximum* present value (wealth) is reached at $R^*$, *which is independent of how much money is borrowed or lent* in the financial market, *present value* can be used as a basis for project selection.

**7.6.2. *The present value criterion for project selection.*** A project is simply an opportunity for the investment of funds by the firm. In the simple two-time, one-period model assumed above, a project can be viewed as a sequence of dated cash flows, $Y_0$ and $Y_1$, at times $t = 0$ and $t = 1$. If $Y_0$ is negative and $Y_1$ is positive, the firm is simply sacrificing present income for future income, and the project is called an *investment* project. The firm can also divest itself of a project already in existence. In this case, $Y_1$ would be negative and $Y_0$ would be positive—i.e., a future cash inflow entitlement is being sacrificed in favor of a present actual cash inflow. Such a project is called a *divestment* project and would result, for example, if a firm sold an existing producing facility for cash now.

In either case (i.e., *in*vestment or *di*vestment), the *present value*, $P_0$, of a project is defined as

$$P_0 = Y_0 + \frac{Y_1}{(1 + i)}. \tag{7.7}$$

Present value, $P_0$, is regarded as a wealth increment associated with a project, and in conjunction with perfect capital markets and the Separation Theorem, then the objective of all decisions concerning investment in (or divestment from) intermediate productive goods is wealth maximization. This reasoning leads to the following decision rule:

*Present Value Rule 1:* Accept any project for which present value, $P_0$, is positive; reject any project for which $P_0$ is negative. (Note that the rule applies to both investment and divestment projects.)

While we are not concerned here with more than a single project, the present value rule can be easily extended to apply to multiple projects, some of which may not be independent. It is possible, for example, for the cash flows of one project to affect those of another. The solution is to form independent *sets* of projects and then choose the set with the maximum present value. For example, Projects *A*, *B*, and *C* may not be independent. The *mutually exclusive* sets *A*, *B*, *C*, *AB*, *AC*, *BC*, and *ABC* can be formed by combining the cash flow streams as indicated, however, and then the present value rule can be applied to the mutually exclusive *sets*. The applicable decision rule in this case can be stated as follows:

> *Present Value Rule 2:* If two projects (or combinations of projects) are mutually exclusive, accept that which has the greater present value, $P_0$.

**7.6.3. Multiperiod analysis.** The same general principles, developed in Sections 7.6.1 and 7.6.2 for the $t = 0, 1$ case, also apply to intertemporal project selection decisions involving more than one period. For example, to go to the two-period case, indifference curves (in the one-period model) become indifference *shells* in the two-period model, and the financial market *line* becomes a financial market *plane* (as in Section 3.1.3). Again, however, the *optimal productive opportunity* is determined at the point of tangency of the financial market *plane* with the productive opportunity *surface*, independent of the choice of the firm to borrow or lend. Hence, the Separation Theorem again applies, and the present value rules stand. In a similar manner, the method can be extended by analogy so that finally Eqs. (3.2) and (3.3), repeated at the beginning of Section 7.6, become the bases for the present value decision rules stated above.

**7.6.4. Characteristics of net present value.** Some of the more important aspects of net present value can be developed by examining Eq. (3.3) in detail. Suppose we drop the subscript on $P_0$ so that $P$ now stands for net present value and we recognize that the form of Eq. (3.3) is a function of the interest rate, $i$, and the project life $N$ as well as the series of project cash flows $Y_0, Y_1, Y_2, \ldots, Y_N$. Thus, we have that $P$, as a function of $i$, is now

$$P(i) = \sum_{t=0}^{N} \frac{Y_t}{(1 + i)^t}. \tag{7.8}$$

If we let $Y_0 < 0$ and all other $Y_t > 0$, with $N$ finite and known, then $P(i)$ can be expanded to

$$P(i) = -Y_0 + Y_1(1 + i)^{-1} + Y_2(1 + i)^{-2} + \cdots + Y_N(1 + i)^{-N}. \tag{7.9}$$

If, as we assume, $i$ is a continuous variable, then $P(i)$ is a continuous function in $i$ and is differentiable. The first derivative of $P(i)$ is

$$\frac{dP(i)}{d(1 + i)} = -\frac{Y_1}{(1 + i)^2} - \frac{2Y_2}{(1 + i)^3} - \frac{3Y_3}{(1 + i)^4} - \cdots - \frac{NY_N}{(1 + i)^{N+1}}, \tag{7.10}$$

which is *negative* for all values of $-1 < i < \infty$. Furthermore, the second derivative is

$$\frac{d^2P(i)}{d(1+i)^2} = +\frac{2Y_1}{(1+i)^3} + \frac{6Y_2}{(1+i)^4} + \frac{12Y_3}{(1+i)^5} + \cdots + \frac{N(N+1)Y_N}{(1+i)^{N+2}}, \quad (7.11)$$

which is always positive for all values of $-1 < i < \infty$. Thus, in the range of $i$ from $-1$ to infinity, the present value function of this simple project is *monotonic decreasing*—simply because it has a negative first derivative, which indicates the function value decreases as $i$ increases, but at a decreasing rate since the second derivative is positive (the function *is* convex). A typical trace of $P(i)$ for a *simple* project is shown in Fig. 7.4.

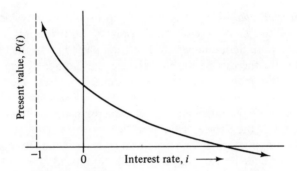

**Fig. 7.4.** Trace of $P(i)$ for a simple investment.

We should note that the interest rate $i$ was restricted to the range $-1 < i < \infty$ in order for Eqs. (7.10) and (7.11) to be valid. The reasons are as follows. If we let $i \longrightarrow \infty$, then the limit in Eq. (7.9) is

$$\lim_{i \to \infty} P(i) = -Y_0$$

so that $P(i)$ is asymptotic to this constant investment value and the derivatives disappear. On the other hand, the future value, $F(i)$, can be found by multiplying Eq. (7.9) by $(1 + i)^N$ so that

$$F(i) = -Y_0(1 + i)^N + Y_1(1 + i)^{N-1} + Y_2(1 + i)^{N-2} + \cdots + Y_N \quad (7.12)$$

and if $i \equiv -1$ is assumed, then $F(i) = Y_N$. Since

$$F(i) = P(i) \cdot (1 + i)^N,$$

however, we have that

$$P(i)\Big|_{i=-1} = \frac{F(i)}{(1+i)^N} = \frac{Y_N}{(1+i)^N} \to 0$$

so that $P(i)$ is indeterminate at $i = -1$ since the division of $Y_N$ by zero is not defined. The usual interpretation of this phenomenon is that an interest rate of $i = -1$ corresponds to a complete loss of capital (loss of $Y_0$) since regardless of the length of the cash flow stream (provided it is finite) it can always be shown that $F(i) \equiv Y_N = 0$ when $i = -1$, which says that *any* future value of $Y_0$ at $i = -1$ is zero—that is, a complete loss of $Y_0$.

A simple investment project, such as we have just described, should be accepted whenever $P(i) > 0$. When this is true, then the *present value* of the cash *in*flows exceeds the *present value* of the cash *out*flows, and Rule 1 applies. Since $P(i)$ is a function of $i$, then how far can we let $i$ advance? Obviously, $i$ can advance in value until $P(i) \equiv 0$, at which point the net present value is zero and the marginal acceptance point is reached; beyond this point $P(i) < 0$ and the project should be rejected by Rule 1. The special point at which $P(i) \equiv 0$ is defined as the *internal rate of return*, designated by the symbol $i^*$ and will be more fully discussed later in this chapter.

The usual procedure for determining net present value for an independent project is to calculate $P(i)$ for some known (or assumed) interest rate. The principle of opportunity costing requires that only those projects be accepted that will not make the firm worse off financially in the future, and this principle dictates the *minimum* interest rate as being the *marginal cost of capital, k*, under our assumed conditions of certainty.

One should be aware that the net present value function, $P(i)$, is not always a monotonic decreasing function in $i$. Depending on the magnitudes of the end-of-period cash flows and their directions ($+$ or $-$) and on the project life, the present value function may assume the shape of an $N$th degree polynominal in $i$. For example, the development of oil or gas producing fields frequently generate cash flow streams in which *net* cash *out*flows (from the firm to the project) occur during the early years of the project due to initial developmental expenditures, then again at some intermediate period when the oil field is converted from primary recovery (natural gas or water drive in the reservoir) to secondary recovery (forced injection of water or other fluid into the reservoir to raise the producing pressure), and again at the end of the project life because of abandonment expenses. All three stages, namely development, conversion, and abandonment, frequently require short-term expenditures in excess of cash inflows. The result is a series of negative net cash flows interspersed with positive cash flows.

An example of such a cash flow stream is the following:

| End of Year, $t$ | Net Cash Flow, $Y_t$ |
|:---:|:---:|
| 0 | $-1,000 |
| 1 | + 800 |
| 2 | + 800 |
| 3 | − 200 |
| 4 | + 350 |
| 5 | − 100 |

Figure 7.5 displays the $P(i)$ function for this cash flow stream over the range of $-0.80 \leq i \leq 10.00$. Note that $P(i)$ tends asymptotically toward $P_0 = -1,000$ as $i$

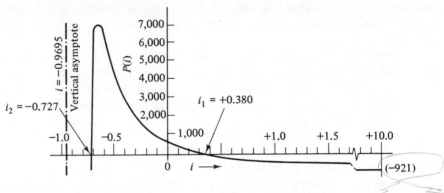

**Fig. 7.5.** Present value function, $P(i)$.

becomes large and that a second root occurs at approximately $i_2 = -0.727$ (the first root, $i_1 = 0.380$). Since this is a fifth-degree polynomial, the remaining three roots (not shown here) are $i_3 = -1.915$, and $i_4 = i_5$ are imaginary, occurring at the vertical asymptote $i = -0.9695$.

Since the imaginary roots are not usable, and $i_3 < -1$, the region of interest for $P(i)$ occurs in the range $-0.9695 < i < \infty$. Accordingly, the project would be accepted if the cost of capital for the firm were in the range $0 < k \leq 0.380$ and rejected otherwise. Obviously, the cost of capital would not be less than zero, and beyond $k = 0.380$ the net present value of the project is negative implying non-recovery of the investment and interest at the cost of capital rate.

## 7.7. The Benefit-Cost Ratio Criteria

Aside from a particular form called *Eckstein's benefit-cost ratio* (discussed in Footnote 3), there are two formulations for the project selection criterion generally known as the *benefit-cost ratio* $(B/C)$. Bernhard [4] uses the terms *benefit-cost ratio* and *net benefit-cost ratio* to distinguish the formulations. Other authors (particularly in the more modern engineering economy texts) use the same terminology. In older texts and in the research literature, however, other names are used to describe similar criteria, such as *profitability index* and *excess present value index*.[6]

---

[6]Other authors use different terminology to describe the same basic measurement. For example, the term "*excess* present value index" is used by Moore and Jaedicke [19] to describe (presumably) the simple *gross* benefit-cost ratio $[(P_j/C_j) + 1]$, because their ratio is required to be ". . . better than 1-to-1 . . ." for acceptance of the project, and they use the ". . . present value of the cash *flows* . . ." in their numerator. On the other hand, Horngren [12] uses the same words, "excess present value index," to describe Bernhard's *net* index [Eq. (7.14)]. Lindsay and Sametz [15] use "profitability index," and Barish [1] uses "premium worth percentage" to describe the *net* index [Eq. (7.14)]. Hence, one must be careful in reading the literature to distinguish exactly the author's meaning in every instance.

The difference between benefit-cost ratio and *net* benefit-cost ratio can be illustrated simply. Let $P_j$ be the *net* present value of the cash flows of Project $j$ at time $t = 0$ and $C_j$ be its present cost at $t = 0$. Then, total benefits (at $t = 0$) is $P_j + C_j$, and the following definitions may be stated:

1. *Benefit-cost ratio* $(B/C)$ is the ratio of *total benefits* to present cost:

$$(B/C) = \frac{P_j + C_j}{C_j} = \frac{P_j}{C_j} + 1 \tag{7.13}$$

2. *Net benefit-cost ratio* $(NB/C)$ is the ratio of *net present value* to present cost:

$$NB/C = \frac{P_j}{C_j}. \tag{7.14}$$

It is obvious that the difference between Eqs. (7.13) and (7.14) is simply unity so that the following decision rules are the result:

| If $B/C$ | or | If $NB/C$, | Rule Is |
|---|---|---|---|
| >1 |  | >0 | Accept |
| =1 |  | =0 | Indifferent |
| <1 |  | <0 | Reject |

These criteria were advanced by some of the early writers in the project selection field based on an argument that the net present value method did not discriminate among large and small investments—what was needed, they said, was a criterion that would provide a ranking of projects based on the net present value *per dollar outlay* (or, alternatively, on the present value of cash inflows per dollar outlay). In this way, it was argued, the most *efficient* projects could be chosen first, regardless of dollar outlay, to be followed by the *less efficient* projects.

As it turns out, this criterion is not an acceptable one for ranking projects under constrained conditions. It suffers from the same faults as the other criteria that preselect or rank projects, such as internal rate of return. These will be examined in Chapter 8. In the *absence of constraints*, however, it serves adequately as a selection criterion but is no more informative than net present value itself. Hence, there is no particular advantage in using benefit-cost over NPV since the calculation of NPV is straightforward and somewhat simpler.

A theoretical examination of the *NB/C* criterion has been made by Weingartner [31], who derives this criterion from the dual of the project selection problem stated in a linear programming format (see Chapter 8). Weingartner indicates that *NB/C*, under unconstrained conditions, will accept and reject the same projects as NPV, with no apparent advantage residing in the longer *NB/C* method. When capital expenditures are limited in the *current* period, it is possible for *NB/C* to rank projects correctly in the order of descending efficient use of capital, but it should *not* be used as a selection criterion because it does not provide a means for aggregating several small projects into a package to displace one large project, thereby perhaps using the total available capital more effectively (the "lumpiness" effect). When cash outflows occur in periods *later* than the current period, then $NB/C$ is completely ineffective as a selection criterion and must be redefined. Finally, Weingartner shows that $NB/C$ is an inaccurate criterion when used with interdependent projects (e.g., mutually exclusive alternatives) and that choices under such conditions must be made only with some knowledge of the (opportunity) cost of capital.

Since the benefit-cost criteria (in both forms) really do nothing to increase our knowledge beyond what the NPV criterion already tells us, it is somewhat superfluous to calculate a present value *per dollar outlay* when we already know that a positive net present value signifies *accept* and a negative one signifies *reject*. We shall not consider the criterion again for single, *un*constrained projects; however, we shall reexamine it for the constrained case in Chapter 8.

## 7.8. Internal Rate of Return

Both the net present value and benefit-cost methods (both forms) just described depend on the knowledge of an external interest rate for their application (i.e., external to the project, such as the firm's cost of capital). The internal rate of return (IRR) method is closely related to the NPV method, in that it also is a discounted cash flow method, but it seeks to avoid the arbitrary choice of an interest rate. Instead, it attempts to find some interest rate, initially unknown, that is *internal* to the project. The procedure is to find an interest rate that will make the present value of the cash flow stream of a project zero—that is, some interest rate that will cause the present value of cash inflows to equal the present value of cash outflows. Mathematically, IRR is defined as the interest rate $i^*$ that will cause the net present value, $P(i)$, to become zero. Thus, IRR is the value, $i^*$, such that

$$P(i) = \sum_{t=0}^{N} Y_t(1 + i^*)^{-t} \equiv 0. \tag{7.15}$$

The IRR must be found by trial and error or by a computer search technique since it is an unknown root (or roots) of a polynomial in $i$. This can be demonstrated by letting $R^t = (1 + i^*)^{-t}$ and writing Eq. (7.15) in expanded form in terms of $R$:

$$Y_0 R^0 + Y_1 R^1 + Y_2 R^2 + \cdots + Y_N R^N = 0,$$

which is a polynomial of degree $N$ in terms of $R$. Thus, if we start with known values of each flow, we can (possibly) find one or more values of $i^*$ that will made Eq. (7.15) true. These values, if they exist as real numbers, are known as the *internal* rates of return, or the *yield* of the project. The selection criterion is *select the project if* $i^*$ *(the IRR) is greater than the firm's marginal investment rate; otherwise, reject.*

Internal rate of return (IRR) has long been advocated as a project acceptance criterion because in this criterion the interest rate is the *unknown* value that relates project returns to outlays. In the sense that it is the functional value *to be established* by the expected cash outlays and inflows of the project itself, it has been called the *internal* rate of return—entirely dependent on the parameters of the project itself. In some instances this is true, but the internal rate of return, as a single, real number, does not always exist mathematically.[7] This, of course, poses problems.

Also, most persons who use IRR as a project selection criterion do not understand its fundamental economic meaning. To clarify these points, the balance of this section is devoted to the use of IRR as a selection criterion for *un*constrained projects.

**7.8.1. *The fundamental meaning of internal rate of return.*** An economic interpretation of internal rate of return is not immediately obvious from Eq. (7.15). To develop the economic interpretation, consider first a numerical example. Suppose a single project has estimated cash flows as follows:

| End of Period, $t$ | Cash Outflow $(-)$ or Cash Inflow $(+)$, $Y_t$ |
|:---:|:---:|
| 0 | $-10,000$ |
| 1 | $+ 2,000$ |
| 2 | $+ 4,000$ |
| 3 | $+ 7,000$ |
| 4 | $+ 5,000$ |
| 5 | $+ 3,000$ |

For the *un*discounted case (an assumed interest rate $i = 0$), the graphical representation of the cash flow stream is depicted in Fig. 7.6. Note in Fig. 7.6 that any resultant vector (ordinate), from the zero cash level, defines either an unrecovered or an over-recovered investment at any time $t$. For example, at time 2 the unrecovered investment is $\$-4,000$, and at time 3 the overrecovery is $\$+3,000$.

---

[7]There are a number of interesting papers that are addressed to the problem of whether a *unique* internal rate of return for a project can be predicted by the cash flow stream. One method that is useful to predict an *upper limit* on the number of positive roots of a polynomial [e.g., Eq. (7.15)] is to apply Descartes' Rule of Signs to the number of sign changes in the cash flow stream. This is discussed in several elementary engineering economy texts (e.g., Newnan [20], pp. 128–132). Soper [36] develops a sufficient condition for a unique root to exist in the interval of interest $(-1 < i^* < \infty)$, but the determination of uniqueness requires a trial-and-error search for the single root. Kaplan [13] demonstrates how Sturm's Theorem (1829) can be applied to find the *exact* number of *distinct* roots in the interval $(-1, \infty)$. The Sturm-Kaplan method can also be used (most effectively with a computer) to find the numerical values of the roots (e.g., see [14]). Note that if the function $P(i^*)$ has repeated roots, they are counted as one in the Sturm-Kaplan method (see Kaplan [13] and Turnbull [29]). Norstrøm [21] develops a simpler condition for uniqueness of the root, *but in the interval* $(0 < i^* < \infty)$. Norstrøm shows that if the *cumulative* cash flow stream (undiscounted) changes sign only once and if the final cash flow is positive, this is a *sufficient* (but not necessary) condition for a unique root, $i^*$, to exist. Bernhard [34] shows that even if Norstrøm's sufficiency condition holds in the $(0, \infty)$ interval, Soper's condition *may* be violated in the $(-1, 0)$ interval with a consequence that the root is not unique and hence $P(i) > 0$ is not guaranteed. Finally, Bernhard [35] provides a more general method for detecting uniqueness in the $(-0, \infty)$ interval.

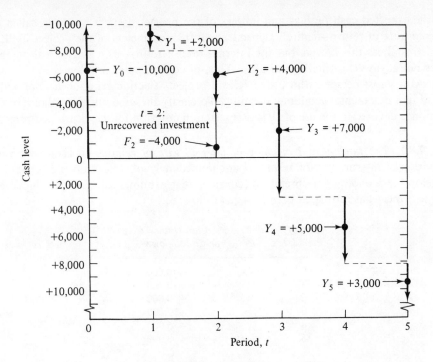

**Fig. 7.6.** Undiscounted cash flow stream.

Economically meaningful interest rates must lie in the range $(-1 < i < \infty)$ and, for practical purposes, in the range $(0 < i < \infty)$, since a negative interest rate implies either partial or complete nonrecovery of capital. When a positive interest rate, say $i^* > 0$, modifies the cash flow stream in the foregoing example, each *un*recovered investment balance, $F_t$ at time $t$, earns compounded interest at the rate $i^*$ during the following period. This increases (in the negative sense) the unrecovered investment balance, $F_{t+1}$, just before the cash inflow, $Y_{t+1}$, is applied at time $t + 1$. After applying the cash inflow vector, $Y_{t+1}$, the new unrecovered investment balance is $F_{t+1}$. This sequence of events is illustrated in Fig. 7.7 for the numerical example.

In general terms, the unrecovered investment at time $t + 1$ can be found from the recursive relationship

$$F_{t+1} = F_t(1 + i) + Y_{t+1} \tag{7.16}$$

where $F_t$ = unrecovered investment at time $t$.
   $F_{t+1}$ = unrecovered investment at time $t + 1$.
   $Y_{t+1}$ = cash flow at time $t + 1$.
      $i$ = applicable interest rate.

To motivate an economic interpretation of internal rate of return we first note, on solving Eq. (7.15) for the foregoing example, that $i^* = 28.35\%$, which can be verified from the following:

$$-10,000 + 2,000(1.2835)^{-1} + 4,000(1.2835)^{-2} + 7,000(1.2835)^{-3}$$
$$+ 5,000(1.2835)^{-4} + 3,000(1.2835)^{-5} = 0.$$

By definition, then, the internal rate of return for this cash flow stream is $i^* = 28.35\%$. Now, let this same interest rate be applied to the unrecovered investments $F_0$, $F_1$, ..., $F_4$ at the end of periods $t = 0, 1, \ldots, 4$, to calculate the interest earned by each unrecovered investment during the succeeding periods $t = 1, 2, \ldots, 5$. The model for these calculations is Eq. (7.16). The calculations are given in Table 7.2, and Fig. 7.7 illustrates the sequence of events to scale.

**Table 7.2.** UNRECOVERED INVESTMENTS, $i^* = 28.35\%$

| End of Period, $t$ | Unrecovered Investment at Beginning of Period $t$: $F_t$ | Interest Earned from $t$ to $t+1$, $F_t i^*$ | Cash Flow at End of Period $t$ (Time $t+1$): $Y_{t+1}$ | Unrecovered Investment at Beginning of Period $t+1$: $F_{t+1} = F_t(1.2835) + Y_{t+1}$ |
|---|---|---|---|---|
| 0 | — | — | $-10,000 | $-10,000 |
| 1 | $-10,000 | $-2,835 | + 2,000 | -10,835 |
| 2 | -10,835 | -3,072 | + 4,000 | - 9,907 |
| 3 | - 9,907 | -2,809 | + 7,000 | - 5,716 |
| 4 | - 5,716 | -2,621 | + 5,000 | - 2,337 |
| 5 | - 2,337 | - 663 | + 3,000 | 0 |

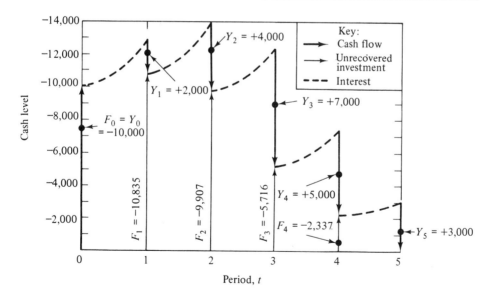

**Fig. 7.7.** Cash flow stream discounted at IRR $= i^* = 28.35\%$.

One should note particularly in Table 7.2 that the unrecovered investment balance at the end of Period 5 (beginning of Period 6) is now zero. It should thus be evident that the IRR as calculated by Eq. (7.15), $i^* = 28.35\%$, is not only the interest rate that causes the net present value of the cash flow stream to be zero in accordance with Eq. (7.15), but it is also the interest rate that causes exact recovery of investment over the life of the project *plus* a return on the unrecovered investment balances during the life of the project.

A common misinterpretation of IRR is that it is an interest rate expressing a rate of return on the *initial* investment. This is not so, and that fact can be demonstrated by an example. Consider the cash flow stream in the example given above. If the IRR, $i^* = 28.35\%$, is applied periodically to the initial investment only, then the interest earned in each period is $\$-2,835$. This considerably changes the unrecovered balances of the investment at the end of each period, and indeed the positive cash flows fail to recover the initial investment plus interest at the assumed rate of $28.35\%$, at the end of the project life. Table 7.3 gives the applicable calculations.

**Table 7.3.** INITIAL INVESTMENT RECOVERY, $i^* = 28.35\%$.

| End of Period, $t$ | Unrecovered Investment at Beginning of Period $t$: $F_t$ | Interest Earned on Initial Investment from $t$ to $t+1$: $I_t = F_0 i^*$ | Cash Flow at End of Period $t$ (Time $t+1$): $Y_{t+1}$ | Unrecovered Investment at Beginning of Period $t+1$: $F_{t+1} = F_0(1.2835) + Y_{t+1}$ |
|---|---|---|---|---|
| 0 | — | — | $\$-10,000$ | $\$-10,000$ |
| 1 | $\$-10,000$ | $\$-2,835$ | $+\ 2,000$ | $-10,835$ |
| 2 | $-10,835$ | $-2,835$ | $+\ 4,000$ | $-\ 9,670$ |
| 3 | $-\ 9,670$ | $-2,835$ | $+\ 7,000$ | $-\ 5,505$ |
| 4 | $-\ 5,505$ | $-2,835$ | $+\ 5,000$ | $-\ 3,340$ |
| 5 | $-\ 3,340$ | $-2,835$ | $+\ 3,000$ | $-\ 3,175$ |

The fundamental economic meaning of internal rate of return should now be apparent. It is the rate of interest earned on the *time-varying, unrecovered* balances of an investment, such that the final investment balance is zero (complete and exact recovery) at the end of the project life.

To complete the exposition, we shall now demonstrate generally that a unique interest rate, $i^*$, applied to the *unrecovered investment balances*, $F_t$, over the life of the project, will define the internal rate of return for a conventional cash flow stream.[8] Let $F_t =$ the unrecovered investment balance at any time $t$ ($t = 0, 1, \ldots, N$), $i^* =$ an interest rate ($-1 < i^* < \infty$), $Y_t =$ cash flow at time $t$, and $N =$ the life of the

---

[8] A conventional cash flow stream is one in which the initial cash flow is negative (an investment) and all others are positive (cash inflows).

project. Recognizing that $F_0 = Y_0$ at $t = 0$, then from the recursive relationship [Eq. (7.16)] one obtains

$$F_0 = Y_0$$
$$F_1 = F_0(1 + i^*) + Y_1 = Y_0(1 + i^*) + Y_1$$
$$F_2 = F_1(1 + i^*) + Y_2 = Y_0(1 + i^*)^2 + Y_1(1 + i^*) + Y_2$$

$$\begin{matrix} \cdot & & \cdot & & \cdot \\ \cdot & & \cdot & & \cdot \\ \cdot & & \cdot & & \cdot \end{matrix}$$

$$F_N = F_{N-1}(1 + i^*) + Y_N = Y_0(1 + i^*)^N + Y_1(1 + i^*)^{N-1}$$
$$+ Y_2(1 + i^*)^{N-2} + \cdots + Y_N. \qquad (7.17)$$

For exact capital recovery, $F_N = 0$. After setting Eq. (7.17) to zero and dividing by $(1 + i^*)^N$, one obtains

$$0 = Y_0 + Y_1(1 + i^*)^{-1} + Y_2(1 + i^*)^{-2} + \cdots + Y_{N-1}(1 + i^*)^{1-N} + Y_N(1 + i^*)^{-N}$$

or

$$P(i^*) = \sum_{t=0}^{N} Y_t(1 + i^*)^{-t} = 0,$$

which defines $i^*$ as the internal rate of return.

Since the internal rate of return does *not* measure the return on initial investment, one should realize that the internal rates of return from two or more projects should not be compared in order to establish a preference ordering among projects. The IRR for a given project merely states the rate of interest earned on the time-varying *un*recovered investment balances for *that* project with *that* cash flow stream. Moreover, it is independent of the absolute level of investment in the project; that is, it has meaning only when the level of investment is considered along with the other cash inflows. Thus, a comparison of IRR's for two or more projects ignores the absolute investment levels in the projects. This can be demonstrated by a simple example in which two projects, *A* and *B*, have cash flow streams as follows:

| End of Period, $t$ | Project A Cash Flow | Project B Cash Flow |
|---|---|---|
| 0 | $-1,000 | $-10,000 |
| 1 | 475 | 4,380 |
| 2 | 475 | 4,380 |
| 3 | 475 | 4,380 |

The internal rate of return for *A* is 20% and for *B*, 15%. In the absence of budget or other constraints, it should be obvious that Project *B* should logically be preferred over *A* in spite of its lower rate of return since in the same span of time it provides the firm with an increase in wealth of 3($4,380) − $10,000 = $3,140; whereas *A* provides only 3($475) − $1,000 = $425.

## 7.9. Internal Rate of Return as a Criterion for Investment (Single Projects)

Under the assumptions of certainty and perfect capital market conditions, it is sometimes possible to use internal rate of return as a *figure of merit* for determining whether a particular project should be undertaken. It is the purpose of this section to determine the conditions under which the IRR may be used as a selection figure and *when it may not*. The development of the presentation begins with a statement of some of the problems encountered in using IRR as a criterion and then proceeds to an explanation of why these problems exist.

**7.9.1.** *Multiple and indeterminate rates of return.* As Lorie and Savage [16] pointed out in 1955, it is possible on solving for internal rates of return with certain forms of the cash flow stream to find that a unique solution does not exist for the IRR but rather that more than one interest rate will satisfy the mathematical definition $\sum_t Y_t(1 + i)^{-t} = 0$. Another case is that no real value of the interest rate will satisfy the definition. When more than one solution exists mathematically, the cash flow stream is said to yield *multiple rates of return*, and when no solution exists, it is said to have an *indeterminate rate of return*.

To illustrate the multiple rates of return case, consider Lorie and Savage's famous "pump problem." The decision required in that problem is whether or not to install a larger pump costing $1,600 in an existing oil well. The larger pump will pump a fixed amount of oil in a shorter period of time than the existing pump. The decision is thus a rational choice between *two* alternatives (Renshaw, [22]), which yield the prospective cash flows given in Table 7.4.

**Table 7.4.** OIL PUMP CASH FLOWS

| End of Year | Cash Flow with Existing Pump | Cash Flow with Larger Pump | Incremental Cash Flow |
|---|---|---|---|
| 0 | 0 | − 1,600 | − 1,600 |
| 1 | +10,000 | +20,000 | +10,000 |
| 2 | +10,000 | 0 | −10,000 |

In other words, by an investment of $1,600 in a larger pump now, the $10,000 cash flow at the end of year 2 can be realized one year earlier. The question is, should the investment in the larger pump be made?

The problem of choosing between two *alternative* courses of action usually can be solved by examining the *incremental* cash flows between the two alternatives. The reasoning is that if the *incremental* cash flow stream from two projects has a rate of return greater than the firm's marginal investment rate, then the incremental investment is desirable and justified. On solving the incremental cash flow stream of the pump problem, however, we discover that the internal rate of return formulation yields two values, 25 % and 400 %.[9] Thus, a dilemma is present: Which interest rate, if either, is the internal rate of return on the incremental investment of $1,600? The answer is not immediately obvious, although an interpretation will be provided for this problem in a later section.

Turning now to an example of a cash flow stream that results in an indeterminate rate of return, consider the cash flows in Table 7.5. On solving the mathematical

**Table 7.5.** CASH FLOWS WITH
INDETERMINATE IRR

| End of Year | Cash Flow at End of Year |
|:---:|:---:|
| 0 | 0 |
| 1 | 50 |
| 2 | 50 |
| 3 | 50 |
| 4 | 50 |
| 5 | -650 |
| 6 | 100 |
| . | . |
| . | . |
| . | . |
| 15 | 100 |

relationship that defines IRR, we find that the only real values of $i^*$ that satisfy the relationship are $-177.5$ % and $-314.0$ %, all other values of $i^*$ being infinite or imaginary. Thus, there are no real values of the interest rate, $i^*$, in the region of interest $(-1 < i^* < \infty)$, and the internal rate of return is said to be *indeterminate*. Obviously, if the IRR is indeterminate, then it cannot be used as a figure of merit to evaluate the worth of an investment to the firm.

While cash flow streams of the type illustrated in the foregoing examples may not occur often in practice, the possibility of obtaining multiple or indeterminate rates of return definitely exists. When more than one sign change occurs in the cash flow stream, the possibility of an anomalous rate of return (multiple or indeterminate) must be admitted. A fairly common occurrence is a stream of $N + 1$ cash flows at times $t$ $(t = 0, 1, \ldots, N)$ with the first cash flow at $t = 0$ being negative (an investment), followed by $N - 1$ positive cash flows, and then the $N$th cash flow being negative. This corresponds to an investment situation in which abandonment expen-

---

[9]By the mathematical definition of IRR,

$$-1,600 + 10,000(1 + i^*)^{-1} - 10,000(1 + i)^{-2} = 0.$$

Multiplying through by $(1 + i^*)^2$ and by $-1$, we have the polynomial

$$1,600(1 + i)^2 - 10,000(1 + i) + 10,000 = 0,$$

which has two roots, $1 + i = 1.25$ and $1 + i = 5.0$.

ditures in the last year of a project exceed the positive revenues in that year. Examples of this kind of occurrence would be the abandonment of an oil field, the disposal of radioactive wastes, and the restoration of strip-mined lands.

The foregoing examples illustrate the need for specifying the conditions under which internal rate of return, if it exists in fact, can be used as a valid figure of merit for judging the worth of a project. While the problems of multiple and indeterminate rates of return have been known to exist for a considerable span of years,[10] no clearly *general* method of solution to these problems was available until 1965, when two significant articles were published by Teichroew, Robichek, and Montalbano [26], [27]. In developing the necessary and sufficient conditions under which internal rate of return may properly be used as a vaild index of worth, we rely heavily on the analysis given by those articles.

## 7.10. Classification of Investments

The existence of an internal rate of return for a project *and* its interpretation depend on two factors, both of which are related to the cash flow stream. One factor is the form of the cash flow stream itself, that is, the number and arrangement of the changes in sign of the net cash flows as a function of time. The other factor is the form of the unrecovered investment balance stream, that is, the number of alternations in sign of the *unrecovered* project balances (*not* the incremental cash flows).

**7.10.1.** *Conventional and nonconventional investments.* As to the form of the cash flow stream itself, we need to distinguish between *conventional* and *nonconventional* investments.[11] A *conventional* investment (viewed from the firm's standpoint) has one or more negative-signed cash outflows *followed* by one or more positively signed cash inflows. A *nonconventional* investment (from the standpoint of the firm) has one or more negative-signed cash outflows *interspersed* with positive-signed cash inflows. The different investment possibilities may be illustrated as follows:

| *Type of Investment* | *Sign of Cash Flow at Time =* | | | |
|---|---|---|---|---|
| | 0 | 1 | 2 | 3 |
| Conventional | − | + | + | + |
| Conventional | − | − | + | + |
| Nonconventional | − | + | + | − |
| Nonconventional | + | − | + | − |

---

[10]See, for example, Bernhard [3], Bierman and Smidt [5], Hirshleifer [11], Lorie and Savage [16], Renshaw [22], Solomon [24], and Mao [18].

[11]This is the terminology of Bierman and Smidt [5]. It is believed to be more descriptive than that of Teichroew, *et al.* ([26], p. 396), who use the terms *simple* and *nonsimple* to describe essentially the same conventions.

**7.10.2. *Pure and mixed investments*.** Investment projects may be further classified as *pure* and *mixed* investments, where this distinction depends on the form of the *unrecovered investment balance* stream.[12] To make the distinction between pure and mixed investments we use the definition of unrecovered investment balance developed earlier in Section 7.8.1.

Recalling that the unrecovered investment balance at the end of period $t$ ($t = 0$, $1, \ldots, N$), with interest earned at rate $i$, is given by the expression

$$F_t(i) = Y_0(1 + i)^t + Y_1(1 + i)^{t-1} + \cdots + Y_t, \qquad (7.18)$$

we examine the case in which $Y_0 < 0$ and all other $Y_j$ ($j = 1, 2, \ldots, t$) are unrestricted as to sign. In this case, except for $F_0(i)$ at $t = 0$, the unrecovered investment balance $F_t(i)$ can be positive, negative, or zero at any time $t \neq 0$. If the unrecovered investment balance is *negative* at time $t$, then the firm has committed ("lent") funds in the amount of $-F_t(i)$ dollars to the project for the *next* period from time $t$ to time $t + 1$. In other words, the firm has money invested in the project from time $t$ to time $t + 1$. On the other hand, if the unrecovered investment balance is *positive* at time $t$, then the firm has in effect overrecovered its investment and is actually "overdrawn" on the cash returns from the project during the period from $t$ to $t + 1$. In effect, the firm owes money to the project during the period $t$ to $t + 1$ and stands as a borrower from the project. Finally, $F_t(i) = 0$ means that the firm has exactly recovered its invested funds at time $t$ together with interest at rate $i$ on the unrecovered investment balances up to time $t$, and the firm is neither borrowing from nor investing in the project during the period $t$ to $t + 1$.

We are now in a position to define pure and mixed investments. A *pure* investment is defined as one in which the project investment balances, calculated at the internal rate of return of the project, are either zero or negative throughout the life of the project. In symbolic terms the investment is pure if, and only if,

$$F_t(i^*) = \sum_{j=0}^{t} Y_j(1 + i^*)^{t-j} \leq 0 \quad \begin{pmatrix} j = 0, 1, \ldots, t \\ t = 0, 1, \ldots, N - 1 \end{pmatrix}$$

*and*

$$F_N(i^*) = \sum_{t=0}^{N} Y_t(1 + i^*)^{N-t} = 0 \quad (t = 0, 1, \ldots, N)$$

$$\qquad (7.19)$$

where $N$ is the life of the project and $i^*$ is the project internal rate of return. Interpreted, these equations state that a pure investment is one in which the firm does not "borrow" from the project *at any time* during the life of the project and exactly recovers its investment [$F_N(i^*) = 0$] at the end of the project life, earning interest at the IRR value, $i^*$, in the interim periods.

A *mixed* investment, in contrast to a pure investment, may be defined as any investment that is not a pure one. Thus, a mixed investment is a project for which $F_t(i^*) > 0$ for *some* values of $t$ and $F_t(i^*) \leq 0$ for all other values of $t$. A mixed investment is one, therefore, that contains both *un*recovered investment balances *and* over-

---

[12]Teichroew, *et al.* [26] call this the *project balance*.

recovered investment balances. At some times during the project life the firm stands as an investor in (or "lender" to) the project (there are unrecovered investment balances), and at other times the firm stands as a "borrower" from the project (there are overrecovered investment balances).

Using the definitions developed above, we can now classify any investment the firm makes into one of four categories:

conventional, pure investment
conventional, mixed investment
nonconventional, pure investment
nonconventional, mixed investment

As we shall demonstrate shortly, all conventional investments are also pure investments, so there is no need for a classification for *conventional, mixed* investment —there is no such condition. The final classification scheme is illustrated in Fig. 7.8, which forms the basis for the study of investments and their internal rates of return as investment criteria.

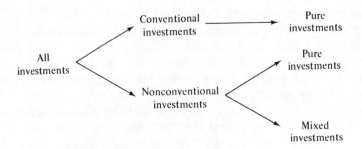

**Fig. 7.8.** Classification of the firm's investments.

**7.10.3.** *Conventional, pure investments.* It will be demonstrated here that all conventional investments are also pure investments for positive values of internal rate of return. The demonstration proceeds by assumption and contradiction. It should also be noted that, while conventional investments are pure investments, the converse is not true—all pure investments are not necessarily conventional investments. The demonstration that conventional investments are pure investments goes as follows.

A conventional investment is defined as one in which the initial $Y_\tau < 0$ ($\tau = 0$, $1, \ldots, m$), successive $Y_\theta \geq 0$ ($\theta = m + 1, m + 2, \ldots, N - 1$), and $Y_N > 0$. Let $i^*$ be the internal rate of return for the investment,[13] where $i^* > 0$ is assumed. Since the investment balance at any time $t$ at interest $i$ is given by Eq. (7.18), then it is obvious

---

[13]A conventional investment yields a unique IRR. For proof of this statement, see Teichroew, *et al.* [26], p. 397, Corollary IC.

that the investment balance at any time $\tau$ with interest $i^*$ is

$$F_\tau(i^*) = \sum_{t=0}^{\tau} Y_t (1 + i^*)^{\tau - t} < 0,$$

since $i^* > 0$ and all $Y_\tau < 0$ in the region $(\tau = 0, 1, \ldots, m)$ are assumed. Now, suppose that under the influence of some positive $Y_\theta$ in succeeding periods the investment balance, $F_\theta(i^*)$, becomes positive in the region $(\theta = m + 1, m + 2, \ldots, N - 1)$. It follows that if any intermediate balance $F_\theta(i^*) > 0$ at any time $\theta \neq N$, then $F_{\theta+1}(i^*) > 0$ also, since $i^* > 0$ and $Y_\theta \geq 0$ have been assumed. Similarly, if $F_{\theta+1}(i^*) > 0$, then $F_{\theta+2}(i^*) > 0$, and so forth until ultimately the final end-of-project investment balance $F_N(i^*) > 0$ also. The implication that $F_N(i^*) > 0$ contradicts the requirement that $F_N(i^*) = 0$ in order for $i^* > 0$ to exist (see Section 7.8.1). Hence, we must conclude that *no* $F_t(i^*)$ in the intermediate region $(0 \leq t \leq N - 1)$ can be positive. This conclusion is identical to the first requirement of a pure investment, and since $F_N(i^*) = 0$ is also required for $i^* > 0$ to exist, a conventional investment thus conforms four-square to the definition of a pure investment [Eq. (7.19)]. We conclude, therefore, that all conventional investments are pure investments (however, the converse is not true). By elimination then, there is no such classification as *conventional mixed* investments.

**7.10.4. Numerical examples.** At this point, it will be helpful to the reader to introduce numerical examples of the three investment classifications, in order to highlight their differences. Four examples will be presented. Investment Project $A$ is an example of a conventional investment.[14] Project $B$ is an example of a nonconventional, pure investment, and Projects $C$ and $D$ are examples of nonconventional, mixed investments. Project $C$ has a unique real root to the internal rate of return equation $F(i^*) = 0$, while Project $D$ has two real roots in the region $(-1 < i^* < \infty)$. All may be considered to be *investment-type* projects because $Y_0 < 0$ for each, but not all are pure investments. The cash flows are given in Table 7.6.

**Table 7.6.** CASH FLOWS FOR FOUR PROJECTS

| End of Period | Net Cash Flows | | | |
|---|---|---|---|---|
| | Project A | Project B | Project C | Project D |
| 0 | −3,605 | −100 | −100 | − 1,600 |
| 1 | +1,000 | + 60 | + 80 | +10,000 |
| 2 | +1,000 | + 50 | + 80 | −10,000 |
| 3 | +1,000 | −200 | −200 | — |
| 4 | +1,000 | +150 | +150 | — |
| 5 | +1,000 | +100 | +100 | — |

---

[14]Since all conventional investments are also pure investments, the adjective *pure* is now redundant.

For the conventional investment (Project *A*), $Y_0 = -\$3{,}605$ and $Y_t = +\$1{,}000$ ($t = 1, \ldots, 5$). On solving the IRR equation $F(i^*) = 0$ we obtain one real root, IRR $= i^* = 12\%$. Setting $i = i^* = 0.12$ in Eq. (7.19), we obtain investment balances for the project as follows:

$$F_0(0.12) = -3{,}605$$
$$F_1(0.12) = -3{,}605(1 + 0.12) + 1000 = -3{,}037$$
$$F_2(0.12) = -3{,}037(1 + 0.12) + 1000 = -2{,}402$$
$$F_3(0.12) = -2{,}402(1 + 0.12) + 1000 = -1{,}690$$
$$F_4(0.12) = -1{,}690(1 + 0.12) + 1000 = -\phantom{0}893$$
$$F_5(0.12) = -\phantom{0}893(1 + 0.12) + 1000 = \phantom{000}0$$

All the intermediate investment balances from $t = 0$ to $t = (N - 1) = 4$ are negative, which means that these are *un*recovered investment balances (the firm has unrecovered funds committed to the project continuously from $t = 0$ *through* time $t = 4$ and *into* the fifth period). The end-of-life investment balance $F_5(0.12) = 0$, which means that the firm finally recovers the balance of the investment only at $t = 5$, as a part of the last cash flow $Y_5 = \$1{,}000$. Since these investment balances conform to Eq. (7.19), Project *A* is a pure investment.

The interspersing of negative and positive cash flows in the cash flow stream for Project *B* identify it as a nonconventional investment. On solving the IRR equation $F(i^*) = 0$ for this project, two imaginary roots and three real roots are obtained: $i_1 = 0.129$, $i_2 = -2.30$, and $i_3 = -1.42$. Since we are interested only in the region $(-1 < i^* < \infty)$ for valid internal rates of return, we shall consider $i_1 = i^* = 0.129$ to be the IRR for this project. Then, by Eq. (7.19) we obtain the investment balances for the project, as follows:

$$F_0(0.129) = -100$$
$$F_1(0.129) = -100(1.129) + 60 = -52.97$$
$$F_2(0.129) = -52.97(1.129) + 50 = -9.85$$
$$F_3(0.129) = -9.95(1.129) - 200 = -211.12$$
$$F_4(0.129) = -211.12(1.129) + 150 = -88.52$$
$$F_5(0.129) = -88.52(1.129) + 100 = 0$$

Again, the intermediate investment balances are all negative and the final balance is zero, so Project *B* is a pure investment. A warning should be particualrly noted as a result of this example: The fact that there is more than one sign change in the cash flow stream does *not* necessarily indicate a *mixed* investment, nor does it indicate that the cash flow stream has more than one real value for IRR in the region $(-1 < i^* < \infty)$.

For Project *C*, the interspering of negative and positive cash flows identifies it also as a nonconventional investment. It is not a pure investment, however, as we shall see. On solving $F(i^*) = 0$, we obtain five real roots, of which three are identical:

$i_1 = i_2 = i_3 = 0.285$, $i_4 = -2.30$, and $i_5 = -1.41$. Thus, there is one real root of interest in the region $(-1 < i^* < \infty)$, namely, $i_1 = i^* = 0.285$. Using this value for $i^*$, we obtain from Eq. (7.19) the investment balances:

$$F_0 = -100$$
$$F_1 = -100(1.285) + 80 = -48.50$$
$$F_2 = -48.50(1.285) + 80 = +17.67$$
$$F_3 = +17.67(1.285) - 200 = -177.29$$
$$F_4 = -177.29(1.285) + 150 = -77.82$$
$$F_5 = -77.82(1.285) + 100 = 0$$

The discounted cash flow stream and unrecovered investment balances are illustrated in Fig. 7.9. Note that the investment balance at time $t = 2$ is positive, whereas all other investment balances are zero or negative. The significance of this is that the firm has committed ("lent") funds to the project *during* the periods *following* $t = 0$, 1, 3, and 4 but has overdrawn ("borrowed") excess funds from the project during the period from $t = 2$ to $t = 3$. The project is a *mixed* investment since it involves aspects of both investing ("lending" to the project) and financing ("borrowing" from the project). The project is both a *user* of the invested capital supplied by the firm *and* a

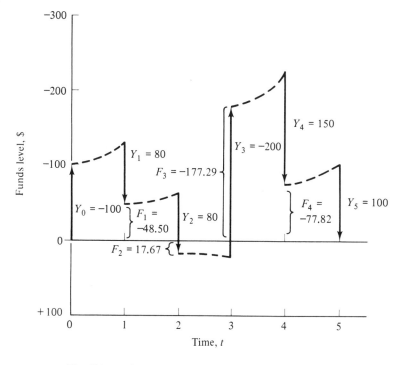

**Fig. 7.9.** Project *C* unrecovered investment balances.

*source* of excess funds for the firm to use elsewhere (during one period only, $t = 2$ to $t = 3$).

*Herein lies the crux of the problem concerning the interpretation of* $i^*$ *for a mixed investment:* Should the firm impute an interest cost for the excess funds "borrowed" from the project at the *same* interest rate that the project yields (the IRR) or should it be some *other* interest rate (e.g., the *cost of money* or *cost of capital*) that is representative of the cost incurred in obtaining money from the free capital market? If the firm imputes the interest cost for "borrowed" funds at the IRR of the project, then the IRR of the project is that given from solving $F(i^*) = 0$ for $i^*$. On the other hand, if some other rate, say the marginal attractive rate of return, $\rho$, is imputed to the excess funds "borrowed" from the project, *then the yield of the investment in the project is no longer the value of* $i^*$ *given by solving* $F(i^*) = 0$ but rather some *other* interest rate, which we shall call the *return on invested capital*. In mixed investments, the return rate yielded on the money invested *in* the project, that is, the return on invested capital, is a function of the interest *cost* rate imputed to the excess funds "borrowed" from the project. The proof of this statement follows in later paragraphs. For now, the important things to be learned from this example are (1) mixed investments involve aspects of both borrowing and lending, (2) multiple sign changes in the cash flow stream are a necessary but not a sufficient condition to identify a mixed investment, and (3) mixed investments can have a unique real value of $i^*$ in the region $(-1 < i^* < \infty)$ as a solution to $F(i^*) = 0$, *but for mixed investments the existence and value of* $i^*$ *is* **not** *to be interpreted as the existence and value of internal rate of return* (yield) of the investment; that is, *in general* $i^* \neq$ IRR for mixed investments. Strictly speaking, the yield of a mixed investment is not *internal* to the project at all; it is a function of another external, imputed interest rate.

The fourth numerical example is the "pump problem," a nonconventional investment. On solving $F(i^*) = 0$, we obtain two values for $i^*$: 0.25 and 4.00. Calculating the investment balances with these rates gives two solutions, as follows:

*Investment Balances at*

|  | $i^* = 0.25$ | $i^* = 4.00$ |
|---|---|---|
| $F_0(i^*) =$ | $-1{,}600$ | $-1{,}600$ |
| $F_1(i^*) =$ | $+8{,}000$ | $+2{,}000$ |
| $F_2(i^*) =$ | $0$ | $0$ |

In both cases the investment balances indicate a mixed investment: The intermediate balances of \$8,000 and \$2,000 are not zero or negative, even though both end-of-life balances are zero. The important things to be learned here are that nonconventional investments *may* have more than one solution for $i^*$ on solving $F(i^*) = 0$ and that we are again in doubt about the interpretation of $i^*$ for a mixed investment, not only because of the dependence of $i^*$ on an external, imputed interest rate but also because there may be multiple values of $i^*$.

We now face a dilemma: When does the *internal* rate of return exist and when does it not? We have seen in Projects $A$ and $B$, for example, that a rate of return *internal to the project itself* exists (even though we accepted someone else's word for it), but for Projects $C$ and $D$ a rate of return *internal to the project* does not exist. From these examples we intuitively associate the existence of IRR's with pure investments and the lack of their existence with mixed investments, *even though* we are able to calculate a *value* for $i^*$ from $F(i^*) = 0$ in all cases illustrated. Having posed this dilemma, we now proceed to analyze it and find some rational rules for using $i^*$ as a basis for evaluating single, independent projects.

## 7.11. The Analysis of an Investment

Except for the case in which the solution is indeterminate, we can always find some value of the interest rate $i$ such that $F(i) = 0$. This interest rate (or in the case of multiple roots, these interest rates) we call $i^*$. They are to be regarded simply as solutions to $F(i) = 0$; that is, we do *not* call them *internal rates of return*. The question of whether $i^*$ can be interpreted as the internal rate of return hinges on whether the investment is pure or mixed. If the investment is pure, then $i^*$ is *internal* to the project and may be interpreted as an internal rate of return for the project. On the other hand, if the investment is mixed, then $F(i)$ is a function of *two* interest rates, one external to the project, and $i^*$ cannot be interpreted as an *internal* rate of return for the project. Thus, we need a consistent rule for distinguishing pure and mixed investments. Such a rule will be developed below.

In addition, we need to know how to proceed in calculating a figure of merit for mixed investments when $i^*$ cannot be used. This procedure will involve the calculation of a *return on invested capital* (RIC) that can be used as a figure of merit for mixed investments. In succeeding paragraphs, it will be shown that the future value function is a function of two interest rates, $r$ and $k$, so that when the RIC, $r^*$, is obtained by the solution of $F(r^*, k) = 0$, $r^*$ is seen to be a function of the other interest rate, $k$.

In the following development, we assume positive interest rates $(0 < i < \infty)$ and an initial negative cash flow $(Y_0 < 0)$. All other cash flows may be zero, negative, or positive, except that the last cash flow $Y_N \neq 0$ (since, of course, if $Y_N = 0$, the project could be shortened by one or more periods to make $Y_N \neq 0$). The development is somewhat simpler by using only positive interest rates, in that we can use intuitive proofs, but the method can be extended to the entire region $(-1 < i < \infty)$, as Teichroew, *et al.* [27] point out.

**7.11.1.** *A test for pure and mixed investments.* Whether a particular investment $(Y_0 < 0)$ is a pure investment or a mixed investment depends on the discounting rate. In fact, since $Y_0 < 0$, we can make any investment satisfy the nonpositivity condition for pure investments, that is, so that the investment balances $F_t(i) \leq 0$ for $(t = 0,$

$1, \ldots, N-1$). We do this simply by raising the interest rate so large that in the recursive expressions

$$F_0(i) = Y_0$$
$$F_1(i) = F_0(1+i) \quad + Y_1$$
$$F_1(i) = F_1(1+i) \quad + Y_2$$
$$\cdot \qquad \cdot \qquad \cdot$$
$$\cdot \qquad \cdot \qquad \cdot$$
$$\cdot \qquad \cdot \qquad \cdot$$
$$F_t(i) = F_{t-1}(1+i) + Y_t$$

the terms $F_0(1+i)$, $F_1(1+i)$, $\ldots$, $F_{N-2}(1+i)$ are large enough to make $F_1(i)$, $F_2(i)$, $\ldots$, $F_{N-1}(i)$ all nonpositive. Thus, there exists some minimum interest rate, which we denote $i_{\min}$, such that the nonpositivity condition is *just* satisfied; that is, $i_{\min}$ is the smallest value that makes $F_t(i) \le 0$ true. For example, for Project $D$ in the preceding section, $i_{\min} = 525\%$, and the investment balances are

$$F_0(5.25) = -1{,}600$$
$$F_1(5.25) = \qquad 0$$
$$F_2(5.25) = -10{,}000$$

We should point out here that if all $F_t(i_{\min}) \le 0$ for some value $i_{\min}$, then at any other value of $i > i_{\min}$ the investment balances $F_t(i) \le 0$ also, since all the $F_t$'s are already zero or negative and any increased $i$ will only make them more so. Now, if $i_{\min}$ is taken as the compounding rate for the entire cash flow stream, then the end-of-life future value of the investment, $F_N(i_{\min})$, may be positive, negative, or zero. If $F_N(i_{\min}) > 0$, there exists some rate $i^* > i_{\min}$ that will make $F_N(i^*) = 0$. This is true because the intermediate investment balances, $F_t(i_{\min})$ ($t = 0, 1, \ldots, N-1$) were all zero or negative for $i_{\min}$, and any larger rate $i^* > i_{\min}$ serves only to intensify the negativity of these balances, while at the same time causing $F_N(i^*)$ to become zero. Such projects are *pure* investments by Eq. (7.19). Project $B$ in the foregoing examples illustrates this point. The investment balances for this project are given in Table 7.7 for $i_{\min} = 0.068$ and $i^* = 0.130$, and the cash flow streams compounded at these rates are illustrated in Fig. 7.10:

**Table 7.7.** INVESTMENT BALANCES FOR PROJECT $B$

| End of Period | Investment Balance at | |
|---|---|---|
| | $i_{\min} = 0.068$ | $i^* = 0.130$ |
| 0 | $-100.00$ | $-100.00$ |
| 1 | $-\ 46.81$ | $-\ 52.97$ |
| 2 | $0$ | $-\ 9.85$ |
| 3 | $-200.00$ | $-211.12$ |
| 4 | $-\ 63.62$ | $-\ 88.52$ |
| 5 | $+\ 32.04$ | $0$ |

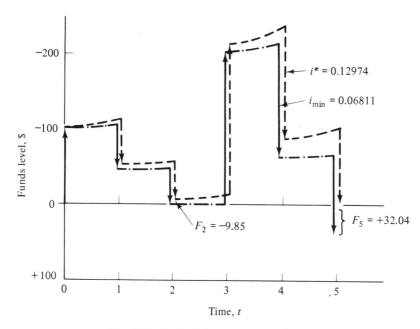

**Fig. 7.10.** Project $B$ investment balances.

It is readily apparent from Table 7.7 and Fig. 7.10 that the higher interest rate, $i^* > i_{min}$, has simply made the intermediate investment balances more negative while converting $F_N(i_{min}) > 0$ to $F_N(i^*) = 0$, thus satisfying the conditions for a pure investment [Eq. (7.19)].

For the second possibility when $F_N(i_{min}) < 0$, there exists some value $i^* < i_{min}$, which will cause some $F_t(i^*) > 0$, and $F_N(i^*) = 0$. We can say this because $i_{min}$ is defined as the *minimum* value for which $F_t(i_{min}) \leq 0$ $(t = 0, 1, \ldots, N - 1)$, and $i^* = i < i_{min}$. In general, since by definition *some* intermediate investment balance $F_t(i_{min}) = 0$ at $i_{min}$, then any $i < i_{min}$ will cause that $F_t(i < i_{min}) > 0$. In particular, if $i^* < i_{min}$, then some one (or more) $F_t(i^*) > 0$ $(t = 0, 1, \ldots, N - 1)$, while the end-of-life balance $F_N(i^*) = 0$. Such investments are *mixed* investments since $F_t(i^*) > 0$ when $F_N(i^*) = 0$ [Eq. (7.19)]. This case is exemplified by Project $C$, whose investment balances are given in Table 7.8 and illustrated in Fig. 7.11 for $i_{min} = 0.380$ and $i^* = 0.285$.

It is apparent here that the lower interest rate $i^* < i_{min}$ has made one intermediate balance, $F_2$, positive while converting the end-of-life balance from $F_5(i_{min}) = -73.80$ to $F_5(i^*) \doteq 0$. Thus, Project $C$ is a mixed investment.

For the third possibility when $F_N(i_{min}) = 0$, then $i^* = i_{min}$ since $F_N(i^*) = 0$ is the condition for $i^*$ to be a root. The situation $i^* = i_{min}$ satisfies both the nonpositivity condition and the end-of-life balance condition in Eq. (7.19), and hence such investments are pure.

We can now summarize the test for pure and mixed investments as follows. On solving $F_N(i^*) = 0$, if $i^* \geq i_{min}$, then the investment is a pure investment; if $i^* <$

**Table 7.8.** INVESTMENT BALANCES FOR PROJECT $C$

| End of Period | Investment Balances at | |
|:---:|:---:|:---:|
| | $i_{min} = 0.380$ | $i^* = 0.285$ |
| 0 | −100.00 | −100.00 |
| 1 | − 57.98 | − 48.50 |
| 2 | 0 | + 17.67 |
| 3 | −200.00 | −177.29 |
| 4 | −125.96 | − 77.82 |
| 5 | − 73.80 | 0 |

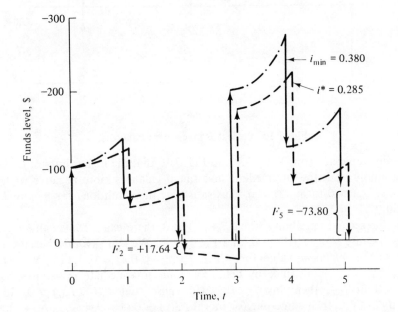

**Fig. 7.11.** Project $C$ investment balances.

$i_{min}$, the investment is a mixed one. Alternatively, if $F_N(i_{min}) \geq 0$, then the investment is pure; if $F_N(i_{min}) < 0$, the investment is mixed.

**7.11.2. *Algorithm for finding $i^*$ and $i_{min}$.*** A simple algorithm for finding $i^*$ and $i_{min}$ is (1) solve $F_N(i) = 0$ for $i^*$, (2) calculate the investment balances $F_t(i^*)$, (3) truncate the cash flow stream so as to include only those values of $Y_t$ occurring at times equal to or earlier than the time when $F_t(i^*)$ is least negative or most positive in value, and (4) solve the truncated cash flow stream $F'_N(i) = 0$ for its root, $i_{min}$.

The method will be illustrated by an example below, but first we need to consider the question of whether or not multiple $i^*$ can occur in the region $i > i_{min}$ since if this were possible, then we would still be left in doubt as to the value of IRR to use for pure investments. Teichroew, *et al.* [26] prove that for all values of $i > i_{min}$ the present value function $P(i)$ is monotonic decreasing for cash flow streams in which $Y_0 < 0$ and that there can be no more than one solution to $P(i) = 0$ for $i > i_{min}$. Hence, no more than one $i^*$ can occur when $i^* > i_{min}$, and we are assured that the problem of multiple $i^*$ for pure investments does not occur. (In fact, the existence of multiple values of $i^*$ in the region $(0 < i^* < \infty)$ is *prima facie* evidence of a mixed investment.)

The algorithm for finding $i^*$ and $i_{min}$ will now be demonstrated. The first step is to find the roots, $i_j^*$ $(j = 1, 2, \ldots, N)$, of the polynomial

$$F_N(i^*) = Y_0(1 + i^*)^N + Y_1(1 + i^*)^{N-1} + \cdots + Y_{N-1}(1 + i^*) + Y_N = 0$$

by any computer root-finding algorithm, such as the POLRT subroutine in the IBM Scientific Subroutine Package (SSP) [33] or by an algorithm in PL/I developed by Dejon and Nickel ([6], pp. 1–35). All roots $i_j^*$, both real and imaginary, should be obtained. For Project *B*, these roots are

$$i_1^* = 0.130$$

$$i_2^* = -2.300$$

$$i_3^* = \text{imaginary}$$

$$i_4^* = \text{imaginary}$$

$$i_5^* = -1.424.$$

The second step is to calculate the investment balances $F_t(i^*)$ $(t = 0, 1, \ldots, n)$ using the largest value of $i^* > 0$ found in the first step. For Project *B*, these balances are given in Table 7.7.

The third step is to truncate the cash flow stream at the *least negative* or *most positive* value of $F_t(i^*)$, that is, at the *maximum* value of $F_t$ when the cash flow stream is compounded with $i^*$. For Project *B* the least negative $F_t(i^*)$ occurs at $t = 2$ (Table 7.7), so the cash flow stream would be truncated to include only $Y_0$, $Y_1$, and $Y_2$, for example. As another example, for Project *C* the most positive $F_t(i^*)$ in Table 7.8 occurs at $t = 2$; hence, this cash flow stream would be truncated at $t = 2$.

The fourth step is to solve the *truncated* cash flow stream, $F_n'(i_0) = 0$, for its root $i_0$ using the POLRT subroutine or an equivalent method. The root thus found is $i_{min} = i_0$, since

1. Truncating the cash flow stream at MAX $[F_t(i^*)]$ $(t = 1, 2, \ldots, N-1)$ is equivalent to forcing $F_N'(i_0) \equiv 0$ in the truncated stream.
2. $i_0$ is the value that causes $F_N'(k_0) = 0$ in the truncated stream and, equivalently, $F_t(i_0) = 0$ in the parent stream.

For Project *B*, the truncated cash flow stream is $Y_0 = -100$, $Y_1 = +60$, and $Y_2 = +50$. On solving the truncated $F_N'(i_{min}) = 0$ with these coefficients, we obtain the root $i_{min} = 0.068$ in the region $(0 < i_{min} < \infty)$. The investment balances for the entire (nontruncated) project cash flow stream can then be calculated using $i_{min}$ as the compounding rate, in order to verify that $i_{min}$ is the rate that causes $F_t(i_{min}) \leq 0$

$(t = 0, 1, \ldots, N - 1)$. For Project $B$, these investment balances (at $i_{min} = 0.068$) are given in Table 7.7.

When implemented on a computer, this algorithm provides a rapid evaluation of the test to discriminate pure and mixed investments. The test is necessary and preliminary to the decision as to whether IRR or RIC should be used as the figure of merit for the project, and a discussion of this decision is the subject of the following paragraphs. The characteristics of mixed investments will be discussed first, and then pure investments will be shown to be a special case of mixed investments.

## 7.12. Mixed Investments and Return on Invested Capital

As we have seen, a mixed investment is partly an investment and partly a source of funds for the firm. Part of the time the firm has funds invested in the project, and part of the time it has funds "borrowed" from the project. To analyze the mixed case we need to introduce the concept that the investment balance stream is a function of *two* interest rates since it is questionable whether a firm would borrow money at the same rate of interest that it earns on its investments. Thus, let $r$ be the rate at which return is realized on invested capital, that is, when the investment balances are negative. This rate we denote the *return on invested capital* (RIC).[15] Also, let $k$ be the rate of interest the firm imputes as its cost for the use of "borrowed" money, that is, when the project is a source of capital: when investment balances are positive. (The rate $k$ might be interpreted, for example, as the firm's cost of capital or the minimum acceptable discount rate. We do not wish to restrict the interpretation of $k$ at this point, however, and thus define it only as an *imputed* cost for the use of money by the firm.)

What we seek is a functional relationship between $r$ and $k$ for a given project cash flow stream. One way of finding this relationship is (1) to write out the expressions for the investment balances of the project, period by period, in terms of $r$ and $k$; (2) to apply the end condition that $F_N(r, k) = 0$ (the firm is assumed to recover its investment exactly at rate $r$ at the end of $N$ years, given an imputed cost $k$); and then (3) to solve $F_N(r, k) = 0$ for $r$ in terms of $k$. Note that the end condition $F_N(r, k) = 0$ defines an implicit relationship between $r$ and $k$, which is the function we seek.

The algorithm for determining the return on invested capital, $r$, as a function of $k$, is as follows:

*Step 1:* Apply the test previously given for distinguishing mixed and pure investments. If $i^* < i_{min}$, the investment is mixed. Proceed with Step 2.

*Step 2:* Recursively calculate $F_t(r, k)$ $(t = 0, 1, 2, \ldots, N)$ according to the rule

---

[15]Teichroew, *et al.* [27] call this the *project investment rate*.

$$F_0(r, k) = Y_0$$

$$F_1(r, k) = \begin{cases} F_0(1 + r) + Y_1 & \text{if } F_0 < 0 \\ F_0(1 + k) + Y_1 & \text{if } F_0 > 0 \end{cases}$$

$$\vdots \qquad\qquad\qquad \vdots$$

$$F_t(r, k) = \begin{cases} F_{t-1}(1 + r) + Y_t & \text{if } F_{t-1} < \\ F_{t-1}(1 + k) + Y_t & \text{if } F_{t-1} > 0 \end{cases}$$

$$\vdots \qquad\qquad\qquad \vdots$$

$$F_N(r, k) = \begin{cases} F_{N-1}(1 + r) + Y_N & \text{if } F_{N-1} < 0 \\ F_{N-1}(1 + k) + Y_N & \text{if } F_{N-1} > 0 \end{cases}$$

*Step 3:* Solve the equation $F_N(r, k) = 0$ for r.

In applying the algorithm, the question arises in Step 2 as to whether an unknown $F_t(r, k)$ is positive or negative since one rule must be chosen if it is negative and another if it is positive. This question can be resolved by recognizing that the unknown $r$ can never be negative (by assumption) and can never exceed $r_{min}$ for a mixed investment, so in effect upper and lower bounds exist on the terms compounded by the $1 + r$ factor, thus defining limits of negativity for these terms. This point can best be made by an example.

The algorithm will be applied to the mixed investment exemplified in Project *D* (the Lorie-Savage "Oil-Pump Problem").

*Step 1:* The project has values of $i_1^* = 0.25$, $i_2^* = 4.00$, and $i_{min} = 5.25$. Since the $i_{max}^* < i_{min}$, the project is a *mixed investment*.

*Step 2:* Recursively calculate $F_t(r, k)$:
    (a) $F_0(r, k) = Y_0 = -1,600.$
    (b) $F_1(r, k) = -1,600(1 + r) + 10,000 \quad (F_0 \leq 0)$
                $= 8,400 - 1,600r.$
    (Since $r$ can never exceed $i_{min} = 5.25$, $1,600r < 8,400$ always and $F_1(r, k)$
    $\geq 0$. Hence, $F_1(r, k)$ is compounded with $(1 + k)$ in the next step.)
    (c) $F_2(r, k) = (8,400 - 1,600r)(1 + k) - 10,000 \quad (F_1 \geq 0).$

*Step 3:* Solve $F_N(r, k) = 0$ for $r(k)$ and, since $F_N(r, k) = F_2(r, k)$,

$$F_N(r, k) = F_2(r, k) = (8,400 - 1,600r)(1 + k) - 10,000 = 0;$$

$$\therefore \quad r = 5.25 - \frac{6.25}{1 + k}. \tag{7.20}$$

Equation (7.20) defines the desired implicit relationship between the return on invested capital, $r$, and the imputed cost of source funds, $k$. As is now evident, for mixed investments *the return on invested capital is not independent of the interest cost rate imputed by the firm to a project for the use of the project's excess funds.* Acceptance or rejection of the project is contingent upon the value of the *external* interest rate, $k$. A graphical solution of Eq. (7.20) is illustrated in Fig. 7.12.

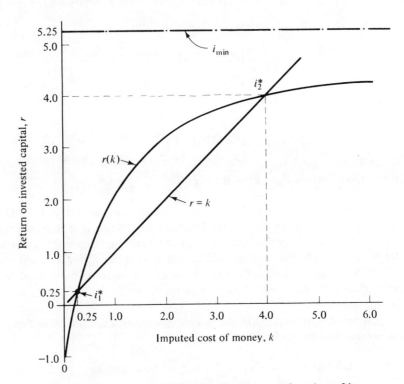

**Fig. 7.12.** Return on invested capital ($r$) as a function of imputed cost of money ($k$), for Project $D$. (*Source:* Teichroew, *et al.* [27], p. 169.)

Four conclusions can be drawn from the functional relationship established between $r$ and $k$. First, the return on invested funds, $r$, is a monotonically increasing function of $k$, the imputed cost of using excess funds. This is not an unexpected result since the higher the cost that is placed on the use of excess funds by the firm, the higher will be the return on the invested funds. That is, a higher credit to the project for the use of its excess funds will result in a higher return realized on the invested funds. *Second,* if we set $k - r$ in Eq. (7.20), then $k = r = i^* = (0.25, 4.00)$, which are the values found by solving $F_N(i^*) = 0$. In Fig. 7.12 the function $r(k)$ crosses the straight line $r = k$ at two points, labeled $i_1^*$ and $i_2^*$. Along the line $k = r = i$, the final value function in Eq. (7.20) reduces to the form of

$$F_N(i, i) = Y_0(1 + i)^N + Y_1(1 + i)^{N-1} + \cdots + Y_N,$$

which is exactly the form of Eq. (7.18), from which $i^*$ can be obtained when $F_N(i, i) = 0$. *For mixed investments, therefore, the roots, i\*, are the values of the return on invested* capital, r, *when the cost of money*, k, *is assumed to be equal to* r. Alternatively, if one considers $i^*$ for a mixed investment to be the *internal* rate of return, then *one implicitly assumes* k = r.

*Third*, the project should be accepted if $r \geq k$ and rejected if $r < k$. For Project D, if the firm's imputed cost of money $k = p$, then the project should be accepted when $r \geq p$. The acceptance region for Project D is defined as $(0.25 \leq k \leq 4.00)$ because here $r \geq k$ [the function $r(k)$ lies *above* the line $r = k$ in Fig. 7.12]. When the cost of money $k < 0.25$ or $k > 4.00$, the project should be rejected, since in these regions, $r < k$.

*Fourth*, the function $r(k)$ approaches $i_{min}$ asymptotically. This can be shown as follows. From Eq. (7.20),

$$r(k) = 5.25 - \frac{6.25}{1+k}.$$

Then, taking the limit as $k \longrightarrow \infty$,

$$\lim_{k \to \infty} r(k) = 5.25,$$

which is the value of $i_{min} = 5.25$ found earlier.

The decision indicated by comparing the return on invested capital, r, to the firm's imputed cost of money, k, removes the ambiguity of two *internal* rates of return. In fact, *the RIC method for mixed investments yields exactly the same decision that the net present value method does*. This can be exemplified by considering the net present value function for D:

$$P(k) = -1,600 + 10,000(1+k)^{-1} - 10,000(1+k)^{-2}, \qquad (7.21)$$

which is illustrated in Fig. 7.13. The net present value function in Fig. 7.13 has three

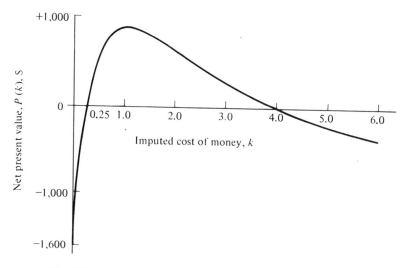

**Fig. 7.13.** Present value function for Project D. (*Source:* Teichroew, *et al.* [17], p. 159.)

noteworthy aspects. *First*, there are two roots of $P(k) = 0$, one at $k_1 = 0.25$ and the other at $k_2 = 4.00$, since the definition of $i^*$ is $i: P(i) = 0$. *Second*, $P(k)$ reaches a maximum value of $+900$ at $k = 1.0$, but one should not infer from this that the difference between return on invested capital, $r$, and cost of money, $k$, is also maximized at $k = 1$. *Third*, since $P(k)$ is positive only in the range $(0.25 < k < 4.0)$, *the net present value method gives the same indications for acceptance and rejection as does the RIC criterion;* i.e., in Fig. 7.13, $P(k) > 0$ in exactly the same region (of $k$) in which $r(k) > k$ in Fig. 7.12.

## 7.13. Pure Investments and Internal Rate of Return

A pure investment is a special case of the more general mixed investment case, in that the investment balance stream contains no positive values. In fact, the mixed investment algorithm can be used for writing the expression for $F_N(r, k) = 0$ for pure investments, but since pure investments contain only zero or negative intermediate investment balances, the form of $F_N(r, k)$ for pure investments is independent of $k$; thus:

$$F_N(r, k) = Y_0(1 + r)^N + Y_1(1 + r)^{N-1} + \cdots + Y_{N-1}(1 + r) + Y_N. \qquad (7.22)$$

The present value of a pure investment is exactly analogous to Eq. (7.22), as demonstrated by multiplying Eq. (7.22) by $(1 + r)^{-N}$; then

$$P(r) = \frac{F_N(r, k)}{(1 + r)^N} = Y_0 + Y_1(1 + r)^{-1} + Y_2(1 + r)^{-2} + \cdots + Y_N(1 + r)^{-N}. \qquad (7.23)$$

It can be shown that Eq. (7.23) for pure investments has at most one positive root in the region $(0 \leq r \leq \infty)$. The case for $Y_0 < 0$, $Y_t \geq 0$ $(t = 1, 2, \ldots, N)$ will be proved, although the more general case for $Y_\tau < 0$ $(\tau = 0, 1, \ldots, m)$, $Y_\theta \geq 0$ $(\theta = m + 1, m + 2, \ldots, N)$ can be proved by the same method but with more labor. Let $v = 1 + r > 1$. Then from Eq. (7.23)

$$\frac{dP(r)}{dv} = -Y_1 v^{-2} - 2Y_2 v^{-3} - \cdots - NY_N v^{-(N+1)}, \qquad (7.24)$$

which is always $<0$ since $Y_t \geq 0$ $(t = 1, 2, \ldots, N - 1)$ and $Y_N > 0$ by assumption, and $v > 0$. Moreover,

$$\frac{d^2 P(r)}{dv^2} = 2Y_1 v^{-3} + 6Y_2 v^{-4} + \ldots + N(N + 1)Y_N v^{-(N+2)}, \qquad (7.25)$$

which is always $>0$ for the same reasons. The function, $P(r)$, is thus strictly decreasing (the first derivative is negative) and is strictly convex (the second derivative is positive) for $Y_0 < 0$, $Y_t \geq 0$ $(t = 1, 2, \ldots, N - 1)$, $Y_N > 0$, and $r > 0$. Furthermore, from Eq. (7.23),

$$\lim_{r \to \infty} P(r) = P(\infty) = Y_0,$$

which is negative by assumption, and since

$$P(0) = \sum_{t=0}^{N} Y_t \quad (r = 0),$$

then the strictly monotonic decreasing function $P(r)$ will provide at most one positive root, $r^*$, between the limits $0 \le r \le \infty$ when the coefficients $Y_0 < 0$ and $Y_t \ge 0$ $(t = 1, 2, \ldots, N)$ are taken such that $\sum_t Y_t > 0$.

We conclude from this reasoning that pure investments have at most one real value of $i^* = r^*$ in the region $(0 \le r \le \infty)$, and since $r^*$ is independent of the cost of money, $k$, then we are justified in considering $i^*$ to be the *internal* rate of return for the project. The decision based on the rate of return criterion for pure investments is, therefore, accept the project if $i^* \ge \rho$ and reject it if $i^* < \rho$.


## 7.14. Summary

Under the *essential assumptions of certainty* and *perfect capital markets*, we have examined four criteria for evaluating the economic acceptability of a single project, given no constraints on the problem. These criteria are (a) payback, (b) net present value, (c) benefit-cost ratio, and (d) internal rate of return.

As a special case of the payback method, the "payback rate of return" has a rational interpretation (an imputed interest rate) under certain special conditions. It is the interest rate that would be earned by a project whose cash inflows are level over time and whose salvage value is zero. Other than this highly limiting interpretation, early payback probably expresses only a subjective preference for early liquidity for the firm.

Net present value is shown, via the Separation Theorem, to be the logical criterion for project selection under perfect capital market conditions. Not only can the investment decision be made separately from the financing decision (thus resulting in an optimal *production* decision), but the financing decision can thereafter be made so as to maximize the utility of the decision-maker also. Further consideration of the characteristics of NPV led us to the conclusion that if the interest (discounting) rate can be specified or secured, then NPV can be calculated for any series of real cash flows.

The benefit-cost ratio *for a single project* is shown to be only a special case of net present value and involves merely added calculational effort without an increase in informational content.

Internal rate of return is examined in detail. The fundamental meaning of *internal* rate of return (IRR) is developed, i.e., that it is an interest rate earned on the time-varying, unrecovered balances of an investment, such that complete and exact recovery of the last increment of investment occurs at the end of the project life. It is demonstrated that **IRR** is **NOT** a rate of interest on the *initial* investment. Furthermore, it is demonstrated that in some types of cash flow streams, in which there are certain types of alternations in signs and cash flow magnitudes, pathologic cases result in which there is no *unique* internal rate of return procurable. In those cases where *multiple* rates of return exist, the problem is shown to be the result of an *over*recovery of the investment in one or more periods prior to the end of the project life. In such cases, *internal* rates of return (i.e., internal to the project) do not exist; rather, the return on invested capital (in the project) is a function of an external interest rate. Finally, it is shown that pure investments are a special case of the mixed investment (external interest rate) case and will exhibit a unique return on investment (i.e., an internal rate of return).

## REFERENCES

[1] BARISH, NORMAN N., *Economic Analysis for Engineering and Managerial Decision-Making* (New York: McGraw-Hill Book Co., 1962), pp. 142–43, 234–35.

[2] BERANEK, WILLIAM, "A Note on the Equivalence of Certain Capital Budgeting Criteria," *The Accounting Review*, XXXIX(4) (October, 1964), pp. 914–16.

[3] BERNHARD, RICHARD H., "Discount Methods for Expenditure Evaluation—A Clarification of Their Assumptions," *Journal of Industrial Engineering*, XVIII(1) (January–February, 1962), pp. 19–27.

[4] ———, "A Comprehensive Comparison and Critique of Discounting Indices Proposed for Capital Investment Evaluation," *The Engineering Economist*, 16(3) (Spring, 1971), pp. 157–186.

[5] BIERMAN, H., JR., and S. SMIDT, *The Capital Budgeting Decision*, 2nd ed. (New York: Macmillan, 1971).

[6] DEJON, B., and KARL NICKEL, "A Never-Failing Fast Convergent Root-Finding Algorithm," in Dejon and Henrici, ed., *Constructive Aspects of the Fundamental Theorem of Algebra* (Proceedings of a Symposium Conducted at IBM Research Laboratory, Zürich, June 5–7, 1967) (New York: Wiley-Interscience, John Wiley & Sons, 1969).

[7] DRYDEN, MYLES, "The MAPI Urgency Rating as an Investment Ranking Criterion," *Journal of Business*, XXXIII(4) (October, 1960), pp. 327–41.

[8] ECKSTEIN, OTTO, *Water Resource Development: The Economics of Project Evaluation* (Cambridge, Mass.: Harvard University Press, 1958).

[9] FISHER, IRVING, *The Theory of Interest* (New York: Macmillan, 1930; reprinted, Kelley and Millman, Inc., 1954).

[10] GORDON, MYRON, "The Payoff Period and the Rate of Profit," *Journal of Business*, XXVIII(4) (October, 1955), pp. 253–60.

[11] HIRSHLEIFER, J., "On the Theory of Optimal Investment Decision," *Journal of Political Economy*, 66(5) (August, 1958), pp. 329–352; reprinted in Ezra Solomon, ed., *The Management of Corporate Capital* (Glencoe, Ill.: The Free Press, 1959), pp. 205–28.

[12] HORNGREN, CHARLES T., *Cost Accounting: A Managerial Emphasis* (Englewood Cliffs, N. J.: Prentice-Hall, Inc., 1962), pp. 409–15.

[13] KAPLAN, S., "A Note on a Method for Precisely Determining the Uniqueness or Nonuniqueness of the Internal Rate of Return for a Proposed Investment," *Journal of Industrial Engineering*, XVI(1) (January–February, 1965), pp. 70–71.

[14] ———, "Computer Algorithms for Finding Exact Rates of Return," *Journal of Business*, **40**(4) (October, 1967), pp. 389–92.

[15] LINDSAY, ROBERT, and ARNOLD W. SAMETZ, *Financial Management: An Analytic Approach* (Homewood, Ill.: Richard D. Irwin, Inc., 1963). pp. 73–75.

[16] LORIE, J., and L. J. SAVAGE, "Three Problems in Capital Rationing," *Journal of Business*, **XXVIII**(4) (October, 1955).

[17] LUTZ, FRIEDRICH, and VERA LUTZ, *The Theory of Investment of the Firm* (Princeton, N. J.: Princeton University Press, 1951).

[18] MAO, J. C. T., *Quantitative Analysis of Financial Decisions* (Toronto: Macmillan, 1969), Chapter 6.

[19] MOORE, CARL L., and ROBERT K. JAEDICKE, *Managerial Accounting* (Cincinnati: South-Western Pub. Co., 1963), p. 524.

[20] NEWNAN, DONALD G., *Engineering Economic Analysis* (San Jose, Calif.: Engineering Press, 1976).

[21] NORSTRØM, CARL J., "A Sufficient Condition for a Unique Nonnegative Internal Rate of Return," *Journal of Financial and Quantitative Analysis*, **7**(3) (June, 1972), pp. 1835–39.

[22] RENSHAW, E., "A Note on the Arithmetic of Capital Budgeting Decisions," *Journal of Business* (July, 1957).

[23] SMITH, VERNON L., *Investment and Production* (Cambridge, Mass.: Harvard University Press, 1961), Chapter IX, pp. 219–41.

[24] SOLOMON, E., "The Arithmetic of Capital Budgeting Decisions," *Journal of Business*, **XXIX**(2) (April, 1956).

[25] SWALM, RALPH O., "On Calculating the Rate of Return on an Investment," *Journal of Industrial Engineering*, **IX**(2) (March–April, 1958), pp. 99–103.

[26] TEICHROEW, D., A. A. ROBICHEK, and M. MONTALBANO, "Mathematical Analysis of Rates of Return Under Certainty," *Management Science*, **11**(3) (January, 1965), pp. 395–403.

[27] ———, "An Analysis of Criteria for Investment and Financing Decisions Under Certainty," *Management Science*, **12**(3) (November, 1965), pp. 151–79.

[28] TERBORGH, GEORGE, *Business Investment Policy* (Washington, D.C.: Machinery and Allied Products Institute, 1958).

[29] TURNBULL, H. W., *Theory of Equations*, 5th ed. (Edinburgh: Oliver and Boyd, 1952).

[30] WEINGARTNER, H. MARTIN, *Mathematical Programming and the Analysis of Capital Budgeting Problems* (Englewood Cliffs, N. J.: Prentice-Hall, Inc., 1963); reprinted under the same title as the "Markham Edition" by Markham Publishing Co., Chicago, 1967.

[31] ———, "The Excess Present Value Index: A Theoretical Basis and Critique," *Journal of Accounting Research*, **1**(2) (Autumn, 1963), pp. 213–24.

[32] ———, "Some New Views on the Payback Period and Capital Budgeting Decisions," *Management Science*, **15**(12) (August, 1969), pp. B594–B607.

[33] "System/360 Scientific Subroutine Package (360A-CM-03X) Version III Programmer's Manual," Document H20-0205-3, 5th ed. (August, 1970), International Business Machines Corp., White Plains, N.Y.

[34] BERNHARD, RICHARD H., "Unrecovered Investment, Uniqueness of the Internal Rate, and the Question of Project Acceptability," *Journal of Financial and Quantitative Analysis*, **XII**(1) (March, 1977), pp. 33–38.

[35] ———, "A More Generalized Sufficient Condition for a Unique Non-negative Internal Rate of Return." (Private communication from the author, September, 1977; also submitted for publication.)

[36] SOPER, C. S., "The Marginal Efficiency of Capital: A Further Note," *The Economic Journal*, **69**(273) (March, 1959), pp. 174–77.

## PROBLEMS

**7-1.** An *investment-type* project has the following cash flows:

| End of Period, $t$ | Net Cash Flow, $Y_t$ |
|:---:|:---:|
| 0 | $\$-3,000.00$ |
| 1 | 791.39 |
| 2 | 791.39 |
| 3 | 791.39 |
| 4 | 791.39 |
| 5 | 791.39 |

(a) By examining the unrecovered investment balances, determine the type of this investment.

(b) Determine the internal rate of return if it exists; otherwise, find $R(k)$.

**7-2.** For each of the following cash flow streams, calculate the net present value, given that the minimum attractive rate of return is 15%.

*Project Cash Flows*

| EOY | A | B | C | D | E |
|:---:|:---:|:---:|:---:|:---:|:---:|
| 0 | $\$-2,000$ | $\$-2,000$ | $\$-2,000$ | $\$-2,000$ | $\$-2,000$ |
| 1 | $+\ \ 597$ | $+\ \ 425$ | $+\ \ 500$ | — | — |
| 2 | 597 | 525 | 500 | — | $+1,000$ |
| 3 | 597 | 625 | 927 | — | 1,424 |
| 4 | 597 | 725 | 527 | — | 1,000 |
| 5 | 597 | 825 | 127 | $+3,525$ | — |

**7-3.** Determine the *payback period* for each project cash flow stream in Problem 7-2. What projects would be desirable investments if the payback period is not to exceed 3 years?

**7-4.** (a) Calculate the *payback rate of return* for each project in Problem 7-2.

(b) Calculate the *internal rate of return* for each project in Problem 7-2.

**7-5.** For the cash flow streams in Problem 7-2, calculate the NPV's for each using nominal interest rates of 0%, 5%, 10%, 12%, 15%, 20%, and then using the IRR's determined previously, plot net present value versus interest rate for each cash flow stream.

**7-6.** Tests indicate that a proposed oil well, if completed, will probably produce 30 barrels of oil per day for the next 10 years. It will cost $100 dollars a day to pump the well.

The oil company must pay the landowner $3 for every barrel of oil pumped. Crude oil is expected to sell for $13 per barrel for the next 10 years. The well will cost $100,000 to drill. This is a first cost and will be amortized on a straight-line basis with a life of 10 years and no salvage value. The installed cost of the pumping equipment at time $t = 0$ is $75,000. This cost will be depreciated on a straight-line basis with a life of 10 years and no salvage value. What is the net present value, internal rate of return, and payback period if the company's tax rate is 52% and the minimum attractive rate of return is 8%? Assume that profits and expenses that occur during a year occur at the end of the year and that amortization of the $100,000 cost of the well is in lieu of allowable depletion expense.

**7-7.** A company has an opportunity to increase its production of Widgets. The price of Widgets will remain at $10 apiece for the next 10 years. The additional operating expenses include a fixed amount of $40,000 for overhead expenses plus $5 per Widget in production and selling costs. The project will last 10 years. To execute this project the company must purchase a new Widget machine for $300,000. This machine will be depreciated using straight-line depreciation with a life of 10 years and no salvage value. How many Widgets must be sold each year so that the project will have an internal rate of return of 10%? Assume an effective tax rate of 48%.

**7-8.** Given the following cash flow stream, (a) demonstrate that it is a pure investment, and (b) find the internal rate of return, $i^*$.

| End of Period, $t_j$ | Net Cash Flow, $Y_j$ |
| --- | --- |
| 0 | $-50,000 |
| 1 | -32,000 |
| 2 | - 1,500 |
| 3 | 25,000 |
| 4 | 35,000 |
| 5 | 45,000 |
| 6 | 40,000 |
| 7 | 35,000 |

**7-9.** An investment is assumed to produce the following cash flows:

| End of Year, t | $Y_t = $ Cash Flow |
| --- | --- |
| 0 | $-19,000 |
| 1 | 10,000 |
| 2 | 17,000 |
| 3 | - 7,000 |
| 4 | - 6,000 |
| 5 | 12,000 |
| 6 | 10,000 |

(a) Solve this cash flow system for its internal rate(s) of return.

(b) Is the investment conventional or nonconventional? Pure or mixed? Why?

(c) If the firm's minimum attractive rate of return (MARR) is 15%, should it select this investment based on a comparison of the project rate with the MARR?

**7-10.** The Stripper Petroleum Company has an opportunity to purchase an oil well from another company. The well is being sold because it doesn't produce enough oil to make it profitable for the present owner to operate it. Stripper can purchase the well for $500, and for an additional expenditure at the time of purchase of $1,500, the following net cash flows from the produced oil can be realized:

| Time, $t =$ | Net Cash Flow, $Y_t$ |
|---|---|
| 1 | $+ 100 |
| 2 | +10,000 |
| 3 | + 100 |
| 4 | + 200 |
| 5 | + 100 |

At the end of the fifth year, however, Stripper will be required to spend an additional $11,900 to plug the well and restore the premises. (a) Can Stripper make a decision based on the *internal rate of return* criterion, assuming their minimum attractive rate of return is 14%? If so, what is their decision? (b) If the answer to (a) is "no," write the recursive end-of-period unrecovered balance equations and determine the return on invested capital.

**7-11.** The Rolling Wheels Harvester Company would like to decide whether it should accept a project with the following cash flows:

| End of Year, $t$: | 0 | 1 | 2 | 3 | 4 | 5 |
|---|---|---|---|---|---|---|
| Cash Flow, $Y_t$: | $-500 | +100 | +400 | +500 | +200 | -600 |

(a) Solve the problem by the internal rate of return (IRR) method if the IRR is procurable. Otherwise, solve for the return on invested capital (RIC) function.

(b) If the company's minimum attractive rate of return is 15%, should the project be accepted based on RIC? Why?

(c) If the company's minimum attractive rate of return is 24%, should the project be accepted? Why?

**7-12.** (a) For the cash flows of Project $C$ in Table 7.6, calculate the implicit relationship between the return on invested capital ($r$) and the cost of external capital ($k$) by recursively examining $F_t(r, k)$. [*Note:* This problem involves setting an arbitrary upper bound on $k$ and a moving lower bound, $r_{min}$, on $r(k)$, in order to establish the rates at which $F_3(r, k)$ and $F_4(r, k)$ are to be compounded.] (b) Plot $r$ versus $k$, and net present value versus $k$. Plot $i_{min}$, $r = k$, $i^*$, and the upper and lower bounds established in (a).

**7-13.** What is the Separation Theorem? Under what conditions does it apply? What might happen if it were not applicable?

**7-14.** What are the present value rules? Under what conditions will the application of the present value rules always lead decision-makers to correct choices of projects? When might the present value rules fail?

**7-15.** Advocates of the internal rate of return method of project selection often state that IRR "does not require the use of an externally determined interest rate" in order for a decision-maker to select or reject a project. Why is this a false statement?

# MULTIPLE PROJECTS AND CONSTRAINTS I
## (The Lorie-Savage Problem)

## 8.1. Introduction

As long as the firm is able to consider projects individually and needs only to decide whether to accept or reject a given project on its own merits, any of the rational criteria—net present value, internal rate of return, return on invested capital, or benefit-cost ratio—will signal the correct decision if applied correctly. In practice, however, the prerequisite conditions of project independence, project indivisibility, and lack of capital rationing generally do not exist. What one usually finds is that many of the projects in the candidate set are dependent and that there is insufficient capital available to undertake all acceptable projects. Under these limitations the selection problem becomes more complicated, and the rational criteria by themselves no longer necessarily signal the *correct* decisions.

To introduce the subject of project selection under constraints, we shall discuss in this chapter a simple constrained problem known as the *Lorie-Savage* problem. Named after the investigators Lorie and Savage [11], who first attempted a solution to it, this simple type of project selection problem sometimes develops what is known as a *ranking inconsistency* when the same set of projects is ranked by two different criteria, e.g., net present value and internal rate of return. Because of the ranking inconsistency phenomenon, serious questions arise about the ranking methods. This chapter will probe the reasons why project ranking is not a satisfactory method of project selection

# 8

and then demonstrate that the mathematical programming formulation provides an optimal solution.

## 8.2. Project Dependence

Two projects are said to be *economically independent* if the acceptance or rejection of one does not measurably alter the cash flow stream or does not affect the acceptance or rejection of the other. Two independent projects would be a manufacturing firm's prospective investment in a special-purpose milling machine and its prospective investment in some office equipment.

Two (or more) projects are said to be *economically dependent* if the acceptance or rejection of one measurably alters the cash flow stream of any other *or* if the acceptance or rejection of any other project is affected. The most obvious type of dependency occurs among *mutually exclusive* projects. Mutual exclusivity in a set of projects exists if the acceptance of any one project automatically (technically or economically) excludes acceptance of all other projects in the set. In economic terms, mutually exclusive projects are *substitutes* for each other. An example of a set of mutually exclusive projects would be alternative uses for a particular land site. Another example would be the alternative designs for a building since only one alternative could be built. A third example would be alternative heights for a water impoundment dam. Obviously, two mutually exclusive projects cannot both be accepted.

Two (or more) projects may be economically dependent even if they are not mutually exclusive substitutes for each other. In this case the degree of substitutability, while less than that of mutually exclusive projects, nevertheless causes economic dependence. In general, this type of substitution dependence occurs when the existence of two projects together causes changes in the cash flow streams of each, as opposed to the cash flows that would be experienced if either project existed by itself. An excellent illustration of this type of economic dependence is given by Bierman and Smidt ([3],p.76): It would be technically feasible, for example, to build a toll bridge (Project *A*) between two points on the opposite sides of a river *and* to operate a toll ferry (Project *B*) between the two points also. The two projects are dependent because the revenues of one will be affected by the presence of the other. This type of economic dependence is sometimes called *partial dependence*.

A third type of dependence, called economic *complementarity*, sometimes occurs between projects. If the undertaking of one project will increase the benefits expected from another project (either by increasing revenues or decreasing investments or costs), then the projects are said to be economic *complements*. If each project complements the other, the dependency relationship is said to be symmetrical. In practice, however, symmetrical dependence is not often found. What is usually found is *a*symmetrical dependence: The acceptance of, say, Project *A* benefits Project *B*, but the acceptance of *B* in no way benefits *A*. An example is a proposed investment in an additional long boom for a crane (Project *A*) and a proposed investment in the crane itself with a short boom (Project *B*). Without the long boom (*A*), the crane (*B*) may be profitable, but with the long boom, the earnings of the crane might be enhanced. Another example is an investment in an air-conditioning system (*A*) and an investment in a building (*B*). The building itself may be profitable, but the addition of the air-conditioning system might make it more so. Generally, asymmetric economic dependence also involves *technical contingency* between projects. As the two examples imply, it would be technically meaningless to acquire a long boom without a crane or an air-conditioning system without a building. In both examples, the acceptance of Project *A* implies the acceptance of Project *B*, but not vice versa.

## 8.3. Capital Rationing

*Rationing* of capital occurs whenever the funds available for investment are insufficient to permit the firm to accept all otherwise acceptable candidate projects. (The reader will recall that *acceptability* is determined by one of the rational criteria—positive NPV, IRR > marginal investment rate, RIC > marginal investment rate, or $B/C > 1.0$.) Restrictions on funds for investment occur because of limitations imposed either by management (internal to the firm) or by the capital market (external to the firm).

Internal capital rationing occurs (a) when management decides to limit the total amount of funds available for capital expenditures to a fixed amount in a given period or (b) when managment sets a cutoff rate for investments that is higher than the firm's imputed cost of money, that is, when it establishes a marginal investment rate (MIR) or a marginal attractive rate of return (MARR) that is greater than the cost of capital. In either case, the effect of internal capital rationing is to cause the rejection of some projects from the candidate set that would otherwise be acceptable from a profitability standpoint if sufficient capital were available.

External capital rationing occurs when the firm cannot obtain funds from the capital market in sufficient amounts at a price the firm considers economical. In actuality, the unlimited availability of funds as postulated in a *free* capital market simply does not exist, and the firm must compete for available funds. Several authors[1] postulate an upward sloping supply curve for capital; that is, beyond a certain critical amount of capital, the weighted average cost of capital increases with the amount of capital raised, as in Fig. 8.1.

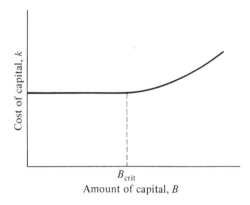

**Fig. 8.1.** Capital supply curve.

An increasing cost of capital curve implies that the firm cannot raise an unlimited amount of capital at one time at a constant cost. The increased usage premium (interest) demanded by the financial market, beyond $B_{crit}$ in Fig. 8.1, is probably due to the increased risk the firm's investors feel they take in supplying large amounts of capital at one time. This reflects as an increased cost of capital to the firm. After a "digestion" period of time during which the firm demonstrates to its creditors and investors its ability to generate satisfactory returns on its investments, however, the risk premium disappears and the firm is then able again to raise capital at the lower constant rate up to some new level, $B_{crit}$.

The rising capital supply curve has implications for the investment decision. Certain marginal projects with IRR's close to the increased cost of capital rate will no longer be acceptable. Thus, the firm must postpone or abandon these marginal projects. An illustration of this situation is shown in Fig. 8.2. Here, projects using incre-

---

[1]For example, see Duesenberry [6], Chapter 5; Lindsey and Sametz [10], Chapters 19 and 20.

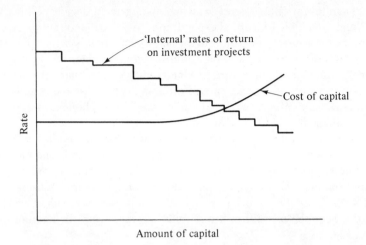

**Fig. 8.2.** Marginal rates of return for investment projects and the marginal cost of capital.

mental amounts of capital are cumulated according to decreasing IRR's (or RIC's), with the results plotted on the same axes as the capital supply curve. The capital demand curve gives the incremental (marginal) rate of return for each increment of investment added. The intersection of the incremental rate of return curve with the marginal cost-of-capital curve determines the amount of capital to be raised and the amount of funds to be invested for the period. The significant point of this discussion is that the external capital market can cause limitations to be placed on the capital available for investment, and the firm consequently must *choose* between investment opportunities, accepting some and rejecting others.

In general then, whether capital is rationed externally or internally, the firm must *select* some investment projects from the candidate set and *reject* others that on their own merits would be otherwise perfectly acceptable. The selection process under capital rationing involves the same kind of *comparison among projects* as does mutual exclusivity, except that under rationing the reason is different. The important point is that investment opportunities must be *compared* with each other, in order to make the decision to accept some and reject others.

## 8.4. Project Indivisibility

It is unlikely that the capital requirements of the entire candidate set of projects will *exactly* match the investment funds available. Some large projects may require the use of a large proportion of the funds available, while many smaller projects individually will require only a small fraction of the funds available. Thus, the possibility arises for a trade-off in the selection process between, say, a single large project and several smaller projects. Put another way, the acceptance of a single large project may, because of rationed funds, automatically exclude the acceptance of several smaller projects. This is because investment projects are considered to be indivisible—that is, a project *as an entity* is accepted or rejected in its entirety. It is assumed that partial projects or "pieces" of a complete project should not be undertaken only to be abandoned by rejection in a later decision process.

As an example, consider three indivisible investments, $C, D$, and $E$, which cost $100, $80, and $80, respectively, and which yield NPV's of $30, $20, and $20, respectively. If the firm's available capital is rationed to $160, the acceptance of the largest project $(C)$, with the highest individual NPV = $30, might cause rejection of $D$ and $E$ that together would yield $40 in net present value. Hence, the indivisibility of projects again necessitates the *comparison of projects* in order to decide which should be accepted and which should be rejected.

## 8.5. Comparison Methodologies

Whenever two or more investment projects must be compared, with the goal being to accept some and reject others—for whatever reason: mutual exclusivity, economic or technical dependence, capital rationing, or project indivisibility—then the firm needs a rational methodology for making the comparison and deciding which projects should be selected and which should be rejected, so as to select an optimal portfolio of investments. There are two basic approaches to the problem of selecting an optimal investment portfolio: (1) the method of ranking and (2) the method of mathematical programming. In the first methodology, all candidate projects are ranked in decreasing order according to their individual IRR's, RIC's, NPV's, or $B/C$ ratios. Projects are then accepted in that order until the capital budget (the firm's available funds) is exhausted. In the second methodology, an optimal set of projects is selected by a mathematical programming procedure, such as 0–1 integer programming or a branch-and-bound procedure, so as to maximize some criterion of interest to the firm subject to a number of feasibility constraints (budget, manpower, liquidity, etc.).

The ranking methodology, originally proposed by Joel Dean [5], is beset by a number of difficulties. First, it is often observed in a given set of candidate projects that the preference ranking obtained by using the IRR criterion is different from the ranking obtained when NPV is the criterion used. Selection in descending order of merit, therefore, results in a different set of projects being accepted under the IRR criterion than those that would be accepted under the NPV criterion. An analogous phenomenon occurs when benefit-cost ratio is used as the ranking criterion. This has been called the *ranking-error problem* (see, for example, Bernhard [1]) and can be illustrated by a simple example.

**Example 8.5.1.** Consider five projects $(F, G, H, I$, and $J)$ with required investments, expected cash flows, and project lives given in Table 8.1 below.[2]

---

[2]In this chapter all investments are assumed to be pure investments unless otherwise stated, so that the IRR criterion is applicable. This avoids having to consider the cost of capital as a variable, which would unduly complicate the presentation in its simplest form.

Salvage values of all investments are considered to be zero. We wish to rank these investments by three different criteria: internal rate of return, net present value, and benefit-cost ratio.

**Table 8.1.** CHARACTERISTICS OF FIVE PROJECTS

| Project | Investment Required at $t = 0$ | Annual Cash Flow, $Y_t$ $(t = 1, \ldots, N)$ | Project Life, $N$ |
|---------|--------------------------------|---------------------------------------------|-------------------|
| F | $-12,000 | $4,281 | 5 |
| G | -17,000 | 5,802 | 10 |
| H | - 5,000 | 1,866 | 15 |
| I | -14,000 | 2,745 | 20 |
| J | -19,000 | 5,544 | 20 |

The ranking by internal rate of return is accomplished by calculating the IRR for each project; thus:

| Project | IRR | Rank |
|---------|-----|------|
| F: | $0 = -12,000 + 4,281(P/A, i, 5) \Rightarrow (P/A, i, 5) = 2.81$ $\Rightarrow i^* = 0.23$ | 4 |
| G: | $0 = -17,000 + 5,802(P/A, i, 10) \Rightarrow (P/A, i, 10) = 2.93$ $\Rightarrow i^* = 0.32$ | 2 |
| H: | $0 = - 5,000 + 1,866(P/A, i, 15) \Rightarrow (P/A, i, 15) = 2.68$ $\Rightarrow i^* = 0.37$ | 1 |
| I: | $0 = -14,000 + 2,745(P/A, i, 20) \Rightarrow (P/A, i, 20) = 5.09$ $\Rightarrow i^* = 0.19$ | 5 |
| J: | $0 = -19,000 + 5,544(P/A, i, 20) \Rightarrow (P/A, i, 20) = 3.43$ $\Rightarrow i^* = 0.29$ | 3 |

Assuming that the marginal investment rate specified by the firm is 15%, the ranking by net present value is accomplished by calculating the NPV of each project; thus:

| Project | NPV | Rank |
|---------|-----|------|
| F: | $P_F = -12,000 + \overset{(P/A,15\%,5)}{4,281(3.352)} = + 2,350$ | 5 |
| G: | $P_G = -17,000 + \overset{(P/A,15\%,10)}{5,802(5.019)} = +12,120$ | 2 |
| H: | $P_H = - 5,000 + \overset{(P/A,15\%,15)}{1,866(5.847)} = + 5,910$ | 3 |
| I: | $P_I = -14,000 + \overset{(P/A,15\%,20)}{2,745(6.259)} = + 3,181$ | 4 |
| J: | $P_J = -19,000 + \overset{(P/A,15\%,20)}{5,544(6.259)} = +15,700$ | 1 |

The ranking by benefit-cost ratio is established in a similar manner:

| Project | Benefit-Cost Ratio | Rank |
|---|---|---|
| F: | $B/C = \dfrac{4,281(\overset{(P/A,15\%,5)}{3.352})}{12,000} = 1.195$ | 5 |
| G: | $B/C = \dfrac{5,802(\overset{(P/A,15\%,10)}{5.019})}{17,000} = 1.713$ | 3 |
| H: | $B/C = \dfrac{1.866(\overset{(P/A,15\%,15)}{5.847})}{5,000} = 2.182$ | 1 |
| I: | $B/C = \dfrac{2,745(\overset{(P/A,15\%,20)}{6.259})}{14,000} = 1.227$ | 4 |
| J: | $B/C = \dfrac{5,544(\overset{(P/A,15\%,20)}{6.259})}{19,000} = 1.826$ | 2 |

It is now obvious that the three criteria (IRR, NPV, and $B/C$) rank the projects differently. If capital is not rationed, then all projects could be accepted by all three criteria and no harm is done. If capital *is* rationed, however, then a different decision is obtained from each criterion. For example, suppose the firm's capital expenditure budget is limited to $40,000. The IRR criterion would accept Projects $H$ and $G$, the NPV criterion would accept Projects $G$ and $J$, and the benefit-cost criterion would accept Projects $H$ and $J$. The question then is, which criterion gives the "correct" decision? Other collateral questions are, why do the apparent inconsistencies in ranking exist, and what is the explanation for them? The ranking inconsistency problem is one originally pointed out by Lorie and Savage [11], and the difficulty can be traced to the differing *implicit* assumptions that the three ranking criteria make concerning reinvestment of cash flows. If a common reinvestment rate is assumed, the ranking inconsistencies disappear.

The second problem associated with the ranking methodology is that of project indivisibility. As pointed out in Section 8.4, the acceptance of, say, a single large project under a capital budget constraint may exclude the acceptance of several smaller projects that potentially have more aggregate value to the firm. If, as Lorie and Savage point out ([11], p. 231), the majority of investment projects have investment requirements that are *small* in relation to the total capital budget, then the problems created by project indivisibility can be safely disregarded with only minor consequences. If there are several indivisible investments that are *large* in comparison to the total capital budget, however, then indivisibility becomes a serious problem in the ranking methodology since the acceptance of a single large investment can exclude the acceptance of several smaller ones that; taken together, provide better profitability for the firm. Probably the most expeditious way of dealing with the indivisibility problem is some form of 0–1 integer programming; however, even programming methods tend to become unwieldy in the computer for large selection problems.

## 8.6. The Reinvestment Rate Problem

Whenever investment projects must be compared one with another, with the objective of accepting some in the candidate set and excluding (rejecting) others, we are faced with the problem of how the projects should be compared. This is true if the projects are mutually exclusive, if they are dependent, if they are indivisible, or if capital is rationed. The *reason* for comparison is immaterial. If certain ones of the otherwise acceptable candidate set are to be rejected, then comparison is inevitable, and the *method* of comparison becomes relevant.[3]

*Internal* rate of return is favored among some businessmen because it is (they think) easily understood. They tend to think of it as a return on initial investment, although this is an incorrect economic interpretation (see Chapter 7). Net present value requires that a marginal investment rate be established *ex ante* before NPV can be calculated for an investment project. The same is true of the benefit-cost method. As we have already seen in Chapter 7, net present value provides for a means of maximizing shareholder wealth under perfect capital market conditions. Benefit-cost ratio possesses a further advantage in certain cases; namely, it relates net present value to cost as a ratio measure, so in effect it measures the *relative* efficiency of providing future wealth per dollar of present investment.[4] Proponents of any given method advocate the superiority of that method over the others by citing methodological advantages, such as those given above. Yet in the face of these purported advantages, the ranking inconsistency problem remains. That is, as we have seen in Example 8.5.1, the three criteria give different rankings to projects in the candidate set. This inconsistency of ranking is called the *reinvestment rate problem* since the inconsistencies can be traced to differing assumptions made about the *rate at which cash flows from projects are reinvested in alternative uses.*[5] If a *common* reinvestment rate is assumed, the ranking inconsistencies disappear.

**Example 8.6.1.** An example by Solomon [14] illustrates the nature of the reinvestment rate problem. Here, the candidate set exists in its simplest nontrivial form, as it consists of only two projects, one of which is to be accepted and the other rejected.[6] The firm must choose between two projects, each costing $100

---

[3]See Bierman and Smidt [4].

[4]See Schwab and Lusztig [13].

[5]Some writers strongly insist, contrary to this statement, that the reinvestment rate has no place in economic studies of alternatives. See Jeynes [9], for example. The weight of the theoretical evidence, however, appears to be in support of the reinvestment rate explanation of the ranking inconsistency problem. See, for example, Solomon [14], Bernhard [1], and Mao [12].

[6]Solomon [14] uses this example to illustrate mutual exclusivity between projects. As Bierman and Smidt [4] point out, however, it is not necessary that economic or technical mutual exclusivity be the *sole* reason for the acceptance of one and the exclusion of the other. All that is necessary is that a requirement be imposed that one of the two projects be accepted and the other rejected; and this could result, in other instances, for example, from the imposition of capital budget and project indivisibility constraints. Hence, Solomon's example is valid in any instance in which two projects are compared, with one to be accepted and the other rejected. The same reasoning can be used to extend the reinvestment rate problem to a candidate set of $m$ ($m = 2, 3, \ldots$) projects in which some are to be accepted and others rejected since all can be compared in pairs.

at time $t = 0$. Project $K$ returns \$120 at the end of 1 year ($t = 1$), and Project $L$ returns \$201.14 at the end of 5 years ($t = 5$).

Application of the IRR method gives the following internal rates of return:

$$K: \quad 0 = -100 + 120(P/F, i^*, 1) \Rightarrow (P/F, i^*, 1) = 0.833 \Rightarrow i_K^* = 0.20$$

$$L: \quad 0 = -100 + 201.14(P/F, i^*, 5) \Rightarrow (P/F, i^*, 5) = 0.4972 \Rightarrow i_L^* = 0.15$$

Since $i_K^* = 0.20$ is greater than $i_L^* = 0.15$, it is thus argued that $K$ should be accepted and $L$ rejected.

Suppose also that the firm's capital availability is limited and that management has imposed a marginal investment rate of 10%. At a discount rate of 10%, the projects have net present values as follows:

$$\overset{(P/F,10\%,1)}{K: \quad P_K = -100 + 120(0.9091)} = +9.09$$

$$\overset{(P/F,10\%,5)}{L: \quad P_L = -100 + 201.14(0.6209)} = +24.89$$

Thus, if the firm maximizes net present value, it should accept $L$ and reject $K$. This decision, of course, is the direct opposite of that signaled by the IRR criterion; and hence, it is argued, the IRR method does not guarantee maximization of net present value (or its related measure, the future wealth of shareholders). This has serious implications for the project selection problem, for if the IRR criterion is chosen without qualification as the method of project selection, it is possible that the firm may not in fact attain its goal of maximization of shareholder wealth.

## 8.7. The Reinvestment Assumption Underlying the Net Present Value Criterion

The basic reason that the projects cannot be compared directly, without consideration of an external reinvestment rate, is that the cash inflows of the two projects ($K$ and $L$) do not occur *at the same point in time*. The fundamental question to be answered is, given a present investment of \$100, is it better from the firm's standpoint to receive \$120 at the end of 1 year (Project $K$) or \$201.14 at the end of 5 years (Project $L$)? This question cannot be answered in an economic sense until a *value* is placed on the *earlier* receipt of \$120. This value can be established *only* when the firm decides what it intends to *do* in the interim period with the earlier receipt of \$120, in comparison to the later receipt of \$201.14. Thus, the firm needs to consider its possible alternative uses of the \$120 *before* it can place a value on its earlier receipt. Once an alternative is specified for *using* the \$120 after it is received, the firm can then compare the desirability of receiving \$120 at the end of 1 year versus receiving \$201.14 at the end of 5 years.

The principle of opportunity costing requires that the firm utilize the \$120 cash inflow at $t = 1$ in its best alternative use. To illustrate this point, the firm has at least four alternative uses for the \$120 when it is received at $t = 1$: (1) It can pay \$120 in dividends to its shareholders immediately; (2) it can retain the $120 in cash or a noninterest-bearing bank account; (3) it can invest the $120 in interest-bearing securities[7] at a rate of interest less than the firm's marginal investment rate, say 8%; or (4) it can reinvest the $120 in another new candidate project at the firm's marginal investment rate of 10%. Obviously, alternatives 2 and 3 are inferior uses of the $120 compared to alternative 4 under conditions of certainty, since alternative 2 provides no return on the retention of the money and alternative 3 provides a return less than that provided by alternative 4. Furthermore, the imputed *cost* to the firm of alternative 1—paying out dividends—is the value of the best return opportunity foregone, that is, the foregone opportunity of retaining the $120 within the firm and utilizing it at 10% under alternative 4. The best alternative use of the $120 receipt, therefore, is reinvestment in another new project that will provide a rate of return of at least the marginal investment rate. This assumes, of course, that such a new project is available at time $t = 1$.

Another way of looking at the cost to the firm of paying out dividends is provided by considering the firm's cost of capital. For example, if the $120 were actually paid out to the shareholders and then simultaneously reobtained by the firm (through borrowing or new equity capital), the firm would thereby incur a *cost* of obtaining the new $120. One could logically assume, in the absence of specifying the mode of obtaining the money, that the new $120 would be obtained at a cost equal to the firm's cost of capital. In any event, the payment of dividends has an imputed cost associated with it, and if the firm's marginal cost of capital is assumed to be its marginal investment rate, then alternatives 1 and 4 are equivalent uses of the $120 receipt from Project $K$.

From this line of reasoning, the firm must consider reinvesting the $120 from Project $K$ at a rate of interest that is at least equal to the marginal investment rate, from time $t = 1$ to time $t = 5$, in order to compare the desirability of receiving $120 at $t = 1$ to the alternative of receiving $201.14 at $t = 5$. The reinvestment act places a *value* on the receipt of the earlier cash inflow and makes the comparison possible. When the act of investing $100 in Project $K$ is *combined* with the act of reinvesting the $120 inflow at a reinvestment rate of at least 10%, the effective return on invested capital for $K$ is

$$0 = -100 + 120 \overset{(F/P,10\%,4)}{(1.464)}(P/F, i^*, 5)_K;$$

$$\therefore \quad (P/F, i^*, 5)_K = 0.569 \Longrightarrow i_K^* = 0.1193.$$

Comparing $i_K^* = 0.1193$ to $i_L^* = 0.15$, we see that now $L$ is ranked ahead of $K$, which is the same ranking given by the NPV method.

Now, to demonstrate that an external reinvestment assumption is implicit in the NPV method when projects with *unequal lives* are compared, we give a generalized proof for two pure investments similar to the example. Consider two competing projects, $M$ and $N$, one of which is to be accepted and the other rejected. Let $M$ cost

---

[7]It is assumed that the risk class of the interest-bearing securities is equal to or lower than that of the investments that would be accepted at the firm's marginal investment rate.

$a_0$ dollars at $t = 0$, and let $N$ cost $a_0'$ dollars at $t = 0$. Let $M$ return $Y_m$ dollars at the end of $m$ years and $N$ return $Y_n$ dollars at the end of $n$ years, with the lives of $M$ and $N$ assumed to be $n > m$. Also, let $k =$ the firm's marginal investment rate and $j =$ the firm's available reinvestment rate, where now it is assumed initially that $j \neq k$.

For the net present value method, *with* reinvestment occurring for the shorter-lived project, the NPV's of $M$ and $N$ are

$$M: \quad P_M = \frac{Y_m(1 + j)^{n-m}}{(1 + k)^n} - a_0$$

or

$$P_M = \frac{Y_m(1 + j)^{n-m}}{(1 + k)^{n-m}(1 + k)^m} - a_0 = \frac{Y_m}{(1 + k)^m}\left(\frac{1 + j}{1 + k}\right)^{n-m} - a_0; \qquad (8.1)$$

and

$$N: \quad P_N = \frac{Y_n}{(1 + k)^n} - a_0'. \qquad (8.2)$$

Now, if the NPV's of $M$ and $N$ are stated *without* reinvestment being applied to the shorter-lived project cash flows, then we obtain the net present values as they are conventionally stated; thus, for

$$M: \quad P_M = \frac{Y_m}{(1 + k)^m} - a_0 \qquad (8.3)$$

and

$$N: \quad P_N = \frac{Y_n}{(1 + k)^n} - a_0'. \qquad (8.4)$$

It is obvious that Eq. (8.4) is exactly the same as Eq. (8.2), so that reinvestment is not a factor in the longer-lived project. The two equations for Project $M$, Eqs. (8.1) and (8.3), are not the same, however: They differ by the factor $[(1 + j)/(1 + k)]^{n-m}$ in Eq. (8.1). The *only* way in which Eq. (8.1) can be made equivalent to Eq. (8.2), with $(n, m > 0)$, is for

$$\left(\frac{1 + j}{1 + k}\right)^{n-m} \equiv 1,$$

which defines an implicit relationship between $j$ and $k$, namely, that $j \equiv k$. In other words, *when we compare the NPV's of two unequal-lived projects by the conventional definition of NPV* [Eqs. (8.3) and (8.4)], *we implicitly assume that the reinvestment rate, j, is applied to the cash flows of the shorter-lived project and that j is equal to the marginal investment rate, k, of the firm.*

It will now be demonstrated that if a *common* reinvestment rate is assumed for both the IRR and the NPV methods, then the ranking inconsistency is removed. For projects $L$ and $K$ in Example 8.6.1, we assume that the cash flows of Project $K$ are reinvested at the firm's *marginal investment rate* of $10\%$ at the ends of years 2,3,4, and 5. Then, from Eqs. (8.1) and (8.2) the net present values are

$$P_K = -100 + \frac{120}{(1.10)^1}\left(\frac{1.10}{1.10}\right)^4 = +9.09$$

$$P_L = -100 + \frac{201.14}{(1.10)^5} = +24.89,$$

which ranks the projects in the order $L, K$. Also, from Eqs. (8.1) and (8.2) we calculate the effective rates of return, $i^*$, with reinvestment at the rate $j = k = 0.10$, by setting NPV $= 0$, as follows:

$$K: \quad \frac{120}{(1 + i_K^*)}\left(\frac{1.10}{1 + i_K^*}\right)^4 - 100 = 0$$

or

$$(1 + i_K^*)^5 = 1.2(1.10)^4 = 1.758$$

from which

$$i_K^* = (1.758)^{0.2} - 1 = 0.119;$$

and for $L$:

$$\frac{201.14}{(1 + i_L^*)^5} - 100 = 0$$

$$(1 + i_L^*)^5 = 2.0114$$

from which

$$i_L^* = (2.0114)^{0.2} - 1 = 0.150,$$

which also rank the projects in the order $L, K$. Thus it is apparent that if a reinvestment rate *common* to both methods is assumed, then competing projects have identical rankings by both methods.

The conclusion that needs to be drawn from this example is that two *unequal-lived* projects are *strictly* noncomparable, unless it is specified how the investment from the shorter-lived project is to be managed during the *entire* period from its inception to the termination of the longer-lived competing project. For the shorter-lived project, management of the investment includes the initial cash outflow (the investment), the intervening returns and capital recovery (the cash inflows), *and* the reinvestment of the cash inflows. The principle of opportunity costing requires reinvestment at a rate at least equal to the firm's marginal investment rate.

The reinvestment problem is not limited in scope merely to competing projects that have unequal lives. As the following example demonstrates, reinvestment is a necessary consideration when two *equal-lived* projects are compared, *if their cash flow streams differ.*

**Example 8.7.1.** Consider two 5-year investments, $X$ and $Y$, with the following cash flow streams:

| EOP | NCF $(X)$ | NCF $(Y)$ |
|---|---|---|
| 0 | $\$-3{,}790$ | $\$-3{,}790$ |
| 1 | $+1{,}000$ | $+\ \ 200$ |
| 2 | $1{,}000$ | $600$ |
| 3 | $1{,}000$ | $600$ |
| 4 | $1{,}000$ | $1{,}000$ |
| 5 | $1{,}000$ | $2{,}800$ |

The internal rates of return are $i_X^* = 10\%$ and $i_Y^* = 8\%$. Thus, $X$ is a more desirable investment if the IRR criterion is to be believed. If the firm's marginal investment rate is $3\%$, however, then the net present values are $P_X = \$790$ and

$P_Y =$ \$823, and thus the NPV criterion ranks $Y$ as the more desirable investment. Although the projects have identical investments and identical lives, *they do not generate cash inflows at the same rate.* Again, the *timing* of the cash inflows creates the reinvestment problem. It is the necessity for placing a *value* on the earlier receipt of money versus later receipt that introduces the problem of how the excess funds are to be used in the interim periods, which is the essence of the reinvestment problem.

In conclusion, the reinvestment problem is present *whenever* two or more projects must be compared, with the objective being to select some and reject others. The question is *not* whether reinvestment is a consideration, but rather what are the specific reinvestment assumptions that are implicit in the several comparison criteria.

## 8.8. The Reinvestment Assumption Underlying the Internal Rate of Return Criterion: Fisher's Intersection

We have seen in Section 8.7 that if a common reinvestment rate is applied to both the IRR and the NPV methods, then these criteria rank competing projects in the same order. The reinvestment rate that is made common to both methods is the marginal investment rate since it is implicit already in the NPV criterion. We may now ask the question, is there perhaps some reinvestment rate higher than the marginal investment rate that would cause a reversal of the ranking? That is, is there some higher reinvestment rate (or rates) that would cause the IRR and NPV methods to rank projects in the *same* order without explicitly incorporating a reinvestment assumption? The answer is that there may be such a rate, provided that certain conditions exist. If this rate does exist, then we can say that the IRR criterion will correctly[8] rank the projects in order of merit.

To see this, we first graphically compare the NPV's of the two projects, $K$ and $L$ in Example 8.6.1, as a function of the marginal investment rate, $k$ (see Fig. 8.3). The bases for Fig. 8.3 are Eqs. (8.3) and (8.4). As the figure illustrates, the NPV method ranks Project $L$ more desirable than $K$ *if* the firm's marginal investment rate (and hence, its reinvestment rate) is less than 13.8%. If the firm's MIR or reinvestment rate is greater than 13.8%, however, then the NPV method ranks $K$ more desirable than $L$. This second ranking is the same as that yielded by the conventional IRR ranking method. Hence, the IRR and NPV methods are consistent in their rankings *if* there is a reinvestment rate at which the firm is *indifferent* between the two projects. The indifference point is labeled $A$ in Fig. 8.3, and is the reinvestment rate at which the net present values of the two projects are equal.

The indifference point is called *Fisher's Intersection* because its concept and method of determination is exactly equivalent to Irving Fisher's [7] *rate of return over*

---

[8]*Correctly,* in the sense that both the IRR and NPV criteria will rank the projects in the same order.

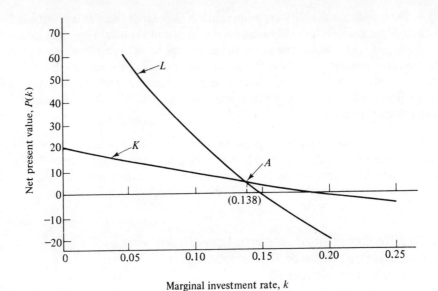

**Fig. 8.3.** Fisher's intersection for two projects.

*cost.* This can be demonstrated as follows: Suppose Project $P$ generates net cash flows of $Y_0, Y_1, \ldots, Y_n$ and Project $Q$ generates net cash flows of $Y_0', Y_1', \ldots, Y_n'$ at the ends of years $0, 1, \ldots, n$, respectively. Then the Fisherian rate of return over cost, $r_f$, is defined by

$$\sum_{t=0}^{n} \frac{Y_t - Y_t'}{(1 + r_f)^t} = 0 \tag{8.5}$$

(see [7], pp. 151–155).

Applying Eq. (8.5) to our example Projects $K$ and $L$, we have the following cash flows and determination of $r_f$:

| End of Year | Cash Flow for $L$ $(Y_t)$ | Cash Flow for $K$ $(Y_t')$ | $Y_t - Y_t'$ |
|:---:|:---:|:---:|:---:|
| 0 | −100 | −100 | 0 |
| 1 | — | +120 | −120 |
| 2 | — | — | — |
| 3 | — | — | — |
| 4 | — | — | — |
| 5 | 201.14 | — | +201.14 |

from which we set

$$-\frac{120}{(1 + r_f)} + \frac{201.14}{(1 + r_f)^5} = 0,$$

resulting in $r_f = 0.138$. This is exactly the reinvestment rate at which we saw that the firm was indifferent between $K$ and $L$ on the basis of net present value. This should be apparent from the Fisherian formulation also since $r_f$ is the rate that makes the incremental outflow ($Y_1 - Y_1' = -120$) exactly equivalent to the incremental inflow ($Y_5 - Y_5' = +201.14$), which is another way of saying that the firm is indifferent when marginal cost equals marginal revenue, that is, when they are made equivalent by $r_f$.

The conclusion is, therefore, that if the firm's marginal investment rate and, hence, its reinvestment rate is greater than the Fisherian intersection, then the IRR and NPV methods give consistent rankings. Another way of looking at the Fisherian intersection is to realize that *if two competing projects are compared by the IRR criterion, then the implicit assumption is that cash inflows the projects are reinvested at a reinvestment equal to or higher than the Fisherian rate*, since this is the region of the reinvestment rate (marginal investment rate) in which IRR and NPV give consistent rankings.

To summarize our findings in Sections 8.7 and 8.8, we may now say that

1. The comparison of two competing projects by the net present value criterion implicitly assumes reinvestment of the positive cash flows from the projects, for the period(s) between the time of their receipt and the end of life of the longer-lived project, *at the firm's marginal investment rate.*
2. The comparison of two such projects by the internal rate of return criterion implicitly assumes reinvestment of the cash flows *at a rate equal to or greater than the Fisherian rate of return over cost.*
3. If the firm's reinvestment rate is less than the Fisherian rate of return over cost, then the IRR and NPV methods will give inconsistent rankings, but the inconsistency can be removed by using a common reinvestment rate for both methods, namely, the firm's marginal investment rate.
4. The ranking inconsistency problem is traceable to the differing assumptions concerning reinvestment that are made by the two methods.

It should also be noted that the Fisherian rate of return over cost may or may not exist. That is, the net present values of two competing projects, $P_j(k)$, ($j = 1, 2$), as functions of the marginal investment rate, $k$, may not intersect (hence, Fisher's intersection would not exist), or they may intersect more than once. If they do not intersect, then the IRR and NPV criteria signal identical rankings regardless of the marginal investment (reinvestment) rate. If multiple intersections exist, the firm is indifferent between the projects at more than one reinvestment rate, and interpretation is difficult. Mao [12] has investigated the problem of the existence of Fisher's intersection extensively, and the reader is referred to his investigative report for the details since they lie beyond the scope of this chapter.

## 8.9. The Reinvestment Assumption Underlying the Benefit-Cost Criterion

In Section 7.7 two forms of the *benefit-cost* criterion were defined. One is the *raw*, or *aggregate*, form, which Bernhard calls simply the *benefit-cost criterion* and which is defined by Eq. (7.13), repeated here:

$$B/C = \frac{P_j + C_j}{C_j} = \frac{P_j}{C_j} + 1, \tag{7.13}$$

where $B/C$ = the benefit-cost ratio.

$P_j$ = *net* present value of the entire cash flow stream at time $t = 0$.

$C_j$ = present cost $(t = 0)$.

The other criterion is called the *net benefit-cost* ratio since it employs the *net* present value, $P_j$, in the numerator:

$$NB/C = \frac{P_j}{C_j}, \tag{7.14}$$

where $NB/C$ = the net benefit-cost ratio.

For our present purposes we need to modify these definitions slightly, but in doing so we shall continue to restrict ourselves to the *pure investment* case. The modification is, however, that we shall now consider several cash outflows to occur in the first $\tau$ periods ($\tau = 0, 1, \ldots, m$) instead of just the first period, and net cash inflows in the successive periods, so that we may define the present value of the cash outflows (investments) as a present *cost*, thus:

$$P(C) = \sum_{\tau=0}^{m} Y_\tau (1 + i)^{-\tau} \quad (Y_0 < 0;\ Y_\tau \leq 0 \text{ for } \tau = 1, 2, \ldots, m)$$

and the present value of the net cash inflows as a present *benefit*, thus:

$$P(B) = \sum_{\theta=m+1}^{n} Y_\theta (1 + i)^{-\theta} \quad (Y_\theta \geq 0 \text{ for } \theta = m + 1, \ldots, n - 1;\ Y_n > 0).$$

Then the benefit-cost ratio, $R_N$ (since it uses only *benefits* in the numerator), may now be defined as

$$R_N = \frac{P(B)}{|P(C)|}, \tag{8.6}$$

which is the form we shall now be concerned with. Note that if $R_N > 1$, the project is accepted; if $R_N < 1$, it is rejected; and if $R_N = 1$ the firm is indifferent. These are the rules developed in Section 7.7.

The $B/C$ criterion, $R_N$, which purports to measure the present worth of cash inflows per present-worth dollar of investment, was the one used in Example 8.5.1. There, the rankings were inconsistent between the NPV and $B/C = R_N$ criteria. To discover why this inconsistency exists we need to probe the implicit reinvestment assumption of the $R_N$ criterion. To pursue this objective we follow generally the development given by Schwab and Lusztig [13], except in the final stages where reinvestment rates are postulated. To motivate the development, we may restate project benefits, $P(B)$, as a function of *net* present value, thus:

$$P(B) = P + |P(C)| \qquad [P(C) < 0], \tag{8.7}$$

where $P$ is the net present value of the project cash flow stream. Similarly, from Eq. (8.6), the project benefits are

$$P(B) = R_N |P(C)| \qquad [P(C) < 0]. \tag{8.8}$$

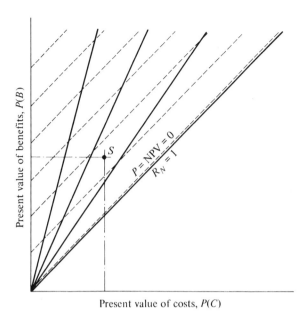

**Fig. 8.4.** Project benefits as a function of project costs.

Equations (8.7) and (8.8) are straight-line functions on $P(B)$, $P(C)$ coordinates, as in Fig. 8.4.

In Fig. 8.4, the present value of project benefits, $P(B)$, at *constant* values of net present value, $P$, are determined from Eq. (8.7) with $P = $ constant, and the family of functions thus determined is represented by dashed lines. Note that as $P$ increases, the function $P(B)$ moves parallel to the $P = 0$ line. With the $R_N$ criterion, however, the present value of project benefits, $P(B)$, is a multiplicative function of $P(C)$, which follows from Eq. (8.8). With the $R_N$ criterion, the decision is that if $R_N > 1$ [thus, $P(B) > P(C)$], then the project should be undertaken. The $R_N$ criterion, therefore, is represented by a family of solid lines radiating from the origin. It should also be noted that for $R_N = 1$, then $P(B) = |P(C)|$ and $P = P(B) - |P(C)| = 0$; hence, the functions $P = 0$ and $R_N = 1$ coincide and have tangents $P(B)/P(C) = R_N = 1$ (they are sloped 45°).

It is clear that any pure investment project with a present-valued benefit, $P(B)$, and a present-valued investment, $P(C)$, can be represented by a point, such as $S$, in Fig. 8.4, and that this point lies on the intersection of two functions, one giving its net present value and the other its net benefit-cost ratio.

The net present value function and the benefit-cost function that pass through a given project [$S$: $P(B)$, $P(C)$] divide the feasible area of comparison for other projects into four sectors, as illustrated in Fig. 8.5 and labeled I through IV. Projects in Sector I (e.g., Project $T$) are preferred to $S$ according to both criteria. Projects in Sector III (e.g., Project $U$) are not preferred to $S$ because both $P_U < P_S$ and $(R_N)_U < (R_N)_S$. Projects such as $V$ in Sector II are preferred to $S$ by the net present value criterion,

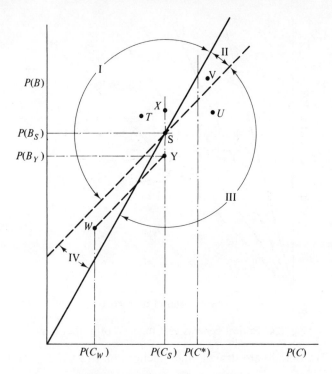

**Fig. 8.5.** Comparison of projects.

however, while $S$ is preferred according to the $R_N$ criterion. Also, projects such as $W$ in IV are preferred to $S$ according to the $R_N$ criterion, while $S$ is preferred over these projects by the net present value criterion. The ranking inconsistency, therefore, occurs in Sectors II and IV.

Under capital rationing, the projects selected by an investor would be constrained by an upper limit on $P(C)$, such as $P(C^*)$ in Fig. 8.5. With the simplest nontrivial candidate set of projects in the inconsistent area, say $S$ and $W$, the capital rationing constraint, $P(C^*)$, in Fig. 8.5 operates to constrain $P(C_S) + P(C_W) \leq P(C^*)$. We now assume that $P(C_S) + P(C_W) > P(C^*)$, so that only $S$ or $W$ can be selected. This assumption sets up the necessary situation for our analysis, namely, that the two criteria give differing rankings and both projects cannot be selected.

The set of feasible investment alternatives for such an investor is given by all investments on the constraint, $P(C^*)$. For the simple case in which we have assumed that only two projects, $S$ and $W$, comprise the candidate set of projects, then it is equivalent to say that $P(C^*) = P(C_S)$, effectively. That is, for this simple two-project case we need not consider a budget constraint greater than the present-valued cost of the costlier project, $S$.

It should be obvious from the geometry of Fig. 8.5 that if other projects, such as $X$ and $Y$, were also available with present-valued costs equal to $S$, then $X$ would be preferred to $S$, and $S$ would be preferred to $Y$, by *both* criteria (since $X$ and $Y$ lie in Sectors I and III, respectively). In effect, both criteria establish the same preference ordering for all projects lying on a vertical cost line through a given project since for identical input, $P(C)$, the system with the higher (lower) ratio productivity, $R_N$, is also the system with the higher (lower) level of difference output (net present value), $P$.

Now, the firm is to choose between Projects $S$ and $W$. Project $W$ requires a lower present-valued capital expenditure than $S$, and if we wish to make a valid comparison, then we have to decide how the firm would use the difference in investment capital, $P(C_S) - P(C_W)$, which would be available if $W$ were chosen. That is, in order to make a *valid* comparison of $W$ with $S$ we shall have to consider an investment *portfolio* containing $W$ and some other investment(s) funded with the difference in available capital, $P(C_S) - P(C_W)$. This investment porfolio will then yield a point on the vertical line, $P(C_S)$, which, as we have seen, will be preferred (or not preferred) to $S$ depending on whether this point lies above or below $S$ on this line. From this line of reasoning, $W$ will be preferred to $S$, or vice versa, *depending on the use which can be made of the funds freed by choosing* W.

We are now back in the reinvestment wicket. The minimum *best alternative use* of otherwise idle capital funds is for the firm to reinvest these funds at the marginal investment rate, as we have previously deduced in the introductory paragraphs of Section 8.7. If this is done, then the *portfolio* mentioned above, for example, would consist of Project $W$ plus reinvestment of released funds at the marginal investment rate. In such a case, the portfolio consisting of $W$ plus reinvestment of available cash flows would produce a *portfolio* benefit, such as $P(B_Y)$ in Fig. 8.5. Whether $Y$ lies above $S$, below $S$, or at $S$, that is, whether $P(B_Y) \gtreqless P(B_S)$, depends on the reinvestment rate. If the reinvestment rate is the marginal investment rate, then the portfolio benefit $P(B_Y)$ is less than $P(B_S)$ for all projects in Sector IV since investment of idle funds at the marginal investment rate does not alter the *net* present value of the portfolio but *does* alter the benefit-cost ratio. This can be illustrated by a numerical example.

**Example 8.9.1.** Consider two projects, $S$ and $W$, whose cash flows and other characteristics are given in Table 8.2. The firm's marginal investment rate is assumed to be 15%. Note that the $R_N$ and NPV criteria give opposite rankings.

**Table 8.2.** CHARACTERISTICS OF TWO COMPETING PROJECTS

| *Characteristic* | *Project S* | *Project W* |
|---|---|---|
| Cash flows at $t = 0$ | $-100. | $-40. |
| 1 | — | +92. |
| 2 | — | — |
| 3 | — | — |
| 4 | — | — |
| 5 | +321.76 | — |
| $P(B) =$ | $+160. | $+80. |
| $P(C) =$ | -100. | -40. |
| $P = P(B) - \|P(C)\|$ | +60. | +40. |
| $R_N = P(B)/\|P(C)\|$ | 1.60 | 2.00 |

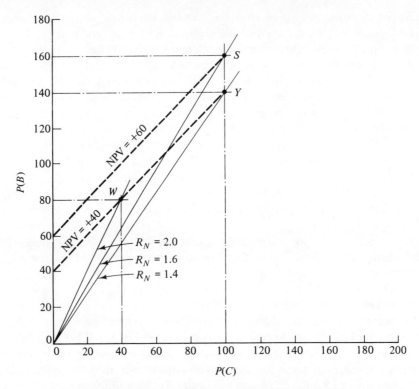

**Fig. 8.6.** Graphical illustration of Projects $S$ and $W$.

The two projects are represented in Fig. 8.6 on $P(B)$, $P(C)$ coordinates by their present values. of benefits, $P(B)$, and investments, $P(C)$. Note that the net present value function, $P = \$60$, passes through $S$ and that $P = \$40$ passes through $W$. Note also that the benefit-cost ratio, $R_N = 1.60$, passes through $S$, while $R_N = 2.00$ passes through $W$.

Now, if project $W$ is accepted, there will be at time $t = 0$ an excess of $\$100 - (\$40) = \$60$ available for reinvestment. Also, at time $t = 1$ an additional $\$92$ is made available for investment since $W$ pays back its original investment plus return at that time. If these two cash availabilities are reinvested at the firm's marginal investment rate, then the *net* present value of the portfolio, consisting of $W$ plus reinvestment, is

$$P_Y = [60(\underbrace{2.011}_{\substack{(F/P,15\%,5)}}) + 92(\underbrace{1.749}_{\substack{(F/P,15\%,4)}})](\underbrace{0.4972}_{\substack{(P/F,15\%,5)}}) - 100 = 140 - 100 = \$+40.$$

$\underbrace{\phantom{60(2.011)}}_{\substack{\text{Future value}\\\text{of excess}\\\text{funds reinvested}}}$    $\underbrace{\phantom{92(1.749)}}_{\substack{\text{Future value}\\\text{of Project } W\\\text{cash inflow}\\\text{reinvested}}}$

$\underbrace{\phantom{60(2.011)+92(1.749)}}_{\substack{\text{Present value of cash}\\\text{inflows from } (W + \text{excess}\\\text{funds reinvested})}}$      $\underset{\substack{\text{Present value,}\\P(C_Y), \text{ of}\\\text{portfolio investment}\\\text{(cash outflow)}}}{\downarrow}$

Thus, the net present value of the portfolio ($P_Y = \$40$) is *not* changed by reinvestment at the MIR from that of Project $W$ alone ($P_W = \$40$; see Table 8.2). However, the benefit-cost ratio, $R_N$, of the portfolio *is* changed. Thus,

$$(R_N)_Y = \frac{P(B_Y)}{|P(C_Y)|} = \frac{\$140}{\$100} = 1.40.$$

Note that the effect of reinvestment of excess funds *at the marginal investment rate* is to shift point $Y$ along the *same* net present value line as $W$ but to a *lower* value of $R_N$. Note particularly that the two criteria now rank Project $S$ and the portfolio of $W$ plus reinvestment in the *same* preference order:

|  | $S$ | $W$ + Reinvestment |
|---|---|---|
| Net Present Value: | \$+60 | \$+40 |
| Benefit-Cost, $R_N$: | 1.60 | 1.40 |

Hence, the ranking inconsistency displayed by the NPV and $B/C$ criteria can be removed by assuming reinvestment of idle funds at the firm's marginal investment rate. This is the rate that is implicitly assumed in the NPV case (see Section 8.7), and we are thus justified in stating that if a reinvestment rate *common to both methods* (the MIR) is applied to the $B/C$ criterion, then the ranking inconsistency is removed. The ranking inconsistency problem, then, is caused by the *failure* of the $B/C$ criterion to assume reinvestment at the firm's MIR.

The question then is, if the $B/C$ criterion fails to assume reinvestment at the firm's MIR, does it in fact assume reinvestment at all, and if so, at what rate? This question can be answered by an analysis of the incremental cash flow stream between $W$ and $S$. The incremental cash flows of $S$–$W$ are as follows:

| $t =$ | $S$ | $W$ | $S$–$W$ |
|---|---|---|---|
| 0 | \$$-$100 | \$$-$40 | \$ $-$60 |
| 1 | — | $+92$ | $-92$ |
| 2 | — | — | — |
| 3 | — | — | — |
| 4 | — | — | — |
| 5 | $+321.76$ | — | $+321.76$ |

The *incremental* interest rate that makes the cash flows of $S$–$W$ equivalent is the reinvestment interest rate at which the firm becomes indifferent between $S$ and $W$, that is, the rate at which $P_W = P_S$, which is found thus:

$$0 = -60 - 92(1 + i^*)^{-1} + 321.76(1 + i^*)^{-5},$$

which upon solving for $i^*$ gives $i^* = 18.5\%$. This is the same format as that given earlier for Fisher's intersection (marginal rate of return over cost). Thus, if the firm's marginal investment rate were greater than 18.5% instead of 15% in this example, the $B/C$ and NPV criteria would signal the same ranking. Hence, when the net $B/C$ criterion is used to rank projects, *the implicit assumption* *underlying the ranking is that reinvestment is assumed at a rate greater than the Fisherian rate of return over cost.*

It is also possible for the $B/C$ criterion to rank projects *wrongly* even when there is no time value of money involved.[9] Consider two projects $Q$ and $R$, whose cash flows occur *instantly*, i.e., at time $t = 0$:

| Project, $j$ | Benefit, $B_j$ | Cost, $C_j$ | $NPV = B_j - C_j$ | $B_j/C_j$ |
|---|---|---|---|---|
| $Q$ | 70 | 50 | 20 | 1.40 |
| $R$ | 83 | 60 | 23 | 1.38 |

Here, the NPV criterion indicates Project $R$ should be accepted, whereas the $B/C$ ratio indicates Project $Q$. What is the reason? It is because the $B/C$ ratio, which is a measure of benefits *per dollar expended*, does not guarantee an increase in the *wealth* of the firm, whereas net present value does. It is not so important to the firm what the *rate* of benefit acquisition per dollar expended is as it is what the *net* benefit acquisition, *in total*, is, i.e., net present value.

In general, then, accepting or rejecting projects by the $B/C$ criterion is neither desirable nor correct, under conditions of certainty and a perfect capital market, since this criterion does not guarantee an increase in the *wealth* of the shareholders.

## 8.10. Marginal Rate of Return on Marginal Investment

Making decisions that are consistent with the economic principle of equating marginal benefits to marginal costs will usually result in an optimal, or near optimal, choice of investment alternatives. This was the principle invoked in Section 8.3 when capital rationing was discussed, and the application of the principle was illustrated in Fig. 8.2. As it is applied to the project selection problem, the marginal principle requires that projects be accepted *at the investment margin* until the last project included in the accepted set provides a marginal (incremental) rate of return just equal to the firm's marginal investment rate. Under perfect capital market conditions, the firm's marginal investment rate is also its marginal cost of capital. The words accepted *at the investment margin* mean *with the next increment of added investment*. This method is often called the *incremental rate-of-return method*. The incremental method is applicable when we are deciding which of several *mutually exclusive alternatives* should be accepted. The incremental method can best be presented by an example.

**Example 8.10.1.** Five mutually exclusive alternative designs for a building, $A,B,C,D$, and $E$, are to be compared, and the one having the greatest incremental

---

[9]I am indebted to Richard H. Bernhard, who pointed out this possibility to me.

rate of return in excess of the firm's assumed marginal cost of capital of 15% is to be accepted. The characteristics of the designs are as follows:

| Design | A | B | C | D | E |
|---|---|---|---|---|---|
| Total investment ($t = 0$) | $335,000 | $500,000 | $725,000 | $885,000 | $940,000 |
| Annual after-tax net cash inflow per year | 50,000 | 110,000 | 149,000 | 170,000 | 184,000 |
| Life | 15 yr | 15 yr | 15 yr | 15 yr | 15 yr |
| Salvage value | 0 | 0 | 0 | 0 | 0 |

The solution for the incremental rates of return proceeds stepwise, as follows.

*Step 1:* Calculate the internal rate of return for each alternative and eliminate from further consideration any alternative having an IRR less than the marginal cost of capital. Thus:

A: $(P/A, i_A^*, 15) = 335,000/50,000 = 6.700$
$\therefore \quad i_A^* = 12.4\%$
(Since $i_A^* = 12.4\%$ is less than $i_{cc} = 15\%$, alternative A is eliminated from further consideration—if accepted, it would not return the firm's desired marginal cost of capital rate.)

B: $(P/A, i_B^*, 15) = 500,000/110,000 = 4.455$
$\therefore \quad i_B^* = 22.3\%$
(Conditionally accept B into the candidate set.)

C: $(P/A, i_C^*, 15) = 725,000/149,000 = 4,866 \Rightarrow i_C^* = 19.05\%$
(Conditionally accept C into the candidate set.)

D: $(P/A, i_D^*, 15) = 885,000/170,000 = 5.206 \Rightarrow i_D^* = 17.50\%$
(Conditionally accept D into the candidate set.)

E: $(P/A, i_E^*, 15) = 940,000/184,000 = 5.109$
$i_E^* = 17.92\%$
(Conditionally accept E into the candidate set.)

*Step 2:* Arrange the conditionally accepted projects in order of ascending investment and, beginning with the lowest investment, calculate the incremental rate of return on each *added* increment of investment. If the *incremental* rate of return for a competing project is greater than the firm's marginal cost of capital, conditionally retain the competing project as the current most desirable one; otherwise, reject it, and proceed stepwise to the next larger increment of investment.

Arranging the conditionally accepted projects in order of ascending investment we have

| Design | Total Investment | Cash Inflow per Year |
|---|---|---|
| B | $500,000 | $110,000 |
| C | 725,000 | 149,000 |
| D | 885,000 | 170,000 |
| E | 940,000 | 184,000 |

To calculate the first incremental rate of return, we look at the first increment of added investment, $\$725,000 - \$500,000 = \$225,000$, which is required if $C$ is accepted over $B$. Associated with this investment increment is an increase in net cash inflow per year, $\$149,000 - \$110,000 = \$39,000$, if $C$ is accepted over $B$. The incremental rate of return is then found by identifying some $i^*_{C-B}$, such that the incremental cash inflow is equivalent to the incremental investment; thus:

$$(P/A, i^*_{C-B}, 15) = \frac{725,000 - 500,000}{149,000 - 110,000} = 5.769$$

$$i^*_{C-B} = 15.28\%$$

Since the incremental rate of return, $i^*_{C-B} = 15.2\%$, is greater than the firm's marginal cost of capital rate, $i_{CC} = 15\%$, the added increment of investment is justified, and we tentatively accept Project $C$ as being more desirable than $B$.

*Step 3:* Recursively calculate incremental rates of return for each successive project, basing the increments of investment and cash inflows on the last conditionally accepted most desirable alternative.

To calculate the next incremental rate of return, we now compare Project $D$ with Project $C$ (the last conditionally accepted most desirable alternative). Thus:

$$(P/A, i^*_{D-C}, 15) = \frac{885,000 - 725,000}{170,000 - 149,000} = 7.619$$

$$\therefore \quad i^*_{D-C} = 9.97\%.$$

Since $i^*_{D-C} = 10\%$ is less than $i_{CC} = 15\%$, the increment of investment between $C$ and $D$ is not justified by the added cash inflow. For this reason, Project $D$ is eliminated, leaving $C$ as the last conditionally accepted most desirable alternative.

We now compare Project $E$ with Project $C$, the last conditionally accepted most desirable alternative, to determine if the added investment between $C$ and $E$ can be justified. Thus:

$$(P/A, i^*_{E-C}, 15) = \frac{940,000 - 725,000}{184,000 - 149,000} = 6.143$$

$$\therefore \quad i^*_{E-C} = 14.00\%$$

Since $i^*_{E-C} = 14\%$ is less than $i_{CC} = 15\%$, the increment of investment between $C$ and $E$ is not justified, which eliminates $E$ as a less desirable alternative. The final decision, therefore, is to choose $C$ as the most desirable of the mutually exclusive alternatives since it supplies the opportunity for investing the last increment at a marginal rate of return greater than the firm's marginal cost of capital.

It should be noted that the *same* decision can be reached by choosing the alternative with the greatest *net present value*. To demonstrate this, calculate the net present values for the design alternatives:

$$P_j = Y_{0j} + A_j(P/A, i_{CC}, 15) \quad (j = A, B, C, D, E),$$

which is done in tabular form, as follows:

| Design, $j$ | $Y_{0j}$ | $A_j$ | $(P/A,15\%,15)$ $A_j(\quad 5.847\quad)$ | $P_j$ |
|---|---|---|---|---|
| A | −335,000 | 50,000 | 292,000 | −43,000 |
| B | −500,000 | 110,000 | 642,000 | +142,000 |
| C | −725,000 | 149,000 | 870,000 | +145,000 ⟵ Max. |
| D | −885,000 | 170,000 | 994,000 | +109,000 |
| E | −940,000 | 184,000 | 1,075,000 | +135,000 |

The alternative having the maximum net present value is Design $C$, for which $P_C = +145,000$. In this instance, ranking by NPV provides the same result as ranking by the incremental rate of return method. (The same result also would have been reached if we had calculated *incremental* benefit-cost ratios instead of incremental rates of return.) The incremental method, while being theoretically correct from an economic standpoint, *fails in general*, however, if the *incremental* cash flow stream between two mutually exclusive projects provides *no answer* or a *multiple answer* to the incremental rate of return problem, as demonstrated in Section 7.9.1. Hence, as Bernhard [2] points out, to avoid the *no answer* and *multiple answer* phenomena, as well as to simplify the computations, it is probably more desirable to use the NPV procedure directly even though the incremental procedure is widely recommended.

**8.10.1. *Incremental rate of return applied to the constrained project selection problem.*** The principle of marginality can be extended to certain *constrained* project selection problems, even when some of the projects themselves are not mutually exclusive. A method of handling dependencies among projects by integer programming procedures was proposed by Weingartner ([16], pp. 11–12, 32–33). The "hand" version of doing this, devised by Fleischer [8], will be described here. All that needs to be done with *dependent* projects, Fleischer proposes, is to group the projects into *financially* (economically) *mutually exclusive bundles* and then calculate incremental rates of return on the increments of investment between bundles. The bundle providing the last *incremental* rate of return greater than the firm's cost of capital will be the optimal bundle, and it will contain the optimal subset of projects. Fleischer's application of the marginality principle to the project selection problem will be illustrated by example.

**Example 8.10.2.** Consider three projects, $F$, $G$, and $H$, with investments, cash inflows, and lives as follows:

| Project | Investment ($t = 0$) | Net Cash Inflows per Year | Life, Years |
|---|---|---|---|
| F | $−12,000 | $+4,281 | 5 |
| G | −10,000 | +4,184 | 5 |
| H | −17,000 | +5,802 | 10 |

The firm's marginal investment rate is assumed to be 15%, and initially we shall consider the three projects to be economically independent of each other. The problem to be solved is, what projects should be selected if successively smaller budget ceilings are imposed, so that all three projects cannot be selected? The solution proceeds stepwise, following the same procedure outlined in Example 8.10.1.

*Step 1:* Identify the investments and cash inflows for all feasible combinations of the projects, where each combination is an economically mutually exclusive bundle.

To execute this step, we consider all possible combinations[10] of Projects *F*, *G*, and *H*, namely, by taking the projects one at a time, two at a time, and so forth:

| Bundle No. | Component Projects | Investment of Bundle | Cash Inflow of Bundle |
|---|---|---|---|
| 1 | *F* | −12,000 | +4,281 for years 1–5 |
| 2 | *G* | −10,000 | +4,184 for years 1–5 |
| 3 | *H* | −17,000 | +5,802 for years 1–10 |
| 4 | *F, G* | −22,000 | +8,465 for years 1–5 |
| 5 | *F, H* | −29,000 | $\begin{cases} +10,083 \text{ for years } 1\text{–}5 \\ +\ 5,802 \text{ for years } 6\text{–}10 \end{cases}$ |
| 6 | *G, H* | −27,000 | $\begin{cases} +\ 9,986 \text{ for years } 1\text{–}5 \\ +\ 5,802 \text{ for years } 6\text{–}10 \end{cases}$ |
| 7 | *F, G, H* | −39,000 | $\begin{cases} +14,267 \text{ for years } 1\text{–}5 \\ +\ 5,802 \text{ for years } 6\text{–}10 \end{cases}$ |

*Step 2:* Arrange the economically mutually exclusive bundles in order of ascending investment:

---

[10]For a candidate set of *m* projects, the total number of combinations, *M*, taken *r* at a time, where $r = 0, 1, 2, \ldots, m$, is

$$M = \sum_{r=0}^{m} \binom{m}{r} = \frac{m!}{0!\,m!} + \frac{m!}{1!\,(m-1)!} + \cdots + \frac{m!}{m!\,0!}$$

$$= \binom{m}{0} + \binom{m}{1} + \binom{m}{2} + \cdots + \binom{m}{m}.$$

The binomial theorem may be stated as

$$(a + x)^m = \binom{m}{0}a^m + \binom{m}{1}a^{m-1}x + \binom{m}{2}a^{m-2}x^2 + \cdots + \binom{m}{m}x^m$$

and by choosing $a = 1$ and $x = 1$ we have

$$(1 + 1)^m = \binom{m}{0}(1) + \binom{m}{1}(1)(1) + \binom{m}{2}(1)(1) + \cdots + \binom{m}{m}(1)$$

or

$$2^m = \binom{m}{0} + \binom{m}{1} + \binom{m}{2} + \cdots + \binom{m}{m}.$$

Hence, the number of combinations of *m* projects is $M = 2^m$, and excluding the alternative $\binom{m}{0} =$ "do nothing," the number of candidate project bundles is $M' = 2^m - 1$. Note that for even a "small" number of projects, say $m = 30$, the number of possible combinations (bundles) becomes *very* large (i.e., $M = 2^{30} = 1,073,741,824$)!

| Bundle No. | Component Projects | Investment of Bundle | Cash Inflow of Bundle |
|:---:|:---:|:---:|:---|
| 2 | G | −10,000 | +4,184 for years 1–5 |
| 1 | F | −12,000 | +4,281 for years 1–5 |
| 3 | H | −17,000 | +5,802 for years 1–10 |
| 4 | F, G | −22,000 | +8,465 for years 1–5 |
| 6 | G, H | −27,000 | $\begin{cases} +9,986 \text{ for years 1–5} \\ +5,802 \text{ for years 6–10} \end{cases}$ |
| 5 | F, H | −29,000 | $\begin{cases} +10,083 \text{ for years 1–5} \\ + 5,802 \text{ for years 6–10} \end{cases}$ |
| 7 | F, G, H | −39,000 | $\begin{cases} +14,267 \text{ for years 1–5} \\ + 5,802 \text{ for years 6–10} \end{cases}$ |

*Step 3:* Calculate the incremental rates of return on each increment of investment, from bundle to bundle. Eliminate from further consideration
any bundle that does not justify the added investment by providing
an incremental rate of return at least equal to the firm's marginal
investment rate. Conditionally accept the bundle that provides an
incremental rate of return, *on the last added increment of investment*,
that is greater than the firm's marginal investment rate. Make comparisons among bundles by comparing successive bundles with the
bundle that last conditionally justified the largest investment of funds.

As an example of this step, we first compare bundle 1 to bundle 2 to see if the
added investment, $-12,000 - (-10,000) = -2,000$, is justified. Hence, comparing 1 to 2 results in

$$(P/A, i^*_{1-2}, 5) = \frac{12,000 - 10,000}{4,281 - 4,184} = 20.6$$

$$\therefore \quad i^*_{1-2} = -34.06\% \quad \text{(This incremental } R/R \text{ is negative because the investment increment of \$2,000 is never recovered by five cash flows of \$97 each.)}$$

Since $i^*_{1-2}$ is less than $i_{\text{MIR}} = 15\%$, bundle 1 is eliminated as a basis for further
incremental comparisons. (*Note*: Instead of calculating the unknown incremental
rate of return for each bundle comparison, the same decision result can be reached
by calculating the *incremental* net present value for the comparison. Thus, in
comparing the added investment of bundle 1 to bundle 2, we could have calculated the incremental present value, $\Delta P$, using the *known* marginal investment
rate; thus:

$$\Delta P_{1-2} = -2000 + 97(\overset{(P/A,15\%,5)}{3.352}) = -1,675.$$

Recalling that for *pure* investments $P(i)$ is a monotonically decreasing function
of $i$, then a negative $\Delta P$ (e.g., $\Delta P_{1-2} = -1675$) signals that the incremental rate
of return (i.e., at $P(i^*_\Delta) = 0$) is *less than* $i_{\text{MIR}} = 15\%$. Conversely, a positive $\Delta P$
signals a $i^*_\Delta > i_{\text{MIR}}$. Since all we need to know is whether or not a particular
bundle provides an incremental rate of return greater than (or less than) the firm's

$i_{MIR} = 15\%$, we need not actually calculate $i_\Delta^*$ but can infer it much easier from the *sign* of $\Delta P$. This decision method will be used in the remainder of the example.)

To proceed, we continue with Step 3. Since bundle 1 has been eliminated as a basis for further comparison, we next compare the bundle having the next larger investment (3) with bundle 2:

$$P_3 = -17,000 + 5,802( \overset{(P/A,15\%,10)}{5.0188} ) = +12,120.$$

$$P_2 = -10,000 + 4,184( \overset{(P/A,15\%,5)}{3.3522} ) = \quad 4,025.$$

$$\Delta P_{3-2} = \qquad\qquad\qquad\qquad\qquad +8,095. \Rightarrow i_{3-2}^* > i_{MIR}.$$

Since $i_{3-2}^* > i_{MIR} = 15\%$, the added investment is justified, and we accept bundle 3 as being more desirable than bundle 2. The basis for the comparison of the next increment of investment is, therefore, bundle 3.

Continuing in the same manner, we ultimately obtain the following results:

| Bundle Number | Component Projects | Investment in Bundle | Incremental $\Delta(NPV)$ | Decision — Incremental $i_\Delta^*$ | Action |
|---|---|---|---|---|---|
| 0 | None | -0- | — | — | — |
| 2 | G | −10,000 | $4,025 | $i_{2-0}^* = 31.0\%$ | Accept |
| 1 | F | −12,000 | −1,675 | $i_{1-2}^* < 15\%$ | Reject |
| 3 | H | −17,000 | +8,095 | $i_{3-2}^* > 15\%$ | Accept |
| 4 | F, G | −22,000 | −5,745 | $i_{4-3}^* < 15\%$ | Reject |
| 6 | G, H | −27,000 | +4,025 | $i_{6-3}^* > 15\%$ | Accept |
| 5 | F, H | −29,000 | − 675 | $i_{5-6}^* < 15\%$ | Reject |
| 7 | F, G, H | −39,000 | +2,350 | $i_{7-6}^* > 15\%$ | Accept |

We may now determine which project bundles to accept at differing investment budget levels. For example, if the available budget is less than $10,000, no bundle will be accepted. If the budget is at least $10,000 and less than $17,000, then bundle 2 is preferred. In a similar manner, the decision rules are

| For Investment Budget (B) in the Range | Select Bundle | Component Projects |
|---|---|---|
| $B < \$10,000$ | 0 | (None) |
| $\$10,000 \leq B < \$17,000$ | 2 | G |
| $\$17,000 < B < \$27,000$ | 3 | H |
| $\$27,000 \leq B < \$39,000$ | 6 | G, H |
| $B \geq \$39,000$ | 7 | F, G, H |

Again, the same decision results can be obtained directly by choosing the bundle having the maximum net present value among competing bundles. To show this, rank the projects again by bundles in order of increasing total investment, along with the net present values of the bundles:

| Bundle Number | Component Projects | Total Investment | Net Present Value of Bundle |
|---|---|---|---|
| 2 | G | −10,000 | +4,025 |
| 1 | F | −12,000 | 2,350 |
| 3 | H | −17,000 | 12,120 |
| 4 | F, G | −22,000 | 6,375 |
| 6 | G, H | −27,000 | 16,145 |
| 5 | F, H | −29,000 | 14,470 |
| 7 | F, G, H | −39,000 | 18,495 |

The following decision table is obtained by applying the same budget ranges as in the incremental method, and maximizing NPV within the budget:

| Budget Range | Decision Method | Decision |
|---|---|---|
| $B < \$10,000$ | — | Reject all |
| $\$10,000 \le B < \$17,000$ | MAX $(P_2, P_1)$ | Accept 2 $(G)$ |
| $\$17,000 \le B < \$27,000$ | MAX $(P_2, P_1, P_3, P_4)$ | Accept 3 $(H)$ |
| $\$27,000 \le B < \$39,000$ | MAX $(P_2, P_1, P_3, P_4, P_6, P_5)$ | Accept 6 $(G, H)$ |
| $B \ge \$39,000$ | MAX [all $P_j$] | Accept 7 $(F, G, H)$ |

Thus, it is seen here, in this example, that maximization of the net present value of economically mutually exclusive sets(bundles) of projects signals the *same* decisions as does the theoretically correct *marginal* rate of return method. Note, however, that Fleischer's method of defining mutually exclusive bundles, and determining incremental rates of return among bundles ranked by increasing investment, breaks down in the *general* case for two reasons, as demonstrated by Bernhard [2]. First, it is possible that the *incremental* cash flow stream between two projects may default to the *no answer* or *multiple answer* cases when a solution for incremental rate of return is attempted. Second, if some of the projects have expenditures at times other than $t = 0$, it is not possible to order the projects by *increasing investment*, as the incremental method requires. The consequence is again that the required incremental rate of return cannot be procured.

An important conclusion, however, is that under certain conditions (i.e., pure investments and single expenditures at time $t = 0$ for all projects), project selection by the net present value criterion *chooses the same projects* as the marginal rate of return method does, in which the assumption is that marginal rate of return equals marginal cost. This is an important economic consequence.

**8.10.2. Inclusion of constraints.** The effect of constraints, both budgetary and physical, is to reduce the size of the feasible set of projects. After the feasibility constraints are applied, the optimization criterion is applied to the remaining feasible set of projects in the same manner that we used above. The application of constraints can best be illustrated by example at this point in the development, so we proceed again with Example 8.10.2.

**Example 8.10.2 (continued).**

a. Because real firms usually do not have unlimited funds available for investment, a capital expenditures limit, or *capital budget* as it is often termed, is applied to the overall expenditures for new projects. The capital budget often takes the form of a fixed sum of money. For example, in the selection of the project bundles, a capital budget might be applied, say, of $28,000. The question then is, which economically mutually exclusive bundle should be selected so as to retain feasibility, that is, so that the budget of $28,000 is not exceeded? The solution is as follows. Referring to the NPV ranking previously developed, the effect of the budget is to eliminate bundles 5 and 7 from the feasible set; thus:

| Bundle Number | Component Projects | Total Investment | Net Present Value of Bundle |
|---|---|---|---|
| 2 | G | −10,000 | + 4,025 |
| 1 | F | −12,000 | 2,350 |
| 3 | H | −17,000 | 12,120 |
| 4 | F, G | −22,000 | 6,375 |
| 6 | G, H | −27,000 | 16,145 ⟵ MAX |
| ---- | ---- | Budget = −28,000 | ---- |
| 5̶ | F̶,̶H̶ | −29,000 | 14,470 |
| 7̶ | F̶,̶G̶,̶H̶ | −39,000 | 18,495 |

Applying the criterion of maximization of net present value, we would select bundle 6, consisting of Projects G and H, and having $P_6 = \$16,415$ as the optimal choice.

b. Another type of constraint easily handled is the mutual exclusivity constraint. Suppose, for example, that Projects G and H were mutually exclusive alternatives and that the same budget constraint of $28,000 still applies. Since G and H are mutually exclusive, no bundle containing both G and H is now feasible. This eliminates bundle 6 from the feasible set, and the remaining feasible set now contains only bundles 2, 1, 3, and 4. Applying the criterion of maximization of net present value, we now see that the optimal solution is bundle 3, consisting of only Project H since $P_3 = \$12,120$ is the maximum value of net present value in the feasible set.

c. Economic complementarity, as we saw in Section 8.2, expresses a conditional relationship between two projects. This type of dependence can be handled by a constraint that also reduces the feasible set. Suppose, for example, that the execution of Project G also requires the execution of F, but not vice versa. That is, F may be done alone without G. The effect of this condition is to remove from the feasible set any and all bundles that contain G without F. Thus, we would remove bundle 2 (contains G only), and bundle 6 (contains G without F). With this constraint and the budget constraint, we would have as a feasible set only bundles 1, 3, and 4. The optimal choice is then bundle 3 since it provides maximum net present value.

While other types of constraints can be designed to reflect more realistic situations, these three illustrate the function of all such constraints, namely, to reduce the size of the feasible set of projects over which optimization is to take place. They also illustrate the basic nature of the project selection problem—that of selecting an optimal subset of projects from a larger, constrained set of candidate projects, so that some objective of primary interest to the firm will be optimized.

We have come by a rather roundabout route to this point, principally to show some of the problems involved with the ranking method of project selection. These problems are inevitably bound up with the central reinvestment problem, with the problem of dependencies and constraints, and with the problem of project indivisibility. Except for Fleischer's *bundling* method of creating *economically* mutually exclusive alternatives, the method of direct ranking of projects does *not* lead to the selection of an optimal set of projects, as Weingartner [16] showed in 1963 in his pioneer work on the application of mathematical programming to the capital budgeting problem. The more promising approach is to use mathematical programming techniques to select an optimal set of projects from the larger constrained candidate set. This important method was originally proposed by Weingartner [16], and all the important present-day project selection methods are modifications and extensions of his basic work. As we shall see, the 0–1 integer form of linear programming will successfully handle *simultaneously* the problems of capital rationing, project dependency, and project indivisibility, for the simple deterministic (certainty) model under perfect capital market assumptions.

We should at once note that the Lorie-Savage type of project selection problem, if it incorporates only *monetary* budget constraints, is a trivial selection problem under perfect capital market assumptions. The reason is that the firm can borrow all the funds it needs to execute all projects having positive net present values, and hence, monetary budget constraints are meaningless. As Weingartner points out, however, other types of "budget" limits may be imposed, such as limitations of space, manpower, throughput, machine capacity, and managerial availability. Since these constraints are formulated in exactly the same manner as monetary budget constraints, *but not in money terms*, the nature of the Lorie-Savage formulation may not be changed, but its *interpretation* is. From this point of view, the Lorie-Savage formulation, therefore, may not be trivial—indeed, it may be of considerable interest.

One of Weingartner's major contributions was to demonstrate ([16], Chapters 3,4, and 5) that the *integer* form of mathematical programming rationally and correctly solves the Lorie-Savage problem, whereas the solution method provided by Lorie and Savage themselves [11] fails under certain conditions. Lorie's and Savage's solution method calls for the trial-and-error choice of positive-valued parameters, $p_1, p_2, \ldots, p_t$, such that the quantity

$$P_j - \sum_{t=1}^{T} p_t C_{tj} \qquad (8.9)$$

is positive or zero for chosen projects and negative for the remaining ones, where $P_j$ = the net present value of Project $j$ ($j = 1, 2, \ldots, M$), and $C_{tj}$ is the present value of the outlays for Project $j$ in period $t$ ($t = 1, 2, \ldots, T$). The cause for failure of the criterion, Eq. (8.9), is that no solution to it may be obtainable, as Weingratner demonstrated by example.

## 8.11. The Weingartner Formulation

**8.11.1.** *Objective function.* The basic Weingartner [16] formulation of the Lorie-Savage resource allocation problem employs an objective function that maximizes a *linear function of the net present values* of the cash flows associated with individual projects. In our terminology, the objective is

$$\text{MAX}_{\forall j} \sum_{j=1}^{m} \sum_{t=0}^{n} Y_{t,j}(1 + i)^{-t}(x_j) \tag{8.10}$$

where $Y_{t,j}$ = cash inflow (outflow) from (to) the *j*th project at the end of the *t*th period; $(j = 1, 2, \ldots, m), (t = 0, 1, \ldots, n)$; cash flows are $+$ if inward from the project, $-$ if outward to the project.

  $m$ = the number of projects in the candidate set.

  $n$ = the life of the *j*th project.

  $i$ = the firm's marginal investment rate.

  $x_j$ = the decision variable (which takes on values of 0 or 1 only).

This objective states, in words, that a subset of projects is to be selected by the decision variables, $x_j$, from a set of $m$ candidate projects so that the selected set will maximize the *net* present value of the future economic contributions from the projects to the firm, in absolute measure.

The choice of net present value as a selection criterion is deliberate, not fortuitous. It provides, under certain conditions, the same answer as does the incremental method. Moreover, under assumptions of certainty and a perfect capital market (such as we have here), those projects that maximize the firm's net present value will also maximize the firm's wealth. This fact follows from the Fisher-Hirshleifer derivation given in Chapter 7. Neither of the other rational criteria (internal rate of return and benefit-cost ratio) will insure wealth maximization.

One disadvantage is inherent, however, in the net present value solution to the Lorie-Savage problem. This disadvantage is that the discount rate [called the *marginal investment rate* in Eq. (8.10)] must be specified from sources *external to the model*. The usual procedure is to use the firm's marginal cost of capital, as calculated in Chapter 6, as a *base* for estimating the marginal investment rate, which is then used to calculate the net present values required by Eq. (8.10). When this is done, then a conservative *reinvestment* policy is also established since, as we have seen in Section 8.7, the comparison of projects by NPV implicitly assumes reinvestment of released funds at the discount rate used for calculating the net present values in the first place, i.e., the firm's marginal cost of capital. The practical import of this implicit assumption is simply that the firm can, hopefully, *continue* to originate and adopt other new projects in the future that will absorb the released funds and in turn provide positive present values. This is not a stringent assumption, although in reality it implicitly requires constant monitoring of ongoing activities to make certain that they, in fact, *do* provide rates of return greater than the firm's cost of capital or succumb to cancellation (i.e., divestment of projects that fail to do this).

It should also be mentioned here that if the assumption of a perfect capital market is modified, so that borrowing and lending interest rates are no longer equal, then the net present value formulation of the objective becomes meaningless. How this problem is handled, and how certain other relationships in the assumptions affect the capital allocation model, will be discussed in Chapter 9.

### 8.11.2. Constraints.

a. The first set of constraints of interest in the selection problem is represented by a *series* of inequalities, such as Eq. (8.11) below, which express the limitations imposed by a resource availability:

$$\sum_{j=1}^{m} c_{tj}(x_j) \leq B_t \qquad (8.11)$$

were $c_{tj}$ = the consumption of the resource $B_t$ by Project $j$ in the $t$th period.

$B_t$ = the resource availability of the specified resource.

Other symbols are as defined previously.

This type of constraint is often called the *budget* constraint since it is used to express the limited availability of investment capital for executing investment projects. For example, if only \$100,000 and \$75,000 in investment capital were available for expenditure for all projects in periods 1 and 2, respectively, then the selection problem would be constrained by two such *budget* constraints; thus:

$$\sum_{j=1}^{m} c_{1j}(x_j) \leq 100,000; \qquad \sum_{j=1}^{m} c_{2j}(x_j) \leq 75,000$$

where $c_{1j}$ is the *cost* (or consumption of invested capital) of the $j$th project in period 1 and $c_{2j}$ is the corresponding cost in period 2.

*Budget* constraints need not be limited to the availability of money alone. They can also be used, for example, to express the limited availability of manpower, construction crews, materials, and equipment (see Weingartner [16], pp. 125–127).

b. If several alternatives for a project or projects exist, then the selection problem needs to be constrained by one or more mutual exclusivity constraints. Inequality of Eq. (8.12) below expresses the fact that the projects included within it are mutually exclusive ways of accomplishing the same end and that only one may be selected:

$$x_a + x_b + \cdots + x_k \leq 1 \qquad (8.12)$$

where $a, b, \ldots, k \in j$. Thus, if $a, b, \ldots, k$ are all alternative methods of *doing* a project, then each is made a separate project $(a, b, \ldots, k)$ and the inequality in Eq. (8.12) permits at most one of them to be selected. Thus, if any decision variable, say $x_a$, in the set of mutually exclusive projects $a, b, \ldots, k$ takes on the value of 1 in the selection process, then all others in this mutually exclusive set must have decision variables $(x_b, \ldots, x_k) = 0$.

As an example, suppose that in a candidate set of 25 projects $(j = 1,$

2, . . . , 25) Projects 9, 16, and 22 are alternative ways, say, of developing a given tract of land. Only one can be done. Hence, the mutual exclusivity constraint would be $x_9 + x_{16} + x_{22} \leq 1$, which permits at most only one of the three projects to be selected. Note, however, that all three decision variables *may* take on values of zero simultaneously and still satisfy the constraint. Thus, the mutual exclusivity constraint permits at most one, or alternatively none, of the mutually exclusive projects to enter the optimal set of selected projects.

c. Two projects are said to be contingent when there is a conditional dependency between them. A project is conditionally dependent on another when its execution, although optional in itself, is operationally, functionally, or economically dependent on the execution of the other. The idea of conditional dependency, therefore, embraces the concept of economic complementarity described in Section 8.2 as well as other types of operational or functional dependency. As an example of contingency, take two projects identified as Project 8 and Project 7. If Project 8 were an optional project (that is, it could or could not be executed) but *if* selected it could be executed if, and only if, Project 7 were also executed, then Project 8 is said to be *contingent* (or conditionally dependent) upon Project 7.

Such dependencies are formulated thus:

$$x_a \leq x_b$$

or, upon subracting $x_b$ from both sides,

$$x_a - x_b \leq 0 \tag{8.13}$$

where $a$ is the dependent project and $b$ is the one depended on. In the example above, $a = 8$ and $b = 7$ defines the constraint

$$x_8 - x_7 \leq 0,$$

which permits Project 8 to be done if, and only if, Project 7 is done also since if $x_7 = 1$ (acceptance of 7), then either $x_8 = 0$ or $x_8 = 1$ is permitted, thus satisfying the constraint. With $x_7 = 0$ (rejection of 7), however, $x_8 = 0$ is also required, since $x_8 = 1$ is prohibited by the constraint. Thus, 8 is accorded conditional acceptance, the condition being that 7 is accepted simultaneously. Neither, however, is *required* to be accepted (both $x_7 = 0$ and $x_8 = 0$ is a solution).

d. Sometimes two projects are strict complements of one another, whether this is because of economic complementarity or for other technical reasons. Two projects are said to be *strictly complementary* when the execution of one *requires* the execution of the other. Thus, if Projects $c$ and $d$ were strict complements of each other, then we would write the strict complementarity constraint

$$x_c - x_d = 0,$$

which requires that $x_c$ and $x_d$ both be zero-valued (neither accepted) or both unit-valued (both accepted) for the combined project. Including this kind of constraint in the selection problem unnecessarily increases the size of the programming problem, however, and it is better to include the combined project, $cd$, in the objective function as an independent project and omit the component projects $c$ and $d$. Thus, the constraint written above can be eliminated and the problem shortened, with the decision taken care of by the decision variable $x_{cd}$ in the objective.

e. It sometimes happens that projects are complements of one another but strict complementarity is not required. Thus, we say, for example, that if Projects $e$ and $f$ can be undertaken together as Project $ef$ and if there is a net economic benefit from undertaking both together, then $e$ and $f$ are complementary, but strict complementarity is not required. With this condition, Projects $e, f,$ and $ef$ are mutually exclusive—that is, we do not simultaneously undertake $e$ and $ef$ or $f$ and $ef$. Less than strict complementarity can be formulated into the selection problem by including mutual exclusivity constraints of the form

$$\left. \begin{aligned} x_e + x_{ef} &\leq 1 \\ x_f + x_{ef} &\leq 1 \end{aligned} \right\} \tag{8.14}$$

to express the requirement that at most one of $e$ or $f$ or $ef$ may be done. In essence, $ef$ is created with a new cash flow stream that expresses the economic savings or benefits to be realized from undertaking the combined project, and then this combined project is made mutually exclusive with the parent projects.

For computational purposes, it is more desirable to create the combined project, $ef$, include it in the candidate set with its decision variable, $x_{ef}$, and then make the combined project and its parents mutually exclusive by the constraint $x_e + x_f + x_{ef} \leq 1$. This results in fewer constraints being included in the computer model.

f. The last constraint of interest is the project indivisibility constraint

$$x_j = 0, 1 \quad (j = 1, 2, \ldots, m). \tag{8.15}$$

This constraint requires that all of a project be selected ($x_j = 1$) or that none of a project be selected ($x_j = 0$). Fractions or partial acceptance of projects are not permissible under this constraint.

The indivisibility constraint has two effects in the selection problem, one technical and the other economic. First, this constraint converts what would otherwise be a linear programming problem into an integer programming one in which the decision variables, $x_j$, are required to take on one of only two integer values, 0 and 1. This has implications for the solution methodology to be used, for integer programming is *much* more difficult to handle in a computer than linear programming. Second, from an economic standpoint, this constraint permits the substitution of, say, two smaller projects for one larger project so that it is possible for the firm to be figuratively better off in maximizing future wealth by the relation in Eq. (8.10) than if it merely accepted the larger project.

To show this substitution effect, consider three projects, $g, h,$ and $k$, whose net present values are $P_g = \$+5,000, P_h = \$+3,500,$ and $P_k = \$+2,000$. Assume that the present investments required are $C_g = \$100,000, C_h = \$50,000,$ and $C_k = \$50,000$. It would obviously be better for the firm that maximizes net present value to select $h$ and $k$ for a total investment of \$100,000 rather than $g$ since $h$ and $k$ provide together a total NPV of \$5,500, whereas $f$ provides only \$5,000. If the risk level is the same for all

three projects, then $h + k$ should be selected over $g$. The project indivisibility constraint permits this kind of project substitution, which is the *basic economic advantage*
enjoyed by mathematical programming models over ranking models as a method of
project selection.

**8.11.3.** *The completed Weingartner formulation.* The mathematical programming
selection problem of the Lorie-Savage type can be formally stated by combining Eqs.
(8.10) through(8.15); thus:

$$\text{MAX}_{\forall j} \sum_{j=1}^{m} \sum_{t=0}^{n} Y_{tj}(1 + i)^{-t}(x_j)$$

subject to

$$\left.
\begin{aligned}
&\text{(a)} \ \sum_{j=1}^{m} c_{tj}(x_j) \leq B_t && \text{(resource constraints; } c_{tj} \geq 0\text{)} \\
&\text{(b)} \ x_a + x_b + \cdots + x_k \leq 1 && \text{(mutual exclusivity constraints; } a, b, \\
& && \ldots, k \text{ being mutually exclusive proj-} \\
& && \text{ects in the candidate set, } j\text{)} \\
&\text{(c)} \ x_c - x_d \leq 0 && \text{(contingent projects; } c, d, \in j\text{)} \\
&\text{(d)} \ x_e + x_f + x_{ef} \leq 1 && \text{(complementary projects; } e, f, ef, \in j\text{)} \\
&\text{(e)} \ x_j = 0, 1.
\end{aligned}
\right\} \quad (8.16)$$

This is a 0–1 integer programming problem in which all relationships are linear.
It can be solved by any of the solution methods that are available for integer linear
programming problems, all of which guarantee an optimal solution in a finite number
of steps, if one exists. The most efficient solution methods are some type of branch-
and-bound procedure since the 0, 1 requirement in the Lorie-Savage problem converts
it into a special case of the integer programming problem, namely, the binary problem.
The necessary assumptions underlying this formulation of simple capital budgeting
problem are

1. All cash flows, $Y_{tj}$, and resource usages, $c_{tj}$, are deterministic (expected values
   measured with zero variance).
2. The discount rate, $i$, is the assumed known marginal investment rate of the
   firm; it is estimated by the firm's marginal cost of capital.
3. *Risk* is the same (i.e., zero) for all projects in the candidate set, $j = 1, 2, \ldots, m$.
4. There is no alteration of a project in the optimal set once the optimal set is
   determined (selected).
5. Reinvestment of cash flows from the shorter-lived projects, or from projects
   having differing cash flow streams, occurs at the firm's marginal investment
   rate (assumed to be the firm's marginal cost of capital, used for discounting the
   $Y_{tj}$ to present values).

## 8.12. Summary

In Chapter 8, we have considered some of the fundamental problems involved in
selecting an optimal set of projects from a larger set of candidate projects. Dependencies among projects, budget and other resource limitations, and project indivisibil-

ity all introduce complications. We have demonstrated that the three rational criteria (internal rate of return, net present value, and benefit-cost ratio) all lead to potential ranking inconsistencies when two (or more) projects are compared with each other and that the ranking inconsistency problem is traceable to the differing assumptions concerning reinvestment of idle funds made by the three criteria. With the proper choice of a *common* reinvestment rate, the ranking inconsistency problem is resolved.

This latter finding leads to the rational choice of the net present value method as the preferred method of project selection. This led to the Weingartner formulation of the simple, constrained Lorie-Savage type of project selection problem as an integer programming problem, in which the objective is to maximize the net present value of a set of candidate projects, subject to the feasibility constraints. Under assumptions of certainty and perfect capital markets, this formulation leads to an optimal choice of projects, if the firm's discount rate for future funds is its assumed known marginal cost of capital (determined by the methods developed in Chapter 6).

## REFERENCES

[1] BERNHARD, RICHARD H., "Discount Methods for Expenditure Evaluation: A Clarification of Their Assumptions," *Journal of Industrial Engineering*, **XIII**(1) (Jan.–Feb., 1962), pp. 19–27.

[2] _____, "A Comprehensive Comparison and Critique of Discounting Indices Proposed for Capital Investment Evaluation," *The Engineering Economist*, **16**(3) (Spring, 1971).

[3] BIERMAN, HAROLD, and SEYMOUR SMIDT, *The Capital Budgeting Decision*, 3rd ed. (New York: The Macmillan Company, 1971).

[4] _____, and _____, "Capital Budgeting and the Problem of Reinvesting Cash Proceeds," *Journal of Business* (October, 1957), pp. 276–79.

[5] DEAN, JOEL, *Capital Budgeting* (New York: Columbia University Press, 1951).

[6] DUESENBERRY, JAMES S., *Business Cycles and Economic Growth* (New York: McGraw-Hill Book Company, 1958).

[7] FISHER, IRVING, *The Theory of Interest* (New York: The Macmillan Company, 1930; reprinted, New York: Kelley and Millman, Inc., 1954), p. 151–55.

[8] FLEISCHER, GERALD A., "Two Major Issues Associated with the Rate of Return Method for Capital Allocation: The 'Ranking Error' and 'Preliminary Selection,'" *Journal of Industrial Engineering*, **XVII**(4) (April, 1966), pp. 202–8.

[9] JEYNES, PAUL H., "The Significance of Reinvestment Rate," *The Engineering Economist*, **11** (Fall, 1965), pp. 1–9.

[10] LINDSAY, J. ROBERT, and ARNOLD W. SAMETZ, *Financial Management: An Analytic Approach* (Homewood, Ill.: Richard D. Irwin, Inc., 1967).

[11] LORIE, JAMES H., and LEONARD J. SAVAGE, "Three Problems in Rationing Capital," *Journal of Business*, **XXVIII**(4) (October, 1955) (also reprinted in [15]).

[12] MAO, JAMES C. T., "The Internal Rate of Return as a Ranking Criterion," *The Engineering Economist*, **11**(4) (Summer, 1966), pp. 1–13.

[13] SCHWAB, BERNHARD, and PETER LUSZTIG, "A Comparative Analysis of the Net Present Value and the Benefit-Cost Ratio as Measures of the Economic Desirability of Investments," *Journal of Finance*, **24** (June, 1969), pp. 507–16.

[14] SOLOMON, EZRA, "The Arithmetic of Capital-Budgeting Decision," *Journal of Business*, **XXIX**(2) (April, 1956) (also reprinted in [15]).

[15] SOLOMON, EZRA, ed., *The Management of Corporate Capital* (Chicago: The University of Chicago Press, 1959).

[16] WEINGARTNER, H. MARTIN, *Mathematical Programming and the Analysis of Capital Budgeting Problems* (Ford Foundation Award-Winning Dissertation). (Englewood Cliffs, N.J.: Prentice-Hall, Inc., 1963; also Chicago: Markham Publishing Co., 1967).

## PROBLEMS

**8-1.** Three projects, $A$, $B$, and $C$, are assumed to develop the following net cash flows:

| Time, $t =$ | Net Cash Flow | | |
|:---:|:---:|:---:|:---:|
| | $A$ | $B$ | $C$ |
| 0 | $-12,000 | $-6,000 | $-6,000 |
| 1 | + 3,180 | +2,200 | +2,070 |
| 2 | ↑ | +2,228 | +2,100 |
| 3 | | +2,257 | +2,128 |
| 4 | | +2,286 | +2,157 |
| 5 | | +2,315 | +2,185 |
| 6 | | +2,343 | +2,214 |
| 7 | ↓ | +2,372 | +2,241 |
| 8 | + 3,180 | +2,401 | +4,270 |

(a) Using an incremental cash flow method, calculate the Fisherian intersection rates for Projects $A$-$C$, $A$-$B$, and $B$-$C$.

(b) Calculate the internal rates of return (IRR) for each project.

(c) For several values of the interest discounting rate, $i$, in the interval $0 \le i \le 0.40$, calculate representative values of the net present value, $P(i)$, for each project; plot the results on a graph of $P(i)$ versus $i$ and show the Fisherian rates and IRR's obtained in (a) and (b) above.

(d) On the graph, indicate the ranges of $i$ in which projects should be accepted and, for each range, designate the dominant (accepted) project.

**8-2.** Four proposed projects, $A$, $B$, $C$, and $D$, are estimated to develop initial investments, net cash inflows, and project lives as follows:

| Project | Initial Investment at Time $t = 0$ | Net Cash Flow, $ per Year (for $t = 1, 2, \ldots, N$) | $N =$ Project Life, Years |
|:---:|:---:|:---:|:---:|
| $A$ | $20,000 | $+10,000 | 3 |
| $B$ | 25,000 | +16,000 | 3 |
| $C$ | 40,000 | +30,000 | 5 |
| $D$ | 50,000 | +20,000 | 10 |

(a) Assume the firm's marginal investment rate is 15%. Formulate the capital allocation decision as an integer programming model in which net present value is maximized, subject to the following constraints: (i) the available budget at $t = 0$ is $80,000; (ii) each project is indivisible, and multiples of projects cannot be executed.

(b) Using the Fleischer *bundling* technique, solve the problem defined in (a) to obtain the optimal solution.

**8-3.** For the data and constraints defined in Problem 8-2, do the following:

    (a) Assume that Projects *A*, *B*, and *C* are alternative methods of accomplishing the same objective (e.g., three possible locations for a sales warehouse, only one of which will be built). Write the necessary constraint(s) to insure mutually exclusive adoption of *A*, *B*, or *C*. With this constraint operative, which project(s) should be chosen in order to maximize net present value?

    (b) Suppose that the budget constraint and the 0, 1 constraint in Problem 8-2 are the only operative constraints. Also, suppose that the execution of Project *C* is conditioned upon the execution of Project *B* but the acceptance of *C* is not mandatory. Write the necessary constraint to show this conditionality, and then construct a decision tree showing which project bundles, if any, should be eliminated from the feasible set of project combinations. With this constraint operative, which project combination should be selected? Is this constraint *tight* or *loose*, and why?

**8-4.** Five projects are available to a company for an investment opportunity (see table below). The company has a budget limit of $75,000 at time $t = 0$ for this investment and a marginal investment rate of 15%. The five projects are assumed to be economically independent of each other. There is a mutual exclusivity constraint between *B* and *C*, however, and the execution of Project *A* requires execution of Project *D*, but the complement of this does not hold true; i.e., *D*, does not require acceptance of *A*.

*Data for Candidate Projects*

| Project: | A | B | C | D | E |
|---|---|---|---|---|---|
| Total investment at $t = 0$ | $5,000 | $15,000 | $20,000 | $25,000 | $50,000 |
| Annual net cash flow, $/yr | 1,000 | 2,500 | 6,500 | 5,000 | 15,500 |
| Life, years | 10 | 10 | 5 | 10 | 5 |
| Salvage value | 0 | 0 | 0 | 0 | 0 |

    (a) Enumerate the $2^5$ possible combinations of projects, and then apply the constraints to define the feasible set of project combinations. For each feasible combination, calculate the total initial investment for the combination (use a tabular form).

    (b) Using the incremental rate-of-return method, rank the feasible combinations and determine the optimal project combination.

    (c) Repeat (b), using the net present value criterion.

**8-5.** Two projects are being considered by a firm as investment opportunities, and only one can be selected. The expected cash flow streams are given in the table below. Using the net benefit-cost ratio and net present value as the selection methods, select the best project. If there is an inconsistency between the two decision methods, resolve it. The firm's marginal investment rate is 15%.

| End of Period, $t =$ | Net Cash Flows Project A | Project B |
|---|---|---|
| 0 | $-350 | $-100 |
| 1 | -100 | -50 |
| 2 | +200 | +100 |
| 3 | +250 | +150 |
| 4 | +450 | +200 |
| 5 | +500 | +150 |

**8-6.** A company must choose between two investment proposals for making repairs to a building. Proposal *A* requires an initial investment of $10,000 with a return of $3,200 for 5 years. Proposal *B* requires an initial investment of $30,000 with a return of $9,300 for 5 years. The marginal investment rate is 15%.
(a) Evaluate the alternatives using the NPV method.
(b) Evaluate the alternatives using the benefit-cost criterion.
(c) Do the two methods yield conflicting results? If so, why?

**8-7.** A firm is faced with four projects competing for the funds available for investment. Project *A* is a coil steel cut-to-length production line. This line will feed steel from a coil, straighten it, shear it, and stack it. Project *B* is an electric furnace for the foundry. Project *C* is a gas furnace for the foundry. Project *D* consists of an electric trolley car, to be used to load coil steel onto the proposed cut-to-length line, rather than using an existing crane. Management has restricted capital investments to $850,000 in the current year. Next year's limit on capital investments is expected to be $750,000. The marginal investment rate is 15%. The expected cash flows related to the projects are as follows:

*Cash Flows ($10^3$ dollars)*

| Time, $t =$ | Project A | Project B | Project C | Project D |
|:---:|:---:|:---:|:---:|:---:|
| 0 | $-500 | $-250 | $-400 | $-100 |
| 1 | -600 | -100 | 50 | -40 |
| 2 | 200 | 150 | 200 | 20 |
| 3 | 500 | 350 | 200 | 180 |
| 4 | 700 | 0 | 100 | 100 |
| 5 | 300 | 0 | 100 | 0 |

(a) Formulate the project selection problem as an integer programming problem, with the decision variables limited to binary values (0, 1), and solve it using maximization of net present value as a criterion.

**8-8.** The "Wichita Worms" are a professional sports team. They are currently in a rundown arena. Attendance is dropping and the franchise appears headed for financial difficulty. Several alternatives are available to the owner: (i) leave the arena as is; (ii) remodel the present arena; (iii) build a new arena; (iv) make a trade for Joe Jock, superstar; (v) sell the franchise to a franchise-hungry Texas oilman. The owner has stated that if he leaves the arena as is, he will make a trade for Joe Jock. The following are the *cost* data (at times $t = 0$ and $t = 1$):

| Project | Cash Expenditures ($10^3$ dollars) | |
|:---:|:---:|:---:|
| | $t = 0$ | $t = 1$ |
| 1 | $ 10 | $ 20 |
| 2 | 60 | 40 |
| 3 | 200 | 150 |
| 4 | 125 | 130 |
| 5 | 200 | 200 |

A financial consultant has estimated that the net present values of the alternatives are, respectively, (1) $100,000, (2) $175,000, (3) $275,000, (4) $150,000, and (5) $300,000. The capital budget available in the next 2 years is expected to be limited to $200,000 for each year. (a) Write an equation to maximize net present value, subject to the applicable constraints. (b) Generate the feasible solutions and find the optimal solution by maximizing net present value.

**8-9.** The Midwest Manufacturing Company is preparing its capital budget for the next 2 years. It has the following projects available:

| Project | Investment at Time $t = 0$ | Investment at Time $t = 1$ | Expected Cash Flows |
|---------|---------------------------|---------------------------|---------------------|
| A | $-35,000 | $ — | $ 9,000 for $t = 1$ through $t = 9$; |
| B | -50,000 | -30,000 | $17,000 for $t = 2$ through $t = 16$; |
| C | — | -30,000 | $ 8,000 for $t = 2$ through $t = 8$; |
| D | -30,000 | -30,000 | $14,000 for $t = 2$ through $t = 10$; |
| E | -10,000 | — | $ 4,500 for $t = 1$ through $t = 6$ |

Company financial analysts have determined that Midwest can provide $90,000 (at $t = 0$) and $70,000 (at $t = 1$) in the next 2 years for capital investment. The marginal investment rate is estimated to be 15%. (The cash flow generated from any of the projects above, if accepted, will not be available for investment in other projects of this set.) The design engineers have specified that Project C is an extension of Project B and hence cannot be undertaken separately from B. Decide which project(s) Midwest should accept by using the maximum net present value criterion.

**8-10.** Economists generally advocate the use of *marginal rate of return on marginal investment* as an effective and theoretically correct method for ranking investment opportunities (projects) in decreasing order of merit, in order to determine project acceptability. The ranking of acceptable projects is generally cut off with the project whose marginal rate of return is equal to the firm's marginal investment rate. Explain why it may not always be possible to use this method and, if used, why it may not result in an optimal set of projects.

**8-11.** Under what assumptions will the IRR, NPV, and *B/C* criteria rank all projects in the same order of priority?

**8-12.** If the projects in Problems 8-2 and 8-3 are all independent and there is no budget constraint, how would you qualify your answers in Problem 8-3(a) and (b)?

# MULTIPLE PROJECTS AND CONSTRAINTS II
## (Extended Deterministic Formulations)

## 9.1. Introduction

In Chapter 7, under assumptions of certainty and a perfect capital market, we demonstrated the superiority of net present value as a criterion for the acceptance or rejection of single, unconstrained projects. In Chapter 8, this concept was extended to include multiple projects under simply constrained conditions, in order to demonstrate what is known as the *Lorie-Savage* type of problem. In Chapter 8, we also presented Weingartner's mathematical programming formulation of this problem and indicated that it could be solved by integer programming methods.

As we noted, however, the Lorie-Savage problem is a nontrivial one only when it contains *non*monetary budget constraints (e.g., limitations on manpower, space, and similar items). When it contains only monetary budget restrictions, the Lorie-Savage resource allocation problem is trivial under perfect capital market conditions since the firm can borrow the funds necessary to accept *all* projects whose net present values are positive. Likewise, it is assumed to lend cash recoveries from the projects in the capital market at the same interest rate.

The assumption of *perfection* in the capital market is a fairly restrictive one, even though there is now some evidence that the market may not be so imperfect as it once was thought to be (e.g., see Fama [10]). Nevertheless, there is still sufficient disagreement on the subject to warrant a discussion of how the capital allocation problem

# 9

can be modeled under an assumption of an imperfect capital market. There are a number of factors in the economy that call into question the existence of a perfect capital market. For example, trading costs and personal income taxes can upset the assumption of perfection. Similarly, it is not difficult to show that the Separation Theorem (developed in Chapter 7) is destroyed when borrowing and lending interest rates become different, as they do in real markets. When this happens, the net present value criterion is invalidated, and maximization of NPV can no longer be used to select an optimal set of projects.

It was principally this problem that led Weingartner to develop alternative formulations of the constrained project selection problem ([23], pp. 139–178) rather than just to be content with the mathematical programming solution to the Lorie-Savage problem. Since 1963, when Weingartner's original work was published, a great deal of development has taken place in project selection modeling. For purposes of convenience, nearly all this work can be classified as being either *deterministic* or *stochastic*. Stochastic models of the project selection problem have, in general, been based on the Bernoulli Principle, or Expected Utility Hypothesis, which we shall develop in Chapter 10 and apply in Chapters 11 and 12. On the other hand, determininstic modeling has likewise undergone a fruitful development, some of which we shall consider in this chapter. Beginning with Weingartner's *basic horizon model* ([23], pp. 141–155), additional valuable contributions have been made by that author and others.[1] Most of this later research can be contained, as special cases, within a generalized model developed by Bernhard [3], which we shall examine. Since Bernhard's work was published in 1969, other important developments have been made using a modeling technique known as *goal programming*, which we shall also briefly consider.

The introduction above thus suggests the organization of this chapter. *First*, as a representative case of market imperfection, we shall assume that borrowing and lending interest rates differ and then summarize Hirshleifer's demonstration that net present value and the Separation Theorem break down in the imperfect capital market. *Second*, we shall consider the generalized alternative formulation of the deterministic capital allocation problem due to Bernhard, some of the simpler forms of which may be made operational. *Third*, we shall introduce and demonstrate the method of *goal programming* as a means of formulating the capital allocation problem and obtaining interpretable results. This last methodology is particularly attractive from an operational point of view since a solution to the problem can be procured even in the face of several conflicting goals.

## 9.2. Invalidation of the Separation Theorem

When capital market imperfections exist, as they probably do in most *real* markets, the Separation Theorem developed in Chapter 7 is invalidated, and as a result the net present value criterion may no longer be defined. What happens is that the act of choosing an optimal set of projects is no longer independent of the method of financing the projects. For example, to determine net present value, we need to know the *market* rate of interest, but this is dependent (in imperfect markets) on the financing method used. In turn, the market rate of interest for the firm is dependent on the set of projects chosen. Hence, when NPV cannot be defined, the mathematical programming formulation of the Lorie-Savage type problem becomes useless. This is an unfortunate but direct consequence of relaxing the perfect capital market assumption.

Hirshleifer demonstrated this result by extending the Fisherian investment analysis to a general case in which market borrowing and lending rates differ ([12], pp. 333–337). We shall summarize the demonstration here. As in Chapter 7 where the Separation Theorem was developed (Sections 7.6.1 and 7.6.2), we assume a two-time, one-period model ($t = 0, 1$) in which present income, $Y_0$, at time $t = 0$, can be traded off for future income, $Y_1$, at time $t = 1$. Also, we assume a *set* of intertemporal indifference curves (e.g., an expected utility of consumption function) for the firm,[2] and we assume a generalized type of production opportunity set (i.e., with decreasing marginal productivity, but otherwise not of specific mathematical shape).

---

[1]See, for example, Weingartner [24], Baumol and Quandt [2], Bernhard [3], Byrne, Charnes, Cooper, and Kortanek [6], Manne [19], Näslund [21].

[2]As in Chapter 7, we assume no distinction between an individual and a firm, so that whoever *acts* for the firm simply represents the owners as a fiducial agent.

Now, with reference to Fig. 9.1, we may describe *three* different situations in which a productive opportunity maximum may be reached, but in only *two* of these cases [Fig. 9.1(a) and (b)] can specified types of financial trading be used to reach an optimal choice solution. In the third case [Fig. 9.1(c)], the interest rate is found only after the optimal productive set is procured, and it is this case that deals the net present value method its death blow.

To describe the three situations more fully, consider Fig. 9.1(a). Here, the firm possesses a rather mediocre potential productive opportunity set, represented by the curve $WX$, and it operates in a financial market where the lending rate of interest is $i_l$. We also take it that the lending interest rate is less than the borrowing rate of interest, $i_b$, since this is in accord with what we usually understand about borrowing and lending rates of interest in real (imperfect) markets. In its choice of productive opportunity set, the firm will move upward from point $W$ (the assumed initial endowment) to $R$, the point of tangency between the *lending* rate of interest and the productive opportunity curve, so as to increase its net present value. In doing this, the firm will invest ($Y_W - Y_R$) dollars. But it can improve its desired position with respect to intertemporal cash flows and increase the expected utility without decreasing its NPV, by thereafter lending ($Y_R - Y_A$) dollars at the *lending* rate of interest, finally arriving at point $A$ (the point of tangency of the lending market live with the indifference curve set), which is the point of maximum utility.

Suppose now, instead of the mediocre productive opportunity set in Fig. 9.1(a), the firm can choose from a really superior set of production opportunities, such as those represented by the curve $W'X'$ in Fig. 9.1(b). The firm will now invest ($Y_W - Y_{R'}$) dollars of its present endowment in order to reach point $R'$, which is the point of tangency of the market *borrowing* line with the productive opportunity curve, thereby reaching the point of maximum exchange of present for future funds by investing in productive assets. Thereafter, the firm will *borrow*, at the market *borrowing* rate of interest, to reach point $A'$, the point of maximum utility, without changing its NPV, $Y_{P'}$.

The point to be made in Fig. 9.1(a) is that with *some* productive opportunity sets the firm clearly should invest part of its present funds in the potential productive assets and lend some more in the capital market at the *lending* rate of interest; whereas in Fig. 9.1(b), with *some* productive opportunity sets, the firm should invest a great deal of its funds in the productive assets and then recover its liquidity by borrowing in the capital market at the *borrowing* rate of interest.

There is a third case, however, in which it is not nearly so clear what interest rate the firm should use or how the projects should be financed. Consider Fig. 9.1(c). Here, the firm is assumed to be able to choose from a set of productive opportunities represented by the curve $W''X''$, which is itself tangent to the indifference curves, with some angle $\theta_i = \tan^{-1}(1 + i^*)$ defined between the tangent and the horizontal axis, where now

$$[\theta_l = \tan^{-1}(1 + i_l)] < \theta_i < [\theta_b = \tan^{-1}(1 + i_b)]$$

or, in other words, where the actual, effective rate of interest, $i^*$, lies somewhere

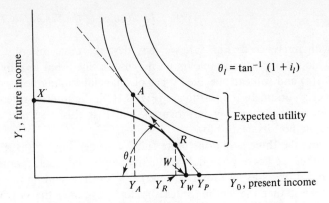

(a) Productive-exchange alternatives requiring lending

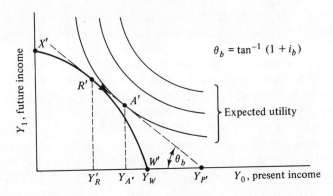

(b) Productive-exchange alternatives requiring borrowing

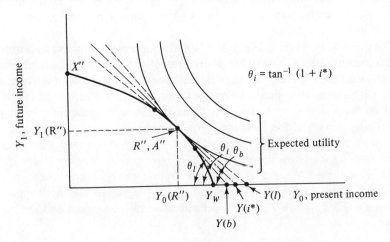

(c) Productive-exchange alternatives internally financed

**Fig. 9.1.** Production-financing relationships in imperfect capital markets.

between the market borrowing and lending rates; i.e., $i_l < i^* < i_b$. Now, in this case, the rate to be used for discounting $Y_1$ to a present equivalent value is unclear. In fact, this rate ($i^*$) *cannot be discovered until the optimal solution is attained and so is of no assistance in reaching the solution.* Because the discounting rate, $i^*$, is not known in advance of determining the optimal solution set of projects, the net present value methodology cannot be used to discover the optimal set, since NPV depends on a prior knowledge of the discount rate. Thus, abandonment of the perfect capital market assumption leads to an inability to use the NPV method for optimizing over a set of project investments.

A final result is that the Separation Theorem is invalidated by abandoning the perfect capital market assumptions. Because the discounting rate is not an *a priori* known value but rather is an *ex post product* of the optimal solution, one cannot say in advance how the optimal set of projects should be financed. In fact, determining the optimal set of projects *and* its method of financing is a *joint* problem in imperfect capital markets. "One hand washes the other"—the optimal set of projects determines the discount rate, and the discount rate determines the optimal set. The optimal discount rate fixes the method of financing. In an imperfect capital market, the present value of the firm [i.e., $Y(i^*)$ in Fig. 9.1(c)] is the result of the *joint* determination of the optimal set of projects and its method of financing. In short, it is the joint time-preference *expectancies* of the firm (as a proxy for its owners) that fix both the optimal set of investments and the method of financing that set. These expectancies are completely contained in the mathematical form of the expected utility functions (indifference curves). Operationally, however, this is not much help since one cannot easily determine the firm's indifference curves for intertemporal exchanges.[3]

## 9.3. Alternative Models of the Selection Problem

**9.3.1.** *Weingartner's horizon models.* The demonstrable breakdown of the net present value criterion and the associated invalidation of the Separation Theorem led Weingartner to develop alternative formulations of the project selection problem, which he called the *horizon* models, and in which he used a mathematical programming format ([23], pp. 139–178). In these formulations, he utilized the earlier lead of Charnes, Cooper, and Miller [8], who, instead of starting with discounted cash flow streams and expenditure limitations (as did Lorie and Savage), used instead the fundamental cost and revenue *relations* of the firm as data inputs, leaving some of the elements of the stream *and* the internal discounting factors to be determined by the model. Weingartner's formulations were intermediate between the Lorie-Savage and Charnes-Cooper-Miller approaches, however, and concentrated on defining the cash

---

[3]Bernhard [4] investigates the implications of using a utility function as an alternative to the discount rate. He demonstrates by a linear programming model that an optimal solution can be obtained in this manner, but the optimal use of resources (via the dual) is dependent on the original specification of the utility function.

flow stream relationships of the firm, on a period-by-period basis, up to a finite time in the future that he called the *horizon*. Instead of maximizing the present worth of the firm, Weingartner took as his objective the maximization of the firm's value as of the *future* terminal *horizon*, and the models were built using *current* (not present) values of the cash flows and resource constraints.

Using this method of approach, Weingartner developed two basic forms of the capital allocation problem under the assumptions of certainty. One he called the *basic horizon model*, and in this model he maximized the terminal wealth of the firm subject to restrictions on the intertemporal transfer of funds at an assumed constant, but *unknown*, interest rate. Using only independent projects and by examining the dual of the linear programming model, he demonstrated that this formulation was formally equivalent to maximizing net present value (i.e., under the assumed constant but unknown borrowing and lending rate of interest). A surprising result of the basic horizon model formulation is that, if mutually exclusive and contingent projects are considered, however, it may accept in the optimal solution some project(s) with *negative* net present value, while rejecting some other project(s) with *positive* net present values. The reason is that the time *availability* of internally generated funds is an important consideration in the model.

The second form of the horizon model developed by Weingartner was an extension of the *basic* model. In these latter models, Weingartner demonstrated some effects of *relaxing the assumptions of a perfect capital market*, by formulating terminal wealth models in which he (1) incorporated absolute limits on borrowing, (2) demonstrated that the financial structure of the firm is not independent of its dividend policy when capital is restricted, (3) provided for a borrowing rate of interest that is a rising function of the amount of funds borrowed, and (4) applied constraints on short-term borrowing to force (and determine) an optimal equity financing policy.

These are all important extensions to the theory of optimal resource allocation, and this is especially so since Weingartner provided numerical examples and solution methods for all his models, both with and without interdependencies between projects. Even though each of these models is worth reviewing in its own right from a historical standpoint, we refrain from doing so for two reasons: (1) They are special cases of a more general model we shall examine below, and (2) we are limited by space. (Interested readers are referred to the Weingartner manuscript [23]). Thus, we shall proceed to the more general model formulated by Bernhard.

**9.3.2. The Bernhard generalized horizon model.** In his paper, "Mathematical Programming Models for Capital Budgeting—A Survey, Generalization, and Critique," Bernhard [3] does three significant things. *First*, he formulates a generalized deterministic mathematical programming model for capital budgeting purposes, which we shall summarize below. *Second*, he demonstrates that the deterministic models of Weingartner and others mentioned in Footnote 1 are either special cases of or in some way closely related to the generalized model. We shall repeat some of Bernhard's special-case findings to demonstrate the properties of the general model. *Third*, Bernhard gives consideration to the introduction of uncertainty into the general model through the use of chance-constrained programming. This topic is beyond the scope of this chapter, and we shall not examine it here.

Bernhard's generalized mathematical programming model has an objective function, (0), and a constraint, (5), which are not necessarily linear. Unless (0) and (5) are linear, the generalized model will be quite difficult to solve. In certain circumstances, however, (0) and (5) can either be made linear or at least made monotonic non-decreasing (so they can be approximated by piecewise linearization techniques). In these cases, it would be theoretically possible to obtain solutions. Nevertheless, even in the absence of a solution, by examining the model's Kuhn-Tucker conditions,[4] several meaningful economic interpretations can be found regardless of the form of (0) and (5). Because any optimal solution of a model is known to comply with the model's Kuhn-Tucker conditions, we may use this method to infer characteristics of the optimal solutions, even though the solution itself might not be directly procurable. Thus, Bernhard is enabled to make statements about some of the *characteristics* of the optimal solutions of certain special-case models, some of which we shall repeat in the present exposition.

**9.3.3. *Notation.*** The following notation, differing in some symbol forms from Bernhard's, is used hereafter in this development:

$Y_{tj}$ = net cash flow obtainable from a unit of Project $j$ at time $t$ ($j = 1, 2, \ldots, m$); ($t = 1, 2, \ldots$); $+$ is a cash inflow to the firm; $-$ is a cash outflow from the firm.

$\hat{Y}_j$ = time $T$ *present worth* of post-$T$ cash flows from a unit of Project $j$ ($j = 1, 2, \ldots, m$).

$M'_t$ = amount of cash made available from projects outside this analysis and from other outside sources at time $t$ ($t = 1, 2, \ldots$).

$M'$ = time $T$ *present worth* of post-$T$ cash flows from these outside projects and other outside sources.

$l_t = 1 + r_{lt}$, where $r_{lt}$ = lending rate of interest from time $t$ to time $t + 1$.

$b_t = 1 + r_{bt}$, where $r_{bt}$ = borrowing rate of interest from time $t$ to time $t + 1$.

$b_t \geq l_t$ for $t = 1, 2, \ldots, T - 1$; $b_t = l_t = \lambda_t = 1 + r_t$ for $t = T, T + 1, \ldots$.

$B_t$ = maximum value of $w_t$ ($t = 1, 2, \ldots, T - 1$), where $w_t$ is defined below.

$d$ = total amount of scarce resource available.

$d_j$ = amount of scarce resource required by a unit of project $j$.

---

[4]Optimal solutions to certain types of mathematical programming problems are characterized by what are known as the *Kuhn-Tucker conditions*. These conditions are a series of partial differential relationships, derived by differentiating the objective function of the programming problem. They are somewhat analogous to the *dual constraints* of linear programming, and they have a comparable economic interpretation. The existence of the *K-T conditions*, as the differential relationships are often called, does not necessarily guarantee the *existence* of an optimal solution, but an optimal solution will always comply with the K-T conditions. Hence, they are helpful in identifying the characteristics and properties of the optimal solution. For those unfamiliar with the K-T conditions as a concept and methodology, a simple exposition of the general case is presented in Hillier and Lieberman ([11], pp. 723–728).

The variables in the general model are

$x_j =$ number of units of Project $j$ to be undertaken ($j = 0, 1, 2, \ldots, m$).

$W_t =$ cash dividend to be paid to owners at time $t$ ($t = 1, 2, \ldots, T$).

$w_t =$ cash to be borrowed from time $t$ to time $t + 1$ ($t = 1, 2, \ldots, T$); assume $w_0 \equiv 0$.

$v_t =$ cash to be lent from time $t$ to time $t + 1$, above and beyond what must be lent to satisfy the liquidity requirement (1), below; ($t = 1, 2, \ldots, T$); $v_0 \equiv 0$.

$G =$ the firm's time $T$ *terminal wealth*, after payment of $W_T$.

Optimal levels of these variables are indicated by an asterisk on the respective symbols; e.g., $x_j^*$ for the optimal level of $x_j$. Other notation will be introduced as needed.

**9.3.4. Objective function.** Most programming models developed prior to the publication of Bernhard's model assumed that a desirable objective of the firm was the simple maximization of the firm's terminal wealth, $G$, at time $T$. Bernhard noted, however, that widespread agreement existed in the literature on the mathematics of finance that an appropriate objective of the firm, in planning its productive investment and financial policy, was the maximization of some function (usually a discounted sum) of all anticipated dividend payments to the firm's present shares. Combining the two concepts, Bernhard reasoned that if a stream of dividends were to be truncated at some finite horizon, $T$, then it would be reasonable to include the time $T$ terminal wealth, $G$, in the objective function as a proxy for the post-$T$ stream of dividends. Based on this reasoning, he adopted as an objective the maximization of a function of the finite dividend payments stream, $W_1, W_2, \ldots, W_T$, *plus* the terminal wealth, $G$. Formally, the objective is to

$$\text{(0)} \qquad \text{MAXIMIZE} \quad f(W_1, W_2, W_3, \ldots, W_T, G). \qquad \text{(9.1)}$$

To give more definition to this objective, the assumptions are made that $\partial F / \partial W_t \geq 0$ for $t = 1, 2, \ldots, T$; and $\partial F / \partial G \geq 0$; that is, $f(\ )$ is a nondecreasing function.

**9.3.5. Constraints.** The model is constrained by a set of five restrictions, which are described below. For each restriction, the associated Kuhn-Tucker (K-T) variable is indicated in brackets at the right of the restriction. The general meaning and interpretation of the K-T variables are indicated later in the subsection on the K-T conditions. The five restrictions are as follows:

*1. Cash Balance Restrictions Including Liquidity Requirements.*

A requirement is made that the firm carry, *in cash*, an amount of at least ($C_t + c_t w_t$), where $C_t \geq 0$ and $0 \leq c_t < 1$. This requirement applies from any time $t$ to $t + 1$, with the exception of $t = 0$, when it is assumed that $C_t = c_t = 0$. Thus, the cash requirement at any time $t$ consists of a constant, $C_t$ (which may vary from period to period), plus a fraction of the outstanding debt, $w_t$, which is the liquidity portion of the requirement. (The latter requirement for liquidity is a typical one made by lending institutions.) The entire amount, $(C_t + c_t w_t)$, is assumed to earn interest from time $t$ to $t + 1$ at the *lending* rate of interest.

From the foregoing, the general form of the cash balance restrictions may be deduced, as follows:

$$-\sum_{j=1}^{m} Y_{tj} x_j - l_{t-1}(v_{t-1} + c_{t-1}w_{t-1} + C_{t-1}) + (v_t + c_t w_t + C_t)$$

$$+ b_{t-1}w_{t-1} - w_t + W_t \leq M_t'; \quad \text{for } t = 1, 2, \ldots, T. \quad (9.2a)$$

Taking the terms in order from the left, this relationship says that, at time $t$, the net cash outflow to projects $(-\sum_{j-1}^{m} Y_{tj}x_j)$; minus the cash inflow from time $t-1$ loans, $l_{t-1}(v_{t-1} + c_{t-1}w_{t-1} + C_{t-1})$; plus the cash outflow for time $t$ loans, $(v_t + c_t w_t + C_t)$; plus the cash outflow for repayment of time $t-1$ borrowing, $(b_{t-1}w_{t-1})$; minus the cash inflow from time $t$ borrowing, $w_t$; plus the cash outflow for time $t$ dividend payments, $W_t$, must as a sum be less than or equal to the cash available from outside sources, $M_t'$, at time $t$. For convenience, the constant values of the cash requirement are transposed to the right side so that Eq. (9.2a) may be rewritten as

$$(1) \qquad -\sum_{j=1}^{m} Y_{tj}x_j - l_{t-1}v_{t-1} + v_t + (b_{t-1} - l_{t-1}c_{t-1})w_{t-1}$$

$$- (1 - c_t)w_t + W_t \leq M_t; \quad \text{for } t = 1, 2, \ldots, T \quad [p_t] \quad (9.2b)$$

where now $M_t = M_t' + l_{t-1}C_{t-1} - C_t$.

### 2. Group Payback Restriction.

To allow for the starting of projects at times other than $t = 0$, Byrne, *et al.* [6] imposed a *group* payback restriction. Bernhard follows the same rule and requires that the net outlays *to date* (time $= t'$) on the *group* of executed projects be zero or negative; i.e.,

$$(2) \qquad -\sum_{j=1}^{m} \sum_{t=1}^{t'} Y_{tj}x_j \leq 0, \quad \text{for some integer, } t', \text{ such that } 1 \leq t' \leq T. \quad [\psi] \quad (9.3)$$

In addition, Bernhard notes, one could add a set of such restrictions for several values of $t'$, or a payback requirement on *individual* executed projects, such as

$$-\sum_{t=1}^{t'} Y_{tj}x_j \leq 0, \quad \text{for } j = 1, 2, \ldots, m.$$

### 3. Scarce Resource Restriction.

Weingartner ([23], p. 126) imposed a "manpower" restriction on his programming formulation of the funds flow model, to illustrate the manner in which a scarce resource restraint is included. Bernhard uses the same general form to typify many such constraints that could be written to limit the use of scarce resources:

$$(3) \qquad \sum_{j=1}^{m} d_j x_j \leq d. \qquad [v] \quad (9.4)$$

It should be noted that many such constraints could be written as needed, e.g., for any given resource, or different restrictions in different periods.

*4. Terminal Wealth Restriction.*

The firm's time $T$ terminal wealth, following payment of dividend, $W_T$, is defined to be

$$G \equiv M' + \sum_{j=1}^{m} \hat{Y}_j x_j + v_T + c_T w_T + C_T - w_T.$$

Here, as defined above, $M'$ is the time $T$ present worth of post-$T$ cash flows from outside projects and other outside sources. $\sum_{j=1}^{m} \hat{Y}_j x_j$ is a similar time $T$ present worth of post-$T$ cash flows from projects chosen for execution by our current analysis. The sum, $v_T + c_T w_T + C_T$, is, as in the case for general $t$ in Eq. (9.2b), the amount lent out at time $T$. From all these, $w_T$, the amount borrowed at time $T$, must be deleted.

It is convenient to rewrite the terminal wealth definition restriction as

(4) $$-\sum_{j=1}^{m} \hat{Y}_j x_j - v_T + (1 - c_T)w_T + G = M, \qquad [\phi] \quad (9.5)$$

where $M \equiv M' + C_T$.

*5. Terminal Wealth Horizon Posture Restriction.*

It is also assumed that the terminal wealth, $G$, is constrained such that $G \geq K + g(W_1, W_2, \ldots, W_T)$ where $K$ is a constant $\geq 0$ and $g$ is a function $\geq 0$. That is, the firm is not allowed to have a negative terminal wealth. The function, $g$, allows the possibility of requiring a positive minimum terminal wealth, the level of which is related to the levels of past dividends. It is thus guaranteed that the firm will be able to pay post-$T$ dividends in some way comparable to those paid at $T$ and earlier.

As before, it is convenient to rewrite the horizon posture restriction as

(5) $$-G + g(W_1, W_2, \ldots, W_T) \leq -K. \qquad [\theta] \quad (9.6)$$

**9.3.6.** *Problems in the measurement of terminal wealth.* There are some problems associated with Restrictions 4 and 5 above. The problems have to do with establishing the level of the time $T$ terminal wealth of the firm. One problem is concerned with the *borrowing* status of the firm at time $T$ (i.e., whether it is a borrower, lender, or neither) and the applicable interest rate. The other problem is whether or not there is a restriction on the amount of funds borrowed at time $T$. Taking these problems in order, we paraphrase Bernhard's analysis ([3], pp. 118–119):

Consider the time $T$ present worth of post-$T$ cash flows, which is $M' + \sum_{j=1}^{m} (\hat{Y}_j x_j)$. For periods beginning at $T$, if each period has only one market rate, $\lambda_t = 1 + r_t$, at which both borrowing and lending can take place, then we have no difficulty in converting future cash flows to a time $T$ present value. For example, if $h$ is a cash receipt assumed to occur at time $T + 1$, then $h$'s equivalent at time $T$ is simply $h\lambda_T^{-1}$. The firm could borrow $h\lambda_T^{-1}$ and repay it with $h$ at time $T + 1$. Alternatively, lending $h\lambda_T^{-1}$ at time $T$ would result in an inflow of $h$ at $T + 1$. In general, if all post-$T$ cash flows are included, then

$$M' = \sum_{t=T+1}^{\infty} \left[ M'_t \prod_{\tau=T+1}^{t} \lambda_{\tau-1}^{-1} \right] \quad \text{and} \quad \hat{Y}_j = \sum_{t=T+1}^{\infty} \left[ Y_{tj} \prod_{\tau=T+1}^{t} \lambda_{\tau-1}^{-1} \right],$$

and hence both $M'$ and $\hat{Y}_j$ are defined beyond time $T$.

If the borrowing rate exceeds the lending rate (i.e., $b_t > l_t$) at time $T$, however, problems are encountered. The rate, of course, depends on whether the firm is a borrower or a lender at $T$. If the firm is in a borrowing position at time $T$, it may borrow funds in the amount of $hb_T^{-1}$ (the then present equivalent of $h$) and pay off the debt at $T + 1$ with $h$. But if the firm is in a lending position at $T$, the time $T$ equivalent of $h$ is $hl_T^{-1}$, which will be recovered by $h$ at time $T + 1$. Comparing the two cases for any value $h \neq 0$, we obtain the fact that the time $T$ value of $h$ is either $hb_T^{-1}$ or $hl_T^{-1}$ and that $hl_T^{-1} > hb_T^{-1}$ (since both $l$ and $b$ are in the denominator and $l < b$). Therefore, the time $T$ value of $h$ cannot be known until one establishes the post-$T$ lending and borrowing states and amounts. To avoid this necessity, Bernhard simply assumes that there is a *single* market interest rate for both borrowing and lending; i.e., $\lambda_t = b_t = l_t = (1 + r_t)$, for all post-$T$ periods.

The assumption of a constant interest rate for all post-$T$ periods does not, however, remove another obstacle. The second one is encountered if the time $T$ borrowing, $w_T$, is restricted. Weingartner ([23], p. 162) suggests such a restriction, in which $w_T < B_T$, where $B_T \geq 0$. Suppose, for example, the restriction *at time $T$* is *tight*; i.e., no funds are permitted to be borrowed at $T$. Hence, $w_T = B_T = 0$. Suppose also that the firm is a "would be" borrower at time $T + 1$—that is, even though no funds are borrowed at time $T$, it *anticipates* borrowing $h$ at time $T + 1$. What is the worth of $h$ at time $T$? It could be interpreted as $hl_T^{-1}$ if it saves some lending at time $T$, but otherwise it is zero. So, in any event the time $T$ value of $h$ again depends on the post-$T$ financing pattern, which Bernhard notes is a *product of the mathematical programming analysis* rather than an *a priori* assumption. Thus, if one wants to define $M'$ and $\hat{Y}_j$ in advance, restrictions of the form $w_T \leq B_T$ must be avoided.

**9.3.7. *Additional restrictions.*** In addition to the five constraints placed on the Bernhard model, three others are added. Two of these are standard ones for capital budgeting programming models, and the third is an upper limit on borrowing. These restrictions are as follows.

*6. Upper Bounds on Borrowing.*

In all but highly unusual instances, lending institutions will limit the total amount of funds *borrowed* by the firm to a fractional part (say 60%) of the firm's equity. Assuming the equity capital of the firm remains constant over time, as the Bernhard model does, the upper bound on borrowing can be represented by

(6) $$w_t \leq B_t \quad \text{for } t = 1, 2, \ldots, T - 1, \qquad [\beta_t] \quad (9.7)$$

which is of the same form used by Weingartner ([22], p. 162).

*7. Prohibition of Multiple Projects.*

In the other models we have heretofore discussed, we have required that mutually exclusive projects (or bundles of projects) be either rejected or accepted (i.e., $x_j = 0$,

1). This requirement imposes great difficulties on solving, or even interpreting, Bernhard's model (see, for example, a discussion of these problems in Weingartner [23], Chapter 5).

To relieve the model of this integer requirement, Bernhard simply prohibits the undertaking of multiple projects by requiring that

(7) $$0 \leq x_j \leq 1 \quad \text{for } j = 1, 2, \ldots, m. \qquad [\mu_j] \quad (9.8)$$

In the event some $x_j$ become fractional in the optimal solution, it is assumed here that the binding constraint can be simply *loosened* to make the fractional project into a complete one. This will not result in an optimal solution, but it may be near-optimal and probably quite realistic since constraints in reality are not rigidly fixed at *deterministic values*.

### 8. Nonnegativity Restrictions.

The final restriction is one usually included in programming models, namely, that all the decision variables be nonnegative. This restriction permits the use of mathematical programming algorithms to solve the problem. While some of the variables have already been required to be nonnegative above, others should be added, thus:

(8) $$v_t, w_t, W_t \geq 0 \quad \text{for } t = 1, 2, \ldots, T. \qquad (9.9)$$

In summary, the Bernhard generalized model requires the maximization of the objective function (0), subject to constraints (1) through (8). In general the model will be difficult to solve unless the objective (0) and the terminal wealth "posture" restriction (5) are linear, which is a special case. Some pertinent economic features of the optimal solution may be discovered by examining the model's Kuhn-Tucker conditions, however, even if the model cannot be solved. We shall consider some of Bernhard's findings below.

**9.3.8. The Kuhn-Tucker conditions.** The Kuhn-Tucker (K-T) *conditions* are a set of constraints, one for each of the variables in the model, plus certain other restrictions on the values of the K-T variables that are added into the problem. The K-T *variables*, one per *original* constraint, are a generalized form of Lagrangian multiplier and have the same economic interpretation. In general (for maximization problems) if a K-T variable has a value other than zero in the optimal solution, it signals the fact that the corresponding constraint in the original problem is *tight*, and it expresses the amount the objective could be increased if the right-hand-side value of the constraint were loosened by one unit.

We shall demonstrate the *steps* for obtaining the K-T conditions for Bernhard's model, although the complete procedure will not be presented because it is quite lengthy. Analogous to the formulation of a Lagrangian function, the K-T conditions are obtained by a procedure in which the *first step* is to convert all constraints into equalities (by adding or subtracting slack variables), and then add converted constraints into the objective by using the appropriate K-T variables as multipliers. For example, the *method* we would use to form a new Lagrangian function, $L(\cdot)$, consists of writing the *original objective* (0), reduced[5] by *each* constraint, (1) through (8), multiplied by its own K-T variable, thus:

$$L(v_t, w_t, x_j, W_t, G, \rho_t, \psi, v, \phi, \theta, \beta_t, \mu_j)$$

$$= \underbrace{f(W_t, G)}_{\substack{\text{Original} \\ \text{objective (0)}}} - \underbrace{\rho_t}_{\substack{\text{K-T} \\ \text{No. 1}}} \underbrace{\left[ -\sum_{j=1}^{m} Y_{tj}x_j - l_{t-1}v_{t-1} + v_t + (b_{t-1} - l_{t-1}c_{t-1})w_{t-1} \right.}_{\text{First constraint, (1)}}$$

$$\underbrace{\left. - (1 - c_t)w_t + W_t - M_t + \mu_{1t}^2 \right]}_{} - \underbrace{\psi}_{\substack{\text{K-T} \\ \text{No. 2}}} \underbrace{\left[ -\sum_{j=1}^{n} \sum_{t=1}^{t'} Y_{tj}x_j + \mu_{2t}^2 \right]}_{\text{Second constraint, (2)}}$$

$$- v \text{ [times constraint (3)]} - \phi \text{ [times constraint (4)]}$$

$$- \theta \text{ [times constraint (5)]} - \beta_t \text{ [times constraint (6)]}$$

$$- \mu_j \text{ [times constraint (7)]}.$$

(9.10)

The *second step* is then to differentiate the Lagrangian with respect to *each* of its argument variables, thereby obtaining a set of partial derivatives in terms of these variables. Each partial derivative equation is then set to zero (this is the necessary condition for an optimum to exist). The *third step* is to solve the system of simultaneous equations, created in the second step, for the optimal solution. As Bernhard remarks, however, unless the objective (0) and the terminal wealth posture restriction (5) are linear, the model would be difficult to solve.

If the objective (0) is assumed to be concave and differentiable and if the left-hand side of (5) is convex, however, we may combine the system of simultaneous equations procured in the second step, above, to obtain a set of K-T *conditions* that are descriptive of the optimal solution, even if it is not easily obtainable. Finding the K-T conditions, by combining the differential equations obtained in the second step above, is itself a tedious task that we shall not repeat here. Bernhard provides the results in his paper, which we shall use. The K-T conditions for the model are as follows. In each case, the associated *original* variable is indicated in brackets at the right of the constraint.

(9)      $-\rho_t + l_t\rho_{t+1} \leq 0$   for $t = 1, 2, \ldots, T - 1$     $[v_t]$   (9.11)

(10)   $[1 - c_t]\rho_t - [b_t - l_tc_t]\rho_{t+1} - \beta_t \leq 0$   for $t = 1, 2, \ldots, T - 1$   $[w_t]$   (9.12)

(11)                  $-\rho_T + \phi \leq 0$                  $[v_t]$   (9.13)

(12)           $[1 - c_T]\rho_T - [1 - c_T]\phi \leq 0$           $[w_t]$   (9.14)

(13)   $\sum_{t=1}^{T} Y_{tj}\rho_t + \hat{Y}_j\phi - d_jv + \sum_{t=1}^{t'} Y_{tj}\psi - \mu_j \leq 0$   for $j = 1, 2, \ldots, m$   $[x_j]$   (9.15)

---

[5]If the sign of the multiplier (in general, $\lambda$), is taken as negative in the formulation of the Lagrangian for *maximization* problems, and the associated requirement $\lambda \geq 0$ is made, then the optimal solution will contain $\lambda$'s that are either zero or of the correct sign $(+)$, so as to indicate an increase of the objective [i.e., $\lambda = \partial f(\cdot)/\partial b$] if the constraint is *tight*.

(14)
$$\left.\frac{\partial f}{\partial W_t}\right|_{W_t} - \rho_t - \theta \left.\frac{\partial g}{\partial W_t}\right|_{W_t} \leq 0 \quad \text{for } t = 1, 2, \ldots, T \qquad [W_t] \quad (9.16)$$

(15)
$$\left.\frac{\partial f}{\partial G}\right|_G - \phi + \theta \leq 0. \qquad [G] \quad (9.17)$$

For a discussion of these K-T conditions and the optimal solution, we quote Bernhard:

> In the optimal solution, both for these K-T inequalities, (9) through (15), and for the original inequalities, (1) through (3) and (5) through (7), if the level of the associated variable, shown in brackets at the right, is greater than zero, the corresponding constraint must be satisfied as a strict equality. On the other hand, if the level of the associated variable is exactly zero, the corresponding constraint may or may not be satisfied as a strict equality. These relationships between variables and associated constraints are referred to by the term "complementary slackness."
>
> For a given constraint in the original model, the optimal level of the associated K-T variable represents, on the margin, the rate at which the objective function (0) could be increased if there were a small increase in the constant at the right-hand side of the constraint in question.
>
> As in the case of the original variables, all of the K-T variables are constrained to be $\geq 0$, except for $\phi$, which, due to its association with a strict equality, (4), is, by that criterion, unconstrained in sign. But, from (11), $\phi \leq \rho_T$, and from (12), $\phi \geq \rho_T$. So,

(16)
$$\phi = \rho_T. \qquad (9.18)$$

From above, we know that $\rho_T \geq 0$. Hence, $\phi \geq 0$.

> Again, as in the case of the original variables, we will also use asterisks to indicate optimal levels of the K-T variables. So, inserting (16) into (13), we find that:

(17)
$$\mu_j^* \geq A_j^* \quad \text{for } j = 1, 2, \ldots, n, \qquad (9.19)$$

where:

(18)
$$A_j^* \equiv \sum_{t=1}^{t'} Y_{tj}(\rho_t^* + \psi^*) + \sum_{t=t'+1}^{T-1} Y_{tj}\rho_t^* + (Y_{Tj} + \hat{Y}_j)\rho_T^* - d_j\nu^*. \qquad (9.20)$$

Note, in passing, that if there is no payback restriction or if it is not binding, $\psi^* = 0$, and similarly, if there is no scarce resource restriction or if it is not binding, $\nu^* = 0$. So, for the simpler case where these two restrictions are nonexistent or at least non-binding,

(19)
$$A_j^* = \sum_{t=1}^{T-1} Y_{tj}\rho_t^* + (Y_{Tj} + \hat{Y}_j)\rho_T^*. \qquad (9.21)$$

Returning to the general case, from conditions (7) and (13) and the "complementary slackness" relationships discussed above:

(20)
$$\text{if} \begin{cases} x_j^* = 1, & \text{then } \mu_j^* = A_j^* \geq 0; \\ 0 < x_j^* < 1, & \text{then } \mu_j^* = A_j^* = 0; \\ x_j^* = 0, & \text{then } \mu_j^* = 0 \geq A_j^*. \end{cases} \qquad (9.22)$$

That is, if, for a given project $j$, $A_j^* > 0$, that project should be accepted in full; if $A_j^* < 0$, the project should be completely rejected; and if $A_j^* = 0$, it does not make any difference in the objective function whether the project is accepted or rejected.

So, given the values of $Y_{tj}$, $\hat{Y}_j$, and $d_j$ for Project $j$, if we can also learn the optimal values of the K-T variables, i.e., the $\rho_t^*$'s, $\psi^*$, and $v^*$, we may determine whether Project $j$ should be undertaken. Unfortunately, knowledge of the magnitudes of these K-T variables will, in general, require a complete programming solution. However, as illustrated below, some of their properties may, with less effort, be determined using the K-T conditions. Indeed, in some simple cases, a complete solution is possible using this latter approach.

**9.3.9. *Properties of $\rho_t^*$.*** The Lagrangian multiplier, $\rho_t$, is related to the cash balance and liquidity restriction, Eq. (9.2b), via the K-T restrictions (9.11) through (9.17). It is important that the nature of this multiplier variable be understood, so we shall summarize Bernhard's statements concerning it. If $\rho_t^* > 0$ in the optimal solution, then the *objective* will be *increased* in amount at time $t$ at the margin if $M_t'$, the amount of cash made available from outside sources, is increased by \$1; *or* if the liquidity requirement at time $t - 1$, $C_{t-1}$, is increased by \$1; *or* if the liquidity requirement at time $t$, $C_t$, is decreased by \$1; *or* if any combination of the above occurs. This reasoning follows from Eq. (9.2b), from which (in essence) the dual variable $\rho_t^*$ is related to the right-hand side of Eq. (9.2b) via

$$\rho_t^* \simeq \frac{\partial(\text{objective})}{\partial(M_t'; C_{t-1}; C_t)}.$$

Ordinarily, $\rho_t^* > 0$ will be true for all time periods, thus rendering Eq. (9.2b) an equality. In this case, Bernhard shows that an extra dollar available in the earlier periods can always be lent through to a later period when it has utility (for distribution to the shareholders), so it has utility in the earlier periods as well.

Conversely, if for the pathologic case when some $\rho_t^* = 0$, then $\rho_{t+1}^* = 0$, as well, and a consequence is that an increase in terminal wealth $G$, will *not* increase the objective function value. A second consequence when some $\rho_t^* = 0$ is that an increase in the dividend, $W_t$, will also *not* increase the objective; and the final consequence is that if any $\rho_t^* > 0$, then Eq. (9.12) reduces to $\rho_t^* \leq \hat{\beta}_t^*$, so it must be that $\beta_t^* > 0$ also, which requires that the upper bound on borrowing be binding [Eq. (9.7)]. The consequence of this pathologic case is that extra dollars beyond time $t$ have no utility in *any* period since if they have no utility beyond time $t$, neither do they *at time $t$*, which can be any instant between $t = 0$ and $t = T$.

**9.3.10. *Special cases.*** In the second section of his article, Bernhard examines three special cases of the general model, which are of interest to us. Summaries of the findings in these cases are presented here.

Case 1 is the case in which the upper bound on borrowing, Eq. (9.7), is either absent or nonbinding. Case 2a is one in which the borrowing and lending rates of interest in the same time period are equal; that is $b_t = l_t = \lambda_t$; and Case 2b is the more restrictive one in which the borrowing and lending rates in all periods are equal (i.e., $b_t = l_t = \lambda_t = \lambda$). In both of these subcases, borrowing constraints are imposed. Case 3a is one in which the borrowing and lending rates are equal in a given period (i.e., $b_t = l_t = \lambda_t$), but borrowing constraints are absent or nonbinding. Finally, Case 3b is similar to 3a, except that the interest rates are assumed constant; i.e., $b_t = l_t = \lambda_t = \lambda$.

For Case 1, in which borrowing constraints are inactive or absent, it is shown that the optimal solution will be characterized as follows: (1) All the cash balance constraints [Eq. (9.2b)] will be equalities; (2) Excess funds from an earlier period can be freely lent into a later period; (3) Funds can be freely borrowed from a later period into an earlier period; (4) Due to the assumption that the borrowing rate exceeds the lending rate ($b_t > l_t$), then the firm can engage in borrowing to maintain liquidity, but the value of a time $t$ dollar is *increased* relative to a time $t + 1$ dollar.

In Case 2a, when the borrowing and lending rates are equal for any given period and when there is a restriction on borrowing in a given period and, in Case 2b, when the borrowing and lending rates are all assumed set to a constant value, $\lambda$, it can be shown for the simple case in which payback and resource restrictions are omitted that the optimal solution *can* contain projects that have a negative present value (or horizon value). That is, a project *need not* be rejected merely because it has a negative NPV (or negative horizon value) based on the *market* rate of interest only (Weingartner [23], pp. 165–166). The intuitive reason is that such a project may indeed generate cash inflows *at times when they are most needed.* The converse is also true: A project with *positive* NPV may be rejected when its cash inflows are *least* needed. Note that Case 2b is a *perfect capital market* model (borrowing and lending rates equal and invariant among periods); yet it may give different results (pick different projects) from the Lorie-Savage model because funds are permitted to be shifted from one period to another (which the Lorie-Savage model does not allow).

In both of the Cases 3a and 3b, when borrowing constraints are absent or nonbinding, the optimal solution contains the following characteristics. When borrowing and lending rates are equal in a given period (Case 3a), the firm may borrow to satisfy the liquidity constraint even though it has already lent funds elsewhere at the same rate. Thus, the firm can accept *any* project whose net present value calculated at the market rate, $\lambda$, is positive, and it rejects any project whose NPV $< 0$. In Case 3b, when $\lambda_t = \lambda$ for all periods, the existence of a capital restriction is meaningless since the firm can borrow as much money as necessary at the market rate, $\lambda$, to accept all projects whose NPV $> 0$. This confirms the NPV criterion for *single* projects developed in Chapter 7, together with its assumptions.

In addition to the above, Bernhard continues on to demonstrate how several of Weingartner's models are simply special cases of the generalized model and then shows that the rate of discount, used in the Lorie-Savage model to find net present value, is not *internally* procurable from the model itself. In doing this, he confirms and extends the earlier work of Baumol and Quandt [2], who made this assertion after an abortive attempt to establish the appropriate discount within their model by using the dual.

It should be mentioned also that Bernhard's generalized model is the basis of another paper by the same author [4], which refutes the claims of Mao ([20], p. 241) and of Lusztig and Schwab [18], who recommend the *internal* determination of the discount rate. Exact knowledge of the discount rate exists only in *perfect* capital markets; if net present value or internal rate of return is used as a selection criterion, then the discount rate must be *estimated* from *external* sources (i.e., for use as a discount rate in the NPV method, or as a comparison standard for acceptance if the IRR method is used). Thus, Bernhard's model again confirms Hirshleifer's finding that in *im*perfect capital markets, the Separation Theorem collapses and optimal project selections cannot be made without considering the future *utility* of intertemporal funds exchange.

## 9.4. Project Selection by Goal Programming Methods

*Goal Programming* (hereafter called GP) is a type of mathematical programming for solving optimization problems that contain *multiple conflicting objectives*, or *goals*. The principal restrictions in applying GP methodology are (1) the decision-maker must state an absolute priority, or ordinal *preference ordering* among his goals, and (2) he must provide a *target value* (i.e., a desired level of attainment) for each of his goals. The GP rationale then provides a solution to the programming problem that minimizes the *absolute deviations* from the stated objectives, *in the specified priority order of goal attainment*. Otherwise, GP is simply a "first cousin" to linear or quadratic programming methods. For example, GP problems can be linearly constrained, they can be formulated and solved as integer [even binary (0, 1)] problems, they require the same nonnegativity constraints on the variables, and they use a modified form of the simplex procedure to obtain solutions.

The GP model was first introduced by Charnes and Cooper [7] and later considerably extended by Ijiri [15], Lee [16], and Ignizio [13]. The present state of the art is fairly summarized in the preceding paragraph. We note particularly that Ignizio has succeeded in combining the GP methodology with a Dakin algorithm for solving the 0, 1 case [14]. This should be of considerable interest to those involved in project selection problems.

To present an exposition of GP methodology and its application to the project selection problem, first we shall give a brief description of the GP concept and format, second we shall illustrate how a GP problem is solved by the modified simplex algorithm, and third we shall show the formulation of a simple project selection problem and summarize its solution.

**9.4.1.** *Goal programming format.* Unlike linear programming problems, the GP model has a multidimensional objective function that seeks to minimize certain *selected absolute deviations* from a set of stated goals, usually within an additional set of given constraints. Each of the selected deviations in the GP objective carry *ordinal* priority weights so that goals are attained (or approached as nearly as possible) in strict order of priority. In general, the format of the GP problem can be stated as follows:

*Find* $\mathbf{X} = (x_1, x_2, \ldots, x_j, \ldots, x_n)$ so as to

$$\text{MIN: } \mathbf{Z} = f(\mathbf{d}^+, \mathbf{d}^-) \qquad (9.23)$$

subject to

$$(1) \qquad \mathbf{AX} = \mathbf{B} + \mathbf{d}^+ - \mathbf{d}^- \qquad (9.24)$$

$$(2) \qquad \mathbf{CX} \leq \mathbf{D} \qquad (9.25)$$

$$(3) \qquad \mathbf{X}, \mathbf{d}^+, \mathbf{d}^- \geq \mathbf{0} \qquad (9.26)$$

where

(a) $\mathbf{X} = (x_1, x_2, \ldots, x_j, \ldots, x_n)$ is the solution vector;
(b) Equation (9.23) is the *goal programming* objective of the problem, in which it is desired to minimize a function of the deviations from the stated goals,
(c) Equation (9.24) states the *original* problem objectives, converted into *goals* by the inclusion of *intentionally* permissible deviations $(d_i^+, d_i^-)$ from the right-hand-side *targets* $(B_i)$; $i = 1, 2, \ldots m$,
(d) Equation (9.25) show the absolute constraints on the problem, corresponding to conventional linear programming constraints; $k = m + 1, m + 2, \ldots,$ $M$,
(e) $f(\mathbf{d}^+, \mathbf{d}^-)$ is a *linear, prioritized* function of the permissible deviation variables from the objectives (goals) in Eq. (9.24),
(f) $\mathbf{d}^+$ is a vector of nonnegative variables that represent the permissible *positive* deviations from the associated objectives, Eq. (9.24),
(g) $\mathbf{d}^-$ is a vector of nonnegative variables that represent permissible *negative* deviations from the associated objectives, Eq. (9.24),
(h) $\mathbf{B}$ is a vector of right-hand-side (RHS) *target* values, or aspiration levels, associated with the objectives, Eq. (9.24),
(i) $\mathbf{C}$ is a matrix of *resource* consumption coefficients,
(j) $\mathbf{A}$ is a matrix of activity coefficients,
(k) $\mathbf{D}$ is the vector of RHS bounds on the absolute constraints.

Quite often, the objective, Eq. (9.23), takes the form

$$\text{MIN } Z = \{P_1[g_1(d_1^+, d_1^-)], P_2[g_2(d_2^+, d_2^-)], \ldots, P_i[g_i(d_i^+, d_i^-)]\}$$

where $g_i(d_i^+, d_i^-)$ is a linear function of the deviation variables,
  $P_i$ is the ordinal priority level associated with $g_i(d_i^+, d_i^-)$,
  $i \leq m$; i.e., the number of ordinal priorities is equal to or less than the total number of objectives.

In goal programming, it should be noted particularly that the priority levels, $P_1, P_2, \ldots, P_i$, have a strict interpretation. The interpretation is as follows. $P_i$ is the preemptive priority associated with the $i$th set of objectives. Thus, $P_1$ is the top priority that is associated with the top priority objective or objectives. (It should be noted that all objectives within a given priority level must have a common measure of effectiveness.) Furthermore, if $P_i$ is the preemptive priority associated with a given set of objectives, then

$$P_i \gg P_{i+1} \gg P_{i+2} \cdots.$$

That is, the satisfaction of a given set of objectives at priority level $i$ is *immeasurably* preferred to the satisfaction of any other set of objectives at a lower priority level. This concept is at the heart of goal programming. As a result, the solution procedure does not *find* a global optimum satisfying all constraints, as in linear programming. Rather, the GP solution procedure *finds* a feasible set of "optimal" solutions to the Priority 1 level subproblem; then *within* this set of solutions it finds *another subset* of optimal solutions (if possible) to the Priority 2 level subproblem, and so forth.

Another assumption in goal programming that is fundamental to understanding the GP method is that *intentional* deviations away from the numerically valued goals are allowed to occur. Deviations can thus be considered either positive-, negative-, or zero-valued movements away from goals. As in linear programming, however, the solution procedures for GP require all variables to be nonnegative; and for this reason all deviations must be structured in the GP problem as nonnegative variables. This might pose a problem, but it is easily circumvented by a simple transformation. For example, if $d_i \gtreqless 0$ is a deviation from a goal, the deviation may be replaced by the difference between two nonnegative variables, thus:

$$d_i = (d_i^+ - d_i^-)$$

where

(a) $-\infty < d_i < +\infty$.
(b) $d_i^+ \geq 0$.
(c) $d_i^- \geq 0$.
(d) $(d_i^+)(d_i^-) = 0$.

Requirement (d) exists in the simplex solution procedure; that is, both $d_i^+$ and $d_i^-$ cannot take on positive values at the same time in the simplex procedure. Hence, only $d_i^+$ or $d_i^-$ can be *in solution* (i.e., $> 0$) in the same tableau of the problem.

The two requirements stated above, namely, the preemptive prioritization within the objective function and the existence of permissible deviations, permit the GP procedure to "work" even when some (or all) of the goals are incompatible. The result is that some of the goals will be attained (or even overattained) while others will be underattained (usually in the lower priority goals). If a goal is overattained, the corresponding $d_i^+$ variable will be in solution (i.e., $d_i^+ > 0$ and $d_i^- = 0$); whereas, if the goal is underattained, then $d_i^+ = 0$ and $d_i^- > 0$. It is in this manner that the GP solution signals which goals are attained and which are not. A simple example will illustrate the method of formulating and solving a goal programming problem.

**9.4.2.** *An example of formulating and solving a goal programming problem.* To motivate an exposition of how goal programming methods may be applied, consider the following simple *mix* problem, in which the firm seeks an operating policy that will optimally allocate its resources to the production of its products (i.e., *optimally* in the sense that its *prioritized but conflicting* goals are met as nearly as possible).

The Chop-N-Block Company[6] produces two products, a cheese knife and a wooden cutting board. Each product requires the following inputs and results in the sales prices noted:

|                                       | Knife  | Board  |
| ------------------------------------- | ------ | ------ |
| Direct Material Cost                  | $0.50  | $1.00  |
| Direct Labor Cost                     | 0.50   | 1.00   |
| Machine Time Required (hours)         | 0.50   | 0.25   |
| Assembly Time Required (man-hours)    | 1.00   | 1.00   |
| Sales Price per Unit                  | $3.00  | $5.00  |

In order to keep the example simple, we shall make some assumptions:

1. Consumer demand is strong so that all products that can be produced can be sold at the prices indicated.
2. One production period is involved; i.e., time $t = 0, 1$.
3. Production is assumed to be limited by two absolute restrictions: (a) Machine capacity is 8 hr per period, and (b) assembly capacity is 20 man-hours per period.
4. Initial values of the firm's cash balance in the bank and its accounts receivable are $20 and $30, respectively. At time $t = 0$, a bank loan to the firm of $10 is outstanding, and long-term bonds in the amount of $30 are owed.
5. Fixed expenses of $5 per period will be incurred in operating the firm, which must be paid in cash.
6. Cash dividends of $2.50 (total )are to be paid in the first period, and $2.50 is to be spent for equipment replacement.
7. The firm sells its products on a one-period credit basis; i.e., receivables for a prior period are collected in the period following the date of sale. Labor costs, materials, and other expenses are paid in cash in the period used.
8. Taxes are assumed nonexistent, and inventory balances are zero since all products can be sold as produced.
9. The Board of Directors of the firm has approved a budget for plant expansion in Period 2 (i.e., $t = 1$ to $t = 2$). Part of the funds for this budget will be obtained by the sale of new bonds and part by sale of new equity stock, both sales to take place in Period 2. In order to command a good market price for its proposed stock sale and to negotiate a favorable bond sale, however, the management of the firm judges that the firm must (a) continue to pay its current dividends of $2.50 (total) and (b) make a satisfactory profit in Period 1. The Board feels that investors would judge a *net* profit of $45 in Period 1 to be satisfactory, and it feels the firm can attain that amount. Since the *total* of fixed expenses, dividends, and expenditures for equipment is $5 + $2.50 + $2.50 = $10 in Period 1, the corresponding contribution to profit and overhead from production is the *net* profit plus $10, or $55 in Period 1, from the production and sale of cheese knives and cutting boards.

---

[6]This problem is adapted from Baumgarten [1].

10. The president of the firm has established a policy of maintaining an end-of-period cash balance that is at least $2 greater than the sum of the short-term liabilities. In this case, the short-term liability is the bank loan of $10 so the policy goal for the cash balance is $10 + $2 = $12.

11. The contractual conditions of the long-term bonds require that the firm's net working capital at the end of Period 1 be at least twice the face value of the *bond* debt. *Net working capital* is defined as

(cash + accounts receivable + inventory − short-term liabilities)

at the end of the period.

We now define the structural variables of the problem as

$X_1$ = number of units of knives to be produced,

$X_2$ = number of units of cutting boards to be produced.

On the basis of the preceding information, we may now formulate the constraints and the goals of the problem. First, the technical constraints due to machine and assembly capacity restrictions are

$$0.5X_1 + 0.25X_2 \leq 8 \quad \text{(machine capacity)}$$
$$1.0X_1 + 1.0X_2 \leq 20 \quad \text{(assembly capacity)} \qquad \Bigg\} \quad (9.27)$$

The contribution to profit and overhead (P & O) *goal* is generated from the sales prices and variable expenses per unit of each product, thus:

Contribution to P & O (knives) = $3.00 − $0.50 − $0.50
                                              Sales       Direct      Direct
                                              price     material    labor

= $2.00 per knife manufactured.

Contribution to P & O (boards) = $5.00 − $1.00 − $1.00

= $3.00 per board manufactured.

We want the contribution to profit and overhead to equal or exceed the P & O goal of $55 so we require

$$2.00X_1 + 3.00X_2 \geq 55.$$

To put this requirement into canonical form, as required by Eq. (9.24), we include the deviation variables on the right-hand side, thus:

$$2.00X_1 + 3.00X_2 = 55 + d_1^+ - d_1^-, \qquad (9.28)$$

and upon transposing the deviations we have the contribution to profit and overhead goal stated as follows:

$$2.00X_1 + 3.00X_2 - d_1^+ + d_1^- = 55. \qquad (9.29)$$

Note that if $(d_1^+ > 0, d_1^- = 0)$ in the optimal solution, the P & O goal of $55 is *over-attained*, and if $(d_1^+ = 0, d_1^- > 0)$, then it is *underattained*.

The end-of-period cash balance goal is determined by the beginning cash balance, the cash inflows and outflows during the period, and the desired end-of-period cash balance. We may write the requirement as follows:

$$\underset{\substack{\text{Beginning}\\\text{cash}\\\text{balance}}}{\$20} + \underset{\substack{\text{Beginning}\\\text{accounts}\\\text{receivable}\\\text{collected}}}{\$30} - \underset{\substack{\text{Cash fixed}\\\text{expenses +}\\\text{equipment}\\\text{expenditures}\\\text{+ dividends}\\\text{paid}}}{\$10} - \underset{\substack{\text{Cash production}\\\text{costs for direct}\\\text{labor and material}}}{\$(1.0X_1 + 2.0X_2)} \geq \underset{\substack{\text{Desired}\\\text{end-of-period}\\\text{cash balance}}}{\$12.} \tag{9.30}$$

Combining terms and adding the required deviation variables, we have

$$-1.00X_1 - 2.00X_2 = -28 + d_2^+ - d_2^-$$

and upon multiplying by $-1$ and transposing the deviation variables to the left side, the end-of-period cash balance *goal* becomes

$$1.00X_1 + 2.00X_2 + d_2^+ - d_2^- = 28. \tag{9.31}$$

We should pause here to comment on the necessity for being consistent with the *signs* attached to the structural variables when goals are formed from the cash flow relationships. If cash flows are always signed $(+)$ to represent inflows and $(-)$ for outflows and if the desired relationship is *always* placed in the form

$$\mathbf{AX} \geq \mathbf{B},$$

then the canonical form of Eq. (9.24) can be used to convert the desired relationship into a *goal*. When this is done, Table 9.1 gives the necessary procedures for forming the *GP* objective.

**Table 9.1.** PROCEDURES FOR ACHIEVING OBJECTIVES

| If the Objective Is To | Procedure | |
|---|---|---|
| | Add on LH Side | Goal Objective |
| (a) Equal or exceed $B_i$ | $-d_i^+ + d_i^-$ | Min $d_i^-$ |
| (b) Equal or be less than $B_i$ | (same) | Min $d_i^+$ |
| (c) Equal $B_i$ | (same) | Min $(d_i^+ + d_i^-)$ |

Turning now to the third goal, we shall formulate the net working capital goal required by Assumption 11. This requirement is first formulated as follows: From Eq. (9.31), the *ending* cash balance is $1.00X_1 + 2.00X_2$. Hence, the end-of-period net working capital is calculated by the following relationship:

$$\underset{\substack{\text{Beginning}\\\text{cash}\\\text{balance}}}{20} + \underset{\substack{\text{Beginning}\\\text{accounts}\\\text{receivable}}}{30} + \underset{\substack{\text{Net contribution}\\\text{to profit and}\\\text{overhead}}}{(2X_1 + 3X_2)} - \underset{\substack{\text{Bank}\\\text{loan}}}{10} - \underset{\substack{\text{Cash fixed}\\\text{expenses,}\\\text{equipment}\\\text{expenditures,}\\\text{and dividend}\\\text{payment}}}{10} \geq \underset{\substack{\text{Twice the}\\\text{bond debt}}}{2(30)}$$

Combining terms and adding the deviation variables to the RHS, we have

$$2.00X_1 + 3.00X_2 = 30 + d_3^+ - d_3^-$$

and upon transposing the deviations, the net working capital goal becomes

$$2.00X_1 + 3.00X_2 - d_3^+ + d_3^- = 30. \tag{9.32}$$

We now consider the GP objective function. Suppose the management of the Chop-N-Block Company desires first and foremost, with Priority 1, to attain a net profit of \$45 (see Assumption 9). This net profit corresponds to a contribution to profit and overhead of \$55, via the goal stated in Eq. (9.29). Suppose also that management only secondarily desires to satisfy the working capital goal [Eq. (9.32)], at a Priority 2 level, and the end-of-period cash balance goal [Eq. (9.31)] at a Priority 3 level. In addition, management considers overattainment of the end-of-period working capital goal to be equally satisfactory as just meeting this goal exactly but that the working capital goal must not be underattained, if possible. Also, management wishes to use the firm's cash as fully as possible so that there is neither an excess nor a deficiency in the \$12 end-of-period cash goal. Finally, management requires that the profit goal not be underattained.

To formulate these preferences into a *goal programming* objective, we let $P_1$, $P_2$, and $P_3$ be ordinal priorities (i.e., $P_1 \gg P_2 \gg P_3$, such that there is no number $k$, given $k > 0$, that can make $kP_2 \geq P_1$ or $kP_3 \geq P_2$). Then, using these ordinal priorities, the GP objective can be written as

$$\text{MIN } Z = P_1 d_1^- + P_2 d_3^- + P_3(d_2^+ + d_2^-) \tag{9.33}$$

where $d_1^- =$ possible underattainment of profit goal.

$d_2^+ =$ possible overattainment of cash goal.

$d_2^- =$ possible underattainment of cash goal.

$d_3^- =$ possible underattainment of working capital goal.

The objective in Eq. (9.33) can be more fully interpreted as follows:

1. Management has set profit goal attainment as its primary and overriding goal. Exceeding the profit goal is equally acceptable as just meeting it, but underattainment is considered unacceptable with Priority 1—hence, the inclusion of $P_1 d_1^-$ in the objective.
2. After the profit goal has been satisfied or exceeded, management wants to equal or exceed the minimum working capital balance. This is expressed by adding the term $P_2 d_3^-$ in the objective to be minimized.
3. Finally, after both of the goals above have been approached or satisfied, management wants cash to be used as fully as possible, with no excess or deficiency in the required end-of-period cash balance. This is assigned Priority 3, however, and the term $P_3(d_2^+ + d_2^-)$ is included in the objective.

The multiple-goal problem can now be stated formally as follows:

$$\text{MIN } Z = P_1 d_1^- + P_2 d_3^- + P_3(d_2^+ + d_2^-)$$

subject to

(1) $2.0X_1 + 3.0X_2 - d_1^+ + d_1^- = 55$ (profit and overhead goal)

(2) $1.0X_1 + 2.0X_2 + d_2^+ - d_2^- = 20$ (cash balance goal)

(3) $2.0X_1 + 3.0X_2 - d_3^+ + d_3^- = 30$ (working capital goal)

(4) $0.5X_1 + 0.25X_2 \qquad\qquad \le 8$ (machine constraint)

(5) $1.0X_1 + 1.0X_2 \qquad\qquad\quad \le 20$ (assembly constraint)

(6) $X_i, d_i^+, d_i^- \qquad\qquad\qquad \ge 0$ (nonnegativity constraints)

The graphical solution of this problem is illustrated in Fig. 9.2. Some features of this solution should be noted. First, the feasible area is circumscribed by the absolute machine and assembly capacity constraints [Eq. (9.27)] and the nonnegativity conditions ($X_1 \ge 0$, $i = 1, 2$). Second, the "optimum" occurs at ($X_1 = 0$, $X_2 = 20$), which is a result of the Priority 1 minimization of the negative deviation from the profit and overhead goal—in fact, $d_1^- = 0$ and $d_1^+ = \$5.00$ in the optimal solution since no

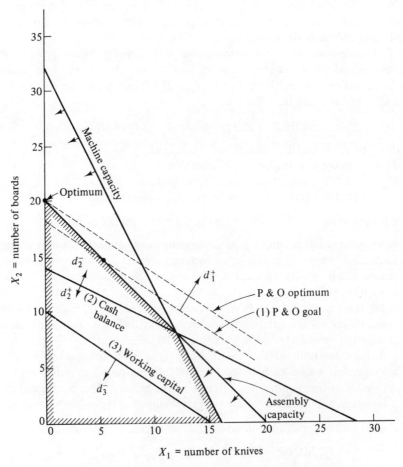

$X_1$ = number of knives

**Fig. 9.2.** Graphical solution to goal programming problem.

restriction was placed on $d_1^+$ except that it be nonnegative. Thus $d_1^-$ was not only driven to its minimum (zero) as $P_1$ required in the objective, but $d_1^+ = 5$ ($>0$) came into solution, indicating that the profit and overhead goal was overattained.

As a result of this superordinate requirement, one of the other goals was acheived while the other was not. The Priority 2 working capital goal was overachieved, as seen by solving Eq. (9.32):

$$2.00(0) + 3.00(20) - d_3^+ + 0 = 30$$

or

$$\left.\begin{array}{l} d_3^+ = 30 \\ d_3^- = 0 \end{array}\right\}.$$

Since $d_3^+ = 30 > 0$, the working capital goal was overachieved by $30. The Priority 3 cash balance goal was underachieved, however, as seen by solving Eq. (9.31):

$$1.0(0) + 2.0(20) + 0 - d_2^- = 28$$

or

$$\left.\begin{array}{l} d_2^- = 12 \\ d_2^+ = 0 \end{array}\right\}.$$

This negative deviation indicates that the ending cash balance is zero since the goal was $12, and it was underachieved by $12. Finally, the "optimal" solution indicates that there is excess machine capacity. This can be seen by defining $S_4$ as the slack activity for the machine constraint, rewriting the constraint as an equality, and then solving it for $S_4$ in terms of $X_1 = 0$, $X_2 = 20$:

$$0.5X_1 + 0.25X_2 \qquad \leq 8$$
$$0.5(0) + 0.25(20) + S_4 = 8$$

or

$$S_4 = 3.$$

A more general method of solving the goal programming problem is the modified simplex procedure. The solution methodology is essentially the same as the simplex procedure for linear programming problems, except that *multiple* objectives appear in the objective *row*, ordered by priorities. The objective variables with the highest priority are brought into solution first and are *thereafter left in solution*. Next, the Priority 2 objective is then optimized by bringing into solution the Priority 2 deviations, however, subject to the solution (deviation) variables from the Priority 1 objective *remaining in solution*. In turn, the lower priority objectives are treated in the same manner until all objective rows are optimized. This method of solution is illustrated in Appendix 9A for the Chop-N-Block Company example. Computer algorithms exist for larger and more complex problems (e.g., see Ignizio [13], pp. 227–247, 256; also [9]).

**9.4.3. *Project selection by goal programming.*** To demonstrate how goal programming can be applied to the project selection problem under imperfect capital market conditions, we shall use an example in which the candidate set consists of 15 possible projects (some of which are interrelated), subject to acceptance in the face of nine goals (some of which are conflicting).[7] Although cash flows and project lives are assumed to be known with certainty, the market rates of discount for both borrowing and lending are not known. The problem for our hypothetical company is to select an "optimal" set of projects from the 15 available ones. For our purposes we assume that the company's planners have established nine specific objectives and that these goals can be ranked in a preference ordering. In addition, since a discounting rate is unavailable in an imperfect capital market, all we are able to do is establish a *preference ordering* for the flow of funds—i.e., we may say that funds flowing at time $t = 1$ are ordinally more valuable than similar amounts at $t = 2$, and so forth. (Baumol and Quandt [2] and Bernhard [4] suggest the use of a utility function of temporal funds flows in lieu of using a discount rate. Here, we have essentially done this.)

The undiscounted *costs* of the 15 projects are given in Table 9.2, along with brief descriptions of certain of the projects that figure in specific goals to be described later. At this point, it is not important that the costs in Table 9.2 be studied carefully, but the projects having specific descriptions should be noted and remembered, as we shall later write equations dealing with these projects.

**Table 9.2.** ESTIMATED ANNUAL COSTS OF PROJECTS

| Project, j | Description | Cost in Year $t$ ($\$ = \$10^4$) | | | |
|:---:|:---|:---:|:---:|:---:|:---:|
| | | $t = 1$ | $t = 2$ | $t = 3$ | $t = 4$ |
| 1 | Internal project | $ 50 | $ 10 | $ 5 | $ 0 |
| 2* | Build foreign factory | 100 | 0 | 0 | 8 |
| 3† | Noise pollution control project | 20 | 20 | 0 | 0 |
| 4† | Noise pollution control project | 75 | 2 | 2 | 1 |
| 5 | Internal project | 200 | 0 | 55 | 0 |
| 6* | Foreign distribution project | 0 | 150 | 0 | 0 |
| 7 | Internal project | 0 | 90 | 30 | 0 |
| 8 | Internal project | 0 | 100 | 0 | 10 |
| 9‡ | Clean air project | 0 | 60 | 5 | 0 |
| 10 | Internal project | 0 | 10 | 86 | 4 |
| 11 | Internal project | 0 | 0 | 180 | 0 |
| 12‡ | Clean air project | 0 | 0 | 80 | 0 |
| 13 | Internal project | 0 | 0 | 30 | 30 |
| 14 | Internal project | 0 | 0 | 2 | 70 |
| 15* | Foreign advertising project | 0 | 0 | 0 | 100 |

*Project 15 is conditioned upon acceptance of Projects 2 and 6.
†Projects 3 and 4 are mutually exclusive.
‡Projects 9 and 12 are mutually exclusive.

---

[7]This example is adapted from Lee and Lerro [17], Run 11; however, their estimated net present value objective (*D* in their Appendix) has been eliminated and an ordinal priority goal substituted in its place (since here the interest rate is unknown due to imperfect capital market conditions). Also, we have reordered some of their priorities. Hence, our solution is not the same as theirs.

The estimated annual income and annual cash flows from each of the projects are given in Table 9.3. The annual incomes are displayed because one of the goals stated by management is a 50 % increase in annual income (this goal will be described later).

**Table 9.3.** ESTIMATED ANNUAL INCOME AND CASH INFLOWS

| Project, j | ($ = $10⁴) Estimated Annual Income | | | | ($ = $10⁴) Estimated Annual Cash Inflow | | | |
|---|---|---|---|---|---|---|---|---|
| | $t = 1$ | $t = 2$ | $t = 3$ | $t = 4$ | $t = 1$ | $t = 2$ | $t = 3$ | $t = 4$ |
| 1 | $ 0 | $ 25 | $ 30 | $ 0 | $ 75 | $ 100 | $ 100 | $ 100 |
| 2 | 10 | 100 | 70 | 105 | 150 | 150 | 150 | 300 |
| 3 | 0 | 1 | 5 | 5 | 5 | 10 | 20 | 40 |
| 4 | −100 | 5 | 0 | − 2 | 0 | 140 | 50 | 40 |
| 5 | − 10 | 65 | − 15 | 26 | 200 | 200 | 50 | 200 |
| 6 | 0 | −115 | 0 | 40 | 0 | 60 | 70 | 80 |
| 7 | 0 | − 75 | − 45 | 385 | 0 | 30 | 0 | 450 |
| 8 | 0 | −140 | 97 | 58 | 0 | 0 | 120 | 150 |
| 9 | 0 | 95 | − 10 | 0 | 0 | 160 | 0 | 0 |
| 10 | 0 | − 13 | − 12 | 80 | 0 | 0 | 100 | 110 |
| 11 | 0 | 0 | 50 | 200 | 0 | 0 | 250 | 295 |
| 12 | 0 | 0 | −100 | 190 | 0 | 0 | 0 | 240 |
| 13 | 0 | 0 | 30 | − 55 | 0 | 0 | 114 | 187 |
| 14 | 0 | 0 | 6 | 62 | 0 | 0 | 38 | 194 |
| 15 | 0 | 0 | 0 | 290 | 0 | 0 | 0 | 550 |
| $\Sigma =$ | $−100 | $ −52 | $ 106 | $1,384 | $ 430 | $ 820 | $1,062 | $2,936 |

The following verbal description will assist in understanding the formulation of the goal programming problem. First, the firm has established an expenditure (capital) budget for each year: $B_1 = \$200$; $B_2 = \$250$; $B_3 = \$260$; $B_4 = \$120$ (where $B_t$ = budget limit, tens of thousands of dollars; $t = 1, 2, 3, 4$). If the firm maintains strict control over capital expenditures, four budget constraints can be written as follows:

$$\sum_{j=1}^{15} C_{tj}x_j \leq B_t \qquad (9.34)$$

where $C_{tj}$ = the cost of the $j$th project in the $t$th year, obtained from Table 9.2, where $t = 1, 2, 3, 4$.

$x_j$ = the proportion of the $j$th project accepted; i.e., $0 \leq x_j \leq 1$.

Casting these constraints into *goal* form, we rewrite Eq. (9.34) as *budget goals*; thus:

$$\sum_{j=1}^{15} C_{tj}x_j + d_t^- - d_t^+ = B_t \qquad (9.35)$$

where now $d_t^-$ = an underachievement of the budget goal (underspending the budget) in year $t$.

$d_t^+ =$ an overachievement of the budget goal in year $t$ (spending more than the budgeted amount).

In this goal, the *positive* deviation is minimized to approach satisfaction of the established budget amounts.

Second, a corollary of the budget *limits* allows for transfer of funds between periods. The *cumulative* funds available for capital allocation is simply the sum of the budgeted amounts. Thus, for the second year, if no funds are spent in the first year, there would be available $B_1 + B_2 = \$200 + \$250 = \$450$ for allocation; in the third year, $B_1 + B_2 + B_3 = \$710$; and so forth. Likewise, cumulative allocations are subjected to these limits. This flexibility allows the firm to take advantage of opportunities regardless of their timing. The generalized goal expression for funds mobility between years is

$$\sum_{j=1}^{15} \sum_{t=1}^{t'} C_{tj}x_j + d_{t'}^- - d_{t'}^+ = \sum_{t=1}^{t'} B_t \qquad (9.36)$$

where $t' = 2, 3, 4$ (time at the end of the second, third, and fourth periods, respectively).

Thus, *three* goals are written representing, respectively, transfer of funds from $t = 1$ to $t = 2$; from $t = 1$ and $t = 2$ to $t = 3$; and from $t = 1$, $t = 2$, and $t = 3$ to $t = 4$. The objective associated with each of these is to minimize the positive deviational variables, which, in effect, expresses management's goal that the *cumulative* expenditures for accepted projects be equal to or less than the cumulative budgeted amounts, as of the same point in time ($t = 2, 3$, or $4$).

Third, the firm is assumed to be faced with public regulatory pressure to control the noise from one of its plants and also to abate some serious air pollution problems. Mutually exclusive alternatives are available for solving both of these problems. Projects 3 and 4 are mutually exclusive methods of solving the noise problem, and Projects 9 and 12 are the mutually exclusive alternatives for abating the air pollution problem. Normally, the formulation of these objectives would be as constraints, such as

Solve noise pollution $\left\{ \begin{array}{llll} x_3 = 1 & \text{or} & x_3 = 0 \\ x_4 = 0 & \text{or} & x_4 = 1 \end{array} \right.$

Air pollution $\left\{ \begin{array}{llll} x_9 = 1 & \text{or} & x_9 = 0 \\ x_{12} = 0 & \text{or} & x_{12} = 1 \end{array} \right.$

In the present formulation, however, it has been decided to investigate only the combination ($x_3 = 1$, $x_9 = 1$). The corresponding deviations are minimized in order to achieve this choice in the final solution.

Foreign-based manufacturing and distribution operations have become more profitable and attractive in recent years. A plan has been advanced for constructing a new captive manufacturing plant in a foreign country (Project 2), to open up new markets and introduce the company's products both there and in adjacent countries. Plans have also been advanced for selecting and establishing new distribution channels in the foreign countries (Project 6), as well as undertaking an advertising campaign

(Project 15). Neither the distribution plan nor the advertising campaign should be undertaken, however, if the plant is not built. These limitations can be expressed by conditional constraints; thus:

$$\left.\begin{aligned} x_{15} - x_6 - d^+ + d^- = 0 \\ x_6 - x_2 - d^+ + d^- = 0 \end{aligned}\right\} \quad (9.37)$$

in which the positive deviations $(d^+)$ would be minimized. Thus, with sufficiently high priority, the $d^+$ values would be zero, and the following results could take place:

| $x_2$ | $x_6$ | $x_{15}$ | Decision |
|---|---|---|---|
| 0 | 0 | 0 | Execute nothing |
| 1 | 0 | 0 | Build plant |
| 1 | 1 | 0 | Build plant; distribute |
| 1 | 1 | 1 | Build plant; distribute, advertise |

(This assumes that the $d^- = 0$ also.)

The remaining objectives are ones that contribute to cash flow, growth, and total value of the firm.

Since a discount rate for the intertemporal transfer of funds is not *a priori* known in an imperfect capital market, a workable substitute for discounting is to place a higher utility on the flow of funds that occur in early time periods than on those that occur in later time periods.[8] The goal programming format allows us to do this since we can assign arbitrary *weights* to deviations within a particular priority class. To incorporate this concept, four objectives are written, one for each period. For example, for $t = 1$, we would write the cash inflow objective as

$$75X_1 + 150X_2 + 5X_3 + 200X_5 + d_{t=1}^- - d_{t=1}^+ = 430 \qquad (9.38)$$

where the coefficients of the $X_j$ are the *cash flows* for $t = 1$ in Table 9.3 and the RHS value, 430, is simply the sum of the coefficients on the LHS. Similar objectives are written for years $t = 2, 3, 4$. In the achievement function of the GP problem, however, one wishes to minimize the *weighted negative* deviations; thus:

$$\text{MIN } S = P_i(W_1 d_{t=1}^- + W_2 d_{t=2}^- + W_3 d_{t=3}^- + W_4 d_{t=4}^-) \qquad (9.39)$$

where        $P_i$ = priority level of the funds flow objectives;

$W_1, \ldots, W_4$ = arbitrary weights (utilities) assigned to the negative deviations $d_t^-$;

where $W_1 > W_2 > W_3 > W_4$ to imply greater utility attachment to early funds flow. Thus, a system of goals of the form of Eq. (9.37) expresses the objective of achieving a set of cash *in*flow goals, and the inclusion of the *weighted* negative deviations [Eq. (9.39)] assures incorporation of a value weighting on each of the annual cash inflows. A similar weighting process is used with cash *out*flows to express a time-value preference.

To maximize the chances for market growth, the firm is assumed to desire a 50 %

---

[8]See Baumol and Quandt [2]; also Bernhard [4].

growth rate in its *income* over time (not cash flows). As a result, the planning staff is assumed to have established the following income goals for each year: $t = 1$, \$15.0; $t = 2$, \$22.5; $t = 3$, \$34.0; $t = 4$, \$51.0. Four constraints, corresponding to each year ($t = 1, 2, 3, 4$) in the planning horizon, express this growth requisite:

$$\sum_{j=1}^{15} (NI)_{tj} X_j + d_t^- - d_t^+ = (TI)_t \qquad (9.40)$$

where

$(NI)_{tj}$ = net income from Project $j$ in Period $t$ (Table 9.3.).

$X_j$ = decision variable, $0 \leq X_j \leq 1$.

$(TI)_t$ = total income for year $t$ ($t = 1$, \$15; $t = 2$, \$22.5; $t = 3$, \$34; $t = 1$, \$51).

When the negative deviations, $d_t^-$, are minimized, the objective is approached as closely as possible on the underachievement side; if a $d_t^+$ comes into solution, the corresponding growth goal is exceeded.

The firm expects a large required cash outflow near the end of year 3, as a result of a contractual obligation with its union. In order to minimize external financing, management desires the internal cash inflow during year 3 to be at least \$5 million. This goal is formulated as

$$\sum_{j=1}^{15} Y_{3j} X_j + d^- - d^+ = 500 \qquad (9.41)$$

where $Y_{3j}$ = cash inflow from Project $j$, accepted in year 3. Minimization of the negative deviation variable will tend to achieve the goal of \$5 million (minimum).

In addition to the foregoing, management desires to maintain a minimum liquidity level for each of the four periods, as follows: $t = 1$, \$300; $t = 2$, \$500; $t = 3$, \$500; $t = 4$, \$1,700. In the same manner as the cash inflow was maximized for year 3 above [Eq. (9.41)], four additional goals can be written for the minimum liquidity requirements, as follows:

$$\sum_{j=1}^{15} Y_{tj} X_j + d_t^- - d_t^+ = (TCF)_t \qquad (9.42)$$

where $(TCF)_t$ = the minimum liquidity levels (total cash flows) at times $t$, as given above. When the negative deviations are minimized, the liquidity goals will be most closely approached from the underachievement side.

Last, it is strongly desired that no multiples of projects be permitted. The 15 constraints that prevent the occurrence of multiple projects are of the form

$$X_j \mid d_j^- \quad d_j^+ = 1$$

where the positive deviations, $d_j^+$, are minimized with a high priority.

The formulation of the *objectives* of the goal program is now complete, and an annotated summary of the model can be found in Appendix 9B.

The GP *achievement function* is formulated as follows. We assume that management has reached a consensus and has assigned relative priorities ($P_1 > P_2 > \cdots > P_k$) to the objectives structured above; where required *within* a priority class, arbitrary weights (e.g., $W_1 > W_2 > W_3 > W_4$) have also been assigned to designated deviation variables. The priorities and weights for the deviation variables are assumed to follow the following rationale:

1. With *Priority 1*, it is desired to
   A. First, prohibit multiples of projects.
   B. Second, minimize annual budget overruns, incorporating a utility-of-money ordering to express time preference.
2. With *Priority 2*, it is desired to
   A. Accept pollution control Projects 3 and 9.
   B. Reject pollution control Projects 4 and 12.
   C. Maximize cash inflow in year 3 (for union contract obligations).
   D. Value A and B, above, twice as important as C.
3. With *Priority 3*, it is desired to
   A. Achieve early funds (cash) inflow, incorporating a utility-of-money ordering to express time preference.
4. With *Priority 4*, it is desired to
   A. Maintain 50 % growth rate on total income.
5. With *Priority 5*, it is desired to
   A. Minimize the shifting of projects from one period to another [i.e., minimize intertemporal transfer of funds via Eq. (9.36)].
   B. Assure foreign investment in new foreign plant, distribution system, and/or advertising.
   C. The foreign investments (B) are considered three times as important as the shifting of funds objective (A).
6. With *Priority 6*, it is desired to
   A. Minimize *excess* liquidity of the firm in each of the four periods.

The foregoing considerations result in the following *achievement function* for the GP problem:

$$\text{MIN } Z = P_1\{\underbrace{10(d_{25}^+ + d_{26}^+ + \cdots + d_{39}^+)}_{\substack{\text{Deviations permitting} \\ \text{multiples of projects}}} + \underbrace{4d_1^+ + 3d_2^+ + 2d_3^+ + 1d_4^+\}}_{\substack{\text{Excess budget overruns,} \\ \text{incorporating utility-of-} \\ \text{money weights}}}$$

$$+ P_2\{\underbrace{2(d_8^- + d_8^+ + d_9^- + d_9^+)}_{\substack{\text{Accept pollution control} \\ \text{Projects 3 and 9}}} + \underbrace{d_{40}^- + d_{40}^+ + d_{41}^- + d_{41}^+}_{\substack{\text{Reject pollution control} \\ \text{Projects 4 and 12}}} + \underbrace{d_{14}^-\}}_{\substack{\text{Underachievement} \\ \text{of year 3 cash flow} \\ \text{goal}}}$$

$$+ P_3\{\underbrace{4d_{19}^- + 3d_{20}^- + 2d_{21}^- + 1d_{22}^-\}}_{\substack{\text{Underachievement of funds inflow,} \\ \text{incorporating utility-of-money function}}} + P_4\{\underbrace{d_{10}^+ + d_{11}^+ + d_{12}^+ + d_{13}^+\}}_{\substack{\text{Maintain 50\% income} \\ \text{growth rate}}} \quad (9.43)$$

$$+ P_5\{\underbrace{3d_{23}^+ + 3d_{24}^+}_{\substack{\text{Assure foreign} \\ \text{investment at} \\ \text{weight} = 3}} + \underbrace{d_5^+ + d_6^+ + d_7^+\}}_{\substack{\text{Prevent excess} \\ \text{transfer of funds} \\ \text{from period to} \\ \text{period}}} + P_6\{\underbrace{d_{15}^+ + d_{16}^+ + d_{17}^+ + d_{18}^+\}}_{\substack{\text{Minimize excess liquidity} \\ \text{in each of the 4 years}}}.$$

This project selection problem was solved by a modified linear *goal* programming code developed by Bershader [5] and reported in Ignizio [13]. (The modifications consisted principally of expanding the algorithm to accommodate 65 variables, 60 objectives, and 10 priority levels.) Bershader's coding follows the modified simplex procedure outlined in Appendix 9A, so that the *optimum* is the result of a stagewise optimization procedure in which successive suboptima are sought in order of a decreasing priority scheme. For this problem, the following projects were selected at the levels indicated:

| Project No. | Description | Acceptance Level |
|:-----------:|:------------|:----------------:|
| 1 | Internal project | 0.224 |
| 2 | Foreign factory | 1.000 |
| 3 | Noise pollution control | 1.000 |
| 5 | Internal project | 0.344 |
| 8 | Internal project | 0.600 |
| 9 | Clean air project | 1.000 |
| 13 | Internal project | 1.000 |
| 14 | Internal project | 1.000 |

The first highest priority goals were satisfied exactly, or exceeded. Under Priority 1, no multiples of projects were accepted, and no budget overruns were allowed (budgets in years 1, 2, and 3 were used exactly, and the budget in year 4 was underutilized by $2.21). Under Priority 2, the designated pollution control projects were selected,[9] which were Projects 3 and 9. Also under Priority 2, the cash inflow goal in year 3 was exceeded by a positive deviation of $143.94.

Beginning with the Priority 3 goal and succeeding ones, some were underachieved and others were partially achieved. The Priority 3 goals of maximizing early funds inflows, weighted according to an assumed utility ordering, were all underachieved. For year 1, the underachievement was $279.4; for year 2, $418.8; for year 3, $342; and for year 4, $1,390.7. Hence, in essence, the utility equivalent of maximum net present value was not achieved. The Priority 4 goal of maintaining a 50% growth rate in income was underachieved in years 1 and 2 ($-9.2 and $-35.2, respectively) but overachieved in years 3 and 4 ($181.1 and $424.2, respectively). The Priority 5 goal of building the foreign factory was achieved, but the proposed distribution system and advertising program were rejected. Also under Priority 5, the minimization of intertemporal transfer of funds was achieved for years 1–2 and 2–3 but failed for years 3–4. Finally, the liquidity goal (Priority 6) was underachieved in years 1, 2, and 4 but overachieved in year 3. The complete numerical solution to the problem is presented in Appendix 9B.

---

[9]The other pollution control projects could just as well have been eliminated from the candidate set for our purposes. The entire problem, however, was adapted from one reported by Lee and Lerro [17], who permitted alternative selections of two sets of pollution control projects for comparative purposes. We wished to disturb the problem formulation as little as possible and hence made our problem comparable to only *one* of theirs by restricting selection.

Quite obviously, the foregoing solution is not the only one possible for this problem. A simple reordering of priorities, or change in the conceptual formulation of one or more of the objectives, would completely change the solution pattern. Since this kind of *restructuring* of the problem format is exactly equivalent conceptually to restating the decision-maker's *preferences*, it is simply a demonstration of the principle enunciated so clearly by Hirshleifer, Bernhard, and others who have followed in their footsteps: In an imperfect capital market, the "optimal" project selection solution is the result of the decision-maker's *choices*. If these can be rationally ordered, consistent decisions can be made. An example of a correct step in this direction is Lee and Lerro's article [17], in which they examine eight decisional permutations of a capital budgeting problem. Such an approach permits management to examine the solutions and ask *what if* questions *beforehand*.

## 9.5. Summary

In this chapter, we have done essentially three things. *First*, using a simple case developed by Hirshleifer in which capital market (interest) rates differ for borrowing and lending, we demonstrated that the familiar maximization of net present value model collapses, and the Separation Theorem is invalidated. No longer can the choice of an *optimal* set of projects be made separately from the method of financing them. *Second*, using the Bernhard generalized horizon model, we demonstrated some methods of *alternative* formulations of the selection problem, when interest rates are not procurable internally from the model. These models are basically undiscounted flow-of-funds models *of the firm* that comply with some terminal wealth restriction, or *posture*, at the end of an assumed finite length of time. Using some of Bernhard's results, obtained by deriving the Kuhn-Tucker conditions for certain cases, we repeated some of Bernhard's findings concerning capital budgeting models. One of the most important of these is a substantiation of Baumol and Quandt's finding that the interest rate, used in a net present value model to find NPV, is not internally procurable from the model. In other words, the *source of funds and its cost* must be assumed known in order to use NPV.

Finally, to demonstrate that the project selection problem can be put into an operational form in imperfect capital markets, we summarized the goal programming approach and then illustrated how a 15-project problem could be formulated, subjected to prioritized goals, and "solved."

### APPENDIX 9.A. MODIFIED SIMPLEX PROCEDURE
### FOR GOAL PROGRAMMING

The reader who is familiar with linear programming techniques will recognize the GP procedure as basically an extension of Wagner's *Two-Phase Method* [22] for driving artificial variables to zero. In the GP format, the several objective functions are formed in the same manner as the *phases* of Wagner's method, and the solution procedure is nearly identical except for the way of choosing incoming variables and maintaining feasibility. To commence a demonstration of the method, the Chop-N-Block problem can be stated thus:

$$\text{MIN} \quad Z = \{P_1 d_1^-; P_2 d_3^-; P_3(d_2^+ + d_2^-)\}$$

subject to:

$$(1) \quad 2.0X_1 + 3.0X_2 \;- d_1^+ + d_1^- = 55$$

$$(2) \quad 1.0X_1 + 2.0X_2 \;+ d_2^+ - d_2^- = 28$$

$$(3) \quad 2.0X_1 + 3.0X_2 \;- d_3^+ + d_3^- = 30$$

$$(4) \quad 0.5X_1 + 0.25X_2 \qquad\qquad\quad \leq 8$$

$$(5) \quad 1.0X_1 + 1.0X_2 \qquad\qquad\qquad \leq 20$$

$$(6) \qquad\qquad X_1, X_2, d_i^+, d_i^- \qquad\quad \geq 0$$

The activity coefficient matrix is formed in the same manner as for a linear programming problem, simply by detaching the coefficients and writing them beneath the associated variable column heading. Slacks are provided where needed to convert inequalities to equalities. *Each* revised objective row ("bottom line") corresponds to a *fixed* priority; these priorities are established by the achievement function, and *within a given priority*, a revised objective row is obtained by the relationship

$$z_j - c_j = \sum_i c_{iB} a_{ij} - C_j$$

where $z_j - c_j$ = value in the revised objective row.

$\qquad c_{iB}$ = initial *basis* variable.

$\qquad a_{ij}$ = activity coefficient.

$\qquad C_j$ = coefficients in the original *achievement function*.

Hence, by these rules, the initial tableau for our problem becomes

**I. First Tableau**

| | | | $P_3$ | 0 | 0 | 0 | 0 | +1 | +1 | 0 | 0 | 0 | 0 | | |
| | | | $P_2$ | 0 | 0 | 0 | 0 | 0 | 0 | 0 | +1 | 0 | 0 | | |
| | | | $P_1$ | 0 | 0 | 0 | +1 | 0 | 0 | 0 | 0 | 0 | 0 | | |
| $(c_{iB})_3$ | $(c_{iB})_2$ | $(c_{iB})_1$ | $X_1$ | $X_2$ | $d_1^+$ | $d_1^-$ | $d_2^+$ | $d_2^-$ | $d_3^+$ | $d_3^-$ | $S_4$ | $S_5$ | $b_i$ | $\theta_i$ |
|---|---|---|---|---|---|---|---|---|---|---|---|---|---|---|
| 0 | 0 | +1 | 2.0 | 3.0 | −1 | +1 | | | | | | | 55 | 18.33 |
| 1 | 0 | 0 | 1.0 | 2.0 | | | +1 | −1 | | | | | 28 | 14.00 |
| 0 | 1 | 0 | 2.0 | (3.0) | | | | | −1 | +1 | | | 30 | ⌊10.00⌋ |
| 0 | 0 | 0 | 0.5 | 0.25 | | | | | | | +1 | | 8 | 32.00 |
| 0 | 0 | 0 | 1.0 | 1.0 | | | | | | | | +1 | 20 | 20.00 |
| | | $P_1'$ | 2.0 | ⌊3.0⌋ | −1 | 0 | 0 | 0 | 0 | 0 | 0 | 0 | 55 | |
| | | $P_2'$ | 2.0 | 3.0 | 0 | 0 | 0 | 0 | −1 | 0 | 0 | 0 | 30 | |
| | | $P_3'$ | 1.0 | 2.0 | 0 | 0 | 0 | 0 | 0 | 0 | 0 | 0 | 28 | |

Optimization commences by examining the revised objective rows, $P'_1$, $P'_2$, and $P'_3$, at the *Priority 1* ($P'_1$) level. Here we notice that the objective can be improved (minimized) by bringing into solution the variable corresponding to MAX $\partial Z/\partial X = -(z_j - c_j)$, or $X_2 = 3$, since this variable will reduce the objective by three units for each unit of $X_2$ brought into solution. Hence, $X_2$ is the entering variable. The leaving variable is identified, as in linear programming, as the one that will just retain feasibility when a maximum of $X_2$ is brought into solution. The leaving variable is identified as the one having a *minimum* value of $\theta_i = b_i/a_{ik}$, where $a_{ik}$ = the activity coefficients in the key column (identified by the incoming variable $X_2$). Thus, $\theta_1 = 55/3.0 = 18.33$; $\theta_2 = 28/2.0 = 14.0$; etc. The minimum value of $\theta_i = 10$ occurs in the third row. The key, or pivot element, then becomes $a_{32} = 3.0$ (circled), i.e., the element at the intersection of the key row and key column.

Thereafter, iterations are made by the simplex procedure until the elements of the revised objective, $P'_1$, are driven to zero or negative. *At this point, the Priority 1 achievement function is satisfied*, and we abandon further iterations with $P'_1$. The next operation commences with $P'_2$, and iterations are thereafter made with $P'_2$ until it, in turn, is optimized. This process is continued with the other prioritized revised objectives, until a final "optimal" solution is reached.

For the Chop-N-Block problem, the final solution is

$$X_1 = 0 \quad \text{(number of knives)}$$

$$X_2 = 20 \quad \text{(number of blocks)}$$

$$\left.\begin{array}{l} d_1^+ = 5 \\ d_1^- = 0 \end{array}\right\} \quad \text{(profit and overhead goal exceeded by \$5)}$$

$$\left.\begin{array}{l} d_2^+ = 0 \\ d_2^- = 12 \end{array}\right\} \quad \text{(cash balance goal underachieved by \$12)}$$

$$\left.\begin{array}{l} d_3^+ = 30 \\ d_3^- = 0 \end{array}\right\} \quad \text{(working capital goal exceeded by \$30)}$$

$$S_4 = 3 \quad \text{(3 hr excess machine capacity)}$$

$$S_5 = 0 \quad \text{(zero slack assembly capacity)}$$

For those who wish to know more about the modified simplex algorithm for solving linear *goal programs*, a rather complete discussion can be found in Ignizio ([13], Chapter 3).

## APPENDIX 9.B. COMPILATION OF PROJECT SELECTION PROBLEM

The model used here is Lee and Lerro's [17] *Model 4*, with certain modifications (chief among which are the elimination of the net present value objective and substitution of an ordered utility-of-money function applied to the cash flows).

The formulations of the objectives are as follows:

A. *Budget Objectives (Priority 1)*:

(First year):  $50X_1 + 100X_2 + 20X_3 + 75X_4 + 200X_5 + d_1^- - d_1^+ = 200.0$

(Second year):  $10X_1 + 20X_3 + 2X_4 + 150X_6 + 90X_7 + 100X_8$
$$+ 60X_9 + 10X_{10} + d_2^- - d_2^+ = 250.0$$

(Third year):  $5X_1 + 2X_4 + 55X_5 + 30X_7 + 5X_9 + 86X_{10}$
$$+ 180X_{11} + 80X_{12} + 30X_{13} + 2X_{14} + d_3^- - d_3^+ = 260.0$$

(Fourth year):  $8X_2 + X_4 + 10X_8 + 4X_{10} + 30X_{13} + 70X_{14}$
$$+ 100X_{15} + d_4^- - d_4^+ = 120.0$$

B. *Permissible Interperiod Transfer of Funds (Priority 5)*:

(Year 2):  $60X_1 + 100X_2 + 40X_3 + 77X_4 + 200X_5 + 150X_6 + 90X_7$
$$+ 100X_8 + 60X_9 + 10X_{10} + d_5^- - d_5^+ = 450.0$$

(Year 3):  $65X_1 + 100X_2 + 40X_3 + 79X_4 + 255X_5 + 150X_6 + 120X_7$
$$+ 100X_8 + 65X_9 + 96X_{10} + 180X_{11} + 80X_{12} + 30X_{13} + 2X_{14}$$
$$+ d_6^- - d_6^+ = 710.0$$

(Year 4):  $65X_1 + 108X_2 + 40X_3 + 80X_4 + 255X_5 + 150X_6 + 120X_7$
$$+ 110X_8 + 65X_9 + 100X_{10} + 180X_{11} + 80X_{12} + 60X_{13} + 72X_{14}$$
$$+ 100X_{15} + d_7^- - d_7^+ = 830.0$$

C. *Accept Pollution Control Projects 3 and 9*:

$$X_9 + d_8^- - d_8^+ = 1$$
$$X_3 + d_9^- - d_9^+ = 1$$

D. *Maintain 50% Income Growth (Priority 4)*:

$$10X_2 - 100X_4 - 10X_5 + d_{10}^- - d_{10}^+ = 15.0$$

$$25X_1 + 100X_2 + X_3 + 5X_4 + 65X_5 - 115X_6 - 75X_7$$
$$- 140X_8 + 95X_9 - 13X_{10} + d_{11}^- - d_{11}^+ = 22.5$$

$$30X_1 + 70X_2 + 5X_3 - 15X_5 - 45X_7 + 97X_8 - 10X_9$$
$$- 12X_{10} + 50X_{11} - 100X_{12} + 30X_{13} + 6X_{14} + d_{12}^- - d_{12}^+ = 34.0$$

$$105X_2 + 5X_3 - 2X_4 + 26X_5 + 40X_6 + 385X_7 + 58X_8$$
$$+ 80X_{10} + 200X_{11} + 190X_{12} - 55X_{13} + 62X_{14} + 290X_{15} + d_{13}^- - d_{13}^+ = 51.0$$

E. *Maximize Cash Flow in Year 3 (Priority 2)*:

$$100X_1 + 150X_2 + 20X_3 + 50X_4 + 50X_5 + 70X_6 + 120X_8 + 100X_{10}$$
$$+ 250X_{11} + 114X_{13} - 38X_{14} + d_{14}^- - d_{14}^+ = 500.0$$

F. *Minimize Excess Liquidity (Priority 6)*:

(Year 1):  $75X_1 + 150X_2 + 5X_3 + 200X_5 + d_{15}^- - d_{15}^+ = 300.0$

(Year 2):  $100X_1 + 150X_2 + 10X_3 + 140X_4 + 200X_5 + 60X_6$
$$+ 160X_9 + d_{16}^+ - d_{16}^- = 500.0$$

(Year 3):  $100X_1 + 150X_2 + 20X_3 + 50X_4 + 50X_5 + 70X_6 + 120X_8$
$$+ 100X_{10} + 250X_{11} + 114X_{13} + 38X_{14} + d^-_{17} - d^+_{17} = 500.0$$

(Year 4):  $100X_1 + 300X_2 + 40X_3 + 40X_4 + 200X_5 + 80X_6 + 450X_7$
$$+ 150X_8 + 110X_{10} + 295X_{11} + 240X_{12} + 187X_{13} + 194X_{14}$$
$$+ 550X_{15} + d^-_{18} - d^+_{18} = 1{,}700.0$$

G. *Place Utility Ranking on Funds Flow* (*Priority 3*):

(Year 1, $W = 4$):  $75X_1 + 150X_2 + 5X_3 + 200X_5 + d^-_{19} - d^+_{19} = 430.0$

(Year 2, $W = 3$):  $100X_1 + 150X_2 + 10X_3 + 140X_4 + 200X_5 + 60X_6$
$$+ 160X_9 + d^-_{20} - d^+_{20} = 820.0$$

(Year 3, $W = 2$):  $100X_1 + 150X_2 + 20X_3 + 50X_4 + 50X_5 + 70X_6$
$$+ 120X_8 + 100X_{10} + 250X_{11} + 114X_{13} + 38X_{14} + d^-_{21} - d^+_{21} = 1{,}062.0$$

(Year 4, $W = 1$):  $100X_1 + 300X_2 + 40X_3 + 40X_4 + 200X_5 + 80X_6$
$$+ 450X_7 + 150X_8 + 110X_{10} + 295X_{11} + 240X_{12} + 187X_{13}$$
$$+ 194X_{14} + 550X_{15} + d^-_{22} - d^+_{22} = 2{,}936.0$$

H. *Increase Foreign Investment* (*Priority 5*):
$$X_{15} - X_6 + d^-_{23} - d^+_{23} = 0$$
$$X_{15} - X_2 + d^-_{24} - d^+_{24} = 0$$

I. *Define Range of Project Acceptance* (*Priority 1*):
$$X_1 + d^-_{25} - d^+_{25} = 1$$
$$X_2 + d^-_{26} - d^+_{26} = 1$$
$$\begin{matrix} \cdot & \cdot & \cdot \\ \cdot & \cdot & \cdot \\ \cdot & \cdot & \cdot \end{matrix}$$
$$X_{15} + d^-_{39} - d^+_{39} = 1$$

(Min $d^+_j$ forces nonmultiples of projects.)

J. *Reject Two Pollution Control Projects* (*Priority 2*):
$$X_4 + d^-_{40} - d^+_{40} = 0$$
$$X_{12} + d^-_{41} - d^+_{41} = 0$$

The solution to the GP problem, using the objective in Eq. (9.43), is as follows:

Projects:

$$X_1 = 0.2237 \qquad X_9 = 1.000$$
$$X_2 = 1.0000 \qquad X_{10} = 0$$
$$X_3 = 1.0000 \qquad X_{11} = 0$$
$$X_4 = 0 \qquad X_{12} = 0$$
$$X_5 = 0.3441 \qquad X_{13} = 1.0000$$

$$X_6 = 0 \qquad\qquad X_{14} = 1.0000$$
$$X_7 = 0 \qquad\qquad X_{15} = 0$$
$$X_8 = 0.6008$$

*Deviations* [listed as they appear in the objective, Eq. (9.43)]:

1.A. Multiples of projects:
$$d_{25}^+, d_{26}^+, \ldots, d_{39}^+ = [0].$$

   B. Budget goals:
$$d_1^+, \ldots, d_4^+ = [0]; \qquad d_1^-, \ldots, d_3^- = [0]; \qquad d_4^- = 2.2095.$$

2.A. Accept pollution control Projects 3, 9:
$$d_8^+, d_8^- = 0; \qquad d_9^+, d_9^- = 0.$$

   B. Reject pollution control Projects 4, 12:
$$d_{40}^+, d_{40}^- = 0; \qquad d_{41}^+, d_{41}^- = 0.$$

   C. Achieve cash inflow in year 3:
$$d_{14}^+ = 143.9418, \qquad d_{14}^- = 0.$$

3.A. Achieve early cash inflows:
$$d_{19}^+, \ldots, d_{22}^+ = [0]; \qquad d_{19}^- = 279.3921; \qquad d_{20}^- = 418.8652;$$
$$d_{21}^- = 342.0579; \qquad d_{22}^- = 1{,}390.7168.$$

4.A. Maintain 50% growth rate on income:
$$d_{10}^+ = 0, d_{10}^- = 9.1168; \qquad d_{11}^+ = 0, d_{11}^- = 35.1549;$$
$$d_{12}^+ = 181.0716, d_{12}^- = 0; \qquad d_{13}^+ = 424.1506, d_{13}^- = 0.$$

5.A. Minimize intertemporal transfer of funds:
$$d_5^+ = 0, d_5^- = 0; \qquad d_6^+ = 0, d_6^- = 0; \qquad d_7^+ = 0, d_7^- = 2.2105.$$

   B. Assure foreign investment:
$$d_{23}^+ = 0, d_{23}^- = 0; \qquad d_{24}^+ = 0, d_{24}^- = 1.0000.$$

6.A. Minimize excess liquidity:
$$d_{15}^+ = 0, d_{15}^- = 66.2921; \qquad d_{16}^+ = 0, d_{16}^- = 98.8659;$$
$$d_{17}^+ = 219.9418, d_{17}^- = 0; \qquad d_{18}^+ = 0, d_{18}^- = 154.7171.$$

*Achievement Function:*

The summation of terms in the achievement function are as follows:

$$P_1: \quad \sum Wd_i = \quad 0.$$
$$P_2: \quad \sum Wd_i = \quad 0.$$
$$P_3: \quad \sum Wd_i = 4{,}449. \quad (\Rightarrow \text{underachievement}).$$
$$P_4: \quad \sum Wd_i = \quad 605.22 \quad (\Rightarrow \text{underachievement}).$$
$$P_5: \quad \sum Wd_i = \quad 0.$$
$$P_6: \quad \sum Wd_i = \quad 219.94 \quad (\Rightarrow \text{underachievement}).$$

# REFERENCES

[1] BAUMGARTEN, EDWIN 0., "An Investigation of the Goal Programming Method," (unpublished M. S. Thesis, Kansas State University, Manhattan, Kan., 1973).

[2] BAUMOL, WILLIAM J., and RICHARD E. QUANDT, "Investment and Discount Rates Under Capital Rationing—A Programming Approach," *The Economic Journal*, **75**(298) (June, 1965), pp. 317–29.

[3] BERNHARD, RICHARD H., "Mathematical Programming Models for Capital Budgeting—A Survey, Generalization, and Critique," *Journal of Financial and Quantitative Analysis*, **4**(2) (June, 1969), pp. 111–58.

[4] ——, "Some Problems in the Use of a Discount Rate for Constrained Capital Budgeting," *AIIE Transactions*, **III**(3) (September, 1971), pp. 180–84.

[5] BERSHADER, PAULA S., "Linear Goal Programming Package," University Park, Pennsylvania: The Pennsylvania State University (Spring 1975) (reproduced in Ignizio [13], pp. 227–42).

[6] BYRNE, R., A. CHARNES, W. W. COOPER, and K. KORTANEK, "A Chance-Constrained Approach to Capital Budgeting with Portfolio Type Payback and Liquidity and Horizon Posture Controls," *Journal of Financial and Quantitative Analysis*, **II**(4) (December, 1967), pp. 339–64.

[7] CHARNES, A., and W. W. COOPER, *Management Models and Industrial Applications of Linear Programming* (New York: John Wiley & Sons, Inc., 1961).

[8] CHARNES, A., W. W. COOPER, and M. H. MILLER, "Application of Linear Programming to Financial Budgeting and the Costing of Funds," *Journal of Business*, **XXXII**(1) (January, 1959), pp. 20–46.

[9] DAUER, J. P. and R. J. KRUEGER, "An Iterative Approach to Goal Programming," *Operational Research Quarterly*, **28**(3ii), 1977, pp. 671–81.

[10] FAMA, EUGENE, F., "Efficient Capital Markets: A Review of Theory and Empirical Work," *Journal of Finance*, **35** (May, 1970), pp. 383–417.

[11] HILLIER, FREDERICK S., and GERALD J. LIEBERMAN, *Operations Research*, 2nd ed. (San Francisco, Calif.: Holden-Day, Inc., 1974).

[12] HIRSHLEIFER, J., "On the Theory of Optimal Investment Decision," *Journal of Political Economy*, **66**(5) (August, 1958), pp. 329–52; reprinted in Ezra Solomon, ed., *The Management of Corporate Capital* (Glencoe, Ill.: The Free Press, 1959).

[13] IGNIZIO, JAMES P., *Goal Programming and Extensions* (Lexington, Mass.: Lexington Books, D. C. Heath and Company, 1976).

[14] ——, "An Approach to the Capital Budgeting Problem with Multiple Objectives," *The Engineering Economist*, **21**(4) (Summer, 1976), pp. 259–72.

[15] IJIRI, YUJI, *Management Goals and Accounting for Control* (Amsterdam: North-Holland Publishing Company, 1965).

[16] LEE, SANG M., *Goal Programming for Decision Analysis* (Philadelphia: Auerbach Publishers, Inc., 1972).

[17] LEE, SANG M., and A. J. LERRO, "Capital Budgeting for Multiple Objectives," *Financial Management*, **3**(1) (Spring, 1974), pp. 58–66.

[18] LUSZTIG, PETER, and BERNHARD SCHWAB, "A Note on the Application of Linear Programming to Capital Budgeting," *Journal of Financial and Quantitative Analysis*, **3**(4) (December, 1968), pp. 426–31.

[19] MANNE, ALAN S., "Optimal Dividend Policies for a Self-Financing Business Enterprise," *Management Science*, **XV**(3) (November, 1968), pp. 119–29.

[20] MAO, JAMES C. T., *Quantitative Analysis of Financial Decisions* (New York: The Macmillan Company, 1969).

[21] NÄSLUND, BERTIL, "A Model of Capital Budgeting Under Risk," *Journal of Business*, **XXXIX**(20) (April, 1966), pp. 257–71.

[22] WAGNER, HARVEY M., "A Two-Phase Method for the Simplex Tableau," *Operations Research*, **4**(4) (1957), pp. 443–47.

[23] WEINGARTNER, H. MARTIN, *Mathematical Programming and the Analysis of Capital Budgeting Problems* (Englewood Cliffs, N.J.: Prentice-Hall, Inc., 1963; reprinted by Markham Publishing Company, Chicago, 1967).

[24] _____, "Capital Budgeting of Interrelated Projects: Survey and Synthesis," *Management Science*, **12**(7) (March, 1966).

[25] _____, "Capital Rationing: *n* Authors in Search of a Plot," *The Journal of Finance*, **XXXII** (5) (December, 1977).

# PROBLEMS

**9-1.** In what manner is the Separation Theorem invalidated by a difference in the borrowing and lending rates of interest in the capital market?

**9-2.** What other factors in the real capital market can cause the Separation Theorem to be invalidated?

**9-3.** What are some possible consequences of *im*perfect capital market conditions on the project selection problem?

**9-4.** Using the necessary variables defined in Section 9.3.3 and the additional variables defined in Section 9.3.5 ("1. Cash Balance Restriction, etc."), write the fundamental cash inflow and outflow expressions for the firm, and then derive Eq. (9.3b) as a cash balance equation at time $t$.

**9-5.** (Bernhard Generalized Model.) A certain firm is considering four new projects whose cash flow streams are independent of each other. The projects have various lives, but the planning horizon is 5 years from now and is the same for all projects. The availability of managerial resources in the firm is considered to be a limiting factor, and at any time the total managerial resources available to all new projects is expected to be limited to 30 "executive units." New projects (Numbers 1 through 4) will require the use of 10, 8, 5, and 15 executive units, respectively. The expected cash flows to and from the projects are as follows:

| Time, $t =$ | Project 1 | Project 2 | Project 3 | Project 4 |
|---|---|---|---|---|
| 1 | $-500 | $-300 | $-300 | $-500 |
| 2 | + 50 | +100 | +100 | - 50 |
| 3 | 100 | 100 | 150 | + 50 |
| 4 | 100 | 100 | 100 | 100 |
| 5 | 100 | - 50 | 100 | 300 |
| "Present" worth (time $T = 5$) of post-$T$ cash flows: | $ 400 | $ 200 | –0– | $ 400 |

Cash throw-offs for other projects (in which the firm has already invested) will be available for the use of the firm in the following amounts:

| Year | Amount |
|------|--------|
| 1 | $1,000,000 |
| 2 | 25,000 |
| 3 | 50,000 |
| 4 | 50,000 |
| 5 | 100,000 |

Also, it is estimated that these other projects will continue to generate cash inflows for the firm after the planning horizon ($T = 5$ years), and the present value of these cash inflows at time $T = 5$ will be $2,000,000.

The firm's borrowing and lending rates of interest are estimated to be 12% and 6% per year, respectively. The maximum debt in any 1 year is $300,000. Also, the firm must maintain a cash balance at all times of at least $5,000 plus 10% of its outstanding debt. In order to attract new shareholders, the Board of Directors has decided that dividends over the next 5 years should be paid in years 1–5 in amounts of *at least* $50,000; $55,000; $61,000; $67,000; and $74,000, respectively.

(a) Formulate the project selection problem as a funds flow programming problem using the Bernhard generalized model. In doing so, maximize terminal wealth plus the discounted dividend stream (use a discount rate of 6% on dividend amounts), and include the following constraints: (1) cash balance restrictions, (2) scarce resource restriction, (3) terminal wealth restriction, (4) upper bound(s) on borrowing, (5) lower bound(s) on payment of dividends, (6) prohibition of multiple projects ($0 \leq x_j \leq 1$; $j = 1, 2, 3, 4$).

(b) Write the Lagrangian corresponding to (a), and derive the properties of the optimal solution by taking partial derivatives and setting the results equal to zero.

(c) Solve (a) by a computer-based linear programming code. Use the *numerical* values obtained from the LP optimal solution to back-substitute into the system of simultaneous linear equations obtained in (b) to demonstrate that the Lagrangian method in (b) correctly describes the LP optimal solution.

(This problem was contributed by Michael D. Chatham.)

9-6. (Bernhard special case 2b, in which the borrowing and lending rates are equal and timewise invariant.) Consider four independent projects, not mutually exclusive, with expected cash flows as follows:

*Expected Cash Flows, $Y_{tj}$*

| End of Period, $t =$ | Project Identification, $j =$ | | | |
|---|---|---|---|---|
| | 1 | 2 | 3 | 4 |
| 1 | $-20,000 | $-25,000 | $-45,000 | $-35,000 |
| 2 | - 1,500 | + 2,000 | + 3,000 | -25,000 |
| 3 | + 1,000 | 5,000 | 5,000 | 10,000 |
| 4 | 1,500 | 15,000 | 10,000 | 7,500 |
| 5 | 1,500 | 15,000 | 15,000 | 7,500 |
| 6 | 750 | 4,000 | 2,000 | 5,000 |
| 7 | 250 | 2,000 | 2,000 | 1,000 |
| 8 | –0– | 500 | –0– | –0– |

Other assumptions are as follows: The planning horizon is at time $T = 3$ (i.e., at the end of Period 3). Borrowing and lending rates of interest are both 10% per year and remain at that value in all periods. The upper limits on borrowing for Periods 1 and 2 are $B_1 = \$20,000$ and $B_2 = \$25,000$. Cash inflows to the firm from other projects outside this study are as follows:

| Time, $t =$ | 1 | 2 | 3 | 4 | 5 | 6 | 7 |
|---|---|---|---|---|---|---|---|
| Amount, $ | 15,000 | 10,000 | 5,000 | 5,000 | 3,000 | 2,000 | –0– |

There is a manpower restriction on the total number of employees available for use on the new projects. The total availability is 100 persons. The number of employees required for each project is as follows:

| Project, $j =$ | 1 | 2 | 3 | 4 |
|---|---|---|---|---|
| Persons | 20 | 25 | 45 | 30 |

A constant cash balance requirement of $5,000 is necessary in all periods (except that at time $t = 0$ the requirement of $C_0 = 0$). In addition, 50% of the outstanding debt at any time must be kept liquid (as cash). A minimum dividend of $30 must be paid during each period up to the planning horizon (i.e., $D_1, D_2, D_3 \geq \$30$).

(a) *Formulate* this problem as a mathematical programming problem in which the objective is to maximize the sum of the annual dividend payments and the terminal wealth at time $t = 3$, subject to the following constraints: (i) cash balance restrictions including liquidity constraints, (ii) scarce resource restriction(s), (iii) terminal wealth restriction, (iv) terminal wealth *posture* restriction, (v) upper bound(s) on borrowing, (vi) prohibition of multiple projects, (vii) lower bounds(s) on dividends, (viii) nonnegativity restrictions.

(b) Solve the problem by a computer-based linear programming code, and give economic interpretations of the optimal solution.

(This problem was contributed by Krishna Lakshminarayan.)

**9-7.** Using the Bernhard model for special case 2a ($l_t = b_t = \lambda_t$) and the absence of payback and resource restrictions, prove (analytically) that a project may still be accepted, even if discounting at the market rate of interest indicates it has a *negative* net present value, provided that restraints on borrowing are binding. [*Hint:* Consider the *meaning* of the selection criterion, $A_j^*$, in Eq. (9.21), and also the Kuhn-Tucker conditions in Eq. (9.11) through (9.14) when $B_t^* = 0$ and when $B_t^* > 0$.]

(This problem was contributed by Robert W. Schmidt, Jr.)

**9-8.** Consider a hypothetical problem in which the A-B-C Company is studying the desirability of adopting one or more of four independent projects. The expected cash flows from the projects and budget limits are as follows:

| Project Number | Time, $t =$ | | |
|---|---|---|---|
| | 0 | 1 | 2 |
| 1 | $−1. | $ 3. | 0 |
| 2 | −1. | 2. | +1.5 |
| 3 | 0 | −1. | 2. |
| 4 | 0 | −2. | 3.5 |
| Budget limit | $ 1. | $ 2. | 0 |

.For simplicity, it may be assumed that the cash flows are zero after time $t = 2$ and that the market borrowing and lending rates of interest are equal and constant over the lives of the projects. Amounts available for investment, however, are from *external sources* and are constrained as shown in the table above. The firm is required to retain, at all times, 20% of its borrowings in liquid form (cash or quick, marketable securities). The firm can borrow only at time $t = 1$, up to a maximum of $1; but it may lend money at any time. There are no other scarce *resources* that restrict the problem. The expected terminal wealth posture at time $t = 2$ is $2 more than the sum of the dividends paid in Periods 1 and 2. Neither multiple nor partial projects are acceptable.

(a) Formulate the problem as a mathematical programming problem, writing the objective function in generalized form as MAX $F = f(W_1, W_2, G)$, where $W_1, W_2 =$ dividends to be paid in Periods 1 and 2, respectively, and $G =$ terminal wealth of the firm at time $t = 2$.

(b) Incorporate your constraints into the objective by using the generalized Lagrangian multiplier technique. Find the Kuhn-Tucker conditions.

(c) By rewriting and simplifying the Kuhn-Tucker conditions, demonstrate that the optimal decision set of projects ($\mathbf{X}^*$) cannot be ascertained simultaneously with the market discount rate of interest, $\lambda_t$. (*Hint:* Show that the values of the K-T variables are dependent on the interest rate).

(This problem was contributed by S. R. Paidy.)

**9-9.** (Goal Programming Problem.) EMPCO Carburetion, Inc., is a gas carburetion equipment manufacturer. The State Air Pollution Control Board has recently issued regulations for more stringent emission controls. EMPCO has designed an emission control device, No. EC-1, to meet these requirements. Because of the Federal government's energy policy, however, an additional project concerning the manufacture of dual-fuel carburetors for small cars is also under consideration. This project is independent of the EC-1 project. The U.S. market for gas carburetion equipment is still somewhat limited; hence EMPCO plans to market its products in foreign countries also. This is the third project under consideration. The undiscounted cash outflows due to the three projects are given in the table below.

|  | Time | | |
|---|---|---|---|
|  | $t = 1$ | $t = 2$ | $t = 3$ |
| Dual-fuel project | $50K* | $10K | $ 0K |
| Foreign project | 10K | 15K | 20K |
| EC-1 emission project | 50K | 0K | 0K |

*K = $1,000.

The cash inflows from these projects are estimated as follows:

|  | $t = 1$ | $t = 2$ | $t = 3$ |
|---|---|---|---|
| Dual-fuel project | $10K | $50K | $60K |
| Foreign project | 5K | 20K | 40K |
| EC-1 emission project | 5K | 30K | 45K |

The company has allocated a capital budget of $110K for the first year, $30K for the second year, and $15K for the third year. Management has assigned the following priorities toward the accomplishment of the projects:

Priority 1—Minimize annual budget overruns (incorporate an ordinal weighting to express a higher preference for early funds flow).

Priority 2—Subpriorities within Priority 2:
(a) Accept EC-1 emission control project (weight = 3).
(b) Assure foreign marketing campaign (weight = 2).
(c) Accept the dual-fuel project (weight = 1).

Priority 3—Assure early cash inflows (incorporate an ordinal weighting to express a higher preference for early funds flow).

*Requirement:* Formulate this problem as a goal programming problem, using the priorities and weights given above to establish the multiple-term achievement function. Obtain a solution to this GP problem (if a computer algorithm is available). (This problem was contributed by S. F. Hoda.)

**9-10.** (Goal Programming Problem.) A company is considering the undertaking of three projects. A project must be either selected or rejected. A partially funded project is infeasible. The expected net profits, personnel needed, and project costs are given in the following table.

| Project | Net Profit (Units) | Number of Personnel (Units) | Cost in Year 1 (Units) | Cost in Year 2 (Units) |
|---------|--------------------|-----------------------------|------------------------|------------------------|
| A | 3 | 12 | 8 | 6 |
| B | 4 | 15 | 12 | 10 |
| C | 2 | 10 | 5 | 6 |

The allowable total budget for year 1 is 20 units and 18 units in year 2. Total number of employees in that company is currently 25 units. The desired priorities are as follows:

With Priority 1, the total costs should not exceed the total budget allowable each year.

With Priority 2, maximize net profit.

With Priority 3, minimize new employment (weighting = 2) and maximize utilization of employees (weighting = 1) in order to minimize the labor turnover. (This problem was contributed by Hoon B. Lee.)

**9-11.** A company is considering the undertaking of three projects. The capital available over the 3-year life of these projects appears insufficient to support all three projects; however, a project can be partially accepted. It is estimated that each project will yield a return in terms of its net profit and a minimum dividend to the shareholders. These expected profits, minimum dividends, and projected costs are given in the following table:

| Project | Net Profit in Year t ($ thousand) | | | Dividend in Year t ($ thousand) | | | Cost in Year t ($ thousand) | | |
|---|---|---|---|---|---|---|---|---|---|
| | t = 1 | t = 2 | t = 3 | t = 1 | t = 2 | t = 3 | t = 1 | t = 2 | t = 3 |
| 1 | $70 | 40 | 20 | $ 6 | 9 | 10 | $60 | 30 | 10 |
| 2 | 6 | 60 | 80 | 5 | 4 | 10 | 50 | 40 | 10 |
| 3 | 20 | 40 | 60 | 3 | 6 | 9 | 30 | 30 | 30 |
| Total | $96 | 140 | 160 | $14 | 19 | 29 | $140 | 100 | 50 |

The capital availability for investment in each year is year 1: $100,000; year 2: $50,000; and year 3: $20,000. The company's goals are listed below in order of priority:

$P_1$:  A. Multiple units of the same project are prohibited.

    B. Capital allocation for each year cannot be exceeded.

$P_2$:  Maximize profit.

$P_3$:  Maximize dividends paid.

$P_4$:  Minimize the shifting of project funds from one period to another.

Formulate the problem, and if a GP computer code is available, find the optimal solution.

(This problem was contributed by Joe M. Tiao.)

part three

INVESTMENT ANALYSIS
UNDER RISK
AND UNCERTAINTY

# PREFERENCE-ORDERING THEORY

## 10.1. Introduction

In the preceding three chapters we examined the deterministic project selection problem. Beginning with the basic assumptions of *certainty* and *perfect capital markets*, we examined first the unconstrained selection problem, from which we essentially concluded that projects with positive net present values should be accepted and those with negative net present values should be rejected. Proceeding on through constrained Lorie-Savage type of selection problem in Chapter 8, we concluded there that Lorie-Savage problems involving only expenditure-of-funds limitations are trivial under perfect capital market conditions but that Lorie-Savage type problems with other types of budget constraints can be quite realistic and useful for analytic purposes. Then in Chapter 9 we relaxed some of the perfect capital market assumptions and discovered that the project selection problem becomes very difficult even to formulate, since under imperfect capital market conditions there is the unanswered question of what is the appropriate criterion to be maximized. In certain special cases, however, it was demonstrated that solutions can be obtained by mathematical programming methods.

Now it is our purpose to relax the *certainty* conditions in a different manner. We want to talk about the *uncertainty* that is inherent in all project planning and selection methodology. Obviously, in a *real* world all possible future outcomes of a project, or

# 10

a group of projects, are *not* known with certainty. We simply cannot know *all* future values of sales, expenses, labor to be utilized, machinery needed, power consumed, raw materials converted, and the host of other items entering the decision model. Furthermore, we *do* know that outside the firm's boundaries (in the real world) a *perfect* capital market does not exist—a firm's borrowing rate of interest is generally higher than its lending rate. As a final clincher, in spite of an army of accountants that a firm might employ to keep its records, we really do not *know* the profitability of a project until it has been brought into existence, actually operated over its economic life, and then finally shut down and *all* its assets sold off in the market place. Only when a project is finally liquidated and its creditors reimbursed for their debts and investment can we tell with *some* degree of certainty what its profitability was. Even then, this *final* determination must be made on the basis of arbitrary accounting rules.

As Haley and Schall point out,[1] when we depart from the conditions of assumed certainty and perfect capital markets into the world of uncertainty, we can think of these departures as being of two kinds—(1) departures that are the result of *changes in the actual cash flow stream* from the predicted values and (2) departures due to *changes in the discount rates* that apply to those flows. To the first kind, Haley and Schall give the name *stream effect*, and to the second, the name *rate effect*. Under perfect

---

[1]Haley and Schall [21], pp. 339–40.

capital market conditions, the *stream effect* (as we saw demonstrated in Chapter 8) does not necessarily invalidate the net present value method. That is, even though several projects may have differing cash flows and lives and be subjected to certain constraints, the choice of an optimal set of projects *can* be accomplished by maximizing net present value—for which the basis is the *existence* and *additivity properties* of the parameter, NPV. However, capital market imperfections introduce *rate effects* (e.g., simply a difference in borrowing and lending interest rates will suffice), which immediately invalidates the NPV criterion since the Separation Theorem (Chapter 9) is thereby destroyed.

The direction we now propose to depart from *certainty* is via the *stream effect* concept. In this departure, we shall no longer assume that future conditions are known with certainty, even though we shall continue (for a time) with the assumption of a perfect capital market. Thus, we shall look at the occurrence and magnitudes of the cash flows themselves as being *uncertain*.

All of these more advanced topics in project selection under uncertainty require a basic knowledge of statistical theory. The concepts of variation, random variables, sampling, and other topics in basic statistical theory are used repeatedly in the remainder of the book. It is felt that by the time the student reaches the level of sophistication required by this text, he will already have been exposed to at least one course in statistical methods and, preferably, one in statistical theory. Therefore, we shall omit a review chapter on statistical methodology and simply assume that the reader is proficient in this area or can become so by his own efforts.

Now, a further paragraph or two on the words *risk* and *uncertainty*. Many authors differentiate the two words as having diverse cognitive and mathematical meanings. This differentiation arises because of the divergence between the underlying concepts of *objective* and *subjective* probabilities. It is relatively easy to visualize the difference.

Historically, we are taught that a probability, objectively determined, is the *limit* of the relative frequency with which a certain event occurs out of a finite set of events in a series of repeated trials. Thus, if we have a black bag containing 60 white balls and 40 red balls and if we perform many *repeated* experiments in which we draw balls successively (with replacement between draws) from the bag, we should obtain, *as a limit*, the probability of drawing a white ball equal to six-tenths. This value, six-tenths, is the value which the calculated relative frequency of successive trials *approaches in the limit*. Thus, objective probabilities depend on the existence of two conditions. which may be stated briefly as follows:

1. There is a finite number of outcomes to an experiment,
2. The experiment is repeatable a large number (perhaps an infinity) of times under *identical conditions*.

The *objectivist* is happy to talk about probabilities in connection with *repeatable* events: the tossing of a coin or the manufacture of a mass-produced item. He can easily conceptualize the idea of many light bulbs being produced and of the probability of a good light bulb being produced as the long-run ratio (limit) of the number of good bulbs to the total number produced. But he draws the line at *unique* events. He would not, for example, want to talk about the *probability* that Leif Ericsson landed in Maine or that Canada and the United States would unite in a single nation. Thus, a large class of problems is shunted aside by the objectivist as being inappropriate for the application of the laws of probability because there is no opportunity for repeated trials and, hence, no long-run approach to a *limit* by which his concept of probability is defined. Hence, the term *risk*, as conceived by the objective probabilist, is simply the *probability* (a long-run limit of relative frequency) that an event will fail to happen— that is, *risk* is defined by the objective probabilist in the same terms he uses to define probability: the long-run limit of a given event *not* happening in a series of repeated trials.

The other school of thought concerning probability is the *subjective* school or, as it is sometimes called, the *personalistic* school. The *subjectivist* regards probability much in the same sense that the man in the street thinks of it: a measure of personal belief in a particular proposition, such as the proposition that it will rain tomorrow. He believes that different *reasonable* individuals may differ in their degrees of belief, even when offered the same evidence; hence, their probability estimates for the same event may differ. The subjectivist will apply the rules of probability to all the problems studied by the objectivist and to many more. For example, the subjectivist wouldn't hesitate to state a probability that Leif Ericsson landed in Maine (given that he had such a belief).

Instead, the whole topic of subjectively determined probabilities has not been con-jured up merely to confound the objectivist; it rests upon rather good evidence. James Bernoulli, in his *Ars Conjectandi* (1713), first formulated the subjective alternative to objective probabilities. Bernoulli suggested that *probability* is a "degree of confidence" (later writers state "degree of belief") that an individual *attaches to an uncertain event* and that this degree depends on the individual's knowledge and can vary from indi-vidual to individual. This theme was further developed by Laplace [27] and DeMorgan [15], but the formal concept of subjective probability as an operational *theory* was first formulated by Ramsey [35] in 1926, according to Raiffa [36]. In this theory, Ramsey went beyond prior subjectivists; he conceived of *probability* as an outright expression of a subjective degree of belief to be interpreted as operationally meaningful in terms of willingness to act or of overt betting behavior. Later, de Finetti [14] was able to assess a person's degree of belief *by observing his overt betting behavior*, requiring as a prior condition only that his bets be internally consistent. From this work, de Finetti was able to demonstrate that a person's *degrees of belief*—i.e., his subjective probability assignments—*obey the usual laws of objective probabilities*. Armed with this kind of definitive work, the subjective probabilist argues that, in the absence of better informa-tion (such as prior trials), *subjective* estimates of probability are not only valid but preferable to no estimates at all. Moreover, he maintains, subjective probabilities may be used in the same manner as objective probabilities. Thus we come around to the idea of *uncertainty*, which is a term assigned by both the objectivist and the subjectivist to the *unknown outcomes* of future events but which the subjectivist maintains can be treated the same as *risk* if one uses subjective probability estimates.

So it is that we now "throw our lot in" with the subjective probabilist and suggest (with good reason) that we can use subjectively determined probability estimates in solving project selection problems. Indeed, Ackoff, Gupta, and Minas [1] maintain that the decision-maker possesses *more* information regarding the decision environment than an assumption of outright uncertainty would require, merely by being able to specify the subjectively *probable* outcomes of a prospective action.

The succeeding chapters are thus based on the generality and legitimacy of *subjective* probabilities. The terms *risk* and *uncertainty*, being connected in project selection work with unbeknown *future* events and probabilities of those events, are essentially·undifferentiable. This is the foundation on which the models that consider *risk* and *uncertainty* are built, and for the reason that we cannot differentiate the two we shall hereafter refer to the phenomenon simply as *uncertainty*.

## 10.2. Choices under Uncertainty: The St. Petersburg Paradox

Under conditions of absolute certainty, the problem of deciding between two alternatives is usually a trivial one. For example, let us assume we must choose between two alternatives, neither of which costs us any money or effort:

Alternative *A* pays us $10;

Alternative *B* pays us $20.

We obviously select *B*, on the grounds of common sense that "more is better," as most people seem to believe and act. (The economist takes this rationale for granted).

Let us suppose now, however, that

*A* pays us $10 with certainty;

*B* pays us $50 if the flip of a fair coin turns heads up and nothing if it is tails.

It is now not so obvious that *B* is preferred to *A*. Obviously, receiving $10 without any outlay is good but is this better (or worse) than a 50–50 chance of getting $50? We don't know. There is no *objective* way of making this choice—each must decide for himself.

To emphasize the essentials of this new problem, Karl Borch [7] uses an ingenious example. It goes somewhat as follows. Suppose we must decide on *one* of the actions $A_0, A_1, \ldots, A_n, \ldots$, in an experiment. If we decide on $A_n$, we shall receive (at no cost to us)

either $S_n$ dollars with probability $P_n$,

or nothing with probability $(1 - P_n)$.

If $S_n$ and $P_n$ are given by the relationships

$$P_n = \frac{10}{10 + n}; \qquad S_n = 10\left(\frac{n}{10}\right)^{0.9}$$

we can obtain the results given in Table 10.1 (and we can also interpolate and extrapolate if we think we need to).

**Table 10.1.** HYPOTHETICAL PAYOFFS

| Action | $P_n$ | $S_n$ |
|--------|-------|-------|
| $A_0$ | 1. | $ \quad 0 |
| $A_1$ | 0.9 | 2 |
| $A_{10}$ | 0.5 | 10 |
| $A_{20}$ | 0.33 | 19 |
| $A_{30}$ | 0.25 | 27 |
| $A_{40}$ | 0.20 | 35 |
| $A_{90}$ | 0.10 | 72 |
| $A_{190}$ | 0.05 | 140 |
| $A_{990}$ | 0.01 | 625 |
| $A_{9990}$ | 0.001 | 5,000 |
| $A_{99990}$ | 0.0001 | 40,000 |
| $A_{999990}$ | 0.00001 | 250,000 |
| . | . | . |
| . | . | . |
| . | . | . |

The only obvious thing *not* to do is chose $A_0$, for which we are assured of obtaining nothing. If we do not choose $A_0$, then how far down the table do we go? If we choose $A_1$, we can get $2 with probability 0.9, but if we choose $A_{20}$, we can get $19 with probability 0.33. So, as we proceed, the payoffs become much greater but only as the probabilities of *success* become much smaller. The question is, what criterion do we use to judge *the* proper action? Where do we stop?

The answer is that, *if we expect* the experiment *to be repeated many times*, say 100,000 or so, then we should choose the *one* action that *maximizes the expected gain*, or the *mathematical expectation* of the series. In Borch's example, this means we should pick the action $A_n$ for which the product $P_n S_n$ takes on its greatest value. Thus, the expectation in general is

$$E_n = P_n S_n = \frac{100}{10 + n} \left(\frac{n}{10}\right)^{0.9} = \frac{10^{1.1} n^{0.9}}{10 + n}$$

and taking this as a continuous function, then $(E_n)_{max}$ is found where $dE_n/dn = 0$,

$$\frac{dE_n}{dn} = \frac{10^{1.1}}{n^{0.1}(10 + n)^2} (9 - 0.1n) = 0$$

from which $(E_n)_{max}$ occurs at $n = 90$. This corresponds to action $A_{90}$—receive $72 with a chance of 1 in 10.

The substance of this criterion arises from the *law of large numbers* in statistics. If we repeated the experiment many times, say 100,000, then $A_{90}$ is very close to the *average* gain we should expect to receive—i.e., a *consistent and repeated* choice of $A_{90}$ over the whole number of trials will give us (with almost certainty) a gain of $P_{90}S_{90}$ = $7.20. Thus, in the long run, we shall do the best we can by choosing the action that gives the greatest *expected* gain.

When we try to apply this principle of maximizing *expected gain* to the capital allocation problem, however, we run into a serious snag. The snag lies in the words *in the long run.* If we undertook the same project over and over, say 100,000 times, then the law of large numbers would undoubtedly apply. Unfortunately, in real life we seldom (if ever) get this opportunity—we are usually restricted to *doing* a project only once. Hence, the law of large numbers most likely will not apply. What happens, apparently, is that people make a one-shot decision on some basis *other* than the law of large numbers.

To show that this is the case, Daniel Bernoulli [6] pointed out as early as 1738 that the *maximum expected gain* criterion is not always literally followed by all decision-makers, especially in situations where they believe the law of large numbers would *not* apply. In what is now a classical counter-example, known as the *St. Petersburg Paradox*, Daniel Bernoulli reported the shortcomings of the expected gain criterion by citing a game devised by his cousin, Nicolas Bernoulli. The game goes somewhat as follows. A coin is tossed until it finally falls *heads*. If heads occurs for the first time on the $n$th toss, the player gets a prize of $2^{n-1}$ ducats (dollars in our currency), and the game is over. The probability that the coin falls heads for the first time on the $n$th toss is $(\frac{1}{2})^n$ since the trials (tosses) are independent and Prob(tails) $=$ Prob(heads) $= \frac{1}{2}$ for a fair coin. Hence, the *expected gain* in this game is

$$E = \sum_{n=1}^{\infty} 2^{n-1} \left(\frac{1}{2}\right)^n = \frac{1}{2} + \frac{1}{2} + \frac{1}{2} + \cdots = \infty,$$

since it is theoretically possible for the game to go on forever.

Now, since this game has a theoretical expectation of an *infinite gain*, then a decision-maker who maximizes expected gain should be willing to pay *any finite amount*, say $100,000, for the opportunity of playing it. Yet we know from common sense that people do not decide things this way. Indeed, Levy and Sarnat ([30], p. 196) report that this experiment, conducted with a group of students, revealed that most were prepared to pay only two or three dollars for a chance to play, and a few were willing to pay as much as eight dollars, but no one offered more than that. This contradiction between the *infinite mathematical expectation* of the game and the amounts that *reasonable* people are willing to pay for the opportunity of playing it is what constitutes the St. Petersburg Paradox. People apparently do not decide, *always*, on the basis of maximizing expected (mathematical) gain.

## 10.3. The Bernoulli Principle: Expected Utility

**10.3.1.** *The Bernoulli solution.* To explain why people do not decide in accordance with the expected gain principle, at least two solutions to the problem were proposed early. One was given by Daniel Bernoulli himself [6], and the other was provided by Gabriel Cramer,[2] a mathematician and contemporary of the Bernoulli's. (The two solutions differ principally in the form of the mathematical function used to describe

---

[2] Quoted by Daniel Bernoulli in his famous paper [6].

the decision-maker's choices.) We shall describe the essential aspects of the Bernoulli solution, which leads us ultimately to the generalized notion of the *Bernoulli Principle*, or *Expected Utility*.

Bernoulli's solution is based on the assumption that an individual is concerned with the usefulness, or *utility value*, rather than the actual *money value*, of the alternative prizes and that the additional utility afforded by additional money increments *decreases* as the money value of the prize increases. (We recognize the latter assumption as being the modern economist's principle of diminishing marginal utility of money.) Hence, while *total* utility continually increases as monetary gain increases, it does so at a diminishing rate. Bernoulli's assumption was that the utility of the money return is a *logarithmic* function of the amount of the *money* prize, in the following form:

$$U(x) = b \log \frac{x}{a} \qquad (10.1)$$

where  $U(x) =$  the utility assigned to a money prize of $x$ dollars,

$a,b =$ positive coefficients.

We note, in passing, that the function in Eq. (10.1) is *non*decreasing and that its second derivative is negative.[3] Hence, the *marginal* utility is always positive but *decreases* with increasing wealth ($x$)—thus satisfying the modern concept of positive but diminishing marginal returns.

Using the logarithmic function, Bernoulli asserted that an individual would consider the *utility* afforded by the prizes rather than their monetary amounts; as a consequence, the amount of *money* he would be willing to pay for the opportunity of playing the game would be at most a dollar amount corresponding to the *expected utility* of the game rather than its *expected monetary value*. If we let $n =$ the number of tosses of the coin until *heads* first appears ($n = 1, 2, 3, \ldots, \infty$) and $U(x) =$ the utility derived from the prize awarded after $n$ tosses, the amount of the money prize will be $2^{n-1}$, and the *utility* of this prize is given by Eq. (10.1); thus:

$$U(x) = b \log \frac{2^{n-1}}{a} = b \log 2^{n-1} - b \log a$$

$$= b[(n - 1) \log 2 - \log a]. \qquad (10.2)$$

According to Bernoulli's assertion that the individual will be willing to pay at most the money equivalent of the *expected utility* of the game, we calculate the expected

---

[3]Since both $a, b > 0$, then first derivative

$$U'(x) = \frac{dU(x)}{dx} = \frac{b}{x} \geq 0,$$

thus showing the function $U(x)$ to be nondecreasing and to have positive marginal utility. Also, the second derivative is

$$U''(x) = \frac{d^2U(x)}{dx^2} = -\frac{b}{x^2} \leq 0,$$

which is (weakly) negative, thus indicating that the marginal utility *decreases* as wealth ($x$) increases.

value of Eq. (10.2):

$$E[U(x)] = \sum_{n=1}^{\infty} P(x)U(x) = \sum_{n=1}^{\infty} P(x)b[(n-1)\log 2 - \log a]. \tag{10.3}$$

Now, the probability of the game lasting for $n$ tosses is $(\frac{1}{2})^n$, so that Eq. (10.3) becomes

$$E[U(x)] = \sum_{n=1}^{\infty} \left(\frac{1}{2}\right)^n b[(n-1)\log 2 - \log a]$$
$$= b\log 2 \sum_{n=1}^{\infty} (n-1)\left(\frac{1}{2}\right)^n - b\log a \sum_{n=1}^{\infty} \left(\frac{1}{2}\right)^n. \tag{10.4}$$

However, since

$$\sum_{n=1}^{\infty} \left(\frac{1}{2}\right)^n = 1 \quad \text{and} \quad \sum_{n=1}^{\infty} (n-1)\left(\frac{1}{2}\right)^n = 1$$

also,[4] then the *expected* utility of the game is

$$E[U(x)] = b\log 2 - b\log a = b\log\left(\frac{2}{a}\right). \tag{10.5}$$

We note, however, from Eq. (10.1) that this is *also* the *utility* of a specific game whose *money prize* is \$2; that is,

$$U(x) = b\log\frac{x}{a} = b\log\frac{2}{a}.$$

Thus, Bernoulli's *expected utility criterion* places an expected *utilitarian* value of \$2 on the game rather than the expected monetary value of infinity, as required by the *expected monetary criterion*. Another way of saying this is that an individual who chooses according to Bernoulli's utility function will pay at most \$2 to play the coin game. Alternatively, we can say that he is also *indifferent* between playing the game and a perfectly certain promise of a gain of \$2. [As a matter of interest, Cramer used the utility function $U(x) = \sqrt{x}$, where $x$ is the monetary gain. For his utility function, the expected utility of the game, in dollar equivalent, is \$2.93.] While Bernoulli's interest lay simply in providing an answer to the paradox and demonstrating the superiority of the expected utility criterion over the simple expected monetary criterion, the economic consequences of the Bernoulli-Cramer result were not appreciated until 200 years later.

---

[4]The series

$$\sum_{n=1}^{\infty} \left(\frac{1}{2}\right)^n = \frac{1}{2} + \frac{1}{4} + \frac{1}{8} + \cdots$$

is an infinite geometric series that converges when the common ratio, $r$, is fractional (i.e., $0 < r < 1$). The sum is unity. Similarly, the second series

$$\sum_{n=1}^{\infty} (n-1)\left(\frac{1}{2}\right)^n$$

is equivalent to

$$\sum_{n=2}^{\infty} \left(\frac{1}{2}\right)^n + \sum_{n=3}^{\infty} \left(\frac{1}{2}\right)^n + \sum_{n=4}^{\infty} \left(\frac{1}{2}\right)^n + \cdots = \frac{1}{2} + \frac{1}{4} + \frac{1}{8} + \cdots = \sum_{n=1}^{\infty} \left(\frac{1}{2}\right)^n = 1.$$

**10.3.2. *Modern preference theory: the von Neumann-Morgenstern hypothesis.*** The Bernoulli-Cramer solutions to the paradox were not well proved from a behavioral point of view—i.e., the expected utility principle was not established from a *behavioral standpoint*, in a rigorous enough manner, so that it could be taken as a criterion of human action. This defect was remedied nearly 200 years later, when attention was turned again to the subject of utility measurement. In 1931, a paper by Frank Ramsey [35], British logician and mathematician, was published shortly after his death. The paper laid the axiomatic foundations and gave the necessary derivation of the expected utility principle as a preference criterion. Ramsey's paper went without notice, however, apparently because no economist of that day thought the results important. Somewhat later, the world-renowned British mathematician, John von Neumann, and the economist, Oskar Morgenstern, published their famous collaborative work, *Theory of Games and Economic Behavior* in 1944. In connection with their study of games, they needed and independently derived (in an appendix to the second edition of their book [34]) the expected utility hypothesis directly from a set of behavioral axioms. While, at the time, the expected utility hypothesis was important as a basis for explaining certain types of behavior in connection with the theory of games, the criterion is of *much* more general application now—and it is somewhat unfortunate that the Neumann-Morgenstern development is intuitively associated with games.

In any event, what Neumann and Morgenstern (N-M) provided us with is a method of ordering choices over a set of *prospects* rather than over just a set of commodities. In traditional utility theory, we add up a set of finite *commodities* to make a *market basket*, to which we assign a relative value, or *utility*. This poses no problems since we always talk about *finite* things—i.e., market baskets and commodities. In N-M preference theory, however, we need to pass from the world of finite things into a world that is infinitely divisible—a world expressed in terms of probabilities that exist in infinite number on a scale of zero to one, each one of which is a prospect. We need to be able to *convolute* the probability functions of compound events and assign utility values to the convoluted probabilities. The Neumann-Morgenstern expected utility hypothesis allows us to do this. In the N-M framework, we are able to talk about a *preference ordering over a set of probabilistic money returns*, just as the traditional economist talks about a preference ordering over a set of market baskets. This is the fundamental and powerful tool provided us by Neumann and Morgenstern. Since the *expected utility* hypothesis of preference ordering is so important to an understanding of the economics of uncertainty, we shall outline below (and in Appendix 10.A) one method of showing that the expected utility criterion derives directly from some rather simple axioms of rational human behavior.

**10.3.3. *The axiomatic basis of expected utility.*** The fundamental contribution of Neumann and Morgernstern lies in showing that utility functions can be introduced into decision problems in such a way that an individual who acts *solely* in accordance with the criterion of *expected utility* is also acting in accordance with his true preferences. To show this, let us proceed as follows.

Assume that an individual is faced with alternative risky options (alternative lotteries), which we shall call *A*, *B*, and *C*, from which he has to choose one. We also assume that the individual makes choices in accordance with the following six axioms of behavior:

*Axiom 1* (Comparability): Any two alternatives may be compared, and either the individual prefers one to the other or he is indifferent between them. In other words, we assume a person can arrive at a choice between two alternative options, or he is indifferent between them.

*Axiom 2* (Transitivity): Both the indifference and preference relations in Axiom 1 are transitive. That is, if the individual prefers option *A* to option *B* and *B* to *C*, then he prefers *A* to *C* also. Likewise, if he is indifferent between *A* and *B* and also between *B* and *C*, then he is indifferent between *A* and *C*.

*Axiom 3* (Decomposition Axiom): Where a risky option has as one of its prizes another risky option, the first option is *decomposable* into its more basic elements. (An example would be the French roulette wheels that yield, in turn, tickets in the French National Lottery as prizes.) The decomposition axiom can be illustrated as follows: Let *G* be a lottery that includes two other lotteries, $L_1$ and $L_2$, as prizes. In abstract notation,

$$G = [qL_1, (1-q)L_2] \tag{10.6}$$

and

$$\left. \begin{array}{l} L_1 = [P_1A_1, (1-P_1)A_2] \\ L_2 = [P_2A_1, (1-P_2)A_2] \end{array} \right\} \tag{10.7}$$

where $q$ = probability of winning lottery $L_1$.

$L_1$ = a lottery with probability $P_1$ of winning prize $A_1$ and probability $(1-P_1)$ of winning prize $A_2$.

$L_2$ = a similar lottery with respect to prizes $A_1$ and $A_2$ but with probabilities $P_2$ and $(1-P_2)$.

Axiom 3 makes it possible for us to decompose the compound lottery, *G*, into its more basic form. If we take the sign $\sim$ to mean *equivalent to*, then we have from Axiom 3 that

$$G = [qL_1, (1-q)L_2] \sim \{q[P_1A_1, (1-P_1)A_2],$$
$$(1-q)[P_2A_1, (1-P_2)A_2]\}$$

or

$$G = [qL_1, (1-q)L_2] \sim \{[qP_1 + (1-q)P_2]A_1,$$
$$[q(1-P_1) + (1-q)(1-P_2)]A_2\}$$

or

$$G \sim [P^*A_1, (1-P^*)A_2] \tag{10.8}$$

where $P^* = qP_1 + (1-q)P_2$. The significance of this axiom, as expressed in Eq. (10.8), is that the compound lottery *G* can be decomposed (or reduced) to a simple lottery, which includes as its outcomes the tangible prizes $A_1$ and $A_2$ with compound probabilities $P^*$ and $(1 - P^*)$.

*Axiom 4* (Substitution Axiom): If an individual is indifferent between two risky options, they are interchangeable as alternatives in any compound option. Axiom 4 states simply that equally preferable payoffs may be substituted for each other in any decision-making problem. This axiom also justifies the expression of nonmonetary consequences (payoffs) in terms of their *certainty* or *cash equivalents*, where the cash equivalent is determined such that the decision-maker is indifferent between the nonmonetary payoff and the cash equivalent. To illustrate, consider the lottery $Q$:

$$Q = (P_1 \cdot 6, P_2 \cdot 8, P_3 \cdot 12). \tag{10.9}$$

Now if another lottery, say $B$, has a certainty equivalent of 8, so that the indifference relationship

$$B = (\tfrac{1}{4} \cdot 1, \tfrac{3}{4} \cdot 9) \sim 8$$

holds, then $B$ can be substituted in Eq. (10.9) for its certainty equivalent, 8, and the following *indifference* relationship then also holds:

$$Q_1 = [P_1 \cdot 6, P_2(\tfrac{1}{4} \cdot 1, \tfrac{3}{4} \cdot 9), P_3 \cdot 12] \sim [P_1 \cdot 6, P_2 \cdot 8, P_3 \cdot 12] = Q.$$

The result is that the indifference relationship between $Q_1$ and $Q$ is established by substitution of another indifference relationship, $B$.

*Axiom 5* (Monotonicity Axiom): If two risky options involve the same two alternatives, then the option in which the more preferred outcome has the higher probability of occurrence is itself preferred. This axiom is often referred to as the one that expresses a *desire for a high probability of success*. For example, if $Q_1 = (\tfrac{1}{3} \cdot 5, \tfrac{2}{3} \cdot 12)$ and $Q_2 = (\tfrac{1}{2} \cdot 5, \tfrac{1}{2} \cdot 12)$ and if the individual prefers getting 12 to 5, he will prefer $Q_1$ instead of $Q_2$ since the probability of getting 12 in $Q_1$ is higher than in $Q_2$.

*Axiom 6* (Continuity Axiom): If $A$ is preferred to $B$ and $B$ to $C$, then some lottery can be defined involving $A$ and $C$, for which the individual expresses indifference to $B$. For example, assume an individual prefers \$20 to \$10, and \$10 to \$1. The continuity axiom assures us that some value of probability, $P$, can be found in the range $0 < P < 1$, such that the following indifference relationship holds for the individual:

$$P \cdot 20 + (1 - P) \cdot 1 \sim 10.$$

The foregoing six axioms are sometimes called the N-M *axioms of rational behavior* since in essence they formally express the manner in which a rational (i.e., consistent) person would make his decisions concerning risky options. If we are willing to accept these axioms, *it can be shown that the optimal investment policy under conditions of uncertainty is the policy that gives maximum expected utility* (see Appendix 10.A). This is the *Bernoulli Principle*. In other words, the selection criterion of maximum *expected utility* can be derived *directly* from the axioms.

While the N-M axioms provide a basis for obtaining an interval-scale preference-ordering function (the utility function), not all mathematical functions, even though they seem to be of "proper" shape, are admissible as N-M preference-ordering functions. The class of admissible functions comprises only those functions that provide the *same ranking* for a given set of risky alternatives. Beyond the sole necessity for *ranking*, no significance is attached to the absolute levels of the utilities of alternatives. The class of utility functions that has the requisite property of keeping the rank order intact is composed of utility functions that are *linear* transformations of one another. Hence, the N-M preference-ordering function, in general, has neither an absolute (true) zero nor a unique unit of measure and can, therefore, be transformed by any linear transformation (e.g., by multiplying or dividing every value by a positive constant or by adding or subtracting a constant). For example, consider three utility functions

$$U_1(x) = x^{1/2}$$

$$U_2(x) = 100x^{1/2}$$

$$U_3(x) = 10 + 100x^{1/2}$$

For several values of $x$, the corresponding utilities are

| $x$: | 1 | 40 | 81 | 400 |
|---|---|---|---|---|
| $U_1(x)$: | 1 | 7 | 9 | 20 |
| $U_2(x)$: | 100 | 700 | 900 | 2,000 |
| $U_3(x)$: | 110 | 710 | 910 | 2,010 |

While the *values* of $U_j(x)$ change for a given value of $x$, notice that all three utility functions *rank* the utilities in the same order as $x$ itself is ranked—i.e., they preserve the rank-ordering of $x$.

Stronger measures of preferential utility (e.g., a proportional scale with rational zero) have been proposed by Shuford, Jones, and Bock [39] and by Restle [37], but the decision environment considered here does not require absolute measurement. For the capital budgeting problem, all that is required is that one be able to determine whether or not one project (or set of projects) has a greater utility to the decision-maker than another; it is not necessary to know *how much* greater. Thus, a proportional (or ratio) scale utility with rational zero is a refinement not required by the selection model.

## 10.4. Procuring a Neumann-Morgenstern Utility Function

**10.4.1. *The standard lottery method.*** The method usually used to ascertain a person's utility function is to present him with a series of hypothetical lotteries, one at a time, each involving different payoffs, and to ask him to choose between pairs of lotteries. The method can be illustrated as follows.

The first step is to choose arbitrarily two widely separated points on the proposed utility function, in order to fix the range of the scale. Thus, we might choose the utility of zero dollars, $U(0)$, as being zero *utiles* (the fictitious unit *utiles* is assigned to the numerical values of the utility function merely to describe the fact that the functional has units of *value* or *worth* and is not simply dimensionless). We also choose an upper scale value, say $U(\$100,000) = 10$ utiles.

The second step is to present what is called a *standard lottery* to the decision-maker, so that he has a choice of two alternative payoffs with different probabilities; say, as follows:

| Alternative A | Alternative B |
|---|---|
| Payoff = $25,000 with probability $p_1 = 1.0$ | (a) Payoff of $100,000 with probability $p_2$, or (b) payoff of $0 with probability $(1 - p_2)$ |

The decision-maker is asked to establish the value of $p$ at which he is indifferent between alternatives $A$ and $B$. Since most persons are not accustomed to thinking in terms of varying probabilities, however, it is customary to precalculate several versions of alternative $B$ using a range of values of $p_2$ and then to ask the decision-maker to establish his preference between $A$ and $B_1$, or $A$ and $B_2$, or $A$ and $B_3$, and so forth. At the point where he becomes undecided, or reverses his preference ordering, his *indifference probability* is established.

The third step is to calculate the value of the lottery, or $U(L)$, at the point of the indifference probability. (This is possible because of Axiom 6.) Suppose, for example, that the decision-maker's indifference probability $p = 0.5$ for alternative $A$ and $B$, above. Then the utility of the lottery would be $U(A) = U(B)$ at the point of indifference, or

$$p_1 U[(\$25,000)] = p_2[U(\$100,000)] + (1 - p_2)[U(0)]$$

or

$$1.0U(\$25,000) = 0.5(10 \text{ utiles}) + (1 - 0.5)(0 \text{ utiles})$$

$$\therefore \quad U(\$25,000) = 5.0 \text{ utiles.}$$

Negative values of utility are also needed to establish the utility function. To obtain these, the decision-maker is presented with a lottery involving a probable loss:

| Alternative C | Alternative D |
|---|---|
| Payoff = $0 with $p_1 = 1.0$ | (a) Payoff = $+100,000 with $p_2$, or (b) payoff = $- 30,000 with $(1 - p_2)$ |

Suppose his indifference probability is $p_2 = 0.5$. Then,

$$(1.0)U(0) = 0.5U(\$100,000) + (1 - 0.5)U(\$ - 30,000)$$

or

$$0 = 0.5(10) \qquad + 0.5U(\$ - 30,000)$$

$$\therefore \quad U(\$ - 30,000) = \frac{-0.5(10)}{10} = -10.0 \text{ utiles.}$$

This procedure, repeated many times, gives a series of points that maps $U(x)$ versus $x$, and a line that fits the data then describes the decision-maker's utility function for money increments. The data derived in the example above are plotted in Fig. 10.1 to indicate the result.

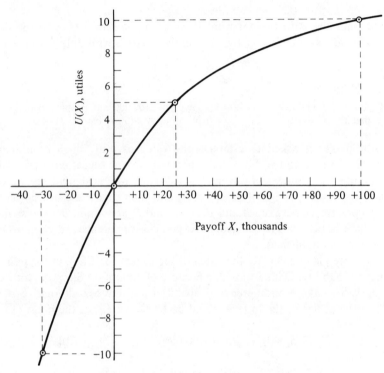

**Fig. 10.1.** Typical utility of money function.

**10.4.2. *Empirical determinations of utility functions.*** The von Neumann-Morgenstern utility theory has been utilized by several investigators as a basis for the empirical determination of utility functions of *individuals*. Mosteller and Nogee [33] were the first investigators (1951) to establish utility functions for individuals, using overt betting behavior in a gambling game to gather data for the construction of the utility curves. Davidson, Suppes, and Siegel [13] made additional determinations in 1957. Grayson [18], using the standard lottery technique, determined the utility functions of 11 principal decision-makers in the petroleum exploration and development business, several of which are shown in Figs. 10.2 and 10.3. Green [19] reported (1963) the determination of utility functions of 16 middle management personnel in a large chemical company, representing the four major divisions of the firm (production, sales, finance, and research). Swalm [41] reported (1966) the empirically determined utility functions of 13 executives, 12 of whom were from one company. Several of Swalm's functions are illustrated in Fig. 10.4. Cramer and Smith [12], also using the

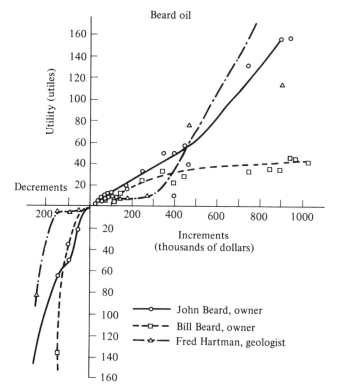

**Fig. 10.2.** Utility functions of three individuals in the petroleum exploration industry (Reproduced from Reference [18], by permission).

standard lottery method, reported (1964) the determination of the utility functions of 8 executives of a leading U.S. corporation, some of whom were from the research department and others from the manufacturing department.

There are several reasons for illustrating several *types* of utility functions, such as those depicted in Figs. 10.1 to 10.3. *First*, it will be noticed that a *unique* function seems to be associated with each *individual* decision-maker. There is good reason for this. Obviously, a utility function expresses a ranking of *personal* choices unique to the individual. But even from a different standpoint, a utility function cannot always be determined (as far as we know) for a *group*. Arrow [4] demonstrated by his *voting paradox* that the Transitivity Axiom can be violated by *circular preferences* in a group, thereby preventing the establishment of a rank ordering by group *choice*.

*Second*, we note that some of the utility functions in the figures are, in general, concave downward (e.g., Fig. 10.3), while others are convex, at least over a portion of the function in the first quadrant (e.g., Fig. 10.2 and Fred Hartman's and John Beard's functions in Fig. 10.1). As we shall see later, the concavity or convexity of the utility function can be interpreted as indicative of risk-avoiding or risk-seeking behavior on

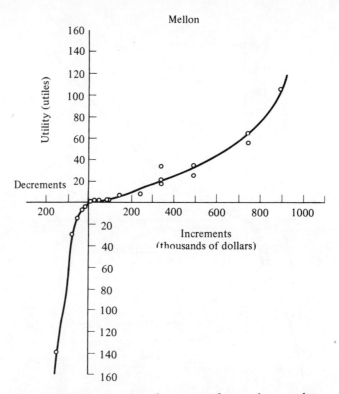

**Fig. 10.3.** Utility function of an owner of a petroleum exploration company (Reproduced from reference [18] by permission).

the part of the decision-maker. Risk avoiders have concave-downward utility functions, while risk seekers display some convexity in the first quadrant.

*Third,* we note that all the utility functions are generally concave downward in the
third quadrant (where payoff is negative—i.e., a loss). This phenomenon expresses an
aversion (disutility) for losses. In fact, most of the functions become rather steep at
small negative values of return, thereby expressing a pronounced dislike for large
losses.

Some other observations concerning N-M utility functions are in order. There is,
in general, no one form of mathematical function that will fit the individual's observed
data points exactly. To be more precise, one cannot specify *from theory* any particular
mathematical function that *is* a utility function for an individual. We can sometimes
disqualify certain functions (i.e., those that do not provide for the required linear
transformation property—see Section 10.3.3); but we cannot specify from theory what
*the* utility function of an individual is. One is never assured that any chosen mathematical function is theoretically *correct* for the individual. The best we can do is
*assume* one, although the choice of function can be somewhat narrowed by using
regression and analysis of variance techniques (e.g., see Bussey [8]).

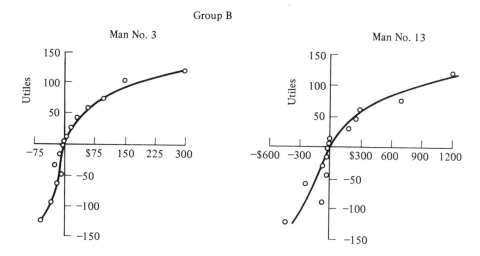

Group B

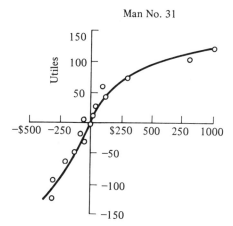

**Fig. 10.4.** Three risk-avoiding utility functions (Reproduced from reference [41] by permission).

## 10.5. Properties of Utility Functions: Indifference Curves and Risk Attitudes

**10.5.1.** *The quadratic utility function.* Mathematical expressions for expected utility are derived from *mathematical expressions* of the utility function, the form of which (in reality) is unknown. One can proceed on that basis, however, if necessary. A simple method of deriving a mathematical function for a simple utility curve (as in Fig.

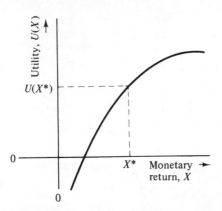

**Fig. 10.5.** General concave-downward utility function.

10.5) will be demonstrated below. The method we use, however, results in a mathematical function that has some rather severe limitations (as we shall see), but it is useful as a teaching device to illustrate how the risk attitudes and indifference curves of a decision-maker can be obtained from a mathematical function.

If the *true* form of the utility function in Fig. 10.5 is not known, it can be approximated by a Taylor series expansion if it is assumed to be a continuous function and at least twice differentiable. Further, it is assumed that the true function is a quadratic in $X$, the return. Now, consider some value of return, say $X^*$, and expand by a Taylor series about $X^*$:

$$U(X^* + h) = U(X^*) + h \frac{\partial U}{\partial X}\bigg|_{X=X^*} + \frac{h^2}{2!} \frac{\partial^2 U}{\partial X^2}\bigg|_{X=X^*} + \cdots \quad (10.10)$$

where $h$ is the perturbation away from $X^*$. Now, let $h = -X^*$, so that the function $U(X^* + h)$ will be evaluated at $X = 0$. Then, using the first three terms of the expansion to approximate the quadratic (the remainder will then vanish), the expansion becomes

$$U(X^* + h) = U(X^* - X^*) = U(0) = U(X^*) - X^* \frac{\partial U}{\partial X}\bigg|_{X=X^*} + \frac{X^{*2}}{2!} \frac{\partial^2 U}{\partial X^2}\bigg|_{X=X^*}.$$

$$(10.11)$$

Now, define $U(0) = 0$. This forces the function to pass through the point $[U(0) = 0, X = 0]$ since the values of $h$ and $U(0)$ were chosen to accomplish this end. From the foregoing, then

$$U(0) = 0 = U(X^*) - X^* \frac{\partial U}{\partial X}\bigg|_{X=X^*} + \frac{X^{*2}}{2!} \frac{\partial^2 U}{\partial X^2}\bigg|_{X=X^*}. \quad (10.12)$$

Now, letting

$$A = \frac{\partial U}{\partial X}\bigg|_{X=X^*} \quad \text{and} \quad B = \frac{1}{2} \frac{\partial^2 U}{\partial X^2}\bigg|_{X=X^*},$$

which are constants, we substitute and solve Eq. (10.12) for $U(X^*)$, so that we have

$$U(X^*) = A(X^*) - B(X^*)^2, \quad (10.13)$$

which is upward sloping and concave downward because of the signs of the terms.

To find the *expected* utility, take expectations of both sides of Eq. (10.13), thus:

$$E[U(X^*)] = AE[X^*] - BE[X^{*2}];$$

but

$$E[X^*] = \mu$$

and

$$E[X^{*2}] = V[X^*] + (E[X^*])^2 = \sigma_{X^*}^2 + \mu^2;$$

hence,

$$E[U(X^*)] = A\mu - B(\sigma_{X^*}^2 + \mu^2); \tag{10.14}$$

where  $\mu$  = the mean of the random variable  $X^*$.

$\sigma_{X^*}^2$  = the variance of  $X^*$.

Equation (10.14) is the expression for the *expected utility* of a random variable $X^*$, *when the utility function is of the form of Eq. (10.13)*. Note that the expected utility is stated in terms of the *mean* and the *variance* of the random variable, when the utility function is of quadratic form.

It follows, then, that if the random variable $X^*$ in Eq. (10.14) is the *distributed* return, $X$, of a proposed lottery, then the *expected utility* of the return is merely Eq. (10.14) and is the *selection criterion* by which the individual expresses *his* expectation of the lottery's utility for him, *when it is assumed* that he possesses a utility function of quadratic form. Note, however, that there is an upper limit to the applicability of this criterion. That is, since the utility function is a quadratic polynomial, it possesses a relative maximum, $U(X')$, at some value of $X = X'$, and the utility function is invalid when $X > X'$. This can be shown as follows.

Since the utility function was assumed to be continuous and at least twice differentiable, the necessary and sufficient conditions for a relative maximum are obtained, thus:

$$\frac{dU(X)}{d(X)} = A - 2B(X) = 0; \tag{10.15}$$

$$\frac{d^2U(X)}{d(X)^2} = = -2B \tag{10.16}$$

from which $X' = A/2B$. Now, the marginal utility, $U'(X) = dU(X)/d(X)$, is required to be everywhere positive for a valid utility function, and this requirement restricts the valid range of the quadratic utility function to values of $X \leq A/2B$. From a theoretical standpoint this is an undesirable limitation since marginal utility (from a classical economic standpoint) is usually assumed to be everywhere positive up to $X < \infty$.

The expected utility, $E[U(X)]$, serves as a basis for making inferences about the risk attitudes of the decision-maker who possesses a quadratic utility function. Referring to Eq. (10.14), if $E[U(X)]$ is assumed to remain constant, then the right-hand side of Eq. (10.14) describes a family of *indifference curves* in the parameters $\mu$ and $\sigma$, the shape of which can be inferred by differentiating Eq. (10.14). Thus,

$$0 = A\frac{d\mu}{d\mu} - 2B\sigma\frac{d\sigma}{d\mu} - 2B\mu\frac{d\mu}{d\mu}$$

or, solving for $d\sigma/d\mu$,

$$\frac{d\sigma}{d\mu} = \frac{A - 2B\mu}{2B\sigma}. \tag{10.17}$$

The expression $2B\sigma$ is clearly positive. Since $X$ and, therefore, $\mu$ must be less than $A/2B$ for a valid quadratic utility function, then the numerator of Eq. (10.17) is positive. Hence, $d\sigma/d\mu > 0$. Also, the second derivative of Eq. (10.14) is

$$\frac{d^2\sigma}{d\mu^2} = -\frac{1}{\sigma} - \frac{(\sigma')^2}{\sigma} \tag{10.18}$$

where $\sigma' = d\sigma/d\mu = (A - 2B\mu)/2B\sigma$, from Eq. (10.17). Since both $\sigma'$ and $\sigma$ are positive, then $d^2\sigma/d\mu^2 < 0$ by Eq. (10.18). Thus, Eqs. (10.17) and (10.18) indicate that the indifference curves, $E[U(X)] = \text{constant}$, are both upward sloping and downward concave on $\sigma$-$\mu$ coordinates, which corresponds to the classical economic interpretation of indifference analysis. Moreover, it should be observed that

$$A - 2B\mu = \frac{\partial E[U(X)]}{\partial \mu} > 0 \quad \text{and} \quad -2B\sigma = \frac{\partial E[U(X)]}{\partial \sigma} < 0$$

for valid values of $X$ and $\mu$, thus indicating that the decision-maker's expected utility varies directly with $\mu$ and *inversely* with $\sigma$. It can thus be inferred that the decision-maker whose utility function is quadratic *avoids* deviations ($\sigma$) of the return $X$ and hence is said to be a *risk avoider*, since he dislikes variation in the random return, which is interpreted as uncertainty. A typical set of risk-avoiding indifference curves is illustrated in Fig. 10.6.

The role of the indifference curves and the expected utility as a selection criterion can be illustrated by reference to Fig. 10.6. The means and standard deviations of return for three hypothetical lotteries $A$, $B$, and $C$ are superimposed on the indifference curves. Since the decision-maker's expected utility increases with $\mu$ and decreases with increasing risk, $\sigma$, then he prefers lotteries in the following manner. For two lotteries, $A$ and $B$, that have the same variance (or standard deviation) of return, he prefers the lottery $B$, with the greater expected return. For two lotteries, $B$ and $C$, that have the same expected return, he prefers the one with the smaller risk ($B$) since it has greater utility for him.

If investment funds were limited so that only one lottery could be purchased, then the decision-maker would choose Lottery $B$ because it has the highest expected utility of the three. If two lotteries could be undertaken, then he would (rationally) choose Lotteries $B$ and $C$ since these two lotteries yield the greatest expected utility. If, however, there were no capital limitation, then the decision-maker might still choose only Lotteries $B$ and $C$. The rationale for this decision can be demonstrated by the method of *certainty equivalents*. The certainty equivalent of an available opportunity is that value of return that has the *same expected utility* as the opportunity, but with zero variance. Thus, the certainty equivalent for Lottery $A$ is the intersection of the iso-utility curve with the abscissa, or point $C_A$. Now, the return on *cash* is zero since an investment of cash into cash provides no return. Likewise, the investment of cash into cash is (presumably) without risk, thus the variance of cash is zero. Hence, the cer-

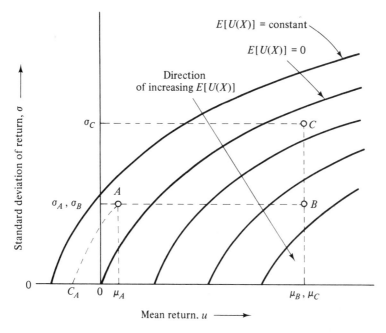

**Fig. 10.6.** Indifference curves for a risk-avoiding decision-maker.

tainty equivalent of cash is the point ($\mu = 0, \sigma = 0$). Because the certainty equivalent of Lottery $A$, $C_A$, is less than the certainty equivalent of cash, Lottery $A$ would not be undertaken. An alternative way of demonstrating the same result is to examine Eq. (10.14); if both $\mu$ and $\sigma$ are zero-valued, then $E[U(X)]$ is zero also. Thus, the isoutility curve, $E[U(X)] = 0$, passes through the origin on the indifference curve plot, and by inspection Lottery $A$ has a negative expected utility. *Investments with negative expected utilities are not undertaken.* Even though such investments may have a positive *expected monetary returns*, their utility becomes negative because of excessive risk to the risk-avoiding decision-maker or, conversely, because of insufficient expected return to offset the risk inherent in the investment. This type of risk-avoiding decision-making would be expected from individuals whose utility functions are concave downward— for example, the three executives whose utility functions are illustrated in Fig. 10.4.

In summary, the following inferences can be made for the *quadratic* utility function:

1. The quadratic formulation of a utility function for concave downward data points is valid when relevant values of mean return, $\mu_X$, are less then the constant $A/2B$.
2. The decision-maker who possesses a quadratic utility function is risk-averse. That is, for investments with equal risk, he prefers the one with the highest expected return; for investments with equal expected return, he prefers the one

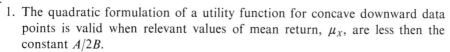

with the least risk. Furthermore, he will not accept investments with negative expected utility since cash has a greater utility for him.

3. Between investments with equal expected utility, the decision-maker with a quadratic utility function is indifferent.

The quadratic utility function has a definite advantage from a teaching standpoint because it is mathematically simple and leads easily to the concepts of indifference curves and risk avoidance. It is, however, not a very good utility function from an economic standpoint, and much criticism has been leveled at it. For example, it is valid only when the range of returns $X \leq A/2B = K$, where $K$ is some constant. Since the function is valid only up to $K$, it can be argued (given that the coefficient $A$ remains constant) that if one increases $K$ to a very large number, so as to encompass a large span of admissible returns ($X \leq K$), the effect is to reduce $B$ to a very small number. In other words, as $K \rightarrow \infty$, then $B \rightarrow 0$; and in the limit, the quadratic utility function reduces to the linear function $U(X) = AX$ since $B(X)^2$ in Eq. (10.13) vanishes. At least, as $K$ becomes large, then $B$ becomes very small, and the quadratic utility function can become insensitive to risk, especially at small values of return.

A second difficulty with the quadratic utility function is that it leads to *circular* (concentric) indifference curves, which is not consistent with observed economic behavior. Sharpe ([38], pp. 198–199) demonstrates this fact by showing that the equation for expected utility, Eq. (10.14), is the equation of a series of concentric *circles*, whose center is located at $\mu_X = A/2B$ and $\sigma_X = 0$, as shown in Fig. 10.7.

On the face of it, circular indifference curves do not seem to be too bad a choice, if one submits to the limitation $X \leq A/2B$; however, further examination proves otherwise. For example, there is not much freedom for expressing a decision-maker's attitudes concerning risk-versus-expectancy trade-offs via circular-shaped indifference

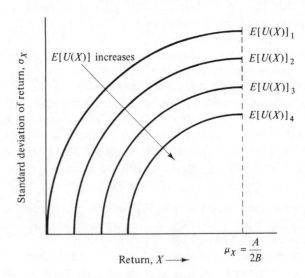

**Fig. 10.7.** Quadratic indifference curves.

curves. For example, as soon as only *two* equally desirable alternatives have been identified for the individual, *then **all** other choices are predictable*. The reason is that two equally desirable alternatives can be described as two points, $(\bar{X}_1, \sigma_{X_1})$ and $(\bar{X}_2, \sigma_{X_2})$ on the same indifference curve, and when they become known, *these two points fix the center of the indifference circle*,[5] given that $\sigma_X = 0$. As soon as the center is fixed, then all other indifference curves are merely concentric circles, and *all* the decision-maker's choices become ascertainable. This is a *substantial* reduction in flexibility of the indifference curve concept.

Aside from this, however, Sharpe ([38], pp. 200–201) also shows that normal risk-avoiding investor behavior in the stock market cannot be adequately described by *concentric* indifference curves, which is a weighty piece of evidence against the use of *quadratic* utility functions *in practice*. Their best use seems to be as a teaching device to show the principles of expected utility derivation, risk-versus-expectation trade-off, isoquant (indifference curve) analysis, and the economic meaning of certainty equivalents.

**10.5.2.** *Other risk-avoiding utility functions.* There are many other mathematical functions that can be used to overcome the limitations of the quadratic utility function. In general, for risk-avoiding utility functions, the requirements are (1) the function be continuous, (2) the first derivative be everywhere positive (thus providing for an increase in utility with an increase in return), (3) the second derivative be everywhere negative (thus providing for decreasing marginal utility), and (4) the function be capable of linear transformation without destroying its relative ordering properties. In essence, the risk-avoiding utility function, $U(X)$, must be continuous, monotonic increasing, and concave downward with respect to its argument (return), $X$.

Hillier ([23], pp. 37–43) specifies the necessary models and values of the coefficients in the models so that certain classes of *hyperbolic* and *exponential* functions can be used as risk-avoiding utility functions. Expected utility can be approximated from the Hillier models, and if Normality is assumed in the exponential model, then expected utility can be derived directly. For both the hyperbolic and the exponential models, the problem of subjectively estimating the utility function is reduced to one of subjectively estimating the asymptotes of $U(X)$.

---

[5]Two points, equally distant from a third (the center), are sufficient to define the equation of an indifference circle. By definition, the center of the indifference circles lies on the $\sigma_X = 0$ axis. The points $(\bar{X}_1, \sigma_{X_1})$ and $(\bar{X}_2, \sigma_{X_2})$, since they express indifference, are equally distant from the center and thus have equal radii. From algebra, by equating the radii of the two points from the location of the center at $(\mu_X, \sigma_X = 0)$, we obtain the distance from $X = 0$:

$$\mu_X = \frac{\sigma_{X_2}^2 - \sigma_{X_1}^2 + \bar{X}_2^2 - \bar{X}_1^2}{2(\bar{X}_2 - \bar{X}_1)}.$$

The center of the indifference curves lies at $(\mu_X, \sigma_X = 0)$. The reader should note also that $\mu_X \equiv A/2B$, and thus knowledge of two points of indifference establishes the *entire* utility function by fixing the constants $A$ and $B$, or vice versa: Knowledge of $A$ and $B$ fixes the entire indifference map of the decision-maker.

Freund [16] develops a model of the form $U(X) = 1 - \exp(-BX)$, which has the desired properties of a risk-avoiding utility function when $X$ is normally distributed, plus the added advantage that only the risk-avoidance constant, $B$, need be estimated from an individual's responses to the standard lottery. The Freund model is given in detail in Appendix 10.B since the original article [16] merely outlines the method of proof but does not give it.

**10.5.3.** *Linear utility functions: Expected monetary value.* A linear utility function is a special case of the risk-avoiding utility functions. A decision-maker with a linear utility function is indifferent to risk, and as a consequence he maximizes *expected monetary value* (EMV) instead of expected utility. The expected monetary value principle is but a special case of the Bernoulli principle, and thus there is no conceptual contradiction between a person who follows the St. Petersburg Paradox (maximizes expected utility) and another who follows the EMV principle. One has a risk-avoiding utility function, and the other simply ignores risk.

To demonstrate (informally) how this result can be obtained, consider again Eqs. (10.14) and (10.16). In Eq. (10.16) the *rate* at which the *marginal* utility [Eq. (10.15)] declines is determined by the constant, $B$. For this reason, $B$ is often called the *coefficient of risk aversion*. Now, if the decision-maker is not averse to risk—in fact, if risk is simply not a consideration for him—then $B = 0$. With this condition, the expected utility criterion, Eq. (10.14), reduces to

$$E[U(X)] = A\mu = AE[X],  \tag{10.19}$$

which is merely the equation of a straight line passing through the origin $\{X = 0, E[U(X)] = 0\}$ with a slope, $A$, times the expected *monetary* value of the return, $E[X]$. Hence, a person who is indifferent to risk $(B = 0)$ will simply maximize expected *monetary* value.

This result is of considerable practical importance in decentralizing the process of decision-making. Even if the principal decision-maker's utility function is nonlinear (e.g., risk avoiding), it is possible to represent it over a series of ranges of return by a *piecewise-linear* model. Then, if the linear segments "predict" the nonlinear decision results without serious error, the EMV principle can be used within a given range of return. This is the fundamental basis of using, for example, expected net present values and equivalent annual amounts in engineering economy studies as criteria for comparing investment alternatives. The delegation process involves simply a determination of a *range* of returns over which a linear approximation to the utility function can be used satisfactorily and then delegating the appropriate decision-making. For example, a policy might be established that "go no go" decisions on investments involving a net return of less than $100 can be made at the work-unit level; decisions concerning investments involving net returns of $100 to $1,000 are to be made at the superintendent level; and decisions on investments over $1,000 net return are to be made at the vice-president level. In each case, EMV criteria could be used but perhaps with different discount rates to reflect the different trade-off rates between expected return and risk, which are implied by the *nonlinear* parent utility function.

**10.5.4. *Complex utility functions: Risk seekers and insurance buyers.*** Many decision-makers do not always behave strictly in accordance with the rational risk-avoiding behavior that is implied by the concave-downward utility functions examined in Section 10.5.1. A simple example is the business executive who *gambles* in prospecting for petroleum and simultaneously buys fire and casualty insurance to avoid loss of his physical assets. If he were strictly a risk avoider, he would not necessarily engage in a business activity where the uncertainties are great (the ratio of "dry holes" to successful wells varies from about 10 : 1 to perhaps 30 : 1 in unproved territory) and where payoffs, if attained, sometimes may be disappointingly small in relation to the sums expended for development. On the other hand, if he were a risk seeker, then why would he purchase insurance, as many do, against a loss of other physical assets that could very well result in financial ruin, the same as if he drilled too many "dry holes" in succession?

Questions such as this were used by opponents of the von Neumann-Morgenstern utility theory to discredit the theory shortly after it was proposed. Such behavior, the critics said, is irrational and shows that the theory is sterile and incapable of predicting the choices of a decision-maker. To counter these allegations, Friedman and Savage [17] demonstrated that a decision-maker with a complex utility function—that is, one that is concave downward (risk avoiding) over certain ranges of payoff and concave upward (risk seeking) over others—would explain the simultaneous acceptance of an unfair gamble and the purchase of insurance to avoid loss in another quarter. To understand how such behavior can occur, consider the utility function in Fig. 10.8.

First, consider a case in which insurance would be purchased by the decision-maker in order to avoid a large loss. Suppose, for example, that the one-time premium for insurance to insure against a loss of $10,000 is $550 and that the actuarial probability of such a loss is 0.005. Now, from Fig. 10.8, the utility of a payment of $-\$550$ is $-3$ utiles, and the utility of a loss of $-\$10,000$ is $-800$ utiles. The alternative actions available are (1) purchase the insurance and (2) self-insure (carry no insurance). Thus, the expected monetary value (EMV) and the expected utility of each of the alternatives are

*Carry Insurance:*

$$\text{EMV} = 0.005(-\$550) + 0.995(-\$550) = -\$550$$
$$E(U) = 0.005(-3) + 0.995(-3) = -3 \text{ utiles}$$

*Self-Insure:*

$$\text{EMV} = 0.005(-\$10{,}000) + 0.995(0) = -\$500$$
$$E(U) = 0.005(-800) + 0.995(0) = -4 \text{ utiles.}$$

Thus, if the decision-maker maximized expected utility, he would purchase the insurance since this alternative has greater utility ($-3$ utiles) than the self-insurance alternative ($-4$ utiles). (Incidentally, note that this is the opposite decision than would have been made had he maximized expected monetary value.)

Next, consider that the same decision-maker has been offered an opportunity to invest in an oil-drilling venture in which the geologist has estimated that there is only 1

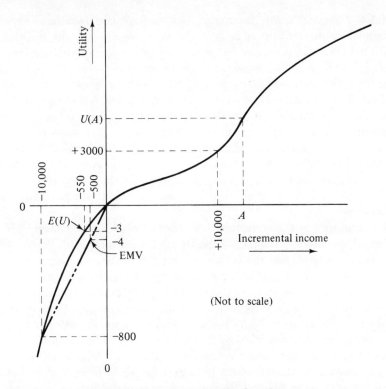

**Fig. 10.8.** Hypothetical utility function.

chance in 200 ($p = 0.005$) of striking a commercial well and a probability of 0.995 of finding a dry hole and losing the investment of $550. If the venture is successful, the decision-maker can anticipate a payoff of $10,000. Suppose also that the utility of a net payoff of $9,450 is +2,997 utiles. The alternative actions available are (1) invest in the venture and (2) do not invest. The expected monetary value and expected utilities of the alternatives are

*Invest in the Venture:*

$$\text{EMV} = 0.995(-550) + 0.005(10,000 - 550) = -\$500$$

$$E(U) = 0.995(-3) + 0.005(2,997) = 12.0 \text{ utiles}$$

*Do Not Invest:*

$$\text{EMV} = 0.995(0) + 0.005(0) = \$0$$

$$E(U) = 0.995(0) = 0.005(0) = 0 \text{ utiles.}$$

Again, the decision-maker who maximizes expected utility would invest in the venture —and note that his cost of accepting the alternative is $550, exactly the same as his cost for the insurance that he also purchased. Note also that had he maximized expected monetary value, he would not have invested in the risk-taking venture.

Markowitz ([32], p. 218) also points out that the complex utility function is consistent with the investor's behavior in diversifying his investments, when important money is at stake. That is, such an investor will insure against large losses, take small bets, and diversify his portfolio of important money investments. Even more theoretical evidence for the existence of complex utility functions is added by the work of Sidney Siegel [40], from the field of psychology. Working from Lewin's level of aspiration theory, Siegel showed (1957) that, with very little difference in terminology, the psychological *level of aspiration* is equivalent to the inflection point ($A$, in Fig. 10.8) of the utility function and that the individual will take risks in order to obtain a return of at least the utility of $A$. Siegel substantiated his derivation by a simple experiment involving 20 students and their semester grades, in which the levels of aspiration for the utility of a grade were measured and correlated with their risk preferences. Chernoff and Moses [11] also used, but did not explain or amplify their choice, utility curves of sigmoid shape (e.g., S-shaped, as in Fig. 10.8) in explaining insurance purchase behavior (1959).

An alternative explanation for the S-shaped utility function, as shown in Fig. 10.8, can be provided by an assumption that the utility function orders over a set of *subjective* probabilities instead of objective probabilities. A number of economic theorists (e.g., Yaari [42] and Hirshleifer [24]) strongly object to the *convex* portions of complex utility functions, not only on the ground that marginal utility be everywhere positive but also that it *must* be everywhere *de*creasing (i.e., the second derivative must be negative). Such a requirement is appropriate for risk avoiders, but how can it apply to risk seekers—i.e., those whose utility functions *may* be convex over certain range(s) of return? Yaari has hypothesized that an individual's subjective estimates of probability tend to be higher than the corresponding objective values when the latter are low, and vice versa. If this hypothesis is correct, then the phenomenon of risk *seeking* can be contained within the overall risk-avoidance model—i.e., without postulating the existence of a convex segment in the utility function.

**10.5.5.  *Empirical determination of a complex utility function.*** In this section, we shall outline a method used by the author [8] to determine the coefficients in a polynomial expression of a decision-maker's utility function. Figures 10.2 and 10.3 depict the utility functions of four decision-makers of the Beard Oil Company, as reported by Grayson [18]. Three of these men display utility functions that are, over some portion of the monetary return scale, convex—and thus indicate some preference for risk. (It should also be noted that not all of Grayson's *tabulated* data for R. F. Mellon's curve are plotted in Grayson's counterpart of our Fig. 10.3—hence, there may be a tendency to view Mellon's utility function in Fig. 10.3 as risk seeking in the range of return greater than about $300,000. When all of Grayson's data points are considered, however, there is some ambiguity as to whether Mellon is a risk seeker or risk avoider at returns greater than about $600,000.) To demonstrate the regression approach to determining a utility function, we shall use Grayson's data [18] but as modified by the author [8].

Fortunately, since Grayson overlapped his standard lotteries [i.e., made multiple determinations of response at repeated (constant) levels of payoff], it is possible to estimate the inherent sampling error for an individual and to perform an analysis of variance on the regression. Then, by using the Grayson data ([18], p. 300) as raw data, the utilities in Table 10.2 were calculated by writing the expected utility identity for

**Table 10.2.** UTILITY FUNCTION DATA: R. F. MELLON

| Investment (thousands) (I) | Utility of Investment U(I) | Net Payoff (thousands) (NPV) | Indifference Probability P (gamble) | Utility of Payoff U (NPV) |
|---|---|---|---|---|
| 10 | − 2.2 | 20 | 0.70 | 0.95 |
| | | 30 | 0.50 | 2.2 |
| | | 50 | 0.40 | 3.3 |
| | | 90 | 0.25 | 6.6 |
| 20 | − 4.6 | 20 | 0.90 | 0.5 |
| | | 30 | 0.90 | 0.5 |
| | | 100 | 0.60 | 3.1 |
| | | 150 | 0.40 | 6.9 |
| 50 | − 27.5 | 50 | 0.90 | 3.1 |
| | | 100 | 0.90 | 3.1 |
| | | 350 | 0.40 | 41.3 |
| | | 750 | 0.20 | 110. |
| 75 | − 56.2 | 90 | 0.90 | 6.2 |
| | | 350 | 0.60 | 37.5 |
| | | 750 | 0.30 | 131. |
| | | 925 | 0.20 | 225. |
| 100 | −112.5 | 250 | 0.90 | 12.5 |
| | | 350 | 0.80 | 28.1 |
| | | 500 | 0.75 | 37.5 |
| | | 900 | 0.60 | 75.0 |
| 150 | −150. | 150 | No | — |
| | | 350 | 0.80 | 37.5 |
| | | 500 | 0.80 | 37.5 |
| | | 850 | 0.70 | 64.3 |

*Source* (Columns 1, 3, and 4): Grayson [18], p. 300. The data in Column 2 were assumed so that best overlap of individual curves resulted.

each data point. That is, if Mellon's response to the standard lottery were, for example, an indifference probability of 0.70 between a net payoff of $850,000 and an investment of $150,000 to obtain the gamble, then the expected utility of the net gamble is zero and the utility of $850,000 can be determined, thus:

$$E(U) = 0 = 0.70U(850,000) + 0.30U(-150,000)$$
$$0 = 0.70U(850,000) + 0.30(-150)$$

from which
$$U(850,000) = 64.3 \text{ utiles.}$$

The remaining data points in Table 10.2 were obtained in the same manner.

Using these data, a multiple linear regression was performed, in which the regression equation was assumed to be of the form

$$\hat{U} = \beta_0 + \beta_1 X + \beta_2 X^2 + \beta_3 X^3 + \beta_4 X^4, \tag{10.20}$$

where $\hat{U} =$ the regressed response variable (utility).

$\beta_i =$ the regression constants ($i = 0, \ldots, 4$).

$X =$ the independent variable, return.

The regression constants were evaluated by a computer-programmed regression technique, yielding a function of least-squares approximation to the data in Table 10.2. The resulting regression estimate is

$$\hat{U} = -17.63 + 48.74X - 17.967X^2 + 2.721X^3 - 0.123X^4, \tag{10.21}$$

where $X$ has units of dollars $\times 10^{-5}$. This equation is exactly analogous to a utility function of the same form, namely,

$$U(X) = K + AX - BX^2 + CX^3 - DX^4$$

where the coefficients $K$, $A$, $B$, $C$, and $D$ are, for the Mellon data, those of Eq. (10.21).

The adequacy of fit for the regression model can be determined by analysis of variance procedures, where one has available (as in this case) repeated measures on the independent variable—e.g., see Table 10.2, for net payoffs of 90, 100, 350, 500, and 750. Such repeated measures permit one to estimate the sampling error variance and thus estimate goodness of fit. In our case, all coefficients $\beta_i$ ($i = 0, 1, \ldots, 4$) were significantly different from zero at the 1 % level, and the values of the coefficients satisfied the conditions for positive marginal utility (up to a limiting return of $X^* = 1,049.8$). (See Bussey and Stevens [9], [10] for a method of determining $X^*$ and for conditions that satisfy the marginality requirements.) The regressed utility function of R. F. Mellon, using Grayson's data shown in Table 10.2, is depicted in Fig. 10.9.

One may ask, "Why use 'higher-order' functions to approximate utility functions?" The answer is that several articles on the theory of investment suggest merit in the use of mathematical functions more complex than a quadratic, for the purpose of approximating utility functions. While earlier investigations in essence merely suggest the use of complex utility functions of unspecified form, the more recent works suggest the use of specific mathematical functions, such as the cubic polynomial. When the assumption is made that the utility approximating function is an $n$th degree polynomial and that the decision-maker selects by maximizing expected utility, then these complex functions, in effect, require that $n$ moments of the return distribution be considered in the analysis of the problem.[6] Thus, Levy [28] develops the case for a cubic utility function approximation from a theoretical standpoint. While not strictly to this point, Arditti [3] used the third central moment of the return distribution to explain empirical

---

[6]See Bussey and Stevens [9].

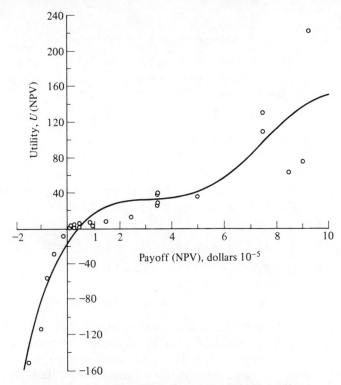

**Fig. 10.9.** Regressed utility function for R. F. Mellon.

findings concerning investor behavior. More recently, Hanoch and Levy [22] developed criteria for efficient selection based on cubic utility functions; Alderfer and Bierman [2] presented empirical evidence tending to show that cubic utility functions may exist; and Jean [25] shows (in effect) that a positively skewed (positive third movement) distribution of new income would be logically preferred to a symmetrical one by corporations whose capital structure is leveraged (i.e., in which senior securities have prior right to distributions of new income). Also, Levy and Sarnat [29] show that the selection criteria previously developed by Hanoch and Levy [22] and Hadar and Russell [20] remain valid even when the present level of the investor's wealth becomes a random variable, in particular, when restrictions are not placed on the shape of the utility function. Thus, the sense of recent investigations is that utility function approximations, which use mathematical polynomials of higher degree than the quadratic, may be of greater value in describing actual investor preferences in portfolio and project selection, namely a cubic or quartic polynomial. The conditions necessary for the existence of a cubic utility function have been reported by Levy [28] and are obtained by relatively straightforward methods. The quartic polynomial case is handled by Bussey and Stevens [9].

## 10.6. Summary

When certainty assumptions are relaxed in the project selection problem, the departures from certainty occur in two directions—(1) departures that are the result of *changes in the cash flow stream* away from predicted values and (2) departures that are due to *changes in the discount rates* that apply to the cash flows. The first is termed the *stream effect*, and the latter is termed the *rate effect*. Under conditions of *un*certainty, as when one estimates the worth of a future project, both effects usually occur in practice. In this chapter, however, we have introduced as a means of handling the *stream* effect the modern theory of preference ordering, which is based upon the Expected Utility Principle (the Bernoulli Principle), derived from the von Neumann-Morgenstern axioms of rational behavior. The *rate* problem has not been considered here.

We note particularly that the expected utility criterion is essentially a *present-time* device. This is because it is derived from the von Neumann-Morgenstern behavioral axioms, which describe a rational decision-maker's behavior when he considers a lottery, which is a set of probabilistic returns in *present time*. That is, there is an assumption of no delay in payoff once a lottery is selected. The N-M axioms do *not* consider, for example, the case of an investor who makes a present-time outlay (to purchase a lottery, for example) and who must then wait for one or more periods of sensible time for his payoff, during which the time value of money ought to be considered.

Furthermore, most authorities recognize that a decision-maker's utility function for money returns is not generally stable along a time axis. People become older, their level of wealth changes, and their risk attitudes change.

For these reasons, it is not possible to apply N-M utility methods *directly* to future money returns. To do so would mean the *present-time* utility function would have to be applied to *future* sums (returns) of money, which is a nonsequitur. Hence, the multiperiod project selection problem, under conditions of uncertainty, cannot be solved by the direct application of N-M utility theory to the future cash flow streams of the project. Nevertheless, considerable insight can be gained by the limited application of expected utility methods, and we shall consider some of the simpler models in Chapter 11.

The special case of a linear utility function, we have seen here, leads to the criterion of expected monetary value (EMV), thus resolving any possible inconsistency between persons who maximize EMV and those who maximize expected utility via the Bernoulli Principle. They simply possess different utility functions.

Finally, we demonstrated in this chapter how the apparent inconsistency between insurance buyers and risk seekers can be resolved and how an empirical utility function for an individual can be procured.

In Chapter 11 we shall consider some applications of utility theory to simple multiperiod models of the project selection problem under uncertainty.

## APPENDIX 10.A. PROOF OF THE EXPECTED
## UTILITY HYPOTHESIS[7]

Based on the risk axioms given in Chapter 10, it is our purpose here to demonstrate that the Bernoulli Principle (expected utility) can be derived directly from the axioms. We assume the investor is faced with two lotteries:

$$L_1 = (p_1 A_1, p_2 A_2, \ldots, p_n A_n)$$
$$L_2 = (q_1 A_1, q_2 A_2, \ldots, q_n A_n)$$
$$\left. \right\} \quad \text{(A10.1)}$$

where $A_i = $ a possible prize (payoff).

$p_i = $ the probability of receiving $A_i$ under Lottery 1.

$q_i = $ the probability of receiving $A_i$ under Lottery 2.

We take $p_i, q_i \geq 0$, and $\sum_{i=1}^{n} (p_i) = \sum_{i=1}^{n} (q_i) = 1$.

Let us assume (via Axiom 1) that the prizes can be ordered so that

$$A_1 \succ A_2 \succ A_3 \succ \cdots \succ A_n$$

where $\succ$ means *is preferred to*.

From Axiom 6 (the continuity axiom), we can fix some lottery $A_i^*$, consisting solely of the prizes $A_1$ and $A_n$, so that the investor will be indifferent between the lottery $A_i^*$ and its certainty equivalent (the prize $A_i$). That is,

$$A_i^* = [u_i A_1 + (1 - u_i)A_n] \sim A_i$$

where the symbol $\sim$ means *indifferent to* or *equivalent to*, and $u_i$ is some number.

Now, if $A_i \succ A_j$, then we expect $u_i > u_j$ since we have to give greater value to lottery $A_i^*$ than lottery $A_j^*$. We can accomplish this result by assigning the following values, which cause $A_i^*$ to be expressed in terms of probability:

$$u(A_1) = u_1 = 1$$

$$u(A_i) = u_i \qquad \text{(given that } 0 < u_i < 1 \text{ for } i = 2, 3, \ldots, n - 1)$$

$$u(A_n) = u_n = 0.$$

(We are allowed to do this because the utility function is determined *up to a linear transformation*; hence we may multiply each $u_i$ by a positive number and add a constant number to each $u_i$ without changing the preference ordering.)

Now, by Axiom 4 (substitution axiom) we can substitute some $A_i^*$ in $L_1$ and $L_2$ for the equivalent $A_i$. Since transitivity relations apply (Axiom 2), we can continue this process until we finally obtain the equivalent lotteries

$$L_1 = [p_1 A_1^*, p_2 A_2^*, \ldots, p_n A_n^*]$$
$$L_2 = [q_1 A_1^*, q_2 A_2^*, \ldots, q_n A_n^*]$$
$$\left. \right\} \quad \text{(A10.2)}$$

---

[7]This proof generally follows the method given by Luce and Raiffa [31]. Another approach can be found in Baumol [5].

Via Axiom 3, the two lotteries in Eq. (A10.2) can be reduced to simpler forms since we can write, for example,

$$L_1 = \{P_1[u_1 A_1, (1 - u_1)A_n], \ldots, P_n[u_n A_1, (1 - u_n)A_n]\}$$

$$= \left[\left(\sum_{i=1}^{n} P_i u_i\right) A_1, \left(1 - \sum_{i=1}^{n} P_i u_i\right) A_n\right] \qquad (A10.3)$$

$$= [\bar{P} A_1, (1 - \bar{P})A_n]$$

where $\bar{P} = P_1 u_1 + P_2 u_2 + \cdots + P_n u_n =$ expected value of $u$ in $L_1$. In a similar manner we can reduce $L_2$, so that we obtain

$$\left.\begin{array}{c} L_1 = [\bar{P} A_1, (1 - \bar{P})A_n] \\ L_2 = [\bar{Q} A_1, (1 - \bar{Q})A_n] \end{array}\right\} \qquad (A10.4)$$

in which $\bar{P} = \sum_{i=1}^{n} P_i u_i =$ expected value of $u$ in $L_1$.

$\bar{Q} = \sum_{i=1}^{n} Q_i u_i =$ expected value of $u$ in $L_2$.

Since $A_1 \succ A_n$ (via Axiom 5, monotonicity), then Lottery $L_1$ will be preferred to Lottery $L_2$ *if and only if* $\bar{P} > \bar{Q}$. Now $\bar{P}$ and $\bar{Q}$ are the *expected values* of a sequence of numbers, $u_1, u_2, \ldots, u_i, \ldots, u_n$, which we call *utilities* and which are ordered *in the same order sequence* as the prizes $A_1, A_2, \ldots, A_i, \ldots, A_n$ are preferred to each other. That is to say, if Lottery $L_1$ is preferred to Lottery $L_2$, then there is a sequence of numbers, $u_i$, constituting a *utility function*, such that

$$E[U(L_1)] \equiv \sum_{i=1}^{n} P_i u_i > E[U(L_2)] \equiv \sum_{i=1}^{n} Q_i u_i.$$

This is the Bernoulli Principle; however, it is here derived from six axioms of *rational behavior*.

## APPENDIX 10.B. THE FREUND RISK-AVOIDING MODEL

Freund [16] developed a similar risk-avoiding utility model that avoids the upper-limit difficulty ($X^*$) in the quadratic model; however, it assumes that the return is a *normally* distributed variable. (This may not be a poor assumption for many capital budgeting problems.)

Freund's utility function is of the form:

$$U(X) = 1 - \exp(-BX) \qquad (B10.1)$$

where $X$ is what Freund calls the *net revenue*. We may take it to be the *return*.

The function in Eq. (B10.1) is concave downward for positive values of $B$ (a constant) and indicates a risk-avoiding decision-maker. Then, Freund says, if $X$ is *normally* distributed (with mean, $\mu$, and standard deviation, $\sigma$), the expected utility is

$$E[U(X)] = \int_{-\infty}^{\infty} [1 - \exp(-BX)] \frac{1}{\sigma\sqrt{2\pi}} \exp\left[-\frac{1}{2}\left(\frac{X - \mu}{\sigma}\right)^2\right] dX, \qquad (B10.2)$$

which is the selection function to be maximized. This form of the selection function is somewhat intractable, however, and can be simplified as follows.

Expanding Eq. (B10.2) and separating the resulting integrals, the problem becomes

$$\text{Max } E[U(X)] = \frac{1}{\sigma\sqrt{2\pi}} \int_{-\infty}^{\infty} \exp\left[-\frac{1}{2}\left(\frac{X-\mu}{\sigma}\right)^2\right] dX$$

$$- \frac{1}{\sigma\sqrt{2\pi}} \int_{-\infty}^{\infty} \exp\left[-\frac{1}{2}\left(\frac{X-\mu}{\sigma}\right)^2 - BX\right] dX, \qquad \text{(B10.3)}$$

from which one recognizes that the first integral is merely the cumulative normal distribution which integrates to unity. Now, make the substitution $z = (X - \mu)/\sigma$, and Eq. (B10.3) becomes

$$\text{Max } E[U(X)] = 1 - \frac{1}{\sigma\sqrt{2\pi}} \int_{-\infty}^{\infty} \sigma \exp\left[-\frac{1}{2}(z)^2 - B\sigma z - B\mu\right] dz. \qquad \text{(B10.4)}$$

Complete the square in the exponent by adding and subtracting the quantity $B^2\sigma^2/2$, obtaining

$$\text{Max } E[U(X)] = 1 - \frac{1}{\sigma\sqrt{2\pi}} \int_{-\infty}^{\infty} \sigma \exp\left[-\frac{1}{2}(z + B\sigma)^2\right]$$

$$\cdot \exp\left[-\frac{1}{2}(2B\mu - B^2\sigma^2)\right] dz. \qquad \text{(B10.5)}$$

Now, the second exponential is a constant and can be brought outside the integral sign and by back-substituting for $z$ its equivalent $(X - \mu)/\sigma$, one obtains

$$\text{Max } E[U(X)] = 1 - \exp\left[-\frac{1}{2}(2B\mu - B^2\sigma^2)\right]\frac{1}{\sigma\sqrt{2\pi}}$$

$$\cdot \int_{-\infty}^{\infty} \exp\left[-\frac{1}{2}\left(\frac{X + B\sigma^2 - \mu}{\sigma}\right)^2\right] dx. \qquad \text{(B10.6)}$$

Now, the quantity $B\sigma^2$ in the exponent of the second exponential is a constant and by defining a new random variable $X^* = X + B\sigma^2$, one obtains $dX^* = dX$, and thus an equivalent statement of the problem is

$$\text{Max } E[U(X^*)] = 1 - \exp\left[-\frac{1}{2}(2B\mu - B^2\sigma^2)\right]$$

$$\cdot \frac{1}{\sigma\sqrt{2\pi}} \int_{-\infty}^{\infty} \exp\left[-\frac{1}{2}\left(\frac{X^* - \mu}{\sigma}\right)^2\right] dX^*. \qquad \text{(B10.7)}$$

The second exponential, under the integral in Eq. (B10.7), is recognized as being merely the cumulative normal distribution of the random variable $X^*$, which integrates to unity. Hence, the equivalent selection problem is to

$$\text{Max } E[U(X^*)] = 1 - \exp\left[-\frac{1}{2}(2B\mu - B^2\sigma^2)\right], \qquad \text{(B10.8)}$$

which can be done by *minimizing* the exponential term. This is accomplished by *max*imizing the quantity $\frac{1}{2}(2\mu - B\sigma^2)$ since $B$ can be factored and the exponent is negative. Hence, if a new variable $Y^* = \frac{1}{2}(2\mu - B\sigma^2)$ is defined, then the equivalent selection problem is to

$$\text{Max } E[U(X^*)] \approx \text{Max } [Y^*] = \text{Max } \left[\mu - \frac{B}{2}\sigma^2\right], \tag{B10.9}$$

which yields the same result (the same set of optimal choices) as if Eq. (B10.8) has been used as the selection criterion.

While Freund does not carry his analysis past this point, one can go on to an indifference curve analysis (as done for the quadratic utility function) and show that the indifference curves obtained from Eq. (B10.9) are similar in form to those obtained from the quadratic function but without the limitations associated with the quadratic. Thus, if $E[U(X^*)]$, and hence $Y^*$ also, is a constant, then by differentiation of Eq. (B10.9) one obtains

$$0 = 1 - B\sigma \frac{d\sigma}{d\mu}$$

from which

$$\frac{d\sigma}{d\mu} = \frac{1}{B\sigma} > 0 \tag{B10.10}$$

and

$$\frac{d^2\sigma}{d\mu^2} = -\frac{1}{B^2\sigma^3} < 0. \tag{B10.11}$$

Thus, the indifference curves on $\sigma$-$\mu$ coordinates will slope upward and to the right and will be concave downward (similar to Fig. 10.6). Moreover, since

$$\frac{dY^*}{d\mu} = 1 \quad \text{and} \quad \frac{dY^*}{d\sigma} = -B\sigma,$$

the decision-maker's expected utility increases with increasing expected return and decreases with increasing risk, $\sigma$. Hence, the decision-maker with an exponential utility function is also a risk-avoiding one. The same risk attitudes can be inferred for such a person as for one who possesses a risk-avoiding quadratic utility function, except that in the exponential case, *there is no upper limit* on the applicability of the utility function since the first derivative (the marginal utility) of Eq. (B10.1) merely approaches zero as an asymptote in the limit as the return, $X$, approaches infinity.

## REFERENCES

[1] ACKOFF, R. L., S. GUPTA, and J. S. MINAS, *Scientific Method: Optimizing Applied Research Decisions* (New York: John Wiley & Sons, Inc., 1962).
[2] ALDERFER, CLAYTON P., and HAROLD BIERMAN, JR., "Choices With Risk: Beyond the Mean and Variance," *The Journal of Business*, 43(3) (July, 1970), pp. 341–53.
[3] ARDITTI, FRED, "Risk and the Required Return on Equity," *Journal of Finance* (March, 1967), pp. 19–36.
[4] ARROW, KENNETH J., *Social Choice and Individual Values* (New York: John Wiley & Sons, Inc., 1951).

[5] BAUMOL, WILLIAM J., *Economic Theory and Operations Analysis*, 3rd ed. (Englewood Cliffs, N.J.: Prentice-Hall, Inc., 1972).

[6] BERNOULLI, DANIEL, "Exposition of a New Theory of the Measurement of Risk," *Econometrica* (1954), pp. 23–36. Translation of a paper "Specimen Theoriae Novae de Mensura Sortis," *Papers of the Imperial Academy of Sciences in Petersburg*, V, 1738.

[7] BORCH, KARL HENRIK, *The Economics of Uncertainty* (Princeton, N.J.: Princeton University Press, 1968).

[8] BUSSEY, LYNN E., "Capital Budgeting Project Analysis and Selection with Complex Utility Functions." (Unpublished Ph.D. Dissertation, Oklahoma State University, Stillwater, 1970).

[9] ——, and G. T. STEVENS, JR., "Quartic Polynomials as Approximations to Complex Utility Functions: A Technical Note," *The Engineering Economist*, **19**(2) (Winter, 1974), pp. 127–38.

[10] ——, and ——, "A Solution Methodology for Probablistic Capital Budgeting Using Complex Utility Functions," *The Engineering Economist*, **21**(2) (1975), pp. 89–109.

[11] CHERNOFF, HERMAN, and LINCOLN E. MOSES, *Elementary Decision Theory* (New York: John Wiley & Sons, Inc., 1959).

[12] CRAMER, ROBERT H., and BARNARD E. SMITH, "Decision Models for the Selection of Research Projects," *The Engineering Economist*, **9**(2) (1964), pp. 1–20.

[13] DAVIDSON, D., P. SUPPES, and S. SIEGEL, *Decision-Making: An Experimental Approach* (Stanford, Calif.: Stanford University Press, 1957).

[14] DE FINETTI, BRUNO, "Foresight: Its Logic Laws, Its Subjective Sources," in H. E. Klyberg and H. E. Smokler, ed., *Studies in Subjective Probability* (New York: John Wiley & Sons, Inc., 1964).

[15] DE MORGAN, AUGUSTUS, *Formal Logic: or The Calculus of Inference, Necessary and Probable* (London: Taylor and Walton, 1847).

[16] FREUND, RUDOLF J., "The Introduction of Risk into a Programming Model," *Econometrica*, **24**(3) (July, 1956), pp. 253–63.

[17] FRIEDMAN, MILTON, and L. J. SAVAGE, "The Utility Analysis of Choices Involving Risk", *Journal of Political Economy* (April, 1948), pp. 279–304.

[18] GRAYSON, C. JACKSON, JR., *Decisions under Uncertainty: Drilling Decisions by Oil and Gas Operators* (Boston: Harvard University, Division of Research, Graduate School of Business Administration, 1960).

[19] GREEN, PAUL, E., "Risk Attitudes and Chemical Investments Decisions," *Chemical Engineering Progress*, **59**(1) (January, 1963), pp. 35–40.

[20] HADAR, J., and W. R. RUSSELL, "Rules of Ordering Uncertain Prospects," *American Economic Review*, **59**(7) (March, 1969), pp. 25–34.

[21] HALEY, CHARLES W., and LAWRENCE D. SCHALL, *The Theory of Financial Decisions* (New York: McGraw-Hill Book Company, 1973).

[22] HANOCH, GIORA, and HAIM LEVY, "Efficient Portfolio Selection with Quadratic and Cubic Utility," *The Journal of Business* (April, 1970), pp. 181–89.

[23] HILLIER, F. S., *The Evaluation of Risky, Interrelated Investments* (Amsterdam: North-Holland Publishing Co., 1969).

[24] HIRSHLEIFER, J., "Investment Decisions under Uncertainty: Choice-Theoretic Approaches," *The Quarterly Journal of Economics*, **75**(4) (November, 1965), pp. 510–36.

[25] JEAN, WILLIAM H., "The Extension of Portfolio Analysis to Three or More Parameters," *Journal of Financial and Quantitative Analysis*, **6**(1) (January, 1971), pp. 505–15.

[26] KLYBERG, H. E., and H. E. SMOKLER, ed., *Studies in Subjective Probability* (New York: John Wiley & Sons, Inc., 1964).

[27] LAPLACE, PIERRE SIMON DE, *A Philosophical Essay on Probabilities*, English translation of 5th (1825) ed. (Dover: Truscott & Emory, 1952).

[28] LEVY, HAIM, "A Utility Function Depending upon the First Three Moments," *The Journal of Finance*, **24**(4) (September, 1969), pp. 715–20.

[29] ——, and MARSHALL SARNAT, "A Note on Portfolio Selection and Investors' Wealth," *Journal of Financial and Quantitative Analysis*, **6**(1) (January, 1971).

[30] ——, and ——, *Investment and Portfolio Analysis* (New York: John Wiley & Sons, Inc., 1972), pp. 639–42.

[31] LUCE, R. D., and H. RAIFFA, *Games and Decisions* (New York: John Wiley & Sons, Inc., 1957).

[32] MARKOWITZ, HARRY M., *Portfolio Selection: Efficient Diversification of Investments.* Cowles Foundation Monograph 16 (New York: John Wiley & Sons, Inc., 1959).

[33] MOSTELLER, FREDERICK, and PHILIP NOGEE, "An Experimental Measurement of Utility," *The Journal of Political Economy*, **59**(5) (October, 1951), pp. 371–404.

[34] NEUMANN, JOHN VON, and OSKAR MORGENSTERN, *Theory of Games and Economic Behavior*, 2nd ed. (Princeton, N.J.: Princeton University Press, 1947).

[35] RAMSEY, F. P., "Truth and Probability," in *The Foundations of Mathematics and Other Logical Essays* (London: Kegan Paul, Trench, Trusner and Co., 1931; also reprinted in [26]).

[36] RAIFFA, HOWARD, *Decision Analysis* (Reading, Mass.: Addison-Wesley, 1968).

[37] RESTLE, F., *Psychology of Judgement and Choice: A Theoretical Essay.* (New York: John Wiley & Sons, Inc., 1961).

[38] SHARPE, WILLIAM, F., *Portfolio Theory and Capital Markets* (New York: McGraw-Hill Book Co., 1970).

[39] SHUFORD, E., LYLE V. JONES, and R. DARREL BOCK, "A Ratio Scale for Utility" (Unpublished paper presented at the 1959 meeting of the American Psychological Association).

[40] SIEGEL, SIDNEY, "Level of Aspiration and Decision Making," *Psychological Review*, **64** (1957), pp. 253–62.

[41] SWALM, RALPH O., "Utility Theory: Insights into Risk Taking," *Harvard Business Review* (November-December, 1966), pp. 123–36.

[42] YAARI, MENAHEM E., "Convexity in the Theory of Choice Under Risk," *Quarterly Journal of Economics*, **75**(4) (May, 1965), pp. 278–90.

## PROBLEMS

**10-1.** What is meant, in mathematical terms, when one states that a utility function is defined *up to a linear transformation*?

**10-2.** The expected utility criterion was derived in Section 10.3.1 using Bernoulli's form of the decision-maker's assumed utility function, namely, $U(x) = b \log (x/a)$. Compare Bernoulli's solution to Cramér's solution, which uses a utility function of the form $U(x) = x^{1/2}$.

**10-3.** Define the mathematical form of a utility function which expresses risk aversion on the part of the decision-maker and which applies over the range of the argument from $x = -1$ to $x = +\infty$. The function passes through the point $[(U(x), x)] = (0, 0)$. What is the expectation of this function if the probability of any value is 0.5?

**10-4.** A person may estimate the expected cash flow in a particular year to be $10,000. If this figure is ued in project analysis, what assumption(s) is (are) being made?

**10-5.** The following are the coordinate points of a decision-maker's utility function:

| Dollars | Utility Measure |
|---|---|
| $-3 000 | -3,000 |
| -1,000 | -1,000 |
| - 600 | - 500 |
| - 500 | - 350 |
| 0 | 0 |
| 100 | 100 |
| 500 | 150 |
| 1,000 | 200 |
| 2,000 | 350 |
| 4,000 | 500 |
| 10,000 | 11,000 |

(a) What is the utility measure of a gamble in which the decision-maker would win $10,000 in cash with probability 0.5 or lose nothing with probability 0.5?

(b) What is the amount the decision-maker would accept *for certain*, in order to cause him to be indifferent between the two choices?

(c) What is the expected *monetary* value of the gamble?

**10-6.** Assume an investor has a utility function with the following coordinate points:

| Dollars | Utility Measure |
|---|---|
| $-20,000 | -400 |
| -10,000 | -100 |
| 0 | 0 |
| 7,200 | 80 |
| 8,600 | 90 |
| 10,000 | 100 |
| 18,600 | 140 |
| 20,000 | 150 |
| 30,000 | 190 |
| 35,800 | 200 |
| 40,000 | 220 |
| 60,000 | 240 |

(a) Should the investor accept an investment that requires an outlay of $10,000 and will result in the complete loss of investment with probability 0.5 or will generate a cash inflow of $30,000 within a week (probability 0.5)?

(b) Should the investor undertake the following investment? Assume that a 5% discount rate for money is applicable.

| End of Period | Cash Flow |
|---|---|
| 0 | $-10,000 |
| 1 | $\begin{cases} 0 & \text{with probability 0.5} \\ +30,000 & \text{with probability 0.5} \end{cases}$ |

(c) What would be your recommendation if the probabilities were 0.6 for failure (cash flow $= 0$ at end of Period 1)?

**10-7.** Which of the von Neumann-Morgenstern axioms is most likely to fail under conditions of reality?

**10-8.** For an assumed utility function of the form $U(x) = x^{1/2}$, fit a series of piecewise-linear functions of the form $U_1(x) = A_1 + B_1 x$ ($A$ and $B$ are constants), so that the maximum relative error, $|U_1(x) - U(x)|/U(x)$, is 5% or less, over the interval $+1 \leq x \leq +4$.

**10-9.** What is the significance of the *two* inflection points in a quartic utility function of the form $U(x) = Ax - Bx^2 + Cx^3 - Dx^4$?

**10-10.** An investor expresses indifference between two one-period projects whose characteristics are as follows:

|  | Investment A | Investment B |
|---|---|---|
| Mean net return | $100 | $200 |
| Standard deviation of return | $ 10 | $ 30 |

(a) Define the investor's utility function if it is assumed to be of the form $U(x) = Ax - Bx^2$. What are the limitations applying to this utility function?

(b) Define a utility function for this investor that will (i) pass through the given *expected* utility coordinates and *also* through the origin $[(U(x), x)] = (0, 0)$ and (ii) have a marginal utility that is always nonnegative.

**10-11.** For any value of wealth $x$, given that $0 \leq x < \infty$, the local *risk aversion function*, $r(x)$, is defined as

$$r(x) = \frac{-U''(x)}{U'(x)} = \frac{-\partial^2 U(x)/\partial x}{\partial U(x)/\partial x}.$$

For quadratic utility functions, the risk aversion function is simply Eq. (10.16) divided by Eq. (10.15), or

$$r(x) = \frac{2B}{A - 2Bx}.$$

Since $r(x)$ obviously increases as $x$ increases (assuming $A/2B \geq x$), comment on the desirability of using a quadratic utility function to describe the choices of a decision-maker whose wealth ($x$) is increasing over time.

# EXPECTED UTILITY MODELS
# OF PROJECT SELECTION

## 11.1. Introduction

In Chapter 10 we derived the Bernoulli, or Expected Utility, Principle as a basis for deciding among lotteries when the outcomes are uncertain. We also indicated, from the nature of the Neumann-Morgenstern axioms and from the fact that payoffs on the lotteries are not *delayed*, that the Expected Utility Principle is a *present-time* decision criterion—i.e., it does not account for the time value of money if payoffs are delayed. Thus, the Expected Utility Principle is a decision device for judging *stream* effects rather than *rate* effects.

In this chapter, we shall continue to use expected utility as a criterion for judging stream effects, although we shall also introduce rate effects in a limited manner. That is, as we did in the certainty case, we shall consider a cash flow *stream* going to or emanating from a project, with the stream consisting of a series of discrete cash flows assumed to occur at time $t$ ($t = 0, 1, \ldots, N$), where $N$ is the life of the project; however, when we consider the *value* of this stream, we shall discount it at some interest rate(s), $i_t$. For the present, *we shall assume perfect capital market conditions*, so that we may have knowledge of $i_t$. Moreover, we shall assume that $i_1 = i_2 = \cdots = i_t = i$, where $i$ is an assumed known market rate of interest, so that the net present value criterion developed in Chapter 7 applies. Under these conditions, we may discount a present value stream to time $t = 0$, thereby obtaining its present equivalent, or net present value.

# 11

Now, under conditions of *un*certainty in *payoff*—i.e., a lottery—the payoff[1] may be viewed as a *random* variable. In other words *each* of the *cash flows* to or from a project may be considered to be a *random variable*, with mean and variance, and possibly higher moments as well. The stream of cash flows, representing the project, is conceptually just a time sequence of random variables in the uncertainty model of the project. The idea of a *mean cash flow*, or perhaps some linear combination of mean cash *flows*, conveys the concept of expected value of (net) cash flow(s) of the project; hence, we may find usefulness for the *expectation* of the cash flows of a project or some function of it. The *variance* of the project's cash flows, or some function of the variance, however, does not *in itself* convey any meaning that would be of value to a decision-maker.

Recalling from Section 10.5.1 that we derived some *risk* attitudes for the decision-maker from the expected utility criterion, we can, from this point of view, attach meaning to the cash flow *variance* (or standard deviation). For the case of the quadratic utility function used in Section 10.5.1, we found the decision-maker to prefer (have positive utility for) more *expected value* of a return to less, but to avoid (have disutility for) more standard deviation of return, $\sigma$, to less. Moreover, we found the *trade-off* between expected return and standard deviation of return to be nonlinear (i.e., indiffer-

---

[1]*Payoff* can be positive or negative, i.e., a return from the project or an investment in it.

ence curves are nonlinear; see Fig. 10.6).[2] Thus, we associate *variation* in the cash flows with *risk*—or, in our present terminology concerning the future, *uncertainty*. Hence, we take it in this and subsequent chapters that uncertainty about future cash flows can be measured by the *variances* of the cash flows or some function of the variances.

This short discussion concerning stream effects, random cash flows, and their principal statistics (mean and variance of cash flows) now brings us to the organization of this chapter. We shall first discuss the random variable basis of single, risky projects and how we may obtain and use a probability distribution (or its moments), in *present time*, to judge the worth of a project. This is the *net present value* method. Counter to this method, we shall develop the *certainty-equivalent* model as an alternative. Then, moving to multiple projects, we shall introduce the utility concept more specifically and develop a model in which mutually exclusive sets of projects are ordered by the Expected Utility (Bernoulli) Principle. Counter to this method, the multiple-project certainty-equivalent model will be described. Finally, we shall indicate that a combined model, in which both *stream* and *rate* effects are considered, is the time-state-preference (TSP) model—which, as a practical matter, is insoluble at the present time, especially if imperfect capital market conditions obtain.

## 11.2. Single Risky Projects—Random Cash Flows[3]

**11.2.1.** *Estimates of cash flows.* A *project*, under conditions of uncertainty, may be characterized by its *random* cash flows. Let us consider a stream of such cash flows, $Y_{tj}$, generated by a particular project $j$ ($j = 1, 2, \ldots, m$) at the end of present and future time periods $t$ ($t = 0, 1, 2, \ldots, n$), where $n$ is the life of the project. We note that $Y_{tj}$ may be positive in sign (an inflow to the firm), negative (an outflow from the firm, i.e., an investment in the project), or zero. We also note that $Y_{tj}$ is the *net* cash flow, resulting from all possible inflows and outflows at any particular time $t$, and also that the project life, $n$, may (at times) be a random variable also. For the present, however, we assume $n$ is fixed and known.

In probablistic cash flow streams each periodic cash flow increment, $Y_{tj}$, for a particular period and project will be a random variable. This means that the actual values taken on by $Y_{tj}$ will be governed by a *random* process. In random processes, one would expect that some values will occur relatively more often than others or, alternatively, that some have greater probabilities of occurrence. Thus, the relative frequencies of the random values taken on by the cash flow increment, $Y_{tj}$, can usually be represented by probability or density functions such as those illustrated in Fig. 11.1. In

---

[2]Obviously, the quadratic utility model yields implied risk attitudes that are unique to that model. Similar risk-avoiding attitudes can be inferred *in general*, however, from any concave downward utility function (e.g., see Markowitz [24], Chapters 8 and 9; Levy and Sarnat [23], Chapter 8).

[3]Portions of this chapter are adapted from three articles by Bussey and Stevens [4], [5], [6], reprinted here by permission of the copyright owner.

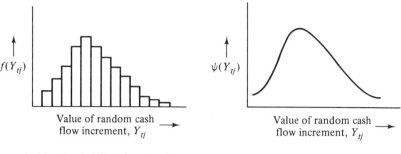

(a) Mass (probability) function for a
discrete random cash flow increment

(b) Density function for a continuous
random cash flow increment

**Fig. 11.1.** Distributions of random cash flow increments.

Fig. 11.1(a), the relative frequency of each *discrete* value of cash flow is described by the mass function $f(Y_{tj})$, while in Fig. 11.1(b) the relative frequency over a small *range* of cash flows for a *continuously* distributed $Y_{tj}$ is given approximately by the expression

$$p(Y_{tj})_{a,b} = \int_{Y=a}^{b} \psi(Y_{tj})\, dY, \tag{11.1}$$

where $\psi(Y_{tj})$ is the probability density function of the random cash flow increment.[4] Thus for the probabilistic case each periodically generated net cash flow increment is conceived of as a *random* variable, either discretely or continuously distributed over the range of interest or applicability rather than as a *known* constant value for any given period. The consequence of this distributional assumption is that each random cash flow increment, $Y_{tj}$, for each project, $j$, and each time period, $t$, will have at least a *mean* and a *variance* associated with it, and possibly higher central moments as well. For the present exposition, however, we confine the development to the case in which only the means and variances of the cash flow increments are of interest.

The question arises, then, how does one determine the probability distribution (or at least the mean and the variance) of each of the cash flow increments, $Y_{tj}$, for a project? In general, cash flow data for future projects must be *estimated* by analysts possessing the necessary subjective expertise. The analyst can, for example, examine various schemes or checklists such as the one shown in Fig. 11.2, to determine the source elements that contribute to cash outflows and inflows. By applying subjective

---

[4]Strictly, for the discrete case, $f(Y_{tj})$ takes on values in the range $0 \leq f(Y_{tj}) \leq 1$ such that

$$F(Y_{tj}) = \sum_{Y_{tj}} f(Y_{tj}) = 1;$$

for the continuous case, $\psi(Y_{tj})$ takes on values in the range $0 \leq \psi(Y_{tj}) \leq 1$ such that

(1) $$F(Y_{tj}) = \int_{-\infty}^{\infty} \psi(Y_{tj})\, dY_{tj} = 1$$

(2) $$\text{Prob}\,[a \leq Y_{tj} \leq b] = \int_{a}^{b} \psi(Y_{tj})\, dY_{tj}.$$

378

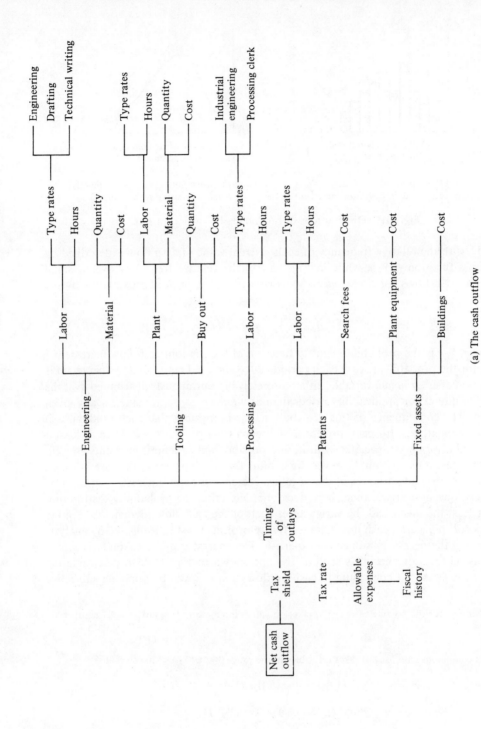

**Fig. 11.2.** Schematic origins of periodic cash flow increments. (After Murray [26], reprinted with permission.)

(a) The cash outflow

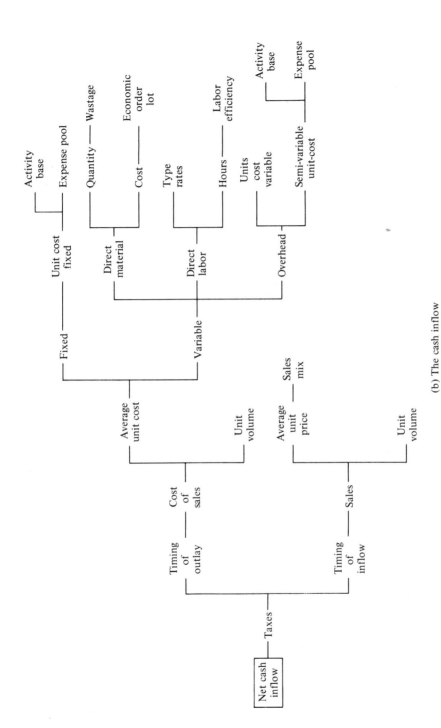

(b) The cash inflow

**Fig. 11.2.** (Continued)

379

(or predictive) estimates to each of the source elements, the analyst can develop a *mean* (expected value) estimate for the net cash flow in a given period. In the probabilistic model, however, the analyst must do more than this. He also must somehow realistically (albeit subjectively) evaluate the *variance* of the net cash flow increment for each period of interest or, alternatively, specify the probability or density function of each net cash flow increment.

One rather straightforward way of obtaining the mean and variance for each cash flow increment is based on the properties of the Beta distribution, used extensively in PERT methodology. This method, proposed by Wagle [33] and summarized by Hillier ([19], p. 87–89), requires that the analyst make an *optimistic* estimate, a *pessimistic* estimate, and a *most likely* estimate for each cash flow increment. These three estimates are assumed to correspond, respectively, to the upper bound, the lower bound, and the mode of the $\beta$ distribution. A typical $\beta$ distribution defined in this manner somewhat resembles a normal distribution, the principal exceptions being that (1) the $\beta$-density function is truncated in the tails (instead of continuing indefinitely as does the normal) and (2) it may be skewed right or left (instead of being symmetrical as is the normal). The $\beta$-density function will be skewed whenever the mode (most likely value) is not midway between the extreme bounds; thus the analyst's most likely estimate for cash flow may take on any value between the pessimistic and optimistic estimates, depending on his expert judgment.

Each optimistic cash flow estimate should typify the cash flow that would occur if everything goes as well as reasonably possible, and the pessimistic estimate should typify the cash flow that would occur if everything goes as poorly as reasonably possible (in both cases, say, with one chance in several hundred). The most likely estimate of cash flow is just what this description implies: The subjectively determined value of cash flow deemed by the analyst most likely to occur. One word of caution should be noted. In establishing values for optimistic and pessimistic cash flows, these are taken to be the slightly probable *extremes* of the cash flow increment *itself* and not the smaller range over which the most likely cash flow value might fluctuate—that is, approximately six standard deviations should exist between the optimistic and pessimistic cash flow estimates.

With the foregoing procedure, and by assuming that the $\beta$ distribution represents the underlying cash flow density function with six standard deviations between the bounds, the mean and the variance of the cash flow increment in any period $t$ can be found by

$$E[Y_{t,j}] = \tfrac{1}{6}[\text{Est}\,(Y_p) + 4\,\text{Est}\,(\tilde{Y}) + \text{Est}\,(Y_o)] \tag{11.2}$$

and

$$V[Y_{t,j}] = \{\tfrac{1}{6}[\text{Est}\,(Y_o) - \text{Est}\,(Y_p)]\}^2 \tag{11.3}$$

where $E[Y_{t,j}]$ = mean cash flow increment for period $t$.

$V[Y_{t,j}]$ = variance of the cash flow increment for period $t$.

$\text{Est}\,(\tilde{Y})$ = most likely estimate of cash flow in period $t$.

Est $(Y_p)$ = pessimistic estimate of cash flow in period $t$.
Est $(Y_o)$ = optimistic estimate of cash flow in period $t$.

To demonstrate the application of this technique, assume that expert subjective analysis has yielded the optimistic, pessimistic, and most likely estimates of cash flow for a project as shown in Table 11.1. One can verify, by the application of Eqs. (11.2) and (11.3) to these data, that the mean cash flows and the variances of the cash flow increments for each year are those given in Table 11.1.

**Table 11.1.** MEANS AND VARIANCES OF $\beta$-DISTRIBUTED CASH FLOW INCREMENTS FOR A HYPOTHETICAL PROJECT

| Year, $t$ | Pessimistic Estimate | Most Likely Estimate | Optimistic Estimate | Mean Cash Flow, $E[Y_{tj}]$ | Variance of Cash Flow, $V[Y_{tj}]$ |
|---|---|---|---|---|---|
| 0 | $-20,000 | $-10,000 | $- 6,000 | $-11,000 | $5.44 \times 10^6$ ($\$^2$) |
| 1 | - 6,000 | + 2,000 | + 6,000 | + 1,333 | $4.00 \times 10^6$ |
| 2 | + 6,000 | +12,000 | +18,000 | +12,000 | $4.00 \times 10^6$ |
| 3 | +12,000 | +18,000 | +28,000 | +18,667 | $7.11 \times 10^6$ |

**11.2.2. Expectation of project net present value.** The net present value for a project is simply the sum of the discounted periodic cash flow increments occurring in each of the periods throughout the project life so that the sum is expressed in equivalent present-time dollars. In the deterministic case, each periodic cash flow increment is assumed to be known with certainty and, therefore, each can take on only fixed values in the summation. In contrast, the assumption in the probabilistic case is that each periodic cash flow increment takes on an *unknown* value, $Y_{tj}$ but, because of the central tendencies underlying the statistical distribution of each $Y_{tj}$, the *effect* of the randomness can be expressed through the mean and variance of the distribution $Y_{tj}$. Thus, in the probabilistic case, the summation of the discounted periodic *random* cash flow increments to obtain the project net present value must result in the fact that the project net present value itself is *also* a random variable. That is,

$$P_j = Y_{0j} + \frac{Y_{1j}}{(1+i)} + \frac{Y_{2j}}{(1+i)^2} + \cdots + \frac{Y_{ij}}{(1+i)^i} + \cdots + \frac{Y_{nj}}{(1+i)^n}, \qquad (11.4)$$

where $P_j$ is the *random* net present value for project $j$ $(j = 1, 2, \cdots, n)$; $Y_{tj}$ is the *random* cash flow increment in the $t$th period $(t = 0, 1, \ldots, n)$ for the $j$th project; and $i$ is the known rate of discount (e.g., the minimum attractive rate of return). Hence, in the probabilistic case the determination of net present value for any project will result in $P_j$ being a *random* variable, with some mean, $E[P_j]$, and some variance, $V[P_j]$.

The random net present value for the project will possess a *mean net present value*, $E[P_j]$, *and a variance of net present value*, $V[P_j]$. These are the *keys* that permit us to relate the unknown $P_j$ to the random cash flow increments of the project. The *mean* net present value of the project is simply the sum of the discounted *mean* cash flow increments occurring in the project or, symbolically,

$$E[P_j] = E[Y_0] + \frac{E[Y_{1j}]}{(1+i)} + \frac{E[Y_{2j}]}{(1+i)^2} + \cdots + \frac{E[Y_{nj}]}{(1+i)^n},$$

or

$$E[P_j] = \sum_{t=0}^{n} \frac{E[Y_{tj}]}{(1+i)^t}. \tag{11.5}$$

Thus, a knowledge of the *mean* values of the cash flow increments (e.g., those in Table 11.1) and a fixed discount rate, $i$, lead directly to the *mean* net present value for the project via Eq. (11.5).

**11.2.3. *Variance of project net present value.*** It is not so easy to establish the variance of net present value as it is to find the mean. Essentially, one of three types of relationships may exist between cash flow increments from a project: (1) complete independence, (2) complete dependence, or (3) partial dependence. Cash flow increments from a project are said to be completely independent if there is no causative or consequential relationship between any two cash flow increments in the cash flow stream. That is, if any given cash flow increment can be determined *solely* from causative events occurring within that period and if these events bear *no* relationship to or dependency on events in prior or succeeding periods, then the cash flow increments are said to be independent among periods. If, on the other hand, there is some relationship between events in one period to those of another, then the cash flow increments are dependent. For example, if operating expenses trend upward in succeeding years as a result of action taken in a prior year or if sales exceed estimates in early years, then they are likely to exceed estimates in succeeding years. These are fairly common phenomena and if such conditions do exist in the formulation of cash flows, then the cash flow increments cannot be assumed independent.

Complete dependence between cash flow increments exists if there is a *one-to-one* relationship among events in succeeding periods, and partial dependence exists if there is a relationship on less than a one-to-one basis. In evaluating the *variance* of project net present value the exact relationship among cash flow relationships must be specified.

For the *independent* case, the variance of project net present value is found as follows. Let $(1+i)^{-t} = k_t$, a constant. Since the cash flow increments, $Y_{tj}$, are random variables, then

$$V\left[\frac{Y_{tj}}{(1+i)^t}\right] = V[k_t Y_{tj}] = k_t^2 V[Y_{tj}], \tag{11.6}$$

and these variances for the $n$ periods are additive, so that

$$V[P_j] = \sum_{t=0}^{n} V\left[\frac{Y_{tj}}{(1+i)^t}\right] = \sum_{t=0}^{n} k_t^2 V[Y_{tj}] = \sum_{t=0}^{n} \left[\frac{\sigma_{Y_{tj}}^2}{(1+i)^{2t}}\right], \tag{11.7}$$

where $\sigma_{Y_{tj}}^2$ is the variance of the $t$th cash flow increment. It is to be noted that the exponent for the discounting factor in the variance formulation is $2t$, compared with simply $t$ for the mean in Eq. (11.5).[5]

If the relationships between the cash flow increments do not permit an assumption of complete independence, then the cash flow increments can be conceived as being statistically correlated, either perfectly or partially, by the causative relationships. Perfect correlation of cash flow increments results in the one-to-one complete dependency mentioned earlier, and partial correlation results in cases intermediate between perfectly correlated and mutually independent cash flow streams.

For the *dependent* cases, the project mean net present value, $E[P_j]$, is found from Eq. (11.5) in exactly the same manner as for independent cash flow streams since this equation depends solely on the properties of the expected value operator, $E$, and not on dependence-independence assumptions in the linear combinations of random cash flow increments.

To determine the variance of project net present value in dependent cases, a useful approach is to assume that cash flows form an autocorrelated time series and that the autocorrelation coefficient matrix among cash flow increments or, alternatively, the autocovariance matrix can be obtained. When the cash flows are correlated, one can derive an expression for the variance of net present value, as described below.

Dropping the subscript $j$ for clarity but recognizing that the development is for a single project, let $Y_t$ be the distributed random cash flow increment for period $t$ ($t = 0, 1, \ldots, n$), with mean $E[Y_t]$ and variance $V[Y_t] = \sigma_{Y_t}^2$. Let $P$ be the project net present value (a distributed random variable) with mean $E[P]$ and variance $V[P]$.

---

[5]The proof of the variance formulation is as follows. Let $(1 + i)^{-t} = k_t$, a constant. For independence among the $Y_t$, then

$$\underbrace{V\left[\frac{Y_{tj}}{(1 + i)^t}\right]}_{\substack{\text{Random} \\ \text{variable}}} = \underbrace{V[k_t Y_{tj}] = k_t^2 V[Y_{tj}]}_{\substack{\text{Constant} \\ \text{times a} \\ \text{random} \\ \text{variable}}}. \tag{1}$$

Hence, for a *sum* of independent random variables,

$$V[P_j] = \sum_{t=0}^{N} V[k_t Y_{tj}] = \sum_{t=0}^{N} k_t^2 V[Y_{tj}] = \sum_{t=0}^{N} \frac{\sigma_{Y_{tj}}^2}{(1 + i)^{2t}}. \tag{2}$$

The proof of (1) above is as follows. Let $Y_i = $ a random variable with finite mean and variance and $k = $ a constant. Then

$$V[k Y_i] = \text{expected value of the mean-square deviation}$$

$$= E\left[\frac{1}{n} \sum_{i=1}^{n} (k Y_i - k \bar{Y})^2\right]$$

$$= E\left[\frac{k^2}{n} \sum_{i=1}^{n} (Y_i - \bar{Y})^2\right] = k^2 E\left[\frac{1}{n} \sum_{i=1}^{n} (Y_i - \bar{Y})^2\right] \tag{3}$$

$$= k^2 \cdot V[Y_i].$$

Let $Y_\tau$ and $Y_\theta (\tau \in t; \theta \in t; \tau \neq \theta)$ be correlated cash flow increments in periods $\tau$ and $\theta$, such that the covariance between $Y_\tau$ and $Y_\theta$ is defined by the relationship

$$\text{Cov}\,(Y_\tau Y_\theta) = \rho_{\tau\theta}\sigma_\tau\sigma_\theta \quad (\tau \neq \theta), \tag{11.8}$$

where $\rho_{\tau\theta}$ is the simple correlation coefficient $(-1 \leq \rho_{\tau\theta} \leq +1)$ and $\sigma_\tau$ and $\sigma_\theta$ are the standard deviations in the $\tau$th and $\theta$th periods, respectively. Symmetry among the correlation coefficients is assumed $(\rho_{\tau\theta} = \rho_{\theta\tau})$. Then, the variance of project net present value is found as follows:

$$V[P] = V[Y_0] + \frac{V[Y_1]}{(1+i)^2} + \frac{V[Y_2]}{(1+i)^4} + \cdots + \frac{V[Y_n]}{(1+i)^{2n}}$$

$$+ \frac{2\,\text{Cov}\,[Y_0 Y_1]}{(1+i)} + \frac{2\,\text{Cov}\,[Y_0 Y_2]}{(1+i)^2} + \cdots + \frac{2\,\text{Cov}\,[Y_1 Y_2]}{(1+i)^3}$$

$$+ \cdots + \frac{2\,\text{Cov}\,[Y_\tau Y_\theta]}{(1+i)^{\tau+\theta}} + \cdots + \frac{2\,\text{Cov}\,[Y_{n-1} Y_n]}{(1+i)^{2n-1}} \tag{11.9}$$

or, on substituting Eq. (11.8) and $\sigma_t^2 = V[Y_t]$,

$$V[P] = \sum_{t=0}^{n} \frac{\sigma_t^2}{(1+i)^{2t}} + 2 \sum_{\tau=0}^{n-1} \sum_{\substack{\theta=1 \\ \tau<\theta}}^{n} \frac{\rho_{\tau\theta}\sigma_\tau\sigma_\theta}{(1+i)^{\tau+\theta}}. \tag{11.10}$$

An alternative form of Eq. (11.10) exists when only the covariance matrix is defined:

$$V[P] = \sum_{t=0}^{n} \frac{\sigma_t^2}{(1+i)^{2t}} + 2 \sum_{\tau=0}^{n+1} \sum_{\substack{\theta=1 \\ \tau<\theta}}^{n} \frac{\text{Cov}\,(Y_\tau Y_\theta)}{(1+i)^{\tau+\theta}}. \tag{11.11}$$

One may now define what is meant in a statistical sense by *complete dependence* and *partial dependence* in the cash flow stream. When cash flows are completely dependent, the correlation is perfect and *all* values of $\rho_{\tau\theta}$ in the correlation coefficient matrix will be either $-1$ or $+1$. If the correlation coefficients, $\rho_{\tau\theta}$, take on values intermediate between $-1$ or $+1$ (excepting zero), then the correlation is partial, and the cash flow increments will be partially dependent. Note that if all $\rho_{\tau\theta} = 0$ exactly, then the second summation term in Eq. (11.10) is equal to zero. This is the case for an *in*dependent cash flow stream.

When either partial or complete dependencies exist among the periodic cash flow increments, the variance of project net present value, therefore, can be found by either Eq. (11.10) or Eq. (11.11). Both of these require a mathematical statement of the relationships that exist among the cash flow increments, either by specification of the autocorrelation coefficients, $\rho_{\tau\theta}$, or by specification of the autocovariances, Cov $(Y_\tau Y_\theta)$.

**11.2.4.** *Autocorrelations among cash flows (same project).* If the cash flows from a proposed project are correlated across time (autocorrelated), the analyst has two choices: (1) He must in effect decompose each cash flow, $Y_t$, into its contributing elements, such as gross sales, operating expense, and depreciation, and determine the autocorrelations between these elements. (2) He can examine the cash flow stream itself as a time series, hypothesize a correlative model for it, and statistically test for goodness of fit between the hypothesized model and the cash flow data.

The first method is tedious and may, in many cases, be so clumsy that no satisfactory estimate of a correlation coefficient can be obtained. The second method is straightforward and will usually result in a satisfactory estimate of the correlation coefficient in a correlated time series, i.e., between a series of cash flows, $Y_t$ and $Y_{t-1}$, to or from a project under consideration.

The time-series approach was first suggested by Hillier ([19], pp. 93–94), who offered a simple proof that the correlation coefficient between two time-related variables, say $Y_t$ and $Y_{t-1}$, could be estimated by regression techniques. Later, Bussey and Stevens [4], [5] expanded and exemplified this concept by using time-series analysis.[6]

To motivate an exposition of the time-series method of determining the autocorrelation coefficient, we shall first present an algorithm of the process and then illustrate it by a numerical example.[7] The solution algorithm is as follows:

*Step 1:* It is assumed that the optimistic, most likely, and pessimistic estimates of the cash flow for each period have been prepared by expert estimators and are known to the analyst. Thus these estimates become the *parameters* of $N + 1$ $\beta$-distributed random variables, $Y_t$, whose parameters are

$$Y_0(t) = \text{optimistic cash flow in the } t\text{th period}$$

$$\tilde{Y}(t) = \text{modal (most likely) cash flow in the } t\text{th period}$$

$$Y_p(t) = \text{pessimistic cash flow in the } t\text{th period}$$

(for $t = 0, 1, \ldots, N$, where $N = $ life of the project).

*Step 2:* Using a pseudo-random number generator and a mathematical model for generating random $\beta$ deviates, generate a sufficient number of cash flow stream *samples* using the $\beta$-distribution *parameters* established in Step 1. A sufficient number of samples implies, in statistical terminology, a "large" number; e.g., $n \geq 30$.

*Step 3:* From time-series theory, hypothesize an appropriate mathematical time-series model or models for analyzing the samples generated in Step 2 (e.g., a Markovian or other time-series model).

*Step 4:* Using time-series regression analyses, analyze the pseudo samples until the investigator is confident that autocorrelation is demonstrated or not. If it is demonstrated to the investigator's satisfaction, then he has an estimate of the autocorrelation coefficient, and the correlated variance of net present value can be calculated via Eq. 11.10.

**Example 11.2.1.** The method can be demonstrated most easily by an example. Consider a hypothetical project whose pessimistic, modal, and optimistic

---

[6]Two excellent texts on time-series analysis are Box and Jenkins [3] and Nelson [28].

[7]This algorithm and method of exploiting Hillier's method appears in full in Bussey and Stevens [4], [5].

**Table 11.2.** $\beta$-DISTRIBUTED CASH FLOW INCREMENTS FOR A HYPOTHETICAL
PROJECT

| Year, $t$ | Pessimistic, $Y_p(t)$ | Modal, $\tilde{Y}(t)$ | Optimistic, $Y_o(t)$ | Mean, $\bar{Y}_t$ | Variance, $V[Y_t]$ |
|---|---|---|---|---|---|
| 0 | $-30,000 | $-22,000 | $-14,000 | $-22,000 | 7.11 $(10^6)$ |
| 1 | -32,000 | -26,000 | -20,000 | -26,000 | 4.00 $(10^6)$ |
| 2 | - 8,000 | - 3,000 | + 2,000 | - 3,000 | 2.78 $(10^6)$ |
| 3 | + 6,000 | +12,000 | +18,000 | +12,000 | 4.00 $(10^6)$ |
| 4 | +12,000 | +20,000 | +28,000 | +20,000 | 7.11 $(10^6)$ |
| 5 | +12,000 | +20,000 | +28,000 | +20,000 | 7.11 $(10^6)$ |
| 6 | +14,000 | +23,000 | +32,000 | +23,000 | 9.00 $(10^6)$ |
| 7 | +16,000 | +25,000 | +34,000 | +25,000 | 9.00 $(10^6)$ |
| 8 | +17,000 | +26,500 | +36,000 | +26,500 | 10.31 $(10^6)$ |
| 9 | +18,000 | +29,000 | +40,000 | +29,000 | 13.44 $(10^6)$ |
| 10 | +20,000 | +30,000 | +40,000 | +30,000 | 11.11 $(10^6)$ |

cash flows are given in Table 11.2. In making these estimates it has been decided by the analyst that cash flows in successive years are possibly autocorrelated according to a one-period lag Markovian model. He wishes to estimate the autocorrelation coefficients and then, using a discount rate of 15%, the mean and variance of net present value are to be determined.

At this point, the *parameters* of 11 $\beta$-distributed cash flow variables, $Y_t$ ($t = 0, 1, \ldots, 10$), are now fixed and known. All we need do now is generate a reasonably sized *random* sample of the $Y_t$, say $n = 30$ sets, and analyze the *random* $Y_t$ values. Recognizing that the optimistic and pessimistic values in Table 11.2 are in reality upper and lower boundary values on the random $Y_t$ and that the mean is known, one has only to generate standardized random $\beta$ deviates and apply them to the mean values in order to obtain *random* realizations (values) of $Y_t$. This is easily done by computer. For this problem, we could obtain, for example, $n = 30$ sets of pseudo-random $\beta$-distributed $Y_t$ (330 values in all). Five of these realizations of random cash flows, along with the upper and lower optimistic and pessimistic boundaries, are illustrated in Fig. 11.3. One should realize that we are working here with a sample of *random cash flow values* themselves rather than with the *parameters* of the $\beta$ distributions.

Since we now have $n = 30$ samples, each consisting of 11 random values of $Y_t$, we should now be able to analyze these data for possible timewise covariation. The analysis takes the form of an assumed mathematical model or models, plus regression analyses to test the models. Consistent with our fictitious investigator's assumption, we assume a linear first-order autoregressive (Markovian) model of the form

$$Y_t = \phi_1 Y_{t-1} + \delta + \epsilon_t \qquad (11.12)$$

where  $Y_t$ = the $t$th realization (observation) of the cash flow time series at time
$t = 0, 1, \ldots$.
$\phi_1$ = the one-period lag coefficient, $|\phi_1| < 1$.

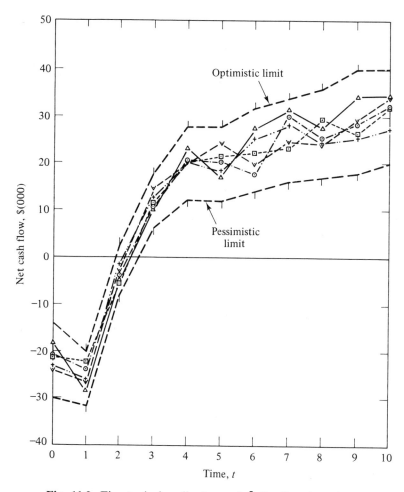

**Fig. 11.3.** Five typical realizations of $\beta$-distributed random cash flows.

$\delta$ = trend or drift constant.

$\epsilon_t$ = random variable with mean zero and variance $\sigma_\epsilon^2$.

Using this model in a standard regression package on the computer with the 330 values of random $Y_t$, we obtained the following estimates of the model parameters and their analysis of variance:

| Parameter | Parameter Estimate | Mean Square | Test | |
|---|---|---|---|---|
| | | | F Value | d.f. |
| $\delta$ | 7,499.5 | — | — | 1 |
| $\phi_1$ | 0.7769 | 6.783 $(10^{10})$ | 1,197.4 | 1 |
| Residual | — | 5.664 $(10^7)$ | — | 298 |

These estimates result in a hypothesized model:

$$\hat{Y}_t = 7,499.5 + 0.7769\, Y_{t-1}. \tag{11.13}$$

For Eq. (11.13) to represent the hypothesized Markovian autoregressive process, we must now demonstrate time stationarity. This can be done by calculating the *first differences* of the random cash flows

$$w_t = Y_t - Y_{t-1} \quad (t = 1, 2, \ldots, 10) \tag{11.14}$$

and then regressing $w_t$ against $w_{t-1}$ for $t = 1, 2, 3, \ldots, 10$. If the process is stationary, then the slope $\hat{\beta}_1$ of the model

$$w_t = \hat{\beta}_0 + \hat{\beta}_1 w_{t-1}$$

should be indistinguishable from zero.

As tested on the computer, the first-difference model yielded an estimate of $\hat{\beta}_1 = 0.018$, with an $F$-test value, $F(1; 268) = 0.096$. With this small value of the $F$ statistic, we may conclude at almost any level of confidence that we fail to reject the null hypothesis that $\beta_1 = 0$, and therefore we conclude that $\beta_1 \equiv 0$ as far as we can tell. The substance here is that the *first differences*, $w_t$, of the cash flow stream are constant at a value $\hat{\beta}_0$, and hence the processes in Eqs. (11.12) and (11.13) are apparently time stationary.

Having concluded that the model in Eq. (11.12) displays time stationarity with our data, we are free to conclude (in the absence of further analyses of the data) that the one-period lag coefficient $\hat{\phi}_1 = 0.777$ and then, assuming that the process is Markovian as hypothesized, the autocorrelation coefficients are given by

$$\rho_{\tau\theta} = \phi_1^{|\theta-\tau|} \tag{11.15}$$

where $\tau, \theta = 1, 2, 3, \ldots, n$ are the periods of interest. With $\hat{\phi}_1 = 0.777$, the autocorrelation coefficient matrix is that given in Table 11.3.

**Table 11.3.** AUTOCORRELATION COEFFICIENT MATRIX, $\rho_{\tau\theta}$, FOR CASH FLOWS $Y_\tau$.

| $\theta =$ | 0 | 1 | 2 | 3 | 4 | 5 | 6 | 7 | 8 | 9 | 10 |
|---|---|---|---|---|---|---|---|---|---|---|---|
| $\tau =$ | | | | | | | | | | | |
| 0 | 1.0 | 0.777 | 0.604 | 0.469 | 0.364 | 0.283 | 0.220 | 0.171 | 0.133 | 0.103 | 0.080 |
| 1 | | 1.0 | 0.777 | 0.604 | 0.469 | 0.364 | 0.283 | 0.220 | 0.171 | 0.133 | 0.103 |
| 2 | | | 1.0 | 0.777 | 0.604 | 0.469 | 0.364 | 0.283 | 0.220 | 0.171 | 0.133 |
| 3 | | | | 1.0 | 0.777 | 0.604 | 0.469 | 0.364 | 0.283 | 0.220 | 0.171 |
| 4 | | | | | 1.0 | 0.777 | 0.604 | 0.469 | 0.364 | 0.283 | 0.220 |
| 5 | | | | | | 1.0 | 0.777 | 0.604 | 0.469 | 0.364 | 0.283 |
| 6 | | | | | | | 1.0 | 0.777 | 0.604 | 0.469 | 0.364 |
| 7 | | (Symmetrical) | | | | | | 1.0 | 0.777 | 0.604 | 0.469 |
| 8 | | | | | | | | | 1.0 | 0.777 | 0.604 |
| 9 | | | | | | | | | | 1.0 | 0.777 |
| 10 | . | | | | | | | | | | 1.0 |

The last step is to calculate the variance of net present value, $V[P_j]$, using the correlation and variance data in Tables 11.2 and 11.3 and Eq. (11.10), repeated here:

$$V[P_j] = \sum_{t=0}^{n} \frac{V[Y_t]}{(1+i)^{2t}} + 2 \sum_{\substack{\tau=0 \\ \tau<\theta}}^{n-1} \sum_{\theta=1}^{n} \frac{\rho_{\tau\theta}\sigma_\tau\sigma_\theta}{(1+i)^{\tau+\theta}},$$

which results in the estimate, $\hat{V}[P_j] = 433.4(10^6)$.

The final step is to calculate the mean net present value by Eq. (11.5) as

$$E[P_j] = -22,000 + \frac{-26,000}{(1.15)} = \frac{-2,333}{(1.15)^2} + \cdots + \frac{30,000}{(1.15)^{10}}$$

$$= 26,056.$$

The reader should note that the effect of a *positively* correlated cash flow stream is to *increase* the project net present value variance. In this example, the *autocorrelated* variance is 433.4($10^6$), which is almost *20 times* the variance in the *independent* model, where the variance is 23.34($10^6$), determined by simply discounting the independent variances in Table 11.2. Conversely, if the correlation coefficients are net *negative*, then the effect is to *reduce* the net present value variance. (Negatively autocorrelated cash flow streams are not the usual case in practical situations, however, since negative autocorrelation coefficients are symptomatic of cash flow increments that oscillate rapidly in time about a mean value—a situation not often encountered in practice.)

In summary, the methodology described here is simple:

1. Use the estimator's values of optimistic, pessimistic, and most likely values as *parameters* to generate pseudo-random cash flows.
2. Generate a sufficient number of pseudo-random cash flow stream samples (say, $n = 30$ samples) for analysis.
3. Hypothesize an appropriate time series model or models for analyzing the samples.
4. Using time-series regression analyses, analyze the samples until one is confident that autocorrelation exists or not, and if it apparently does, then it is probable that one can identify a satisfactory model for estimating purposes.
5. If there is an apparent autocorrelational model that fits the pseudo-random data, then the correlated variance of net present value can be calculated.

**11.2.5 *Probability statements about net present value.*** It should be noted that in establishing the values of the net present value mean, $E[P]$, in Eq. (11.5) and the variance, $V[P]$, in Eq. (11.10), we do so without specifying the *form* of the resulting statistical distribution of $P$, except to require that it have finite mean and variance. Alternatively, we can say that Eqs. (11.5) and (11.10) are not dependent on any assumptions concerning the *form* of the distributions of the random cash flow elements, $Y_{tj}$, since it can be shown that these equations are obtained by the application of the expected value operator, which is a distribution-free operator. As Hillier [17] states, these equations can be used to estimate $E[P]$ and $V[P]$ for any *linear combination* of $Y_{tj}$, regardless of distribution. Thus, having found the mean and variance of net present value, we possess more information than we had, but now we need to put it to use.

If we can make certain distributional assumptions concerning net present value, then it is possible to make probability statements concerning the NPV for a particular project. For example, if the cash flows themselves ($Y_{tj}$) are *normally* distributed, then net present value ($P_j$) is also a normally distributed variable with mean $E[P_j]$, and variance $V[P_j]$, and probability statements about $P_j$ can be made from standard normal tables. This is possible because the *sum* of a series of normally distributed variables is also a normally distributed variable, via the Central Limit Theorem. Moreover, if the $Y_{tj}$ are not normally distributed, then it may still be possible that $P_j$ can be approximated by a normal distribution if one or more of the several special versions of the Central Limit Theorem is applicable (see Hillier [19], pp. 24–29), which would also permit normal probability statements to be made. Finally, if no distributional assumptions concerning the random $Y_{tj}$ can be made, it is still possible to make certain weak probability statements via the Chebyshev inequality or via a stronger form of this inequality investigated by Grosh and Bussey [11]. Numerical examples will illustrate these principles.

**Example 11.2.2.** A proposed project has an estimated mean investment of $800,000, and the standard deviation of the investment is $250,000. The cash flows at the ends of years 1 and 2 are

| End of Year | Mean Net Cash Flow, $Y_t$ | Standard Deviation of Cash Flow, $\sigma_{Y(t)}$ |
|---|---|---|
| 1 | $+1,000,000 | $450,000 |
| 2 | +1,000,000 | 600,000 |

Assuming that the cash flows are independent and the net present value, $P$, is distributed $N(\bar{P}, \sigma_P^2)$, that is, normal with mean $\bar{P}$ and variance $\sigma_P^2$, and if the minimum attractive rate of return is 15%, what is the probability that the net present value will be

a. $210,000 or less?
b. Zero or less (i.e., that the internal rate of return $i^* \leq 0.9059$)?
c. $1,000,000 or greater?

*Solution: Let* K = $1,000, then

$$\bar{P} = -800K + 1,000K(\overset{(P/F,15\%,1)}{0.8696}) + 1,000K(\overset{(P/F,15\%,2)}{0.7561})$$

$$= +826K.$$

$$\sigma_P^2 = (250K)^2 + (450K)^2(\overset{(P/F,15\%,2)}{0.7561}) + (600K)^2(\overset{(P/F,15\%,4)}{0.5718})$$

$$= 422,000K^2;$$

$$\sigma_P = (422,000K^2)^{1/2} = 650K.$$

a. Assuming $P \sim N(\bar{P}, \sigma_P^2)$:

$$Z_\alpha = \frac{P - \bar{P}}{\sigma_P} = \frac{210\text{K} - 826\text{K}}{650\text{K}} = -0.947;$$

$$\therefore \quad \alpha = 0.173 \text{ (from Normal tables)}.$$

b.

$$Z_\alpha = \frac{0 - 826\text{K}}{650\text{K}} = -1.27;$$

$$\therefore \quad \alpha = 0.102, \text{ or } 10.2\%.$$

c.

$$Z_\alpha = \frac{1{,}000\text{K} - 856\text{K}}{650\text{K}} = +0.268;$$

$$\therefore \quad \alpha = 0.605 = \text{Prob}\,[P \le 1{,}000{,}000].$$

Hence,

$$\text{Prob}\,[P \ge 1{,}000{,}000] = 1 - \alpha = 0.395.$$

**Example 11.2.3.** Using the same data presented in Example 11.2.2, except that we now stipulate that no distributional assumptions can be made,

a. What is the probability that the net present value is zero or negative? (Note that this is equivalent to asking the question, "What is the probability that the internal rate of return is equal to or less than 0.906?")[8]

*Solution:* From Ref. [11], we have a strong form of the Chebyshev inequality applying to *single-tail* probabilities, so that

$$\text{Prob}\,[(P - \bar{P}) \le -t\sigma_P] \le \frac{1}{1 + t^2}$$

or, equivalently, that $\alpha = 1/(1 + t^2)$, where $t = (P - \bar{P})/\sigma_P$. Hence,

$$t = \frac{0 - 826\text{K}}{650\text{K}} = -1.27;$$

$$\therefore \quad t^2 = 1.61,$$

---

[8]Some difficulties are attached to equating the probability that NPV $\le 0$ with the probability that the IRR (e.g., $i^*$) is equal to or less than some value $i'$. In an original development, Hillier [17] asserted that the two probabilities are identical. As pointed out later by Kaplan and Bernhard, however, Hillier erred in this assumption and corrected his error [18]. Bernhard commented further on this phenomenon in [2]. *In general*, the identity holds only if the following relationship is satisfied with probability one, or nearly one:

$$\text{Prob}\,[i^* < i'] = \text{Prob}\,[\text{NPV} < 0\,|\,i']. \qquad (4)$$

For example, the relationship holds only if the investment is a simple one [only one root, $i^*$, and initial cash flow(s) $< 0$; hence, NPV$(i)$ is a monotonic decreasing function of $i$]. If, as assumed in the present example, the cash flows, $Y_t$, are assumed *normally* distributed, then *some* of the $Y_t$ can become negative at *some* time, thereby possibly invalidating the monotonic decreasing requirement for NPV$(i)$, and thus invalidating the rule given in (4), above. The remedy, as Kaplan suggests, is to assume that all the $Y_t$ have small variances compared to their $\bar{Y}_t$, so that Prob $[Y_t < 0]$ is very small. Then requirement (4) above will be satisfied (nearly).

and

$$\text{Prob}\,[P \le 0] \le \frac{1}{1+t^2} = \frac{1}{2.61} = 0.383.$$

b. If it is known that the net present value, $P$, is distributed unimodal and symmetrical about the mean but otherwise nothing is known about the distribution of $P$, then the Camp-Meidell inequality ([10], p. 75) applies:

$$[(\bar{P} - t\sigma) \le P \le (\bar{P} + t\sigma)] \le 1 - \frac{1}{2.25t^2}$$

so that, with $t = -1.27$ [as in (a) above], then (assuming symmetry)

$$2\alpha = 1 - \text{Prob}\,[(\bar{P} - t\sigma) \le P\,(\bar{P} + t\sigma)]$$

$$= \frac{1}{2.25t^2},$$

which is obvious from the sketch below:

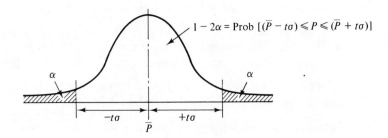

Hence,

$$\alpha \le \frac{1}{(2)(2.25)t^2} = 0.138 \quad \text{and} \quad \text{since Prob}\,[P \le 0] = \alpha,$$

we have that

$$\text{Prob}\,[P \le 0] = \text{Prob}\,[\text{IRR} \le 15\%] \le 0.138.$$

**11.2.6. *Procuring NPV distribution by simulation.*** It is frequently desirable to know not only the mean and variance of the cash flow (or net present value) distribution but also the *form* of the distribution itself. The reason for this is that the NPV distribution may be skewed or abnormally peaked, due to the interaction of economic factors that establish the cash flows. If the NPV distribution is abnormally skewed or peaked, then probability statements about NPV using Normal tables will be in error. One method of resolving this problem is to use Monte Carlo simulation to obtain repeated samples from an assumed economic model of the project. This method results in a sampling distribution of NPV.

Hess and Quigley [16] and Hertz [14], [15] were among the first to demonstrate the use of Monte Carlo simulation techniques for the construction of NPV distributions. Hess and Quigley assumed complete independence among all cash flows, and while Hertz stated that some of the cash flows *might* be correlated, he did not report how correlational effects could be taken into account. One of the possible problems, therefore, in using simulation techniques to procure a distribution of NPV is correlation in the cash flow stream. Bussey and Stevens [6] reported on a simulation model (using the GPSS simulation language [34] on an IBM/360 computer) that took into account some rather complex internal dependencies and interactions, resulting in correlative effects. No generalizations can be made concerning correlative phenomena, however, since the degree of correlation affecting the variance of the NPV distribution is model-dependent.

To illustrate the *method* of procuring a sampling distribution for net present value, a simple numerical example will be used in which independence among variables is assumed. More complex models can be constructed, but the sampling methodology (either manually or via computer) does not change.

**Example 11.2.4.** Consider a project whose estimated investment (at time $t = 0$), life (at $t = N$), and salvage value are independent random variables, distributed according to the probability functions shown in Fig. 11.4. (Such probability functions would in reality be developed by expert estimators or by the analyst himself using forecasting techniques and data supplied by estimators.)

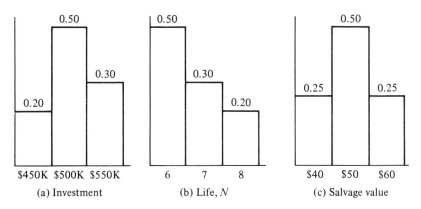

**Fig. 11.4.** Density functions of project investment, life, and salvage value.

We assume also that the annual gross income, annual cash operating expense, and effective income tax rate that obtain in any given year ($t = 1, 2, \ldots, N$) are independent random variables, whose density functions are shown in Fig. 11.5. In the simulation, each of these values will change (independently) with each year $t$ in the project life.

The firm's marginal cost of capital, at which the annual cash flows are to be discounted to present time ($t = 0$), is also taken as an independent random variable, whose density function is given in Fig. 11.6.

Depreciation expense per year is assumed to follow the straight-line method

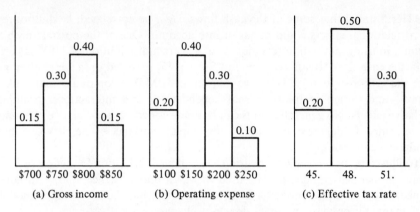

(a) Gross income     (b) Operating expense     (c) Effective tax rate

**Fig. 11.5.** Density functions of gross income, operating expenses, and effective tax rate.

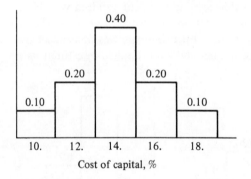

Cost of capital, %

**Fig. 11.6.** Cost of capital (discount rate).

so that for each year in which positive cash flows occur ($t = 1, 2, \ldots, N$), the depreciation amount is calculated by

$$D_t = \frac{\text{investment} - \text{salvage value}}{\text{life}}.$$

The annual cash flow, $Y_t$, for this example is calculated by the equations

$$\left.\begin{array}{l} Y_0 = \text{investment (negative valued)}, \quad \text{for } t = 0 \\ Y_t = (\text{gross income} - \text{operational expense} - D_t)(1 - \text{tax rate}) \\ \qquad + D_t, \qquad \text{for } t = 1, 2, \ldots, N, \end{array}\right\} \quad (11.16)$$

which is a simplified form of Eq. (5.4).

The process of procuring a distribution of net present value for this example is, in general, a simple one. One randomly estimates a sample of the input data for investment, salvage value, life, gross income, expenses, tax rate, and discounting rate and calculates a *realization* of net present value by successively applying Eq. (11.16) and discounting the $Y_t$ to $t = 0$. Such a realization is a sample of size *one* from the unknown NPV distribution. The process is repeated many times to obtain repeated sample values of the random NPV. These sample NPV's are tabulated into a frequency histogram, which, after many iterations, becomes a sampling distribution (i.e., an estimated density function) of the random net present value. The simulation process is illustrated by the flow chart in Fig. 11.7.

The simulation process is usually executed on a computer since the number of iterations must be quite large—on the order of several hundred to perhaps a thousand or more. The reason for this is that we often wish to test the sampling distribution of NPV against a theoretical distribution to see if it is statistically different from the theoretical distribution (e.g., a Normal distribution, with mean and standard deviation equal to the sampling distribution). We make such a test to determine if it is safe to use the theoretical distribution in lieu of the actual sample distribution; for example, to make probability statements about NPV. If, at an assumed level of confidence (say, $\alpha = 5\%$), we can "see" no statistical difference between the sampling distribution and the theoretical distribution, then it may be easier to use the theoretical distribution for prediction purposes, such as establishing confidence intervals on NPV.

A sampling distribution can be compared to an *assumed* theoretical distribution by statistical goodness-of-fit tests. One such test is the $\chi$-square goodness-of-fit test. For details in the application of this test, see Hahn and Shapiro ([12], pp. 302–307), for example. In using the $\chi$-square test, however, the number of sample values of NPV must be quite large,[9] probably on the order of 500 or more for the NPV distributions we have experimented with [6]. An alternative distributional test is the Kolmogorov-Smirnov test, which is a nonparametric test that is probably more powerful than the $\chi$-square test in rejecting untrue hypotheses concerning the assumed theoretical distribution, especially when the sample size is small. For the details of this test, see Siegel ([31], pp. 47–52).

For our numerical Example 11.2.4 here, the 500-sample output histogram of net present value is shown in Fig. 11.8. This sampling distribution was obtained by simulating the example in the GPSS-V simulation language,[10] a computer language system that is quite adaptable to performing discrete-event simulations (e.g., a net present value problem in discrete random variables, such as the $Y_t$, is a discrete-event simulation problem). The cumulative NPV sampling distribution, as a series of unconnected points, is shown in Fig. 11.9, along with an assumed Normal distribution (solid line), whose mean $\overline{\text{NPV}} = 970.6(10^3)$ and $\sigma_{\text{NPV}} = 137(10^3)$, the sampled values of the empirical histogram. Also shown in Fig. 11.9 are the $\alpha = \pm 0.05$ confidence limits on the assumed Normal distribution, as determined by the Kolmogorov-Smirnov statistic. Since the sampling distribution lies within the upper and lower confidence limits, we may conclude without serious consequences that the net present value for our example can be adequately approximated by a Normal distribution, with mean $\overline{\text{NPV}} =$

---

[9]The large sample size assists in compliance with some theoretical requirements concerning the $\chi$-square test, i.e., that fewer than 20% of the histogram cells contain expected frequencies of less than 5, and no cell contains an expected frequency of zero (e.g., see Conover [7], p. 178).

[10]"GPSS-V" = General-Purpose Simulation System Five. See [34] for an introduction to this language. For other simulation methods and languages, see Mize and Cox [25] and Schmidt and Taylor [30].

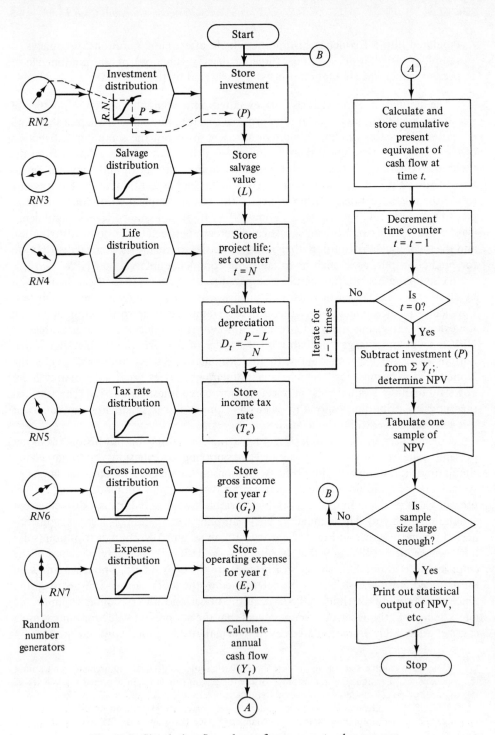

**Fig. 11.7.** Simulation flow chart of net present value process.

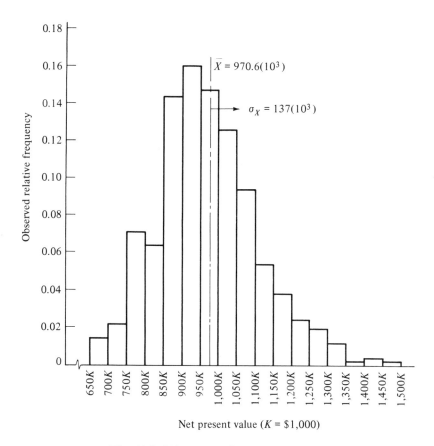

Net present value ($K = \$1,000$)

**Fig. 11.8.** Histogram of net present value.

$970.6(10^3)$ dollars and standard deviation $\sigma_{\text{NPV}} = 137(10^3)$ dollars. Thus, it becomes a simple matter to make probability statements about the realizations of NPV by the firm, in the same manner that was demonstrated in Section 11.2.5. It should be noted, however, that if the empirical distribution of NPV could not be satisfactorily fitted with a theoretical distribution, then the *sampling* distribution of NPV should be used to make probability statements about NPV.

**11.2.7. *Method of certainty equivalents.*** One of the fundamental difficulties one encounters in using the expected utility approach, when present value variances are estimated by *rational* means (e.g., Sections 11.2.3 and 11.2.4), is that the cash flow terms are discounted to present time by factors $(1 + i)^{-kt}$, where $k = 2$, at least. In the correlated cases, the covariance terms are usually additive, and $k$ is some other value in the range $1 < k < 2$ so that the final effect is to give an exponent $k > 2$. In most practical cases, the interest rate, $i$, is the estimated marginal cost of capital and will already contain an implicit allowance for the riskiness of the firm's securities (see

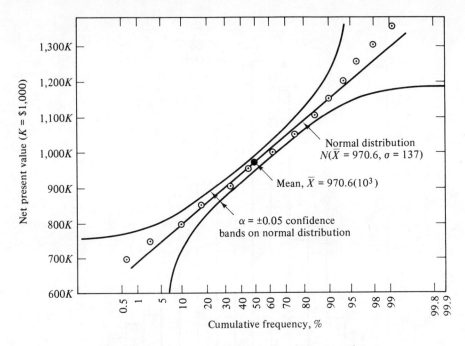

**Fig. 11.9.** Sampling distribution of net present value.

Chapter 6). There are valid theoretical objections to discounting the *risk* portion of the marginal cost of capital, and especially so when the exponent of the discount term becomes greater than simply *t*. There is no rational basis for assuming that future riskiness is reduced [by the $(1 + i)^{-kt}$ factor] simply because it is translated to present time. This is what is required, however, by the *rational* formulas for variance of net present value in Sections 11.2.3 and 11.2.4. The simulation approach in Section 11.2.6 avoids this problem by discounting each *random* cash *flow*, $Y_t$, by the factor $(1 + i)^{-t}$.

Another method of obtaining a present equivalent amount that also avoids double counting of risk is the *certainty equivalent method*. The general procedure here is (1) to assume that the decision-maker's utility function is applicable to *future* amounts as well as *present* amounts, (2) then to find the certainty equivalent of each of the expected future cash flows of the project, and (3) to discount the certainty equivalent amounts to a present value using a *riskless* (*or default-free*) *rate of interest*. The result is a *present* expectation for the project, but risk has not been either *single-counted* or *double-counted* since the default-free interest rate discount factor is applied to *certainty* amounts that are simply equivalent to future uncertain cash flows. As a decision criterion for single projects, if the *present-time* certainty equivalent is positive, the project would be accepted. Again, the certainty equivalent method can best be illustrated by example.

**Example 11.2.5.** For simplicity, consider a project whose random cash flows are characterized by the means and standard deviations given in Table 11.4

below. (We assume these have been obtained by some appropriate estimating procedure; e.g., the PERT methodology described in Section 11.2.1.)

**Table 11.4.** MEANS AND VARIANCES OF PROJECT CASH FLOWS FOR EXAMPLE 11.2.5

| End of Year, t | $E(Y_t)$, Expected Cash Flow, $Y_t$ | $[V(Y_t)]^{0.5} =$ Standard Deviation of Cash Flow, $Y_t$ |
|---|---|---|
| 0 | − 9.0 | 10.5 |
| 1 | + 6.0 | 14.0 |
| 2 | 15.0 | 9.4 |
| 3 | 22.0 | 23.5 |
| 4 | 15.0 | 22.0 |

We also assume the decision-maker exhibits a utility function of the form of Eq. (B10.1) (the Freund exponential utility function in Appendix 10.B):

$$U(Y) = 1 - e^{-BY}$$

in which the constant $B$ now has a value $B = 0.05$. Then, from Eq. (B10.8), the expected utility, $E[U(Y)]$, is

$$E[U(Y)] = 1 - e^{-0.5(2B\mu - B^2\sigma^2)}$$
$$= 1 - e^{-0.5(0.1\mu - 0.0025\sigma^2)}. \qquad (11.17)$$

We use Eq. (11.17) to calculate coordinate points for the $\mu - \sigma$ indifference curves. For example, if the curve $E[U(Y)] = 0$ is desired, then the exponent of $e$ in Eq. (11.17) must be zero so that $E[U(Y)] = 1 - e^0 = 1 - 1 = 0$. For this condition to obtain, the argument of the exponent $(0.1\mu - 0.0025\sigma^2) = 0$. This is the implicit equation in $\mu, \sigma$ values for the curve $E[U(Y)] = 0$. Other indifference curves can be found in a similar manner {e.g., for $E[U(Y)] = -1, +0.2, +0.4, \ldots$}. Figure 11.10 illustrates the family of expected utility indifference curves in the range $-1.2 \le E[U(Y)] \le +0.8$. This family of indifference curves forms the framework on which the certainty equivalent method is based.

The expected cash flows, $Y_t (t = 0, 1, \cdots, 4)$, for our example project are plotted as point values of $[\mu(Y_t), \sigma(Y_t)]$ on Fig. 11.10. The five values are denoted by circled points, labeled $t = 0, 1, \ldots, 4$. Recalling the definition of *certainty equivalent* developed in Section 10.5.1, we note that the certainty equivalents. $C_0, C_1, C_2, C_3$, and $C_4$ of the parameters $[\mu(Y_t), \sigma(Y_t)], (t = 0, 1, \ldots, 4)$, are simply the values of *expected* cash flow, $\mu(Y_t)$, at which the *expected utility* of $[\mu(Y_t), \sigma(Y_t) \equiv 0]$ is identical to that of $[\mu(Y_t), \sigma(Y_t)]$. In other words, for example, the cash flow $Y_0 = (\mu = -9, \sigma = 10.5)$ lies on the expected utility curve $E[U(Y)] = -0.8$, and the certainty equivalent of $Y_0$ is the value at $C_0$, or $C_0 = (\mu = -11.75, \sigma = 0)$, which also lies on the curve $E[U(Y)] = -0.8$, *but at the*

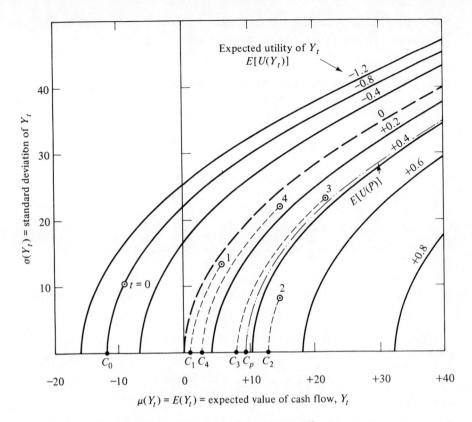

**Fig. 11.10.** Certainty equivalents and indifference curves.

*point where* $\sigma(Y_t) \equiv 0$. Thus, $C_0, C_1, \ldots, C_4$ are the *certainty equivalents* of the cash flows whose means and variances are $[\mu(Y_0), \sigma(Y_0); \mu(Y_1), \sigma(Y_1); \cdots; \mu(Y_4), \sigma(Y_4)]$. The values of the certainty equivalents are given in Table 11.5, Column 4.

If we now assume a perfect capital market in which funds can be borrowed

**Table 11.5.** CERTAINTY EQUIVALENTS AND PRESENT VALUES OF CE'S

| End of Year, $t$ | $E(Y_i)$ | $\sigma(Y_t)$ | Certainty Equivalent, $C_t$ | Discount Factor, $(1 + 0.06)^{-t}$ | $P(C_t)$ |
|---|---|---|---|---|---|
| 0 | $- 9.0$ | 10.5 | $-11.8$ | 1.000 | $-11.8$ |
| 1 | $+ 6.0$ | 14.0 | 1.1 | 0.943 | 1.0 |
| 2 | $+15.0$ | 9.4 | 12.8 | 0.890 | 11.4 |
| 3 | $+22.0$ | 23.5 | 8.2 | 0.840 | 6.9 |
| 4 | $+15.0$ | 22.0 | 2.9 | 0.792 | 2.3 |
| | | | | $\sum P(C_t) =$ | $+ 9.8$ |

and lent at the same *default-free* interest rate (since we are now working with *certainty* equivalents), say 6% per year, then we may discount each annual certainty equivalent amount, $C_t$, by the appropriate discount factor, $(1 + 0.06)^{-t}$, to obtain the present equivalent, $P(C_t)$. This has been done in Taple 11.5 (Columns 5 and 6), and the final certainty equivalent of the project, $C_p = \sum P(C_t)$, is +9.8. Since this is positive, we would accept the project—i.e., it represents a *positive expected utility* of approximately $E[U(P)] = +0.39$, where $E[U(P)]$ is the expected utility of the certainty equivalent.

The significance of the positive expected utility for the project can be more clearly depicted by aid of Fig. 11.11. Note in Fig. 11.10 that the certainty equivalent $C_p = 9.8$ occurs at $\sigma_p = 0$; but this value of $(C_p, \sigma_p)$ for the project is but *one* such value of *possible* project present values, $[P(Y_p), \sigma_p]$, lying on the indifference curve $E[U(P)] = 0.39$. Hence, *any* combination of $[P(Y_p), \sigma_p]$ for the project that lies on the indifference curve $E[U(P)] = 0.39$ will be of equal utility for the decision-maker. Thus, in Fig. 11.11, all the combinations of $[P(Y_p), \sigma_p]$ have equal expected utility for the decision-maker, and he will accept any one of them. Conversely, these *realizations* of the project are all equally acceptable to him.

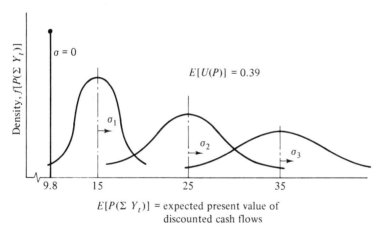

$E[P(\sum Y_t)]$ = expected present value of discounted cash flows

**Fig. 11.11.** Equivalent realizations of the certainty equivalent of a project.

If we now calculate the expected net present value of the project,

$$E[\text{NPV}] = P(\sum Y_t) = \sum [E(Y_t)](1 + i)^{-t},$$

using the default-free discount rate, $i = 6\%$, we obtain the mean net present value of the project:

$$E(\text{NPV}) = -9.0 + 6.0(1.06)^{-1} + 15.0(1.06)^{-2} + \cdots + 15.0(1.06)^{-4} = 40.36.$$

Using the expected utility criterion, Eq. (11.17), we can calculate the value of the variance of NPV corresponding to this value of $E(\text{NPV}) = 40.36$, since the expected utility is constant {i.e., $E[U(P)] = +0.39$}, thus:

$$E[U(P)] = +0.39 = 1 - e^{-0.5(0.1\mu_p - 0.0025\sigma_p^2)}$$

or

$$0.39 = 1 - e^{-0.5[0.1(40.36) - 0.0025\sigma_p^2]}$$

from which we obtain, after some algebraic manipulations, that $\sigma_p^2 = 1,220$ or that the standard deviation of the present equivalent is $(\sigma_p^2)^{0.5} = 34.90$. If now we are willing to assume that the net present value, $P[\sum Y_t(1.06)^{-t}]$, is Normally distributed with parameters

$$E[\text{NPV}] = 40.4 \quad \text{and} \quad \sigma[\text{NPV}] = 34.9,$$

then we may make probability statements about the occurrences of net present values in the same manner as illustrated in Section 11.2.5.

There are three observations that should be noted concerning the applicability of the certainty equivalent model. *First*, in reducing *future* random cash flows to their certainty equivalents before discounting, the *same utility function was used for all periods of time*—i.e., the same expected utility indifference curves were used (Fig. 11.10). This implies that the decision-maker's utility-of-money function does *not* vary with time. This is hardly to be expected; in fact, most theorists agree that one's utility function does change over time, and with other factors as well (for example, level of wealth). *Second*, the certainty equivalent method incorporates the desirable feature of *not* discounting the risk measures, as explicitly stated by the $\sigma(Y_t)$. Instead, risky cash flows (i.e., the random $Y_t$) are converted to *certainty* equivalent amounts, which are then discounted to present time by a default-free interest rate. *Third*, the *present time* certainty equivalent is then reconverted to an *equivalent project*, whose mean is the sum of the discounted mean cash flows of the project (i.e., discounted at the default-free rate) and whose standard deviation (equivalent risk) is found by the Expected Utility (Bernoulli) Principle. The major disadvantage to the whole procedure, obviously, is the assumption of time-stationarity in the decision-maker's utility function.

It should be noted in passing that the certainty equivalent procedure described above is different from the usual presentation in most textbook discussions of the subject. In the usual presentations of the certainty equivalent model,[11] the value of the certainty equivalent, $C_t$, is taken as a multiple of the expected value of cash flow, $E(Y_t)$, thus:

$$C_t = \alpha_t E(Y_t) \tag{11.18}$$

where $\alpha_t$ is some positive constant and $Y_t > 0$ is assumed. Now, the *only* way in which this relationship can hold is for the indifference curve {$E[U(Y)] = $ constant} to be a *straight line*, passing through the points $(C_t, \sigma = 0)$ and $[Y_t, \sigma(Y_t)]$. This situation is shown graphically in Fig. 11.12. Such a linear indifference curve will have an intercept on the $\sigma$ axis at some value $\sigma_0 < 0$.

---

[11]See, for example, Robichek and Myers [29], pp. 80–82 and Van Horne [32], pp. 127–31.

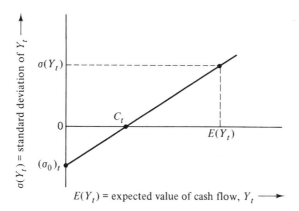

**Fig. 11.12.** Linear certainty equivalent diagram.

Now, by similar triangles we obtain the result that

$$\frac{C_t}{E(Y_t)} = \frac{(\sigma_0)_t}{(\sigma_0)_t + \sigma(Y_t)},$$

but

$$\alpha_t = \frac{C_t}{E[Y_t]}, \quad \text{so} \quad \alpha_t = \frac{(\sigma_0)_t}{(\sigma_0)_t + \sigma(Y_t)}. \tag{11.19}$$

Thus, as we should have suspected, the multiplier, $\alpha_t$, is a function of $\sigma(Y_t)$, the standard deviation of cash flow at time $t$ and of the intercept, $(\sigma_0)_t$. As time changes (e.g., from $t$ to $t+1$), we should expect, with nonlinear indifference curves, that both $\sigma(Y_{t+1})$ and $(\sigma_0)_{t+1}$ would be different from the corresponding values at time $t$. Hence, we should expect, *in general*, that $\alpha_t \neq \alpha_{t+1}$, from Eq. (11.19). Moreover, we should suspect that $\alpha_t$ and $\alpha_{t+1}$ are not necessarily related at all!

Attempts have been made to justify this finding (e.g., see Robichek and Myers [29], pp. 82–83). The explanations are not entirely satisfactory because they posit a functional relationship between the $\alpha_t$, and such may not be the case. The curious aspect about the whole procedure that seems to have gone unnoticed and unchallenged, however, is that in order to use Eq. (11.18) *at all*, one *must* implicitly assume the existence of *linear* indifference curves, as shown in Fig. 11.12. Such indifference curves imply a special form of the investor's utility function; hence Eq. (11.18) *cannot* be used in the *general* case, in any event!

In contrast to the foregoing method [Eq. (11.18)] and its crippling assumption, we have used the perfectly general approach of deriving the expected utility function (the indifference curve) from the decision-maker's utility function and then using the *derived* indifference curve to specify the certainty equivalent of $[E(Y_t), \sigma(Y_t)]$. This procedure not only takes into account the facts (1) that $\sigma(Y_t)$ may vary from period to period, (2) that each $\sigma(Y_t)$ is associated with a specific value of $E(Y_t)$—which Eq. (11.18) does not admit—but also (3) that there may be *no* functional relationship at all among the proportional constants, $\alpha_t$, whereas the usual textbook explanations seem to require one (e.g., see Robichek and Myers, above). In addition, the more general indifference curve method used here admits the possibility that the indifference curves may be *non*linear (as they usually are with actual risk-expectance trade-offs) but may have *non*uniform spacing as well.

## 11.3. Multiple Risky Projects and Constraints

In Chapter 8, in order to allocate resources optimally, we used Fleischer's [9] *bundling* method to create *mutually exclusive* subsets (bundles) of candidate projects and then applied a selection criterion (e.g., maximization of net present value or incremental rate of return) to obtain *the* single subset of feasible projects that optimally satisfied the selection criterion. Also, we demonstrated that Weingartner's mathematical programming method did this for the constrained Lorie-Savage model under certainty conditions.

The same general approach is valid here, as we consider projects whose cash flows are random variables instead of assumed known values. There is one difference between the deterministic and random cases, however, and it is an *extremely* important difference. In the *deterministic* cases in Chapter 8, we did not need to consider interactions between the cash flows of different projects, except insofar as there might be a synergistic effect (i.e., a complementarity effect). In the case where project cash flows are *random variables*, however, we need to consider possible *correlative effects* between the cash flow streams of two or more projects. The reason for this is that if correlative effects exist, say between two cash flow streams, then the variances (and hence, the risk) of the cash flow distributions for the *combination* of cash flows can be seriously affected by the covariance terms. The practical importance of this is that the right combination of projects can reduce the firm's overall risk, whereas the wrong combination can increase it. For this reason, our attention will first be directed toward methods of estimating the variance of combinations of random cash flows and then at possible selection methods for multiple risky projects.

**11.3.1.** *Variance of cross-correlated cash flow streams.* Sometimes distinct economic factors exist that may affect the cash flows of more than one project. When the cash flow increments, $Y_{tj}$ and $Y_{tk}$, of two projects $j$ and $k$ in the *same* period ($t$) are thus affected, then the net present values of the projects, $P_j$ and $P_k$, will be cross-correlated. In the absence of cross-correlations between the cash flow streams of two projects, then $P_j$ and $P_k$ are independent of each other.

When the cash flow streams of two or more projects are correlated, then it will be necessary to pairwise compose each two sets of statistical parameters into one set (one mean and one variance of net present value) representing each *pair* of correlated cash flow streams. The procedure is as follows. Obtain the expected net present value for each pairwise overall project by merely taking the sum of the $E[P_j]$ of the two net present values of the projects:

$$E[P_{j,k}] = E[P_j] + E[P_k]. \tag{11.20}$$

The method of obtaining the variance of the pairwise overall project, $V[P_{j,k}]$, depends on the relationship between the two cash flow streams. If the two cash flow streams are perfectly correlated year by year, merely *add the cash flow streams* year by year and calculate the resulting variance by the methods given in Section 11.2.4 ("Auto-correlations among Cash Flow Increments").

If the two project cash flow streams are only partially correlated between projects, then a somewhat more complex problem is faced and it becomes necessary again to specify the nature of the relationship. The development is considerably simplified if it can be assumed that the correlation between the two cash flow elements $Y_{tj}$ and $Y_{tk}$ ($j < k$) in the *same* time period is the only relationship between the two elements. This is descriptive of the usual practical situation in which a common causative economic circumstance would tend to push the two cash flow elements up or down simultaneously rather than in different time periods. The development is further simplified if the assumption is made that the partial correlation coefficient relating projects $j$ and $k$, $\rho_{jk}(t)$, is constant over all time periods ($t = 1, 2, \ldots, n$).

The second assumption allows us to regress the cash flow estimates of one project, $Y_{tj}$, against the cash flow estimates of another project, $Y_{tk}$, for $t = 1, 2, \ldots, n$ and obtain an estimate of the correlation coefficient relating the two projects. This method was essentially proposed by Hillier ([19] p. 93–95) using a slightly different approach. The present approach is as follows. If there is systematic correlated behavior between $Y_{tj}$ and $Y_{tk}$, then the regression of $Y_{tk}$ on $Y_{tj}$ will measure the degree of association, and the correlation coefficient $\rho_{jk}(t)$ can be estimated. The estimating model for regressing $Y_{tj}$ on $Y_{tk}$ is

$$\hat{Y}_{tj} = E[Y_{tj}] + \hat{\beta}\{Y_{tk} - E[Y_{tk}]\}, \tag{11.21}$$

where $\hat{Y}_{tj}$ = estimate of $Y_{tj}$.
$\hat{\beta}$ = slope of the linear regression function.

This model is theoretically adequate when the two cash flow elements $Y_{tj}$ and $Y_{tk}$ are assumed to be *normally* distributed. If $Y_{tj}$ and $Y_{tk}$ are not normally distributed, as would be the case when the $\beta$ distributional assumption is made in calculating $E[Y_{tj}]$ or $E[Y_{tk}]$, then Eq. (11.21) does not generally apply. What can be said, however, is that Eq. (11.21) still provides the best *linear estimate* of $Y_{tj}$ via the method of least squares.

When Eq. (11.21) is the accepted model for regressing $Y_{tj}$ on $Y_{tk}$, then the Pearsonian sample correlation coefficient $r_{jk}$ can be found by

$$r_{jk} = \hat{\beta}\left[\frac{s_{tk}}{s_{tj}}\right] = \frac{\sum (X_{tj} - \bar{Y})(Y_{tk} - \bar{Y})}{[\sum (Y_{tj} - \bar{Y})^2 \sum (Y_{tk} - \bar{Y})^2]^{1/2}} \tag{11.22}$$

where $s_{tk}, s_{tj}$ = the sample standard deviations of $Y_{tk}$ and $Y_{tj}$, respectively. Since the sample correlation coefficient, $r_{jk}$, is the *best* estimator of the correlation coefficient, then

$$\hat{\rho}_{jk} = r_{jk}. \tag{11.23}$$

The following example will illustrate the method. Consider the mean cash flow increments for the two projects, $A$ and $B$, given in Table 11.6. Suppose that these two

**Table 11.6.** CASH FLOW STREAMS FOR TWO HYPOTHETICAL PROJECTS

| Year (t) | Cash Flow for Project A ($Y_{tA}$) | Variance, $V[Y_{tA}]$ | Cash Flow for Project B ($Y_{tB}$) | Variance $V[Y_{tB}]$ |
|---|---|---|---|---|
| 1 | 2.0 | 0.20 | 19.0 | 2.0 |
| 2 | 2.0 | 0.24 | 21.0 | 2.2 |
| 3 | 3.0 | 0.31 | 24.0 | 2.6 |
| 4 | 3.0 | 0.35 | 27.0 | 3.0 |
| 5 | 3.0 | 0.40 | 27.0 | 3.2 |
| 6 | 4.0 | 0.42 | 29.0 | 3.3 |
| 7 | 4.0 | 0.46 | 31.0 | 3.2 |
| 8 | 6.0 | 0.62 | 35.0 | 3.6 |
| 9 | 6.0 | 0.64 | 36.0 | 3.8 |
| 10 | 6.0 | 0.68 | 37.0 | 4.0 |
| | $\bar{Y}_A = 3.9$* | $\sum = 4.32$ | $\bar{Y}_B = 28.6$* | $\sum = 30.9$ |

\* $\bar{Y} = (\bar{Y}_A + \bar{Y}_B)/2 = 16.25$.

streams were estimated from common economic considerations that would point to a correlation between the two cash flow streams, year by year.

The estimate of the Pearsonian correlation coefficient, $\hat{\rho}$, comes directly from Eq. (11.22):

$$\hat{\rho}_{AB} = \frac{(2.0 - 16.25)(19.0 - 16.25) + \cdots + (6.0 - 16.25)(37.0 - 16.25)}{[(4.32)(30.9)]^{1/2}}$$

$$= 0.782.$$

For the pairwise overall project, $AB$, the *combined* variance of net present value is found, by methods analogous to Eq. (11.10), as follows; noting, however, that the *cross*-correlation coefficient, $\rho_{AB}(t)$ ($t = 0, 1, 2, \ldots, n$), is now constant among periods.

$$V[P_{AB}] = \sum_{t=0}^{n} \frac{\sigma_{tA}^2}{(1+i)^{2t}} + \sum_{t=0}^{n} \frac{\sigma_{tB}^2}{(1+i)^{2t}} + 2\rho_{AB} \sum_{t=0}^{n} \frac{\sigma_{tA}\sigma_{tB}}{(1+i)^{2t}}. \quad (11.24)$$

Thus, for the example above, with $i = 15\%$ assumed,

$$V[P_{AB}] = \left[\frac{0.20}{(1.15)^2} + \frac{0.24}{(1.15)^4} + \frac{0.31}{(1.15)^6} + \cdots + \frac{0.68}{(1.15)^{20}} + \frac{2.0}{(1.15)^2} + \frac{2.2}{(1.15)^4} \right.$$

$$+ \cdots + \frac{4.0}{(1.15)^{20}}\bigg] + 2(0.782)\left[\frac{(0.2)^{1/2}(2.0)^{1/2}}{(1.15)^2} + \frac{(0.24)^{1/2}(2.2)^{1/2}}{(1.15)^4}\right.$$

$$+ \frac{(0.31)^{1/2}(2.6)^{1/2}}{(1.15)^6} + \cdots + \frac{(0.68)^{1/2}(4.0)^{1/2}}{(1.15)^{20}}\bigg]$$

$$= 12.80.$$

If, however, the two project cash flow streams had been independent, the resulting variance of net present value would simply have excluded the covariance terms so that in this case

$$VP_{AB} = \left[\frac{0.20}{(1.15)^2} + \frac{0.24}{(1.15)^4} + \cdots + \frac{0.68}{(1.15)^{20}} + \frac{2.0}{(1.15)^2} + \frac{2.2}{(1.15)^4} + \cdots + \frac{4.0}{(1.15)^{20}}\right]$$

$$= 8.61.$$

Note that the *positive* correlation ($\rho_{AB} = 0.782$) between the two cash flow streams has in fact increased the NPV variance of the project pair, $V[\text{NPV}_{AB}]$, from 8.61 to 12.80, thereby increasing the risk of undertaking the two correlated projects simultaneously. Also, we can see from Eq. (11.24) that if the correlation coefficient, $\rho_{AB}$, were *negative*, then the result of undertaking the joint project, $AB$, would be to reduce the risk below that of a combination in which the projects were independent.

**11.3.2. *The candidate set of projects.*** The foregoing demonstration of possible correlational effects among the future cash flow streams of candidate projects has important implications for the decision policies of the firm. It also has definite implications concerning the composition of the candidate sets of projects. Consider the following case, for example. Suppose a firm is considering the expansion of a portion of its existing facilities as a candidate project. Suppose also that the firm's analysts predict a high degree of positive correlation between the cash flows of the future project and the anticipated cash flows of the *existing* facilities—i.e., the unchanged "going concern." The adoption of the candidate project would thereby change (actually *increase*) the firm's risk position because of the additive property of the positive correlational effect. Hence, even though the *expected* return would be increased by adoption of the project, the firm's *risk* (standard deviation of return) might be disproportionately increased so as to result in the rejection of the project.

For the going concern, this has two implications. *First*, the concept of correlated cash flows mandates that *existing* undertakings of the firm be included in the candidate set of investments. That is, it becomes necessary in the project selection process to evaluate not only future cash flows of *additional* projects but also the future cash flows of *present* projects. In essence, then, the decision set covers *all* future correlated cash flows of the firm, in *all* feasible combinations, *including the future cash flows anticipated from presently existing projects and investments.*

*Second*, the firm *ought* to undertake future projects that complement its existing investments—i.e., projects that are *negatively* correlated with present activities. In short, this is the basis for *diversification* of activities undertaken by the firm. By doing this, the overall risk position of the firm would be reduced because the negative correlational effect is to reduce the sum of the variances.

A consequence of the diversification argument is that a *merger* with another firm, or the outright *acquisition* of another firm, can be viewed conceptually as a *project*. In either case (merger or acquisition), a present outlay of funds (or their equivalent) will result in future cash inflows to the firm; hence, mergers and acquisitions can be treated as projects by the firm. The advantage of mergers and acquisitions lies in the obvious opportunity for the acquiring firm to reduce its overall risk, while at the same time avoiding the initial expenses of market and product development, start-up, etc. This is an exciting and fruitful area for the application of the theory of investment of the firm but is beyond the scope of this book.[12] In passing, however, we should note that *under the assumptions of a perfect capital market*, Haley and Schall demonstrate ([13], pp. 194–195, 289–290) that the stochastic relationships (i.e., correlational effects) between cash flow streams are irrelevant—that is, the firm's risk stance is *not* affected by correlational affects. The consequence of this argument is that, *under perfect capital market assumptions*, we can again proceed to judge candidate projects on an *incremental* basis with respect to the present investments of the firm—i.e., independently of how the firm has its funds presently invested. Note particularly, however, that if borrowing and lending rates differ or if any other factor destroys the perfect capital market assumptions, then the *entire* scenario, *including present investments of the firm*, must be evaluated for their future consequences.

**11.3.3. *Multiple project selection by maximizing expected utility of net present value.*** The selection of a set of multiple projects by maximizing the expected utility of net present value is a straightforward extension of the methodology demonstrated in Sections 11.2.1 through 11.2.5, for single projects. For multiple projects, the procedure involves finding the means and variances of net present value for all candidate projects and, if the utility function is of higher order, then higher moments of NPV must be found also. (For our purposes, however, we shall restrict the discussion to cases in which only the means and variances of the candidate project NPV's are required.)

Once these values are procured, generally by one of the methods outlined in Section 11.2, then candidate projects are combined into *mutually exclusive* subsets. If correlational effects are present in the cash flow streams of the projects constituting a mutually exclusive subset, then the appropriate adjustments must be made for this effect in the *variance* of the NPV of the specific subset. Constraints are also applied to nullify infeasible subsets.

When the appropriate means and variances of net present value are established for each *feasible* subset (*bundle*), then the paired value, $[E(NPV), \sigma(NPV)]$, for each such subset is converted into its expected utility, and the criterion of maximizing expected utility is applied over the feasible set of bundles. The single, mutually exclusive subset of projects that satisfies the maximum expected utility criterion is the optimal solution.

There are some fundamental objections, however, to using this method for finding an optimal set of projects. *First*, net present value, *even as a random variable*, can exist *only* when perfect capital market conditions obtain. Alternatively, we can *assume* that the NPV for candidate projects exists *if* we are able to hypothesize a marginal cost-of-capital rate for the firm, to be used as the interest discount rate; and *if* we are

---

[12]Readers interested in mergers and acquisitions as methods of reducing the overall risk of the firm are referred to modern texts on financial management and theory. See, for example, Van Horne [32], Chapter 6; and Levy and Sarnat [23], Chapters 15 and 16.

able to assume that *additional new projects* can be made available in the future that will yield a rate at least equal to the assumed cost of capital, to provide a *sink* for funds recovered from projects accepted in the interim. (This latter requirement stems from the reinvestment assumption underlying NPV, which was developed in Chapter 8).

*Second*, the discounting of variances by interest factors with $-2t$ as the exponent is undesirable. As in the case of single projects (Section 11.2.3), the $-2t$ exponent amounts to double counting of risk—once in the interest rate itself (the cost of capital) and again in the exponent. This tends to diminish the present variance of future risk components disproportionately. Alternatively, it can be argued that the *risk* component of the interest rate should not be discounted at all. In any event, the NPV method of discounting variances tampers with the facts that express future risk (variation in future cash flows).

*Third*, the model assumes implicitly that an expected utility indifference function is obtainable for the firm. This may or may not be the case in reality.

*Fourth*, as with other Lorie-Savage–type investment problems, the model does not consider intertemporal transfer and/or reinvestment of idle funds at rates other than the assumed discount rate. Hence, it has limited applicability in practice.

For the foregoing reasons, we shall not exemplify the maximum expected utility of net present value model. The most disabling assumption is the discounting of variances by a factor of $-2t$. Instead, we shall proceed to the certainty equivalent model, which is devoid of this assumption, but carries all the others (perfect capital market, single utility function for the firm, reinvestment of funds at a known rate).

**11.3.4.** *Multiple project selection by maximizing certainty equivalent.* The selection of multiple projects by maximizing the present value of certainty equivalents is a straightforward extension of the single-project certainty equivalent approach described in Section 11.2.7. The multiple project extension of this method embraces the following steps:

1. *Projects* are combined into *mutually exclusive, feasible* subsets by combining their undiscounted expected cash flows, $E[Y_{tj}]$, and undiscounted variances of cash flows, $V[Y_{tj}]$, *year by year*, to obtain a time series of expectations and variances for each mutually exclusive subset; thus:

$$\left.\begin{aligned} E[Y_{tp}] &= \sum_{j=1}^{m} E[Y_{tj}] \\ V[Y_{tp}] &= \sum_{j=1}^{m} V[Y_{tj}] + 2 \sum_{j \neq k} \text{Cov}\,(Y_{tj}, Y_{tk}) \end{aligned}\right\} \quad (11.25)$$

where $E[Y_{tp}]$ = expected cash flow (net) of project subset $P$ at time $t$
$\qquad (t = 0, 1, 2, \ldots, n), [P = 1, 2, \ldots, (2^m - 1)].$
$\quad V[Y_{tp}]$ = variance of net cash flow of project subset $P$ at time $t$.

2. Each of the ordered pairs of expectancies and variances of cash flows, $\{E[Y_{tp}],$ $V[Y_{tp}]\}$, are converted into certainty equivalents by the methods described in

Section 11.2.7. These methods require the application of the expected utility indifference function to find each of the certainty equivalents

$$\{E[Y'_{tp}], 0\} \sim \{E[Y_{tp}], V^{1/2}[Y_{tp}]\}$$

so that the expected utility of each combination of $(E, \sigma)$ is identical.

3. When the certainty equivalents, $E[Y'_{tp}]$, for each period $t$ of each mutually exclusive subset of projects are found, then the $E[Y'_{tp}]$ for a given project subset are discounted at an assumed known *default-free* interest rate to present time and summed.

4. The resulting present-time certainty equivalents for the mutually exclusive project subsets are compared. The project combination subset having the greatest certainty equivalent is the optimal choice.

5. If probability statements need be made concerning the optimal subset of selected projects, the mean net present value of the subset may be found (as demonstrated in Example 11.2.5), and then the variance of NPV corresponding to the mean NPV may be calculated, assuming constant expected utility. With the mean and variance of NPV known, probability statements can be made concerning the *package* investment if distributional assumptions are made.

The certainty equivalent approach to multiple project selection will not be demonstrated by example since the method is exactly analogous to the single-project model, except for the necessity of combining *cash flows* for the projects that form each mutually exclusive, feasible subset. Methods for doing this are explained in detail in Section 11.2.

## 11.4. Time-State Preference (TSP) Models

It is theoretically possible to allow both rate and stream effects to enter in the same model. When such a model is constructed, not only would it be possible for the discounting rate to vary from period to period but also the decision-maker would no doubt have different preferences (i.e., different utility functions) about future cash flows. These are the special properties of the time-state preference (TSP) model. In this model, the value (utility) of money received (or paid) at a future point in time is considered to be not only a function of the length of time from "now" to "then" but also of the *state* of circumstances of the decision-maker when the money is received or paid. For example, 10 years from now the receipt of $1,000 would be viewed differently by a poor man than by a wealthy one, even though *at the present time* both men possesed considerable means. Thus, the critical concept in the TSP model is the *state* of nature *and* the decision-maker *at a given time*.

Briefly, the model assumes a *finite* set of *states*. States occur in a time sequence from the present on into the future (the end of the project), and there may be one, two, several, or many states at any given point in time. It is required, however, that *all* states be specified. Each state includes, as a part of its specification, a particular *sequence of events*, assumed to occur from now to the time $t$ when the state $s$ is defined. Thus, the number of possible states can increase rapidly as the model becomes more complex. Furthermore, all *possible* states must be positively identified—i.e., all possible combinations of prior states and paths must be defined—and then, it is a further requirement (in evaluating the model) that only *one* state can occur at one point in time (i.e., states are mutually exclusive and exhaustive and all possible combinations must be accounted for).

Using such a model, it is possible to define cash flow streams and utility functions that are state-dependent, and probabilities of occurrence for each state. If necessary, the time value of money can be made state-dependent also; thus, this model can tolerate the intertemporal transfer of funds at different interest rates (for borrowing and lending purposes) and with differing *utilities* for borrowing and lending. As a result, the TSP approach to modeling the capital investment decision is an extremely powerful one, and the syntax of the methodology can be made very complex. Very sophisticated models can be built using the TSP concept; however, its extreme generality is also its downfall from a practical standpoint. Because it is so general in its approach, it is *very* difficult not only to formulate the models themselves but also to formulate them in such a manner that solutions can be obtained. Hence, we shall not attempt more than this very brief discussion. For interested readers, however, there is a literature on the TSP approach that extends from Arrow [1], Debreu [8], and Hirshleifer [20], [21], [22] to the present. A TSP model for securities valuation that is very descriptive of the methodology is given by Myers [27].

## 11.5. Summary

In this chapter our main objective was to examine two essentially different models of handling uncertainty connected with the cash flows of projects, both models, however, being based on the Bernoulli Principle of expected utility. One model is based on maximizing the expected utility of net present value, and the other model is based on the certainty equivalent principle. Both models can be used to evaluate single or multiple projects by converting future random cash flows (or their statistics) to present equivalents.

In addition, we examined in considerable detail some specific techniques for estimating future cash flows and their stochastic relationships (i.e., timewise autocorrelations within a project, and cross-correlations between projects). Two typically different methods for procuring estimates of net present value were described and examples given—one, a rational method based on the Central Limit Theorem, in which moments are combined and discounted; the other, discrete-event simulation techniques.

All the models above were assumed to be viable only under perfect capital market conditions—or at least, under conditions in which the *rate* effects were known, or could be reasonably assumed. Finally, a time-state-preference modeling procedure was briefly described, in which it is possible (at least theoretically) to allow both uncertainty and rate effects to play varying roles. This model, however, is typified by its generality and, therefore, is extremely difficult to construct and solve.

# REFERENCES

[1] ARROW, KENNETH J., "The Role of Securities in the Optimal Allocation of Risk-Bearing," *Review of Economic Studies*, **XXXI** (1963–1964), pp. 91–96.

[2] BERNHARD, RICHARD H., "Probability and Rates of Return: Some Critical Comments," *Management Science*, **13**(7) (March, 1967), pp. 598–600.

[3] BOX, GEORGE E. P., and GWILYM M. JENKINS, *Time Series Analysis, Forecasting and Control*, revised ed. (San Francisco: Holden-Day, Inc., 1976).

[4] BUSSEY, LYNN E., and G. T. STEVENS, JR., "Formulating Correlated Cash Flow Streams," *The Engineering Economist*, **18**(1) (1972), pp. 1–30.

[5] ———, "Reply to 'Comment' on 'Formulating Correlated Cash Flow Streams'," *The Engineering Economist*, **20**(3) (1975), pp. 215–21.

[6] ———, "Net Present Value from Complex Cash Flow Streams by Simulation," *AIIE Transactions*, **3**(1) (March, 1971), pp. 81–89.

[7] CONOVER, W. J., *Practical Non-Parametric Statistics* (New York: John Wiley & Sons, Inc., 1971).

[8] DEBREU, GERARD, *The Theory of Value* (New York: John Wiley & Sons, Inc., 1959).

[9] FLEISCHER, GERALD A., "Two Major Issues Associated With the Rate of Return Method for Capital Allocation: The 'Ranking Error' and 'Preliminary Selection," *The Journal of Industrial Engineering*, **XVII**(4) (April, 1966), pp. 202–8.

[10] GRANT, EUGENE L., and RICHARD S. LEAVENWORTH, *Statistical Quality Control*, 4th ed. (New York: McGraw-Hill Book Co., 1972).

[11] GROSH, DORIS, L., and L. E. BUSSEY, "A Generalized Cramér Inequality," *Special Report No. 115, Kansas Engineering Experiment Station* (Manhattan, Kan.: Kansas State University, November, 1973).

[12] HAHN, GERALD J., and SAMUEL S. SHAPIRO, *Statistical Models in Engineering* (New York: John Wiley & Sons, Inc., 1967).

[13] HALEY, CHARLES W., and LAWRENCE D. SCHALL, *The Theory of Financial Decisions* (New York: McGraw-Hill Book Co., 1973).

[14] HERTZ, DAVID B., "Risk Analysis in Capital Investment," *Harvard Business Review* (January-February, 1964), pp. 95–106.

[15] ———, "Investment Policies That Pay Off," *Harvard Business Review* (January-February, 1968), pp. 96–108.

[16] HESS, SIDNEY W., and HARRY A. QUIGLEY, "Analysis of Risk in Investments Using Monte Carlo Techniques," *Chemical Engineering Progress Symposium Series 42: Statistics and Numerical Methods in Chemical Engineering* (New York: American Institute of Chemical Engineering, 1963).

[17] HILLIER, FREDERICK, S., "The Derivation of Probabilistic Information for the Evaluation of Risky Investments," *Management Science* (April, 1963), p. 443.

[18] ———, "Supplement to 'The Derivation of Probabilistic Information for the Evaluation of Risky Investments,'" *Management Science*, **11**(3), (January, 1965), pp. 485–87.

[19] ———, *The Evaluation of Risky Interrelated Investments* (Amsterdam: North Holland Publishing Co., 1969).

[20] Hirshleifer, J., "Efficient Allocation of Capital in an Uncertain World," *American Economic Review*, **LIV** (May, 1964), pp. 77–85.

[21] ———, "Investment Decision Under Uncertainty: Choice-Theoretic Approaches," *Quarterly Journal of Economics*, **LXXIX** (November, 1965), pp. 509–36.

[22] ———, "Investment Decision Under Uncertainty: Application of the State-Preference Approach," *Quarterly Journal of Economics*, **LXXX** (May, 1966), pp. 252–77.

[23] Levy, Haim, and Marshall Sarnat, *Investment and Portfolio Analysis* (New York: John Wiley & Sons, Inc., 1972).

[24] Markowitz, H. M., *Portfolio Selection: Efficient Diversification of Investments* (New York: John Wiley & Sons, Inc., 1959).

[25] Mize, J. H., and J. G. Cox, *Essentials of Simulation* (Englewood Cliffs, N.J.: Prentice-Hall, Inc., 1968).

[26] Murray, John R., "Sensitivity Analysis in the Return on Investment Criterion," *Management Accounting*, **50**(9), (May, 1969), pp. 23–25.

[27] Myers, Stewart C., "A Time-State-Preference Model of Security Valuation," *Journal of Financial and Quantitative Analysis* (June, 1968), pp. 1–33.

[28] Nelson, Charles R., *Applied Time Series Analysis for Managerial Forecasting* (San Francisco, Calif.: Holden-Day, Inc., 1973).

[29] Robichek, Alexander A., and Stewart C. Myers, *Optimal Financial Decisions* (Englewood Cliffs, N.J.: Prentice-Hall, Inc., 1965).

[30] Schmidt, J. W., and R. E. Taylor, *Simulation and Analysis of Industrial Systems* (Homewood, Ill.: Richard D. Irwin, Inc., 1970).

[31] Siegel, Sidney, *Nonparametric Statistics* (New York: McGraw-Hill Book Co., 1956).

[32] Van Horne, James C., *Financial Management and Policy*, 2nd ed. (Englewood Cliffs, N.J.: Prentice-Hall, Inc., 1971).

[33] Wagle, B., "A Statistical Analysis of Risk in Investment Projects," *Operational Research Quarterly*, **18**(1) (March, 1967), pp. 13–33.

[34] International Business Machines Corp., *General Purpose Simulation System V Users Manual*, 2nd ed., Form No. 5H-20-0851-1 (White Plains, N.Y.: International Business Machines Corp., August, 1971).

## PROBLEMS

**11-1.** Dauntless Electric Company is trying to decide whether to invest $1,800,000 in a new plant to expand their output of stereo equipment. Management forecasts indicate that the new plant will generate random net cash flows of $Y_t$ dollars at the end of each year ($t = 1, 2, \ldots, 5$), where each of the $Y_t$ is an independent random variable. The means and standard deviations of the cash flows are estimated as follows:

| End of Year, t | E (NCF) | σ (NCF) |
|:---:|:---:|:---:|
| 0 | $-1,800 (10³) | $ 0 |
| 1 | + 100 (10³) | 10 (10³) |
| 2 | + 300 (10³) | 20 (10³) |
| 3 | + 500 (10³) | 50 (10³) |
| 4 | + 800 (10³) | 60 (10³) |
| 5 | + 800 (10³) | 80 (10³) |

You are to assume a marginal investment rate of 15% for the following questions:

(a) Calculate the mean net present value and the variance of net present value.

(b) If net present value is assumed to be distributed Normally, what is the probability that the firm will fail to recover its investment plus required return?

(c) Assuming Normality, what is the probability that the project's rate of return will be less than 15%? What *assumptions* are implicit in your answer?

(d) If the annual net cash flow amounts are Normally and independently distributed, what is the probability that *no* return will be realized on the investment (i.e., that only the investment itself will be recovered)? (*Hint:* Find $E$ [Net Cash Flows] at an interest rate $i = 0$ and then compare this mean value with net present value $= 0$).

(e) If the distributional form of net present value is unknown, but it nevertheless can be. assumed unimodal, what is the probability that the company will fail to recover its investment plus the required return of 15%?

**11-2.** In a cash flow stream that is correlated across time (autocorrelated), what is the effect on the variance of net present value if the correlation coefficients are positive (i.e., $0 \leq \rho \leq 1$)? What is the effect of cash flow increments that are negatively correlated?

**11-3.** Consult Ref. [3] or [28] and develop an economic interpretation of a cash flow stream in which the annual cash flows are strongly and *negatively* correlated.

**11-4.** Identify some of the possible economic and physical causes of strong, positive autocorrelations in a project's cash flow stream.

**11-5.** Assume that the cash flow stream for a particular project has been synthesized from relevant economic and technical data, with the following estimates of the parameters of the cash flows:

| End of Period | Mean Cash Flow, $E[Y_t]$ | Standard Deviation of Cash Flow, $\sigma(Y_t)$ |
|---|---|---|
| 0 | \$-5.0 | \$0.750 |
| 1 | +2.0 | 0.500 |
| 2 | 4.0 | 1.000 |
| 3 | 3.0 | 1.732 |
| 4 | 3.0 | 2.449 |

(a) If the cash flows, $Y_t$, are Normally and independently distributed and if the firm's marginal investment rate is assumed to be 15%, what is the probability that the net present value of the project will be zero or negative?

(b) If the cash flows, $Y_t$, are Normally distributed and autocorrelated with the autocorrelation coefficients shown in the table below and if the firm's marginal investment rate is assumed to be 15%, what is the probability that the project will fail to return its investment plus the required return rate? (Use net present value method.)

| $\theta =$ | Correlation Coefficients, $\rho_{\tau\theta}$ | | | | |
|---|---|---|---|---|---|
| | 0 | 1 | 2 | 3 | 4 |
| $\tau = 0$ | +1.00 | 0 | 0 | 0 | 0 |
| 1 | | +1.00 | +0.10 | +0.05 | +0.02 |
| 2 | | | +1.00 | +0.15 | +0.12 |
| 3 | | (Symmetrical) | | +1.00 | -0.16 |
| 4 | | | | | +1.00 |

(c) Assuming that the cash flows, $Y_t$, are Normally and independently distributed and using discount rates of 15, 30, 45, 60, 75, and 100%, calculate the *probabilities* that NPV $\leq 0$. Plot these probabilities as a function of the discount rate, $i$, and "fair in" a continuous function of NPV($i$) versus $i$. What relation does this function bear to the function $P(i^* \leq 0)$ versus $i$, where $i^*$ is the internal rate of return of the project?

**11-6.** The cash flows from a contemplated project are assumed to be distributed $\beta$ with the following estimated values:

| End of Year, $t =$ | Cash Flows | | |
|---|---|---|---|
| | Pessimistic, $Y_p$ | Modal, $\tilde{Y}$ | Optimistic, $Y_o$ |
| 0 | $-14,000 | $-12,000 | $-10,000 |
| 1 | 0 | 2,000 | 4,000 |
| 2 | 5,000 | 8,000 | 11,000 |
| 3 | 8,000 | 12,000 | 16,000 |

(a) Calculate the mean cash flows and standard deviations of the cash flows using PERT estimating techniques.
(b) Using a marginal attractive rate of return of 15%, formulate the equations for mean net present value and the standard deviation of net present value, and substitute the necessary numerical values into the equations, including discount factors. Find the numerical values for the expected net present value and the standard deviation of net present value.

**11-7.** A project being proposed for adoption has the following characteristics:

| Investment, C | | Life, N | | Annual Gross Income | |
|---|---|---|---|---|---|
| Amount | Probability | Years | Probability | Amount | Probability |
| $100,000 | 0.15 | 10 | 0.10 | $10,000 | 0.05 |
| 120,000 | 0.70 | 11 | 0.20 | 20,000 | 0.15 |
| 140,000 | 0.15 | 12 | 0.40 | 30,000 | 0.40 |
| | | 13 | 0.20 | 40,000 | 0.25 |
| | | 14 | 0.10 | 50,000 | 0.15 |

| Annual Expense | | Effective Tax Rate | |
|---|---|---|---|
| Amount | Probability | Amount | Probability |
| $ 5,000 | 0.15 | 47% | 0.25 |
| 7,000 | 0.20 | 50% | 0.50 |
| 9,000 | 0.30 | 53% | 0.25 |
| 11,000 | 0.20 | | |
| 13,000 | 0.15 | | |

Assume the estimated marginal investment rate of the firm is 12%.
(a) Convert the probability functions above into cumulative distributions, and using

a random number table (with each of the variates being determined by an independent series of random numbers), make 50 determinations of the random net present value (i.e., procure net present value with a sample size of 50).

(b) Determine the mean and estimated population variance of NPV from the sample.

(c) Fit a cumulative Normal distribution to your sampled distribution by matching the moments of the assumed normal to your empirical distribution. Apply the Kolmogorov-Smirnov test to determine if the Normal distribution is acceptable to you as a fit to your empirical distribution. (Use an $\alpha = \pm 10\%$ confidence level.)

(d) What is the probability that the NPV > 0?

**11-8.** It is found that a decision-maker's utility function can be approximated with an equation of the form

$$U(Y) = \frac{1}{2} \log_e \left(1 + \frac{Y}{1000}\right)^2,$$

where $U(Y)$ is the utility of $Y$, a present-valued random payoff, whose mean is $\mu$ and variance is $\sigma^2$. Derive the expectation of this utility function.

**11-9.** For a utility function whose expectation is

$$E[U(Y)] = \frac{1}{2} \log_e \left[1 + \frac{\mu}{5,000} + \frac{\mu^2 - \sigma^2}{(10,000)^2}\right],$$

determine some representative coordinates of the indifference curve $E[U(Y)] = 0$ over the region $(0 \leq \mu \leq 20{,}000)$, and plot the indifference curve.

**11-10.** For a utility function whose expectation is

$$E[U(Y)] = \frac{1}{2} \log_e \left[1 + \frac{\mu}{5} + \frac{\mu^2 - \sigma^2}{100}\right],$$

calculate a sufficient number of coordinate points and plot the four indifference curves for $E[U(Y)] = -1.0$, 0, $+0.5$, and $+1.0$ for values of $0 \leq \sigma \leq 30$, and $\mu \leq 30$. Plot the four indifference curves on $\sigma$-$\mu$ axes.

**11-11.** The following after-tax cash flows are estimated for a certain pending project:

| Time, t | Net Cash Flow | |
|---|---|---|
| | Expected Value, $\mu$ | Variance, $\sigma^2$ |
| 0 | $-$ 5.0 | 20.0 |
| 1 | $+$ 1.0 | 21.0 |
| 2 | $+$ 5.0 | 49.0 |
| 3 | $+10.0$ | 100.0 |
| 4 | $+15.0$ | 144.0 |
| 5 | $+20.0$ | 64.0 |

(a) Using an effective interest rate of 5%, which is considered to be risk-free, calculate the certainty-equivalent present value of the project for a decision-maker whose expected utility is given in Problem 11.10. What is the variance of this certainty equivalent?

(b) Calculate the *mean* net present value of the project using a discount rate of 5%.

(c) Calculate the expected *utility* of the equivalent project whose certainty equivalent you determined in (a).

(d) Calculate the variance and standard deviation of the equivalent project whose expected utility is the same as you calculated in (c). Why is this *project* equally acceptable to the decision-maker as the one you calculated in (a)?

**11-12.** Four independent projects under consideration have parameters (estimates) as follows:

| Project Number | Expected Net Present Value | Variance of Net Present Value | Initial Cost at Time $t = 0$ |
|---|---|---|---|
| 1 | $2.0 (10^5)$ | $0.25 (10^{10})$ | $ 50,000. |
| 2 | $4.0 (10^5)$ | $1.00 (10^{10})$ | 100,000. |
| 3 | $3.0 (10^5)$ | $3.00 (10^{10})$ | 40,000. |
| 4 | $3.0 (10^5)$ | $6.00 (10^{10})$ | 70,000. |

The budget limitation at time $t = 0$ is $175,000.

(a) If the decision-maker's utility function is

$$U(\text{NPV}) = 48.74(\text{NPV}) - 17.967(10^{-6})(\text{NPV})^2$$

and if he maximizes expected utility, which projects should he select? (*Note:* NPV = net present value.)

(b) What is the probability, $P(\text{NPV} \leq 0)$, for the optimal project set if its net present value is Normally distributed with mean $\mu_{\text{NPV}}$ and variance $\sigma^2_{\text{NPV}}$?

(c) On $\sigma$-$\mu$ axes, plot the coordinate points for each *feasible* project *bundle* (combination) established in (a). Determine the convex set (*efficient frontier*) of projects by connecting the dominant projects with straight lines (assuming risk-avoidance).

(d) One form of utility function, termed the *catastrophe-avoidance* model, was developed by A. D. Roy ["Safety First and the Holding of Assets," *Econometrica*, **20** (July, 1952), pp. 431–49]. When applied to the net present value case, the *expected value form* of Roy's risk-expectation trade-off function becomes $\mu = D + k\sigma$, where $\mu$ = expected net present value, $\sigma$ = standard deviation of net present value, $k$ = a nonnegative constant, and $D$ = the disaster point, or the minimum net present value (with zero variance) that is acceptable to the decision-maker. When the risk-expectation trade-off function is placed in the form $\sigma = (\mu - D)/k$, it is seen to be a straight line on $\sigma$-$\mu$ coordinates, with intercept of $D$ and slope $1/k$. The value of $k$ can be determined by erecting a tangent to the convex feasible set of projects [as in part (c) above], from the intercept $(D, 0)$. For a disaster value of $[D = \$3.0(10^5), \sigma_D = 0]$, determine the slope $(1/k)$ of the tangent, and determine the composition of the optimal bundle of projects and its mean and standard deviation.

(e) In part (d), the slope of the Roy catastrophe-avoidance trade-off function can be interpreted as a probability. That is, $k = (\mu - D)/\sigma$, which is a standardized deviate. Assuming that net present value is distributed Normally, what is the probability of *disaster* (i.e., NPV $\leq D$)?

# PROJECT SELECTION
# USING CAPITAL ASSET PRICING THEORY

## 12.1. Introduction

In previous chapters we have considered two of the three fundamental approaches that can be used for modeling the project selection problem. The first approach, presented in a simplified format in Chapters 7 through 9, is based on the criterion of maximizing an *expected return* (net present value) to the firm, using an assumed known interest rate for discounting future sums to present equivalents. In this approach, *risk* and *uncertainty* are assumed to be zero. The second approach, presented in Chapters 10 and 11, is based on the criterion of maximizing the *expected utility* of a set of future returns, using an assumed known discount rate. This approach introduces the concept of *variability* of project cash flows, thus giving explicit recognition to the uncertainty inherently present in every project selection problem, which is due to the human inability to forecast and control future cash flows exactly.

The third approach, originally conceived by Sharpe [17] and Lintner [11], and extended by Mossin [13], is similar to the utilitarian approach, but with important differences. Called the *capital asset pricing* methodology, this approach to the project selection problem is based in capital market theory and attempts to solve both the capital supply and capital resource allocation problems simultaneously. It differs from the cardinal utility model in two respects. *First*, it assumes a *generalized* risk-avoidance posture on the part of the decision-maker instead of a specific, quantifiable utility

# 12

function, as does the von Neumann-Morgenstern model in Chapter 10. The generalized risk-avoidance posture assumed in the capital asset pricing model merely requires the decision-maker to be a risk avoider—that is, one who requires more than a one-to-one increase in the expected return to risk of a project, if the risk exposure of the firm would be increased as a result of accepting the project. In the capital asset pricing model, this tradeoff of increased return for increased risk is perfectly general; it is not of specific functional form as required by the utility models. *Second,* the capital asset pricing approach to project selection assumes that the firm's marginal cost of capital is a *random variable* instead of a *known* numerical constant, as does the utilitarian approach. In the capital asset pricing model, the firm's random cost of capital has a mean and a variance that are established by two factors; namely, (1) the randomness of the securities market itself, and (2) the corelationships that exist among the firm's dividend policies, the fluctuations in the market price of the firm's shares, and the randomness of the financial market as a whole. The corelationships of these factors are given effect by and through the financial market itself, via the free market pricing mechanism.

From a practical standpoint, the capital asset pricing approach to project selection has several major advantages over the other methodologies. To visualize these advantages, we constrast some of the assumptions and features of the capital asset pricing methodology to those of the deterministic and utilitarian methods previously presented.

**419**

The deterministic (expected return) approach obviously suffers from the defective assumption that *all future events* are known with certainty. This includes complete knowledge of what the projects will be (in all details), what their incomes and expenses *will be*, what depreciation models and income tax rates *will be* effective, what the market rate of interest *will be*, and so forth. While the expected return models supply us with valuable insights into the firm and its investment processes, we have no real assurances that the solutions resulting from these processes will necessarily be any more *optimal* for the firm than a random selection process, although they would likely be *better*. The deterministic models are simply not in accord with what we know to be *reality*.

Moreover, both the utilitarian (expected utility) and deterministic (expected return) models depend on the assumed existence of a known discount rate, which is used to relate cash flows occurring in the future to equivalent present amounts. This discount rate is usually based on a calculation of the cost of capital for the firm, which contains an implicit allowance for risk in addition to the base interest rate (the time value of money). The risk allowance portion of the cost of capital figure is a part of the total rate because of the manner in which the cost of capital figure is calculated—it is based on the market *price* of the firm's equity shares and an estimated stream of future dividends.

The dividend-to-price ratio, being fixed by the securities market, implicitly includes a collective evaluation of the riskiness of the firm's shares, which is established by the pricing mechanism of the market. While it is entirely proper to discount future cash flows to their present-time equivalent amounts by using a compounded *time-value-of-money* interest rate (this is simply Fisher's theory of interest), there are valid and serious objections to a compounding of the *risk* portion of the cost-of-capital rate. The *compounding* of the *risk* portion of the cost-of-capital rate may seriously distort the interpretation of the actual riskiness of future cash flows. Furthermore, in the utilitarian models, when the present equivalent of the *random* net present value is found, the discount factors used for calculating the *variance* of net present value are of the form $(1 + i)^{-2t}$. Valid objections to this procedure are raised in Chapter 9 because the procedure *counts* risk twice: once in the interest rate ($i$) itself, as a result of the cost-of-capital calculation, and then again in the *second*-order exponent ($2t$) of the variance calculation.

Some other rather prominent defects of the utilitarian approach are the assumptions that (1) the utility function must be of known (or assumed known) form, (2) the utility function must be one derived from a single decision-maker (group utility functions can be shown to be the result of collective bargaining or gamesmanship in the group rather than a *preference* ordering), and (3) the utility function remains unchanging in the time dimension (which is contrary to observed empirical results).

All of these limiting assumptions seem to demand some procedure, preferably based in theory, that will satisfactorily model the firm's project selection apparatus from a normative standpoint. While it is a new methodology, capital asset pricing theory appears to provide answers to most of the defects in the previous approaches, even though the theory itself is still incomplete and in a state of continuing development.

The general approach used in capital asset pricing theory is due to Markowitz [12], who first suggested the idea that the return rates on various securities, or portfolios of securities, are correlated with one another pair by pair and that the computational job of calculating these correlative effects could be considerably simplified if a model were to be constructed in which each security is assumed to be correlated solely with a *market-wide* portfolio (or a market "index," as Markowitz termed it ([12], p. 100), rather than with each other pair by pair. The result is a shortened method of calculating an empirical, *market-based* cost of capital, which effectively integrates the long-run project investment *and* dividend policies of the firm—thereby providing a criterion for the selection of future investment projects.

The actual process of comparing the characteristics of a project with the capital asset "price" determined by the market is often called *risk screening* [1]. Risk-screening is fundamentally a *variable* cost of capital technique that allows one to segregate the risk effect in the firm's discount rate from the time-value-of-money effect. Also, since it relates individual security (or project) variance to market variance through a covariance term, the risk-screening method allows us to calculate a relative *volatility* measure for a particular project (or set of projects) that expresses the *explicit* risk involved in making the investment. Then, by combining a risky project with assumed borrowing or lending, a firm can, in effect, establish the necessary conditions for undertaking or rejecting the project *while holding the equivalent risk position of the firm unchanged*. This latter caveat is a necessary prerequisite for maintaining the equity position of the shareholders intact, thereby protecting their per-share investment against devaluation in the market.

Thus, a risk-equalized state for all candidate projects can be established, and once this state is calculated, the actual risk screening process itself involves simply accepting any project that provides (in its risk-equalized state) a return rate greater than that expected by the firm's equity investors. For pure investments, this policy tends also to maximize the future wealth of the equity shareholders, thus making it equivalent as an investment criterion to the maximization of net present value. Since riskiness can be accounted for *explicitly* by the risk-screening technique, there is no need for a discount factor to be inflated for risk effects, or for second-order exponentiation in the discounting of variances.

Capital asset pricing theory, augmented by the risk-screening technique, is an important advance in the art of project selection and capital allocation in the firm. The theory appears to be well grounded. Empirical tests of the theory, while possibly indicating somewhat contradictory findings in some respects at the present time, nevertheless provide new insights into the interactive processes of capital acquisition and investment by the firm. Most importantly, the risk-screening approach can be applied *directly* to the capital allocation problem of the firm, which is of prime practical importance, For these reasons, capital asset pricing theory and the risk-screening techniques will be rather fully developed in this chapter.

The starting point for the development is Markowitz' concept of a securities *portfolio* and how the variance of the portfolio return is affected by *covariation* among the securities comprising the portfolio. Following a brief description of portfolio covariation, the concept of *efficient* portfolios will be developed. In relation to other portfolios, *efficient* portfolios display a dominance effect that is analogous to the dominance found among discrete projects, as described in Chapter 10, that results from using the expected utility criterion. The result of the *dominance* effect is that many of the candidate portfolios can be eliminated, leaving the investor to choose from among only efficient portfolios. Following this, we shall consider how individual securities can be extended to include portfolios of arbitrary composition and then how these can be coupled with borrowing or lending at a risk-free interest rate to establish a *security line*—a locus of choices on which the investor's maximum expected utility choice between the risky, arbitrary portfolio and the riskless security will lie. The next topic will consider Sharpe's market model that establishes the risk trade-off relationship between a given security and an arbitrary portfolio and then the regression model equivalent of the theoretical model will be introduced.

Following these topics, a project selection methodology based on the capital asset pricing model will be introduced. The topics to be covered there are risk equivalency, the reward-to-variability selection criterion, the reward-to-volatility criterion, project selection methods for publicly held firms, and project selection methods for privately held (unlisted) firms.

## 12.2. Portfolio Theory

The fundamental unit in a financial transaction, by which an investor invests his funds and acquires a right to receive future cash inflows, is called a *security*. A security can generally be presumed to be a written, legal instrument (such as a bond or share of stock) that vests in the owner the *right to receive future income*, if and when produced. It may or may not vest ownership in a share of the assets owned by the issuer of the security. Investors usually associate some degree of risk with the ownership of a security because there is no guarantee on the part of the issuer (except his implicit reputation or perhaps the worth of pledged assets underlying the security) for either the *payment of income* on the security or *repayment of the purchase price*, or its future equivalent. Thus, the riskiness of securities, in the eyes of investors, can be a variable that depends largely on who the issuer is. Shares of stock in Flybynight Commuter Airlines would no doubt be considered more risky than shares of General Motors common stock because of the general uncertainty attending the *dividends* and *earnings prospects* of Flybynight compared to General Motors. On the other hand, bonds of the United States Government, compared to General Motors stock, are considered by most investors to be nearly riskless—or, to use better terminology, virtually default-free. The reason is obvious: The Government possesses the authority to tax and the authority to issue money; hence, it can always pay its obligations by collecting a tax on the assets of its owners, the citizens. Since General Motors and Flybynight Commuter

Airlines do not have the authority to tax and issue money, their securities are said to be risky, whereas the Government's securities (some classes of them, at least) are said to be default-free, if not riskless in the theoretical sense.

When an investor invests his funds in several securities, he is said to own (or hold) a *portfolio* of securities that, in the aggregate, represents his right to receive *future incomes* (in the form of interest, dividends, or other benefits) on the securities in his portfolio. The present value of a portfolio is simply the total present market price of its component securities. The ratio of future income to present price is often called the *yield* of the security or portfolio and may be thought of as a return *rate* for the security or portfolio. As commonly known, however, the market prices of most securities fluctuate in response to the pressures of buying demands and selling availabilities in the market place. At any given instant, the price of a security is an equilibrium value resulting from a contract in which a willing buyer and a willing seller agree to exchange commodities (say, money for securities) at an *agreed rate* of *exchange* (price).

Securities prices fluctuate in the market place from time to time: moment by moment, hour by hour, day by day, and over longer intervals of time. Astute observers have noticed, however, that securities prices behave much as time series do; that is, as correlated *random variables*. For analytical purposes, securities prices are often taken as random variables with finite means and variances. Since yields are related to prices, yields on both securities and portfolios are also considered to be random variables with finite means and variances. Thus it follows that the mean yield of a portfolio is simply a function of the yields of the individual securities comprising the portfolio, and the variance of a portfolio yield is another function of the variances of the yields of the component securities, plus a correction in the variance term for any *covariance* among the yields of the securities in the portfolio. In summary, then, we assume we may completely characterize the *random* yield of either a single security or a portfolio by specifying (or determining) the appropriate mean yield and variance of yield for the security or portfolio.

In addition to these considerations, some other assumptions are either explicitly or implicitly incorporated in the capital asset pricing model. These assumptions may be summarized as follows:

1. All investors are single-period expected utility-of-wealth maximizers, who choose among alternative investment opportunities (securities or portfolios) on the basis of mean and variance (or standard deviation) of return. The dollar return is the increment that increases (decreases) net present value.
2. All investors can borrow or lend an unlimited amount in the financial market, at an exogenously fixed (constant) default-free rate of interest, $R_f$, and there are no restrictions on the short sales of any security.[1]

---

[1]A *short* sale is the sale of a security not actually owned at the time of sale. In *actuality*, the seller sells an asset not owned; he does this by *borrowing* the security (usually from a broker), which he plans to replace through purchase in the market at a lower price at some future date, thereby making a profit. In *effect*, the same result can be reached analytically in a risk-free money market by the seller of the security simply borrowing the money and then simultaneously purchasing the security and selling it.

3. All investors have identical estimates of the means, variances, and covariances of return among all securities and portfolios. The import of this assumption is that we need not consider differing *subjective* evaluations of the securities because of a diversity of ownership.
4. All securities and portfolios are perfectly divisible (fractional shares are permissible) and perfectly liquid (i.e., all securities are marketable and there are no transaction costs).
5. There are no taxes on income.
6. All investors are price takers (i.e., the actions of a single investor do not significantly affect the market price of a security).
7. The quantities of all securities holdings are given.

Based on the foregoing discussion and assumptions, we now proceed to the method of calculating mean return rates and variances of return rate for a typical Markowitz-type securities portfolio.

**12.2.1. Mean and variance of a portfolio.** Consider a portfolio consisting of $n$ securities, where $n$ is a finite integer number ($n = 1, 2, \ldots$). Since securities are considered to be perfectly divisible, so that (within practical limits) any desired amount of money can be invested in each security, we may describe any particular portfolio by the *relative* amount of money, $X_i$, invested in each security. For example, a portfolio consisting of $n = 5$ securities might result from relative investments as follows:

| Security No., $i$ | Relative Amount of Funds Invested, $X_i$ |
|:---:|:---:|
| 1 | 0.10 |
| 2 | 0.40 |
| 3 | 0.10 |
| 4 | 0.25 |
| 5 | 0.15 |
| | 1.00 |

The proportion of funds invested in Security 1 is $X_1 = 0.10$; in Security 2, $X_2 = 0.40$; and so forth. Since total funds are committed to the whole portfolio, then the relative amounts invested must sum to one, or

$$\sum_{i=1}^{n} X_i = 1. \tag{12.1}$$

If any $X_i = 0$, the portfolio contains none of Security $i$. If $X_i > 0$, then some of Security $i$ is held in the portfolio; but if $X_i < 0$, then this denotes the *issuance* of Security $i$ by the holder; i.e., the holder of the portfolio has agreed to pay someone else a portion of the portfolio's earnings (he has issued a risky security). A portfolio is defined as a set of $n$ securities, held and issued in proportions $X_i$ (where $X_i \gtreqless 0$), such that Eq. (12.1) is satisfied.

The mean return of a portfolio is simply the weighted average return of the composite securities. Let $\bar{R}_P$ denote the mean return rate on the portfolio and $R_i$ the actual return rate on Security $i$ in the portfolio. Then the mean *portfolio* return rate is given by

$$\bar{R}_P = \sum_{i=1}^{n} X_i R_i. \tag{12.2}$$

The *variance* of the return rate for a portfolio is based on the very realistic assumption (originally proposed by Markovitz) that the return rates of marketed securities are all *pairwise* correlated. Hence, the variance of a portfolio is not found by simply adding the variances of individual securities, as one would do if the returns on the securities behaved independently of one another. Instead, each security is assumed to be correlated with every other security in the market so that the variance of a portfolio is developed as follows. Suppose that $R_i$ and $R_j$ are the return rates from two securities, $i$ and $j$, that are held in the proportions $X_i$ and $X_j$, respectively. Then, from the definition of variance we have

$$\text{Var}\left(\sum_{i=1}^{n} X_i R_i\right) = E\left[\sum_{i=1}^{n} X_i R_i - \sum X_i E(R_i)\right]^2$$

$$= E\left\{\sum_{i=1}^{n} X_i [R_i - E(R_i)]\right\}^2$$

$$= E\left\{\sum_{i=1}^{n} X_i^2 [R_i - E(R_i)]^2 + 2\sum_{i=1}^{n-1}\sum_{\substack{j=2\\j>i}}^{n} X_i X_j [R_i - E(R_i)][R_j - E(R_j)]\right\}$$

$$= \sum_{i=1}^{n} X_i^2 \text{Var}(R_i) + 2\sum_{i=1}^{n-1}\sum_{\substack{j=2\\j>i}}^{n} X_i X_j \text{Cov}(R_i, R_j)$$

and by substitution of $\sigma_P^2 = \text{Var}(R_P)$ we have

$$\sigma_P^2 = \text{Var}(R_P) = \sum_{i=1}^{n} X_i^2 \text{Var}(R_i) + 2\sum_{i=1}^{n-1}\sum_{\substack{j=2\\j>i}}^{n} X_i X_j \text{Cov}(R_i, R_j). \tag{12.3}$$

**12.2.2. *Variance as a measure of risk.*** The variance of a portfolio return is taken to be a measure of the risk, or at least uncertainty, associated with owning the portfolio. There is an economic basis for this measure. The concept can easily be demonstrated by the use of utility theory for a special case, which was done in Chapter 10. For a more general case, Hanoch and Levy [7] and Levy and Sarnat [10] provide a proof. The special case, involving a quadratic utility function, was presented in Section 10.5.1. In this case, the expected utility function is given by Eq. (10.14), which is repeated here:

$$E[U(X)] = A\mu - B(\sigma_X^2 + \mu^2),$$

and that the decision-maker's risk attitudes may be inferred from the directional partial derivatives of Eq. (10.14) as follows:

$$\frac{\partial E[U(X)]}{\partial \mu_X} = A - 2B\mu_X, \tag{10.15}$$

and

$$\frac{\partial E[U(X)]}{\partial \sigma_x} = -2B\sigma_x. \tag{10.16}$$

These partial derivatives define the shape of the *expected utility function* on $\mu$-$\sigma$ coordinates. When $E[U(X)] =$ a constant, we have an isoquant, or indifference curve.

### 12.2.3. *Dominance among portfolios.*

Since a portfolio can be measured in terms of its mean return rate and standard deviation of return rate, any given portfolio can be described as a point in $(\bar{R}_P, \sigma_P)$ coordinates, such as Fig. 12.1. In this figure,

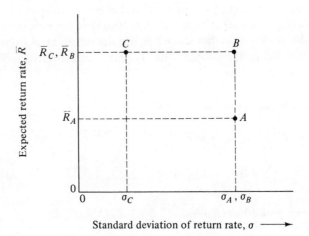

**Fig. 12.1.** Dominance among three securities.

consider the three points labeled $A$, $B$, and $C$, which describe the expected return rates and standard deviations of return rate for three possible securities ($A$, $B$, and $C$). In order to determine which of these securities would be preferred by a typical risk-avoiding decision-maker, the following rules can be invoked. They follow directly from the partial derivatives and reasoning stated in Section 10.5.1:

1. If two securities have the same standard deviation of return rate, such as $A$ and $B$, the one with the larger expected return rate ($B$) is preferred by the risk-avoiding decision-maker since he attaches greater expected utility to the security with the higher expected return rate. This follows from Eq. (10.15).

2. If two securities have the same expected return rate, such as $B$ and $C$, the one with the smaller standard deviation of return rate ($C$) will be preferred since the decision-maker displays a *decrease* in expected utility with an *increase* in standard deviation of return rate. This follows from Eq. (10.16).

Thus, in Fig. 12.1, Security $B$ is preferred to Security $A$ since $B$ has a greater expected return rate than $A$, even though the risk is equal. Hence $B$ is said to *dominate* $A$. Likewise, $C$ would be preferred to $B$ since, although the expected return rate is the same for both, the risk attached to $C(\sigma_C)$ is less than that for $B(\sigma_B)$. Thus, $C$ *dominates* $B$. Furthermore, it should be noted that the commutative rule holds so that if $B$ dominates $A$ and $C$ dominates $B$, then $C$ dominates $A$ also.

In general, securities and portfolios lying upward and to the left on $(\bar{R}_P, \sigma_P)$ coordinates will dominate those represented by points lying downward and to the right. This was shown in Chapter 10 by indifference curve analysis (Section 10.5.1). The graphical concept is presented in Fig. 12.2.

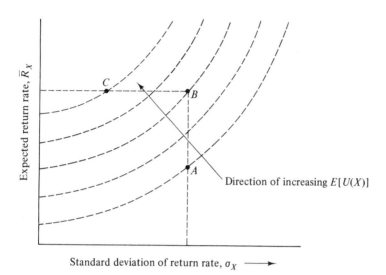

**Fig. 12.2.** Indifference curves displaying dominance.

**12.2.4. Efficient portfolios.** The calculation of the variance of a portfolio return, using Eq. (12.3), is a lengthy process requiring complete knowledge of the pairwise covariations among all component securities. For all possible portfolios, the computing task is impossibly large. Fortunately, the number of portfolios that need to be considered can be reduced greatly because of the dominance effect developed in the previous section. What one eventually discovers is a locus of efficient portfolios in the $(\bar{R}, \sigma)$ plane, on which the efficient portfolios dominate all other possible portfolios.

To develop this concept, consider a portfolio composed of only two securities, say Securities 1 and 2. Let $X_1 =$ the proportion of Security 1 in the portfolio and $X_2 = 1 - X_1 =$ the proportion of Security 2 in the portfolio (note that $\sum X_i = 1$). Let the two securities have return rates of $R_1$ and $R_2$, respectively. Then the expected return rate for the portfolio is

$$\bar{R}_P = \sum_i X_i R_i = X_1 R_1 + X_2 R_2. \tag{12.4}$$

From Eq. (12.3) the variance of the portfolio return rate is

$$\sigma_P^2 = X_1^2 \, \text{Var}(R_1) + X_2^2 \, \text{Var}(R_2) + 2X_1 X_2 \, \text{Cov}(R_1, R_2). \tag{12.5}$$

If we let Cov $(R_1, R_2) = \rho_{12}\sigma_1\sigma_2$, Var $(R_1) = \sigma_1^2$, and Var $(R_2) = \sigma_2^2$, where ,

$\rho_{12}$ = the Pearsonian correlation coefficient $(-1 \leq \rho_{ij} \leq +1)$,

$\sigma_2^2$ = the variance of the return rate on Security 1,

$\sigma_2^2$ = the variance of the return rate on Security 2,

then Eq. (12.5) becomes

$$\sigma_P^2 = X_1^2\sigma_1^2 + 2X_1X_2\rho_{12}\sigma_1\sigma_2 + X_2^2\sigma_2^2. \tag{12.6}$$

Several interesting results flow from this fundamental equation. First, we note that if $\rho_{12} = +1$, then there is perfect positive correlation between $R_1$ and $R_2$, so that Eq. (12.6) reduces to

$$\sigma_P^2 = (X_1\sigma_1 + X_2\sigma_2)^2$$

or

$$\begin{aligned} \sigma_P &= X_1\sigma_1 + X_2\sigma_2 \\ &= X_1\sigma_1 + (1 - X_1)\sigma_2 \\ &= \sigma_2 + X_1(\sigma_1 - \sigma_2). \end{aligned} \tag{12.7}$$

Equation (12.7) together with Eq. (12.4) provide an implicit relationship between $\bar{R}_P$ and $\sigma_P$, depending on the value chosen for $X_1$. Hence, on $(\bar{R}, \sigma)$ coordinates, $\bar{R}_P$ will simply be (for the case in which $\rho_{12} = +1$) a *linear* function of $\sigma_P$, as illustrated in Fig. 12.3, for the line $\rho_{12} = +1$.

As the correlation coefficient, $\rho_{12}$, becomes less than $+1$, however, the relationship between $\bar{R}_p$ and $\sigma_P$ becomes nonlinear, as Fig. 12.3 indicates, until finally it becomes possible for *two* values of expected return rate to occur for the same portfolio standard deviation $(\sigma_P)$. In the case of two possible values, the risk-avoiding investor will always prefer the portfolio with the higher expected return rate, and the portfolio mix $(X_i)$ corresponding to this point is termed the *efficient portfolio* (point $A$ in Fig. 12.3). The other portfolio $(B)$ is referred to as the *inefficient portfolio*. This follows directly from the indifference curve analysis concepts presented in Section 12.2.3 since the expected utility of Portfolio $A$ dominates Portfolio $B$.

In addition to portfolios consisting of only two securities, a third security could be added to the set. In this case, portfolios could be formed, for example, of combinations of Securities 1 and 3 and of Securities 2 and 3, which the solid lines indicate in Fig. 12.4. Furthermore, any intermediate portfolio, say $B$, could be formed of Securities 1 and 3 in Fig. 12.4; and $B$ in turn could be combined with portions of Security 2 to form portfolio combinations of these two components (the dashed line in Fig. 12.4). Since $B$ is a perfectly general combination of Securities 1 and 3, then the combination of $B$ and Security 2 is also general, and the idea can be extended to that an infinity of portfolios can be generated from Securities 1, 2, and 3. This concept is illustrated by the shaded area in Fig. 12.4. Thus, the investor is free to choose any portfolio in the feasible area.

Now, by applying the dominance effect that is generated by a risk-avoider's indifference curve, we are able to eliminate all but a few portfolios from the feasible set.

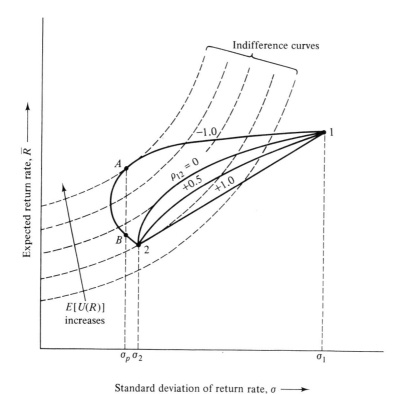

**Fig. 12.3.** Dominance in a two-security portfolio.

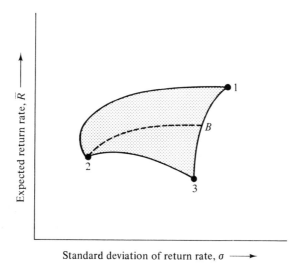

**Fig. 12.4.** Feasible combinations for a three-security portfolio.

**429**

The ones that remain are called *efficient portfolios,* and all others are said to be *inefficient.* To demonstrate this conclusion, consider again the implicit *slope* of the indifference curve given in Eqs. (10.15) and (10.16):

$$\frac{d\mu_X}{d\sigma_X} = \frac{2B\sigma_X}{A - 2B\mu_X}$$

where it is understood now that $\mu_X = \bar{R}_X$. If we take the limit of this slope as the investor's risk-aversion factor, $B$, approaches zero (i.e., as risk becomes completely acceptable to him without trade-off for increased $\mu$), we have

$$\lim_{B \to 0} \left(\frac{d\mu_X}{d\sigma_X}\right) = \lim_{B \to 0} \left(\frac{2B\sigma_X}{A - 2B\mu_X}\right) = \frac{0}{A - 0} = 0, \tag{12.8}$$

which indicates that in the limit the $E[U(X)]$ function is *horizontal* and thus *tangent* to the feasible area, say at point $D$ in Fig. 12.5.

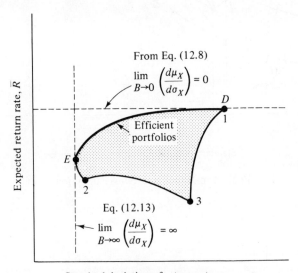

**Fig. 12.5.** *Efficient* portfolios.

Similarly, if we allow the decision-maker to become completely risk averse, then $B \longrightarrow \infty$ in the limit, and

$$\lim_{B \to \infty} \left(\frac{d\mu_X}{d\sigma_X}\right) = \lim_{B \to \infty} \left(\frac{2B\sigma_X}{A - 2B\mu_X}\right). \tag{12.9}$$

In order to take this limit, however, we note that the denominator of Eq. (12.9) is required to be nonnegative in order for the marginal utility of the decision-maker to be positive.

Hence, Eq. (12.9) above is of the form

$$\lim_{B \to \infty} \left(\frac{2B\sigma_X}{A - 2B\mu_X}\right) = \lim_{B \to \infty} \left(\frac{\infty}{\infty - \infty}\right),$$

which is an indeterminate form. This can be remedied by first taking the limit of the reciprocal, or

$$\lim_{B \to \infty} \left( \frac{d\sigma_X}{d\mu_X} \right) = \lim_{B \to \infty} \left( \frac{A - 2B\mu_X}{2B\sigma_X} \right) = \lim_{B \to \infty} \left( \frac{A}{2B\sigma_X} - \frac{\mu_X}{\sigma_X} \right), \quad (12.10)$$

and noting that this is of the form

$$\lim_{B \to \infty} \left( \frac{\infty}{\infty} - k \right) = \lim_{B \to \infty} \left( \frac{\infty}{\infty} \right), \quad (12.11)$$

where $k =$ any *finite* value of $\mu_X/\sigma_X$. Then by applying l'Hôpital's rule to Eq. (12.10), we have

$$\lim_{B \to \infty} \left( \frac{d\sigma_X}{d\mu_X} \right) = \lim_{B \to \infty} \frac{\frac{d}{dc}(A)}{\frac{d}{dx}(2B\sigma_X)} = \frac{0}{2\sigma_X} = 0. \quad (12.12)$$

The fact that the derivative $d\sigma_X/d\mu_X = 0$ in the limit, as $B \to \infty$, implies that the reciprocal $d\mu_X/d\sigma_X$ is undefined or that

$$\frac{d\mu_X}{d\sigma_X} = \frac{1}{d\sigma_X/d\mu_X} = \infty. \quad (12.13)$$

Thus, the expected utility function, $E[U(X)]$, has an infinite slope when the decision-maker is a complete risk avoider ($B = \infty$), and this fact is indicated in Fig. 12.5 by the vertical asymptote at point $E$ on the feasible set of portfolios.

The infinity of portfolios lying on the arc connecting points $D$ and $E$ in Fig. 12.5 will be the efficient portfolios since they dominate all other feasible portfolios for *all* finite values of the risk-avoidance constant ($0 < B < \infty$). This was implicitly proved by examining the limiting conditions of the expected utility function, $E[U(X)]$, for $B = 0$ and $B = \infty$. Along this efficient portfolio set, or *efficiency frontier* as it is sometimes called, the decision-maker will *choose* a portfolio that is consistent with *his* particular risk-aversion factor, $B$, where the possible values of $B$ lie in the range $0 < B < \infty$. Thus, in Fig. 12.6, one decision-maker, say $G$, will maximize *his* expected utility by choosing some portfolio $G_{max}$, while another decision-maker, say $H$, will maximize *his* expected utility by choosing portfolio $H_{max}$.

**12.2.5. Combinations of risky and riskless assets.** The second major assumption of capital market theory permits all investors to borrow or lend an unlimited amount of money in the market at a given risk-free rate of interest. The term *risk free* is not in actuality correct. There is no such thing as a riskless asset. A preferable term is a *virtually default-free* asset. For example, short-term U.S. Treasury bills, usually of no more than 1-year maturity, are considered virtually default free. This is due to the government's power to raise money by taxes and to print currency. Hence, when a *risk-free* rate is used, the term *virtually default free* is implied. The relaxation of this assumption causes no major insurmountable problems. The current value of a default-free rate is assumed to be around 5–6%, but whether such a value can be taken as a constant is arguable. The risk-free interest rate, since it is assumed to have *zero* risk ($\sigma = 0$), can be plotted on $R_P$, $\sigma_P$ coordinates and is a point on the expected return

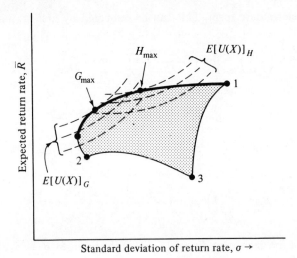

**Fig. 12.6.** Choice of portfolios along efficient frontier by indifference curves.

axis since it is assumed to have zero variance. The risk-free rate is denoted by $R_f$ and is plotted as a point on the $(\bar{R}, 0)$ axis.

Fama [5] points out that borrowing or lending at the risk-free rate, $R_f$, can be coupled with investment in any risky security or portfolio. Consider in Fig. 12.7, for example, some portfolio $C$ involving combinations of a default-free asset returning $R_f$ and an arbitrary Security $A$, with expected return $\bar{R}_A$ and standard deviation of return $\sigma_A$. The expected return and standard deviation of return for the combined Portfolio $C$ are

$$\bar{R}_C = XR_f + (1 - X)\bar{R}_A \qquad (X \leq 1), \qquad (12.14)$$

$$\sigma_C = (1 - X)\sigma_A + X\sigma_f = (1 - X)\sigma_A, \qquad (12.15)$$

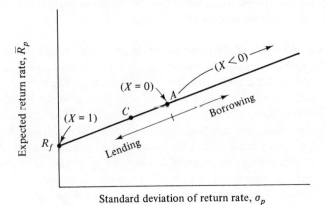

**Fig. 12.7.** Combination of any portfolio and the riskless asset.

where $X$ is the proportion of available funds invested in the risk-free security at the risk-free rate, $R_f$, and $(1 - X)$ is the proportion invested in Security $A$. Applying the chain rule of differentiation to Eqs. (12.14) and (12.15), we obtain

$$\frac{d\sigma_C}{d\bar{R}_C} = \frac{d\sigma_C}{dX}\frac{dX}{d\bar{R}_C} = \frac{\sigma_A}{\bar{R}_A - R_f}. \tag{12.16}$$

The form of this equation implies that all combinations of the riskless asset and the risky Security $A$ will result in a linear trade-off between the risk ($\sigma_C$) of the portfolio and its expected return ($\bar{R}_C$) since Eq. (12.16) is of linear form ($\sigma_A$ and $\bar{R}_A$ are expectations, and $R_f$ is assumed to be a constant). Thus, in Fig. 12.7, portfolios such as $C$ will lie on a straight line connecting $R_f$ and $A$, or an extension of that line. Portfolios lying between $R_f$ and $A$ involve the *lending* of the firm's funds at rate $R_f$ (since $0 \le X \le 1$). That is, an investor (such as the firm) invests a portion of its money in Security $A$ and lends the rest of it by purchasing riskless assets (i.e., default-free bonds). Points lying beyond $A$ involve the borrowing of funds ($X < 0$). An investor will invest all his available funds in Security $A$ and borrow more funds at the risk-free rate by selling default-free bonds and investing these funds in Security $A$. For $X = 0$, the investor invests all his available funds in Security $A$, without borrowing or lending outside funds. For $X = 1$, the investor uses only his own funds to purchase the riskless asset, yielding the return rate $R_f$. This case is the one in which all funds are "lent" at the riskless rate $R_f$.

**12.2.6. *The capital market line.*** Since it is possible to combine borrowing or lending with any arbitrary portfolio (Fama demonstrated this), it is possible to combine borrowing or lending with a portfolio on the efficient frontier of risky portfolios. For example, it is possible to connect the point $(R_f, 0)$ with the efficient frontier of risky portfolios by means of a straight line, as is shown in Fig. 12.8. The line is

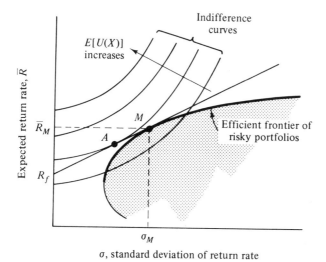

**Fig. 12.8.** The capital market line.

tangent to the efficient frontier at some point $(\bar{R}_M, \sigma_M)$, denoted by $M$ in Fig. 12.8. The point of tangency, $M$, describes an optimal portfolio of risky securities since by the application of indifference curve analysis any combination of the risky portfolio, $M$, plus borrowing or lending at the riskless rate, $R_f$, will dominate all other possible portfolios lying along the efficient frontier. The particular optimal investment for an investor will lie somewhere along the line $\overline{R_f M}$, as dictated by the investor's indifference curves (see Fig. 12.8). His optimal portfolio, consisting of a fraction $X_M$ of portfolio $M$ and a fraction $(1 - X_M)$ of the riskless asset, would be at, say, point $A$ in the diagram. If $X_M = 0$, corresponding to no investment in $M$, then his optimum would be at $R_f$. If $X_M = 1$, however, then his optimum portfolio would be at $(\bar{R}_M, \sigma_M)$, i.e., at point $M$. The concept of concern here is that the *proportion* of funds invested in the risky portfolio $(X_M)$ versus the *proportion* invested in the riskless asset, $(1 - X_M)$, is determined by the investor's indifference function that is tangent to the line $\overline{R_f M}$.

The point $M$ has a special interpretation. It is called the *market portfolio*, whose mean return rate and standard deviation are $(\bar{R}_M, \sigma_M)$. It needs to be demonstrated that $M$ is, in fact, the market portfolio; that is, a portfolio composed of *all* securities in the market, in which the $i$th security is included in the portfolio at a relative level $X_i$, so that when all securities are included, $\sum_i X_i \equiv 1$. This demonstration proceeds as follows.

Recalling from the third assumption of capital asset pricing theory that *all investors are assumed to view all securities in the same way*, we can consequently assert that *all investors will hold equal proportions of all securities in an equilibrium market*. This propostion can be demonstrated by assumption and contradiction. If this assumption were false, so that the optimal combination of securities contained a different proportion of securities than the portfolio representing the entire market, then all investors would try to hold different proportions of securities than those available in the market portfolio. Equilibrium in the market makes it impossible for this to be done. Therefore, portfolio $M$ will be the optimal combination of risky securities that is available in the market and is called the *market portfolio*. The line connecting the risk-free rate, $R_f$, and the market portfolio, $(\bar{R}_M, \sigma_M)$, is called the *capital market line* and represents all linear combinations of portfolios composed of the market portfolio, $M$, and the risk-free asset, $R_f$.

The equation of the capital market line can be written in linear form, as follows:

$$\bar{R}_M = R_f + \lambda \sigma_M \qquad (12.17)$$

where $\lambda = $ a proportionality constant, which we presently interpret as the premium required for incurring additional risk for a finite-variance portfolio; i.e., one having an assessable risk, such as $\sigma_M$.

$\bar{R}_M = $ expected return of the market portfolio.

$\sigma_M = $ standard deviation or risk of the market portfolio.

This equation says simply that the expected return on the *market* portfolio is a linear function of the market portfolio standard deviation (risk); and the function in Eq. (12.17) is referred to as the *capital market line*. Financially, it represents the locus of expected returns and standard deviations of return for all investors who invest a portion of their funds in the market portfolio and the remainder of which are borrowed or lent at the riskless rate, $R_f$.

**12.2.7. *Individual securities and investments.*** While a theoretical capital market line—i.e., one that hypothesizes a linear relationship between the expected return of the *market* portfolio and the standard deviation of the market return rate (the riskiness of the market)—is certainly a simplifying concept in financial theory, it tells us nothing about the prospective behavior of the firm when confronted with decisions concerning prospective investment projects. The reason is that the firm does not invest in the *market* portfolio or in combinations of the market portfolio and riskless assets. On the contrary, the firm invests in *discrete projects*, whose return rates are probably far removed from the leveling effects of the market. Hence, we need to know something about individual investments and specific combinations of individual investments in individual portfolios.

To investigate the behavior of individual securities, consider the following development. Suppose an investor wished to divide his funds in some way between some security $j$ and the market portfolio so as to form a new portfolio, $A$ (see Fig. 12.9). The composition of this new portfolio, $A$, would be represented by some point on a line connecting the point $(\bar{R}_j, \sigma_j)$ for the security and the point $(\bar{R}_M, \sigma_M)$ representing the market portfolio. The shape of the connecting curve would again depend on the value of the correlation coefficient, $\rho_{jM}$, between the security and the market portfolio; and the position of the point value $(\bar{R}_A, \sigma_A)$ of the resultant portfolio would depend on the relative amounts invested.

Equations (12.2) and (12.3) can again be used as functions to define the implicit slope $d\bar{R}/d\sigma$ of the security-market line. The portfolio would be a combination of the

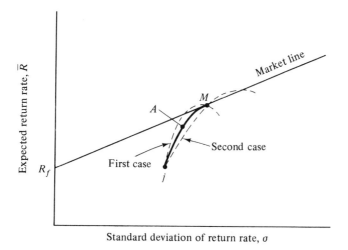

**Fig. 12.9.** Combination of any security and the market portfolio.

market portfolio, $M$, and Security $j$. Let $X_j =$ the amount of resources invested in Security $j$ and $(1 - X_j) =$ the amount invested in the market portfolio, $M$. Using the chain rule and Eqs. (12.2) and (12.3), the slope of the curve, $jM$, can be calculated at any point (such as $A$); thus:

$$\frac{d\bar{R}_A}{d\sigma_A} = \frac{d\bar{R}_A}{dX_j} \cdot \frac{dX_j}{d\sigma_A} \tag{12.18}$$

From Eq. (12.2)[2] we have

$$\frac{d\bar{R}_A}{dX_j} = \bar{R}_j - \bar{R}_M; \tag{12.19}$$

and from Eq. (12.3):[3]

$$\frac{dX_j}{d\sigma_A} = \frac{\sigma_A}{X_j[\sigma_j^2 + \sigma_M^2 - 2\,\text{Cov}\,(R_j, R_M)] + \text{Cov}\,(R_j, R_M) - \sigma_M^2}. \tag{12.20}$$

On substituting Eqs. (12.19) and (12.20) into Eq. (12.18), we have

$$\frac{d\bar{R}_A}{d\sigma_A} = \frac{(\bar{R}_j - \bar{R}_M)\sigma_A}{X_j[\sigma_j^2 + \sigma_M^2 - 2\,\text{Cov}\,(R_j, R_M)] + \text{Cov}\,(R_j, R_M) - \sigma_M^2}.$$

At point $M$ (the market portfolio point), it is known that $X_j = 0$ (by definition) and $\sigma_A^2 = \sigma_M^2$. Hence, at point $M$ the slope of $jM$ is

$$\left.\frac{\partial\bar{R}_A}{\partial\sigma_A}\right|_{X_j=0} = \frac{\sigma_M}{\text{Cov}\,(R_j, R_M) - \sigma_M^2}(\bar{R}_j - \bar{R}_M). \tag{12.21}$$

Now, it is required that the slope of the curve $jM$ be tangent to the market line at point $M$. To see why, consider the following cases. First, if the slope of $jM$ were flatter

---

[2]For the two-component case, $X_j =$ the proportion of funds invested in the $j$th security and $X_M = (1 - X_j) =$ the proportion of funds invested in the market portfolio. Hence, from Eq. (12.2),

$$\bar{R}_P = \bar{R}_A = X_j\bar{R}_j + (1 - X_j)\bar{R}_M$$

and, differentiating,

$$\frac{d\bar{R}_A}{dX_j} = \bar{R}_j - \bar{R}_M,$$

which is Eq. (12.17).

[3]Also, for the two component case, Eq. (12.3) reduces to

$$\sigma_A^2 = X_j^2\sigma_j^2 + (1 - X_j)^2\sigma_M^2 + 2X_j(1 - X_j)C_{JM}$$

where $X_j =$ proportion of funds invested in Security $j$.

$1 - X_j = X_M =$ proportion of funds invested in market portfolio.

$C_{JM} = \text{Cov}\,(R_j R_M) =$ covariance of $j$th security return rate and the market return rate.

By taking the square root, we have

$$\sigma_A = [X_j^2\sigma_j^2 + (1 - X_j)^2\sigma_M^2 + 2X_j(1 - X_j)C_{JM}]^{1/2}$$

and then, by differentiating with respect to $X$, we have

$$\frac{d\sigma_A}{dX} = \frac{X_j(\sigma_j^2 + \sigma_M^2 - 2C_{JM}) + C_{JM} - \sigma_M^2}{\sigma_A}$$

which is the inverse of Eq. (12.20).

than the market line at $M$, the line $jM$ would intersect the market line to the left of $M$, and there would be at least one portfolio on the curve $jM$ that would be *better* than the market line combination of $R_f$ and $M$. This is impossible since all investors would attempt to purchase that combination and the market price would rise. Second, if the slope of $jM$ were steeper than the market line at point $M$, then there would also be a *better* portfolio beyond $M$ that would likewise attract buyers. This situation is also impossible. Hence, the only situation that can obtain *under equilibrium conditions* is for the curve $jM$ to be tangent at point $M$ to the capital market line.

Under these conditions (market equilibrium), the *slopes* of the capital market line and the security portfolio line ($jM$) are equal or, in symbolic terms,

$$\frac{\bar{R}_M - R_f}{\sigma_M} = \frac{\sigma_M(\bar{R}_j - \bar{R}_M)}{\text{Cov}(R_j, R_M) - \sigma_M^2}, \tag{12.22}$$

where the left side of Eq. (12.22) is the slope of the capital market line from Eq. (12.18) and the right-hand side is the slope of the curve $jM$ [from Eq. (12.21)]. By simplifying and rearranging the terms of Eq. (12.22), we have

$$\bar{R}_j - R_f = \frac{\text{Cov}(R_j, R_M)}{\sigma_M^2}(\bar{R}_M - R_f). \tag{12.23}$$

This is the sought-for relationship and *holds in the vicinity of M*. The term on the left is the *reward* for bearing risk—the excess of the $j$th security's return rate over the default-free interest rate. From Eq. (12.23) this reward is simply some constant, $\text{Cov}(R_j, R_M)/\sigma_M^2$, times the expected premium required by the market as a whole, $(\bar{R}_M - R_f)$. The constant multiplier is simply the value of $\lambda$ in Eq. (12.8); hence

$$\lambda = \frac{\text{Cov}(R_j, R_M)}{\sigma_M^2}. \tag{12.24}$$

Thus, the expectation of the risk premium required for investing marginally in some $j$th security is simply a *multiple* of the expected *market* risk premium, where the multiplier is the relative covariance, $\text{Cov}(R_j, R_M)/\sigma_M^2$.

This multiplier, which relates an individual security's expected risk premium to the expected risk premium of the market itself, is called the *volatility* of Security $j$. It is taken to be a constant for a given security and is denoted as $\beta_j$, or $\beta_j = C_{jM}/\sigma_M^2$ where $C_{jM} = \text{Cov}(R_j, R_M)$. On substituting $\beta_j$ into Eq. (12.23), we have

$$\bar{R}_j - R_f = \beta_j(\bar{R}_M - R_f). \tag{12.25}$$

Equation (12.25) is called the *capital asset pricing model*.

$\beta_j$, the volatility constant for the $j$th security, is also the appropriate measure of risk for an *individual security*. This is because of the fact that the individual security is assumed to be correlated *only* with the market portfolio, $M$. $\beta_j$ relates the covariance of each security to the variance of the market portfolio, for a marginal investment in the security. Thus, *the problem of an appropriate measure of risk for an individual security is approached through the use of the volatility concept*.

Since it is an important concept, more should be said of the nature of $\beta_j$, the volatility. The market return, $R_M$, is taken to be a random variable with mean $\bar{R}_M$ and variance $\sigma_M^2$. Hence the market risk premium, $R_M - R_f$, is also a random variable. If a security exhibits a $\beta_j$ greater than 1, an increase in the random market risk premium will mean an even greater increase in the expected premium for the security. Similarly, a decrease of greater magnitude would occur in the expected return of the security when the expected market premium decreases. When $\beta_j < 1$, the increase or decrease in the risk premium for a particular security is less than that of the expected market premium. Thus it is that $\beta_j$ is described as the *volatility* of the *j*th security.

**12.2.8.** *Regression model of the security line.* Equation (12.25), the equation of the *j*th *security* return rate (or, the *j*th portfolio return rate also) in terms of the expected *market* return rate, is unfortunately never observable in actuality, so we cannot assess its validity directly. By statistical methods, however, we can examine it evidentially. To demonstrate how this can be done, we shall discuss the individual factors in Eq. (12.25) and how they are related and measured.

Characteristically, the default-free interest rate ($R_f$) is taken to be a constant. Over long periods of time, it has been observed (via the returns on short-term government bonds) that $R_f$ typically takes on values in the range of 4–6% in the market. Because of its small variability over time, finance theorists generally assume $R_f$ to be a known constant,[4] on the order of about 5%. We shall assume for our purposes that $R_f$ is a constant and that it is either known or can be satisfactorily approximated for a particular span of time of interest.

The other factors in Eq. (12.25) are $R_j$, $R_M$, and $\beta_j$. If $R_j$ and $R_M$ are viewed as correlated *random* variables,[5] for which data are available, then we may estimate $\beta_j$, the volatility of the *j*th security (or portfolio or project). The essentials of the estimating procedure are based on the following premises:

1. Both $R_j$ and $R_M$ are assumed to be bivariate random variables in a time series, with observable (*ex post*) values $R_{jt}$ and $R_{Mt}$ at times $t$ ($t = 1, 2, \ldots, n$). Finite means and variances for both $R_j$ and $R_M$ are assumed, and the two variables are assumed to be correlated with a covariance, Cov ($R_j$, $R_M$).
2. If it is assumed that $R_{jt}$ is distributed conditionally upon assumed *fixed* values of $R_{Mt}$, we may investigate the nature of the corelationship by regression techniques.[6] For our purposes, this is a reasonable requirement since our objective is to predict values for $R_{jt}$ based upon assumed future market values of $R_{Mt}$.

---

[4]There is some evidence that $R_f$ may not be constant over time (see, for example, Breen and Lerner [2]); however, the methodology purporting to show time instability is also in dispute (see Myers [14]).

[5]Note that *random* variables, $R_j$ and $R_M$, have taken the place of the *expected values*, $\bar{R}_j$ and $\bar{R}_M$, in Eq. (12.25). This is not a trivial transformation. It is done in order to use *ex post* data to evaluate basically what is an *ex ante* proposition [Eq. (12.25)]. The explanation of the reason why this transformation can be made is beyond the scope of this chapter but may be found in detail in Jensen [9], pp. 177–82.

[6]This is Case 3, Model 3 of Graybill ([6], pp. 217–20).

Noting that a constant, $R_f$, can be subtracted from the random variables $R_j$ and $R_M$ without changing the fundamental *random* nature of these variables, the time-series regression form of Eq. (12.25) becomes

$$(R_{jt} - R_f) = \alpha_j + \beta_j(R_{Mt} - R_f) + \epsilon_{jt} \tag{12.26}$$

where $R_{jt} =$ random return rate on Security $j$ at time $t$.

$\qquad R_{Mt} =$ random return rate on the market portfolio $(M)$ at time $t$.

$\qquad R_f =$ the fixed default-free interest rate.

$\qquad \alpha_j =$ an unknown intercept parameter.

$\qquad \beta_j =$ the unknown *volatility* of the $j$th return premium to the market premium.

$\qquad \epsilon_{jt} =$ a random error term, assumed normally distributed with mean of zero and variance of $\sigma_\epsilon^2$; also, $\epsilon_{jt}$ has certain special properties described below.

The error term, $\epsilon_{jt}$, in Eq. (12.26) has certain special properties that are of fundamental importance in the Sharpe-Lintner model. In addition to the two general properties that are usually assigned to $\epsilon_{jt}$ in typical regression models (Normal distribution with zero mean and finite variance, $\sigma_\epsilon^2$), the powerful nature of the Sharpe-Lintner model derives from a third property attributed to $\epsilon_{jt}$. All three of these properties will be examined so that the essential basis of the regression model can be fully displayed.

Consider the case involving two securities, $i$ and $j$, whose regression functions with the market return would be given by separate models of Eq. (12.26). The first property of the random error terms, $\epsilon_{it}$ and $\epsilon_{jt}$, is one that is usually assumed in regression models; namely,

$$E(\epsilon_{it}) = 0; \qquad E(\epsilon_{jt}) = 0. \tag{12.27}$$

The second property, also a usual assumption in time-series regressions, is that the error terms are uncorrelated timewise; thus

$$\left.\begin{array}{l} \text{Cov}\,(\epsilon_{i,t}, \epsilon_{i,t-1}) = 0 \\ \text{Cov}\,(\epsilon_{j,t}, \epsilon_{j,t-1}) = 0 \end{array}\right\} \tag{12.28}$$

The third, and special property of $\epsilon_{it}$ and $\epsilon_{jt}$, for our case, is that

$$\text{Cov}\,(\epsilon_{it}, \epsilon_{jt}) = \begin{cases} \text{Var}\,(\epsilon_{it}) = \sigma_\epsilon^2, & \text{for } i = j \\ 0, & \text{for } i \neq j \end{cases}. \tag{12.29}$$

This latter property is the result of an assumption made by Markowitz [12], concerning the covariance of the random returns for two securities, in order to simplify calculations. The nature of this assumption can be developed as follows. For two related securities, $i$ and $j$, the covariance of their return rates ($R_i$ and $R_j$) can be written in expanded form as the expectation of the product of the deviations from their respective means, thus:

$$\begin{aligned} \text{Cov}\,(R_i R_j) &= E[(R_i - \bar{R}_i)(R_j - \bar{R}_j)] \\ &= E[(\alpha_i + \beta_i R_M + \epsilon_i - \alpha_i - \beta_i \bar{R}_M)(\alpha_j + \beta_j R_M + \epsilon_j - \alpha_j - \beta_j \bar{R}_M)] \\ &= E\{[\beta_i(R_m - \bar{R}_M) + \epsilon_i][\beta_j(R_M - \bar{R}_M) + \epsilon_j]\}; \end{aligned} \tag{12.30}$$

and if we let $(R_M - \bar{R}_M) = r_M$, then

$$\text{Cov}(R_i R_j) = E[\beta_i \beta_j r_M^2 + \beta_j r_M \epsilon_i + \beta_i r_M \epsilon_j + \epsilon_i \epsilon_j]$$
$$= \beta_i \beta_j V[R_M] + \beta_j \text{ Cov}(R_M \epsilon_i) + \beta_i \text{ Cov}(R_M \epsilon_j) + \text{Cov}(\epsilon_i \epsilon_j). \tag{12.31}$$

Since the Sharpe-Lintner model assumes that the entire relationship between the random $R_i$ and $R_M$ is contained in Eq. (12.26), then there is no covariance between the error term and the market return; that is, it assumes

$$\text{Cov}(R_M \epsilon_i) = \text{Cov}(R_M \epsilon_j) = 0.$$

As a consequence, Eq. (12.31) reduces to

$$\text{Cov}(R_i R_j) = \beta_i \beta_j V[R_M] + \text{Cov}(\epsilon_i \epsilon_j). \tag{12.32}$$

Now the factor $\beta_i \beta_j V[R_M]$ in Eq. (12.32) expresses the portion of the covariance that is attributable to the market variance itself, and the factor $\text{Cov}(\epsilon_i \epsilon_j)$ expresses the portion of the covariance of $R_i$ and $R_j$ *not accounted for by the market* variability. It is this latter factor, $\text{Cov}(\epsilon_i \epsilon_j)$, that Markowitz ([12], p. 100, footnote) suggested be *assumed equal to zero*, in order to reduce the size of the calculating problem for a portfolio of correlated securities. If this is done, then Eq. (12.32) becomes simply

$$\text{Cov}(R_i R_j) = \beta_i \beta_j V[R_M]. \tag{12.33}$$

Thus, Eq. (12.33) leads to the special property of the error covariance stated in Eq. (12.29); namely,

$$\text{Cov}(\epsilon_i \epsilon_j) = \begin{cases} \text{Var}(\epsilon_i) = \sigma_\epsilon^2, & \text{for } i = j \\ 0, & \text{for } i \neq j \end{cases}.$$

In summary, the substance of this third property attributed to the error term in Eq. (12.33) is that after accounting for the relationship of each security return rate with the market return rate, *no further relationship between any two securities*, say $i$ and $j$, exists.

Returning now to the regression model developed in Eq. (12.26), to simplify notation, let $R'_{jt} = R_{jt} - R_f$ and $R'_{Mt} = R_{Mt} - R_f$. Equation (12.26) then becomes

$$R'_{jt} = \alpha_j + \beta_j R'_{Mt} + \epsilon_{jt}, \tag{12.34}$$

which is simply a straightforward regression model in terms of the *premiums* required by the market and security return rates, respectively.[7] In this model, the parameters $\alpha_j$ and $\beta_j$ are not observable but can be estimated. The estimated linear function corresponding to Eq. (12.34) is

$$\hat{R}'_j = \hat{\alpha}_j + \hat{\beta}_j R'_M \tag{12.35}$$

where $\hat{R}'_j$, $\hat{\alpha}_j$, and $\hat{\beta}_j$ are estimates of the corresponding unknown parameters in Eq. (12.34). The method of least squares leads to unbiased, minimum variance, point estimates of $\alpha_j$ and $\beta_j$ via the normal equations.[8] These estimates are

---

[7]Again, this is Case 3, Model 3 of Graybill [6] and is handled in the same manner as Case 1 (see [6], p. 104), which is commonly called the *linear model of full rank.*

[8]See any good text on linear models; for example, Neter and Wasserman [15], pp. 30–44.

$$\hat{\beta}_j = \frac{\sum (R'_{Mt} - \bar{R}'_M)(R'_{jt} - \bar{R}'_j)}{\sum (R'_{Mt} - \bar{R}'_M)^2} \tag{12.36}$$

and

$$\hat{\alpha}_j = \bar{R}'_j - \hat{\beta}_j \bar{R}'_M. \tag{12.37}$$

The unbiased estimates in Eqs. (12.36) and (12.37) now lead us to an interpretation of the capital asset pricing model in terms of observable data. First we note that $\hat{\alpha}_j$ is an intercept estimate that, if $R_f$ has been chosen correctly and if it remains constant over time, should be zero. A zero value for $\hat{\alpha}_j$ would be evidence tending to support the capital asset pricing model. If a significant nonzero value for $\hat{\alpha}_j$ were found, there would be evidence that the Sharpe-Lintner model (in its simplest form) is not adequate. Significant nonzero values have been found in several empirical tests of the model, which tends to show that the most basic model (which we have examined here) is not a completely descriptive model of securities behavior.[9] Because of its simplicity, however, we shall retain it for consideration as a basis for project selection.

To continue the examination of the regression model, we note that the right-hand side of Eq. (12.36) is simply the estimated covariance of the return rate of the $j$th security and the market return rate, divided by the estimated variance of the market rate itself. That is,

$$\hat{\beta}_j = \frac{\sum (R'_{Mt} - \bar{R}'_M)(R'_{jt} - \bar{R}'_j)}{\sum (R'_{Mt} - \bar{R}'_M)^2} = \frac{\text{Cov}(R'_j R'_M)}{\hat{V}(R'_M)}. \tag{12.38}$$

Since $\hat{\beta}_j$ is an estimator of $\beta_j$ for the $j$th security, $\beta_j$ is often referred to as the *systematic risk* or *volatility* of the $j$th security. It represents the extent to which the return rate on Security $j$ *covaries* with the market rate, or the *system* rate. The balance of the risk associated with the return rate on Security $j$ is represented by the error term in Eq. (12.34) or Eq. (12.26). This is a residual risk, unique to the individual security, which is not priced by the market. Total risk, therefore, is said to be made up of *systematic risk* (security volatility) plus *residual risk*. Systematic risk is generally taken to be the risk associated with fluctuations in the economy on the security market as a whole, whereas residual risk is the remaining risk assumed to be peculiar to and associated with a particular security that is not accounted for by market factors.

In portfolio theory, it is assumed that *residual* risk can be minimized by the choice of a diversified portfolio, in which the residual risk of one security tends to offset (in the opposite direction) the residual risk of another investment. This can be intuitively seen if one realizes that as the diversity of a given portfolio approaches that of the market by including more and more types of securities, then the *residual* risk of the portfolio approaches that of the market itself, which is zero.

On the other hand, it is nearly impossible to eliminate *systematic* risk, or volatility, in a portfolio. The reason is that most securities and projects display returns that are positively correlated with market returns. [One notable exception is the case of gold mining stocks, which typically display return rates that are negatively correlated with market return rates. Such shares have negative values of $\hat{\beta}_j$ (Campanella [3], pp. 28–

---

[9]See Jensen [8], pp. 363–67, for a survey of recent empirical tests of the linear Sharpe-Lintner model.

29), and their return rates typically move opposite to the market trend]. For the reason that systematic risk, or volatility $(\beta_j)$, *cannot* be eliminated by diversification, volatility becomes an attractive measure for valuing a security or project that is a candidate for acquisition. This is the basis of the *project selection aspects* of capital asset pricing theory, which will be examined in the next sections.

## 12.3. Risk Equivalency

One should recall that any Security $j$ can be represented as a point on $(\bar{R}_j, \sigma_j)$ coordinates, where $\bar{R}_j$ is the expected return rate of the $j$th security and $\sigma_j$ is the standard deviation of its return rate. Furthermore, as we have seen, the risky security can be combined in a portfolio with the riskless asset, whose return rate is $R_f$. The resulting portfolio will have an expected return rate that lies on a straight line (see Fig. 12.10) connecting the point $(R_f, 0)$ and the point $J$, representing the risky portfolio with parameters $(\bar{R}_j, \sigma_j)$.

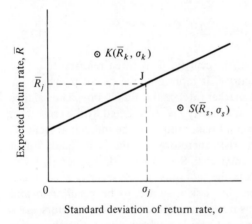

**Fig. 12.10.** Combination of the firm's own security and the riskless asset.

Now, consider that Security $j$ represents the firm's *own* equity shares. That is, if we look at $(\bar{R}_j, \sigma_j)$ as the mean return rate and standard deviation of return rate *of the firm itself*, then the straight line $\overline{RJ}$ in Fig. 12.10 becomes a market-established project selection criterion. All projects, such as $K$, having values $(\bar{R}_k, \sigma_k)$ lying *above* the firm's market line would yield expected return rates greater than those required by the firm's shareholders in the marketplace, and acceptance of such projects would increase the market value of the firm. Conversely, projects such as $S$, with return rate values of $(\bar{R}_s, \sigma_s)$, lying below the firm's market line would tend to reduce the market value of the firm and should be rejected. Hence, the firm's own market line is an *exogenously* determined project selection criterion—its parameters $(\bar{R}_j, \sigma_j)$ are explicitly determined in the financial marketplace by the collective evaluations placed on the stock prices and dividend policies by the firm's investors. From a practical standpoint, the firm's market line is an ideal project selection criterion, but there are some problems also. These are mainly theoretical in nature.

The market develops a current risk level, say $\sigma_0$, on the *equity* return rate for the firm. That is, there is a certain level of $\sigma_0$ established by the market, which is representative of the current pricing of the firm's shares and its current and expected future dividend policies. Furthermore, each individual investment project that is a candidate for acceptance by the firm has its own riskiness. As each project is accepted and invested, the riskiness and equity price structure of the firm would be altered (however slightly), thereby changing the risk level of the firm and, hence, the firm's market trade-off point. This difference between project risk and the firm's risk also forces the need for moving from one indifference function to another in order to determine the desirability of one return-risk combination against another. Tuttle and Litzenberger [20] have proposed a method of risk adjustment to achieve a *risk equivalency* of the proposed project and the firm's residual return to equity. The purpose of this adjustment is to leave the market price of the firm's shares unchanged. This is accomplished by combining borrowing or lending with equity capital to finance the proposed project.

To illustrate this approach, consider a project alternative, *I*, under consideration by the firm, with an expected return rate and estimated standard deviation of return rate. Let

$\bar{R}_z$ = the expected return rate to *equity* from the project.

$\sigma_z$ = the estimated standard deviation of the return rate to equity.

$R_f$ = the risk-free borrowing and lending rate.

$\alpha$ = the financing ratio of the project, i.e., unity plus the project's debt-equity ratio $(1 + D/E)$, where debt is either borrowed or lent.

$\bar{R}_i$ = expected return rate from Project *i*.

$\sigma_i$ = expected standard deviation of return from Project *i*.

The estimate of the risk on the return rate to equity (since $\sigma_f = 0$) is then

$$\sigma_z = \alpha \sigma_i. \tag{12.39}$$

When $\alpha$ dollars per dollar of equity are invested in a project and $(\alpha - 1)$ dollars are borrowed per dollar of equity, the expected return on equity from the project is $\alpha \bar{R}_i$, and the cost of borrowing is $(\alpha - 1)R_f$. From the fact that the total return is composed of the return to equity plus the return to borrowed capital, then the expected return rate to equity is

$$\bar{R}_z = \bar{R}_i + (\alpha - 1)\bar{R}_i - (\alpha - 1)R_f, \tag{12.40}$$

which simplifies to

$$\bar{R}_z = R_f + \alpha(\bar{R}_i - R_f). \tag{12.41}$$

Recalling the form of Eq. (12.39), we can write Eq. (12.41) in the form

$$\bar{R}_z = R_f + (\bar{R}_i - R_f)\left(\frac{\sigma_z}{\sigma_i}\right). \tag{12.42}$$

Differentiating the expected return rate with respect to the standard deviation, $\sigma_z$, we have

$$\frac{d\bar{R}_z}{d\sigma_z} = \frac{(\bar{R}_i - R_f)}{\sigma_i}. \tag{12.43}$$

Now, there exists some factor ($\alpha'$) that, when multiplied by the risk of the investment project, $\sigma_i$, will equate $\alpha'\sigma_i$ with the *current* risk of the firm, $\sigma_0$. Thus, we define

$$\sigma_0 = \alpha'\sigma_i \tag{12.44}$$

and

$$\alpha' = \frac{\sigma_0}{\sigma_i}. \tag{12.45}$$

The risk effect of a project on the firm's return rate to equity may be equalized either through long-term lending of an amount equal to $[(1/\alpha') - 1]$ of the cost of the investment project if $\sigma_i > \sigma_0$, or the long-term borrowing of $[1 - (1/\alpha')]$ of the cost of the project if $\sigma_i < \alpha_0$. The risk-adjusted expected return rate on an investment project, $\bar{R}_i$, is

$$\bar{R}'_i = R_f + \alpha'(\bar{R}_i - R_f) \tag{12.46}$$

or

$$\bar{R}'_i = R_f + \left(\frac{\sigma_0}{\sigma_i}\right)(\bar{R}_i - R_f), \tag{12.47}$$

which is a *linear* relationship.

Figure 12.11 illustrates the risk adjustment procedure of Tuttle and Litzenberger. Point $I$ is the return-risk combination of Project $I$. Point 0 is the current return-risk level of the firm. Through borrowing or lending (in this example, borrowing) at the risk-free rate, $R_f$, the return-risk level of Project $I$ can be equalized with the risk level of the firm. This equalization occurs at point $I'$. Thus in this case, Project I would be accepted as it yields a greater return than the firm is currently receiving on its investments at the firm's current risk level.

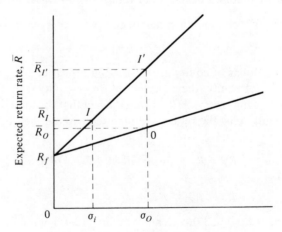

**Fig. 12.11.** Risk adjustment of a project.

## 12.4. Reward-to-Volatility Selection Criterion

As illustrated in Fig. 12.11, a project will be accepted if the *slope* of its risk equal-ization line, connecting the coordinate point $(\bar{R}_i, \sigma_i)$ of the project with the riskless asset point $(R_f, 0)$, exceeds the slope of the firm's security line. Such projects will be preferred by the firm whether or not the projects are risk equalized since all points on the project line would lie on a higher indifference curve than the firm's shares them-selves. The slopes of these lines can be calculated by Eq. (12.43). They can then be compared and used in a decision criterion for the firm. The resulting criterion is

Accept the project if
$$\frac{(R_i - R_f)}{\sigma_i} > \frac{(R_0 - R_f)}{\sigma_0}. \qquad (12.48)$$

If the firm wishes to risk equalize, the criterion becomes

$$\frac{(R_i' - R_f)}{\sigma_i'} > \frac{(R_0 - R_f)}{\sigma_0}. \qquad (12.49)$$

Recalling that $\sigma_i' = \sigma_0$ when the project is risk equalized, Eq. (12.49) reduces to

Accept if
$$R_i' > R_0. \qquad (12.50)$$

These relationships are known as *reward-to-variability* ratios. The ratio was developed by Sharpe [18] and implies simply that a reward above the riskless rate must exist for accepting the risk of such investments; i.e., in order for a project to be acceptable to a firm, its reward-to-variability ratio must be equal to or greater than the ratio the firm currently achieves from its existing projects.

Sharpe [18] questions the application of the reward-to-variability ratio as being the proper measure for evaluating a *single* security or *single* project. He states:

> The reward-to-variability ratio is designed to measure the performance of a portfolio. The investor is presumed to have placed a substantial portion of his wealth in the portfolio in question. Variability is thus the relevant measure of the amount of risk actually borne. To evaluate the performance of a single security, or that of a portfolio constituting only part of an investor's holdings, a different measure is needed. Variability will not adequately represent the risk actually borne. A more appropriate choice is *volatility*. (Italics supplied.)

Originally proposed by Treynor [19] and subsequently developed by Mossin [13], the reward-to-volatility criterion is of similar form to the reward-to-variability crite-rion, except that the volatility, $\beta_i$, replaces the standard deviation, $\sigma_i$, in the denomi-nator. The reward-to-volatility criterion for project selection can be stated as follows:

Accept the project if
$$\frac{\bar{R}_i - R_f}{\beta_i} > \frac{\bar{R}_0 - R_f}{\beta_0}; \qquad (12.51)$$

otherwise, reject the project

where the subscript 0 refers to *present* (i.e., *ex post*) known values for the firm, and $i$ refers to the candidate project. Other symbols are as stated before.

The reward-to-volatility criterion proceeds naturally from the equation of the expected return rate for an individual security (or project), namely, Eq. (12.23) or (12.25):

$$\bar{R}_i - R_f = \frac{\text{Cov}(R_i, R_M)}{\sigma_M^2}(\bar{R}_M - R_f) = \beta_i(\bar{R}_M - R_f),$$

where $\beta_i = \text{Cov}(R_i, R_M)/\sigma_M^2$. If we view the expected market premium, $\bar{R}_M - R_f$, as the (assumed) known multiplying factor, then the risk premium for the $i$th project is a linear function of $\beta_i$, thus:

$$\bar{R}_i - R_f = (\bar{R}_M - R_f)\beta_i. \tag{12.52}$$

Here, $\beta_i$ is the *in*dependent variable—the descriptor that establishes the volatility of the project in relation to the market return rate fluctuations. Also, $(\bar{R}_M - R_f)$ is viewed as a constant since it is an expected value. If Eq. (12.52) is plotted on rectangular coordinates $[(\bar{R} - R_f), \beta]$, as in Fig. 12.12, the slope of the line is simply the constant $(\bar{R}_M - R_f)$ since the slope is $(\bar{R}_i - R_f)/\beta_i = (\bar{R}_M - R_f)$.

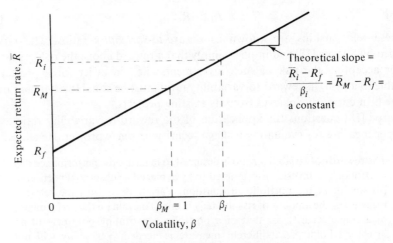

**Fig. 12.12.** Reward-to-volatility diagram.

It should be noted that the *basing point* for comparisons of several $(\beta_i, \bar{R}_i)$ points is the volatility of the market itself, $\beta_M$. Noting that the covariance of the market rate with itself is simply $\text{Cov}(R_M, R_M) = \sigma_M^2$, then the volatility of the market is

$$\beta_M = \frac{\text{Cov}(R_M, R_M)}{\sigma_M^2} = \frac{\sigma_M^2}{\sigma_M^2} = 1.$$

Thus, the expected market return rate is $\bar{R}_M$ when $\beta_M = 1$, as indicated in Fig. 12.12. By comparison, securities or projects whose values of $\beta_t > 1$ are more volatile than the market; i.e., they exhibit greater swings in expected return rates than the market itself. On the other hand, projects with $\beta_t < 1$ provide smaller swings in expected return rates than the market.

There is an important feature about the reward-to-volatility criterion that needs to be examined. We need to show that the acceptance of a candidate project in accordance with Eq. (12.51) will in fact *result in an increase in the expected net present value of the firm.* This proof is actually the "clincher" that qualifies Eq. (12.51) as a bona fide project selection criterion. Originally given by Mossin [13], the present version of this proof was outlined by Rubenstein (see [16], footnotes 10 and 14, pp. 172–174), but not in detail. Since it is of fundamental importance to project selection methodology when using capital market theory, the proof is given in Appendix 12.A in detail.

From the appendix, the reward-to-volatility criterion with respect to the *market* is

$$\frac{E(R_i) - R_f}{\beta_i} > E(R_M) - R_f. \tag{12.53}$$

This criterion suggests that if the *project's* reward-to-volatility ratio is greater than the constant slope of the market line, then the project should be accepted. This suggestion is illustrated in Fig. 12.13. Thus, the criterion suggests that Projects *A* and *C* be accepted and Project *B* be rejected. This is not quite in accord with all the facts, however, as we shall see.

We need to recall that the selection criterion in Eq. (12.53) was based on an initial assumption that the price of the firm's equity shares, *P*, was in equilibrium with the market. It is entirely possible—indeed, it is the general occurrence—that the price of a single firm's shares will stabilize in equilibrium so that the expected risk premium for

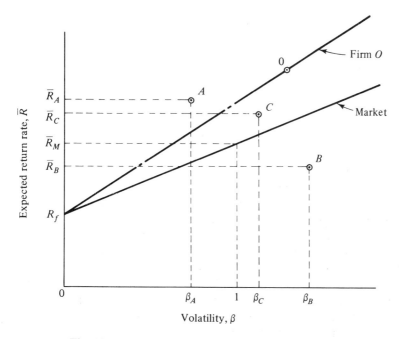

**Fig. 12.13.** Reward-to-volatility for three projects.

the firm, $[E(R_0) - R_f]$, equalized for the firm's volatility, $\beta_0$, *does not fall on the market line*. The explanation of this phenomenon is that individuals who purchase a firm's equity shares *think and act as if* the firm will provide an expected return premium, $E(R_0) - R_f$, greater or smaller than the market itself, in relation to the volatility involved $(\beta_0)$, and carry out their beliefs in terms of the equilibrium price of the shares, which they are willing to pay. Hence, it is the usual case that the *firm itself* will exhibit some coordinate pair, $[E(R_0), \beta_0]$, away from the market line as illustrated at 0 in Fig. 12.13, representing the market's historical evaluation of the firm's ability to generate a higher expected return than the market. In the case shown in Fig. 12.13, Firm $O$ has consistently outperformed the market since

$$\frac{E(R_0) - R_f}{\beta_0} > \frac{E(R_M) - R_f}{1}. \tag{12.54}$$

In such a case, Firm $O$ would *not* improve its net worth by using the selection criterion in Eq. (12.53). In fact, the firm's shares are already valued at some $[E(R_0) - R_f]/\beta_0$ greater than the market, probably due to the repeated successful application of Eq. (12.53) in historically selecting its projects. The proper project selection criterion for Firm $O$ to use, then, is not the market line but rather its own historical performance line, $[E(R_0) - R_f]/\beta_0$. By doing this, it will improve its *current* net worth. Hence, in Fig. 12.13, Firm $O$ should accept Project $A$ and reject Projects $B$ and $C$. The proper project selection criterion for the firm—i.e., one that will increase its *current* net worth —is a combination of Eqs. (12.53) and (12.54), or accept the project ($i$) if

$$\frac{E(R_i) - R_f}{\beta_i} > \frac{E(R_0) - R_f}{\beta_0}, \tag{12.55}$$

which is the same as suggested earlier in Eq. (12.51). Here, however, it is the result of a demonstration that the current net worth of the firm is expected to increase if Eq. (12.55) is applied.

## 12.5. Project Selection in the Public Firm

The reward-to-volatility criterion can be applied quite easily to the project selection problem for firms whose shares are publicly traded on a stock exchange. The public market establishes traded prices for the firm's shares, which tend to evaluate the management, operating, and dividend policies of the firm directly. Dividend payment information is documented in readily available publications, such as the U.S. Department of Commerce publication, *The Biennial Supplement to the Survey of Current Business* [23], and Moody's or Standard and Poors' publications. The theoretical principles of asset expansion were developed in Section 12.4, and this present section describes an application methodology that generally follows one given by Weston [25].

Some historical (*ex post*) data for the return rates on the market portfolio are given below in Table 12.1, and similar data are given for Eastman Kodak Company in Table 12.2. In Table 12.1, the market-wide return rates ($R_{Mt}$), displayed in Column

**Table 12.1.** ESTIMATES OF MARKET PARAMETERS

| (1) Year, $t$ | (2) $R_{Mt}$* | (3) $(R_{Mt} - \bar{R}_M)$ | (4) $(R_{Mt} - \bar{R}_M)^2$ | (5) $R_{ft}$† |
|---|---|---|---|---|
| 1961 | 0.267 | 0.188 | 0.035 | 0.03 |
| 1962 | −0.088 | −0.167 | 0.028 | 0.03 |
| 1963 | 0.226 | 0.147 | 0.022 | 0.03 |
| 1964 | 0.164 | 0.085 | 0.007 | 0.04 |
| 1965 | 0.124 | 0.045 | 0.002 | 0.04 |
| 1966 | −0.099 | −0.178 | 0.032 | 0.05 |
| 1967 | 0.238 | 0.159 | 0.025 | 0.05 |
| 1968 | 0.121 | 0.042 | 0.002 | 0.05 |
| 1969 | −0.104 | −0.183 | 0.033 | 0.07 |
| 1970 | 0.048 | −0.031 | 0.001 | 0.06 |
| 1971 | 0.141 | 0.062 | 0.004 | 0.05 |
| 1972 | 0.178 | 0.099 | 0.010 | 0.05 |
| 1973 | −0.138 | −0.217 | 0.047 | 0.07 |
| 1974 | −0.258 | −0.337 | 0.114 | 0.08 |
| 1975 | 0.369 | 0.290 | 0.084 | 0.06 |
| | $\Sigma = 1.189$ | | $\Sigma = 0.446$ | $\Sigma = 0.76$ |

$$\bar{R}_M = \frac{1.189}{15} = 0.079; \qquad \sigma_M^2 = \frac{\Sigma d^2}{n-1} = \frac{0.446}{14} = 0.0318;$$

$$\bar{R}_f = \frac{0.76}{15} = 0.051$$

---

*Data from *The Biennial Supplement to the Survey of Current Business* [23], calculated according to Eq. (12.56); i.e., including dividend yields but before individual income taxes and individual transaction costs.

†Annual yields on 9- to 12-month U.S. Government securities issues, compiled from *Federal Reserve Bulletin*, various issues.

2, were calculated by the following relationship:

$$R_{Mt} = \frac{P_t - P_{t-1}}{P_{t-1}} + \left(\frac{D_t}{P_t}\right)\left(\frac{P_t}{P_{t-1}}\right) \tag{12.56}$$

where $P_t$ = the closing market price per share of Standard & Poor's 500 Composite Index at the end of year $t$.

$P_{t-1}$ = the same price relative at the end of year $t - 1$.

$D_t/P_t$ = the current dividend-to-price ratio for the market at the end of year $t$, where $D_t$ = the *annualized* dividend ($/share).

This relationship in Eq. (12.56) simply accounts for both price fluctuations and dividend payments on the yield of the Composite Index, which is standard practice in reducing financial data. In the third and fourth columns of Table 12.1, the deviations and deviations squared are calculated, to estimate the variance and standard deviation of the market return rate for the sample. In the fifth column, the default-free return rate is estimated by the average of the default-free return rates of 9- to 12-month U.S.

Government security issues over the previous 10-year period. In summary, these calculations indicate an average market return rate of 8.2%, a variance of approximately 1%, and an estimated default-free interest rate of approximately 4.3%.

In Table 12.2 the second step is presented. Here, the analysis of Eastman Kodak's equity shares is undertaken. The required data on stock prices and dividend yields are readily available in widely used publications and financial services. From such sources, share prices are listed in the second column, and current dividend-to-price ratios $(D_t/P_t)$ are listed in the third column. The yields shown in Column 4 are again calculated by a direct analogy of Eq. (12.56). Column 5 lists the periodic deviations of the corporate return rate from the mean return rate, and Column 6 lists the same deviates for the market (repeated from Table 12.1). Column 7 lists the products of the corporate and market return deviations, which are summed to estimate the covariance of the security's return rate with the market return rate. Calculations for the means, covariances, and volatility $(\beta)$ are given just above the footnotes of the table.

Calculations such as those illustrated in Table 12.2 result in coordinate pairs of

**Table 12.2.** DATA AND CALCULATIONS FOR EASTMAN KODAK COMPANY STOCK

| (1) Year, t | (2) $P_t^*$ | (3) $(D_t/P_t)$† | (4) $R_{Jt}$ | (5) $(R_{Jt} - \bar{R}_J)$ | (6) $(R_{Mt} - \bar{R}_M)$ | (7) $(R_{Jt} - \bar{R}_J)(R_{Mt} - \bar{R}_M)$ |
|---|---|---|---|---|---|---|
| 1960 | 26. | — | — | — | — | — |
| 1961 | 25. | 0.54 | −0.018 | −0.186 | 0.188 | −0.035 |
| 1962 | 27. | 0.58 | 0.103 | −0.065 | −0.167 | 0.011 |
| 1963 | 29. | 0.62 | 0.097 | −0.071 | 0.147 | −0.010 |
| 1964 | 35. | 0.75 | 0.233 | 0.065 | 0.085 | 0.006 |
| 1965 | 60. | 0.90 | 0.740 | 0.572 | 0.045 | 0.026 |
| 1966 | 57. | 1.02 | −0.032 | −0.170 | −0.178 | 0.030 |
| 1967 | 70. | 1.05 | 0.246 | 0.078 | 0.159 | 0.012 |
| 1968 | 78. | 1.14 | 0.131 | 0.063 | 0.042 | 0.003 |
| 1969 | 79. | 1.25 | 0.029 | −0.139 | −0.183 | 0.025 |
| 1970 | 73. | 1.32 | −0.059 | −0.227 | −0.031 | 0.007 |
| 1971 | 92. | 1.34 | 0.279 | 0.111 | 0.062 | 0.007 |
| 1972 | 140. | 1.39 | 0.537 | 0.369 | 0.099 | 0.037 |
| 1973 | 110. | 1.81 | −0.201 | −0.369 | −0.217 | 0.080 |
| 1974 | 60. | 1.99 | −0.436 | −0.604 | −0.337 | 0.204 |
| 1975 | 110. | 2.06 | 0.868 | 0.700 | 0.290 | 0.203 |
| | | | $\sum = 2.517$ | | | $\sum = 0.605$ |

$$\bar{R}_J = \frac{2.517}{15} = 0.1678, \qquad \text{Cov}(R_J, R_M) = \frac{0.605}{14} = 0.043;$$

or approximately 16.8%. $\qquad \hat{\beta}_J = \text{Cov}(R_J, R_m)/\sigma_M^2 = \frac{0.043}{0.0318} = 1.36.$

*Average of calendar year-end closing prices from *Value Line Survey*, adjusted for stock splits and stock dividends.
†Current yields, same source.

$(\bar{R}_j, \hat{\beta}_j)$ values, each pair being descriptive of a particular traded stock. In the case of Eastman Kodak, the coordinate pair is $(\bar{R}_j, \hat{\beta}_j) = (0.168, 1.36)$. Such coordinate pairs can be plotted on $(\bar{R}, \hat{\beta})$ coordinates such as Fig. 12.14. In this figure, Eastman Kodak is plotted along with similar data for 18 other publicly traded firms.

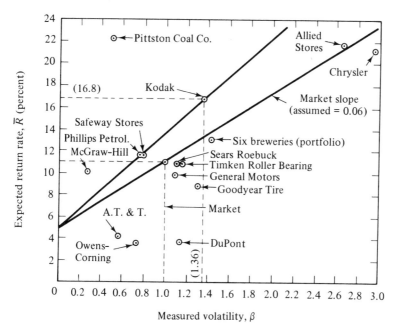

**Fig. 12.14.** Asset expansion criteria.

Theory, of course, predicts that the slope of the *market* line in Fig. 12.14 will be a constant, here estimated as $\bar{R}_M - R_f = 0.06$. The scatter of the coordinate pairs for individual firms around the market line attests, however, to the differential valuation placed on an individual firm's shares by the market. Note, moreover, that the *portfolio* composed of six breweries displays a coordinate pair $(\bar{R}_j = 13.1\%, \hat{\beta}_j = 1.42)$ that is very nearly on the market line. In fact, as more and more securities are included in even larger portfolios, one would expect that a completely diversified portfolio return would approach the market return value, $\bar{R}_M \doteq 11.0\%$, and its volatility would approach the market volatility, $\beta_M = 1.0$. Many empirical tests have been made of this asymptotic phenomenon, and this fact is well documented.[10] For diversified portfolios, the market line can be considered an adequate project selection criterion on a risk-adjusted basis, but for *individual* firms the market line is not the proper criterion, as we discovered in Section 12.4.

The proper project selection criterion is the relationship given in Eq. (12.55). For Eastman Kodak Company, the market-established reward-to-volatility criterion is the slope of the line connecting the riskless security $(R_f, 0)$ and the Kodak coordinate

---

[10]See, for example, Sharpe [18] (pp. 149–50; 177–80).

pair ($\bar{R}_0 = 0.168$, $\hat{\beta}_0 = 1.36$), as illustrated in Fig. 12.15. The slope of the Kodak reward-to-volatility line is

$$\lambda_K = \frac{\bar{R}_0 - R_f}{\beta_0} = \frac{0.168 - 0.050}{1.36} = 0.087;$$

whereas the slope of the market line is

$$\lambda_M = \frac{\bar{R}_M - R_f}{\beta_M} = \frac{0.110 - 0.050}{1.0} = 0.060.$$

Thus, any project such as $A$, whose $(\bar{R}_i, \hat{\beta}_i)$ coordinate pair lies above the *firm's* performance line, should be accepted since it will tend to increase the firm's *present* value (and hence its future value, also) in accordance with the arguments advanced in Section 12.4. Conversely, projects that plot below the firm line, such as $B$, should be rejected, even though they lie above the market line. They tend to reduce the firm's present value as perceived by the market.

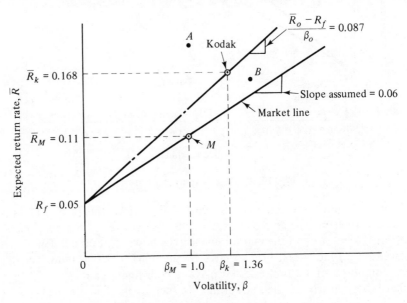

**Fig. 12.15.** Asset expansion criteria for a firm.

The coordinate pair $(\bar{R}_i, \hat{\beta}_i)$ for a particular project under consideration is needed in order to compare it with the firm's project selection criterion (the firm's reward-to-volatility line). To illustrate a fundamental procedure for obtaining coordinate pairs $(\bar{R}_i, \hat{\beta}_i)$ for projects, one might use what is called the *state-of-nature* approach. In the cases following, four states of nature are considered with respect to future prospects for real growth in gross national product. We let State 1 represent a relatively serious recession that we subjectively estimate will occur with a probability $P_s = 0.1$; State 2 is a mild recession that occurs with probability 0.2; State 3 is a mild recovery that occurs with probability of 0.3; and State 4 is a strong recovery that

**Table 12.3.** CALCULATION OF ESTIMATED MARKET PARAMETERS

| (1) State, s | (2) $P_s$ | (3) $R_M^*$ | (4) $P_S R_M$ | (5) $(R_M - \bar{R}_M)$ | (6) $(R_M - \bar{R}_M)^2$ | (7) $P_S(R_M - \bar{R}_M)^2$ |
|---|---|---|---|---|---|---|
| 1 | 0.1 | −0.30 | −0.03 | −0.40 | 0.16 | 0.016 |
| 2 | 0.2 | −0.10 | −0.02 | −0.20 | 0.04 | 0.008 |
| 3 | 0.3 | 0.10 | 0.03 | 0 | 0 | 0 |
| 4 | 0.4 | 0.30 | 0.12 | 0.20 | 0.04 | 0.040 |
|  | 1.0 |  | $\bar{R}_M = 0.10$ |  |  | $\sigma_M^2 = 0.040$ |

*Estimates from historical data corresponding to similar states.

occurs with probability 0.4. The calculations of the *estimated* future market parameters, based on these states and probabilities, are given in Table 12.3.

Suppose now that Kodak is considering four projects in a capital expansion program. The Economic Analysis Staff estimates the single-period return rates for each of the four projects under each of the assumed states of nature to be as follows:

*Project Return Rate*

| State, S | Project A | Project B | Project C | Project D |
|---|---|---|---|---|
| 1 | −0.46 | −0.70 | −0.40 | −0.40 |
| 2 | −0.26 | −0.40 | −0.20 | −0.20 |
| 3 | 0.46 | 0 | 0 | 0.60 |
| 4 | 0 | 0.70 | 0.70 | 0.30 |

In Table 12.4, the calculations for expected return rate and the covariance of each of the four individual projects are presented. The expected project return rate is obtained by multiplying the probability of each state of nature times the associated forecasted return rate. The deviations of the return rate under each state from the expected (mean) return rate are calculated in Column 6, and the deviations of the market return rates are repeated (from Table 12.3) for convenience in Column 7. In Column 9, the deviations of the project return rates are multiplied by the deviations of the market return rate and then weighted by the respective probabilities, to determine the covariance of each of the four projects.

In Table 12.5, the volatility for each project is calculated as the ratio of its covariance (from Table 12.4) to the market return rate variance (from Table 12.3). The expected project return rates ($\bar{R}_j$) are repeated there from Table 12.4. These are the coordinate pairs used to plot the positions of the projects with respect to Kodak's firm performance line in Fig. 12.16. Table 12.5 also includes a column for the calculation of the reward-to-volatility ratio for each project.

The reward-to-volatility criterion accepts projects whose reward-to-volatility ratio is greater than that of the firm (here, Project *B*—in both Table 12.5 and Fig. 12.16) and rejects those with ratios smaller than the firm's (Projects *A*, *C*, and *D*). A

**Table 12.4.** CALCULATION OF EXPECTED RETURNS AND COVARIANCES FOR FOUR HYPOTHETICAL PROJECTS

| (1) Project Number | (2) State S | (3) P(S) | (4) $R_J$ | (5) $P_S R_J$ | (6) $(R_J - \bar{R}_J)$ | (7) $(R_M - \bar{R}_M)$ | (8) $(R_J - \bar{R}_J) \times (R_M - \bar{R}_M)$ | (9) $P_S(R_J - \bar{R}_J) \times (R_M - \bar{R}_M)$ |
|---|---|---|---|---|---|---|---|---|
| A | 1 | 0.1 | −0.46 | −0.046 | −0.50 | −0.40 | 0.200 | 0.020 |
|   | 2 | 0.2 | −0.26 | −0.052 | −0.30 | −0.20 | −0.060 | 0.012 |
|   | 3 | 0.3 | 0.46 | 0.138 | 0.42 | 0 | 0 | 0 |
|   | 4 | 0.4 | 0 | 0 | −0.04 | 0.20 | −0.008 | −0.003 |
|   |   |   |   | $\bar{R}_A = 0.040$ |   |   | Cov $(R_A, R_M) =$ | 0.029 |
| B | 1 | 0.1 | −0.70 | −0.070 | −0.20 | −0.40 | 0.080 | 0.008 |
|   | 2 | 0.2 | −0.40 | −0.080 | −0.21 | −0.20 | 0.042 | 0.008 |
|   | 3 | 0.3 | 0 | 0 | −0.13 | 0 | 0 | 0 |
|   | 4 | 0.4 | 0.70 | 0.280 | 0.15 | 0.20 | 0.030 | 0.012 |
|   |   |   |   | $\bar{R}_B = 0.130$ |   |   | Cov $(R_B, R_M) =$ | 0.028 |
| C | 1 | 0.1 | −0.40 | −0.040 | −0.60 | −0.40 | 0.240 | 0.024 |
|   | 2 | 0.2 | −0.20 | −0.040 | −0.40 | −0.20 | 0.080 | 0.016 |
|   | 3 | 0.3 | 0 | 0 | −0.20 | 0 | 0 | 0 |
|   | 4 | 0.4 | 0.70 | 0.280 | 0.50 | 0.20 | 0.100 | 0.040 |
|   |   |   |   | $\bar{R}_C = 0.200$ |   |   | Cov $(R_C, R_M) =$ | 0.080 |
| D | 1 | 0.1 | −0.60 | −0.060 | −0.71 | −0.40 | 0.284 | 0.028 |
|   | 2 | 0.2 | −0.30 | −0.060 | −0.41 | −0.20 | 0.082 | 0.016 |
|   | 3 | 0.3 | 0.10 | 0.030 | −0.01 | 0 | 0 | 0 |
|   | 4 | 0.4 | 0.50 | 0.200 | 0.39 | 0.20 | 0.078 | 0.031 |
|   |   |   |   | $\bar{R}_D = 0.110$ |   |   | Cov $(R_D, R_M) =$ | 0.075 |

**Table 12.5.** PERFORMANCE CHARACTERISTICS FOR FOUR HYPOTHETICAL PROJECTS

| (1) Project Number | (2) $\hat{\beta}_J = \dfrac{\text{Cov}(R_J, R_M)}{\sigma_M^2}$ | (3) $E[R_J]$ | (4) Reward-to-Volatility $= \dfrac{[E(R) - R_f]}{\hat{\beta}}$ |
|---|---|---|---|
| A | 0.725 | 0.04 | −0.013 |
| B | 0.700 | 0.13 | 0.114 |
| C | 2.00 | 0.20 | 0.075 |
| D | 1.53 | 0.11 | 0.039 |
| Kodak | 1.36 | 0.168 | 0.087 |

comparison with the weighted average cost of capital (WACC) criterion is also facilitated by Fig. 12.16, where the weighted average cost of capital line is shown as a horizontal line at $E(R_w) = 0.14$. Note that the WACC line is a constant value $(\bar{R}_w)$ since it does not change with volatility. Here, it is assumed that Kodak's weighted

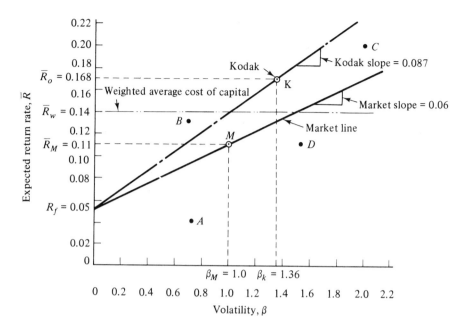

**Fig. 12.16.** Application of the reward-to-volatility project selection criterion.

average cost of capital is 14%, and if the WACC project selection criterion is interpreted as "accept the project if $E(R_j)$ exceeds $E(R_w)$," then conflicting results may be obtained. The WACC criterion would accept Project $C$ and reject Project $B$; whereas the reward-to-volatility criterion does exactly the opposite. It can be argued (correctly, incidentally) that projects with different risk are in different risk classes, and therefore, the WACC line cannot be employed to discriminate projects of differing risk. This exact point emphasizes the fact that direct and appropriate adjustments for risk are provided by the reward-to-volatility measure, thus underscoring the usefulness of the reward-to-volatility criterion.

    It should also be noted that the expected return rate for Project $B$ (Table 12.5, $\bar{R}_B = 0.13$) is considerably smaller than the current expected return for Kodak itself ($\bar{R}_0 = 0.168$). The *relative* risk (volatility) for the project is also smaller (0.700 versus 1.36), however, so that the expected reward *per unit of volatility* for the project is greater (0.114 versus 0.087). This serves to emphasize the need for accepting projects whose return rates are *less* than the firm's current earning capability, provided there is an offsetting lowering of the risk (volatility) also.

    The practical problem in the implementation of the reward-to-volatility method of project selection is the calculation of the volatilities ($\hat{\beta}_j$) for projects or *bundles* of projects. One approach has already been used above—the state-of-nature approach. Estimates are required of alternative future states of nature, and probabilities are attached to them that correspond to return rates in the future alternative states. The prospective return rates on the individual projects or bundles of projects can then be calculated as illustrated above. It should also be recalled from the discussion in Chapter 8 that bundles of projects can be constructed that are mutually exclusive, and also exhaustive of all feasible projects. That is, project bundles that violate budget or manpower constraints can be eliminated from the candidate set, with the remaining bundles being the mutually exclusive and exhaustive set of feasible bundles. Hence, by calculating the expected return rates and volatilities for these bundles, one may apply the firm's reward-to-volatility measure as the project bundle selection criteria in constrained selection problems.

Weston [25] suggests that an alternative procedure devised by Rubenstein [16] can be used to check on such calculations. This procedure involves multiplying three factors: (1) the price, less variable cost margin for the product; (2) the standard deviation of the turnover of operating investment to produce the product, normalized by the standard deviation of the market return rates; and (3) the correlational function between the fluctuations in the economy as a whole and the output of the individual product.

## 12.6. Project Selection in the Private Firm[11]

The reward-to-volatility ratio can be used directly by publicly held firms for use in project selection decisions. Since the reward-to-volatility ratio requires a relationship between the return rate of the firm and the market rate, however, the ratio cannot be used directly for the many privately owned and financed firms that operate in the industrial sector. The concept of volatility for the shares of a private firm is meaningless since there is no market for the firm's stock. This does not, however, eliminate the possibility of *indirectly* applying the reward-to-volatility ratio to the private firm.

There are numerous industries in which private firms are engaged in competition. Often they compete chiefly with publicly owned corporations. In any type of industry, one way of evaluating the success of any firm would be by making a comparison against its competitors. If the firm had a return rate on its investment that was as good or better than its competitors, it is reasonable to assume that the firm is performing well in its investment decisions. Thus, some sort of *average* of the competing publicly owned firms might be calculated and used as a comparative *standard*. This average could serve as a surrogate or pseudo firm, against which the private firm could be compared. The private firm could evaluate all its investment alternatives against a security line constructed from the surrogate firm. A reward-to-volatility ratio could then be used for any private firm that was competing in the same field of endeavor against publicly owned firms.

---

[11]This section is taken from Campbell [4].

A weighted average of the return rates of selected individual public firms is first calculated. Thus, one would calculate the surrogate firm's expected return rate:

$$\bar{R}_i = \sum X_j \bar{R}_j, \tag{12.57}$$

where $X_j$ is the assumed proportion invested in Firm $j$, using the relative net worth of the particular firm as the weighting factor, $X_j$. Larger firms would thus be weighted greater than smaller firms, acknowledging their importance in the industry. The value for $\bar{R}_i$ in Eq. (12.57) could then be calculated for a number of years and these values could be used in a time-series regression model. The estimates for $R_i$ and $\beta_i$ could be used in a reward-to-volatility ratio criterion for the private firm. This results in a *surrogate security line* on $(\bar{R}, \beta)$ coordinates that the private firm could use in its capital budgeting analysis. All projects plotting above the line would be accepted as before, with projects plotting below the line being rejected. That is, all projects with $(\bar{R}_i, \beta_i)$ coordinates above the line are projects that would improve the firm's *expected net worth* position relative to its competition. This is a true test of survival of a firm, i.e., how it performs in relation to its competition.

**Example 12.6.1.** The use of a surrogate security in application of capital asset pricing theory to capital budgeting for the private firm cannot be considered as an all-inclusive method. In industries dominated by conglomerate firms that are diversified in several or many different industries, the concept of a surrogate firm is unrealistic. The return of the surrogate would be distorted by the returns of those divisions of the firms whose products or services are entirely unrelated to the industry for which the surrogate is being developed. This is not necessarily a severe limitation, but an important one. In selecting an industry for the construction of a surrogate firm, certain other requirements might be specified. For example, the industry should have approximately 5 to 20 firms that are publicly owned and should be easily identifiable and familiar to the general public. For illustrative purposes, the brewing industry meets these requirements.

The *Standard Industrial Classification* (S.I.C.) *Manual* [22] categorizes types of industry by function, giving each particular category a unique S.I.C. number. Thus, 2082 is the S.I.C. number for Malt Beverages. Standard & Poor's publishes a list of corporations by S.I.C. number. From this list, six publicly held firms with listings on the New York and American stock exchanges or over-the-counter price information were selected. These six firms are Anheuser-Busch, Carling O'Keefe Ltd., Falstaff Brewing, Pabst Brewing, F & M Schaefer, and Joseph Schlitz Brewing. Closing prices, dividends paid, and net worths for the years 1961–1975 were obtained using issues of the *Wall Street Journal* and *Value Line* [24]. For the market, Standard & Poor's 500 Composite Index was selected as the indicator of market return. The dividend yield of the market was obtained from various issues of the *Federal Reserve Bulletin* [21]. The return rate for each of the firms was then calculated by the relationship below, which is a direct analog of Eq. (12.56):

$$R_{it} = \frac{P_t + D_t - P_{t-1}}{P_{t-1}} \qquad (12.58)$$

where $R_{it}$ = return rate for Security $i$ for year $t$.

$P_t$ = closing price for Security $i$ at year $t$ (dollars).

$P_{t-1}$ = closing price for Security $i$ at year $t-1$ (dollars).

$D_t$ = dollar amount of dividends paid by firm during year $t$.

These returns were weighted by net worth and summed using Eq. (12.57) to obtain a surrogate return rate for the brewing industry. The return rates for the market were calculated for each year by Eq. (12.58), and the results of these and the $R_i$ calculations are summarized in Table 12.6.

Using the information from Table 12.6, a linear regression analysis is then performed, in which the market premium rate $(R_M - R_f)$ is the independent

**Table 12.6.** RETURN RATES FOR INDIVIDUAL SECURITIES, BREWING SURROGATE SECURITY, AND THE MARKET (PERCENT)

|  | 1961 | 1962 | 1963 | 1964 | 1965 | 1966 | 1967 | 1968 |
|---|---|---|---|---|---|---|---|---|
| Anheuser-Busch | 44.27 | −13.64 | 1.79 | 49.37 | 47.06 | 26.30 | 43.93 | 56.00 |
| Carling O'Keefe | 31.49 | − 8.90 | − 5.25 | 11.23 | −15.13 | −12.38 | 13.85 | 68.29 |
| Falstaff | 13.91 | −16.97 | 12.48 | 34.68 | − 5.84 | −30.47 | 4.98 | 32.24 |
| Pabst | 91.43 | −20.15 | 64.08 | 60.00 | 28.08 | − 9.40 | 78.08 | 51.56 |
| F & M Schaefer | — | — | — | — | — | — | — | — |
| Schlitz | — | — | 70.08 | 11.49 | 4.70 | −58.51 | 90.95 | 42.98 |
| Surrogate | 44.39 | −13.33 | 22.47 | 27.00 | 12.66 | −12.44 | 48.85 | 53.24 |
| Market (S & P 500) | 26.66 | − 8.82 | 22.64 | 16.42 | 12.40 | − 9.93 | 23.79 | 12.10 |

|  | 1969 | 1970 | 1971 | 1972 | 1973 | 1974 | 1975 |
|---|---|---|---|---|---|---|---|
| Anheuser-Busch | 15.31 | 5.81 | 48.02 | − 0.30 | −39.40 | −25.18 | 43.29 |
| Carling O'Keefe | −27.24 | − 4.44 | 2.10 | −15.99 | −33.09 | −46.29 | 32.98 |
| Falstaff | −37.82 | −41.54 | 52.75 | −39.65 | −56.14 | −44.44 | — |
| Pabst | − 4.00 | 10.51 | 54.00 | 0.26 | −64.85 | −31.72 | 35.70 |
| F & M Schaefer | — | −47.57 | −38.89 | −46.18 | −57.77 | −36.53 | 21.01 |
| Schlitz | 47.54 | − 6.12 | 60.22 | 62.21 | − 3.03 | −72.02 | 32.07 |
| Surrogate | 6.55 | − 0.47 | 40.62 | 7.43 | −35.81 | −41.36 | 37.03 |
| Market (S & P 500) | −10.35 | 4.82 | 14.10 | 17.80 | −13.83 | −25.79 | 36.96 |

variable, and the surrogate security premium rate $(R_i - R_f)$ is the dependent variable of the analysis. The regression equation is identical to Eq. (12.25):

$$(R_{it} - R_f) = \beta_0 + \beta_1(R_{Mt} - R_f) + \epsilon_{it}$$

in which the risk-free rate, $R_f$, is assumed to be 5%. The results of the regression analysis and the analysis of variance are given in Table 12.7. It is to be noted there that the estimate of $\hat{\beta}_0 = 3.9$ cannot be statistically distinguished from zero at the $\alpha = 0.05$ level so it was assumed that $\beta_0 = 0$ and, consequently, that $R_f = 0.05$. On the other hand, the regression indicates that $\hat{\beta}_1$ for the brewing industry is significantly greater than zero ($\hat{\beta}_1 = 1.43$), due to the large relative value of the $F$ test in the analysis of variance.

Table 12.8 shows the returns for the market and four hypothetical projects, given four states of the world along with the probabilities for these four states.

**Table 12.7.** RESULTS OF REGRESSION ANALYSIS

| Variable | Mean | Std. Dev. | Parameter | Estimate | t (test) | t (α = 0.05) |
|----------|------|-----------|-----------|----------|----------|--------------|
| $R_i - R_f$ | 8.122 | 29.818 | $\hat{\beta}_0$ | 3.900 | 0.92 | 2.13 |
| $R_M - R_f$ | 2.965 | 17.814 | $\hat{\beta}_1$ | 1.425 | — | — |

ANALYSIS OF VARIANCE

| | DF | Sum of Squares | Mean Square | F (test) | F (α = 0.05) |
|---|----|----------------|-------------|----------|--------------|
| Total (uncorrected) | 15 | 13,437.143 | — | — | — |
| Corrections: | | | | | |
| Mean | 1 | 989.503 | 989.503 | — | — |
| Total (corrected) | 14 | 12,447.640 | 889.117 | — | — |
| Due to Regression | 1 | 9,023.363 | 9,023.363 | 34.256 | 4.69 |
| Error | 13 | 3,424.277 | 263.406 | — | — |

$$r^2 = 0.7249$$
$$r = 0.8514$$

**Table 12.8.** RETURN OF THE MARKET AND FOUR PROJECTS, GIVEN FOUR STATES OF THE WORLD

| State of the World (S) | Subjective Probability, $P_S$ | Market Return ($R_M$) | Project Return | | | |
|------------------------|-------------------------------|------------------------|-------|-------|-------|-------|
| | | | $R_1$ | $R_2$ | $R_3$ | $R_4$ |
| 1. Serious recession | 0.05 | −0.30 | −1.00 | −0.20 | −0.05 | −0.48 |
| 2. Mild recession | 0.20 | −0.10 | −0.40 | 0.07 | 0.07 | −0.12 |
| 3. Mild recovery | 0.45 | 0.10 | 0.25 | 0.16 | 0.10 | 0.13 |
| 4. Strong recovery | 0.30 | 0.30 | 0.50 | 0.25 | 0.17 | 0.33 |

Using this information, expected return rates and variances of return rates can be calculated as described in Section 12.5. Using the same information the covariance of the projects with the market can also be estimated. These calculations are summarized in Tables 12.9 and 12.10.

Since the volatility of a project is defined as the covariance of the project

**Table 12.9.** EXPECTED RETURN AND STANDARD DEVIATION OF RETURN FOR THE MARKET

| $S$ | $P_S$ | $R_M$ | $P_S R_M$ | $R_M - \bar{R}_M$ | $P_S(R_M - \bar{R}_M)^2$ |
|---|---|---|---|---|---|
| 1 | 0.05 | −0.30 | −0.015 | −0.40 | 0.008 |
| 2 | 0.20 | −0.10 | 0.02 | −0.20 | 0.008 |
| 3 | 0.45 | 0.10 | 0.045 | 0.00 | 0.000 |
| 4 | 0.30 | 0.30 | 0.09 | 0.20 | 0.012 |
| | | | $\bar{R}_M = 0.10$ | | $\sigma_M^2 = 0.028$ |

**Table 12.10.** EXPECTED RETURN AND COVARIANCE OF RETURN WITH THE MARKET FOR FOUR PROJECTS

| Project | $S$ | $P_S$ | $R_i$ | $P_S R_i$ | $R_i - \bar{R}_i$ | $R_M - \bar{R}_M$ | $P_S(R_i - \bar{R}_i)(R_M - \bar{R}_M)$ |
|---|---|---|---|---|---|---|---|
| 1 | 1 | 0.05 | −1.00 | −0.05 | −1.133 | −0.40 | 0.0223 |
|   | 2 | 0.20 | −0.40 | −0.08 | −0.533 | −0.20 | 0.0214 |
|   | 3 | 0.45 | 0.25 | 0.1125 | 0.118 | 0 | 0 |
|   | 4 | 0.30 | 0.50 | 0.15 | 0.368 | 0.20 | 0.0147 |
|   |   |   |   | $\bar{R}_1 = 0.133$ |   |   | Cov $(R_1, R_M) = 0.0584$ |
| 2 | 1 | 0.05 | −0.20 | −0.01 | −0.351 | −0.40 | 0.007 |
|   | 2 | 0.20 | 0.07 | 0.014 | −0.081 | 0.20 | 0.0032 |
|   | 3 | 0.45 | 0.16 | 0.072 | 0.009 | 0 | 0 |
|   | 4 | 0.30 | 0.25 | 0.075 | 0.099 | 0.20 | 0.0059 |
|   |   |   |   | $\bar{R}_2 = 0.151$ |   |   | Cov $(R_2, R_M) = 0.0161$ |
| 3 | 1 | 0.05 | −0.05 | 0.0025 | −1.55 | −0.40 | 0.0031 |
|   | 2 | 0.20 | 0.03 | 0.006 | −0.075 | −0.20 | 0.0030 |
|   | 3 | 0.45 | 0.10 | 0.045 | 0 | 0 | 0 |
|   | 4 | 0.30 | 0.17 | 0.051 | 0.065 | 0.20 | 0.0026 |
|   |   |   |   | $\bar{R}_3 = 0.105$ |   |   | Cov $(R_3, R_M) = 0.0087$ |
| 4 | 1 | 0.05 | −0.48 | −0.024 | −0.59 | −0.40 | 0.0118 |
|   | 2 | 0.20 | −0.12 | −0.024 | −0.23 | −0.20 | 0.0092 |
|   | 3 | 0.45 | 0.13 | 0.0585 | 0.02 | 0 | 0 |
|   | 4 | 0.30 | 0.33 | 0.099 | 0.22 | 0.20 | 0.0132 |
|   |   |   |   | $\bar{R}_4 = 0.110$ |   |   | Cov $(R_4, R_M) = 0.0342$ |

rate with the market rate divided by the variance of the market rate, an estimate of the volatility for each project can be made. The volatility for each project is shown in Table 12.11. The reward-to-volatility ratio for the projects can then be compared to the reward-to-volatility ratio of the surrogate or the risk equalized return of the projects compared with the current return level of the surrogate.

**Table 12.11.** VOLATILITY FOR FOUR PROJECTS

| *Project* | $Cov\ (R_i, R_M)$ | $\hat{\beta}$ |
|:---:|:---:|:---:|
| 1 | 0.0584 | 2.08 |
| 2 | 0.0161 | 0.57 |
| 3 | 0.0087 | 0.31 |
| 4 | 0.0342 | 1.22 |

The reward-to-volatility ratio for the surrogate is

$$\frac{\bar{R}_0 - R_f}{\hat{\beta}_0} = \frac{13.12 - 5}{1.43} = 5.68.$$

The reward-to-volatility ratio for each of the projects is as follows:

For Project 1: $\quad \dfrac{\bar{R}_1 - R_f}{\hat{\beta}_1} = \dfrac{13.3 - 5}{2.08} = 3.99$

For Project 2: $\quad \dfrac{\bar{R}_2 - R_f}{\hat{\beta}_2} = \dfrac{15.1 - 5}{0.57} = 17.72$

For Project 3: $\quad \dfrac{\bar{R}_3 - R_f}{\hat{\beta}_3} = \dfrac{10.5 - 5}{0.31} = 17.74$

For Project 4: $\quad \dfrac{\bar{R}_4 - R_f}{\hat{\beta}_4} = \dfrac{11.0 - 5}{1.22} = 4.92$

Comparison of these values with the reward-to-volatility ratio of the surrogate results in the acceptance of Projects 2 and 3 and the rejection of Projects 1 and 4.

Figure 12.17 illustrates graphically the reward-to-volatility criterion as a project selection tool in connection with a surrogate security. The $(\bar{R}_i, \beta_i)$ coordinates for each project are plotted and compared with the security line of the surrogate. This line connects the risk-free rate at $\beta = 0$ with the $(\bar{R}_0, \beta_0)$ coordinates for the surrogate. The reward for accepting additional risk for Projects 2 and 3 is greater than the reward for accepting risk currently in effect for the surrogate, resulting in $(\bar{R}_i, \beta_i)$ coordinates above the firm security line. Since the reward-to-volatility ratio for Projects 1 and 4 are less than the ratio of the surrogate, those projects plot below the security line and are rejected.

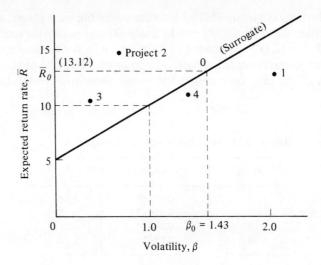

**Fig. 12.17.** The surrogate firm reward-to-volatility criterion.

## 12.7. Summary

In Chapter 12, we have examined the pertinent aspects of capital market theory and the implications of that theory for project selection. The fundamental advantage of a project selection methodology using capital market theory is that it takes explicit recognition of the market-assessed risk of both the firm and the candidate project. Rather than assume a *fixed* weighted average cost of capital as a base return rate for project selection, the capital market methodology tempers the risk premium required of the project by the risk involved. In actuality, the *risk* turns out to be the relative volatility of the project return rate to the market rate, and the comparative risk basis is the market-established counterpart for the firm. It is also demonstrated that the proper selection criterion is the reward-to-volatility ratio of the firm since projects that provide ratios greater than that of the firm will, in general, increase the present net worth of the firm. Thus, the capital market method of project selection solves both the capital availability and capital usage aspects of the resource allocation problem simultaneously, using the market as the mediating mechanism.

The limitations of capital market methodology seem to lie in the area of model inadequacy (the Sharpe-Lintner straight-line, single-variable model may not suffice), and in its fundamental assumption of risk avoidance on the part of the firm. The first inadequacy is being remedied by research into multivariable models (see Jensen [8]), and the second is really not an impediment since most firms seem to fit this general category—namely, that of requiring more than a uniform increase in return rate for increased riskiness in its investments. In any event, capital market theory *seems* to offer the most fertile opportunities for future modeling that will effectively allocate resources for productive investment within the firm, under very special assumptions. As the models and the methodology become more refined, however, the result should be increased validity and predictive capability.

## APPENDIX 12.A. PROOF THAT PROJECT ACCEPTANCE VIA THE REWARD-TO-VOLATILITY RATIO INCREASES THE FIRM'S NET WORTH

The acceptance of a favorable project (i.e., one that will cause an expected increase in the firm's net worth) temporarily throws the pricing of the firm's shares on the market into disequilibrium, with the firm's reward-to-volatility ordered pair $[(R_0 - R_f), \beta_0]$ plotting above the market line as indicated by Eq. (12.25). This increase in $E(R_0)$ causes individuals to demand more of the firm's shares, which bids up the share price. In turn, equilibrium is restored when $E(R_0)$ is reduced due to the increased price paid for the firm's shares. The root cause is the expected (believed) increase in net worth of the firm caused by the acceptance of favorable projects. The following mathematical analysis will help one see this fact.

For simplicity, consider a *one-period* firm whose entire capital structure consists of equity shares.[12] Income taxes are assumed nonexistent. Let

$P =$ the present *equilibrium* price of the firm's shares before acceptance of the new project, $i$.

$P' =$ the revised out-of-equilibrium price of the firm's shares after acceptance of the new project.

$N_0 =$ number of equity shares outstanding before acceptance of the new project.

$N_i =$ the additional shares issued at price $P'$ to finance the project.

$X_0 =$ the (random) dollar value of the firm's cash inflow before acceptance of the new project.

$X_i =$ the (random) dollar value of the cash inflow from the project to the firm, after acceptance of the project.

$C_i =$ the present cost of the project.

$R_0 =$ the present return rate for the firm, $= X_0/N_0 P$.

$R_i =$ the projected return rate for the project.

$R_M =$ the return rate for the market portfolio.

$R_f =$ the default-free interest rate.

Before acceptance of the project, Eq. (12.25) indicates that the expected return rate for the firm is

$$E(R_0) = R_f + \frac{\text{Cov}(R_0 R_M)}{\sigma_M^2}[E(R_M) - R_f];  \qquad (A12.1)$$

---

[12]Rubenstein [16] assumes this; but, as he points out, this assumption is merely convenient, not necessary. Mossin [13], for example, assumes the opposite; namely, that the project is financed entirely by borrowed capital. What is important is the implied assumption in both cases that there are no income taxes.

and by taking the expectation of the definition of the firm's return rate, $R_0$, we have

$$X_0 = R_0 N_0 P$$

$$E(X_0) = N_0 P E(R_0). \tag{A12.2}$$

From Eqs. (A12.2) and (A12.1) we obtain the expected value of the firm's present cash inflow:

$$E(X_0) = N_0 P R_f + N_0 P \frac{E(R_M) - R_f}{\sigma_M^2} \text{Cov} (R_0 R_M)$$

$$= N_0 P R_f + \lambda \text{Cov} (N_0 P R_0, R_M)$$

$$= N_0 P R_f + \lambda \text{Cov} (X_0, R_M) \tag{A12.3}$$

where

$$\lambda = \frac{[E(R_0) - R_f]}{\sigma_M^2}.$$

After acceptance of the project, the firm's cash inflow will be $X_0 + X_i$ so that the balance equation for *before* and *after* acceptance conditions becomes

$$\underbrace{E(X_0 + X_i)}_{\text{After acceptance of project}} - \underbrace{E(X_0)}_{\text{Before acceptance}} = \underbrace{E(X_i)}_{\text{Cash flow due to project}}. \tag{A12.4}$$

Now $E(X_0 + X_i)$, in terms of the new market parameters, becomes

$$E(X_0 + X_i) = R_f(N_0 + N_i)P' + \lambda \text{Cov} (X_0 + X_i, R_M) \tag{A12.5}$$

and by definition the return, $R_i$, on the project itself provides an evaluation of $E(X_i)$, thus:

$$R_i = \frac{X_i}{N_i P'},$$

or

$$E(X_i) = N_i P' E(R_i). \tag{A12.6}$$

Thus, we have in Eqs. (A12.3), (A12.5), and (A12.6) the necessary expressions to incorporate into the balance Eq. (A12.4). Making these substitutions, we obtain

$$R_f(N_0 + N_i)P' - R_f N_0 P + \lambda[\text{Cov} (X_0 + X_i, R_M) - \text{Cov} (X_0, R_M)] = N_i P' E(R_i). \tag{A12.7}$$

Recombining terms to bring the factors containing $(P' - P)$ to the left side, we find

$$R_f N_0(P' - P) = N_i P' E(R_i) - \lambda[\text{Cov} (X_0 + X_i, R_M) - \text{Cov} (X_0, R_M)] - N_i P' R_f. \tag{A12.8}$$

In Eq. (A12.8), consider for the moment the two terms involving the covariances. These can be expanded by the expected value operator into

$$\text{Cov} (X_0 + X_i, R_M) = E\{[(X_0 + X_i) + \mu_{X_0 + X_i}][R_M - \mu_{RM}]\}$$

and

$$\text{Cov} (X_0, R_M) = E[(X_0 - \mu_{X_0})(R_M - \mu_{RM})];$$

but recalling that

$$X_0 = N_0 P R_0$$
$$X_i = N_i P' R_i$$
$$X_0 + X_i = N_0 P R_0 + N_i P' R_i$$

$$\tag{A12.9}$$

and by taking the expectations of these we have expressions for the required means, thus:

$$\mu_{X_0} = E(X_0) = N_0 P E(R_0) = N_0 P \bar{R}_0$$
$$\mu_{X_i} = E(X_i) = N_i P' E(R_i) = N_i P' \bar{R}_i$$
$$\mu_{X_0+X_i} = E(X_0 + X_i) = N_0 P \bar{R}_0 + N_i P' \bar{R}_i.$$

$$\tag{A12.10}$$

The difference in covariances thus becomes

$$\Delta \text{Cov}(\cdot) = \text{Cov}(X_0 + X_i, R_M) - \text{Cov}(X_0, R_M)$$
$$= E\{[(X_0 + X_i) - \mu_{X_0-X_i}]R_M - [(X_0 + X_i) - \mu_{X_0+X_i}]\mu_{R_m}\}$$
$$- E[(X_0 - \mu_{X_0})R_M - (X_0 - \mu_{X_0})\mu_{R_M}],$$

which after substituting Eqs. (A12.9) and (A12.10) and after several steps of algebraic manipulations (omitted here), we obtain

$$\Delta \text{Cov}(\cdot) = E[N_i P'(R_i - \bar{R}_i)(R_M - \bar{R}_M)]$$
$$= N_i P' \text{Cov}(R_i, R_M). \tag{A12.11}$$

Finally, after substitution of Eq. (A12.11), Eq. (A12.8) becomes

$$R_f N_0 (P' - P) = N_i P' E(R_i) - (\lambda N_i P' \text{Cov}(R_i, R_M) + N_i P' R_f); \tag{A12.12}$$

however, on the right-hand side $N_i P'$ is simply the cost of the project (in terms of the new equity stock sold to finance it), so by factoring $N_i P'$ and replacing it by $C_i$, Eq. (A12.12) becomes

$$R_f N_0 (P' - P) = C_i [E(R_i) - (R_f + \lambda \text{Cov}(R_i, R_M)]. \tag{A12.13}$$

By dividing Eq. (A12.13) by $R_f$, we have

$$N_0 (P' - P) = C_i \left[ \frac{E(R_i) - (R_f + \lambda \text{Cov}(R_i, R_M)}{R_f} \right]. \tag{A12.14}$$

We now recognize the left side of Eq. (A12.14), i.e., $N_0(P' - P)$, as the expected increase in the net worth of the firm and note that since $C_i > 0$ and $R_f > 0$, then $N_0(P' - P)$ will be positive whenever the numerator of Eq. (A12.14) is positive. Hence, the criterion for accepting a project that is expected to increase the firm's net worth is

$$E(R_i) - [R_f + \lambda \text{Cov}(R_i, R_M)] > 0$$

or recalling that

$$\beta_i = \frac{\text{Cov}(R_i, R_M)}{\sigma_M^2} \quad \text{and} \quad \lambda = \frac{E(R_M) - R_f}{\sigma_M^2},$$

then the criterion is

$$E(R_i) - R_f > \lambda \operatorname{Cov}(R_i, R_M) = \left[\frac{E(R_M) - R_f}{\sigma_M^2}\right] \operatorname{Cov}(R_i, R_M)$$

or

$$\frac{E(R_i) - R_f}{\beta_i} > E(R_M) - R_f. \tag{A12.15}$$

## REFERENCES

[1] BOWER, RICHARD S., and DONALD R. LESSARD, "An Operational Approach to Risk-Screening," *Journal of Finance*, **28**(2) (May, 1973), pp. 321–37.

[2] BREEN, WILLIAM J., and EUGENE M. LERNER, "On the Use of $\beta$ in Regulatory Proceedings," *The Bell Journal of Economics and Management Science*, **3**(2) (August, 1972), pp. 612–21.

[3] CAMPANELLA, FRANK B., *The Measurement of Portfolio Risk Exposure* (Lexington, Mass.: D. C. Heath and Company, 1972).

[4] CAMPBELL, MARC A., "A Method of Project Selection for the Private Firm," (Unpublished M. S. Thesis, Kansas State University, Manhattan, Kan., 1976).

[5] FAMA, EUGENE, "Risk, Return and Equilibrium: Some Clarifying Comments," *Journal of Finance*, **23**(1) (March, 1968), pp. 29–40.

[6] GRAYBILL, FRANKLIN A., *An Introduction to Linear Statistical Models*, Vol. I (New York: McGraw-Hill Book Co., 1961).

[7] HANOCH, G., and H. LEVY, "The Efficiency Analysis of Choices Involving Risk," *Review of Economic Studies* (July, 1969), pp. 338–41.

[8] JENSEN, MICHAEL C., "Capital Markets: Theory and Evidence," *The Bell Journal of Economics and Management Science*, **3**(2) (Autumn, 1972), pp. 357–98.

[9] _____, "Risk, the Pricing of Capital Assets, and the Evaluation of Investment Portfolios," *Journal of Business*, **42**(2) (April, 1969), pp. 167–247.

[10] LEVY, HAIM, and MARSHALL SARNAT, *Investment and Portfolio Analysis* (New York: John Wiley & Sons, Inc., 1972), pp. 463–65.

[11] LINTNER, JOHN, "Security Prices, Risk, and Maximal Gains from Diversification," *Journal of Finance*, **20**(4) (December, 1965), pp. 587–615.

[12] MARKOWITZ, HARRY, *Portfolio Selection: Efficient Diversification of Investments* (New York: John Wiley & Sons, Inc., 1959).

[13] MOSSIN, J., "Security Pricing and Investment Criteria in Competitive Markets," *American Economic Review*, **59**(5) (December, 1969) pp. 749–56.

[14] MYERS, STEWART C., "On the Use of $\beta$ in Regulatory Proceedings: A Comment," *The Bell Journal of Economics and Management Science*, **3**(2) (August, 1972), pp. 622–27.

[15] NETER, JOHN, and WILLIAM WASSERMAN, *Applied Linear Statistical Models* (Homewood, Ill.: Richard D. Irwin, Inc., 1974).

[16] RUBENSTEIN, MARK E., "A Mean-Variance Synthesis of Corporate Financial Policy," *Journal of Finance*, **28**(1) (March, 1973), pp. 167–81.

[17] SHARPE, WILLIAM F., "A Simplified Model for Portfolio Analysis," *Management Science*, **9**(2) (January, 1963), pp. 277–93.

[18] _____, *Portfolio Theory and Capital Markets* (New York: McGraw-Hill Book Co., 1970).

[19] TREYNOR, JACK L., "How to Rate Management of Investment Funds," *Harvard Business Review*, **43**(1) (January–February, 1965), pp. 63–75.

[20] TUTTLE, DONALD L., and R. H. LITZENBERGER, "Leverage, Diversification, and Capital Market Effects on a Risk-Adjusted Capital Budgeting Framework," *Journal of Finance*, **23**(3) (June, 1968), pp. 427–43.

[21] U.S. Board of Governors of the Federal Reserve System, *Federal Reserve Bulletin* (Washington: Board of Governors, Federal Reserve System, various issues).

[22] U.S. Bureau of the Budget, Office of Statistical Standards, *Standard Industrial Classification Manual* (Washington, D.C.: U.S. Government Printing Office, 1972).

[23] U.S. Department of Commerce, Bureau of Economic Analysis, *Business Statistics: The Biennial Supplement to the Survey of Current Business* (Washington, D.C.: U.S. Government Printing Office, various issues).

[24] *Value Line Investment Survey, The* (New York: Arnold Bernhard, Inc., 1976).

[25] WESTON, J. FRED, "Investment Decisions Using the Capital Asset Pricing Model," *Financial Management*, **2**(1) (Spring, 1973), pp. 25–33.

APPENDICES

# APPENDIX A.1

$1/4\%$ INTEREST FACTORS FOR DISCRETE COMPOUNDING PERIODS

| | SINGLE PAYMENT | | UNIFORM PAYMENT SERIES | | | | GRADIENT SERIES | |
|---|---|---|---|---|---|---|---|---|
| | Compound Amount Factor | Present Worth Factor | Present Worth Factor | Capital Recovery Factor | Compound Amount Factor | Sinking Fund Factor | Gradient Uniform Series | Gradient Present Worth |
| $N$ | Find $F$ Given $P$ $F/P$ | Find $P$ Given $F$ $P/F$ | Find $P$ Given $A$ $P/A$ | Find $A$ Given $P$ $A/P$ | Find $F$ Given $A$ $F/A$ | Find $A$ Given $F$ $A/F$ | Find $A$ Given $G$ $A/G$ | Find $P$ Given $G$ $P/G$ |
| 1 | 1.003 | 0.9975 | 0.9975 | 1.0025 | 1.000 | 1.0000 | 0.0000 | 0.000 |
| 2 | 1.005 | 0.9950 | 1.9925 | 0.5019 | 2.002 | 0.4994 | 0.4994 | 0.995 |
| 3 | 1.008 | 0.9925 | 2.9851 | 0.3350 | 3.008 | 0.3325 | 0.9983 | 2.980 |
| 4 | 1.010 | 0.9901 | 3.9751 | 0.2516 | 4.015 | 0.2491 | 1.4969 | 5.950 |
| 5 | 1.013 | 0.9876 | 4.9627 | 0.2015 | 5.025 | 0.1990 | 1.9950 | 9.901 |
| 6 | 1.015 | 0.9851 | 5.9478 | 0.1681 | 6.038 | 0.1656 | 2.4927 | 14.826 |
| 7 | 1.018 | 0.9827 | 6.9305 | 0.1443 | 7.053 | 0.1418 | 2.9900 | 20.722 |
| 8 | 1.020 | 0.9802 | 7.9107 | 0.1264 | 8.070 | 0.1239 | 3.4869 | 27.584 |
| 9 | 1.023 | 0.9778 | 8.8885 | 0.1125 | 9.091 | 0.1100 | 3.9834 | 35.406 |
| 10 | 1.025 | 0.9753 | 9.8639 | 0.1014 | 10.113 | 0.0989 | 4.4794 | 44.184 |
| 11 | 1.028 | 0.9729 | 10.8368 | 0.0923 | 11.139 | 0.0898 | 4.9750 | 53.913 |
| 12 | 1.030 | 0.9705 | 11.8073 | 0.0847 | 12.166 | 0.0822 | 5.4702 | 64.589 |
| 13 | 1.033 | 0.9681 | 12.7753 | 0.0783 | 13.197 | 0.0758 | 5.9650 | 76.205 |
| 14 | 1.036 | 0.9656 | 13.7410 | 0.0728 | 14.230 | 0.0703 | 6.4594 | 88.759 |
| 15 | 1.038 | 0.9632 | 14.7042 | 0.0680 | 15.265 | 0.0655 | 6.9534 | 102.244 |
| 16 | 1.041 | 0.9608 | 15.6650 | 0.0638 | 16.304 | 0.0613 | 7.4469 | 116.657 |
| 17 | 1.043 | 0.9584 | 16.6235 | 0.0602 | 17.344 | 0.0577 | 7.9401 | 131.992 |
| 18 | 1.046 | 0.9561 | 17.5795 | 0.0569 | 18.388 | 0.0544 | 8.4328 | 148.245 |
| 19 | 1.049 | 0.9537 | 18.5332 | 0.0540 | 19.434 | 0.0515 | 8.9251 | 165.411 |
| 20 | 1.051 | 0.9513 | 19.4845 | 0.0513 | 20.482 | 0.0488 | 9.4170 | 183.485 |
| 21 | 1.054 | 0.9489 | 20.4334 | 0.0489 | 21.533 | 0.0464 | 9.9085 | 202.463 |
| 22 | 1.056 | 0.9466 | 21.3800 | 0.0468 | 22.587 | 0.0443 | 10.3995 | 222.341 |
| 23 | 1.059 | 0.9442 | 22.3241 | 0.0448 | 23.644 | 0.0423 | 10.8901 | 243.113 |
| 24 | 1.062 | 0.9418 | 23.2660 | 0.0430 | 24.703 | 0.0405 | 11.3804 | 264.775 |
| 25 | 1.064 | 0.9395 | 24.2055 | 0.0413 | 25.765 | 0.0388 | 11.8702 | 287.323 |
| 26 | 1.067 | 0.9371 | 25.1426 | 0.0398 | 26.829 | 0.0373 | 12.3596 | 310.752 |
| 27 | 1.070 | 0.9348 | 26.0774 | 0.0383 | 27.896 | 0.0358 | 12.8485 | 335.057 |
| 28 | 1.072 | 0.9325 | 27.0099 | 0.0370 | 28.966 | 0.0345 | 13.3371 | 360.233 |
| 29 | 1.075 | 0.9301 | 27.9400 | 0.0358 | 30.038 | 0.0333 | 13.8252 | 386.278 |
| 30 | 1.078 | 0.9278 | 28.8679 | 0.0346 | 31.113 | 0.0321 | 14.3130 | 413.185 |
| 31 | 1.080 | 0.9255 | 29.7934 | 0.0336 | 32.191 | 0.0311 | 14.8003 | 440.950 |
| 32 | 1.083 | 0.9232 | 30.7166 | 0.0326 | 33.272 | 0.0301 | 15.2872 | 469.570 |
| 33 | 1.086 | 0.9209 | 31.6375 | 0.0316 | 34.355 | 0.0291 | 15.7736 | 499.039 |
| 34 | 1.089 | 0.9186 | 32.5561 | 0.0307 | 35.441 | 0.0282 | 16.2597 | 529.353 |
| 35 | 1.091 | 0.9163 | 33.4724 | 0.0299 | 36.529 | 0.0274 | 16.7454 | 560.508 |
| 36 | 1.094 | 0.9140 | 34.3865 | 0.0291 | 37.621 | 0.0266 | 17.2306 | 592.499 |
| 37 | 1.097 | 0.9118 | 35.2982 | 0.0283 | 38.715 | 0.0258 | 17.7154 | 625.322 |
| 38 | 1.100 | 0.9095 | 36.2077 | 0.0276 | 39.811 | 0.0251 | 18.1998 | 658.973 |
| 39 | 1.102 | 0.9072 | 37.1149 | 0.0269 | 40.911 | 0.0244 | 18.6838 | 693.447 |
| 40 | 1.105 | 0.9050 | 38.0199 | 0.0263 | 42.013 | 0.0238 | 19.1673 | 728.740 |

# APPENDIX A.2

$1/2\%$ INTEREST FACTORS FOR DISCRETE COMPOUNDING PERIODS

| | SINGLE PAYMENT | | UNIFORM PAYMENT SERIES | | | | GRADIENT SERIES | |
|---|---|---|---|---|---|---|---|---|
| | Compound Amount Factor | Present Worth Factor | Present Worth Factor | Capital Recovery Factor | Compound Amount Factor | Sinking Fund Factor | Gradient Uniform Series | Gradient Present Worth |
| N | Find $F$ Given $P$ $F/P$ | Find $P$ Given $F$ $P/F$ | Find $P$ Given $A$ $P/A$ | Find $A$ Given $P$ $A/P$ | Find $F$ Given $A$ $F/A$ | Find $A$ Given $F$ $A/F$ | Find $A$ Given $G$ $A/G$ | Find $P$ Given $G$ $P/G$ |
| 1 | 1.005 | 0.9950 | 0.9950 | 1.0050 | 1.000 | 1.0000 | 0.0000 | 0.000 |
| 2 | 1.010 | 0.9901 | 1.9851 | 0.5038 | 2.005 | 0.4988 | 0.4988 | 0.990 |
| 3 | 1.015 | 0.9851 | 2.9702 | 0.3367 | 3.015 | 0.3317 | 0.9967 | 2.960 |
| 4 | 1.020 | 0.9802 | 3.9505 | 0.2531 | 4.030 | 0.2481 | 1.4938 | 5.901 |
| 5 | 1.025 | 0.9754 | 4.9259 | 0.2030 | 5.050 | 0.1980 | 1.9900 | 9.803 |
| 6 | 1.030 | 0.9705 | 5.8964 | 0.1696 | 6.076 | 0.1646 | 2.4855 | 14.655 |
| 7 | 1.036 | 0.9657 | 6.8621 | 0.1457 | 7.106 | 0.1407 | 2.9801 | 20.449 |
| 8 | 1.041 | 0.9609 | 7.8230 | 0.1278 | 8.141 | 0.1228 | 3.4738 | 27.176 |
| 9 | 1.046 | 0.9561 | 8.7791 | 0.1139 | 9.182 | 0.1089 | 3.9668 | 34.824 |
| 10 | 1.051 | 0.9513 | 9.7304 | 0.1028 | 10.228 | 0.0978 | 4.4589 | 43.386 |
| 11 | 1.056 | 0.9466 | 10.6770 | 0.0937 | 11.279 | 0.0887 | 4.9501 | 52.853 |
| 12 | 1.062 | 0.9419 | 11.6189 | 0.0861 | 12.336 | 0.0811 | 5.4406 | 63.214 |
| 13 | 1.067 | 0.9372 | 12.5562 | 0.0796 | 13.397 | 0.0746 | 5.9302 | 74.460 |
| 14 | 1.072 | 0.9326 | 13.4887 | 0.0741 | 14.464 | 0.0691 | 6.4190 | 86.583 |
| 15 | 1.078 | 0.9279 | 14.4166 | 0.0694 | 15.537 | 0.0644 | 6.9069 | 99.574 |
| 16 | 1.083 | 0.9233 | 15.3399 | 0.0652 | 16.614 | 0.0602 | 7.3940 | 113.424 |
| 17 | 1.088 | 0.9187 | 16.2586 | 0.0615 | 17.697 | 0.0565 | 7.8803 | 128.123 |
| 18 | 1.094 | 0.9141 | 17.1728 | 0.0582 | 18.786 | 0.0532 | 8.3658 | 143.663 |
| 19 | 1.099 | 0.9096 | 18.0824 | 0.0553 | 19.880 | 0.0503 | 8.8504 | 160.036 |
| 20 | 1.105 | 0.9051 | 18.9874 | 0.0527 | 20.979 | 0.0477 | 9.3342 | 177.232 |
| 21 | 1.110 | 0.9006 | 19.8880 | 0.0503 | 22.084 | 0.0453 | 9.8172 | 195.243 |
| 22 | 1.116 | 0.8961 | 20.7841 | 0.0481 | 23.194 | 0.0431 | 10.2993 | 214.061 |
| 23 | 1.122 | 0.8916 | 21.6757 | 0.0461 | 24.310 | 0.0411 | 10.7806 | 233.677 |
| 24 | 1.127 | 0.8872 | 22.5629 | 0.0443 | 25.432 | 0.0393 | 11.2611 | 254.082 |
| 25 | 1.133 | 0.8828 | 23.4456 | 0.0427 | 26.559 | 0.0377 | 11.7407 | 275.269 |
| 26 | 1.138 | 0.8784 | 24.3240 | 0.0411 | 27.692 | 0.0361 | 12.2195 | 297.228 |
| 27 | 1.144 | 0.8740 | 25.1980 | 0.0397 | 28.830 | 0.0347 | 12.6975 | 319.952 |
| 28 | 1.150 | 0.8697 | 26.0677 | 0.0384 | 29.975 | 0.0334 | 13.1747 | 343.433 |
| 29 | 1.156 | 0.8653 | 26.9330 | 0.0371 | 31.124 | 0.0321 | 13.6510 | 367.663 |
| 30 | 1.161 | 0.8610 | 27.7941 | 0.0360 | 32.280 | 0.0310 | 14.1265 | 392.632 |
| 31 | 1.167 | 0.8567 | 28.6508 | 0.0349 | 33.441 | 0.0299 | 14.6012 | 418.335 |
| 32 | 1.173 | 0.8525 | 29.5033 | 0.0339 | 34.609 | 0.0289 | 15.0750 | 444.762 |
| 33 | 1.179 | 0.8482 | 30.3515 | 0.0329 | 35.782 | 0.0279 | 15.5480 | 471.906 |
| 34 | 1.185 | 0.8440 | 31.1955 | 0.0321 | 36.961 | 0.0271 | 16.0202 | 499.758 |
| 35 | 1.191 | 0.8398 | 32.0354 | 0.0312 | 38.145 | 0.0262 | 16.4915 | 528.312 |
| 36 | 1.197 | 0.8356 | 32.8710 | 0.0304 | 39.336 | 0.0254 | 16.9621 | 557.560 |
| 37 | 1.203 | 0.8315 | 33.7025 | 0.0297 | 40.533 | 0.0247 | 17.4317 | 587.493 |
| 38 | 1.209 | 0.8274 | 34.5299 | 0.0290 | 41.735 | 0.0240 | 17.9006 | 618.105 |
| 39 | 1.215 | 0.8232 | 35.3531 | 0.0283 | 42.944 | 0.0233 | 18.3686 | 649.388 |
| 40 | 1.221 | 0.8191 | 36.1722 | 0.0276 | 44.159 | 0.0226 | 18.8359 | 681.335 |

# APPENDIX A.3

| | SINGLE PAYMENT | | UNIFORM PAYMENT SERIES | | | | GRADIENT SERIES | |
|---|---|---|---|---|---|---|---|---|
| | Compound Amount Factor | Present Worth Factor | Present Worth Factor | Capital Recovery Factor | Compound Amount Factor | Sinking Fund Factor | Gradient Uniform Series | Gradient Present Worth |
| N | Find F Given P F/P | Find P Given F P/F | Find P Given A P/A | Find A Given P A/P | Find F Given A F/A | Find A Given F A/F | Find A Given G A/G | Find P Given G P/G |
| 1 | 1.010 | 0.9901 | 0.9901 | 1.0100 | 1.000 | 1.0000 | 0.0000 | 0.000 |
| 2 | 1.020 | 0.9803 | 1.9704 | 0.5075 | 2.010 | 0.4975 | 0.4975 | 0.980 |
| 3 | 1.030 | 0.9706 | 2.9410 | 0.3400 | 3.030 | 0.3300 | 0.9934 | 2.921 |
| 4 | 1.041 | 0.9610 | 3.9020 | 0.2563 | 4.060 | 0.2463 | 1.4876 | 5.804 |
| 5 | 1.051 | 0.9515 | 4.8534 | 0.2060 | 5.101 | 0.1960 | 1.9801 | 9.610 |
| 6 | 1.062 | 0.9420 | 5.7955 | 0.1725 | 6.152 | 0.1625 | 2.4710 | 14.321 |
| 7 | 1.072 | 0.9327 | 6.7282 | 0.1486 | 7.214 | 0.1386 | 2.9602 | 19.917 |
| 8 | 1.083 | 0.9235 | 7.6517 | 0.1307 | 8.286 | 0.1207 | 3.4478 | 26.381 |
| 9 | 1.094 | 0.9143 | 8.5660 | 0.1167 | 9.369 | 0.1067 | 3.9337 | 33.696 |
| 10 | 1.105 | 0.9053 | 9.4713 | 0.1056 | 10.462 | 0.0956 | 4.4179 | 41.843 |
| 11 | 1.116 | 0.8963 | 10.3676 | 0.0965 | 11.567 | 0.0865 | 4.9005 | 50.807 |
| 12 | 1.127 | 0.8874 | 11.2551 | 0.0888 | 12.683 | 0.0788 | 5.3815 | 60.569 |
| 13 | 1.138 | 0.8787 | 12.1337 | 0.0824 | 13.809 | 0.0724 | 5.8607 | 71.113 |
| 14 | 1.149 | 0.8700 | 13.0037 | 0.0769 | 14.947 | 0.0669 | 6.3384 | 82.422 |
| 15 | 1.161 | 0.8613 | 13.8651 | 0.0721 | 16.097 | 0.0621 | 6.8143 | 94.481 |
| 16 | 1.173 | 0.8528 | 14.7179 | 0.0679 | 17.258 | 0.0579 | 7.2886 | 107.273 |
| 17 | 1.184 | 0.8444 | 15.5623 | 0.0643 | 18.430 | 0.0543 | 7.7613 | 120.783 |
| 18 | 1.196 | 0.8360 | 16.3983 | 0.0610 | 19.615 | 0.0510 | 8.2323 | 134.996 |
| 19 | 1.208 | 0.8277 | 17.2260 | 0.0581 | 20.811 | 0.0481 | 8.7017 | 149.895 |
| 20 | 1.220 | 0.8195 | 18.0456 | 0.0554 | 22.019 | 0.0454 | 9.1694 | 165.466 |
| 21 | 1.232 | 0.8114 | 18.8570 | 0.0530 | 23.239 | 0.0430 | 9.6354 | 181.695 |
| 22 | 1.245 | 0.8034 | 19.6604 | 0.0509 | 24.472 | 0.0409 | 10.0998 | 198.566 |
| 23 | 1.257 | 0.7954 | 20.4558 | 0.0489 | 25.716 | 0.0389 | 10.5626 | 216.066 |
| 24 | 1.270 | 0.7876 | 21.2434 | 0.0471 | 26.973 | 0.0371 | 11.0237 | 234.180 |
| 25 | 1.282 | 0.7798 | 22.0232 | 0.0454 | 28.243 | 0.0354 | 11.4831 | 252.894 |
| 26 | 1.295 | 0.7720 | 22.7952 | 0.0439 | 29.526 | 0.0339 | 11.9409 | 272.196 |
| 27 | 1.308 | 0.7644 | 23.5596 | 0.0424 | 30.821 | 0.0324 | 12.3971 | 292.070 |
| 28 | 1.321 | 0.7568 | 24.3164 | 0.0411 | 32.129 | 0.0311 | 12.8516 | 312.505 |
| 29 | 1.335 | 0.7493 | 25.0658 | 0.0399 | 33.450 | 0.0299 | 13.3044 | 333.486 |
| 30 | 1.348 | 0.7419 | 25.8077 | 0.0387 | 34.785 | 0.0287 | 13.7557 | 355.002 |
| 31 | 1.361 | 0.7346 | 26.5423 | 0.0377 | 36.133 | 0.0277 | 14.2052 | 377.039 |
| 32 | 1.375 | 0.7273 | 27.2696 | 0.0367 | 37.494 | 0.0267 | 14.6532 | 399.586 |
| 33 | 1.389 | 0.7201 | 27.9897 | 0.0357 | 38.869 | 0.0257 | 15.0995 | 422.629 |
| 34 | 1.403 | 0.7130 | 28.7027 | 0.0348 | 40.258 | 0.0248 | 15.5441 | 446.157 |
| 35 | 1.417 | 0.7059 | 29.4086 | 0.0340 | 41.660 | 0.0240 | 15.9871 | 470.158 |
| 36 | 1.431 | 0.6989 | 30.1075 | 0.0332 | 43.077 | 0.0232 | 16.4285 | 494.621 |
| 37 | 1.445 | 0.6920 | 30.7995 | 0.0325 | 44.508 | 0.0225 | 16.8682 | 519.533 |
| 38 | 1.460 | 0.6852 | 31.4847 | 0.0318 | 45.953 | 0.0218 | 17.3063 | 544.884 |
| 39 | 1.474 | 0.6784 | 32.1630 | 0.0311 | 47.412 | 0.0211 | 17.7428 | 570.662 |
| 40 | 1.489 | 0.6717 | 32.8347 | 0.0305 | 48.886 | 0.0205 | 18.1776 | 596.856 |

# APPENDIX A.4

| | SINGLE PAYMENT | | UNIFORM PAYMENT SERIES | | | | GRADIENT SERIES | |
|---|---|---|---|---|---|---|---|---|
| | Compound Amount Factor | Present Worth Factor | Present Worth Factor | Capital Recovery Factor | Compound Amount Factor | Sinking Fund Factor | Gradient Uniform Series | Gradient Present Worth |
| $N$ | Find $F$ Given $P$ $F/P$ | Find $P$ Given $F$ $P/F$ | Find $P$ Given $A$ $P/A$ | Find $A$ Given $P$ $A/P$ | Find $F$ Given $A$ $F/A$ | Find $A$ Given $F$ $A/F$ | Find $A$ Given $G$ $A/G$ | Find $P$ Given $G$ $P/G$ |
| 1 | 1.030 | 0.9709 | 0.9709 | 1.0300 | 1.000 | 1.0000 | 0.0000 | 0.000 |
| 2 | 1.061 | 0.9426 | 1.9135 | 0.5226 | 2.030 | 0.4926 | 0.4926 | 0.943 |
| 3 | 1.093 | 0.9151 | 2.8286 | 0.3535 | 3.091 | 0.3235 | 0.9803 | 2.773 |
| 4 | 1.126 | 0.8885 | 3.7171 | 0.2690 | 4.184 | 0.2390 | 1.4631 | 5.438 |
| 5 | 1.159 | 0.8626 | 4.5797 | 0.2184 | 5.309 | 0.1884 | 1.9409 | 8.889 |
| 6 | 1.194 | 0.8375 | 5.4172 | 0.1846 | 6.468 | 0.1546 | 2.4138 | 13.076 |
| 7 | 1.230 | 0.8131 | 6.2303 | 0.1605 | 7.662 | 0.1305 | 2.8819 | 17.955 |
| 8 | 1.267 | 0.7894 | 7.0197 | 0.1425 | 8.892 | 0.1125 | 3.3450 | 23.481 |
| 9 | 1.305 | 0.7664 | 7.7861 | 0.1284 | 10.159 | 0.0984 | 3.8032 | 29.612 |
| 10 | 1.344 | 0.7441 | 8.5302 | 0.1172 | 11.464 | 0.0872 | 4.2565 | 36.309 |
| 11 | 1.384 | 0.7224 | 9.2526 | 0.1081 | 12.808 | 0.0781 | 4.7049 | 43.533 |
| 12 | 1.426 | 0.7014 | 9.9540 | 0.1005 | 14.192 | 0.0705 | 5.1485 | 51.248 |
| 13 | 1.469 | 0.6810 | 10.6350 | 0.0940 | 15.618 | 0.0640 | 5.5872 | 59.420 |
| 14 | 1.513 | 0.6611 | 11.2961 | 0.0885 | 17.086 | 0.0585 | 6.0210 | 68.014 |
| 15 | 1.558 | 0.6419 | 11.9379 | 0.0838 | 18.599 | 0.0538 | 6.4500 | 77.000 |
| 16 | 1.605 | 0.6232 | 12.5611 | 0.0796 | 20.157 | 0.0496 | 6.8742 | 86.348 |
| 17 | 1.653 | 0.6050 | 13.1661 | 0.0760 | 21.762 | 0.0460 | 7.2936 | 96.028 |
| 18 | 1.702 | 0.5874 | 13.7535 | 0.0727 | 23.414 | 0.0427 | 7.7081 | 106.014 |
| 19 | 1.754 | 0.5703 | 14.3238 | 0.0698 | 25.117 | 0.0398 | 8.1179 | 116.279 |
| 20 | 1.806 | 0.5537 | 14.8775 | 0.0672 | 26.870 | 0.0372 | 8.5229 | 126.799 |
| 21 | 1.860 | 0.5375 | 15.4150 | 0.0649 | 28.676 | 0.0349 | 8.9231 | 137.550 |
| 22 | 1.916 | 0.5219 | 15.9369 | 0.0627 | 30.537 | 0.0327 | 9.3186 | 148.509 |
| 23 | 1.974 | 0.5067 | 16.4436 | 0.0608 | 32.453 | 0.0308 | 9.7093 | 159.657 |
| 24 | 2.033 | 0.4919 | 16.9355 | 0.0590 | 34.426 | 0.0290 | 10.0954 | 170.971 |
| 25 | 2.094 | 0.4776 | 17.4131 | 0.0574 | 36.459 | 0.0274 | 10.4768 | 182.434 |
| 26 | 2.157 | 0.4637 | 17.8768 | 0.0559 | 38.553 | 0.0259 | 10.8535 | 194.026 |
| 27 | 2.221 | 0.4502 | 18.3270 | 0.0546 | 40.710 | 0.0246 | 11.2255 | 205.731 |
| 28 | 2.288 | 0.4371 | 18.7641 | 0.0533 | 42.931 | 0.0233 | 11.5930 | 217.532 |
| 29 | 2.357 | 0.4243 | 19.1885 | 0.0521 | 45.219 | 0.0221 | 11.9558 | 229.414 |
| 30 | 2.427 | 0.4120 | 19.6004 | 0.0510 | 47.575 | 0.0210 | 12.3141 | 241.361 |
| 31 | 2.500 | 0.4000 | 20.0004 | 0.0500 | 50.003 | 0.0200 | 12.6678 | 253.361 |
| 32 | 2.575 | 0.3883 | 20.3888 | 0.0490 | 52.503 | 0.0190 | 13.0169 | 265.399 |
| 33 | 2.652 | 0.3770 | 20.7658 | 0.0482 | 55.078 | 0.0182 | 13.3616 | 277.464 |
| 34 | 2.732 | 0.3660 | 21.1318 | 0.0473 | 57.730 | 0.0173 | 13.7018 | 289.544 |
| 35 | 2.814 | 0.3554 | 21.4872 | 0.0465 | 60.462 | 0.0165 | 14.0375 | 301.627 |
| 36 | 2.898 | 0.3450 | 21.8323 | 0.0458 | 63.276 | 0.0158 | 14.3688 | 313.703 |
| 37 | 2.985 | 0.3350 | 22.1672 | 0.0451 | 66.174 | 0.0151 | 14.6957 | 325.762 |
| 38 | 3.075 | 0.3252 | 22.4925 | 0.0445 | 69.159 | 0.0145 | 15.0182 | 337.796 |
| 39 | 3.167 | 0.3158 | 22.8082 | 0.0438 | 72.234 | 0.0138 | 15.3363 | 349.794 |
| 40 | 3.262 | 0.3066 | 23.1148 | 0.0433 | 75.401 | 0.0133 | 15.6502 | 361.750 |

# APPENDIX A.5

| | SINGLE PAYMENT | | UNIFORM PAYMENT SERIES | | | | GRADIENT SERIES | |
|---|---|---|---|---|---|---|---|---|
| | Compound Amount Factor | Present Worth Factor | Present Worth Factor | Capital Recovery Factor | Compound Amount Factor | Sinking Fund Factor | Gradient Uniform Series | Gradient Present Worth |
| $N$ | Find $F$ Given $P$ $F/P$ | Find $P$ Given $F$ $P/F$ | Find $P$ Given $A$ $P/A$ | Find $A$ Given $P$ $A/P$ | Find $F$ Given $A$ $F/A$ | Find $A$ Given $F$ $A/F$ | Find $A$ Given $G$ $A/G$ | Find $P$ Given $G$ $P/G$ |
| 1 | 1.050 | 0.9524 | 0.9524 | 1.0500 | 1.000 | 1.0000 | 0.0000 | 0.000 |
| 2 | 1.103 | 0.9070 | 1.8594 | 0.5378 | 2.050 | 0.4878 | 0.4878 | 0.907 |
| 3 | 1.158 | 0.8638 | 2.7232 | 0.3672 | 3.152 | 0.3172 | 0.9675 | 2.635 |
| 4 | 1.216 | 0.8227 | 3.5460 | 0.2820 | 4.310 | 0.2320 | 1.4391 | 5.103 |
| 5 | 1.276 | 0.7835 | 4.3295 | 0.2310 | 5.526 | 0.1810 | 1.9025 | 8.237 |
| 6 | 1.340 | 0.7462 | 5.0757 | 0.1970 | 6.802 | 0.1470 | 2.3579 | 11.968 |
| 7 | 1.407 | 0.7107 | 5.7864 | 0.1728 | 8.142 | 0.1228 | 2.8052 | 16.232 |
| 8 | 1.477 | 0.6768 | 6.4632 | 0.1547 | 9.549 | 0.1047 | 3.2445 | 20.970 |
| 9 | 1.551 | 0.6446 | 7.1078 | 0.1407 | 11.027 | 0.0907 | 3.6758 | 26.127 |
| 10 | 1.629 | 0.6139 | 7.7217 | 0.1295 | 12.578 | 0.0795 | 4.0991 | 31.652 |
| 11 | 1.710 | 0.5847 | 8.3064 | 0.1204 | 14.207 | 0.0704 | 4.5144 | 37.499 |
| 12 | 1.796 | 0.5568 | 8.8633 | 0.1128 | 15.917 | 0.0628 | 4.9219 | 43.624 |
| 13 | 1.886 | 0.5303 | 9.3936 | 0.1065 | 17.713 | 0.0565 | 5.3215 | 49.988 |
| 14 | 1.980 | 0.5051 | 9.8986 | 0.1010 | 19.599 | 0.0510 | 5.7133 | 56.554 |
| 15 | 2.079 | 0.4810 | 10.3797 | 0.0963 | 21.579 | 0.0463 | 6.0973 | 63.288 |
| 16 | 2.183 | 0.4581 | 10.8378 | 0.0923 | 23.657 | 0.0423 | 6.4736 | 70.160 |
| 17 | 2.292 | 0.4363 | 11.2741 | 0.0887 | 25.840 | 0.0387 | 6.8423 | 77.140 |
| 18 | 2.407 | 0.4155 | 11.6896 | 0.0855 | 28.132 | 0.0355 | 7.2034 | 84.204 |
| 19 | 2.527 | 0.3957 | 12.0853 | 0.0827 | 30.539 | 0.0327 | 7.5569 | 91.328 |
| 20 | 2.653 | 0.3769 | 12.4622 | 0.0802 | 33.066 | 0.0302 | 7.9030 | 98.488 |
| 21 | 2.786 | 0.3589 | 12.8212 | 0.0780 | 35.719 | 0.0280 | 8.2416 | 105.667 |
| 22 | 2.925 | 0.3418 | 13.1630 | 0.0760 | 38.505 | 0.0260 | 8.5730 | 112.846 |
| 23 | 3.072 | 0.3256 | 13.4886 | 0.0741 | 41.430 | 0.0241 | 8.8971 | 120.009 |
| 24 | 3.225 | 0.3101 | 13.7986 | 0.0725 | 44.502 | 0.0225 | 9.2140 | 127.140 |
| 25 | 3.386 | 0.2953 | 14.0939 | 0.0710 | 47.727 | 0.0210 | 9.5238 | 134.228 |
| 26 | 3.556 | 0.2812 | 14.3752 | 0.0696 | 51.113 | 0.0196 | 9.8266 | 141.259 |
| 27 | 3.733 | 0.2678 | 14.6430 | 0.0683 | 54.669 | 0.0183 | 10.1224 | 148.223 |
| 28 | 3.920 | 0.2551 | 14.8981 | 0.0671 | 58.403 | 0.0171 | 10.4114 | 155.110 |
| 29 | 4.116 | 0.2429 | 15.1411 | 0.0660 | 62.323 | 0.0160 | 10.6936 | 161.913 |
| 30 | 4.322 | 0.2314 | 15.3725 | 0.0651 | 66.439 | 0.0151 | 10.9691 | 168.623 |
| 31 | 4.538 | 0.2204 | 15.5928 | 0.0641 | 70.761 | 0.0141 | 11.2381 | 175.233 |
| 32 | 4.765 | 0.2099 | 15.8027 | 0.0633 | 75.299 | 0.0133 | 11.5005 | 181.739 |
| 33 | 5.003 | 0.1999 | 16.0025 | 0.0625 | 80.064 | 0.0125 | 11.7566 | 188.135 |
| 34 | 5.253 | 0.1904 | 16.1929 | 0.0618 | 85.067 | 0.0118 | 12.0063 | 194.417 |
| 35 | 5.516 | 0.1813 | 16.3742 | 0.0611 | 90.320 | 0.0111 | 12.2498 | 200.581 |
| 36 | 5.792 | 0.1727 | 16.5469 | 0.0604 | 95.836 | 0.0104 | 12.4872 | 206.624 |
| 37 | 6.081 | 0.1644 | 16.7113 | 0.0598 | 101.628 | 0.0098 | 12.7186 | 212.543 |
| 38 | 6.385 | 0.1566 | 16.8679 | 0.0593 | 107.710 | 0.0093 | 12.9440 | 218.338 |
| 39 | 6.705 | 0.1491 | 17.0170 | 0.0588 | 114.095 | 0.0088 | 13.1636 | 224.005 |
| 40 | 7.040 | 0.1420 | 17.1591 | 0.0583 | 120.800 | 0.0083 | 13.3775 | 229.545 |

# APPENDIX A.6

## 8 % INTEREST FACTORS FOR DISCRETE COMPOUNDING PERIODS

| | SINGLE PAYMENT | | UNIFORM PAYMENT SERIES | | | | GRADIENT SERIES | |
|---|---|---|---|---|---|---|---|---|
| | Compound Amount Factor | Present Worth Factor | Present Worth Factor | Capital Recovery Factor | Compound Amount Factor | Sinking Fund Factor | Gradient Uniform Series | Gradient Present Worth |
| N | Find F Given P F/P | Find P Given F P/F | Find P Given A P/A | Find A Given P A/P | Find F Given A F/A | Find A Given F A/F | Find A Given G A/G | Find P Given G P/G |
| 1 | 1.080 | 0.9259 | 0.9259 | 1.0800 | 1.000 | 1.0000 | 0.0000 | 0.000 |
| 2 | 1.166 | 0.8573 | 1.7833 | 0.5608 | 2.080 | 0.4808 | 0.4808 | 0.857 |
| 3 | 1.260 | 0.7938 | 2.5771 | 0.3880 | 3.246 | 0.3080 | 0.9487 | 2.445 |
| 4 | 1.360 | 0.7350 | 3.3121 | 0.3019 | 4.506 | 0.2219 | 1.4040 | 4.650 |
| 5 | 1.469 | 0.6806 | 3.9927 | 0.2505 | 5.867 | 0.1705 | 1.8465 | 7.372 |
| 6 | 1.587 | 0.6302 | 4.6229 | 0.2163 | 7.336 | 0.1363 | 2.2763 | 10.523 |
| 7 | 1.714 | 0.5835 | 5.2064 | 0.1921 | 8.923 | 0.1121 | 2.6937 | 14.024 |
| 8 | 1.851 | 0.5403 | 5.7466 | 0.1740 | 10.637 | 0.0940 | 3.0985 | 17.806 |
| 9 | 1.999 | 0.5002 | 6.2469 | 0.1601 | 12.488 | 0.0801 | 3.4910 | 21.808 |
| 10 | 2.159 | 0.4632 | 6.7101 | 0.1490 | 14.487 | 0.0690 | 3.8713 | 25.977 |
| 11 | 2.332 | 0.4289 | 7.1390 | 0.1401 | 16.645 | 0.0601 | 4.2395 | 30.266 |
| 12 | 2.518 | 0.3971 | 7.5361 | 0.1327 | 18.977 | 0.0527 | 4.5957 | 34.634 |
| 13 | 2.720 | 0.3677 | 7.9038 | 0.1265 | 21.495 | 0.0465 | 4.9402 | 39.046 |
| 14 | 2.937 | 0.3405 | 8.2442 | 0.1213 | 24.215 | 0.0413 | 5.2731 | 43.472 |
| 15 | 3.172 | 0.3152 | 8.5595 | 0.1168 | 27.152 | 0.0368 | 5.5945 | 47.886 |
| 16 | 3.426 | 0.2919 | 8.8514 | 0.1130 | 30.324 | 0.0330 | 5.9046 | 52.264 |
| 17 | 3.700 | 0.2703 | 9.1216 | 0.1096 | 33.750 | 0.0296 | 6.2037 | 56.588 |
| 18 | 3.996 | 0.2502 | 9.3719 | 0.1067 | 37.450 | 0.0267 | 6.4920 | 60.843 |
| 19 | 4.316 | 0.2317 | 9.6036 | 0.1041 | 41.446 | 0.0241 | 6.7697 | 65.013 |
| 20 | 4.661 | 0.2145 | 9.8181 | 0.1019 | 45.762 | 0.0219 | 7.0369 | 69.090 |
| 21 | 5.034 | 0.1987 | 10.0168 | 0.0998 | 50.423 | 0.0198 | 7.2940 | 73.063 |
| 22 | 5.437 | 0.1839 | 10.2007 | 0.0980 | 55.457 | 0.0180 | 7.5412 | 76.926 |
| 23 | 5.871 | 0.1703 | 10.3711 | 0.0964 | 60.893 | 0.0164 | 7.7786 | 80.673 |
| 24 | 6.341 | 0.1577 | 10.5288 | 0.0950 | 66.765 | 0.0150 | 8.0066 | 84.300 |
| 25 | 6.848 | 0.1460 | 10.6748 | 0.0937 | 73.106 | 0.0137 | 8.2254 | 87.804 |
| 26 | 7.396 | 0.1352 | 10.8100 | 0.0925 | 79.954 | 0.0125 | 8.4352 | 91.184 |
| 27 | 7.988 | 0.1252 | 10.9352 | 0.0914 | 87.351 | 0.0114 | 8.6363 | 94.439 |
| 28 | 8.627 | 0.1159 | 11.0511 | 0.0905 | 95.339 | 0.0105 | 8.8289 | 97.569 |
| 29 | 9.317 | 0.1073 | 11.1584 | 0.0896 | 103.966 | 0.0096 | 9.0133 | 100.574 |
| 30 | 10.063 | 0.0994 | 11.2578 | 0.0888 | 113.283 | 0.0088 | 9.1897 | 103.456 |
| 31 | 10.868 | 0.0920 | 11.3498 | 0.0881 | 123.346 | 0.0081 | 9.3584 | 106.216 |
| 32 | 11.737 | 0.0852 | 11.4350 | 0.0875 | 134.214 | 0.0075 | 9.5197 | 108.857 |
| 33 | 12.676 | 0.0789 | 11.5139 | 0.0869 | 145.951 | 0.0069 | 9.6737 | 111.382 |
| 34 | 13.690 | 0.0730 | 11.5869 | 0.0863 | 158.627 | 0.0063 | 9.8208 | 113.792 |
| 35 | 14.785 | 0.0676 | 11.6546 | 0.0858 | 172.317 | 0.0058 | 9.9611 | 116.092 |
| 36 | 15.968 | 0.0626 | 11.7172 | 0.0853 | 187.102 | 0.0053 | 10.0949 | 118.284 |
| 37 | 17.246 | 0.0580 | 11.7752 | 0.0849 | 203.070 | 0.0049 | 10.2225 | 120.371 |
| 38 | 18.625 | 0.0537 | 11.8289 | 0.0845 | 220.316 | 0.0045 | 10.3440 | 122.358 |
| 39 | 20.115 | 0.0497 | 11.8786 | 0.0842 | 238.941 | 0.0042 | 10.4597 | 124.247 |
| 40 | 21.725 | 0.0460 | 11.9246 | 0.0839 | 259.057 | 0.0039 | 10.5699 | 126.042 |

# APPENDIX A.7

## $10\%$ INTEREST FACTORS FOR DISCRETE COMPOUNDING PERIODS

| | SINGLE PAYMENT | | UNIFORM PAYMENT SERIES | | | | GRADIENT SERIES | |
|---|---|---|---|---|---|---|---|---|
| | Compound Amount Factor | Present Worth Factor | Present Worth Factor | Capital Recovery Factor | Compound Amount Factor | Sinking Fund Factor | Gradient Uniform Series | Gradient Present Worth |
| $N$ | Find $F$ Given $P$ $F/P$ | Find $P$ Given $F$ $P/F$ | Find $P$ Given $A$ $P/A$ | Find $A$ Given $P$ $A/P$ | Find $F$ Given $A$ $F/A$ | Find $A$ Given $F$ $A/F$ | Find $A$ Given $G$ $A/G$ | Find $P$ Given $G$ $P/G$ |
| 1 | 1.100 | 0.9091 | 0.9091 | 1.1000 | 1.000 | 1.0000 | 0.0000 | 0.000 |
| 2 | 1.210 | 0.8264 | 1.7355 | 0.5762 | 2.100 | 0.4762 | 0.4762 | 0.826 |
| 3 | 1.331 | 0.7513 | 2.4869 | 0.4021 | 3.310 | 0.3021 | 0.9366 | 2.329 |
| 4 | 1.464 | 0.6830 | 3.1699 | 0.3155 | 4.641 | 0.2155 | 1.3812 | 4.378 |
| 5 | 1.611 | 0.6209 | 3.7908 | 0.2638 | 6.105 | 0.1638 | 1.8101 | 6.862 |
| 6 | 1.772 | 0.5645 | 4.3553 | 0.2296 | 7.716 | 0.1296 | 2.2236 | 9.684 |
| 7 | 1.949 | 0.5132 | 4.8684 | 0.2054 | 9.487 | 0.1054 | 2.6216 | 12.763 |
| 8 | 2.144 | 0.4665 | 5.3349 | 0.1874 | 11.436 | 0.0874 | 3.0045 | 16.029 |
| 9 | 2.358 | 0.4241 | 5.7590 | 0.1736 | 13.579 | 0.0736 | 3.3724 | 19.421 |
| 10 | 2.594 | 0.3855 | 6.1446 | 0.1627 | 15.937 | 0.0627 | 3.7255 | 22.891 |
| 11 | 2.853 | 0.3505 | 6.4951 | 0.1540 | 18.531 | 0.0540 | 4.0641 | 26.396 |
| 12 | 3.138 | 0.3186 | 6.8137 | 0.1468 | 21.384 | 0.0468 | 4.3884 | 29.901 |
| 13 | 3.452 | 0.2897 | 7.1034 | 0.1408 | 24.523 | 0.0408 | 4.6988 | 33.377 |
| 14 | 3.797 | 0.2633 | 7.3667 | 0.1357 | 27.975 | 0.0357 | 4.9955 | 36.800 |
| 15 | 4.177 | 0.2394 | 7.6061 | 0.1315 | 31.772 | 0.0315 | 5.2789 | 40.152 |
| 16 | 4.595 | 0.2176 | 7.8237 | 0.1278 | 35.950 | 0.0278 | 5.5493 | 43.416 |
| 17 | 5.054 | 0.1978 | 8.0216 | 0.1247 | 40.545 | 0.0247 | 5.8071 | 46.582 |
| 18 | 5.560 | 0.1799 | 8.2014 | 0.1219 | 45.599 | 0.0219 | 6.0526 | 49.640 |
| 19 | 6.116 | 0.1635 | 8.3649 | 0.1195 | 51.159 | 0.0195 | 6.2861 | 52.583 |
| 20 | 6.727 | 0.1486 | 8.5136 | 0.1175 | 57.275 | 0.0175 | 6.5081 | 55.407 |
| 21 | 7.400 | 0.1351 | 8.6487 | 0.1156 | 64.002 | 0.0156 | 6.7189 | 58.110 |
| 22 | 8.140 | 0.1228 | 8.7715 | 0.1140 | 71.403 | 0.0140 | 6.9189 | 60.689 |
| 23 | 8.954 | 0.1117 | 8.8832 | 0.1126 | 79.543 | 0.0126 | 7.1085 | 63.146 |
| 24 | 9.850 | 0.1015 | 8.9847 | 0.1113 | 88.497 | 0.0113 | 7.2881 | 65.481 |
| 25 | 10.835 | 0.0923 | 9.0770 | 0.1102 | 98.347 | 0.0102 | 7.4580 | 67.696 |
| 26 | 11.918 | 0.0839 | 9.1609 | 0.1092 | 109.182 | 0.0092 | 7.6186 | 69.794 |
| 27 | 13.110 | 0.0763 | 9.2372 | 0.1083 | 121.100 | 0.0083 | 7.7704 | 71.777 |
| 28 | 14.421 | 0.0693 | 9.3066 | 0.1075 | 134.210 | 0.0075 | 7.9137 | 73.650 |
| 29 | 15.863 | 0.0630 | 9.3696 | 0.1067 | 148.631 | 0.0067 | 8.0489 | 75.415 |
| 30 | 17.449 | 0.0573 | 9.4269 | 0.1061 | 164.494 | 0.0061 | 8.1762 | 77.077 |
| 31 | 19.194 | 0.0521 | 9.4790 | 0.1055 | 181.943 | 0.0055 | 8.2962 | 78.640 |
| 32 | 21.114 | 0.0474 | 9.5264 | 0.1050 | 201.138 | 0.0050 | 8.4091 | 80.108 |
| 33 | 23.225 | 0.0431 | 9.5694 | 0.1045 | 222.252 | 0.0045 | 8.5152 | 81.486 |
| 34 | 25.548 | 0.0391 | 9.6086 | 0.1041 | 245.477 | 0.0041 | 8.6149 | 82.777 |
| 35 | 28.102 | 0.0356 | 9.6442 | 0.1037 | 271.024 | 0.0037 | 8.7086 | 83.987 |
| 36 | 30.913 | 0.0323 | 9.6765 | 0.1033 | 299.127 | 0.0033 | 8.7965 | 85.119 |
| 37 | 34.004 | 0.0294 | 9.7059 | 0.1030 | 330.039 | 0.0030 | 8.8789 | 86.178 |
| 38 | 37.404 | 0.0267 | 9.7327 | 0.1027 | 364.043 | 0.0027 | 8.9562 | 87.167 |
| 39 | 41.145 | 0.0243 | 9.7570 | 0.1025 | 401.448 | 0.0025 | 9.0285 | 88.091 |
| 40 | 45.259 | 0.0221 | 9.7791 | 0.1023 | 442.593 | 0.0023 | 9.0962 | 88.953 |

# APPENDIX A.8

## 12% INTEREST FACTORS FOR DISCRETE COMPOUNDING PERIODS

| | SINGLE PAYMENT | | UNIFORM PAYMENT SERIES | | | | GRADIENT SERIES | |
|---|---|---|---|---|---|---|---|---|
| | Compound Amount Factor | Present Worth Factor | Present Worth Factor | Capital Recovery Factor | Compound Amount Factor | Sinking Fund Factor | Gradient Uniform Series | Gradient Present Worth |
| | Find $F$ Given $P$ | Find $P$ Given $F$ | Find $P$ Given $A$ | Find $A$ Given $P$ | Find $F$ Given $A$ | Find $A$ Given $F$ | Find $A$ Given $G$ | Find $P$ Given $G$ |
| $N$ | $F/P$ | $P/F$ | $P/A$ | $A/P$ | $F/A$ | $A/F$ | $A/G$ | $P/G$ |
| 1 | 1.120 | 0.8929 | 0.8929 | 1.1200 | 1.000 | 1.0000 | 0.0000 | 0.000 |
| 2 | 1.254 | 0.7972 | 1.6901 | 0.5917 | 2.120 | 0.4717 | 0.4717 | 0.797 |
| 3 | 1.405 | 0.7118 | 2.4018 | 0.4163 | 3.374 | 0.2963 | 0.9246 | 2.221 |
| 4 | 1.574 | 0.6355 | 3.0373 | 0.3292 | 4.779 | 0.2092 | 1.3589 | 4.127 |
| 5 | 1.762 | 0.5674 | 3.6048 | 0.2774 | 6.353 | 0.1574 | 1.7746 | 6.397 |
| 6 | 1.974 | 0.5066 | 4.1114 | 0.2432 | 8.115 | 0.1232 | 2.1720 | 8.930 |
| 7 | 2.211 | 0.4523 | 4.5638 | 0.2191 | 10.089 | 0.0991 | 2.5515 | 11.644 |
| 8 | 2.476 | 0.4039 | 4.9676 | 0.2013 | 12.300 | 0.0813 | 2.9131 | 14.471 |
| 9 | 2.773 | 0.3606 | 5.3282 | 0.1877 | 14.776 | 0.0677 | 3.2574 | 17.356 |
| 10 | 3.106 | 0.3220 | 5.6502 | 0.1770 | 17.549 | 0.0570 | 3.5847 | 20.254 |
| 11 | 3.479 | 0.2875 | 5.9377 | 0.1684 | 20.655 | 0.0484 | 3.8953 | 23.129 |
| 12 | 3.896 | 0.2567 | 6.1944 | 0.1614 | 24.133 | 0.0414 | 4.1897 | 25.952 |
| 13 | 4.363 | 0.2292 | 6.4235 | 0.1557 | 28.029 | 0.0357 | 4.4683 | 28.702 |
| 14 | 4.887 | 0.2046 | 6.6282 | 0.1509 | 32.393 | 0.0309 | 4.7317 | 31.362 |
| 15 | 5.474 | 0.1827 | 6.8109 | 0.1468 | 37.280 | 0.0268 | 4.9803 | 33.920 |
| 16 | 6.130 | 0.1631 | 6.9740 | 0.1434 | 42.753 | 0.0234 | 5.2147 | 36.367 |
| 17 | 6.866 | 0.1456 | 7.1196 | 0.1405 | 48.884 | 0.0205 | 5.4353 | 38.697 |
| 18 | 7.690 | 0.1300 | 7.2497 | 0.1379 | 55.750 | 0.0179 | 5.6427 | 40.908 |
| 19 | 8.613 | 0.1161 | 7.3658 | 0.1358 | 63.440 | 0.0158 | 5.8375 | 42.998 |
| 20 | 9.646 | 0.1037 | 7.4694 | 0.1339 | 72.052 | 0.0139 | 6.0202 | 44.968 |
| 21 | 10.804 | 0.0926 | 7.5620 | 0.1322 | 81.699 | 0.0122 | 6.1913 | 46.819 |
| 22 | 12.100 | 0.0826 | 7.6446 | 0.1308 | 92.503 | 0.0108 | 6.3514 | 48.554 |
| 23 | 13.552 | 0.0738 | 7.7184 | 0.1296 | 104.603 | 0.0096 | 6.5010 | 50.178 |
| 24 | 15.179 | 0.0659 | 7.7843 | 0.1285 | 118.155 | 0.0085 | 6.6406 | 51.693 |
| 25 | 17.000 | 0.0588 | 7.8431 | 0.1275 | 133.334 | 0.0075 | 6.7708 | 53.105 |
| 26 | 19.040 | 0.0525 | 7.8957 | 0.1267 | 150.334 | 0.0067 | 6.8921 | 54.418 |
| 27 | 21.325 | 0.0469 | 7.9426 | 0.1259 | 169.374 | 0.0059 | 7.0049 | 55.637 |
| 28 | 23.884 | 0.0419 | 7.9844 | 0.1252 | 190.699 | 0.0052 | 7.1098 | 56.767 |
| 29 | 26.750 | 0.0374 | 8.0218 | 0.1247 | 214.583 | 0.0047 | 7.2071 | 57.814 |
| 30 | 29.960 | 0.0334 | 8.0552 | 0.1241 | 241.333 | 0.0041 | 7.2974 | 58.782 |
| 31 | 33.555 | 0.0298 | 8.0850 | 0.1237 | 271.293 | 0.0037 | 7.3811 | 59.676 |
| 32 | 37.582 | 0.0266 | 8.1116 | 0.1233 | 304.848 | 0.0033 | 7.4586 | 60.501 |
| 33 | 42.092 | 0.0238 | 8.1354 | 0.1229 | 342.429 | 0.0029 | 7.5302 | 61.261 |
| 34 | 47.143 | 0.0212 | 8.1566 | 0.1226 | 384.521 | 0.0026 | 7.5965 | 61.961 |
| 35 | 52.800 | 0.0189 | 8.1755 | 0.1223 | 431.663 | 0.0023 | 7.6577 | 62.605 |
| 36 | 59.136 | 0.0169 | 8.1924 | 0.1221 | 484.463 | 0.0021 | 7.7141 | 63.197 |
| 37 | 66.232 | 0.0151 | 8.2075 | 0.1218 | 543.599 | 0.0018 | 7.7661 | 63.741 |
| 38 | 74.180 | 0.0135 | 8.2210 | 0.1216 | 609.831 | 0.0016 | 7.8141 | 64.239 |
| 39 | 83.081 | 0.0120 | 8.2330 | 0.1215 | 684.010 | 0.0015 | 7.8582 | 64.697 |
| 40 | 93.051 | 0.0107 | 8.2438 | 0.1213 | 767.091 | 0.0013 | 7.8988 | 65.116 |

# APPENDIX A.9

## 15% INTEREST FACTORS FOR DISCRETE COMPOUNDING PERIODS

| | SINGLE PAYMENT | | UNIFORM PAYMENT SERIES | | | | GRADIENT SERIES | |
|---|---|---|---|---|---|---|---|---|
| | Compound Amount Factor | Present Worth Factor | Present Worth Factor | Capital Recovery Factor | Compound Amount Factor | Sinking Fund Factor | Gradient Uniform Series | Gradient Present Worth |
| $N$ | Find $F$ Given $P$ $F/P$ | Find $P$ Given $F$ $P/F$ | Find $P$ Given $A$ $P/A$ | Find $A$ Given $P$ $A/P$ | Find $F$ Given $A$ $F/A$ | Find $A$ Given $F$ $A/F$ | Find $A$ Given $G$ $A/G$ | Find $P$ Given $G$ $P/G$ |
| 1 | 1.150 | 0.8696 | 0.8696 | 1.1500 | 1.000 | 1.0000 | 0.0000 | 0.000 |
| 2 | 1.323 | 0.7561 | 1.6257 | 0.6151 | 2.150 | 0.4651 | 0.4651 | 0.756 |
| 3 | 1.521 | 0.6575 | 2.2832 | 0.4380 | 3.472 | 0.2880 | 0.9071 | 2.071 |
| 4 | 1.749 | 0.5718 | 2.8550 | 0.3503 | 4.993 | 0.2003 | 1.3263 | 3.786 |
| 5 | 2.011 | 0.4972 | 3.3522 | 0.2983 | 6.742 | 0.1483 | 1.7228 | 5.775 |
| 6 | 2.313 | 0.4323 | 3.7845 | 0.2642 | 8.754 | 0.1142 | 2.0972 | 7.937 |
| 7 | 2.660 | 0.3759 | 4.1604 | 0.2404 | 11.067 | 0.0904 | 2.4498 | 10.192 |
| 8 | 3.059 | 0.3269 | 4.4873 | 0.2229 | 13.727 | 0.0729 | 2.7813 | 12.481 |
| 9 | 3.518 | 0.2843 | 4.7716 | 0.2096 | 16.786 | 0.0596 | 3.0922 | 14.755 |
| 10 | 4.046 | 0.2472 | 5.0188 | 0.1993 | 20.304 | 0.0493 | 3.3832 | 16.979 |
| 11 | 4.652 | 0.2149 | 5.2337 | 0.1911 | 24.349 | 0.0411 | 3.6549 | 19.129 |
| 12 | 5.350 | 0.1869 | 5.4206 | 0.1845 | 29.002 | 0.0345 | 3.9082 | 21.185 |
| 13 | 6.153 | 0.1625 | 5.5831 | 0.1791 | 34.352 | 0.0291 | 4.1438 | 23.135 |
| 14 | 7.076 | 0.1413 | 5.7245 | 0.1747 | 40.505 | 0.0247 | 4.3624 | 24.972 |
| 15 | 8.137 | 0.1229 | 5.8474 | 0.1710 | 47.580 | 0.0210 | 4.5650 | 26.693 |
| 16 | 9.358 | 0.1069 | 5.9542 | 0.1679 | 55.717 | 0.0179 | 4.7522 | 28.296 |
| 17 | 10.761 | 0.0929 | 6.0472 | 0.1654 | 65.075 | 0.0154 | 4.9251 | 29.783 |
| 18 | 12.375 | 0.0808 | 6.1280 | 0.1632 | 75.836 | 0.0132 | 5.0843 | 31.156 |
| 19 | 14.232 | 0.0703 | 6.1982 | 0.1613 | 88.212 | 0.0113 | 5.2307 | 32.421 |
| 20 | 16.367 | 0.0611 | 6.2593 | 0.1598 | 102.444 | 0.0098 | 5.3651 | 33.582 |
| 21 | 18.822 | 0.0531 | 6.3125 | 0.1584 | 118.810 | 0.0084 | 5.4883 | 34.645 |
| 22 | 21.645 | 0.0462 | 6.3587 | 0.1573 | 137.632 | 0.0073 | 5.6010 | 35.615 |
| 23 | 24.891 | 0.0402 | 6.3988 | 0.1563 | 159.276 | 0.0063 | 5.7040 | 36.499 |
| 24 | 28.625 | 0.0349 | 6.4338 | 0.1554 | 184.168 | 0.0054 | 5.7979 | 37.302 |
| 25 | 32.919 | 0.0304 | 6.4641 | 0.1547 | 212.793 | 0.0047 | 5.8834 | 38.031 |
| 26 | 37.857 | 0.0264 | 6.4906 | 0.1541 | 245.712 | 0.0041 | 5.9612 | 38.692 |
| 27 | 43.535 | 0.0230 | 6.5135 | 0.1535 | 283.569 | 0.0035 | 6.0319 | 39.289 |
| 28 | 50.066 | 0.0200 | 6.5335 | 0.1531 | 327.104 | 0.0031 | 6.0960 | 39.828 |
| 29 | 57.575 | 0.0174 | 6.5509 | 0.1527 | 377.170 | 0.0027 | 6.1541 | 40.315 |
| 30 | 66.212 | 0.0151 | 6.5660 | 0.1523 | 434.745 | 0.0023 | 6.2066 | 40.753 |
| 31 | 76.144 | 0.0131 | 6.5791 | 0.1520 | 500.957 | 0.0020 | 6.2541 | 41.147 |
| 32 | 87.565 | 0.0114 | 6.5905 | 0.1517 | 577.100 | 0.0017 | 6.2970 | 41.501 |
| 33 | 100.700 | 0.0099 | 6.6005 | 0.1515 | 664.666 | 0.0015 | 6.3357 | 41.818 |
| 34 | 115.805 | 0.0086 | 6.6091 | 0.1513 | 765.365 | 0.0013 | 6.3705 | 42.103 |
| 35 | 133.176 | 0.0075 | 6.6166 | 0.1511 | 881.170 | 0.0011 | 6.4019 | 42.359 |
| 36 | 153.152 | 0.0065 | 6.6231 | 0.1510 | 1014.346 | 0.0010 | 6.4301 | 42.587 |
| 37 | 176.125 | 0.0057 | 6.6288 | 0.1509 | 1167.498 | 0.0009 | 6.4554 | 42.792 |
| 38 | 202.543 | 0.0049 | 6.6338 | 0.1507 | 1343.622 | 0.0007 | 6.4781 | 42.974 |
| 39 | 232.925 | 0.0043 | 6.6380 | 0.1506 | 1546.165 | 0.0006 | 6.4985 | 43.137 |
| 40 | 267.864 | 0.0037 | 6.6418 | 0.1506 | 1779.090 | 0.0006 | 6.5168 | 43.283 |

# APPENDIX A.10

20% INTEREST FACTORS FOR DISCRETE COMPOUNDING PERIODS

| | SINGLE PAYMENT | | UNIFORM PAYMENT SERIES | | | | GRADIENT SERIES | |
|---|---|---|---|---|---|---|---|---|
| | Compound Amount Factor | Present Worth Factor | Present Worth Factor | Capital Recovery Factor | Compound Amount Factor | Sinking Fund Factor | Gradient Uniform Series | Gradient Present Worth |
| | Find $F$ Given $P$ $F/P$ | Find $P$ Given $F$ $P/F$ | Find $P$ Given $A$ $P/A$ | Find $A$ Given $P$ $A/P$ | Find $F$ Given $A$ $F/A$ | Find $A$ Given $F$ $A/F$ | Find $A$ Given $G$ $A/G$ | Find $P$ Given $G$ $P/G$ |
| $N$ | | | | | | | | |
| 1 | 1.200 | 0.8333 | 0.8333 | 1.2000 | 1.000 | 1.0000 | 0.0000 | 0.000 |
| 2 | 1.440 | 0.6944 | 1.5278 | 0.6545 | 2.200 | 0.4545 | 0.4545 | 0.694 |
| 3 | 1.728 | 0.5787 | 2.1065 | 0.4747 | 3.640 | 0.2747 | 0.8791 | 1.852 |
| 4 | 2.074 | 0.4823 | 2.5887 | 0.3863 | 5.368 | 0.1863 | 1.2742 | 3.299 |
| 5 | 2.488 | 0.4019 | 2.9906 | 0.3344 | 7.442 | 0.1344 | 1.6405 | 4.906 |
| 6 | 2.986 | 0.3349 | 3.3255 | 0.3007 | 9.930 | 0.1007 | 1.9788 | 6.581 |
| 7 | 3.583 | 0.2791 | 3.6046 | 0.2774 | 12.916 | 0.0774 | 2.2902 | 8.255 |
| 8 | 4.300 | 0.2326 | 3.8372 | 0.2606 | 16.499 | 0.0606 | 2.5756 | 9.883 |
| 9 | 5.160 | 0.1938 | 4.0310 | 0.2481 | 20.799 | 0.0481 | 2.8364 | 11.434 |
| 10 | 6.192 | 0.1615 | 4.1925 | 0.2385 | 25.959 | 0.0385 | 3.0739 | 12.887 |
| 11 | 7.430 | 0.1346 | 4.3271 | 0.2311 | 32.150 | 0.0311 | 3.2893 | 14.233 |
| 12 | 8.916 | 0.1122 | 4.4392 | 0.2253 | 39.581 | 0.0253 | 3.4841 | 15.467 |
| 13 | 10.699 | 0.0935 | 4.5327 | 0.2206 | 48.497 | 0.0206 | 3.6597 | 16.588 |
| 14 | 12.839 | 0.0779 | 4.6106 | 0.2169 | 59.196 | 0.0169 | 3.8175 | 17.601 |
| 15 | 15.407 | 0.0649 | 4.6755 | 0.2139 | 72.035 | 0.0139 | 3.9588 | 18.509 |
| 16 | 18.488 | 0.0541 | 4.7296 | 0.2114 | 87.442 | 0.0114 | 4.0851 | 19.321 |
| 17 | 22.186 | 0.0451 | 4.7746 | 0.2094 | 105.931 | 0.0094 | 4.1976 | 20.042 |
| 18 | 26.623 | 0.0376 | 4.8122 | 0.2078 | 128.117 | 0.0078 | 4.2975 | 20.680 |
| 19 | 31.948 | 0.0313 | 4.8435 | 0.2065 | 154.740 | 0.0065 | 4.3861 | 21.244 |
| 20 | 38.338 | 0.0261 | 4.8696 | 0.2054 | 186.688 | 0.0054 | 4.4643 | 21.739 |
| 21 | 46.005 | 0.0217 | 4.8913 | 0.2044 | 225.026 | 0.0044 | 4.5334 | 22.174 |
| 22 | 55.206 | 0.0181 | 4.9094 | 0.2037 | 271.031 | 0.0037 | 4.5941 | 22.555 |
| 23 | 66.247 | 0.0151 | 4.9245 | 0.2031 | 326.237 | 0.0031 | 4.6475 | 22.887 |
| 24 | 79.497 | 0.0126 | 4.9371 | 0.2025 | 392.484 | 0.0025 | 4.6943 | 23.176 |
| 25 | 95.396 | 0.0105 | 4.9476 | 0.2021 | 471.981 | 0.0021 | 4.7352 | 23.428 |
| 26 | 114.475 | 0.0087 | 4.9563 | 0.2018 | 567.377 | 0.0018 | 4.7709 | 23.646 |
| 27 | 137.371 | 0.0073 | 4.9636 | 0.2015 | 681.853 | 0.0015 | 4.8020 | 23.835 |
| 28 | 164.845 | 0.0061 | 4.9697 | 0.2012 | 819.223 | 0.0012 | 4.8291 | 23.999 |
| 29 | 197.814 | 0.0051 | 4.9747 | 0.2010 | 984.068 | 0.0010 | 4.8527 | 24.141 |
| 30 | 237.376 | 0.0042 | 4.9789 | 0.2008 | 1181.882 | 0.0008 | 4.8731 | 24.263 |
| 31 | 284.852 | 0.0035 | 4.9824 | 0.2007 | 1419.258 | 0.0007 | 4.8908 | 24.368 |
| 32 | 341.822 | 0.0029 | 4.9854 | 0.2006 | 1704.109 | 0.0006 | 4.9061 | 24.459 |
| 33 | 410.186 | 0.0024 | 4.9878 | 0.2005 | 2045.931 | 0.0005 | 4.9194 | 24.537 |
| 34 | 492.224 | 0.0020 | 4.9898 | 0.2004 | 2456.118 | 0.0004 | 4.9308 | 24.604 |
| 35 | 590.668 | 0.0017 | 4.9915 | 0.2003 | 2948.341 | 0.0003 | 4.9406 | 24.661 |
| 36 | 708.802 | 0.0014 | 4.9929 | 0.2003 | 3539.009 | 0.0003 | 4.9491 | 24.711 |
| 37 | 850.562 | 0.0012 | 4.9941 | 0.2002 | 4247.811 | 0.0002 | 4.9564 | 24.753 |
| 38 | 1020.675 | 0.0010 | 4.9951 | 0.2002 | 5098.373 | 0.0002 | 4.9627 | 24.789 |
| 39 | 1224.810 | 0.0008 | 4.9959 | 0.2002 | 6119.048 | 0.0002 | 4.9681 | 24.820 |
| 40 | 1469.772 | 0.0007 | 4.9966 | 0.2001 | 7343.858 | 0.0001 | 4.9728 | 24.847 |

# APPENDIX A.11

| | SINGLE PAYMENT | | UNIFORM PAYMENT SERIES | | | | GRADIENT SERIES | |
|---|---|---|---|---|---|---|---|---|
| | Compound Amount Factor | Present Worth Factor | Present Worth Factor | Capital Recovery Factor | Compound Amount Factor | Sinking Fund Factor | Gradient Uniform Series | Gradient Present Worth |
| $N$ | Find $F$ Given $P$ $F/P$ | Find $P$ Given $F$ $P/F$ | Find $P$ Given $A$ $P/A$ | Find $A$ Given $P$ $A/P$ | Find $F$ Given $A$ $F/A$ | Find $A$ Given $F$ $A/F$ | Find $A$ Given $G$ $A/G$ | Find $P$ Given $G$ $P/G$ |
| 1 | 1.250 | 0.8000 | 0.8000 | 1.2500 | 1.000 | 1.0000 | 0.0000 | 0.000 |
| 2 | 1.563 | 0.6400 | 1.4400 | 0.6944 | 2.250 | 0.4444 | 0.4444 | 0.640 |
| 3 | 1.953 | 0.5120 | 1.9520 | 0.5123 | 3.812 | 0.2623 | 0.8525 | 1.664 |
| 4 | 2.441 | 0.4096 | 2.3616 | 0.4234 | 5.766 | 0.1734 | 1.2249 | 2.893 |
| 5 | 3.052 | 0.3277 | 2.6893 | 0.3718 | 8.207 | 0.1218 | 1.5631 | 4.204 |
| 6 | 3.815 | 0.2621 | 2.9514 | 0.3388 | 11.259 | 0.0888 | 1.8683 | 5.514 |
| 7 | 4.768 | 0.2097 | 3.1611 | 0.3163 | 15.073 | 0.0663 | 2.1424 | 6.773 |
| 8 | 5.960 | 0.1678 | 3.3289 | 0.3004 | 19.842 | 0.0504 | 2.3872 | 7.947 |
| 9 | 7.451 | 0.1342 | 3.4631 | 0.2888 | 25.802 | 0.0388 | 2.6048 | 9.021 |
| 10 | 9.313 | 0.1074 | 3.5705 | 0.2801 | 33.253 | 0.0301 | 2.7971 | 9.987 |
| 11 | 11.642 | 0.0859 | 3.6564 | 0.2735 | 42.566 | 0.0235 | 2.9663 | 10.846 |
| 12 | 14.552 | 0.0687 | 3.7251 | 0.2684 | 54.208 | 0.0184 | 3.1145 | 11.602 |
| 13 | 18.190 | 0.0550 | 3.7801 | 0.2645 | 68.760 | 0.0145 | 3.2437 | 12.262 |
| 14 | 22.737 | 0.0440 | 3.8241 | 0.2615 | 86.949 | 0.0115 | 3.3559 | 12.833 |
| 15 | 28.422 | 0.0352 | 3.8593 | 0.2591 | 109.687 | 0.0091 | 3.4530 | 13.326 |
| 16 | 35.527 | 0.0281 | 3.8874 | 0.2572 | 138.109 | 0.0072 | 3.5366 | 13.748 |
| 17 | 44.409 | 0.0225 | 3.9099 | 0.2558 | 173.636 | 0.0058 | 3.6084 | 14.108 |
| 18 | 55.511 | 0.0180 | 3.9279 | 0.2546 | 218.045 | 0.0046 | 3.6698 | 14.415 |
| 19 | 69.389 | 0.0144 | 3.9424 | 0.2537 | 273.556 | 0.0037 | 3.7222 | 14.674 |
| 20 | 86.736 | 0.0115 | 3.9539 | 0.2529 | 342.945 | 0.0029 | 3.7667 | 14.893 |
| 21 | 108.420 | 0.0092 | 3.9631 | 0.2523 | 429.681 | 0.0023 | 3.8045 | 15.078 |
| 22 | 135.525 | 0.0074 | 3.9705 | 0.2519 | 538.101 | 0.0019 | 3.8365 | 15.233 |
| 23 | 169.407 | 0.0059 | 3.9764 | 0.2515 | 673.626 | 0.0015 | 3.8634 | 15.362 |
| 24 | 211.758 | 0.0047 | 3.9811 | 0.2512 | 843.033 | 0.0012 | 3.8861 | 15.471 |
| 25 | 264.698 | 0.0038 | 3.9849 | 0.2509 | 1054.791 | 0.0009 | 3.9052 | 15.562 |
| 26 | 330.872 | 0.0030 | 3.9879 | 0.2508 | 1319.489 | 0.0008 | 3.9212 | 15.637 |
| 27 | 413.590 | 0.0024 | 3.9903 | 0.2506 | 1650.361 | 0.0006 | 3.9346 | 15.700 |
| 28 | 516.988 | 0.0019 | 3.9923 | 0.2505 | 2063.952 | 0.0005 | 3.9457 | 15.752 |
| 29 | 646.235 | 0.0015 | 3.9938 | 0.2504 | 2580.939 | 0.0004 | 3.9551 | 15.796 |
| 30 | 807.794 | 0.0012 | 3.9950 | 0.2503 | 3227.174 | 0.0003 | 3.9628 | 15.832 |
| 31 | 1009.742 | 0.0010 | 3.9960 | 0.2502 | 4034.968 | 0.0002 | 3.9693 | 15.861 |
| 32 | 1262.177 | 0.0008 | 3.9968 | 0.2502 | 5044.710 | 0.0002 | 3.9746 | 15.886 |
| 33 | 1577.722 | 0.0006 | 3.9975 | 0.2502 | 6306.887 | 0.0002 | 3.9791 | 15.906 |
| 34 | 1972.152 | 0.0005 | 3.9980 | 0.2501 | 7884.609 | 0.0001 | 3.9828 | 15.923 |
| 35 | 2465.190 | 0.0004 | 3.9984 | 0.2501 | 9856.761 | 0.0001 | 3.9858 | 15.937 |

# APPENDIX A.12

| | SINGLE PAYMENT | | UNIFORM PAYMENT SERIES | | | | GRADIENT SERIES | |
|---|---|---|---|---|---|---|---|---|
| | Compound Amount Factor | Present Worth Factor | Present Worth Factor | Capital Recovery Factor | Compound Amount Factor | Sinking Fund Factor | Gradient Uniform Series | Gradient Present Worth |
| N | Find $F$ Given $P$ $F/P$ | Find $P$ Given $F$ $P/F$ | Find $P$ Given $A$ $P/A$ | Find $A$ Given $P$ $A/P$ | Find $F$ Given $A$ $F/A$ | Find $A$ Given $F$ $A/F$ | Find $A$ Given $G$ $A/G$ | Find $P$ Given $G$ $P/G$ |
| 1 | 1.300 | 0.7692 | 0.7692 | 1.3000 | 1.000 | 1.0000 | 0.0000 | 0.000 |
| 2 | 1.690 | 0.5917 | 1.3609 | 0.7348 | 2.300 | 0.4348 | 0.4348 | 0.592 |
| 3 | 2.197 | 0.4552 | 1.8161 | 0.5506 | 3.990 | 0.2506 | 0.8271 | 1.502 |
| 4 | 2.856 | 0.3501 | 2.1662 | 0.4616 | 6.187 | 0.1616 | 1.1783 | 2.552 |
| 5 | 3.713 | 0.2693 | 2.4356 | 0.4106 | 9.043 | 0.1106 | 1.4903 | 3.630 |
| 6 | 4.827 | 0.2072 | 2.6427 | 0.3784 | 12.756 | 0.0784 | 1.7654 | 4.666 |
| 7 | 6.275 | 0.1594 | 2.8021 | 0.3569 | 17.583 | 0.0569 | 2.0063 | 5.622 |
| 8 | 8.157 | 0.1226 | 2.9247 | 0.3419 | 23.858 | 0.0419 | 2.2156 | 6.480 |
| 9 | 10.604 | 0.0943 | 3.0190 | 0.3312 | 32.015 | 0.0312 | 2.3963 | 7.234 |
| 10 | 13.786 | 0.0725 | 3.0915 | 0.3235 | 42.619 | 0.0235 | 2.5512 | 7.887 |
| 11 | 17.922 | 0.0558 | 3.1473 | 0.3177 | 56.405 | 0.0177 | 2.6833 | 8.445 |
| 12 | 23.298 | 0.0429 | 3.1903 | 0.3135 | 74.327 | 0.0135 | 2.7952 | 8.917 |
| 13 | 30.288 | 0.0330 | 3.2233 | 0.3102 | 97.625 | 0.0102 | 2.8895 | 9.314 |
| 14 | 39.374 | 0.0254 | 3.2487 | 0.3078 | 127.913 | 0.0078 | 2.9685 | 9.644 |
| 15 | 51.186 | 0.0195 | 3.2682 | 0.3060 | 167.286 | 0.0060 | 3.0344 | 9.917 |
| 16 | 66.542 | 0.0150 | 3.2832 | 0.3046 | 218.472 | 0.0046 | 3.0892 | 10.143 |
| 17 | 86.504 | 0.0116 | 3.2948 | 0.3035 | 285.014 | 0.0035 | 3.1345 | 10.328 |
| 18 | 112.455 | 0.0089 | 3.3037 | 0.3027 | 371.518 | 0.0027 | 3.1718 | 10.479 |
| 19 | 146.192 | 0.0068 | 3.3105 | 0.3021 | 483.973 | 0.0021 | 3.2025 | 10.602 |
| 20 | 190.050 | 0.0053 | 3.3158 | 0.3016 | 630.165 | 0.0016 | 3.2275 | 10.702 |
| 21 | 247.065 | 0.0040 | 3.3198 | 0.3012 | 820.215 | 0.0012 | 3.2480 | 10.783 |
| 22 | 321.184 | 0.0031 | 3.3230 | 0.3009 | 1067.280 | 0.0009 | 3.2646 | 10.848 |
| 23 | 417.539 | 0.0024 | 3.3254 | 0.3007 | 1388.464 | 0.0007 | 3.2781 | 10.901 |
| 24 | 542.801 | 0.0018 | 3.3272 | 0.3006 | 1806.003 | 0.0006 | 3.2890 | 10.943 |
| 25 | 705.641 | 0.0014 | 3.3286 | 0.3004 | 2348.803 | 0.0004 | 3.2979 | 10.977 |
| 26 | 917.333 | 0.0011 | 3.3297 | 0.3003 | 3054.444 | 0.0003 | 3.3050 | 11.005 |
| 27 | 1192.533 | 0.0008 | 3.3305 | 0.3003 | 3971.778 | 0.0003 | 3.3107 | 11.026 |
| 28 | 1550.293 | 0.0006 | 3.3312 | 0.3002 | 5164.311 | 0.0002 | 3.3153 | 11.044 |
| 29 | 2015.381 | 0.0005 | 3.3317 | 0.3001 | 6714.604 | 0.0001 | 3.3189 | 11.058 |
| 30 | 2619.996 | 0.0004 | 3.3321 | 0.3001 | 8729.985 | 0.0001 | 3.3219 | 11.069 |
| 31 | 3405.994 | 0.0003 | 3.3324 | 0.3001 | 11349.981 | 0.0001 | 3.3242 | 11.078 |
| 32 | 4427.793 | 0.0002 | 3.3326 | 0.3001 | 14755.975 | 0.0001 | 3.3261 | 11.085 |
| 33 | 5756.130 | 0.0002 | 3.3328 | 0.3001 | 19183.768 | 0.0001 | 3.3276 | 11.090 |
| 34 | 7482.970 | 0.0001 | 3.3329 | 0.3000 | 24939.899 | 0.0000 | 3.3288 | 11.094 |
| 35 | 9727.860 | 0.0001 | 3.3330 | 0.3000 | 32422.868 | 0.0000 | 3.3297 | 11.098 |

# APPENDIX A.13

| | SINGLE PAYMENT | | UNIFORM PAYMENT SERIES | | | | GRADIENT SERIES | |
|---|---|---|---|---|---|---|---|---|
| | Compound Amount Factor | Present Worth Factor | Present Worth Factor | Capital Recovery Factor | Compound Amount Factor | Sinking Fund Factor | Gradient Uniform Series | Gradient Present Worth |
| $N$ | Find $F$ Given $P$ $F/P$ | Find $P$ Given $F$ $P/F$ | Find $P$ Given $A$ $P/F$ | Find $A$ Given $P$ $A/P$ | Find $F$ Given $A$ $F/A$ | Find $A$ Given $F$ $A/F$ | Find $A$ Given $G$ $A/G$ | Find $P$ Given $G$ $P/G$ |
| 1 | 1.400 | 0.7143 | 0.7143 | 1.4000 | 1.000 | 1.0000 | 0.0000 | 0.000 |
| 2 | 1.960 | 0.5102 | 1.2245 | 0.8167 | 2.400 | 0.4167 | 0.4167 | 0.510 |
| 3 | 2.744 | 0.3644 | 1.5889 | 0.6294 | 4.360 | 0.2294 | 0.7798 | 1.239 |
| 4 | 3.842 | 0.2603 | 1.8492 | 0.5408 | 7.104 | 0.1408 | 1.0923 | 2.020 |
| 5 | 5.378 | 0.1859 | 2.0352 | 0.4914 | 10.946 | 0.0914 | 1.3580 | 2.764 |
| 6 | 7.530 | 0.1328 | 2.1680 | 0.4613 | 16.324 | 0.0613 | 1.5811 | 3.428 |
| 7 | 10.541 | 0.0949 | 2.2628 | 0.4419 | 23.853 | 0.0419 | 1.7664 | 3.997 |
| 8 | 14.758 | 0.0678 | 2.3306 | 0.4291 | 34.395 | 0.0291 | 1.9185 | 4.471 |
| 9 | 20.661 | 0.0484 | 2.3790 | 0.4203 | 49.153 | 0.0203 | 2.0422 | 4.858 |
| 10 | 28.925 | 0.0346 | 2.4136 | 0.4143 | 69.814 | 0.0143 | 2.1419 | 5.170 |
| 11 | 40.496 | 0.0247 | 2.4383 | 0.4101 | 98.739 | 0.0101 | 2.2215 | 5.417 |
| 12 | 56.694 | 0.0176 | 2.4559 | 0.4072 | 139.235 | 0.0072 | 2.2845 | 5.611 |
| 13 | 79.371 | 0.0126 | 2.4685 | 0.4051 | 195.929 | 0.0051 | 2.3341 | 5.762 |
| 14 | 111.120 | 0.0090 | 2.4775 | 0.4036 | 275.300 | 0.0036 | 2.3729 | 5.879 |
| 15 | 155.568 | 0.0064 | 2.4839 | 0.4026 | 386.420 | 0.0026 | 2.4030 | 5.969 |
| 16 | 217.795 | 0.0046 | 2.4885 | 0.4018 | 541.988 | 0.0018 | 2.4262 | 6.038 |
| 17 | 304.913 | 0.0033 | 2.4918 | 0.4013 | 759.784 | 0.0013 | 2.4441 | 6.090 |
| 18 | 426.879 | 0.0023 | 2.4941 | 0.4009 | 1064.697 | 0.0009 | 2.4577 | 6.130 |
| 19 | 597.630 | 0.0017 | 2.4958 | 0.4007 | 1491.576 | 0.0007 | 2.4682 | 6.160 |
| 20 | 836.683 | 0.0012 | 2.4970 | 0.4005 | 2089.206 | 0.0005 | 2.4761 | 6.183 |
| 21 | 1171.356 | 0.0009 | 2.4979 | 0.4003 | 2925.889 | 0.0003 | 2.4821 | 6.200 |
| 22 | 1639.898 | 0.0006 | 2.4985 | 0.4002 | 4097.245 | 0.0002 | 2.4866 | 6.213 |
| 23 | 2295.857 | 0.0004 | 2.4989 | 0.4002 | 5737.142 | 0.0002 | 2.4900 | 6.222 |
| 24 | 3214.200 | 0.0003 | 2.4992 | 0.4001 | 8032.999 | 0.0001 | 2.4925 | 6.229 |
| 25 | 4499.880 | 0.0002 | 2.4994 | 0.4001 | 11247.199 | 0.0001 | 2.4944 | 6.235 |
| 26 | 6299.831 | 0.0002 | 2.4996 | 0.4001 | 15747.079 | 0.0001 | 2.4959 | 6.239 |
| 27 | 8819.764 | 0.0001 | 2.4997 | 0.4000 | 22046.910 | 0.0000 | 2.4969 | 6.242 |
| 28 | 12347.670 | 0.0001 | 2.4998 | 0.4000 | 30866.674 | 0.0000 | 2.4977 | 6.244 |
| 29 | 17286.737 | 0.0001 | 2.4999 | 0.4000 | 43214.343 | 0.0000 | 2.4983 | 6.245 |
| 30 | 24201.432 | 0.0000 | 2.4999 | 0.4000 | 60501.081 | 0.0000 | 2.4988 | 6.247 |

# APPENDIX A.14

| | SINGLE PAYMENT | | UNIFORM PAYMENT SERIES | | | | GRADIENT SERIES | |
|---|---|---|---|---|---|---|---|---|
| | Compound Amount Factor | Present Worth Factor | Present Worth Factor | Capital Recovery Factor | Compound Amount Factor | Sinking Fund Factor | Gradient Uniform Series | Gradient Present Worth |
| N | Find $F$ Given $P$ $F/P$ | Find $P$ Given $F$ $P/F$ | Find $P$ Given $A$ $P/F$ | Find $A$ Given $P$ $A/P$ | Find $F$ Given $A$ $F/A$ | Find $A$ Given $F$ $A/F$ | Find $A$ Given $G$ $A/G$ | Find $P$ Given $G$ $P/G$ |
| 1 | 1.500 | 0.6667 | 0.6667 | 1.5000 | 1.000 | 1.0000 | 0.0000 | 0.000 |
| 2 | 2.250 | 0.4444 | 1.1111 | 0.9000 | 2.500 | 0.4000 | 0.4000 | 0.444 |
| 3 | 3.375 | 0.2963 | 1.4074 | 0.7105 | 4.750 | 0.2105 | 0.7368 | 1.037 |
| 4 | 5.063 | 0.1975 | 1.6049 | 0.6231 | 8.125 | 0.1231 | 1.0154 | 1.630 |
| 5 | 7.594 | 0.1317 | 1.7366 | 0.5758 | 13.188 | 0.0758 | 1.2417 | 2.156 |
| 6 | 11.391 | 0.0878 | 1.8244 | 0.5481 | 20.781 | 0.0481 | 1.4226 | 2.595 |
| 7 | 17.086 | 0.0585 | 1.8829 | 0.5311 | 32.172 | 0.0311 | 1.5648 | 2.947 |
| 8 | 25.629 | 0.0390 | 1.9220 | 0.5203 | 49.258 | 0.0203 | 1.6752 | 3.220 |
| 9 | 38.443 | 0.0260 | 1.9480 | 0.5134 | 74.887 | 0.0134 | 1.7596 | 3.428 |
| 10 | 57.665 | 0.0173 | 1.9653 | 0.5088 | 113.330 | 0.0088 | 1.8235 | 3.584 |
| 11 | 86.498 | 0.0116 | 1.9769 | 0.5058 | 170.995 | 0.0058 | 1.8713 | 3.699 |
| 12 | 129.746 | 0.0077 | 1.9846 | 0.5039 | 257.493 | 0.0039 | 1.9068 | 3.784 |
| 13 | 194.620 | 0.0051 | 1.9897 | 0.5026 | 387.239 | 0.0026 | 1.9329 | 3.846 |
| 14 | 291.929 | 0.0034 | 1.9931 | 0.5017 | 581.859 | 0.0017 | 1.9519 | 3.890 |
| 15 | 437.894 | 0.0023 | 1.9544 | 0.5011 | 873.788 | 0.0011 | 1.9657 | 3.922 |
| 16 | 656.841 | 0.0015 | 1.9970 | 0.5008 | 1311.682 | 0.0008 | 1.9756 | 3.945 |
| 17 | 985.261 | 0.0010 | 1.9980 | 0.5005 | 1968.523 | 0.0005 | 1.9827 | 3.961 |
| 18 | 1477.892 | 0.0007 | 1.9986 | 0.5003 | 2953.784 | 0.0003 | 1.9878 | 3.973 |
| 19 | 2216.838 | 0.0005 | 1.9991 | 0.5002 | 4431.676 | 0.0002 | 1.9914 | 3.981 |
| 20 | 3325.257 | 0.0003 | 1.9994 | 0.5002 | 6648.513 | 0.0002 | 1.9940 | 3.987 |
| 21 | 4987.885 | 0.0002 | 1.9996 | 0.5001 | 9973.770 | 0.0001 | 1.9958 | 3.991 |
| 22 | 7481.828 | 0.0001 | 1.9997 | 0.5001 | 14961.655 | 0.0001 | 1.9971 | 3.994 |
| 23 | 11222.741 | 0.0001 | 1.9998 | 0.5000 | 22443.483 | 0.0000 | 1.9980 | 3.996 |
| 24 | 16834.112 | 0.0001 | 1.9999 | 0.5000 | 33666.224 | 0.0000 | 1.9986 | 3.997 |
| 25 | 25251.168 | 0.0000 | 1.9999 | 0.5000 | 50500.337 | 0.0000 | 1.9990 | 3.998 |

# INDEX